LAW & ETHICS
in the
BUSINESS ENVIRONMENT

LAW & ETHICS
in the
BUSINESS ENVIRONMENT

SEVENTH EDITION

Terry Halbert, J.D.
Professor of Legal Studies
Temple University Fox School of Business & Management

Elaine Ingulli, J.D., LL.M.
Professor of Business Law
Richard Stockton College of New Jersey

SOUTH-WESTERN
CENGAGE Learning

Australia • Brazil • Japan • Korea • Mexico • Singapore • Spain • United Kingdom • United States

SOUTH-WESTERN
CENGAGE Learning

Law & Ethics *in the* Business Environment, Seventh Edition, International Edition
Terry Halbert and Elaine Ingulli

VP/Editorial Director: Jack W. Calhoun

Editor-in-Chief: Rob Dewey

Senior Acquisitions Editor: Vicky True-Baker

Developmental Editor: Jan Lamar

Editorial Assistant: Patrick Ian Clark

Marketing and Sales Manager: Laura-Aurora Stopa

Senior Art Director: Michelle Kunkler

Senior Media Editor: Kristen Meere

Senior Frontlist Buyer, Manufacturing: Kevin Kluck

Production Manager: Jennifer Ziegler

Content Project Management: PreMediaGlobal

Compositor: PreMediaGlobal

Production Technology Analyst: Emily Gross

Permissions Acquisition Manager, Text: John Hill

Cover Designer: Patti Hudepohl

Internal Designers: PreMediaGlobal

Cover Image: © iStockphoto Images/wsfurlan

For product information and technology assistance, contact us at **Cengage Learning Customer & Sales Support, 1-800-354-9706.**
For permission to use material from this text or product, submit all requests online at **www.cengage.com/permissions.**
Further permissions questions can be e-mailed to **permissionrequest@cengage.com.**

Library of Congress Control Number: 2010942580

International Edition

ISBN-13: 978-0-538-47352-1

ISBN-10: 0-538-47352-5

Cengage Learning International Offices

Asia
www.cengageasia.com
tel: (65) 6410 1200

Australia/New Zealand
www.cengage.com.au
tel: (61) 3 9685 4111

Brazil
www.cengage.com.br
tel: (55) 11 3665 9900

India
www.cengage.co.in
tel: (91) 11 4364 1111

Latin America
www.cengage.com.mx
tel: (52) 55 1500 6000

UK/Europe/Middle East/Africa
www.cengage.co.uk
tel: (44) 0 1264 332 424

Represented in Canada by Nelson Education, Ltd.
tel: (416) 752 9100 / (800) 668 0671
www.nelson.com

Cengage Learning is a leading provider of customized learning solutions with office locations around the globe, including Singapore, the United Kingdom, Australia, Mexico, Brazil, and Japan. Locate your local office at: **www.cengage.com/global**

For product information: **www.cengage.com/international**

Visit your local office: **www.cengage.com/global**

Visit our corporate website: **www.cengage.com**

AVAILABILITY OF RESOURCES MAY DIFFER BY REGION. Check with your local Cengage Learning representative for details.

Printed in the United States of America
1 2 3 4 5 6 7 15 14 13 12 11

In Memory of
Steven Carl Halbert
and
John Bonsigniore, for inspiring the
upending of assumptions

Brief Table of Contents

Table of Contents

This book presents a set of flashpoints where business imperatives, legal and ethical concerns collide. Our goal has been to make these situations vivid and involving. We want to give students practice making the kind of tough decisions they will confront as managers. And we want to expose them to the complex debates that continue to frame broader political decision-making.

If good education is about learning how to live, we hope this book helps students develop the critical habits of mind that will sustain them throughout their lives, supporting them in the various roles they will play—as employees, as friends, as parents, as community members, and as citizens of a globalized world.

Focus on Teaching & Learning

We cannot effectively teach everything about the legal system—even everything about business law—in just one semester. The vast "seamless web" is always in flux, as legislatures and courts channel the cultural, economic, and political forces that impact upon it. Law is, in this sense, a kind of moving target, and we believe in studying why and how it changes. We have selected readings that reveal the process of the law as it evolves—the pressure points where controversy is brewing and where ethical issues surface.

Our students know a good story when they see one. A case is a rich, stylized form of a story, with a protagonist, an antagonist, a dispute, and a resolution. Each one of our chapters starts with a lightly-edited case, selected not just because it is current, or landmark, but because it is likely to provoke reaction and to effectively problematize the theme of the chapter.

We follow that lead case with a mix of readings from scholarly and media sources, from different areas of expertise, and from diverse cultural perspectives, offering a variety of prisms through which students can view the chapter theme. Meanwhile, we demonstrate how the law has evolved in this area, highlighting the latest developments.

We give as much thought to effective teaching tools as to interesting content. After every case and reading, and at the end of every chapter, we include questions, exercises, and projects that we know—based on our combined more than 50 years of experience—work well in the classroom.

New in this Seventh Edition

We have enriched Chapter 1 with a new introduction to ethical theory, analyzing decisions made by BP before, during, and immediately after the 2010 Oil Spill in the Gulf of Mexico. With this searing event as a touchstone, we demonstrate five ethical perspectives in application, providing the tools for students to do their own ethical analyses as they progress through the book.

The theme of sustainability—particularly as it encompasses energy consumption and climate change—is sharply in focus in both Chapter 1 and Chapter 6. It also appears throughout the book, with smaller strands woven into other chapters.

We use the Supreme Court's decision on corporate financing of elections to open our exploration of the relationship between business and government. In later chapters, we prompt students to consider the full spectrum of possibilities, from business resistance to any form of regulation to collaborative strategies yielding responsible policy solutions.

In two Chapter Projects (Chapters 1 and 6) that build on one another, we ask students to actively interrogate corporate social responsibility.

We continue to raise human rights concerns—adding religious tolerance and accommodation to the workplace concerns we address in Chapter 4 (Diversity).

We address Facebook and social media in Chapter 3 (Privacy and Technology), with a complaint that has come before the FTC. Chapter 4 explores developments in the still-unfolding debate about immigration. In Chapter 5 (Worker's Rights) we include Congressional testimony regarding the West Virginia mine disaster. We offer expanded coverage of childhood obesity in Chapter 7 (Marketing) and include a class action complaint arising out of the Toyota recall in Chapter 8 (Product Safety.) The final chapter, Chapter 9 (Intellectual Property Rights), expands coverage of copyright issues related to music and the recent Supreme Court case involving business-method patents.

We are ever in debt to our students and colleagues, whose critical responses to our book push us to make each revision better than the last. In particular: Terry thanks Julie Ragatz, Assistant Professor of Ethics and Associate Director of the Center for Ethics in Financial Services at The American College, for her thoughtful feedback on the ethical analysis of the BP Spill; Elaine thanks Daniel H. Seiders, MBA candidate, for his careful reading of the Sixth Edition and suggestions for this revision. Once again, research librarian Mary Ann Trail came through for us at crunchtime. Temple University library specialist Fred Rowland was also a great help.

We also thank our reviewers for their valuable input:

Brian Bartel	*Mid-State Technical College*
Carolyn Berrett	*Mid-State Technical College*
Jean Cook	*Mid-State Technical College*
G. Howard Doty	*Nashville State Community College*
Raymond L. Hogler	*Colorado State University at Fort Collins*
Robert Woods	*Texas Woman's University*

We thank our colleagues at Cengage Learning: Acquisitions Editor Vicki True-Baker, Developmental Editor Jan Lamar, Editorial Assistant Patrick Clark, Designer Jennifer Ziegler, and Marketing Manager Laura Stopa. Their efforts, along with those of Production Project Manager Prashanth Kamavarapu and Copy Editor Mary Kemper, made this book possible and assured that we finished on time.

We are grateful to our husbands, Brian Ackerman and Bill Coleman, who have learned how to coexist with us while we dive into this task every few years.

And we thank one another, again, for the abiding mutual affection that sustains this project.

Acknowledgments

We thank all of the authors and publishers who have so generously allowed us to reprint their work with permission, including the following:

Excerpts from THE AFFLUENT SOCIETY by John Kenneth Galbraith, Copyright 1958, 1969, 1978, 1984 by John Kenneth Galbraith. Reprinted by permission of Houghton Mifflin Company. All Rights Reserved.

Excerpts from NO LOGO by Naomi Klein. Copyright 1999, Picador USA. Reprinted with permission.

"Exporting Hazards" by Henry Shue is reprinted from BOUNDARIES: NATIONAL AUTONOMY AND ITS LIMITS, Peter Brown and Henry Shue, eds. Copyright 1981 Rowan & Littlefield Publishers, Inc.

"The Functions of Privacy" is reprinted with the permission of Scribner, a division of Simon and Schuster, from PRIVACY AND FREEDOM by Alan F. Westin. Copyright 1967 by the Association of the Bar of the City of New York.

CHAPTER 1

Law, Ethics, Business
An Introduction

Law must be stable, and yet it cannot stand still.

— ROSCOE POUND

Neither fire nor wind, birth nor death, can erase our good deeds.

— BUDDHA

Business has become, in the last half century, the most powerful institution on the planet. The dominant institution in any society needs to take responsibility for the whole.... Every decision that is made, every action that is taken, must be viewed in light of that kind of responsibility.

— DAVID KORTEN

Law is not a static phenomenon, yet in certain ways it appears bounded and clear cut. Where it holds jurisdictional authority, law provides a set of rules for behavior. When these rules are broken, behavior is punishable. If you have been driving carelessly and hit another car, you might pay money damages. If you are caught stealing, you might go to jail. If you are caught polluting, you may be forced to stop. The creation of law and the delivery of sanctions for rule breaking are contested processes. How law is made, how it is enforced, and how it is interpreted are always in dispute, constantly changing, and responsive to the power relations that surround it. Still, we can identify its purposes: law both sets behavioral standards and sets up a system for compliance with them. Within the reach of a legal system, we are on notice that we must meet its standards or risk penalty. Chances are we were not directly involved in the making of the rules—we may even disagree strongly with them—but we understand that the legal system shadows us anyway. It may be the closest we can get to a shared reality.

Ethics, on the other hand, presents a menu of options, often disconnected from official sanctions.[1] While law concerns what we *must* do, ethics concerns what we *should* do. Suppose you work for an advertising agency and have just been offered a chance to work on a new ad campaign for a certain fast-food chain. Burgers, fries, and sodas are legal products. Under the First Amendment of the U.S. Constitution, fast-food companies

---

[1] We distinguish ethics from "professional ethics," which are binding on those with professional licenses for the practice of law or accounting, for example. Indeed, licensing authorities have enforcement powers not unlike those of legal authorities to sanction those who violate their professional codes of ethics.

have the legal right to get their messages out to consumers. But you may believe that their ads are particularly attractive to children, who are at risk of becoming accustomed and even addicted to the empty calories that make them fat and unhealthy. Although no law requires it, you may feel you should decline to participate in the campaign. Or suppose a company manufactures a pesticide that can no longer be sold in the United States because the Environmental Protection Agency has banned its primary ingredient, but that *can* be sold in places like India or Africa, where environmental regulations are far less stringent. Legally, the company is free to sell its pesticide overseas; but should it?

Ethical preferences are not preselected for us by legislators or by judges; they involve critical consciousness, engaging each of us in a process of bringing reason and emotion to bear on a particular situation. The right way to behave is not necessarily a matter of aligning our actions with the norm—a community or religious norm, for instance— although it may be.

The question of what should be done in a given situation, of the right way to live our lives, is complicated by divergent and overlapping cultural inputs. Within the borders of the United States, and globally, we are confronted with a kaleidoscopic array of ethical traditions. Does this mean that there can be no such thing as consensus, no agreement about what is good behavior? While there are differences among communities, we might identify a core set of values rooted in the kind of beings we are: We are all self-conscious, self-aware. We are all equipped to think rationally and to feel emotionally. And we are, by nature, dependent upon one another.

Today, almost half of the 100 largest economies in the world are multinational corporations. Comparing corporate revenues to the gross domestic product of nations, Walmart, BP, Exxon Mobil, and Royal Dutch/Shell all generated more income than Saudi Arabia, Norway, Denmark, Poland, South Africa, and Greece in 2005. The largest 200 companies in the world account for more than one-fourth of the world's economic activity. By 2002, they had twice the economic clout of the poorest four-fifths of humanity. Business has powerful effects on our natural environment. It strongly affects what we eat, how we transport ourselves, what our communities look like, and how we take care of ourselves when we are sick. In many ways, the impact of global business has been beneficial. Multinationals provide new jobs, pay taxes, and produce new or less expensive goods and services. They introduce technology, capital, and skills to their host countries and raise the standard of living. On the other hand, multinationals have been blamed for hastening the collapse of traditional ways of life; for taking advantage of weak and/or corrupt governments to exploit resources in developing countries; for implementing questionable safety, environmental, and financial practices; and for profiting from unsustainable technologies while blocking technologies antithetical to their interests. Multinational corporations are implicated in some of the world's most pressing problems— the growing disparities between rich and poor, for example, and global climate change.

As bearers of a diverse set of cultural achievements, we need to find points of agreement, both in legal and ethical terms, as to how human societies can best flourish. And as participants in the global economy, we need to discover ways of tempering the tremendous power of the market so that the planet and its inhabitants will thrive.

In this chapter we introduce values—and a tension between values—that will thread throughout this book. On the one hand, the value of maximizing individual freedom of choice, our right to think and act as we wish, as long as we don't infringe on someone else's rights to do the same; on the other hand, the value of building community, our duty as interdependent social beings to care about and for one another. We start with a case that raises questions about the relationship between law and ethics. Then we look at the 2010 BP oil spill in the Gulf of Mexico through five different ethical lenses, introducing the basic tools for ethical analysis that you will be using throughout this book. A brief description of the legal structure of corporations is followed by a recent Supreme Court decision establishing a corporate right to freedom of speech in the context of campaign financing. Finally, we read about "strategic" corporate social responsibility and its recognition of the mutually-advantageous linkages between business and society.

Freedom versus Responsibility: A Duty to Rescue?

In this first case, a man is sued for failing to do anything to rescue his drowning friend. While we only know the story as told by the widow—the case is dismissed before the facts can be fully investigated by both sides in a trial setting—we can see how, in this kind of scenario, the law views the conflict between freedom and responsibility.

YANIA v. BIGAN
Supreme Court of Pennsylvania, 1959
155 A.2d 343

JONES, Benjamin R., Justice

… On September 25, 1957 John E. Bigan was engaged in a coal strip-mining operation in Shade Township, Somerset County. On the property being stripped were large cuts or trenches created by Bigan when he removed the earthen overburden for the purpose of removing the coal underneath. One cut contained water 8 to 10 feet in depth with side walls or embankments 16 to 18 feet in height; at this cut Bigan had installed a pump to remove the water.

At approximately 4 p.m. on that date, Joseph F. Yania, the operator of another coal strip-mining operation, and one Boyd M. Ross, went upon Bigan's property for the purpose of discussing a business matter with Bigan, and, while there, [were] asked by Bigan to aid him in starting the pump. Bigan entered the cut and stood at the point where the pump was located. Yania stood at the top of one of the cut's side walls and then jumped from the side wall—a height of 16 to 18 feet—into the water and was drowned.

Yania's widow [sued], contending Bigan was responsible for Yania's death.

She contends that Yania's descent from the high embankment into the water and the resulting death were caused "entirely" by the spoken words … of Bigan delivered at a distance from Yania. The complaint does not allege that Yania slipped or that he was pushed or that Bigan made any physical impact upon Yania. On the contrary, the only inference deducible from the … complaint is that Bigan … caused such a mental impact on Yania that the latter was deprived of his … freedom of choice and placed under a compulsion to jump into the water. Had Yania been a child of tender years or a person mentally deficient then it is conceivable that taunting and enticement could constitute actionable negligence if it resulted in harm. However, to contend that such conduct directed to an adult in full possession of all his mental faculties constitutes actionable negligence is … completely without merit.

[The widow then claims] that Bigan … violated a duty owed to Yania in that his land contained a dangerous condition, i.e., the water-filled cut or trench, and he failed to warn Yania of such condition.… Of this condition there was neither concealment nor failure to warn, but, on the contrary, the complaint specifically avers that Bigan not only requested Yania and Boyd to assist him in starting the pump to remove the water from the cut but "led" them to the cut itself. If this cut possessed any potentiality of danger, such a condition was as obvious and apparent to Yania as to Bigan, both coal strip-mine opera-tors. Under the circumstances herein depicted Bigan could not be held liable in this respect.

Lastly, [the widow claims] that Bigan failed to take the necessary steps to rescue Yania from the water. The mere fact that Bigan saw Yania in a position of peril in the water imposed upon him no legal, although a moral, obligation or duty to go to his rescue unless Bigan was legally responsible, in whole or in part, for placing Yania in the perilous position. "[The deceased] voluntarily placed himself in the way of danger, and his death was the result of his own act.... That his undertaking was an exceedingly reckless and dangerous one, the event proves, but there was no one to blame for it but himself. He had the right to try the experiment, obviously dangerous as it was, but then also upon him rested the consequences of that experiment, and upon no one else; he may have been, and probably was, ignorant of the risk which he was taking upon himself, or know-ing it, and trusting to his own skill, he may have regarded it as easily superable. But in either case, the result of his ignorance, or of his mistake, must rest with himself and can-not be charged to the defendants." The law imposes on Bigan no duty of rescue.

Order [dismissing the complaint] affirmed.

QUESTIONS

1. What happened in this case? If Yania couldn't swim, why did he jump?

2. Identify each of the arguments made by Yania's widow. For each, explain how the judge dealt with it.

3. According to the judge, Bigan would have been liable in this case under certain circum-stances that did not apply here. What are those circumstances?

4. Suppose you could revise the law of rescue. Would you hold people responsible for doing something to help others in an emergency? If so, what circumstances would trigger a duty to rescue? How much would be required of a rescuer?

■ ■ ■

Justifying the "No Duty to Rescue" Rule

The men who wrote the Bill of Rights were not concerned that government might do too little for the people, but that it might do too much to them.

— RICHARD POSNER[2]

The ruling in *Yania v. Bigan* is still valid. While there are some exceptions, in general, in the U.S. legal system, we do not have a duty or responsibility to rescue those who are endangered.

There are both philosophical and practical reasons against imposing a duty to res-cue. Traditionally, our society has tended to grant maximum leeway to individual free-dom of choice. Requiring that people help one another in emergencies would infringe on that freedom by forcing people to act when they might choose not to. Further, imposing an affirmative duty to rescue presupposes that there is agreement that rendering assis-tance is always the right thing to do. Is there really such consensus? Beliefs and opinions about the right way to behave in a given situation might vary widely across our diverse societies. If we are to grant genuine respect to each person's freedom of conscience, shouldn't we insist on legal enforcement of "right" behavior only when it is unavoidable?

---

[2] *Jackson v. City of Joliet*, 715 F. 2d 1200, 1203 (7th Cir. 1983), in which Judge Richard Posner explains why someone in need of emergency assistance has no constitutional right to it.

Shouldn't we reserve punishment or liability for the times when people actively injure others, and allow rescue to be a matter of personal choice? In a sense, those who do not choose to rescue are not behaving badly; rather, they are merely doing nothing. As U.S. Supreme Court Justice Oliver Wendell Holmes once said, "While there is properly in law a duty not to harm, there is not ... a negative duty not to allow harm to happen."

In the next excerpt, nineteenth-century philosopher John Stuart Mill describes the connection between individual freedom of choice and the law of the liberal democratic state.

ON LIBERTY
John Stuart Mill

Over himself, over his own body and mind, the individual is sovereign....

This, then, is the appropriate region of human liberty. It comprises, first, the inward domain of consciousness; demanding liberty of conscience, in the most comprehensive sense; liberty of thought and feeling; absolute freedom of opinion and sentiment on all subjects, practical or speculative, scientific, moral, or theological.... Secondly, the principle requires liberty of tastes and pursuits; of framing the plan of our life to suit our own character; of doing as we like, subject to such consequences as may follow; without impediment from our fellow-creatures, so long as what we do does not harm them, even though they should think our conduct foolish, perverse, or wrong. Thirdly, from this liberty of each individual, follows the liberty, within the same limits, of combination among individuals; freedom to unite, for any purpose not involving harm to others: the persons combining being supposed to be of full age, and not forced or deceived.

No society in which these liberties are not, on the whole, respected, is free, whatever may be its form of government; and none is completely free in which they do not exist absolute and unqualified. The only freedom which deserves the name is that of pursuing our own good in our own way, so long as we do not attempt to deprive others of theirs, or impede their effort to obtain it. Each is the proper guardian of his own health, whether bodily, or mental and spiritual. Mankind are greater gainers by suffering each other to live as seems good to themselves, than by compelling each to live as seems good to the rest.

Creating a legal duty to rescue would not only run into resistance on philosophical grounds. There would also be practical objections. How would we enforce such a rule? Where would we draw the line? Must a person attempt to rescue even if it would be terribly dangerous? Should a rescuer be compensated by the victim for any injuries suffered? Who, in a crowd, are the potential rescuers: The closest witnesses? Anyone at the scene? Anyone aware of the incident?

Radical Change?

Lawgivers make the citizens good by training them in habits of right.... This is the aim of all legislation, and if it fails to do this it is a failure.

— ARISTOTLE, NICHOMACHEAN ETHICS

While the Anglo-American tradition emphasizing individual freedom of choice is a major reason our legal system demands no duty to rescue, law professor Steven Heyman argues that recognition of a duty to rescue is in line with that very tradition. His article appeared in a communitarian journal. Communitarians are concerned with reviving the notion of shared responsibility and interconnectedness at a time when, they believe, too many people view social change solely in terms of defining and enforcing an ever-growing number of personal rights.

He begins his essay by mentioning two famous examples in which bystanders chose to ignore those who desperately needed help. The first incident happened one night in March 1964. Twenty-eight-year-old Kitty Genovese was returning home to her apartment complex in a quiet, respectable neighborhood in Queens, New York. Manager of a bar in another part of Queens, she was arriving late; it was 3:00 a.m. As she left her red Fiat and began walking to her apartment, she saw a man walking towards her. He chased her, caught up with her, and attacked her with a knife. She screamed, "Oh my God, he stabbed me! Please help me! Please help me!" People opened windows, someone called out, "Let that girl alone," and several lights went on. But as more than a half hour passed, none of the witnesses did anything more. The killer had time to drive away, leaving Ms. Genovese collapsed on the sidewalk, and then to drive back to stab her again. Thirty-eight people later admitted they had heard Ms. Genovese's screams, but no one even called the police until after she was dead.[3]

The second incident happened many years later. In 1983, in New Bedford, Massachusetts, a young woman went into a bar to buy a pack of cigarettes. She was gang-raped on the pool table while customers watched and even cheered.[4]

──■■──

THE DUTY TO RESCUE: A LIBERAL-COMMUNITARIAN APPROACH
Steven J. Heyman[5]

Rescue and the Common-Law Tradition

Consider two notorious incidents: the 1964 slaying of Kitty Genovese and the 1983 New Bedford tavern rape. In both cases, neighbors or bystanders watched as a young woman was brutally and repeatedly assaulted, yet they made no effort to intervene or call for help. Under current doctrine, their inaction breached no legal duty, however reprehensible it may have been morally.

Suppose, however, that a police officer had been present at the time. Surely we would not say that the officer was free to stand by and do nothing while the attack took place. The state has a responsibility to protect its citizens against criminal violence. It performs this function largely through its police force. An officer who unjustifiably failed to prevent a violent crime would be guilty of a serious dereliction of duty, which might result in dismissal from the force or even criminal prosecution. Thus the officer would have a legal duty to act. But what if there is no officer on the scene? In that situation, the state can fulfill its responsibility to prevent violence only by relying on the assistance of those persons who are present.

Contrary to the conventional view, there is strong evidence that, for centuries, the common law of England and America did recognize an individual duty to act in precisely such cases. According to traditional legal doctrine, every person was

---

[3] A. M. Rosenthal, Thirty-Eight Witnesses: *The Kitty Genovese Case* (Berkeley, CA: University of California Press, 1999).

[4] This incident is the basis of a film, *The Accused*, with Kelly McGinnis and Jody Foster.

[5] Steven J. Heyman, "The Duty to Rescue: A Liberal-Communitarian Approach" from The Responsive Community 7(3), Summer 1997, pp. 44–49. Reprinted by permission.

entitled to protection by the government against violence and injury. In return for this protection, individuals had an obligation not merely to obey the law, but also, when necessary, to actively help enforce it.... Thus, individuals at the scene of a violent crime had a duty to intervene if they could do so without danger to themselves. If they could not, they were required to notify the authorities.

With the development of modern police forces in the 19th century, this tradition of active citizen participation in law enforcement gradually declined. In recent decades, however, it has become increasingly clear that effective crime prevention requires the efforts of the whole community—a recognition that is reflected, for example, in neighborhood crime watch and community policing programs....

Rescue and the Liberal Tradition

A duty to prevent violence finds support not only in the Anglo-American common-law tradition but also in liberal political theory. According to Locke and other natural rights theorists, individuals enter into society to preserve their lives, liberties, and properties. Under the social contract, citizens obtain a right to protection by the community against criminal violence. In return, they promise not only to comply with the laws, but also to assist the authorities in enforcing those laws. In this way, Locke writes, the rights of individuals come to be defended by "the united strength of the whole Society." In *On Liberty*, John Stuart Mill recognizes a similar duty on the part of individuals.... Mill agrees "that everyone who receives the protection of society owes a return for the benefit," including an obligation to bear one's fair share of "the labours and sacrifices incurred for defending the society or its members from injury."

In addition to endorsing a duty to prevent violence, liberal thought suggests a way to expand that duty into a general duty to rescue. According to liberal writers, the community has a responsibility to preserve the lives of its members, not only against violence but also against other forms of harm. For example, Locke, Blackstone, and Kant all maintain that the state has an obligation to relieve poverty and support those who are unable to provide for their own needs. In Locke's words, both natural right and "common charity" teach "that those should be most taken care of by the law, who are least capable of taking care of themselves." Of course, this is also a major theme in contemporary liberal political thought....

Rescue and Communitarian Theory

Communitarian theory supports and deepens the argument for a duty to rescue. On this view, community is valuable not merely as a means to the protection of individual rights, but also as a positive human good. Human nature has an irreducible social dimension that can be fulfilled only through relationships with others. The community has a responsibility to promote the good of its members. But this can be fully achieved only within a society whose members recognize a reciprocal obligation to act for the welfare of the community and their fellow citizens. A core instance is the duty to rescue.

Of course, some might doubt whether contemporary society is characterized by the kind of community required for a duty to rescue. Community is not simply given, however; it must be created. Common action, and action on behalf of others, plays a crucial role in creating relationships between people. Thus the adoption of a duty to rescue might not merely reflect, but also promote, a greater sense of community in modern society.

The Contours of a Duty to Rescue

Advocates of a duty to rescue usually propose that it be restricted to cases in which one can act with little or no inconvenience to oneself. But this does not go far enough. Because its purpose is to safeguard the most vital human interests, the duty should not be limited to easy rescues, but should require an individual to do anything reasonably necessary to prevent criminal violence or to preserve others from death or serious bodily harm. Rescue should not require self-sacrifice, however. Thus the duty should not apply if it would involve a substantial risk of death or serious bodily injury to the rescuer or to other innocent people.

This responsibility falls on individuals only in emergency situations when no officer is present. Moreover, the duty would often be satisfied by calling the police, fire department, or rescue services....

In performing the duty to rescue, one acts on behalf of the community as a whole. For this reason, one should receive compensation from the community for any expense reasonably incurred or any injury suffered in the course of the rescue. Any other rule would mean that some people would be required to bear a cost that should properly be borne by the community at large, simply because they happened to be at a place where rescue was required....

Far from diminishing liberty, the recognition of a duty to rescue would enhance it by strengthening protection for the most basic right of all—freedom from criminal violence and other serious forms of harm. And by requiring action for the sake of others, a duty to rescue also has the potential to promote a greater sense of community, civic responsibility, and commitment to the common good.

QUESTIONS

1. According to the writer, a change in our law—a new duty to rescue—might change the way people think, heightening their awareness of one another as members of a community, and leading them to be more responsive to one another. Do you think law can have such power? Can you think of any examples where a change in the law seemed to improve the moral climate of our society?

2. Do you think law should be used as a tool for shaping a shared moral climate? Why or why not?

WHEN RESCUE IS REQUIRED

The law recognizes a number of exceptions to the "no duty to rescue" rule. Many states impose criminal penalties, for example, for failing to report child abuse or an accident in which someone is killed. Only a few states—Rhode Island, Vermont, Wisconsin, Hawaii, and Minnesota—impose a more general duty to rescue by statute. In theory, violators would be fined. In fact, however, the statutes are rarely, if ever, invoked.

One means of finding a legal duty to rescue is through contract law. Certain persons assume contractual responsibilities to help others or to prevent them from being harmed. A lifeguard, for instance, cannot ignore a drowning swimmer, nor can a firefighter let a building burn. While a person could be disciplined or fired for refusing to attempt rescue under such circumstances,[6] to commit to a dangerous job such as policing or firefighting is itself a statement of willingness to risk one's life to save lives—to risk rescue as a part of an ordinary day's work. In fact, of the 343 firefighters killed on September 11, 2001, 60 were not on duty that day, but responded to the alarm as if they were.

---

[6] For reasons of public policy, however, civil lawsuits against police, fire, or other government workers are rarely permitted.

When people—trained or not—volunteer to rescue, they become legally bound to take reasonable care in finishing what they have started. In one case, an 80-year-old woman had a stroke while she was shopping at a department store. A sales-clerk led her to the store infirmary and left her unattended for six hours. By the time help arrived, her condition was irreparably aggravated, and the store was held liable for failing to carry through on the rescue attempt.[7] Liability is imposed in this kind of case for making a bad situation worse: The person in trouble may be lulled into a false sense of security, believing they will be helped, and other would-be rescuers may not realize assistance is needed.

Another exception to the "no-duty-to rescue" rule applies when a person has endangered another, even indirectly, or has participated in creating a dangerous sit-uation. When professionals in a mental institution release a violent psychotic with-out taking measures to make certain he will be properly medicated, they may be putting members of the public in danger. When organizers of a rock concert sell general admission tickets to a performance of a wildly popular group and do not provide lane control, they may be held responsible for the fatal result as fans are suffocated in the crush to gain entry.

Finally, a set of exceptions is triggered when there is a "special relationship" be-tween the person who needs help and the person who must take responsible action. Special relationships may be based on their custodial, rather intimate nature, such as that between a parent and child or between a teacher and young pupils. Or such relationships may exist because of an economic connection, such as that between an employer and employees or between a provider of public transportation and its passengers. In either type, the relationship involves a degree of dependency. The law allows those who are dependent to expect reasonable protection from harm and requires the more powerful to provide it. A father must make some effort to save his drowning infant, and a city transportation system must take reasonable steps to protect its subway riders from criminal attacks.

Ethical Decision Making: A Toolkit

We have been looking at the way U.S. law addresses the question of balancing two important values, that of freedom—the freedom of individuals like Mr. Bigan to choose not to help in an emergency, for example—and that of responsibility—the responsibility we might have to respond to one another in certain circumstances.

Suppose a business decision, although legal and profitable in the short term, causes harmful effects on people and on the natural environment. Again, there is interplay between freedom and responsibility, but here we will focus more on ethics than on law.

Ethics and the Gulf Oil Spill of 2010

The tragedy unfolding on our coast is the most painful and powerful reminder yet that the time to embrace a clean energy future is now.

—PRESIDENT BARAK OBAMA, (JUNE 15, 2010)

---

[7] *Zelenko v. Gimbel Bros. Inc.*, 287 N.Y.S. 134 (1935).

BP CEO Tony Hayward said he would just like to get his life back. You know, I say give him life plus 20.

—JAY LENO

While much ethics is indeed about individual behavior, the best even of that has considered individuals as they are situated in various nested relationships such as family, nation, class, gender, and humanity. Any rules for individuals that ignore context and situation are probably well ignored.

—HENRY SHUE

One of the largest oil companies in the world, BP (formerly British Petroleum) is a multinational corporation headquartered in London. It has subsidiaries worldwide, including two in North America. BP possesses drilling rights in the Macondo Prospect, off the coast of Louisiana in the Gulf of Mexico. In order to access the crude oil there, BP leased a rig from Transocean, the world's biggest offshore drilling company. With more than 26,000 employees and a fleet of 136 vessels, Transocean operates in some 30 countries. BP also hired Halliburton, the second largest oilfield services company, to cement and seal off the well once drilling was complete. Halliburton employs more than 50,000 people and provides services in 70 countries.

While all three of these mega-firms would play a part in this scenario, it was BP's responsibility to address safety. And safety was certainly at risk. In recent years, as the world's appetite for oil has grown and as the political complexities of obtaining it in the Middle East have increased, companies like BP have been focusing on new sites and new technologies for oil extraction. Since the 1990s, they have been exploring deep sea drilling in the Gulf of Mexico and elsewhere. Deepwater drilling in the Gulf is particularly hazardous due to the high-pressure mix of oil and natural gas trapped in pockets within a twisted landscape of salt on the seabed. Huge bubbles of gas can move suddenly to the surface with volcanic force. According to geophysicist Roger Anderson of Columbia University's Lamont-Doherty Earth Observatory, many of the ultra-deep wells in the Gulf of Mexico are full of natural gas; the dangerous bubbles that come up the pipes are called "kicks." Anytime a company enters a new deposit, he says, "it's unknown what you're going to find."[8]

So BP had to consider the risk of a "blowout," a destructive gusher of oil and/or natural gas. Industry-wide, the most commonly used safety device is a valve called a "blow-out preventer" (BOP). Located on the sea floor, it is designed to pinch through the well pipe to cut off any leak. BOPs, operated manually or automatically through a system of sensors, are not fool-proof, however. They can fail in extreme weather conditions, and they can clog during the cementing of a well or during an explosion.

BP could have installed a so-called "acoustic cut-off switch," which would activate the BOP remotely in case the rig was damaged or destroyed. Although these switches were legally required in Norway and Brazil, they were not mandated in the United States. In fact, for a decade, while U.S. lawmakers considered this safety option, BP had been lobbying hard against any such regulation, arguing that acoustic switches were too expensive—$500,000 each—and would sometimes cause unnecessary shut-downs. These would be costly too: BP's rental rate for Transocean's rig, for instance, was about $500,000 per day.

---

[8] Faye Flam, "The Dangers of Deep-Sea Oil Drilling," *The Philadelphia Inquirer*, June 7, 2010.

Although Transocean would be drilling at greater than usual depths in the Gulf of Mexico, BP was also aware that blowouts rarely occurred, and that the first line of defense, the BOP, would normally control any blowout.

As we know, the unlikely happened. On April 20, 2010, there was an explosion on *Deepwater Horizon*. The rig burned and sank over the next two days; 11 Transocean workers were killed and 17 others were injured. A leak 5,000 feet below sea level began to gush oil, ultimately releasing an estimated 4.9 million barrels of crude oil into the Gulf of Mexico over 87 days before it was capped. This was the largest marine oil spill in history.[9]

We now ask: Were the decisions made by BP before, during, and after the Gulf Spill ethical?

There are many different ways to answer this question. Ethical analysis, unlike much quantitative analysis, can be a messy, complex business, without a clear and definitive outcome. However, we do have tools at our disposal to help us make these complicated assessments.

First, let's turn to an approach that will be familiar to you. It amounts to the bed-rock principle of strategic management; it underlies the entire free market system. This value system is so embedded in both business theory and business reality that we might fail to recognize it as not only an economic perspective, but also as an ethical one.

Free Market Ethics

A basic assumption of classic microeconomic theory is that the overriding goal of any business is to be profitable. As trustees (**fiduciaries**) of the shareholders, managers have a primary responsibility to try to improve the value of shareholder investment. In fact, under the law of corporations, managers are answerable to the owners of a company—its stockholders—if they fail to take reasonable care in running it.

Milton Friedman, a well-known free market economist and a proponent of this view, has written:

> *In a free enterprise, private property system, a corporate executive is the employee of the owners of the business. He has a direct responsibility to his employers. That responsibility is to conduct the business in accordance with their desires, which generally will be to make as much money as possible while conforming to the basic rules of society, both those embodied in law and those embodied in ethical custom.... In a free society, there is one and only one social responsibility of business—to use its resources and engage in activities designed to increase its profits so long as it stays within the rules of the game, which is to say, engages in open and free competition without deception or fraud.*[10]

Friedman argues it is wrong for managers to use corporate resources to deal with problems in society at large. Decisions regarding what might be best for society should be made in the political arena, and implementation of policies agreed upon there should be funded by tax dollars. For managers to make those kinds of decisions themselves, and to use corporate monies to pay for them, is the equivalent of theft—theft of stockholders' resources.

---

[9] Information for this introductory background has been gleaned from pp. 1–3 of Tim Lemper, Josh Bruce, and Mimi C, "The BP Spill in the Gulf of Mexico: A Case Study in U.S. and International Legal and Ethical Issues," presented at the Academy of Legal Studies in Business, August 2010 in Richmond VA.

[10] "The Social Responsibility of Business is to Increase its Profits," *New York Times*, September 13, 1970.

Let's apply Friedman's thinking and free market ethical theory to BP's decision. First of all we might ask, is deepwater drilling for oil in the Gulf of Mexico likely to be profitable for BP?

Consider demand: At present, global consumption of oil is at 80 million gallons a day, and an upward trend continues, as people in developing nations learn to want what the developed world has—goods and services that are fossil fuel dependent—and are increasingly able to afford those habits of consumption. And while renewable energy is expected to cut into the virtual monopoly of fossil fuels, there remains a great deal of uncertainty as to when and to what extent this will occur.

Consider supply: About ten per cent of the world's more than 1.3 trillion gallons of oil reserves—over 800 billion barrels—lies miles under the ocean floor. Given the combination of strong global demand for hydrocarbons, robust oil prices, and technical advances that have allowed companies to go further offshore and thousands of feet beneath the seabed to extract energy resources, deepwater oil and gas production has expanded rapidly in recent years—up nearly two-thirds since 2000. Most of the new areas for exploration are in the so-called "golden triangle," along the coast of Western Africa, South America, and the Gulf of Mexico—their once-joined geological formations having been separated by the continental drift that became the Atlantic Ocean. And while deepwater oil comprises a fraction of total global production, its potential is vast. Financial analysts forecast a vigorous future for it in the next 10 to 15 years.[11]

With an estimated 30-40 billion barrels in oil and gas reserves, the Gulf of Mexico represents a development opportunity for companies like BP, a place where they can enjoy close proximity to the United States and low offshore tax rates. By 2000-2001, deepwater drilling accounted for the majority of oil production in the Gulf. In 2009, BP announced it had located a giant oil deposit about 200 miles south of Louisiana, one of a dozen such discoveries.[12] BP is the most active oil firm in the area, but it is not alone; by the end of 2009, the deep waters of the Gulf of Mexico were dotted with more than 35 drilling vessels.[13]

Considering overall strategic direction, then, it seems that continuing its deepwater oil exploration and production work in the Gulf will sustain profits and give BP a competitive advantage.

Using Friedman's analysis, we also need to ask whether the BP's actions were legal. Now that the calamitous spill has happened, the regulatory environment is in flux. The Obama administration imposed a moratorium on deepwater[14] drilling in the Gulf of Mexico pending safety studies, in summer 2010. It was lifted in October 2010, as new safety regulations were put in place. However, at the time when BP made its decision not to install the acoustic back-up switch, there was no legal requirement to do so. Milton Friedman would contend that corporations have every right to voice their opinions by, for example, lobbying vigorously—as BP did—against more costly safety mandates. Friedman would point out that corporate political activity should focus on increasing

[11] Manouchehr Takin, a senior analyst at the Centre for Global Energy Studies (CGES), quoted in Sarah Arnott, "Shell defends deepwater oil drilling, as profits soar," *The Independent*, July 30, 2010. *http://www.independent.co.uk/news/business/news/shell-defends-deepwater-oil-drilling-as-profits-soar-2039028.html*. Last visited August 7, 2010.

[12] Deepwater Oil Exploration, Wikinvest *http://www.wikinvest.com/concept/Deepwater_Oil_Exploration*. Last visited August 7, 2010.

[13] Ben Rooney, "BP Biggest Player in Deepwater Oil," June 14, 2010. *http://money.cnn.com/2010/06/11/news/companies/BP_deepwater_drilling/index.htm*. Last visited August 7, 2010.

[14] Defined as drilling more than 1,000 feet under the seabed.

shareholder value. Corporate resources should be deployed solely to increase the value of shareholder investment. The more expensive acoustic switch would only make sense, in this analysis, if it would enhance profits.

With perfect hindsight, we can see that it might have done so. The back-up switch—operated remotely to activate the BOP—might have prevented the explosion—the deaths, the injuries, the lost rig—and might have prevented the spill. Again, with perfect hindsight we can see that such a choice would have saved BP at least $20 billion in clean-up costs, untold amounts in criminal and civil lawsuits, and severe reputational damage with inevitable consequences to the bottom line. Through the summer of 2010, video images of oil spewing into the water were a constant, then-CEO of BP Tony Hayward complained that he "wanted his life back," and as BP's shockingly poor safety record was being uncovered, public outrage reached a tipping point. From boycotts of BP gas stations to Internet contests to rename the company that had recently branded itself as "Beyond Petroleum,"[15] this outrage was palpable. At least in the short term, BP lost stock value as a result of the spill; for the first time the company was unable to pay investors dividends, halting them until 2011.[16] By mid-summer 2010, the company had lost more than $100 billion in market value, the worth of its stock halved since the rig explosion.[17] Although the company has pockets deep enough to pay the legal claims against it and cleanup costs, and although the stock price will probably rebound, the spectacle of the 87-day gusher will leave BP with a lasting stigma. As oil gushed into the Gulf, there was talk of its vulnerability to a takeover by rival Exxon Mobil, and news that the British government would not intervene to prevent such a move.[18]

While these cascading negative effects are now evident, at the time BP made the decision about the back-up switch a catastrophic oil spill was an outside possibility. And even factoring in such an event, BP might have gone ahead as planned. The company had been generating strong profits—$14 billion in 2009—and would survive even an epic disaster. The public's attention span is notoriously short. Outrage can be forgotten; the need for oil is an American mantra. BP management might have noted how Exxon Mobil, responsible in 1989 for (until the Gulf spill) the biggest oil spill in U.S. history, had managed to stave off claims through vigorous defense litigation and had still not made payments to commercial fishermen nearly 20 years later. So even if BP foresaw the possibility of a major spill, moving forward with the *Deepwater Horizon* contract and continuing deepwater oil production in the Gulf of Mexico appeared be an ethical choice in microeconomic terms, well-aligned with shareholder interests.

With the this approach, there would be no need to be concerned with the interests of other stakeholders—except to the extent that these too might impact profits. BP's decision would not be made out of concern for the families whose livelihoods might be dependent on tourism or fishing in Gulf waters, in other words, or out of concern for the thousands of birds and sea creatures at risk should a spill occur. In any case, just before *Deepwater Horizon* exploded, the potential for calamity might have seemed vague and

---

[15] Some entries to the renaming contests: Blame Proof, Bad People, Black Pelican, Best Polluter, Behind Politics, Breaking Promises. For more: *http://www.greenpeace.org.uk/files/tarsands/index.html* Last visited August 8, 2010.

[16] "BP Stops Dividend Payments During Oil Spill," CBS News Business, June 16, 2010, *http://www.cbsnews.com/stories/2010/06/16/business/main6588695.shtml*. Last visited August 8, 2010.

[17] Michael Kunzelman, "BP has lost more than $100B in value since oil spill started," *USA Today*, *http://www.usatoday.com/money/industries/energy/2010-06-25-bp-stock_N.htm*. Last visited August 8, 2010.

[18] James Moore, *Bloomberg Businessweek*, July 12, 2010. *http://www.businessweek.com/globalbiz/content/jul2010/gb20100712_341314.htm*. Last visited August 8, 2010.

unlikely, while what was sharply in focus was the fact that BP was 43 days behind schedule. Delays had already cost the company more than $21 million in rig rental rates. It made sense, according to the free market approach to ethics, to push on.

Notice how this analysis meshes with a belief in expanding freedom of choice for individuals—and in minimizing government interference with that freedom. Such thinking, which we saw supporting the "no duty to rescue" rule, has been key in the development of both our market economy and our legal system. The underlying assumption is that we can best progress as a society if we grant as much leeway as possible to private preference, allowing people (and private associations of people, like corporations) to do what they think best with their own resources—as long as they do not infringe of the rights of others to do the same.

Utilitarianism: Assessing Consequences

Through much of Western history, the most influential ethical reference point has been religious; the rules to be followed were God-authored and were "written on men's hearts." It was a radical break with tradition, then, for eighteenth-century philosopher and social thinker Jeremy Bentham to suggest an entirely new frame of reference. Ethical behavior, he argued, was not a matter of pleasing God, but of bringing about as much happiness as possible for the greatest number of people. According to Bentham, the definitive moral standard is that of "utility," requiring us to consider the consequences of an act (or a social policy) for all those affected by it. One of Bentham's followers, nineteenth-century philosopher John Stuart Mill, would become the best-known proponent of this ethical approach, known as **utilitarianism**.

According to the principle of utilitarianism, the right way to behave in a given situation is to choose the alternative that is likely to produce the greatest overall good. Cost-benefit analysis, the sort of efficiency calculation that is common to business decision making—what BP might have used to assess the profitability of deepwater oil production—is based on notions of utility. As an ethical theory, however, utilitarianism asks us to compare the harms and benefits of an action not just for the decider, but for *all who will be affected by the decision*. In the BP scenario, this would mean, at the least, not only weighing the effects of the decision on BP's investors, but also looking at the consequences to other important *stakeholders*, including, for example, the workers who were killed or injured in the *Deepwater Horizon* explosion, the people living in the coastal areas of the Gulf of Mexico, and the wide array of living creatures contaminated by the oil, and the American public overall.

In a utilitarian analysis, we will want to evaluate both short and long-term consequences to these stakeholders, paying close attention to the size of each group, the nature of the effects on each group, and the likelihood that particular consequences would actually ensue. Ultimately, if the benefits that flow from a decision appear to outweigh the harms, we would identify that decision as ethical. Let's try to make this kind of complex utilitarian calculation in the Gulf scenario.

We have already assessed the consequences for one stakeholder group—BP shareholders—in the discussion above. Certainly this is a significant group, with major investors including large British insurance companies, U.S. money management firms, Norwegian, Kuwaiti, Chinese and Singaporean government-controlled investment funds. Americans own half of BP's stock, and many British pension funds are dependent on the fortunes of the company. Significant loss of stock value would have ripple effects within thousands of individual lives. Yet as we have explained, it is likely that BP's stock will regain value as time goes by. As of mid-July 2010, it was estimated the spill would cost $37 billion in clean up, fines, and compensation claims. Assuming BP alone (and not its partners) pays for all of that, the final sum would be more like $29 billion after tax deductions, an amount that would not strain BP's finances; the company was expected to generate $30 billion in 2010. Its "proven" oil and gas reserves were worth $220 billion, and the company held additional assets and equity worth $40 billion. Clearly, BP will not be going bankrupt, and can withstand the burden of costs related to the spill.[19] In sum, although we cannot forecast them perfectly, the kinds of consequences that shareholders might suffer here are financial, are spread out over thousands of individuals, and may be insignificant in the long-term.

As we turn to other stakeholder groups, we notice that they are affected much more negatively. Most tragically, 11 people were killed and 17 injured as the *Deepwater Horizon* exploded and sank. Although the number of people in this group is small, losses of life and health weigh heavily on the scale as we assess the consequences of BP's decision to forego the back-up switch. Of course at the time the decision was made, the failure of the BOP may have seemed unlikely, and utilitarian analysis would factor that in, but it would also factor in the *extent* of the possible harm, so extreme in this case.

Many have described the post-spill Gulf as a gigantic chemical experiment, with as-yet unknown effects on its delicate ecosystem. We know that, from the well-head 5,000 feet below the surface, nearly 5 million gallons of crude oil gushed into the Gulf for about three months. We also know that BP sprayed 1.8 million gallons of a chemical dispersant on the spill, causing much of it to break into tiny droplets and form several massive "plumes" with oil contaminants spiraling through the water column. As this book was being written, in the summer of 2010, only some of the environmental consequences of this disaster were evident—others had yet to unfold.

By July 2010, one third of the Gulf's fishing area—more than 80,000 square miles—had been closed,[20] affecting the livelihoods of thousands in coastal Louisiana and Mississippi. Here is a glimpse into what happened as nearly 2 million acres of Louisiana's oyster beds were declared off-limits:

> *Hundreds of oystermen have stopped fishing. Processors have shut down. Gulf restaurants have closed, and chains such as Red Lobster have yanked the briny morsels off their menus.... That's only the beginning. Scientists fear generations of larvae and mollusks could be wiped out, destroying harvests for years.*

> *After the Deepwater Horizon rig explosion, ... Louisiana officials decided to use Mississippi River water to push back encroaching oil. Culverts built into the river's levee system were opened, redirecting freshwater into saltwater estuaries. The resulting change in salinity can be fatal to the mollusks. State scientists started checking beds two weeks ago. Their early findings: a wide spread of dead oysters.[21]*

This article goes on to explain how deeply-embedded oyster harvesting (and oyster-appreciating) is in the local culture ("The oyster is to Louisiana what corn is to Iowa or

---

[19] John Schwartz, "Weighing the Possibility of Bankruptcy for BP," *New York Times* July 10, 2010; "Tallying BP's Bill on the Gulf Coast," *New York Times*, July 14, 2010.

[20] Jeff Goodell, "The Poisoning," *Rolling Stone*, July 21, 2010. The impact has been huge on the Gulf's $2.4 billion seafood industry.

[21] P.J. Huffstutter, Nicole Santa Cruz and Ashley Powers, "Oil Spill Threatens Gulf Oyster Industry, Livelihoods, *Seattle Times*, July 18, 2010. *http://seattletimes.nwsource.com/html/nationworld/2012391634_oysters19. html*. Last visited August 11, 2010.

oranges to Florida—part sustenance, part identity."), and how important the $1 billion oyster industry has been to a region recently ravaged by Hurricane Katrina. While loss to livelihood is one of the consequences of the Gulf Spill for which people can make compensable claims, there is some question about how quickly they will be paid. (Recall the decades-long struggle of Alaskan fisheries against Exxon Mobil for recovery costs.) And if fish and seafood supplies are tainted long term—or even perceived to be—consequences will be both profound and impossible to measure. This is one of the challenges of the utilitarian calculus: How do we put a number on the loss of a way of life? These kinds of ripple-effects can be felt most deeply by the most vulnerable. Along the Gulf coast, African American and immigrant communities which have recently been battered by Hurricane Katrina have been hit especially hard, both economically and psychologically; children in the area are suffering higher rates of depression since the Spill.

The Gulf is one of the most productive natural environments on the planet. Every spring, great migrations of fish and birds arrive there to spawn and lay their eggs. The area nurtures 1,200 fish species, millions of migratory birds, mammals like bottlenose dolphins, and endangered creatures like sea turtles. One of the most tragic aspects of the oil spill was its timing, in the middle of "biological spring," just as the Gulf had burst into new life, with birds returning to nest and baby pelicans cracking out of the eggs in their rookeries. The oil spill has already killed hundreds of birds, dolphins, and sea turtles—we know because we have found and counted them.[22] But what we still don't know, and won't know for many years, is how the enormous spill is affecting and will affect the creatures at the lower end of the food chain—the smaller fish, their eggs and larvae, the "filter feeders" like oysters which are nourished by the water they pump through themselves, down to the tiny plankton that is the basis for the entire ecosystem. There is tremendous uncertainty as to the damage that is occurring under the surface, within the huge plumes of water mixed with oil. Experts worry that toxicity will be locked into the food chain for years, doing damage that will be difficult to trace back to BP. As Mark David, director of Tulane University's Institute on Water Resources Law & Policy put it, "If you end up with a bunch of dead fish five years from now, it becomes very hard to prove BP killed them."[23] It is often difficult, in a utilitarian analysis, to untangle the various harms—and the benefits—that flow from a complex situation.[24]

According to Jeremy Bentham, when we evaluate consequences for those affected by an action, we should include all those who are capable of experiencing pain or pleasure. Human beings can experience pain or pleasure, but so can all sentient beings—all are conscious of such feelings. The salient inquiry, according to Bentham, is not "can they reason," but rather "can they suffer?" For the purposes of utilitarian analysis, then, we can

---

[22] As of July 2010, rescue workers had found dead, or alive but oiled, some 4,000 birds, 700 sea turtles, dozens of dolphins and a whale. This count excludes the hundreds of birds that have been left in order to avoid disturbing their nesting areas.

[23] Matthew Brown, "Teams Begin to Tally Losses and Costs of the Oil Spill," *The Philadelphia Inquirer*, July 32, 2010.

[24] In mid summer 2010, scientists detected several plumes between 2,000 and 4,000 feet below the surface. These huge—15 miles long and 5 miles wide, in one instance; 22 miles long and 6 miles wide in another—rivers of oil are likely to affect the Gulf through two mechanisms: The first is oxygen depletion. By May 2010 scientists were estimating 30 percent less oxygen inside the plumes. The second is toxic after-effects. We have no idea how these gigantic oil-contaminated undersea rivers will affect fish and other sea creatures, nor for how long. As Lisa Levin of the Scripps Institution of Oceanography puts it, "All the zones of life interact, and now they're probably all being hammered." Sharon Begley, "What the Spill Will Kill, *Newsweek*, June 14, 2010.

assume that now, and for many years to come, there will be considerable suffering on the part of vast numbers of living creatures related to the oil spill of 2010. Again, measuring that pain would be an impossible exercise, but we can sense its scope and magnitude.

There are a myriad other effects of the Gulf spill that are now or will someday be felt, most of them negatively, by other stakeholders. The tourism business in Florida has taken a big hit, for example, and although BP will eventually pay claims, the damage to perception cannot be easily repaired, and the Florida coast may endure years of economic aftershock.

As we have traced the after-effects of BP's decision not to employ a back-up switch, we see mostly harmful consequences. But if we widen our lens to examine BP's strategic decision to be a major participant in deepwater oil extraction in the Gulf of Mexico, we can detect an array of benefits. The U.S. economy is deeply reliant on energy, and on oil. To the extent that the U.S. oil supply is compromised, the economy itself is compromised. The Gulf is the source of 30 percent of the crude oil consumed in the United States,[25] and as we have seen, BP is the biggest player in the deepwater oil production in the Gulf. There can be no doubt that if BP discontinued its efforts, we would see negative reverberations for millions of U.S. citizens, who would have to pay more to build, heat and cool homes and businesses, to purchase food, and to fill the tanks of their SUVs, for example.

In late May 2010, as BP's pipe was spewing thousands of gallons of crude oil a day, the Obama administration imposed a six-month moratorium on new deepwater projects and suspended operations on more than 30 exploratory wells. In response to industry complaints, on June 22, 2010 District Court Judge Martin Feldman overturned the order, describing the "irreparable harm" it would cause. An excerpt from his opinion gives us a glimpse of the type of injury that might result should BP turn away from its Gulf oil development strategy:

> *Gulf of Mexico drilling activities rely upon a vast and complex network of technology, assets, human capital and experience. Indeed, an estimated 150,000 jobs are directly related to offshore operations. The government admits that the industry provides relatively high paying jobs in drilling and production activities. Oil and gas production is quite simply elemental to Gulf communities. There are currently approximately 3600 structures in the Gulf, and Gulf production from these structures accounts for 31% of total domestic oil production and 11% of total domestic, marketed natural gas production.... [D]eepwater oil exploration and production in the Gulf ... employ[s] over 11,875 people.[26]*

Our utilitarian analysis, as it attempts to address a range of stakeholders and the full range of consequences to them, leaves us with a more fine-grained picture but also with a host of uncertainties. On balance, it is no longer clear that BP's decisions were ethical. The harms to human and environmental stability caused by the spill seem to weigh heavily against the benefits to the local and U.S. economy of deepwater drilling itself.

Deontology: Rights and Duties

In contrast to the utilitarian concern with consequences, and with maximizing social welfare, deontological ethics is marked by steadfastness to universal principles—for example, respect for life, fairness, telling the truth, keeping promises—no matter what

---

[25] Erwin Seba, "Nearly Half Gulf of Mexico Oil Production Shut," *The Economist*, July 25, 2010. *http://www.reuters.com/article/idUSTRE66O24A20100725*. Last visited August 12, 2010.

[26] *Hornbeck Offshore Services et.al. v. Salazar*, 2010 U.S. Dist. LEXIS 61303 (E.D. La., June 22, 2010)

the consequences. At the core of this approach to making ethical choices is the understanding that moral action should be guided by certain overriding rights and duties.

The most famous deontological thinker, eighteenth-century German philosopher Immanuel Kant, believed that human beings could reason their way to a set of absolute rules for right behavior. A person should never lie, according to Kant, even when lying seems to produce a good result. Suppose someone running away from a murderer tells you where he is going to hide, and then the murderer rushes up to ask you where the first person went. Wouldn't this be a good time to lie? Kant would say there is never a good time, even in this example.

Moral behavior, then, is a matter of holding, without exception, to certain principles. Kant believed that each person has the right to be treated with respect as the equal of every other, and that each person has the corresponding duty to treat everyone else with respect as an equal.

He arrived at this by means of his **categorical imperatives**. The first of these states that people should be willing to have the reasons for their actions become universal principles. That is, people should be willing to live in a world where an action they chose to take would be repeated for the same reasons whenever the same situation arose, even if they wound up on the receiving end of such actions.

Think of BP's decision regarding the acoustic back-up switch. If we apply Kant's first categorical imperative, the decision maker should ask: Would I want to live in a world where multinational corporations drilling for oil in sensitive coastal regions cut costs by forgoing the use of safer technology? Perhaps the BP decision makers would defend such decisions, but the Kantian universalizing framework asks the decision-makers to imagine themselves at the short end of the stick. What if BP's then-CEO Tony Hayward found the English Channel—the body of water where he went to watch a yacht race in June 2010–befouled the way the Gulf was? Assuming other BP managers would be similarly upset by pollution in their home waters, in deontological terms, their actions would fall short of being ethical. We might also frame the question more broadly: "Whenever anyone is in a situation where it would be possible to save money by curtailing safety protections, what if they did so?" If BP managers valued their lives, they would not want to live in a world where this was the general rule. How would they feel stepping into a car, a subway, or an airplane?

In another formulation of the categorical imperative, Kant states that we should have respect for the intrinsic value of other people and not just use them as means to achieve our own purposes. By this Kant did not mean that people should *never* use other people at all. People "use" one another in mutually beneficial ways all the time. For example, in a typical contractual transaction, each party to the agreement gives something up to get what it wants. Each party "uses" the other: When you purchase gasoline, you "use" the oil company's product and it "uses" you to pay for it. Kant would have no objection here. Rather, he believed it was unethical for people to use others *only* as a means to accomplishing their own purposes, with no mutual benefit attached. So, if an oil company uses slave labor to build an oil pipeline in Southeast Asia, it would be violating this Kantian categorical. Here one party— the more powerful one—is effectively able to remove the free will of the other, to make it do what it wants the way a puppeteer pulls a marionette's strings. What is lost—of great ethical value in deontology—is the right to autonomy, the right to make fully informed decisions for oneself about how to live one's life.

Let's look at BP's decision-making immediately after the *Deepwater Horizon* explosion. First of all, although the company was using submersible robots to work on and to film the undersea gusher from the start, it would not permit scientists to have access to the site or to any information the company had about the leak. Meanwhile BP announced that the rate at which oil was flowing into the Gulf was relatively minimal; for the first few days after the rig exploded, it claimed the pipe was leaking 1,000 barrels (42,000 gallons) a day. A week into the spill, Sky Truth, a small nonprofit group that uses satellite images to monitor environmental crises, estimated the flow at 5,000 barrels (210,000 gallons) per day.[27] The next day, the government, over BP's objections, raised its estimate of the flow-rate to 5,000 barrels. By May 4, BP was admitting to Congress that the rate could be 60,000 barrels, the equivalent of an Exxon Valdez spill every four days.[28] But throughout this time, BP had much grimmer data in hand. Internal company documents that became public in late June revealed that BP had predicted, in the case of a failure of the BOP, a flow rate "as high as 100,000 barrels per day." Speaking to the media about this, Congressman Ed Markey, chairman of the House Select Committee on Energy Independent and Global Warming, noted that even as BP was telling the government the leak was 5,000 barrels a day it knew better:

> *It was their technology; it was their spill camp, they're the ones that should have known right from the beginning, and either to limit their liability or because they were grossly incompetent, they delayed a full response to … this disaster.*[29]

In deontological terms, the fact that BP withheld accurate and important information, combined with its superior access to it, violated the categorical imperative. In effect, the more powerful entity in this situation was preventing other people from making fully-informed decisions about critical aspects of their lives—with the rescue of the Gulf hanging in the balance.

As BP repeatedly downplayed the size of the spill, it also argued that any attempts to measure it were both impossible and unnecessary.[30] Experts sharply disputed both assertions. Scientists at the Woods Hole Oceanographic Institute in Massachusetts, for instance, have been using ultrasound to measure flow rates at the ocean floor for decades, and were ready to apply the technique to the Gulf spill, but were rebuffed. As for the importance of calculating the size of the spill, scientists say that its size relates directly to the scope of the damage that can be expected onshore and in the ocean. Environmental groups argue that understanding the flow-rate is also the key to understanding how to prepare an appropriate response capacity for the future. An accurate spill-rate number, they say, should be the touchstone of any plan to deal with the next deepwater accident.[31]

As we examine BP's actions from this angle, we see them falling short of several deontological principles. Kantian thinking maintains that certain fundamental rights should not be violated under any circumstances. Just as lying would never be acceptable with this approach, neither would an infringement of one of these basic rights. Primary among these is the right to life and to health. BP, in its decision regarding the acoustic back-up switch, put the lives and health of workers at risk—and as we

---

[27] Julie Cart, "Tiny Group has Big Impact on Spill Estimates," *LA Times*, May 1, 2010.

[28] John M. Broder, Campbell Robertson and Clifford Krauss, "Amount of Spill Could Escalate, Company Admits," *New York Times*, May 4, 2010.

[29] Justin Gillis, "Size of Spill Underestimated, Scientists Say," *New York Times*, May 13, 2010.

[30] As BP spokesperson Tom Mueller put it on May 14, 2010: "We're not going to take any extra efforts to calculate the flow there at this point. It's not relevant to the response effort, and might even detract from it." Doug Suttles. BP COO, Global Exploration said of the leak, "Since the beginning, we've said it's impossible to get a precise number."

[31] *Id.,* Gillis.

know several were killed in the rig explosion. In the aftermath, as the company persisted in withholding spill-rate data, it hampered the response. In essence, BP was lying. Here too, the *right to health* was at stake, as any hope for the health of the Gulf, and of the people who depend on it for a livelihood, would rest on the best possible clean-up and recovery.[32]

In response to the spill, BP made heavy use of a dispersant called Corexit, spraying nearly 2 million gallons on the water's surface and injecting it at the gusher to fragment the oil. This was the first time that chemical dispersants were used over such a vast area, so the whole process was experimental. Again, BP—not the government, and not the environmental scientific community, was in control. Dispersants cause the oil on the surface to form small droplets and sink. The effect is to dramatically reduce the size of an oil slick.[33] According to Jeff Goodell of *Rolling Stone*:

> *BP argued that dispersing the spill reduced the number of brown pelicans and sea turtles coated in oil, and prevented it from reaching fragile shorelines, where it is difficult to clean and deadly to breeding grounds for shrimp and other sea life. But the chemicals also benefited the company by effectively covering up the spill, breaking it up into thousands of smaller slicks that don't look so bad on the nightly news. "It's about PR," says Steiner, the scientist whose expertise helped contain the Valdez disaster. "It's about keeping the oil out of sight, and out of the public mind, so fewer people really understand what is happening in the Gulf and get outraged by it." During the Valdez response, he adds, Corexit earned a telling nickname: "Hides-it."*[34]

To the degree that BP's decision on the dispersants was intended to cover up the extent of the damage to the Gulf, the company's behavior violates Kantian principles.

One difficulty with deontology is the confusion created when different universal rights and duties crop up in the same ethical problem and seem to conflict with one another. How does one decide which absolute value should prevail? Consider the intensity of conflicting beliefs on the question of abortion. Both the right-to-life and the pro-choice factions are convinced that their points of view derive from natural rights; both embrace referents that each of them consider beyond debate, beyond compromise. We can see this kind of conflict playing itself out in the post-spill scenario in the Gulf. While some argue we need a moratorium on deepwater drilling to ensure that safety and environmental concerns are prioritized—in line with the right to life and health—others will argue (on the same grounds) that the Gulf should be re-opened immediately to the fishing and shrimping industries, and to all extractive energy projects.

Virtue Ethics: Habits of Goodness

For some critics, both the utilitarian and deontological frameworks are inadequate in a fundamental sense; while both set forth logical bases for deciding what might be called moral minima—the floor beneath which no one should drop in terms of ethical choices—they are silent on the concept of moral excellence. They also focus on the moral acceptability of

---

[32] Tim Webb and Ed Pilkington, "U.S. Congressman Says Company's Worst-case Assessment of Leak was 20 Times Higher Than Public Estimate," *The Guardian*, June 20, 2010.

[33] Because the surface oil was greatly reduced by the dispersants, collecting it by skimming was more difficult. Only 67,000 barrels were skimmed.

[34] "The Poisoning, July 21, 2010.

actions. Virtue ethics, on the other hand, directs our attention to what human beings are capable of being, on how they can cultivate the habits of good character that will naturally lead them to their fullest potential.

This strand of thinking derives from Aristotle, who argued that people develop their moral abilities, called **virtues**, through training, by being repeatedly exposed to demonstrations of decent behavior within families and communities. We learn to become courageous, generous, just, honest, cooperative, and cheerful gradually, as we become habituated to living in social settings where these qualities are exhibited and valued. Ethics, then, is not a matter of teasing out the correct choice given a series of knotty dilemmas; it is instead a lifelong conditioning process. In harmonious relationship with their communities, people thrive, learning the habits that allow them to excel at everything they are capable of doing. In a sense, they assimilate habits of generosity, temperance, fairness and courage the way a chameleon takes on the colors around itself. People who have been raised within a virtuous community are able to behave virtuously, applying ethical principles to concrete situations in a rather seamless and natural way.

Virtue ethics does raise its own set of questions, however. What does it mean to define moral character in term of one's community? What community? At present, too many people are living in family environments in which relatedness endures in spite of severe economic and psychological stresses. Half the population of the world lives in poverty. If children grow up in hardship, where the natural environment is harshly degraded and the social fabric is weakened, does the transmittal of virtuous habit become a luxury? If families cannot effectively teach virtue to their young, what are the alternatives? Schools? Religious communities? How do we judge which moral community is best?[35] And what do we mean by community in the business context? Where is the community touchstone in the Gulf Spill scenario?

To answer this question about a large company like BP, we must examine what is called "corporate culture." Here one scholar describes what is meant by the culture of an organization:

> *The pattern of basic assumptions that a given group has invented, discovered, or developed in learning to cope with its problems of external adaptation and internal integration, and that have worked well enough to be considered valid, and, therefore, to be taught to new members as the correct way to perceive, think, and feel in relation to those problems.*

More colloquially, a company might describe its culture as "the way we do things around here."

---

[35] Julie Ragatz, Associate Director of the Center for Ethics in Financial Services at The American College, answers the question this way: "The virtuous person is one who thrives mentally, physically and in community with others (socially). [No matter where they have been raised], people who are ungenerous and unjust will not get along with other people. People who lack courage will be anxious and fearful, people who are intemperate will be physically sick. People who are rageful are ill in all aspects. While there are differences among communities, most agree that there is a core set of virtues rooted in the sort of beings we are—namely beings who depend on others, have emotions and a self-consciousness, have physical bodies and can think rationally." Ragatz goes on to talk about conflicts among communities and their effects on virtue development: "Communities overlap in a series of concentric circles, the virtue of integrity demands that a person carry the same moral values and commitments at work, at home and in her community engagement. Fractured people, people who espouse one value in church and a different one in the boardroom cannot by definition flourish."

What forces inside a company determine the type of culture that develops inside it? What forces outside a company might influence that process?

BP is the fourth largest company in the world. It is third largest of the six "super-majors," the giant multinational energy (oil and natural gas) corporations. A quick sketch of its history: In 1908, when a wealthy Englishman struck oil in Iran, the Anglo-Persia Oil Company was formed. This was a colonial operation, partially owned by the British Empire. Eventually, as the countries in the region (and the world) began to shed their colonial status and to nationalize their natural resources, British Petroleum (as it was then called) had to regroup and reset its corporate strategy. The government sold its stake in the company in 1995, and it came under the leadership of John Browne, a bold, charismatic dealmaker.

In the late 1990s, at a cost of $200 million, Browne launched an enormous corporate re-branding exercise, changing the company's name from British Petroleum to BP, coining the slogan "Beyond Petroleum" and redesigning its corporate insignia. Instead of the more than 70-year-old British Petroleum shield, the new logo was a yellow white and green sunburst, suggesting the company was looking past oil and gas toward an eco-friendly future of renewable energy. Billboards announced, for example, that BP was partnering with Urban Park Rangers to release four bald eagles into upper Manhattan, or that BP "believes in alternative energy. Like solar and cappuccino." At the end of each ad, was the sly comment, "It's a start."

Originally conceived as pure public relations, this massive re-imaging seemed to have caught the imagination of CEO Browne. He began consulting with Greenpeace and pledged to spend $1 billion on solar technology. Instead of joining companies like Exxon, who with President Bush were challenging the science behind global warming and calling for more research, Browne argued that the U.S. should sign the Kyoto Protocol, the world's first treaty for addressing greenhouse gas emissions." Companies composed of highly skilled and trained people can't live in denial of mounting evidence gathered by hundreds of the most reputable scientists in the world," he declared, speaking at Stanford University in 2002. Ironically, given BP's core mission, he was advancing the case for reduced consumption of fossil fuels: "Climate change is an issue which raises fundamental questions about the relationship between companies and society as a whole, and between one generation and the next."

At the same time, Browne was building the company up to be the world's second-largest oil company (after Exxon). He presided over a wave of cost-cutting and consolidation, as BP took over some of its American competitors, fired thousands of employees—many of them engineers--and streamlined itself significantly, so that it came to rely more on outside contractors. Browne distinguished himself in the industry as a risk-taker, chasing after some of the most expensive and potentially lucrative projects. He set aggressive profit goals, pushing managers to cut costs sharply in order to meet quarterly targets. By 2002, BP had gross revenues of $174 billion, 15,500 service stations in the United States, and was operating in 100 countries. In seven years, under Browne's leadership, share value had jumped 80 percent. And in the midst of the Beyond Petroleum PR blitz, BP was producing almost 3.5 billion barrels of oil and gas annually.

We can investigate BP's culture by a process of triangulation. We can look at the company's aspirations—at the values it claimed to support. We can find out what employees and experts can tell us about how the company was run, noting how those values were operationalized. And we can observe whether BP's actual track record—its behavior—reflected its values.

First, the aspirations. The company's Web site presents "Our Values:"

> *BP wants to be recognised as a great company—competitively successful and a force for progress. We have a fundamental belief that we can make a difference in the world.*
>
> *We help the world meet its growing need for heat, light and mobility. We strive to do that by producing energy that is affordable, secure and doesn't damage the environment.*
>
> *BP is progressive, responsible, innovative and performance driven.*
>
> - *Progressive: We believe in the principle of mutual advantage and build productive relationships with each other, our partners, and our customers.*
> - *Responsible: We are committed to the safety and development of our people and the communities and societies in which we operate. We aim for no accidents, no harm to people and no damage to the environment.*
> - *Innovative: We push boundaries today and create tomorrow's breakthroughs through our people and technology.*
> - *Performance driven: We deliver on our promises through continuous improvement and safe, reliable operations.*[36]

Now let's look at how the company was run, and how it performed. In 2005, a 20-foot geyser of volatile chemicals ignited at a BP plant in Texas City. Fifteen workers were killed and more than 170 people were injured. The plant, built in 1934, was long overdue for capital investment. Routine maintenance that might have prevented the accident had been delayed due to pressure to cut expenses. And there had been unstable leadership—five managers in six years.[37] Perhaps most telling was this comment from a report completed two months before the explosion, compiled by the Telos Group, a consulting firm: "We have never seen a site where the notion 'I could die today' was so real." A U.S. government investigation found the explosion was "caused by organizational and safety deficiencies at all levels of BP," fining the company a then-record $21 million for more than 300 safety violations.

A year later BP was responsible for another horrific accident: 267,000 gallons of oil leaked in Prudhoe Bay in Alaska, the worst spill in that area—and again, the cause was preventable. Investigators found corrosion throughout miles of BP's pipe network, which was poorly maintained. Here too, the company paid more than $20 million in fines.[38]

In 2005 there were serious problems at Thunder Horse, BP's 15-story offshore production platform in the Gulf of Mexico. This was supposed to be BP's crowning glory, with the potential to produce 20 percent of the Gulf's oil, but because a valve

---

[36] *http://www.bp.com/sectiongenericarticle.do?categoryId=9002630&contentId=7005204*. Last visited August 13, 2010.

[37] According to Tom Kirchmaier, professor at Manchester Business School, Lord Browne ran BP as if it was a financial firm, with managers rotating into new positions, handed challenging profit targets, and rotated out again before the consequences of their decisions were upon them.

[38] In 2009, OSHA inspectors revisited BP's Texas City facility and discovered more than 700 safety violations, proposing a record fine of $87.4 million. Most of this was for the company's failure to abide by the prior Texas City settlement. And in March 2010, just before the Deepwater Horizon explosion, OSHA found yet more safety violations at BP's Ohio refinery, for a $62 million fine. According to one OSHA administrator, "Senior management told us they are very serious about safety, but we observed that they haven't translated their words into safe working procedures and practices, and they have difficulty applying the lessons learned from refinery to refinery or even from within refineries." Sarah Lyall, "In BP's Record, a History of Boldness and Blunders," *New York Times*, July 13, 2010.

had been installed backwards, Hurricane Dennis flooded the vessel. Then other flaws emerged—faulty welding, full of cracks and breaks. Thunder Horse had to be dismantled.

The similarities that run through these instances of failure on the part of BP also showed up in early investigations of the *Deepwater Horizon* explosion of 2010: All were high-risk ventures, marked by rushed and shoddy work, and a disregard for safety. Chairman of the House Energy and Commerce Committee Henry A. Waxman, when questioning former CEO Tony Hayward as the Gulf was gushing BP's oil, said:

> There is a complete contradiction between BP's words and deeds.... BP cut corner after corner to save a million dollars here and a few hours there. And now the whole Gulf Coast is paying the price.

We see a striking dissonance between BP's stated values ("We are committed to the safety and development of our people and the communities and societies in which we operate. We aim for no accidents, no harm to people, and no damage to the environment.") and its relentless sacrifice of safety for the sake of results. As assistant to the Secretary of Labor for OSHA Jordan Barab has said, "BP has systemic safety and health problems. They need to take their intentions and apply them much more effectively on the ground, where the hazards actually lie."[39] Such a strategy seems to have been adopted by BP rival Exxon. Scarred by its own experience of a major spill in Alaska, Exxon is now number one for safety among the oil majors. Before drilling a well, it runs complex modeling programs to forecast whatever obstacles might be encountered. Exxon trains its contractors to recognize risky behavior, and asks employees for suggestions for safety improvement. Contrast this with a confidential survey of rig workers that was taken a month before the *Deepwater Horizon* explosion. Many expressed concern about safety and felt they would be punished for reporting problems or mistakes.[40]

We come away from this analysis of the culture of BP with a sense that the "Beyond Petroleum" campaign and the company's official statements valuing safety and the protecting the environment amount to little more than empty rhetoric. In terms of virtue ethics, then, BP has much to do to close the gap between its aspirations and its ways of doing business. And given these mixed messages, we can imagine how difficult it has been for BP employees to develop the kind of virtuous habits they would need—courage, for example, even heroism—to confront a culture that repeatedly rewards speed and risk-taking over other values.

Ethic of Care

The ethical theories we have looked at so far assume that decisions about the right thing to do are ultimately private, made by individuals in isolation. Whether using their intellectual powers or responding to trained habit, people act as autonomous beings, as free agents in this process. But suppose we began ethical analysis with a different understanding? Suppose we start with the assumption that people are deeply connected to one another in webs of relationships, and that ethical decisions cannot be made outside the context of those relationships? Ethics becomes a matter of nurturing and reinforcing the

---

[39] Jad Mouawad, "Fast-Growing BP Also Has a Mounting List of Spills and Safety Lapses," New York *Times*, May 9, 2010.

[40] Robbie Brown, "Official Denies BP Put Cost Ahead of Safety at Oil Rig," *New York Times*, July 23, 2010. As of June 2010, BP had 760 OSHA fines for "willful" safety violations. Exxon Mobil had only one.

ties we have with one another. This alternative view has become known as the "ethic of care," as it is based on caring for others.

The ethic of care is based on the work of feminist psychologist Carol Gilligan, who studied moral development. Her research initially led her to believe that men and women approached moral issues from different perspectives. While most men had an individualistic focus on abstract rights and justice, women tended to focus on caring, on supporting human interconnectedness—an approach that Gilligan saw as undervalued, and which she characterized as "a different voice." Over time this understanding has shifted: Rather than a split between male versus female ethics, it is thought that both of these approaches can be accessed by either men or women.

To analyze the Gulf Spill from the perspective of the ethic of care, we will want to consider the network of relationships in this complex scenario to try to determine which are the most important, the most fundamental. We will do this by putting the Gulf Spill in context, both widening our lens to include relevant broader circumstances, and narrowing our focus to absorb some of the specifics, the particular details that make this event distinctive. Both macro and micro contextual clues will be useful. Finally, as we get to the point of establishing which are the most crucial relationships, the ethic of care requires us to think about how best to nourish and sustain them. This perspective is less concerned with following a set of abstract principles to avoid harm than with the relatively messy business of proactively caring for others. It asks us to be creative in discovering workable compromises to support the relationships that matter most.

So let's start with the broader context. Starkly evident in the bigger picture surrounding the Gulf Spill is the global hunger for energy—and for oil. Just days before the *Deepwater Horizon* explosion, the International Energy Agency forecasted that global oil demand would hit a record high in 2010 and would continue to rise as world economy recovers,[41] in spite of the recent world financial crisis. The demand for oil has remained strong in the United States since the late 1970s; developing countries are catching up fast. In June 2010 in fact, China overtook the U.S. in energy consumption—posting record crude oil imports of 5.4 million barrels per day. (In terms of per capita rates, the U.S. still leads: The average American still consumes about 10 times as much oil as the average Chinese.)

Meanwhile, obtaining the supply to meet eager demand has become more difficult. "Conventional" (near-shore and shallow) oil reserves are largely depleted, and so extraction has focused on those that are "unconventional," as companies squeeze oil out of rocks like sandstone or drill deep into water and then deep underground. Accessing oil in these locations is something like an extreme sport, rife with environmental and health risks.[42] According to Robert Bea, professor of engineering at the University of California Berkeley who has worked on offshore oil installations:

> *This is a pretty frigging complex system. You've got equipment and steel strung out over a long piece of geography starting at surface and terminating at 18,000 feet below the sea floor. So it has many potential weak points.... The danger has*

---

[41] Susan Lyon, Rebecca Lefton, Daniel J. Weiss, "Quenching Our Thirst For Oil," *Center for American Progress*, April 23, 2010. *http://www.americanprogress.org/issues/2010/04/oil_quench.html*. Last visited August 17, 2010. While the World Energy Outlook projects oil demand will hit 105 million barrels per day by 2030, a recent New York University study found that official projections like these were far too conservative, predicting total demand in 2030 at 138 mbd.

[42] The risks of deepwater drilling for oil is comparable to other fossil fuel energy extraction processes: mountaintop removal mining for coal, or example, or "fracking" (fracturing with water and chemicals under high pressure) into rock for natural gas.

escalated exponentially. We've pushed it to the edge in this very very unforgiving environment, and we don't have a lot of experience.[43]

A prominent feature of the Gulf Spill context, for the major energy firms, includes the pressure of world financial markets, which expect good news on a quarterly basis. So the majors compete fiercely, amidst powerful incentives to cut costs and mount high-risk, potentially lucrative ventures.

Add to this government oversight that was almost the inverse of government oversight.[44] The Minerals Management Service (MMS), a division of the federal Department of the Interior, was charged with issuing leases and regulating drilling on the Outer Continental Shelf. But for decades, it actually functioned to rubberstamp energy projects, disallowing virtually none, and granting exemptions so that firms were not required to provide "environmental impact statements."[45] The MMS, staffed with individuals with industry experience and ties, facilitated a round of back-scratching that had little to do with the public interest, granting leases, collecting payments, and sending them back to Washington. Meanwhile the oil industry kept up a flow of generous political donations: In the 2010 election cycle, for example, oil and gas contributed nearly $13 million to congressional candidates, about 71 percent of them Republicans. And for the part decade, the oil industry has been one of the most powerful lobbying groups in Washington, spending nearly a billion dollars since 1998.[46] These expenditures appear to be producing results. While he campaigned for the presidency with a host of green and alternative energy promises, Barack Obama was the recipient of energy industry support. According to the Center for Responsive Politics, over the past 20 years BP has given more than $3.5 million to federal candidates, with the largest chunk going to Obama. These donations came from both BP employees ($638,000) and from the company's political action committees (BP-related PACs supplied $2.89 million). In the spring of 2010, just three weeks before the *Deepwater Horizon* exploded, President Obama proposed expanding offshore oil exploration.[47]

Now if we examine some of the specific contextual details surrounding the Gulf Spill, we see that the MMS was aware of problems that deepwater drilling operators were having with that key equipment component, the blowout preventer or BOP. The agency had studies from 2002 and 2004 revealing malfunctions of the so-called "blind shear ram" blades inside the BOPs that were designed to slice through pipes and seal

---

[43] Quoted in John McQuaid, "The Gulf Oil Spill: An Accident Waiting to Happen," *Yale Environment 360*, May 10, 2010.

[44] Observers have noted an intriguing similarity: Both the Securities and Exchange Commission and the now-dismantled Minerals and Management Service were rife with anti-government culture. Both operated on the assumption that industry was to be trusted. There were staffers at both agencies who were watching porn on government computers instead of worrying about what might be going on either the trading floor or the ocean floor. Paul M. Barratt, "Surviving the Spill," *Bloomberg Business Week*, June 7-13, 2010.

[45] In 2009, BP's *Deepwater Horizon* lease received such an exemption, based on company analyses downplaying the likely size of an offshore spill, stating the "most likely size" would be 4,600 barrels. The actual spill has been estimated to be about 25 times that size.

[46] David M. Hershzenhorn and Eric Lightblau, "Tricky Balance For Politicians for Oil States," *New York Times*, June 18, 2010.

[47] Erika Lovley, "Obama Biggest Recipent of BP Cash," *Politico*, May 5, 2010. *http://www.politico.com/news/stories/0510/36783.html*. Last visited August 18, 2010. Although Obama was the biggest recipient of BP's support in the 2008 election cycle, Democrats received only 40 percent of their contributions. Moreover commentators have suggested that Obama's willingness to open up offshore drilling was a strategic move to make a federal green energy bill more likely.

blown out well-heads. According to experts, the integrity of the blind shear ram is the key, the most crucial factor for safety in deepwater drilling. In a rare instance of adopting a regulation, the MMS began requiring companies to submit evidence that their blind shear rams would function under high pressure conditions. Yet in 2009, when the agency reviewed BP's application to begin drilling the Macondo well, it ignored its own rules. MMS approved the permit without proof that BP's BOP could actually shear pipe and seal a well at 5,000 feet. It never asked for and never reviewed BP's own data—a report completed in 2000 pointing to vulnerabilities in this critically important piece of equipment.[48]

Another contextual detail surrounding the Gulf Spill is the way decisions had to be made under pressure, and by representatives of different companies with different ways of doing business. As we recall, *Deepwater Horizon* was BP's operation, but the work was done on a Transocean rig leased by BP (for about a half million dollars a day), and Halliburton was hired to provide cementing services, to reinforce and seal off the well as drilling was completed. University of California Berkeley engineer Robert Bea has described a problem with fragmented responsibilities here:

> *Each of these organizations has fundamentally different goals. BP wants access to hydrocarbon resources that feed their refinery and distribution network. Halliburton provides oil field services. Transocean drives drill rigs, kind of like taxicabs. Each has different operating processes.*[49]

And each of them had different orientations. On April 20, 2010, BP was trying to seal the well and move on; its concerns were cost and speed—the project was already more than a month behind schedule. On the rig itself, Transocean workers were more concerned with controlling the well. This culture clash would come to a head shortly before the explosion. At an investigative hearing in May 2010, Douglas H. Brown, chief mechanic for *Deepwater Horizon*, said he witnessed a "skirmish" on the rig the morning of the blast between a BP well site leader and members of Transocean's drilling crew. According to Brown, it was sparked by BP's insistence that they displace protective, heavy drilling mud with lighter saltwater before the well was sealed with a cement plug. "I remember the company man saying 'this is how it's going to be,'" Brown testified.[50] He recalled the Transocean installation manager grumbling as they left this meeting, "Well, I guess that's what we have those pinchers for," referring to the shear rams on the BOP, implying that removing the drilling mud would risk an emergency. Hours later, the rig exploded.

Investigative environmental journalist John McQuaid, writing about the *Deepwater Horizon* disaster as "a classic 'low probability, high impact event,'" points to the assumption that was being made—by BP and by all the big oil companies doing deepwater drilling— that a major catastrophe was so unlikely it was not worth considering.[51] He writes:

> *BP and other companies tend to measure safety and environmental compliance on a day-to-day checklist basis, to the point of basing executive bonuses on those metrics.*

---

[48] David Barstow, Laura Dodd, James Glanz, Stephanie Saul and Ian Urbina, "Between Blast and Spill, One Last, Flawed Hope," *New York Times*, June 21, 2010.

[49] McQuaid, *Ibid.*

[50] Ian Urbina, "BP Used Riskier Method to Seal Well Before Blast," *New York Times*, May 26, 2010.

[51] McQuaid views the government, in the form of the MMS, as complicit in that assumption.

But even if worker accident rates fall to zero, that may reveal nothing about the risks of a major disaster.

Their resistance to planning for possible disaster is rooted, he reports, in a fear of stimulating public resistance their projects. But if the oil majors had created worst-case response plans, they would have had in place mechanisms for addressing the kind of event that occurred on April 20, 2010. They might have had a good strategy for dealing with, for example, the failure of a BOP, or a hurricane blowing into a major spill. Instead, after lobbying hard and successfully against any government requirement that they do formal disaster analyses, the companies all possess absurdly inadequate response documents. They are all the same. They all discuss arrangements to rescue walruses—which do not inhabit the Gulf of Mexico—and they all offer contact information for marine biologist who has been dead since 2005.[52]

Now that we have carefully laid out the context, we can return to the ethic of care and its primary question: Which are the most important relationships in this scenario, and how can we creatively construct ways of sustaining them? There are many different relationships of significance here, between the oil companies and the government, for example, or between the companies and their employees. But we might realize at this point that the most critically important relationships encompass more. One of the most compelling relational connections in the story of the Gulf Spill exists between the people living in the coastal Gulf of Mexico and the Gulf itself. Here are the comments of eighth-generation oysterman Kenneth Voisin, whose oyster harvesting processing company lost more than half of its business during the Spill:

> I don't think much of the nation understands—they think this is about money and jobs," he says. "But it's beyond that. It's about life. It's about who we are.... The Cajun way of life is fiercely independent.... Because we live in a place with the most glorious abundance of food.... We've always been able to turn to our surroundings to support us. Now our surroundings are threatening us because of the oil.

A similar web of relationships is of overriding importance. The scientific evidence is now overwhelming that human activity in burning fossil fuels for energy is driving climate change. This means we can trace a connection from our use of oil to global increases in drought, flooding, storms, and extinctions. It also means we can trace a connection from our use of oil to global increases in pollution, poverty, governmental corruption, and ethnic warfare. As surreal as it seems, we are positioned as a species on a fossil-fuel burning trajectory to irreparably affect the natural environment, and to destroy its ability to support our very existence. Perhaps, then, the most significant relationship we might identify as we think about the Gulf Oil Spill is vast—connecting the people now living on the planet, the planet itself, and humans yet to be born.

How might we keep *that* essential relationship healthy and strong? Depending on where we are, and who we are, and what role we can play, this will vary. The ethic of care encourages compromise and flexibility in knitting valuable relationships closer.

---

[52] Congressional questioners accused the oil companies of "Xeroxing" one another's plans. Tim Webb and Ed Pilkington, "U.S. Congressman Says Company's Worst-case Assessment of Leak was 20 Times Higher Than Public Estimate," *The Guardian*, June 20, 2010.

Here are a few ideas for sustaining the irreplaceable relational network that links humans with the natural world:

> *Corporations, particularly the energy majors, could alter their policies and practices in the light of the BP Spill, coordinating with the scientific community and government regulators to develop responsible energy policies. A level playing field works best for all players. Reasonable standards can stimulate innovative solutions and can complement the incentives of a competitive economy. Responsible energy policies might include appropriate disclosure rules that protect environmental health and safety, well-crafted crisis response plans, and government subsidies for alternative energy research and development.[53] Corporations could also lobby for the U.S. to take a leadership role in reaching the compromises needed to re-energize the world's first treaty to reduce carbon emissions, the Kyoto Protocol.*

Individuals, like you and me, could alter our habits, learning about how to make day-to-day and long-term choices that shrink our carbon footprints. As writer Peter Maass has put it, responding to the question of whether it made sense for consumers to boycott BP in the wake of the BP Spill:

> *It little matters whether we fill our tanks at BP or Exxon stations. What matters is that we visit gas stations less often.[54]*

As we look through the different ethical prisms at the Gulf Oil Spill of 2010, we see a spectrum of indicators for the way we must remake our world. All of us, singly and collectively, will need to engage our moral imaginations to make our futures possible.

Why Ethical Theory?

Having explored several approaches to ethics, we may feel unsettled by the journey, uncertain how useful it has been. Yet this unresolved aftertaste may be exactly appropriate. There are no easy answers at the intersection of law, ethics, and business. The best we can hope for may be a reflective approach, combining one or more frameworks to reach several possible solutions, and then comparing the solutions to see if they "agree."

Ideally, familiarity with these theories will support you in at least two ways as you face business dilemmas in the future. First, the models for analysis can spark creative thinking, as you brainstorm ways of handling the ethical questions that will confront you. Second, they offer you a means of explaining your thinking to others, and of advocating for new ideas. Knowing the theoretical basis for ethical decision making can help you understand your own position, and help you articulate it to your superiors, your co-workers, and those who report to you in the company.

There is a familiar "language" in the business world for most decision-making: cost-benefit analysis. Ethical theory offers you another language, making you "bilingual" in complex situations.

---

[53] As of this writing, the Obama administration had announced a new set of such subsidies. Matthew Wald, "Finding New Ways to Fill the Tank: Federal Money Flows Into Research on Gas Substitutes," *New York Times*, August 19, 2010.

[54] Peter Maass has written *Crude World: The Violent Twilight of Oil*, about the relationships between our relentless search for depleting oil supplies and world poverty, governmental corruption, and strife. This quote is from one of his blog posts: "To BP or Not to BP: Here's Why a Spill-Inspired Boycott Doesn't Make Sense." June 7, 2010.

Corporate Governance

CORPORATE ROLES, RIGHTS, AND RESPONSIBILITIES

Shareholders

Shareholders are, collectively, the owners of a corporation. As their holdings rise in value, they profit; when their shares lose value, shareholders lose. They may be private shareholders—individual investors, both large and small—or they may be institutional shareholders, such as pension funds, mutual funds, insurance companies. The legal liability of shareholders is limited by law to the amount of investment they make in the company. Their rights include:

- Receipt of true and accurate financial reports
- Dividends whenever dividends declared
- Attendance at shareholder meetings
- Vote (by proxy or in person), on:

    Membership of board of directors
    Significant mergers and acquisitions
    Changes in charter or by-laws
    Proposals by management or shareholders

Shareholders can also hold managers and directors accountable by bringing shareholder derivative suits (see below).

Board of Directors

Board members are elected by shareholders from a slate provided by management. They can be "inside directors" with ongoing or previous contractual relationships with the company, or "outside" or "independent directors" with no financial relationship with the company other than as a member of its board. Directors are held by law to a duty of loyalty. They cannot interfere with corporate opportunities, compete with the corporation, take secret profits or engage in other forms of self-dealing at the company's expense. They are also required to abide by a duty of care—to act in good faith and as reasonably prudent persons in their role as directors. These two duties are known as fiduciary duties, to be carried out by those who are entrusted with responsibility for other peoples' investments.

The board may create committees and delegate certain powers to them; since the Sarbanes-Oxley Act of 2002, all public companies must have audit committees made up of independent directors, which hire independent public accountants to supervise the audit of company financial records.

In a broad oversight function, the board sets company policy and goals. In addition, it:

- Presents financial data to shareholders
- Hires and fires management
- Slates membership of the board and of its committees
- Is authorized to file lawsuits on behalf of the corporation to recover damages

Officers and Management

The chief executive officer (CEO or President) of a company and other officers are appointed by the board of directors, and must report to the board about the ongoing operations of the corporation. Like the directors, management is held to both a duty of loyalty and a duty of care, and must.

- Run the company on a day-to-day basis
- Implement decisions made by the board of directors
- Prepare reports for the board of directors and shareholders

Corporations, Public Policy, and Money

[There are two key distinctions between the arena of the market and the arena of politics.] The first is that while markets allow persons to make choices on an individual basis, politics involves a collective process of decision-making. The second is that while choices in the marketplace are transactional in nature, political decision making has a deliberative character.

—JEFFREY NESTERUK[55]

"I was in one board meeting, and I said, 'I started this [company] to do positive things with the world and do good in The Amazon, not necessarily to get a big payout.'... And one of [the angel investors] looked me in the eye and said, 'Well, the problem is, then you went out and took $9 million of other people's money.'"

—GWENDOLYN BOUNDS[56]

Corporations are said to be "creatures of statute;" they exist because state laws allow human beings to organize themselves into entities that separate ownership and management functions as the outline above delineates. Although the legally-defined structure appears to confer a degree of representative democracy to the corporate form, with investors having the ability to vote on proposals and to sue for misconduct of managers and board members, the shareholders of a corporation have limited power to influence or control the decisions of corporate officers and directors. "Minority shareholders"— those who own so little stock with voting rights that they will always be outvoted by other shareholders—have even less control.[57]

Corporate law is structured to protect the ability of officers and directors to run a company as they see fit. According to the **business judgment rule**, there is a presumption is that, in making a business decision, the directors of a corporation act on an informed basis, in good faith and in the honest belief that the action taken is in the best interests of the company. Unless there has been "an abuse of discretion," the business judgment of corporate directors will be respected by the courts. In theory, shareholders can hold directors or officers accountable for a breach of fiduciary duties through what is called a **shareholders derivative** lawsuit. These suits are initiated by individual shareholders on behalf of the corporation as a whole, against persons or entities that have harmed the company—most often one or more of its own directors or

---

[55] Jeffrey Nesteruk, "Response: Enriching Corporate Theory," 42 AM.BUS.L.J. 91 (2005).

[56] Gwendolyn Bounds, "The Perils of Being First," *WSJ*, Mar. 19, 2007, at R 1.

[57] In Chapter 6 you will read about the hurdles shareholders face when they attempt to make proposals and bring them to a vote.

officers for breach of fiduciary duty.[58] In most states, shareholders must first make a "demand," asking the Board if they may sue. These and other pre-conditions limit the frequency of shareholders derivative suits.

Critical to understanding the role of corporations in American society is a legal fiction created by the courts in the late nineteenth century: the idea that a corporation is a "person" entitled to Constitutional protections.

■　■　■

Citizens United, a nonprofit corporation with an annual budget of $12 million, receives support from individual donations and for-profit corporations. In January 2008, Citizens United released to theatres *Hillary: The Movie*, a 90-minute negative documentary about then-Senator Hillary Clinton. Later, the group wanted to make it available through video-on-demand, but feared doing so would violate the Bipartisan Campaign Reform Act of 2002 (BCRA). That federal election law banned corporations and unions both from using general treasury funds to make contributions to candidates and from using independent expenditures for "electioneering communication"—speech that expressly advocates the election or defeat of a candidate within 30 days of a primary or 60 days of a general election. Violations carried both civil and criminal penalties. Citizens United challenged the BCRA in court as a violation of its First Amendment rights. In January 2010, the Supreme Court ruled in favor of Citizens United, overruling precedent cases, including *Austin v. Michigan Chamber of Commerce* (1990). The case turned on differing interpretations of the First Amendment protection for free speech and—as the following excerpts make clear—the role of corporations in the political process.

CITIZENS UNITED v. FEDERAL ELECTION COMMISSION
United States Supreme Court, 2010, 130 S.Ct. 876

Justice KENNEDY delivered the opinion of the Court. He is joined by Chief Justice ROBERTS, Justices SCALIA, ALITO, and THOMAS (in part).

… Speech is an essential mechanism of democracy, for it is the means to hold officials accountable to the people…. The right of citizens to inquire, to hear, to speak, and to use information to reach consensus is a precondition to enlightened self-government and a necessary means to protect it. The First Amendment "has its fullest and most urgent application to speech uttered during a campaign for political office."…

For these reasons, political speech must prevail against laws that would suppress it…. Laws that burden political speech are "subject to strict scrutiny," which requires the Government to prove that the restriction "furthers a compelling interest and is narrowly tailored to achieve that interest."…

If the First Amendment has any force, it prohibits Congress from fining or jailing citizens, or associations of citizens, for simply engaging in political speech….

[The precedent case, *Austin*, justified a Michigan state law that banned corporations from using corporate funds to support electoral candidates, finding a compelling governmental interest in preventing the "corrosive and distorting effects of immense

---

[58] In other words, shareholders attempt to bring a suit that they believe the board of directors should have brought against persons or entities that have harmed the company, including suits individual officers or members of the board guilty of wrongdoing.

aggregations of wealth that are accumulated with the help of the corporate form and that have little or no correlation to the public's support for the corporation's political ideas." Justice Kennedy rejects that reasoning:]

If the anti-distortion rationale were to be accepted ... it would permit Government to ban political speech simply because the speaker is an association that has taken on the corporate form....

[T]he *Austin* majority undertook to distinguish wealthy individuals from corporations on the ground that "[s]tate law grants corporations special advantages—such as limited liability, perpetual life, and favorable treatment of the accumulation and distribution of assets." This does not suffice, however, to allow laws prohibiting speech. "It is rudimentary that the State cannot exact as the price of those special advantages the forfeiture of First Amendment rights."...

Austin interferes with the "open marketplace" of ideas protected by the First Amendment.... It permits the Government to ban the political speech of millions of associations of citizens.[59]...

The censorship we now confront is vast in its reach. The Government has "muffle[d] the voices that best represent the most significant segments of the economy."... And "the electorate [has been] deprived of information, knowledge and opinion vital to its function." By suppressing the speech of ... both for-profit and nonprofit [corporations], the Government prevents their voices and viewpoints from reaching the public and advising voters on which persons or entities are hostile to their interests....

"[T]he First Amendment protects the right of corporations to petition legislative and administrative bodies."... Corporate executives and employees counsel Members of Congress and Presidential administrations on many issues, as a matter of routine and often in private.... When that phenomenon is coupled with [the BCRA] the result is that smaller or nonprofit corporations cannot raise a voice to object when other corporations, including those with vast wealth, are cooperating with the Government. That cooperation may sometimes be voluntary, or it may be at the demand of a Government official who uses his or her authority, influence, and power to threaten corporations to support the Government's policies. Those kinds of interactions are often unknown and unseen. The speech that [the BCRA] forbids, though, is public, and all can judge its content and purpose....

When Government seeks to use its full power, including the criminal law, to command where a person may get his or her information or what distrusted source he or she may not hear, it uses censorship to control thought. This is unlawful. The First Amendment confirms the freedom to think for ourselves....

[After concluding that independent expenditures by corporations do not give rise to corruption or the appearance of corruption, the Court addresses another justification put forward to defend the ban.]

The Government contends further that corporate independent expenditures can be limited because of its interest in protecting dissenting shareholders from being compelled to fund corporate political speech.... There is ... little evidence of abuse that cannot be corrected by shareholders "through the procedures of corporate democracy."...

For the reasons above, it must be concluded that *Austin* was not well reasoned.... *Austin* is undermined by experience since its announcement. Political speech is so ingrained in our culture that speakers find ways to circumvent campaign finance laws.... Corporations, like individuals, do not have monolithic views. On certain topics corporations may possess valuable expertise, leaving them the best equipped to point out errors or fallacies in speech of all sorts, including the speech of candidates and elected officials.

Rapid changes in technology—and the creative dynamic inherent in the concept of free expression—counsel against upholding a law that restricts political speech in certain media

---

[59] Kennedy notes that most of the 5.8 million for-profit corporations filing tax returns in 2006 are "small corporations." More than 75% of them have less than $1 million in receipts per year. Ninety-six percent of the 3 million businesses that belong to the U.S. Chamber of Commerce have fewer than 100 employees.

or by certain speakers. Today, 30-second television ads may be the most effective way to convey a political message. Soon, however, it may be that Internet sources, such as blogs and social networking Web sites, will provide citizens with significant information about political candidates and issues. Yet [the BCRA] would seem to ban a blog post expressly advocating the election or defeat of a candidate if that blog were created with corporate funds.... The First Amendment does not permit Congress to make these categorical distinctions based on the corporate identity of the speaker and the content of the political speech.

Due consideration leads to this conclusion: *Austin* should be and now is overruled. We return to the principle ... that the Government may not suppress political speech on the basis of the speaker's corporate identity. No sufficient governmental interest justifies limits on the political speech of nonprofit or for-profit corporations.

Justice SCALIA, with whom Justice ALITO joins, and with whom Justice THOMAS joins in part, concurring.

...The dissent says that when the Framers "constitutionalized the right to free speech in the First Amendment, it was the free speech of individual Americans that they had in mind." That is no doubt true. All the provisions of the Bill of Rights set forth the rights of individual men and women—not, for example, of trees or polar bears. But the individual person's right to speak includes the right to speak in association with other individual persons. Surely the dissent does not believe that speech by the Republican Party or the Democratic Party can be censored because it is not the speech of "an individual American." It is the speech of many individual Americans, who have associated in a common cause, giving the leadership of the party the right to speak on their behalf. The association of individuals in a business corporation is no different—or at least it cannot be denied the right to speak on the simplistic ground that it is not "an individual American."...

The [First] Amendment is written in terms of "speech," not speakers. Its text offers no foothold for excluding any category of speaker, from single individuals to partnerships of individuals, to unincorporated associations of individuals, to incorporated associations of individuals—and the dissent offers no evidence about the original meaning of the text to support any such exclusion.... [T]o exclude or impede corporate speech is to muzzle the principal agents of the modern free economy. We should celebrate rather than condemn the addition of this speech to the public debate.

Justice STEVENS, with whom Justice GINSBURG, Justice BREYER, and Justice SOTOMAYOR join, concurring in part and dissenting in part

... In the context of election to public office, the distinction between corporate and human speakers is significant. Although they make enormous contributions to our society, corporations are not actually members of it. They cannot vote or run for office. Because they may be managed and controlled by nonresidents, their interests may conflict in fundamental respects with the interests of eligible voters. The financial resources, legal structure, and instrumental orientation of corporations raise legitimate concerns about their role in the electoral process. Our lawmakers have a compelling constitutional basis, if not also a democratic duty, to take measures designed to guard against the potentially deleterious effects of corporate spending in local and national races....

[T]he Framers and their contemporaries ... held very different views about the nature of the First Amendment right and the role of corporations in society. Those few corporations that existed at the founding were authorized by grant of a special legislative charter.... Corporations were created, supervised, and conceptualized as quasi-public entities, "designed to serve a social function for the state." It was "assumed that [they] were legally privileged organizations that had to be closely scrutinized by the legislature because their purposes had to be made consistent with public welfare."...

The individualized charter mode of incorporation reflected the "cloud of disfavor under which corporations labored" in the early years of this Nation. Thomas Jefferson famously fretted that corporations would subvert the Republic. General incorporation statutes, and widespread acceptance of business corporations as socially useful actors, did not emerge until the 1800's....

Unlike our colleagues, [the Framers] had little trouble distinguishing corporations from human beings, and when they constitutionalized the right to free speech in the First Amendment, it was the free speech of individual Americans that they had in mind. While individuals might join together to exercise their speech rights, business corporations, at least, were plainly not seen as facilitating such associational or expressive ends.... [I]t seems to me implausible that the Framers believed "the freedom of speech" would extend equally to all corporate speakers, much less that it would preclude legislatures from taking limited measures to guard against corporate capture of elections....

[O]ver the course of the past century Congress has demonstrated a recurrent need to regulate corporate participation in candidate elections to "'[p]reserv[e] the integrity of the electoral process, preven[t] corruption, ... sustai[n] the active, alert responsibility of the individual citizen,'" protect the expressive interests of shareholders, and "'[p]reserv[e] ... the individual citizen's confidence in government.'"... Continuously for over 100 years, this line of "[c]ampaign finance reform has been a series of reactions to documented threats to electoral integrity obvious to any voter, posed by large sums of money from corporate or union treasuries."...

Austin set forth some of the basic differences [between human beings and corporations]. Unlike natural persons, corporations have "limited liability" for their owners and managers, "perpetual life," separation of ownership and control, "and favorable treatment of the accumulation and distribution of assets ... that enhance their ability to attract capital and to deploy their resources in ways that maximize the return on their shareholders' investments." Unlike voters in U.S. elections, corporations may be foreign controlled. Unlike other interest groups, business corporations have been "effectively delegated responsibility for ensuring society's economic welfare"; they inescapably structure the life of every citizen. "'[T]he resources in the treasury of a business corporation,'" furthermore, "'are not an indication of popular support for the corporation's political ideas.'"..."'They reflect instead the economically motivated decisions of investors and customers. The availability of these resources may make a corporation a formidable political presence, even though the power of the corporation may be no reflection of the power of its ideas.'"

It might also be added that corporations have no consciences, no beliefs, no feelings, no thoughts, no desires. Corporations help structure and facilitate the activities of human beings, to be sure, and their "personhood" often serves as a useful legal fiction. But they are not themselves members of "We the People" by whom and for whom our Constitution was established....

Corporate "domination" of electioneering, can generate the impression that corporations dominate our democracy. When citizens turn on their televisions and radios before an election and hear only corporate electioneering, they may lose faith in their capacity, as citizens, to influence public policy. A Government captured by corporate interests, they may come to believe, will be neither responsive to their needs nor willing to give their views a fair hearing. The predictable result is cynicism and disenchantment: an increased perception that large spenders "'call the tune'" and a reduced "'willingness of voters to take part in democratic governance.'" To the extent that corporations are allowed to exert undue influence in electoral races, the speech of the eventual winners of those races may also be chilled. Politicians who fear that a certain corporation can make or break their reelection chances may be cowed into silence about that corporation. On a variety of levels, unregulated corporate electioneering might diminish the ability of citizens to "hold officials accountable to the people," and disserve the goal of a public debate that is "uninhibited, robust, and wide-open."...

When corporations use general treasury funds to praise or attack a particular candidate for office, it is the shareholders ... who are effectively footing the bill. Those shareholders who disagree with the corporation's electoral message may find their financial investments being used to undermine their political convictions....

At bottom, the Court's opinion is ... a rejection of the common sense of the American people, who have recognized a need to prevent corporations from undermining self-government since the founding, and who have fought against the distinctive corrupting potential of corporate electioneering since the days of Theodore Roosevelt. It is a strange time to repudiate that common sense. While American democracy is imperfect, few outside the majority of this Court would have thought its flaws included a dearth of corporate money in politics.

QUESTIONS

1. What are the primary arguments advanced by Justice Kennedy, writing for the majority, against the reasoning of the *Austin* case and against the restrictions of BCRA? He mentions that shareholders who do not agree with the political views supported by corporate expenditures are protected by "corporate democracy." What might he mean by that? Given what you have read about corporate legal structure, do you agree?

2. Articulate the differing views of the corporation that emerge from the opinions in this case.

3. Elsewhere in this case, Justice Kennedy writes:

   Favoritism and influence are not ... avoidable in representative politics. It is in the nature of an elected representative to favor certain policies, and, by necessary corollary, to favor the voters and contributors who support those policies. It is well understood that a substantial and legitimate reason, if not the only reason, to cast a vote for, or to make a contribution to, one candidate over another is that the candidate will respond by producing those political outcomes the supporter favors. Democracy is premised on responsiveness....

   He goes on to argue that "[t]he appearance of influence or access, furthermore, will not cause the electorate to lose faith in our democracy.... The fact that a corporation, or any other speaker, is willing to spend money to try to persuade voters presupposes that the people have the ultimate influence over elected officials." Does corporate spending on political advertising have the effect of enhancing your faith in the democratic process?

4. Dissenting Justice Stevens notes that some corporations have advocated bans on electioneering because they fear officeholders will "shake them down for supportive ads" and they will find themselves in "an ever-escalating arms race with their competitors, and the public trust in business will be eroded." Do you agree that election spending controls might create limits that corporations might welcome? Why/why not?

■ ■ ■

Corporate Social Responsibility as Strategy

The notion that corporations have a responsibility to their stakeholders—not only their stockholders—is not new. Waves of scandal—defense contracting in the 1970s, insider trading in the 1980s, the financial fraud that bankrupted companies like Enron and WorldCom and led to the mortgage-credit-banking debacles and the recession of 2008—were accompanied by public relations problems for corporations, a certain amount of public soul-searching on their part, and calls, sometimes heeded, for a ratcheting up of government regulation. Most businesses will strive to be ethical in order to stay out of crisis management mode—until and unless the profit imperative simply becomes too strong. Even an organizational culture that supports ethical decision making can be put at risk when the pressures of market competition overwhelm it.

In the second decade of the twenty-first century, business is coming to understand that sustainability requires that it to attend to the triple-bottom line: profits, people, and the planet. Michael E. Porter, professor at Harvard Business School, and Mark R. Kramer, senior fellow at Harvard's Kennedy School of Government, co-founded FSG Social Impact Advisors, an international nonprofit consulting firm. In this article they urge businesses to take a proactive or "strategic" approach to Corporate Social Responsibility (CSR), in which companies can zero in on what they do best to benefit both themselves and the larger society. Strategic CSR, they write, goes beyond philanthropy and beyond mitigating any harmful impacts a firm might have on its surroundings, to take advantage of an important reality: the mutual dependence of business and society.

STRATEGY & SOCIETY: THE LINK BETWEEN COMPETITIVE ADVANTAGE AND CORPORATE SOCIAL RESPONSIBILITY
Michael Porter and Mark R. Kramer[60]

Integrating Business and Society

Successful corporations need a healthy society. Education, health care, and equal opportunity are essential to a productive workforce. Safe products and working conditions not only attract customers but lower the internal costs of accidents. Efficient utilization of land, water, energy, and other natural resources makes business more productive. Good government, the rule of law, and property rights are essential for efficiency and innovation. Strong regulatory standards protect both consumers and competitive companies from exploitation. Ultimately, a healthy society creates expanding demand for business, as more human needs are met and aspirations grow. Any business that pursues its ends at the expense of the society in which it operates will find its success to be illusory and ultimately temporary.

At the same time, a healthy society needs successful companies. No social program can rival the business sector when it comes to creating the jobs, wealth, and innovation that improve standards of living and social conditions over time. If governments, NGOs, and other participants in civil society weaken the ability of business to operate productively, they may win battles but will lose the war, as corporate and regional competitiveness fade, wages stagnate, jobs disappear, and the wealth that pays taxes and supports non-profit contributions evaporates.

Leaders in both business and civil society have focused too much on the friction between them and not enough on the points of intersection. The mutual dependence of corporations and society implies that both business decisions and social policies must follow the principle of shared value. That is, choices must benefit both sides....

[Porter and Kramer identify "inside-out linkages," or points at which businesses can impact society—from waste disposal to hiring practices. Inside-out linkages can exist all along a company's "value chain," the series of operations it performs to produce goods or services. The authors also note "outside-in linkages," or ways in which the external environment impinges on business operations—from the quality of the labor pool, to the nature of consumer demand, to the way government creates and enforces rules and officers incentives. Outside-in linkages, according to Porter and Kramer, provide the "competitive context" for any business.]

---

[60] Michael Porter and Mark R. Kramer, "Strategy & Society: The Link Between Competitive Advantage and Corporate Social Responsibility," *Harvard Business Review* 84(12), December 2006. Used by permission of Harvard Business Publishing.

Choosing Which Social Issues to Address

No business can solve all of society's problems or bear the cost of doing so. Instead, each company must select issues that intersect with its particular business. Other social agendas are best left to those companies in other industries, NGOs, or government institutions that are better positioned to address them. The essential test that should guide CSR is not whether a cause is worthy but whether it presents an opportunity to create shared value—that is, a meaningful benefit for society that is also valuable to the business.

Our framework suggests that the social issues affecting a company fall into three categories that distinguish between the many worthy causes and the narrower set of social issues that are both important and strategic for the business.

Generic social issues may be important to society but are neither significantly affected by the company's operations nor influence the company's long-term competitiveness. **Value chain social** impacts are those that are significantly affected by the company's activities in the ordinary course of business. **Social dimensions of competitive context** are factors in the external environment that significantly affect the underlying drivers of competitiveness in those places where the company operates.

Every company will need to sort social issues into these three categories for each of its business units and primary locations, and then rank them in terms of potential impact. Into which category a given social issue falls will vary from business unit to business unit, industry to industry, and place to place.

Supporting a dance company may be a generic social issue for a utility like Southern California Edison but an important part of the competitive context for a corporation like American Express, which depends on the high-end entertainment, hospitality, and tourism cluster. Carbon emissions may be a generic social issue for a financial services firm like Bank of America, a negative value chain impact for a transportation-based company like UPS, or both a value chain impact and a competitive context issue for a car manufacturer like Toyota. The AIDS pandemic in Africa may be a generic social issue for a U.S. retailer like Home Depot, a value chain impact for a pharmaceutical company like GlaxoSmithKline, and a competitive context issue for a mining company like Anglo American that depends on local labor in Africa for its operations....

Creating a Corporate Social Agenda

[Porter and Kramer argue that companies can and should engage in "responsive CSR," acting as good corporate citizens with philanthropic activity and taking care to address any harmful impacts they might have caused. Such CSR is fittingly "responsive to stake-holders," they write, but "it cannot stop there."]

Strategic CSR

For any company, strategy must go beyond best practices. It is about choosing a unique position—doing things differently from competitors in a way that lowers costs or better serves a particular set of customer needs....

Strategic CSR moves beyond good corporate citizenship and mitigating harmful value chain impacts to mount a small number of initiatives whose social and business benefits are large and distinctive. Strategic CSR involves both inside-out and outside-in dimensions working in tandem. It is here that the opportunities for shared value truly lie.

Many opportunities to pioneer innovations to benefit both society and a company's own competitiveness can arise in the product offering and the value chain. Toyota's response to concerns over automobile emissions is an example. Toyota's Prius, the hybrid electric/gasoline vehicle, is the first in a series of innovative car models that have produced competitive advantage and environmental benefits. Hybrid engines emit as little as 10 percent of the harmful pollutants conventional vehicles produce while consuming only half as much gas. Voted 2004 Car of the Year by Motor Trend magazine, Prius has given Toyota a lead so substantial that Ford and other car companies are licensing the technology. Toyota has created a unique position with customers and is well on its way to establishing its technology as the world standard.

Urbi, a Mexican construction company, has prospered by building housing for disadvantaged buyers using novel financing vehicles such as flexible mortgage payments made through payroll deductions. Crédit Agricole, France's largest bank, has differentiated itself by offering specialized financial products related to the environment, such as financing packages for energy-saving home improvements and for audits to certify farms as organic.

Strategic CSR also unlocks shared value by investing in social aspects of context that strengthen company competitiveness. A symbiotic relationship develops: The success of the company and the success of the community become mutually reinforcing. Typically, the more closely tied a social issue is to the company's business, the greater the opportunity to leverage the firm's resources and capabilities, and benefit society.

Microsoft's Working Connections partnership with the American Association of Community Colleges (AACC) is a good example of a shared-value opportunity arising from investments in context. The shortage of information technology workers is a significant constraint on Microsoft's growth; currently, there are more than 450,000 unfilled IT positions in the United States alone. Community colleges, with an enrollment of 11.6 million students, representing 45 percent of all U.S. undergraduates, could be a major solution. Microsoft recognizes, however, that community colleges face special challenges: IT curricula are not standardized, technology used in classrooms is often outdated, and there are no systematic professional development programs to keep faculty up to date.

Microsoft's $50 million five-year initiative was aimed at all three problems. In addition to contributing money and products, Microsoft sent employee volunteers to colleges to assess needs, contribute to curriculum development, and create faculty development institutes. Note that in this case, volunteers and assigned staff were able to use their core professional skills to address a social need, a far cry from typical volunteer programs. Microsoft has achieved results that have benefited many communities while having a direct—and potentially significant—impact on the company.

Integrating Inside-out and Outside-in Practices

… Activities in the value chain can be performed in ways that reinforce improvements in the social dimensions of context. At the same time, investments in competitive context have the potential to reduce constraints on a company's value chain activities. Marriott, for example, provides 180 hours of paid classroom and on-the-job training to chronically unemployed job candidates. The company has combined this with support for local community service organizations, which identify, screen, and refer the candidates to Marriott. The net result is both a major benefit to communities and a reduction in Marriott's cost of recruiting entry-level employees. Ninety percent of those in the training program take jobs with Marriott. One year later, more than 65 percent are still in their jobs, a substantially higher retention rate than the norm.

Creating a Social Dimension to the Value Proposition

At the heart of any strategy is a unique value proposition: a set of needs a company can meet for its chosen customers that others cannot. The most strategic CSR occurs when a company adds a social dimension to its value proposition, making social impact integral to the overall strategy.

Consider Whole Foods Market, whose value proposition is to sell organic, natural, and healthy food products to customers who are passionate about food and the environment. Social issues are fundamental to what makes Whole Foods unique in food retailing and to its ability to command premium prices. The company's sourcing emphasizes purchases from local farmers through each store's procurement process. Buyers screen out foods containing any of nearly 100 common ingredients that the company considers unhealthy or environmentally damaging. The same standards apply to products made internally. Whole Foods' baked goods, for example, use only unbleached and unbromated flour.

Whole Foods' commitment to natural and environmentally friendly operating practices extends well beyond sourcing. Stores are constructed using a minimum of virgin raw materials. Recently, the company purchased renewable wind energy credits equal to 100 percent of its electricity use in all of its stores and facilities, the only Fortune 500 company to offset its electricity consumption entirely. Spoiled produce and biodegradable waste are trucked to regional centers for composting. Whole Foods' vehicles are being converted to run on biofuels. Even the cleaning products used in its stores are environmentally friendly. And through its philanthropy, the company has created the Animal Compassion Foundation to develop more natural and humane ways of raising farm animals. In short, nearly every aspect of the company's value chain reinforces the social dimensions of its value proposition, distinguishing Whole Foods from its competitors.

Not every company can build its entire value proposition around social issues as Whole Foods does, but adding a social dimension to the value proposition offers a new frontier in competitive positioning....

The Moral Purpose of Business

Corporations are not responsible for all the world's problems, nor do they have the resources to solve them all. Each company can identify the particular set of societal problems that it is best equipped to help resolve and from which it can gain the greatest competitive benefit. Addressing social issues by creating shared value will lead to self-sustaining solutions that do not depend on private or government subsidies. When a well-run business applies its vast resources, expertise, and management talent to problems that it understands and in which it has a stake, it can have a greater impact on social good than any other institution or philanthropic organization.

QUESTIONS

1. How do Porter and Kramer support the claim that business and society are interdependent?

2. According to the writers, how should a business begin to position itself in terms of strategic CSR? How could BP do so?

3. Porter and Kramer write: "For any company, strategy must go beyond best practices. It is about choosing a unique position—doing things differently from competitors in a way that lowers costs or better serves a particular set of customer needs." What does this mean with regard to strategy for CSR?

4. When immigration reform re-appeared on the nation's legislative agenda in 2007, Bill Gates and other leaders in the high tech field entered the debate, advocating changes in the law to make it easier for highly skilled software engineers to gain legal entry to the United States. How would Porter and Kramer characterize their lobbying for changes in the law?

Chapter Problems

1. Analyze this scenario from the standpoint of law and of ethics: For years, Dr. Eddingfield, a licensed physician, had been the Hurley family doctor. When Hurley became dangerously ill, he sent a messenger to Dr. Eddingfield, who told the doctor of Hurley's sickness, explained that no other doctor was available, and offered to pay Eddingfield's fee. At the time, none of his other patients needed attention, and Dr. Eddingfield was free to help the sick man, but he chose not to help. Mr. Hurley died.

2. **Research:**
   a. Although in the United States there is no general "duty to rescue," other countries do have such requirements. In France, Germany, and Russia, for example, bystanders may not legally ignore a fellow citizen who needs help in an emergency. What can you find about laws that require rescue in other parts of the world?
   b. Several states, including Wisconsin, Vermont, Hawaii, Rhode Island, and Minnesota, also have such legislation. Many states require certain persons to report specific kinds of crimes, most often child abuse. Find and compare two state statutes.
   c. While rescue is not required in the United States, it is encouraged by the existence in every state of "Good Samaritan" laws, protecting people who assist in an emergency from liability in most circumstances. Locate the Good Samaritan law in your home state. Describe it in your own words. Does it protect those who do not have medical training?

3. Leslie Bender, professor of law at Syracuse University, has written about the ethic of care and how it might reframe the law of negligence. Instead of the traditional tort standard that measures whether a defendant has behaved "reasonably, or prudently by guarding against foreseeable harm," she imagines a standard that would measure whether a defendant has demonstrated "concern and responsibility for the well-being of others and their protection from harm." Turning to the "no duty to rescue" rule, and the first case in this chapter, *Yania v. Bigan*, Bender would have us look at Yania, the "drowning stranger," in the light of this "new legal perspective, informed by ... notions of caring, responsibility, interconnectedness and cooperation." What matters now, she writes, is that "someone, a human being, a part of us, is drowning and will die without some affirmative action."

The drowning stranger ... no doubt has people who care about him—parents, spouse, children, friends, colleagues; groups he participates in—religious, social, athletic, artistic, political, educational, work-related; he may even have people who depend upon him for emotional or financial support. He is interconnected with others. If the stranger drowns, many will be harmed.... When our legal system trains us to understand the drowning stranger story as a limited event between two people, both of whom have interests at least equally worth protecting, and when the social ramifications we credit most are the impositions on personal liberty of action, we take a human situation and translate it into a cold, dehumanized algebraic equation. We forget that we are talking about human death or grave physical harms and their reverberating consequences....[61]

---

[61] "A Primer of Feminist Theory and Tort," 38 *J. Leg. Educ.* 3 (1988).

Bender goes on to argue that any duty to act would be shaped by the particular context of the situation, in line with the ethic of care. How would a rule like this have played out in Yania? What might Bigan's duty have been? What are the pros and cons of adopting such a rule in other cases where accidental harm was not directly caused by defendants?

4. Writer and investigative journalist Peter Maass has pointed out the devastation caused by the pursuit of oil reserves in the developing world. In Nigeria, throughout some 30 years of oil extraction, the government was "a carnival of corruption," with a series of military dictators siphoning off the oil wealth into foreign bank accounts. Meanwhile, hundreds of spills ruined farmland and fisheries. Social inequalities grew, as did tribal violence. For years the Niger Delta, the heart of the oil-producing region, has been the scene of terrible pollution and of an undeclared and brutal civil war.

How should companies respond to such a situation? Should they try to improve infrastructure (education, environment)? Should they try to influence government policies? Should they consider not operating within a failed state?

5. Part of the financial reform legislation passed by Congress in July 2010 was a requirement that all extractive industries—oil, coal, natural gas, and oil—make public the payments they make to foreign governments for these resources. Any extractive company that is registered with the SEC—including those which are not U.S.-based but operate within the U.S.—will have to publish such figures. Those in the transparency movement are pleased with this new regulation. According to George Soros, founder of Open Society Institute:

This law sets a new, higher global standard for financial transparency. Making public the revenues that governments receive from oil, gas and mining companies will make those governments more open and more accountable to their citizens— and will also make these industries more transparent to investors. This is a victory for everyone who recognizes that financial transparency is essential for government and corporate accountability.

Research: Find out what BP (or any other oil major) has published in response to this transparency rule. For one of the foreign nations for which it has given payment information, what can you find out about the standard of living of ordinary citizens, and the oil-related pollution of their environment?

6. In August 2010, the world's first "green oil" deal was negotiated: Ecuador agreed to leave as much as a fifth of its total oil reserves underground, in exchange for $3.6 billion, to be paid by wealthy nations. The oil lies beneath one of the most bio-diverse rainforests on the planet, the Yasuni National Park, where one hectare contains more tree species than all of North America. The deal, backed by Greenpeace and the World Wildlife Fund, will protect the ecosystem, the indigenous tribes who live there, and will "lock up" fossil fuel that would have added 407 metric tonnes of $CO2$ to the atmosphere. The compensation the Ecuadoran government receives— about half of the value of the oil if it were extracted—will be invested in renewable energy projects. Who are the stakeholders in this scenario? Analyze it by using the five ethical theories that were introduced in this chapter.

7. Environmentalist David Orr says that bringing U.S. energy use within sustainable limits will have two parts. The easy part will be passing laws regulating the use of fossil fuels. More difficult will be the second part: changing the culture of

consumption. Orr says "the frantic search for more money and more stuff" is not making us happier, but is actually "profoundly disquieting." The research on happiness shows that, "beyond some fairly minimal level of comfort, we find satisfaction in our friendships and social relationships. It's what brings us together that makes us really happy and makes life satisfying." What ideas might be at the convergence of the human need for sociability and the planet's need for humans to consume less? Can you make connections between these ideas and ethical theory?

8. Plato believed that the rulers of the ideal society should be paid no more than four times what the lowliest member of that society was paid. In the United States in 1980, CEO compensation was estimated to be 42 times that of average employees; by 2005, it was 411 times. In 2009, the average CEO of a Standard and Poors 500 Company earned $9.25 million in salary and stock options. The $700 billion government bailout of 2008 rescued many major financial institutions whose leaders had steered the U.S. into the worst economic crisis since the Great Depression. While millions of jobs, homes, and retirement savings were lost, senior executives in the financial sector were rewarded with enormous pay packages. In 2009, for example, Thomas Montag CEO of Bank of America received nearly $30 million. Lloyd Blankfein, CEO of Goldman Sachs and Walid Chammah, CEO of Morgan Stanley were each given about $10 million.[62]

   Analyze executive compensation with the ethical toolkit. How would Milton Friedman want to recompense corporate executives? How would a utilitarian? A deontological thinker? What would a virtue ethicist have to say about executive compensation? What would be the response of the ethic of care?

9. The BCRA (the law at issue in *Citizens United*) restricted both corporations and labor unions from making "independent expenditures" to finance elections. Both, however, were free to form Political Action Committees (PACs) that in turn could contribute to political campaigns and/or political advertising.
   a. PACs are highly regulated and must make detailed monthly reports to the Federal Elections Commission. What argument can you make that the right to form PACs should have led to a different outcome in this case?
   b. Consider corporations and labor unions. How are they alike? Different? Should the law treat both the same when it comes to controlling political spending?

10. As part of their commercial due diligence efforts, most major banks already address environmental risk, focusing on potential legal liability that their borrowers may face. But should banks be concerned when borrower activity fall short of being illegal, yet still threatens the environment and/or contributes to climate change? Recently HSBC has limited its relationships with companies that produce palm oil, which is associated with deforestation. Rabobank of Holland uses a checklist of conditions that must be met by oil and gas firms before they are approved for loans, including commitments to protect water quality and to improve environmental performance. And as of August 2010 the U.S.-based banking giant Wells Fargo announced it would curtail its involvement with companies that are engaged in mountaintop removal mining. How would Porter and Kramer react to these practices? Are they in line with strategic CSR?

---

[62] *http://www.aflcio.org/corporatewatch/paywatch/. Last* visited August 23, 2010.

CHAPTER PROJECT

Walking the Talk?[63]

Preparation:

Come to class with the name of a company that claims to be a socially responsible enterprise.

If you have a laptop, be sure to bring it to class. (Your professor may specifically assign some students to bring laptops to be certain there are enough.)

In-class project:

The teacher and/or class will select a number of companies to evaluate, depending on the size of the class. For example, a class of forty-eight students might evaluate four companies with twelve students assigned to each company.

For each company, students will be further divided into four groups for in-class research to assess the degree to which their company "walks the talk."

GROUP A: Company Self-image

- What does the company's Web site say about its commitment to social responsibility?
- Has the company issued any type of report about its social responsibility?
- If so, does it seem to follow the GRI (Global Reporting Initiative) standards? Was the data verified by a third party?
- Does the company mention any awards or recognition it has received?

GROUP B: Outside Rankings

- Is the company listed on any outside rankings lists? If so, how does it rank?
- What can you find out about the entity that made the rankings?
- Has the company received any awards or recognition for its social responsibility?

GROUP C: Government Regulation

- What is the company's record with the relevant government agency? (EPA for environmental impact; EEOC for diversity and civil rights issues; FTC for marketing/consumer relations; FDA for health/medical issues; OSHA for workplace safety concerns) Does the company seem to have had any violations/fines?
- Has the company partnered with any government agency to set standards or make improvements?

GROUP D: News Reports

- Has the company been in the news for a reason that casts a negative light on its "talk?" Can you find any evidence of mismanagement?
- What is the company's record with respected non-governmental Organizations (NGOs)

---

[63] Christina C. Benson, Chapter Project: Walking the Talk. [This chapter project is a shortened variation of a teaching exercise presented by Christina C. Benson to the Academy of Legal Studies in Business Master Teacher Symposium, in August 2010. It has been edited and reprinted with permission of the author.]

De-briefing your findings:

Immediately: The class regroups to share its findings and to compare the snapshot records of different companies. Results should be posted to a class blog, WIKI, or blackboard within 24 hours of class.

Upon reflection: After reading all of the results, each group should re-evaluate its company. Devise a rating scale from "A" to "F," grade your company and explain why you think the company deserves the grade you have assigned. Cite specific evidence and information you relied upon in assessing and grading.

For example, if the company can be commended for progress it has made, then give specific examples of genuine efforts. Highlight those that go beyond compliance with the law and regulations to reflect that the company has a proactive and systematic approach. Conversely, if there are shortcomings in the company's record, give specific examples. Discuss how well you think the company has addressed and resolved prior problems, and what more it could/should do.

CHAPTER 2

The Duty of Loyalty
Whistleblowing

The woods were filled with smart people at Enron, but there were really no wise people, or people who could say "this is enough."

— JOHN OLSON, Energy Industry Analyst

What matters...is not what a person is, but how closely his many personae mesh with the organizational ideal; not his willingness to stand by his actions, but his agility in avoiding blame; not what he stands for, but whom he stands with in the labyrinths of his organization.

— ROBERT JACKALL, Moral Mazes: Bureaucracy and Managerial Work

This chapter is about people who feel morally driven to call attention to problems they see at work—often at the risk of disturbing the status quo, alienating others, and bringing damaging repercussions upon themselves and their families. It is about being caught between conflicting loyalties—to one's employer, and to one's conscience—the dilemma faced by a person who must decide whether to become a "whistleblower."

Whistleblowers are people who decide to report unethical or illegal activities, usually activities under the control of their employers. They may be working for private companies, nonprofit organizations, or for the government. They may disclose information inside or outside their organizations—to supervisors, regulators, or to the media. What unites all whistleblowing is the urge to bring a disturbing situation to light, the urge to bring about some corrective change. The motivating issues range from airline, nuclear, and environmental safety to the kinds of investment practices that led the Securities and Exchange Commission to go after Goldman Sachs for its role in the financial crisis that began in 2007.

This chapter explains the legal doctrine known as **employment-at-will**, which gives employers broad discretion to fire employees "for a good reason, a bad reason, or no reason at all." Although twentieth-century exceptions to this rule have blunted its harshness, the cases demonstrate that whistleblowers often experience retaliation and have little recourse under the common law. Statutes passed in all 50 states provide some protection for employees, but wide variation exists among them; we will look at one of them. We will consider the cultural significance of having a job, and the harsh effects of employment-at-will during tough economic times. We then turn to the Sarbanes-Oxley Act of 2002, passed in the wake of financial and accounting scandals, to assess the degree to which it protects corporate whistleblowers. We consider how First Amendment freedom of speech has been interpreted by the Supreme Court to limit the right of public employees to blow the whistle. We introduce the False Claims Act, which provides financial incentives to report fraud against the government, and we learn about the personal experiences of so-called *qui tam* whistleblowers under that law.

Finally, widening our enquiry to a global perspective, we ask whether multinational corporations with clear and appropriate reporting procedures might positively impact the societies of other countries in which they do business.

Whistleblowing can wreak havoc. Those who insist that bad news must be heard may damage the reputations of their employers, and risk having their own careers destroyed. In this chapter we see that in spite of the costs, we may yet appreciate the role of the dissenters in serving the public interest when the checkpoints of our systems fail us.

■   ■   ■

In 1993, Dr. Donn Milton was hired by a nonprofit scientific research organization, IIT Research Institute (IITRI), to oversee a contract with the federal government. By 1995, his responsibilities widened as he was promoted to vice president of IITRI's Advanced Technology Group. Like other nonprofits, IITRI had been established with a public mission and was classified as tax exempt. As Dr. Milton discovered, however, the organization was "abusing its tax-exempt status by failing to report ... taxable income generated by the substantial portion of ... business that did not constitute scientific research in the public interest."

DONN MILTON, DR., v. IIT RESEARCH INSTITUTE
Fourth Circuit Court of Appeals, 1998
138 F.3d 519

WILKINSON, Chief Judge

Milton voiced his concerns to IITRI management, to no avail. In 1995, after similar allegations by a competitor, IITRI initiated an internal examination of the issue. In connection with this inquiry, IITRI received an outside opinion letter concluding that the IRS could well deem some of IITRI's projects unrelated business activities and that the income from these activities was likely taxable. Milton urged the President of IITRI, John Scott, to take action in response to the letter, but Scott refused. Milton raised the issue with IITRI's Treasurer, who agreed that IITRI was improperly claiming unrelated business income as exempt income and promised to remedy the problem after Scott's then-imminent retirement. However, this retirement did not come to pass [and the treasurer took no action]. Finally, in November 1996, when Scott falsely indicated to IITRI's board of governors that IITRI had no problem with unrelated business income, Milton reported the falsity of these statements to Lew Collens, Chairman of the Board of IITRI, and informed Collens of the opinion letter.

On January 1, 1997, Scott called Milton at home and informed him that he had been relieved of his Group Vice President title and demoted to his previous position as supervisor of TSMI. On February 12, 1997, Milton's attorney contacted IITRI about the demotion, alleging that it was unlawful retaliation for informing management of IITRI's unlawful practices. Two days later ... Milton received a letter from Collens terminating his employment with IITRI.

[The general legal rule is that employees can be fired with or without cause, but there is an exception: Under the tort of "wrongful discharge," an employee can argue that the firing clearly conflicts with "public policy."]

Milton filed suit against IITRI for wrongful discharge....

Maryland has recognized a "narrow exception" to the general rule of at-will employment: "discharge may not contravene a clear mandate of public policy." Maryland courts have found such a mandate only in limited circumstances: (1) "where an employee has been fired for refusing to violate the law..."and (2) "where [an] employee has been terminated for exercising a specific legal right or duty...."

Milton makes no claim that he was asked to break the law. He had no role in preparing IITRI's submissions to the IRS and no responsibility for their content. Instead, Milton claims he was fired for fulfilling his fiduciary duty as a corporate officer to inform IITRI's Board of activities injurious to the corporation's long-term interests....

Maryland law does provide a wrongful discharge cause of action for employees who are terminated because they perform their "statutorily prescribed duty." However, this exception to the norm of at-will employment has been construed narrowly by the Maryland courts and is not available in Milton's case.... [I]n *Thompson v. Memorial Hospital* (D. Md. 1996), the court ... held that, because a hospital employee was not chargeable with the hospital's regulatory duty to report misadministration of radiation, he did not state a claim for wrongful discharge when he was fired for making such a report. By contrast, in *Bleich v. Florence Crittenden Services* (Md. 1993), the court recognized that an educator terminated for filing a report of child abuse and neglect, as she was explicitly required to do by Maryland law, did state a claim for wrongful discharge. These cases indicate that, for Milton to recover, it is not enough that someone at IITRI was responsible for correcting its tax filings or that the corporation may have been liable for tax fraud. This responsibility was never Milton's, nor did he face any potential liability for failing to discharge it, so his claim fails.

Milton argues that his fiduciary obligations as an officer of IITRI supply the legal duty that was missing in *Thompson* and that supported the cause of action in *Bleich*. But in fact Milton labored under no "specific legal duty," to report IITRI's tax fraud to the Board. He points to no statute or other legal source that imposes on him a specific duty to report, and the broad fiduciary obligations of "care and loyalty" he alleges are simply too general to qualify as a specific legal duty that will support the claim that his discharge violates a "clear mandate of public policy." Recognizing whistleblower protection for every corporate officer fired in the wake of a disagreement over an employer's business practices would transform this "narrow exception" into a broad one indeed.

This search for a specific legal duty is no mere formality. Rather it limits judicial forays into the wilderness of discerning "public policy" without clear direction from a legislative or regulatory source.

[Judgment of dismissal affirmed.]

QUESTIONS

1. In legal terms, why did Milton lose?

2. The court here expresses concern that, if Dr. Milton were permitted to win, it would open a "Pandora's box," with "every corporate officer fired in the wake of a disagreement over an employer's business practices" a potential successful plaintiff. Reframe this argument. What is at stake here for employers?

3. This case is about conflicting loyalties. Make a list of the stakeholders (those primarily affected by the situation). Now describe the various links of loyalty—who felt responsible to whom? Analyze the situation using the ethical theories and the information about corporate governance in Chapter 1. Did Milton do the right thing?

■   ■   ■

Employment-at-Will

The right of an employee to quit the services of the employer, for whatever reason, is the same as the right of the employer, for whatever reason, to dispense with the services of such employee.

— JUSTICE HARLAN IN Adair v. U.S., 208 U.S. 161 (1908).

The Law, in its majestic equality, forbids the rich, as well as the poor, to sleep under the bridges, to beg in the streets, and to steal bread.

— ANATOLE FRANCE

Employment-at-will is a legal rule that developed in the nineteenth century, giving employers unfettered power to "dismiss their employees at will for good cause, for no cause, or even for cause morally wrong, without being thereby guilty of a legal wrong."[1] The economic philosophy of laissez-faire provided theoretical support for employment-at-will. Its legal underpinnings consisted mainly of "freedom of contract," the idea that individuals are free to choose how to dispose of what they own, including their labor, as they see fit, and that the voluntary contractual promises they make are legitimately enforceable.

Exceptions to the Rule

The earliest adjustments to the doctrine of employment-at-will were made as workers fought for the right to organize and form unions. In 1935, they were guaranteed these rights, and not long after, the U.S. Supreme Court announced that an employer could not use employment-at-will as a means of "intimidat[ing] or coerc[ing] its employees with respect to their self organization."[2] In other words, employees could not be fired as punishment for attempting to organize themselves into unions. Although at this writing only a fairly narrow slice of the U.S. workforce is unionized,[3] collective bargaining agreements typically cut against employment-at-will, protecting workers from being fired except for "good cause."

Beginning in the 1960s, federal civil rights laws created remedies against employers who fire workers because of their race, national origin, color, religion, sex, age, or disability.[4] In the 1970s and 1980s, federal and state statutes included protection from retaliation for employees who report violations of environmental or workplace safety laws, for example.[5] In the wake of the wave of scandals and the implosion of major firms such as Enron and

---

[1] *Payne v. Webster & Atlantic R.R. Co.*, 81 Tenn. 507, 519–20 (1884).

[2] *NLRB v. Jones & Laughlin Steel Corp.*, 301 U.S. 1, 45–46 (1937).

[3] According to the Bureau of Labor Standards, the union membership rate in 2009 was 12.3%, with some 15.3 million wage and salary workers belonging to unions. If we look at only nongovernmental workers, we see they represent 8 percent of the workforce today, compared with 35 percent in 1950.

[4] For example, *Civil Rights Act of 1964*, 42 U.S.C. Sec. 2000e-2a (1976); *Age Discrimination in Employment Act of 1967*, 29 U.S.C. Sec. 623(a) (1976); *Americans with Disabilities Act*, 42 U.S.C. Sec. 12112(b)(5)(A). Civil rights laws are discussed more fully in Chapter 4. Most states have similar laws, and some of these go further than the federal statutes, protecting employees against discrimination on the basis of family status or sexual orientation, for example.

[5] Federal laws include the *Toxic Substances Control Act*, 15 U.S.C. Sec. 2622(a) (1988); *Occupational Safety and Health Act*, Sec. 660(c)(1) (1988); *Water Pollution Control Act*, 33 U.S.C. Sec. 1367(a) (1988); *Safe Drinking Water Act*, 42 U.S.C.A. Sec. 300j-9(i)(1); *Energy Reorganization Act*, 42 U.S.C. Sec. 5851(a)(3) (1982); *Solid Waste Disposal Act*, 42 U.S.C. Sec. 6971(a) (1982); *Comprehensive Environmental Response, Compensation, and Liability Act*, Sec. 99610(a); *Clean Air Act* Sec. 7622(a).

Worldcom, in 2002 Congress passed corporate fraud reform legislation with whistleblower provisions protecting those who report financial misconduct in publicly traded companies. This law is known as Sarbanes-Oxley, or SOX. As of mid-2010, in response to the housing crisis and the economic meltdown of 2007-2009, another piece of reform legislation appears to be on the verge of passage; it too is likely to contain whistleblower protections related to the financial services sector.

FEDERAL WHISTLEBLOWER PROTECTION LAWS

The Occupational Safety and Health Administration (OSHA) is responsible for enforcing some seventeen whistleblower protection laws, including provisions of the following:

- Clean Air Act
- Occupational Safety and Health Act
- Safe Drinking Water Act
- Sarbanes Oxley Act
- Super Fund

The Equal Employment Opportunity Commission (EEOC) handles retaliation against those who blow the whistle on violations of the civil rights laws, including:

- Age Discrimination in Employment Act
- Americans with Disabilities Act
- Civil Rights Act of 1964 ("Title VII")

The Department of Labor is charged with protecting against whistleblowing or retaliation under various laws, including:

- Fair Labor Standards Act (wage & hour, child labor, minimum wage, overtime)
- National Labor Relations Act
- Patient Protection & Affordable Care Act (new health care reform protects hospital and medical providers)
- Sarbanes Oxley Act

The Whistleblower Protection Act covers federal employees who disclose illegal or improper government activities.

The common law has also evolved to create exceptions to the employment-at-will rule. In some states, courts have set limits by means of contract law. There are two main approaches: 1) to imply a promise of "good faith and fair dealing" in the contract of employment, or (2) to imply contractual terms (not to dismiss except for good cause, for instance) from an employer's handbook, policy statement, or behavior. However, fewer than a dozen states use the first approach. And, although the second approach has been recognized by most states, employers are on notice, and unlikely to make any express or implied promises that might be interpreted to cut against employment-at-will. In fact, they are more likely to promise the reverse, as in the following paragraph, recommended for inclusion in employment handbooks for law firms:

Your employment with the Firm is voluntarily entered into and you are free to resign at any time. Similarly, the Firm is free to conclude an employment relationship with you where it believes it is in the Firm's best interest at any time. It should be recognized that neither you, nor we, have entered into any contract of employment, express or implied. Our relationship is and will be always one of voluntary employment "at will."[6]

Tort law has also made inroads into employment-at-will, offering a plaintiff the chance to convince a jury to award substantial money damages. For almost four decades, most U.S. state courts have been shaping the tort of "wrongful discharge," a firing that contradicts "public policy"—in other words, a dismissal that undermines what is beneficial to society in general.

The problem has been how to define public policy.[7] As with contract law, this exception to employment-at-will developed simultaneously in several states, producing a crazy quilt of varying rules. Most state courts are comfortable looking to the legislature—to laws that have already been passed—for guidance. For instance, they will protect from retaliation employees who have simply exercised their legal rights to file a worker's compensation or a sexual harassment claim,[8] or who have merely performed their legal duty to serve on a jury.[9] And, if employers put their employees "between a rock and a hard place," expecting them to participate in breaking the law or be fired, most courts would again see a violation of public policy, triggering the tort of wrongful discharge.[10] For example, suppose you were an employee of BP in Louisiana, and your supervisor told you to delete safety and engineering files related to the government investigation of the 2010 oil spill in the Gulf of Mexico. Once subpoenas were issued, destroying those files would amount to obstruction of justice. So, if you refused to destroy them and were fired for that, you would succeed in a suit for wrongful discharge.

But some states still do not recognize the tort at all. In New York, for instance, while an employer could be fined for refusing to allow an employee time for jury service, the employee could not then sue for wrongful discharge.[11] As we have seen, other jurisdictions, such as Maryland, are conservative in identifying violations of public policy.

Inconsistencies like these complicate the risk for whistleblowers. They have noticed a troubling situation at work. It may be illegal; it may be "merely" unethical; it may be one they are expected to participate in; it may be one they are expected to ignore; it may involve a statute that carries protection for whistleblowers; it may not. Whistleblowers react first and must worry about the reach of "public policy" later. Characteristically unable to remain passive in the face of what they believe is wrong, they speak out. Research reveals that whistleblowers are typically long-term, highly loyal employees who feel strongly that their companies should do the right thing, and who tend to

---

[6] Victor Schachter, "The Promise of Partnership," *National Law Journal*, October 8, 1984, p. 15.

[7] Public policy is generally understood to mean that which benefits society as a whole. But this is a fuzzy concept indeed and very likely to mirror the personal and political beliefs of individual judges. As one commentator put it, "Public policy is the unruly horse of the law."

[8] *Frampton v. Central Indiana Gas Co.*, 297 N.E.2d 425 (Indiana 1973). Plaintiff fired for filing a worker's compensation claim.

[9] *Reuther v. Fowler & Williams*, 386 A.2d 119 (Pa. 1978). Plaintiff fired for jury service.

[10] For example, in *Petermann v. Int'l. Brotherhood of Teamsters*, 344 P.2d 25 (1969), plaintiff was instructed by his employer to lie when testifying before a legislative investigatory committee. He refused and was fired. The court allowed his suit for wrongful discharge, describing public policy as "that principle of law which holds that no citizen can lawfully do that which has a tendency to be injurious to the public or against the public good." Id. at 27.

[11] *Di Blasi v. Traffax Traffic Network*, 681 N.Y.S.2d 147 (N.Y. App. Div 1998).

disclose to outsiders only after trying to make headway internally.[12] The whistleblower profile is such that, if nothing is done to respond to their internal complaints, they often feel compelled to disclose to authorities outside the company—even to the media. In any case, they are taking the chance that they will not be covered under the wrongful discharge exception to employment-at-will. As one commentator put it, effectively, those who blow the whistle "very often must choose between silence and driving over a cliff."[13]

Conflicting Loyalties: Whistleblowing and Professional Ethics

THE MAYOR: We shall expect you, on further investigation, to come to the conclusion that the situation is not nearly as pressing or as dangerous as you had at first imagined.

DR. STOCKMANN: Oh! You expect that of me, do you?

THE MAYOR: Furthermore we will expect you to make a public statement expressing your faith in the management's integrity and in their intention to take thorough and conscientious steps to remedy any possible defects.

DR. STOCKMANN: But that's out of the question, Peter. No amount of patching or tinkering can put this matter right; I tell you I know! It is my firm and unalterable conviction—

THE MAYOR: As a member of the staff you have no right to personal convictions.

DR. STOCKMANN: (With a start) No right to—?

THE MAYOR: Not as a member of the staff—no! As a private individual—that's of course another matter. But as a subordinate in the employ of the Baths you have no right to openly express convictions opposed to those of your superiors.

DR. STOCKMANN: This is too much! Do you mean to tell me that as a doctor—a scientific man—I have no right to—!

THE MAYOR: But this is not purely a scientific matter; there are other questions involved—technical and economic questions.

DR. STOCKMANN: To hell with all that! I insist that I am free to speak my mind on any and all questions![14]

In the next case, the plaintiff is a doctor caught in a conflict between what her employer expects her to do, and what she feels is in line with her professional ethical responsibilities.

---

[12] Marlene Winfield, "Whistleblowers as Corporate Safety Net," in *Whistleblowing: Subversion or Corporate Citizenship?* 21, 22 (New York: St. Martin's Press: 1994).

[13] Joseph Henkert, "Management's Hat Trick: Misuse of 'Engineering Judgment' in the Challenger Incident," 10 *J. Bus. Ethics* 617, 619 (1991).

[14] Henrik Ibsen, *An Enemy of the People.*

PIERCE v. ORTHO PHARMACEUTICAL CORP.
Supreme Court of New Jersey, 1980
417 A.2d 505

Pollock, J.

This case presents the question whether an employee-at-will has a cause of action against her employer to recover damages for the termination of her employment following her refusal to continue a project she viewed as medically unethical....

Ortho specializes in the development and manufacture of therapeutic and reproductive drugs. Dr. Pierce is a medical doctor who was first employed by Ortho in 1971 as an Associate Director of Medical Research. She signed no contract except a secrecy agreement, and her employment was not for a fixed term. She was an employee-at-will. In 1973, she became the Director of Medical Research/Therapeutics, one of three major sections of the Medical Research Department. Her primary responsibilities were to oversee development of therapeutic drugs and to establish procedures for testing those drugs for safety, effectiveness, and marketability. Her immediate supervisor was Dr. Samuel Pasquale, Executive Medical Director.

In the spring of 1975, Dr. Pierce was the only medical doctor on a project team developing loperamide, a liquid drug for treatment of diarrhea in infants, children, and elderly. The proposed formulation contained saccharin. Although the concentration was consistent with the formula for loperamide marketed in Europe, the project team agreed that the formula was unsuitable for use in the United States.[15] An alternative formulation containing less saccharin might have been developed within approximately three months.

By March 28, however, the project team, except for Dr. Pierce, decided to continue with the development of loperamide [without reducing the amount of saccharin]. That decision was made apparently in response to a directive from the Marketing Division of Ortho. This decision meant that Ortho would file an investigational new drug application (IND) with the Federal Food and Drug Administration (FDA), continuing laboratory studies on loperamide, and begin work on a formulation....

Dr. Pierce continued to oppose the work being done on loperamide at Ortho. On April 21, 1975, she sent a memorandum to the project team expressing her disagreement with its decision to proceed.... In her opinion, there was no justification for seeking FDA permission to use the drug in light of medical controversy over the safety of saccharin.

Dr. Pierce met with Dr. Pasquale on May 9 and informed him that she disagreed with the decision to file an IND with the FDA.... She concluded that the risk that saccharin might be harmful should preclude testing the formula on children or elderly persons, especially when an alternative formulation might soon be available....

After their meeting on May 9, Dr. Pasquale informed Dr. Pierce that she would no longer be assigned to the loperamide project. On May 14, Dr. Pasquale asked Dr. Pierce to choose other projects.... She felt she was being demoted, even though her salary would not be decreased. Dr. Pierce [submitted a] letter of resignation.... [This is called "constructive discharge," the legal equivalent of being fired.]

Dr. Pierce claimed damages for the termination of her employment. Her complaint alleged: "The Defendant, its agents, servants and employees requested and demanded Plaintiff follow a course of action and behavior which was impossible for Plaintiff to follow

---

[15] The group's toxicologist, for instance, noted that saccharin was a "slow carcinogen"; it had produced benign and malignant tumors in test animals after 17 years. The harm it might cause would be obvious only after a long period of time, and "any intentional exposure of any segment of the human population to a potential carcinogen is not in the best interest of public health of the Ortho Pharmaceutical Corporation."

because of the Hippocratic oath she had taken, because of the ethical standards by which she was governed as a physician, and because of the regulatory schemes, both federal and state, statutory and case law, for the protection of the public in the field of health and human well-being, which schemes Plaintiff believed she should honor."

...Under the common law, in the absence of an employment contract, employers or employees have been free to terminate the employment relationship with or without cause....

Commentators have questioned the compatibility of the traditional at-will doctrine with the realities of modern economics and employment practices.... The common law rule has been modified by the enactment of labor relations legislation [prohibiting employers from firing workers because they organize or join a union]....

Recently [many] states have recognized a common law cause of action for employees-at-will who were discharged for reasons that were in some way "wrongful." The courts in those jurisdictions have taken varied approaches, some recognizing the action in tort, some in contract. Nearly all jurisdictions link the success of the wrongful discharged employee's action to proof that the discharge violated public policy....

In recognizing a cause of action to provide a remedy for employees who are wrongfully discharged, we must balance the interests of the employee, the employer, and the public. Employees have an interest in knowing they will not be discharged for exercising their legal rights. Employers have an interest in knowing they can run their businesses as they see fit as long as their conduct is consistent with public policy. The public has an interest in employment stability and in discouraging frivolous lawsuits by dissatisfied employees.

Although the contours of an exception are important to all employees-at-will, this case focuses on the special considerations arising out of the right to fire an employee-at-will who is a member of a recognized profession. One writer has described the predicament that may confront a professional employed by a large corporation: Consider, for example, the plight of an engineer who is told that he will lose his job unless he falsifies his data or conclusions, or unless he approves a product which does not conform to specifications or meet minimum standards...and the predicament of an accountant who is told to falsify his employer's profit and loss statement in order to enable the employer to obtain credit.

Employees who are professionals owe a special duty to abide not only by federal and state law, but also by the recognized codes of ethics of their professions. That duty may oblige them to decline to perform acts required by their employers. However, an employee should not have the right to prevent his or her employer from pursuing its business because the employee perceives that a particular business decision violates the employee's personal morals, as distinguished from the recognized code of ethics of the employee's profession.

We hold that an employee has a cause of action for wrongful discharge when the discharge is contrary to a clear mandate of public policy. The sources of public policy include legislation; administrative rules, regulations or decisions; and judicial decisions. In certain instances, a professional code of ethics may contain an expression of public policy. However, not all such sources express a clear mandate of public policy. For example, a code of ethics designed to serve only the interests of a profession or an administrative regulation concerned with technical matters probably would not be sufficient. Absent legislation, the judiciary must define the cause of action in case-by-case determinations.... [U]nless an employee-at-will identifies a specific expression of public policy, he may be discharged with or without cause.

[B]efore loperamide could be tested on humans, an IND had to be submitted to the FDA to obtain approval for such testing. The IND must contain complete manufacturing specifications, details of pre-clinical studies [testing on animals] which demonstrate the safe use of the drug, and a description of proposed clinical studies. The FDA then has 30 days to withhold approval of testing. Since no IND had been filed here, and even giving Dr. Pierce the benefit of all doubt regarding her allegations, it is clear that clinical testing of loperamide on humans was not imminent.

Dr. Pierce argues that by continuing to perform research on loperamide she would have been forced to violate professional medical ethics expressed in the Hippocratic oath.

She cites the part of the oath that reads: "I will prescribe regimen for the good of my patients according to my ability and my judgment and never do harm to anyone." Clearly, the general language of the oath does not prohibit specifically research that does not involve tests on humans and that cannot lead to such tests without governmental approval.

We note that Dr. Pierce did not rely on or allege violation of any other standards, including the "codes of professional ethics" advanced by the dissent. Similarly, she did not allege that continuing her research would constitute an act of medical malpractice or violate any statute....

The case would be far different if Ortho had filed the IND, the FDA had disapproved it, and Ortho insisted on testing the drug on humans....

[I]mplicit in Dr. Pierce's position is the contention that Dr. Pasquale and Ortho were obliged to accept her opinion. Dr. Pierce contends, in effect, that Ortho should have stopped research on loperamide because of her opinion about the controversial nature of the drug.

Dr. Pierce espouses a doctrine that would lead to disorder in drug research.... Chaos would result if a single doctor engaged in research were allowed to determine, according to his or her individual conscience, whether a project should continue. An employee does not have a right to continued employment when he or she refuses to conduct research simply because it would contravene his or her personal morals. An employee-at-will who refuses to work for an employer in answer to a call of conscience should recognize that other employees and their employer might heed a different call. However, nothing in this opinion should be construed to restrict the right of an employee-at-will to refuse to work on a project that he or she believes is unethical....

Under these circumstances, we conclude that the Hippocratic oath does not contain a clear mandate of public policy that prevented Dr. Pierce from continuing her research on loperamide. To hold otherwise would seriously impair the ability of drug manufacturers to develop new drugs according to their best judgment.

The legislative and regulatory framework pertaining to drug development reflects a public policy that research involving testing on humans may proceed with FDA approval. The public has an interest in the development of drugs, subject to the approval of a responsible management and the FDA, to protect and promote the health of mankind....

[Appellate division judgment for the plaintiff is reversed and the case is remanded.]

Pashman, J., Dissenting

The majority's analysis recognizes that the ethical goals of professional conduct are of inestimable social value. By maintaining informed standards of conduct, licensed professions bring to the problems of their public responsibilities the same expertise that marks their calling. The integrity of codes of professional conduct that result from this regulation deserves judicial protection from undue economic pressure. Employers are a potential source of this pressure, for they can provide or withhold until today, at their whim, job security and the means of enhancing a professional's reputation. Thus, I completely agree with the majority's ruling that "an employee has a cause of action for wrongful discharge when the discharge is contrary to a clear mandate of public policy" as expressed in a "professional code of ethics."

The Court pronounces this rule for the first time today. One would think that it would therefore afford plaintiff an opportunity to seek relief within the confines of this newly announced cause of action. By ordering the grant of summary judgment for defendant, however, the majority apparently believes that such an opportunity would be an exercise in futility. I fail to see how the majority reaches this conclusion. There are a number of detailed, recognized codes of medical ethics that proscribe participation in clinical experimentation when a doctor perceives an unreasonable threat to human health. Any one of these codes could provide the "clear mandate of public policy" that the majority requires.

Three other points made by the majority require discussion.... The first is the majority's characterization of the effect of plaintiff's ethical position. It appears to believe that Dr. Pierce had the power to determine whether defendant's proposed development program would continue at all. This is not the case, nor is plaintiff claiming the right to halt defendant's developmental efforts. [P]laintiff claims only the right to her professional autonomy. She contends that she may not be discharged for expressing her view that the clinical program is unethical or for refusing to continue her participation in the project. She has done nothing else to impede continued development of defendant's proposal; moreover, it is undisputed that defendant was able to continue its program by reassigning personnel. Thus, the majority's view that granting doctors a right to be free from abusive discharges would confer on any one of them complete veto power over desirable drug development, is ill-conceived.

The second point concerns the role of governmental approval of the proposed experimental program. In apparent ignorance of the past failures of official regulation to safeguard against pharmaceutical horrors, the majority implies that the necessity for administrative approval for human testing eliminates the need for active, ethical professionals within the drug industry. But we do not know whether the United States Food and Drug Administration (FDA) would be aware of the safer alternative to the proposed drug when it would pass upon defendant's application for the more hazardous formula. The majority professes no such knowledge. We must therefore assume the FDA would have been left in ignorance. This highlights the need for ethically autonomous professionals within the pharmaceutical industry....

The final point to which I must respond is the majority's observation that plaintiff expressed her opposition prematurely, before the FDA had approved clinical experimentation. Essentially, the majority holds that a professional employee may not express a refusal to engage in illegal or clearly unethical conduct until his actual participation and the resulting harm is imminent. This principle grants little protection to the ethical autonomy of professionals that the majority proclaims. Would the majority have Dr. Pierce wait until the first infant was placed before her, ready to receive the first dose of a drug containing 44 times the concentration of saccharin permitted in 12 ounces of soda?

I respectfully dissent.

QUESTIONS

1. The *Pierce* majority announces a new "cause of action in New Jersey for wrongful discharge when the discharge is contrary to a clear mandate of public policy." Such a mandate, it goes on to say, could be found in a professional code of ethics, yet Dr. Pierce had failed to identify one in her complaint with enough specificity. How does the dissenting judge respond to this point?

2. What is the procedure for obtaining FDA approval of a new drug? Do you agree with the majority that when Dr. Pierce stopped working on the loperamide project, the risk to human test subjects was not "imminent"?

3. Surveying the interests at stake in the case, the *Pierce* majority states:

   [W]e must balance the interests of the employee, the employer, and the public. Employees have an interest in knowing they will not be discharged for exercising their legal rights. Employers have an interest in knowing they can run their businesses as they see fit as long as their conduct is consistent with public policy. The public has an interest in employment stability and in discouraging frivolous lawsuits by dissatisfied employees.

   Are there any important stakeholder interests not mentioned here?

4. The dissent mentions "past failures of official regulation to safeguard against pharmaceutical horrors." There have been more recent failures. Since 2000, the diet drug Fen-Phen led to lung and heart disorders, the antidepressant Paxil caused birth defects in children whose mothers took Paxil while pregnant, and the painkiller Vioxx was found to double the risk of heart attack. In each instance, there was evidence that the pharmaceutical firms had evidence suggesting serious problems with drugs that were

in development or had already been brought to market. By the time Merck recalled Vioxx in late 2004, there were congressional hearings underway. A doctor in the FDA's Office of Drug Safety, David Graham, told Congress that Vioxx may have caused as many as 55,000 deaths. Graham charged his agency with being "incapable of protecting America" against dangerous drugs. A study led by Dr. Graham that looked at the cardiovascular risks of taking Vioxx was supposed to be published in a prestigious medical journal, but was pulled at the last minute after Dr. Graham received a warning from his supervisor. FDA management then began a smear campaign, with anonymous claims that his study could reflect scientific misconduct, and that Graham "bullied" his staff.

Research: Fearing his job was at risk, Graham sought help from the whistleblower support organization, the Government Accountability Project. Find out what happened. What accusations did Graham make against the FDA in 2010, regarding the diabetes drug, Avandia?

5. Agencies such as the FDA (Food and Drug Administration), the FAA (Federal Aviation Administration) or the EPA (Environmental Protection Administration) depend on corporations to generate accurate data to use in analyzing safety risks. Because government resources are limited, it must rely on companies to do their own tests, and to share all relevant results. Business decisions to hold back adverse information from regulators can be both fatal and expensive. Consider the Bridgestone/Ford debacle of 2000. In 1999, both Bridgestone and Ford knew the Wilderness tire on a Ford Explorer was dangerous; there had been dozens of tread separations and SUV rollover deaths abroad, particularly in hot climates. The two companies planned a recall in Saudi Arabia, but then made a joint decision not to alert NHTSA, fearing this would lead to a recall in the United States. By late 2000, after SUV rollovers caused more than 100 fatalities in the United States, Bridgestone was forced to recall more than 6 million tires, and both companies faced countless lawsuits. A similar scenario unfolded in 2009, when Toyota apparently learned of problems with sticking accelerators and dangerous floor mats months before it was forced to recall more than 2.3 million cars and was hit with the largest fine in the history of the NHTSA. Again, action was taken in Europe and Canada before the problem was acknowledged in the United States.

The dissent in *Pierce* mentions the need to protect "professional autonomy." What does this phrase mean? What connection might professional autonomy have with the U.S. safety regulatory scheme?

6. In 1986, responding to the *Pierce* decision of its supreme court, the New Jersey legislature adopted *The Conscientious Employee Protection Act*,[16] shielding from retaliation employees who object to, or refuse to participate in, "any activity, policy or practice which the employee reasonably believes to be incompatible with a clear mandate of public policy concerning the public health, safety or welfare." What would have been the likely outcome had Dr. Pierce sued under this new law?

7. **Research:** By 2000, every state in the United States had adopted whistleblower protection statutes of some type. Locate one such law from your home state. Under what circumstances are whistleblowers protected? Are private sector as well as government employees covered? Does coverage under the statute exclude the possibility of suing in tort?

■ ■ ■

---

[16] *N.J.S.A.* 34:19-1 et. seq.

MONTANA: WRONGFUL DISCHARGE FROM EMPLOYMENT ACT[17]

Purpose

This part sets forth certain rights and remedies with respect to wrongful discharge. Except as limited in this part, employment having no specified term may be terminated at the will of either the employer or the employee on notice to the other for any reason considered sufficient by the terminating party.

Definitions

In this part, the following definitions apply:

(2)"Discharge" includes a constructive discharge...and any other termination of employment, including resignation, elimination of the job, layoff for lack of work, failure to recall or rehire, and any other cutback in the number of employees for a legitimate business reason.

(3) "Employee" means a person who works for another for hire. The term does not include a person who is an independent contractor....

(5)"Good cause" means reasonable job-related grounds for dismissal based on a failure to satisfactorily perform job duties, disruption of the employer's operation, or other legitimate business reason. The legal use of a lawful product by an individual on the employer's premises during nonworking hours is not a legitimate business reason....

(7)"Public policy" means a policy in effect at the time of the discharge concerning the public health, safety, or welfare established by constitutional provision, statute, or administrative rule.

Elements of Wrongful Discharge

A discharge is wrongful only if:

1. it was in retaliation for the employee's refusal to violate public policy or for reporting a violation of public policy;
2. the discharge was not for good cause and the employee had completed the employer's probationary period of employment; or
3. the employer violated the express provisions of its own written personnel policy.

Remedies

1. If an employer has committed a wrongful discharge, the employee may be awarded lost wages and fringe benefits for a period not to exceed four years from the date of discharge, together with interest thereon....
2. The employee may recover punitive damages otherwise allowed by law if it is established by clear and convincing evidence that the employer engaged in actual fraud or actual malice in the discharge of the employee [for refusing to violate public policy or for reporting a violation of public policy].

Exemptions

This part does not apply to a discharge:

1. that is subject to any other state or federal statute that provides a procedure or remedy for contesting the dispute. Such statutes include those that prohibit discharge for filing complaints, charges, or claims with administrative bodies or that prohibit

---

[17] 39 *Montana Code Annotated* Chapter 2, Part 9. Puerto Rico has been the only other U.S. jurisdiction that has passed equivalent legislation.

unlawful discrimination based on race, national origin, sex, age, handicap, creed, religion, political belief, color, marital status, and other similar grounds.

2. of an employee covered by a written collective bargaining agreement or a written contract of employment for a specific term.

Preemption of Common-Law Remedies

Except as provided in this part, no claim for discharge may arise from tort or express or implied contract.

QUESTIONS

1. How would the *Milton* case have been decided had this law been in effect in Maryland? How would Dr. Pierce have fared under it?

2. What parts of this law seem to benefit employees? Employers?

3. The state laws protecting whistleblowers vary enormously, but none of them protect whistleblowers who turn to the media first. Why do you think that is so? Does that seem like sound policy to you? Does it encourage or discourage ethical behavior?

■ ■ ■

Valuing Work

As Marion Crain, law professor and Director of the Center for the Interdisciplinary Study of Work and Social Capital at Washington University, reminds us in the next reading, "Work lies at the core of the American Dream: our cultural belief is that if you are willing to work hard, your family will be secure." She points out that, while for some of us "work is a calling—a labor of love," for most, "work is the means for achieving a better social and economic condition, for ensuring that our children have a better life and more opportunities than we had." In the U.S., she writes, work also has an important ethical dimension. It is a "duty and a demonstration of the virtue of industriousness. Most importantly, work means self-sufficiency and independence." This recognition of the profound economic and cultural significance of work provides a context for Crain's analysis of employment-at-will in a time of recession. She begins by pointing to the effects of the recent economic downturn, with unemployment rates nearly doubling from November 2007 to October 2009. She also notes that the impact was strikingly different either side of the social class divide: "[T]hose at the bottom of the income strata suffered unemployment rates that rivaled or exceeded Depression-era rates, while those at the top of the strata emerged relatively unscathed."

WORK MATTERS
Marion Crain[18]

In the United States, work is mostly defined as having a job (or being self-employed). Jobs are the entry tickets to provision—health insurance, pension benefits, and social security. As feminists and critical race theorists have explained, work also includes homemaking, childcare work, unwaged work, and invisible work. Despite these multiple understandings of work, our political system, our cultural values, and our law are still largely predicated on the assumption that full citizens contribute to the country through waged work. As many scholars have explained, work confers

[18] Marion Crain, "Work Matters," *Kansas Journal of Law & Public Policy* 19(3), Spring 2010. Reprinted by permission.

not only self-sufficiency, then, but also dignity, standing in society, and membership in the social structure....

To work means, then, to participate in the public conversation about democracy, to belong. Senator Robert Wagner, the major proponent of the National Labor Relations Act (articulating the nation's commitment to protecting the right to organize a union and to collectively bargain with one's employer) argued persuasively that collective bargaining promotes democracy by providing an outlet for voice in the context where workers are most likely to learn the positive effects of democratic participation. He believed that work is the bedrock of our democracy. He believed, in short, that work matters....

Work is far more than a market exchange of labor for dollars.... Other than in family relationships, nowhere in life do people invest so much of their time, their passion, and their imagination.

[Yet] U.S. law treats the employment relation as if it were nothing more than a market transaction, as if labor were nothing more than a commodity.... Since the early 1900s, American courts have applied a default rule of employment-at-will to employment relationships of undefined duration. Pursuant to the at-will doctrine, either the employer or the employee may terminate the employment relationship at any time and for any reason without notice.... The rationale behind this doctrine is the policy favoring business flexibility—to maximize the ability of firms to shrink and enlarge their workforces in response to market fluctuations. The rule is further justified by the notion that employees are free to quit at any time to pursue more desirable market alternatives. The law envisions employees as free agents, bargaining at arm's length for the most advantageous terms and moving on to greener pastures as opportunities beckon....

The acceptance of a relatively high unemployment rate in the United States as business-as-usual is philosophically linked to our commitment to the doctrine of employment-at-will. Other countries with lower unemployment rates are not only more committed to job-saving measures in the event of financial downturns, but also have erected a legal architecture that imposes more checks on discharge to begin with.... Most countries outside the United States require just cause for discharge, although they typically permit layoffs for economic reasons as well, usually requiring notice and severance packages, at least for mass layoffs.... Some countries adhere to an even more rigorous standard, limiting employer discretion to discharge. Germany, for example, prohibits discharge except for cause or "urgent social need," reflecting the country's view that job security is a legal entitlement.

Other countries also provide more support for dislocated workers than we do. While the United States provides for benefits covering 35-40 percent of a worker's pay for up to six months, Germany provides for benefits covering 68 percent of a worker's net pay for up to a year; Sweden provides for 80 percent of pay for up to 300 days, or 450 days for workers over age 55; and Japan provides for 60-80 percent of employee wages in unemployment compensation associated with permanent layoffs.

[Crain goes on to describe some of the legal strategies other countries have developed that ease the effects on workers of economic downturns.]

Work-Spreading, Job-Saving Measures

If work is important to social engagement and a healthy democracy, wouldn't it make sense when the economy falters to incentivize work-spreading and work-saving measures instead of layoffs? Other countries have responded to economic downturns by cushioning workers against unemployment, eschewing layoffs in favor of work-sharing, reduced hours, and furloughs. The Netherlands, Germany, and Austria rely on such "labor-hoarding" policies to preserve jobs and keep unemployment low. The Dutch have been particularly successful: their unemployment rate of 3.7 percent near the end of 2009 was one of the lowest among developed nations.

In the Netherlands, "short work" programs allow firms that can demonstrate a 30 percent reduction in revenue over a two-month period to claim a government subsidy for wages lost by workers due to reductions in hours. Workers reduce their hours and are paid at a lower (subsidized) rate for the hours not worked. The subsidy is limited to a six-month period. Many European countries provide for work-sharing or have established relief work programs that allow workers who have exhausted their unemployment benefits to work part-time, yet receive full compensation through government subsidies.

The Center for Law and Social Policy (CLASP) recently surveyed a short-hours compensation system successfully deployed in seventeen states and recommended creation of a federal program based upon it. In states that have adopted "short-time work sharing" programs, employers develop a plan, consult with the union representing their workforce (if any), and submit the plan to the state unemployment insurance agency for approval. If the plan is approved, workers can collect unemployment insurance benefits to compensate them for lost work hours caused by a financial downturn. Thus, workers might work four days out of five and collect unemployment benefits for the fifth day in partial compensation for the lost pay. Such programs encourage job-saving measures by firms, who can choose to cut all workers' hours by 20 percent, rather than laying off 20 percent of the workforce. Employers benefit by maintaining a skilled workforce, avoiding training and hiring costs when the economy recovers, and retain the ability to respond immediately to a change in product markets. Workers benefit by keeping their jobs and maintaining health and pension benefits, as well as continuing to build their skills while working.

The programs are not a panacea in recessionary times: they are available only for relatively short-term reductions in hours, not for permanent reductions; the employer must still bear disproportionate costs of maintaining health and pension insurance; and they tend to benefit more junior employees disproportionately since they might have more likely lost jobs in the event of a layoff along seniority lines. The downside risk of "labor-hoarding" policies is a slow recovery, since job preservation tends to stifle the reallocation of labor from industries that are declining to those that may be growing, and even within industries, it can be difficult to separate the firms that are worth saving from those that should be allowed to fold....

Nevertheless, there is no doubt that work-sparing programs such as short-time compensation achieve significant social gains. Workers displaced during a recession sustain greater income losses even after they find new jobs than workers who are laid-off during good economic times.

Imagine finally how the law might intervene to reshape termination processes: ... [T]he law might provide for notice periods, severance pay, and transitional assistance and retraining, either through government subsidies or a tax on employers who choose layoffs over furloughs.

Investments in Human Capital

Worker training and investment in human capital are perhaps the most important sorts of programs for countries that hope to compete effectively in a global market, and the United States lags far behind its European neighbors in such investments.... European Union countries were most likely to respond to the crisis in labor markets with job-saving measures, particularly work sharing, increased investment in worker re-training programs...and national re-employment centers that assist workers in locating new jobs. The European Union has also embraced "Flexicurity," which couples unemployment benefits with retraining and transitional assistance to help displaced workers adapt to labor market restructuring. Flexicurity reflects a commitment to foster career development and upward mobility for workers, while at the same time serving economic development goals by allowing employers flexibility in employment to maintain productivity and compete effectively in the market. Employers have discretion to hire and fire as necessary to respond to business cycles, but workers enjoy generous unemployment benefits and a commitment to worker training. Flexicurity abandons the older model of rigid protection of job security in a particular position (the

German model) and replaces it with a commitment to employment security—the right to be assured of work, but not necessarily a particular job.

A Matter of Values and Priorities

In countries that see work as a fundamental right, it follows logically that both government and employers owe a responsibility to workers when the right is withdrawn or compromised by market events. By contrast, the American system places responsibility predominantly on the shoulders of individual workers, with only peripheral and short-term support through the unemployment insurance system provided for those who, through no fault of their own, lose jobs.

Countries that conceptualize work as a fundamental right recognize a species of property interest held by the worker in his or her job. Thus, employers must justify interference with the right, and notice and severance pay obligations are triggered where infringement is unavoidable. The U.S. rule clashes with the lived experience of workers, who believe that the jobs in which they have invested blood, sweat, and tears, often over a lengthy period of time, belong to them....

Why does the law treat work as if it does not matter? Because in U.S. work law, property rights trump labor. Capital investment matters; work does not. The human costs of that policy choice have never been clearer.

QUESTIONS

1. Elsewhere in this article, Crain points out that other countries have enshrined in their constitutions the right to work. **Research:** Find one of these provisions. How is it worded? Can you find any litigation under it?

2. When writer and historian Studs Terkel graduated from University of Chicago Law School in 1934, he announced that he wanted to become a concierge in a hotel. Then he joined an acting troupe, and during a stint with the Depression-era Federal Writers Project, became a radio broadcaster. But Terkel is best known for his oral histories of ordinary Americans, including a compilation of interviews of men and women talking about their work. In the introduction to this book, *Working*, Terkel describes how often people were searching for "daily meaning as well as daily bread, for recognition as well as cash, for astonishment rather than torpor ... for a sort of life rather than a Monday through Friday sort of dying." Can you draw connections between this attitude about the meaning of work and ethical theory?

Sarbanes-Oxley and the Corporate Whistleblower

Ms. Watkins is no whistleblower in the conventional sense. She was and is a loyal employee.

— JAMES GREENWOOD (R., PA.) Chairman of Congressional Committee
Investigating the Collapse of Enron

At the crux of the whistleblower's decision is the question of loyalty, and of divided loyalties. An employee such as Dr. Pierce who blows the whistle experiences opposite pulls—allegiance to the employer and allegiance to a professional code of values. In the next reading, law professor Leonard Baynes takes up the example of Sherron Watkins, the best-known whistleblower associated with the fall of Enron Corporation in 2001. Watkins, a certified public accountant, worked directly with Enron's CFO, and from that vantage point discovered accounting improprieties. Fearing retaliation, she did not report these to her immediate boss, but went straight to the president of the company, warning that Enron might "implode in a wave of accounting scandals." She was ignored, Enron collapsed, and Watkins would later appear on the cover of *Time Magazine* as "Person of the Week." But in the way she tried to communicate concerns up the hierarchy, the author views her as the prototypical corporate whistleblower: reporting to her superiors instead of to the government or the media. He uses her story as a means of discussing the difficult position of the corporate insider who chooses to blow the whistle, and asks whether the 2002 Sarbanes-Oxley Act (SOX), the federal law designed to prevent future Enrons, adequately addresses the quandary of employees like Sherron Watkins.

JUST PUCKER AND BLOW: AN ANALYSIS OF CORPORATE WHISTLEBLOWERS
Leonard M. Baynes[19]

You know how to whistle, don't you, Steve? You just put your lips together—and blow.
— LAUREN BACALL TO HUMPHREY BOGART IN *TO HAVE AND TO HAVE NOT*

The Sarbanes-Oxley Act prohibits any public company from discriminating against any employee who lawfully provides information or otherwise assists in an investigation of conduct that the employee "reasonably believes" constitutes a violation of the federal securities laws. This provision was designed from the lessons learned from Sherron Watkins's testimony. As Senator Patrick Leahy stated, "We learned from Sherron Watkins of Enron that these corporate insiders are the key witnesses that need to be encouraged to report fraud and help prove it in court." The legislation protects an employee from retaliation by an employer for testifying before Congress or a federal regulatory agency or giving evidence to law enforcement of possible securities fraud violations....

[Baynes now asks whether the antiretaliation provision of the new law adequately addresses the dilemma of the corporate whistleblower, caught in the "vortex" of the duty of loyalty and the duty of care.]

Undoubtedly, the Sarbanes-Oxley Act provides an extra level of protection for employees. Despite this,... we must be cognizant that federal whistleblowers have low success rates in their suits before government agencies.... Under the Act, the corporate senior executive or employee is likely ... also [to] have a low rate of success under its whistleblowing provisions. First, the statute only affords protection against retaliations based on securities fraud. Whistleblowing of other kinds of wrongdoing remain unprotected under this Act. In these cases, the whistleblower then must rely on the vagaries of state law, which generally give preference to those allegations dealing with public safety. For example, a senior executive may overhear a high-ranking executive make disparaging remarks about a particular racial group and state that he would never hire or promote members of that group. The corporation employs very few members of this particular group and has none in senior management. The senior executive believes that the corporation is engaged in race discrimination. The senior executive has a fiduciary obligation to hold certain corporate information like employee demographics in confidence but has an obligation to resign or object from his position when confronting corporate wrongdoing. The Act provides protection only for those matters that involve security fraud. If this

[19] Source: Leonard M. Baynes, "Just Pucker and Blow: An Analysis of Corporate Whistleblowers," 76 *St. John's L. Rev.* 875, Fall 2002.

senior manager discloses, she would have to rely on the protections of the state laws.

Second, low-level employees are also relatively unprotected. They probably are unaware of these new protections. They may feel particularly oppressed by the many layers of management that may exist in some corporations. Some may be unsophisticated and may not know whether certain actions violate the law. Many of the wrongful or illegal activities that they observe may not rise to the level of securities fraud. For example, an employee at McDonald's may notice that large numbers of pre-packaged hamburgers disappear shortly after delivery. The disappearance may be the result of conversion [stealing] by the store manager. The McDonald's employee might be in the best position to ascertain whether this wrongdoing is occurring, but she is unprotected by the Sarbanes-Oxley Act because this conversion does not involve securities fraud. In addition, many of these employees rely very heavily on their paychecks; a high turnover rate exists in these jobs. Students and those re-entering the workforce hold many of these jobs. These individuals may be particularly reluctant to "rock the boat" and report wrongdoing unless they are guaranteed that their job is protected. The Act does nothing to address this population of whistleblowers.

Third, for both senior executives and low-level employees, the Sarbanes-Oxley Act gives little guidance as to the circumstances under which an employee is to disclose allegations of wrongdoing to her supervisor as opposed to law enforcement authorities. Senior executives also have an obligation to use "reasonable efforts" to disclose to the principal information which is "relevant to affairs entrusted to [the agent]" and which the principal would desire to have... . In some instances, however, the whistleblowing employee who reports wrongdoing to her supervisor might not be doing enough to stem the wrongdoing behavior. For instance, once she has made the report, the wrongdoing supervisor might exclude the employee from access to information that would allow her to continue to observe the wrongful behavior. In those cases, the reporting employee may have breached her duty of care to the corporation by using insufficient actions to stop the wrongdoing.... Conversely, if the whistleblowing employee reports the evidence of wrongdoing immediately to law enforcement authorities, she may be violating her duty of loyalty to the corporation.... She has an obligation to protect certain proprietary and confidential corporate information. Also by going to the law enforcement authorities right away, she may be depriving the corporation of the opportunity to resolve the matter or, in the case of wrongdoing, get the best deal for the corporation. In addition, the employee who jumps the gun and goes to law enforcement authorities may be putting herself in a difficult political situation at her corporation. Even though the terms of her position and employment may remain the same, she will always, to her detriment, be remembered for making that report.

Fourth, the Sarbanes-Oxley Act gives no guidance concerning whether the whistleblowing employee should disclose the information to her direct supervisor or her supervisor's supervisor. Who is the principal of senior executives? Is it the corporation? Is it the board of directors? Is it the senior executive's boss?

Fifth, the legislative history of the Sarbanes-Oxley Act states that the employee's actions have to be reasonable in making reports... .Most cases may not be as clear-cut as the one involving Sherron Watkins. Because she was an accountant, she had a very good idea that Enron's accounting policies were illegal. For most other whistleblowers, they may have only a slight inkling that something might be amiss. In those circumstances, what are they supposed to do?...

Sixth, the Sarbanes-Oxley Act prohibits a corporation from "discharg[ing], demot [ing], suspend[ing], threaten[ing], harass[ing], or in any other manner discriminat[ing] against an employee in the terms and conditions of employment" because she blew the whistle. Senator Leahy conceded, however, that "most corporate employers, with help from their lawyers, know exactly what they can do to a whistle-blowing employee under the law." The types of retaliation that can occur include: (1) "attacking the [whistleblower's] motives, credibility, [or] professional competence"; (2) "build[ing] a damaging record against [the whistleblower]"; (3) threatening the employee with "reprisals for whistleblowing"; (4) "reassign[ing]" the employee to an isolated work location; (5) "publicly humiliat[ing]" the employee; (6) "set[ting] ... up [the whistleblower] for failure" by putting them in impossible assignments; (7) "prosecut[ing the employee] for unauthorized disclosures [of information]"; (8) "reorganiz[ing]" the company so that the whistleblower's job is eliminated"; and (9) "blacklist[ing]" the whistleblower so she will be unable to work in the industry. Of course some methods on this list would clearly violate the Act. A deft supervisor, however, could "set up" the whistleblowing employee for failure. For instance, the employer may place the whistleblower in a job unsuitable to her skill level to ensure her failure. The employer could then document the employee's poor performance. The Act provides protections for whistleblowing employees except in cases where valid business reasons exist for their termination like inferior work performance. In addition, even if the employer refrains from discriminating against the whistleblowing employee in the terms and conditions of her employment, the employer is unlikely to give that employee any opportunities for advancement. By blowing the whistle, she may have "tapped out" her career trajectory....

QUESTIONS

1. Describe the conflict faced by corporate insiders who discover unethical or illegal activities within their organizations.

2. Would the SOX law have protected Dr. Donn Milton? Dr. Grace Pierce? Why, or why not? What kinds of corporate wrongdoing might a senior executive discover that would not be covered by SOX?

3. Suppose Sherron Watkins had been fired by Enron before SOX went into effect. How would she have fared under Maryland law? New Jersey? Montana? Does SOX provide her any basis for a lawsuit?

4. Baynes identifies these weaknesses in the SOX law:
   (a) "non-securities fraud matters are not covered;
   (b) low-level employees may not be aware of the protections;
   (c) no guidance is given as to when to report wrongdoing to outside authorities or to a supervisor;
   (d) no guidance is given as to when the whistleblower should go over his or her supervisor's head to senior management; and
   (e) no protection is given to undercover retaliations that do not quite manifest themselves as a 'discharge, demotion, suspension, threat, or other manner of discrimination.'"

   Working with a group of classmates, tackle each of these issues. How would you amend the law to respond to them? Might some of these concerns be more effectively addressed by changes in corporate policy or culture? If so, what changes would your group recommend?

5. **Research:** In 2010 Congress passed legislation in response to the financial crisis that began in 2007. Find this law. Does it contain whistleblower protections? Does it answer any of the concerns outlined by Baynes in this article?

GROUP THINK

Seven months after the U.S. space shuttle Columbia crashed in August 2003, a report on the causes of the disaster was released. It had been a gargantuan effort. Some 25,000 workers had gathered more than 84,000 pieces of debris evidence by walking slowly across eastern Texas and western Louisiana. According to the final report, the "broken safety culture" inside NASA was at least as much to blame for the crash as the chunk of foam tile that blew a hole in the wing of Columbia just after liftoff. Engineers, hoping a high-risk rescue might be possible, had asked management for outside assistance in getting photos of the damage, but these requests were rejected:

> As much as the foam, what helped to doom the shuttle and its crew, even after liftoff, was not a lack of technology or ability...but missed opportunities and a lack of leadership and open-mindedness in management. The accident "was probably not an anomalous, random event, but rather likely rooted to some degree in NASA's history and the human spacelight program's culture."[20]

Similar problems appear to have affected the CIA in the months leading up to the U.S. invasion of Iraq. According to a scathing Congressional report released in July 2004, key assessments used to justify the war were not supported by the government's own evidence:

> Among the central findings, endorsed by all nine Republicans and eight Democrats on the committee, were that a culture of "group think" in intelligence agencies left unchallenged an institutional belief that Iraq had illicit weapons; ...and that intelligence agencies too often failed to acknowledge the limited, ambiguous and even contradictory nature of their information about Iraq and illicit arms.[21]

Studies have shown that, within large organizations, there is a tendency to go along with the majority. Most people are not likely to challenge the worthiness of the task at hand, or the way in which the task at hand is being accomplished. This reality, combined with the pressures that affect an organization from the outside—time and money pressures in the case of NASA's Columbia shuttle, political pressures in the case of the United States in Iraq—can obscure good judgment.

Public Employees and Freedom of Speech

What I was surprised at was the silence, the collective silence by so many people that had to be involved, that had to have seen something or heard something.

— SGT. SAMUEL PROVANCE, Key Witness in Government
Investigation of Abu Ghraib Prison Abuse

People who work for the government or for any of its branches—such as police officers, air traffic controllers, and those employed by government-supported institutions such as

---

[20] John Schwartz and Matthew Wald, "Report on Loss of Shuttle Focuses on NASA Blunders," *New York Times*, August 27, 2003.

[21] Douglas Jehl, "Senators Assail C.I.A. Judgments on Iraq's Arms as Deeply Flawed, *New York Times*, July 10, 2004.

hospitals or schools—are called public employees. For almost 200 years, public employees were thought to have no greater speech rights than those who worked in the private sector. The leading case, which dates back to the nineteenth century, involved a police officer who was fired for publicly criticizing the management of his department. He sued to get his job back, relying on his free speech rights. Judge Oliver Wendell Holmes refused his claim, stating, "The petitioner may have a constitutional right to talk politics, but he has no constitutional right to be a policeman."[22]

Then, in 1968, the Supreme Court reinterpreted the First Amendment of the U.S. Constitution to give public employees limited speech protections. Marvin Pickering, a public school teacher, was fired for publishing a letter in the local paper critical of the Board of Education's allocation of funds to its athletic program. He sued, losing in the lower courts. On appeal, however, the Court ruled in his favor. In *Pickering v. Board of Education*,[23] the Court weighed "the interests of the teacher, as a citizen, in commenting upon matters of public concern" against the "interest of the State, as an employer, in promoting the efficiency of the public services it performs through its employees." On balance, Pickering's free speech interests were greater. The Court noted that a public employee could not be punished for speaking out on matters of public concern unless the employer could demonstrate that the employee's statements caused substantial interference with the performance of his own duties or with the functioning of the workplace.

In 1983, in *Connick v. Myers*,[24] the Supreme Court clarified and reinterpreted *Pickering*. Sheila Myers had distributed at her place of employment a questionnaire that inquired not only about internal matters, such as an office transfer policy, but also about matters of public concern, including pressure put on employees to work on certain political campaigns. Before applying the *Pickering* balancing test, the Court ruled that it would first have to determine whether a public employee's speech was related to matters of public concern, thus creating a new obstacle for plaintiffs in these cases. Ms. Myers' questionnaire was tinged with just enough public interest to be examined under the *Pickering* test, although a statement limited to internal matters would not be. She lost, however, because the government demonstrated that her questionnaire interfered with working relationships by causing a "mini-insurrection" that could have disrupted the office.

■ ■ ■

In 2006, the Supreme Court revisited the *Pickering* rule, making it even more difficult for public employees to successfully argue their free speech rights had been violated. The facts of the case were as follows: Richard Ceballos began working as a deputy district attorney in Los Angeles County in 1989. By 2000, he was a "calendar" attorney, supervising other lawyers in the DA's office. In February of that year, a defense attorney contacted Ceballos to tell him he would be challenging a search warrant because it was based on "inaccuracies" in the supporting affidavit. Ceballos agreed to investigate. When he went to the location described in the warrant as a "long driveway," he found a separate road. Although the affidavit described tire tracks that led from a stripped-down truck to the premises to be searched, Ceballos found a road surface that would make it difficult or impossible to leave visible tire tracks.

After a telephone conversation with the affiant—a deputy sheriff—Ceballos told his supervisors that the case should be dismissed because there were serious misrepresentations in the affidavit supporting the search warrant. He repeated the same concerns in a

---

[22] *McAuliffe v. Mayor of New Bedford*, 29 N.E. 517 (1892).

[23] 391 U.S. 563 (1968).

[24] *Connick v. Myers*, 461 U.S. 138 (1983).

memorandum. Then, at heated meeting with his supervisors and with the sheriff who had made the statements in the warrant, Ceballos was sharply reprimanded. Later, he claims, he experienced a series of retaliations, including being reassigned, transferred, and denied promotion.

He sued, claiming those actions violated his First Amendment rights.

GARCETTI v. CEBALLOS
U.S. Supreme Court, 2006
547 U.S. 410

Justice KENNEDY Delivered the Opinion of the Court

Pickering and the cases decided in its wake identify two inquiries to guide interpretation of the constitutional protections accorded to public employee speech. The first requires determining whether the employee spoke as a citizen on a matter of public concern. If the answer is no, the employee has no First Amendment cause of action.... If the answer is yes, then the possibility of a First Amendment claim arises. The question becomes whether the relevant government entity had an adequate justification for treating the employee differently from any other member of the general public....

When a citizen enters government service, the citizen by necessity must accept certain limitations on his or her freedom... Government employers, like private employers, need a significant degree of control over their employees' words and actions; without it, there would be little chance for the efficient provision of public services....

At the same time, the Court has recognized that a citizen who works for the government is nonetheless a citizen. The First Amendment limits the ability of a public employer to leverage the employment relationship to restrict, incidentally or intentionally, the liberties employees enjoy in their capacities as private citizens. So long as employees are speaking as citizens about matters of public concern, they must face only those speech restrictions that are necessary for their employers to operate efficiently and effectively...

[T]he First Amendment interests at stake extend beyond the individual speaker... [to include] the public's interest in receiving the well-informed views of government employees engaging in civic discussion... [and] the necessity for informed, vibrant dialogue in a democratic society....

With these principles in mind we turn to the instant case....

The controlling factor in Ceballos' case is that his expressions were made pursuant to his duties as a calendar deputy. That consideration—the fact that Ceballos spoke as a prosecutor fulfilling a responsibility to advise his supervisor about how best to proceed with a pending case—distinguishes Ceballos' case...We hold that when public employees make statements pursuant to their official duties, the employees are not speaking as citizens for First Amendment purposes, and the Constitution does not insulate their communications from employer discipline.

The significant point is that the memo was written pursuant to Ceballos' official duties.... Contrast, for example, the expressions made by the speaker in *Pickering*, whose letter to the newspaper had no official significance and bore similarities to letters submitted by numerous citizens every day.

Ceballos did not act as a citizen when he went about conducting his daily professional activities, such as supervising attorneys, investigating charges, and preparing filings. In the same way he did not speak as a citizen by writing a memo that addressed the proper disposition of a pending criminal case. When he went to work and performed the tasks he was paid to perform, Ceballos acted as a government employee. The fact that his duties sometimes required him to speak or write does not mean his supervisors were prohibited from evaluating his performance.

This result is consistent with our precedents' attention to the potential societal value of employee speech.... First Amendment claims based on government employees' work product does not prevent them from participating in public debate. The employees retain the prospect of constitutional protection for their contributions to the civic discourse.... This prospect of protection, however, does not invest them with a right to perform their jobs however they see fit.

Our holding likewise is supported by the emphasis of our precedents on affording government employers sufficient discretion to manage their operations. Employers have heightened interests in controlling speech made by an employee in his or her professional capacity.... Supervisors must ensure that their employees' official communications are accurate, demonstrate sound judgment, and promote the employer's mission. Ceballos' memo is illustrative. It demanded the attention of his supervisors and led to a heated meeting with employees from the sheriff's department. If Ceballos' superiors thought his memo was inflammatory or misguided, they had the authority to take proper corrective action....

Proper application of our precedents thus leads to the conclusion that the First Amendment does not prohibit managerial discipline based on an employee's expressions made pursuant to official responsibilities. Because Ceballos' memo falls into this category, his allegation of unconstitutional retaliation must fail....

Justice STEVENS, Dissenting

The proper answer to the question "whether the First Amendment protects a government employee from discipline based on speech made pursuant to the employee's official duties," is "Sometimes," not "Never." Of course a supervisor may take corrective action when such speech is "inflammatory or misguided," But what if it is just unwelcome speech because it reveals facts that the supervisor would rather not have anyone else discover?

[P]ublic employees are still citizens while they are in the office. The notion that there is a categorical difference between speaking as a citizen and speaking in the course of one's employment is quite wrong. Over a quarter of a century has passed since then-Justice Rehnquist, writing for a unanimous Court, rejected "the conclusion that a public employee forfeits his protection against governmental abridgment of freedom of speech if he decides to express his views privately rather than publicly." ... [It] is senseless to let constitutional protection...hinge on whether [words] fall within a job description. Moreover, it seems perverse to fashion a new rule that provides employees with an incentive to voice their concerns publicly before talking frankly to their superiors.

Justice SOUTER, Justice STEVENS and Justice GINSBURG Dissenting

Open speech by a private citizen on a matter of public importance lies at the heart of expression subject to protection by the First Amendment.... At the other extreme, a statement by a government employee complaining about nothing beyond treatment under personnel rules raises no greater claim to constitutional protection against retaliatory response than the remarks of a private employee.... In between these points lies a public employee's speech unwelcome to the government but on a significant public issue. Such an employee speaking as a citizen, that is, with a citizen's interest, is protected from reprisal unless the statements are too damaging to the government's capacity to conduct public business to be justified by any individual or public benefit thought to flow from the statements. *Pickering v. Board of Ed. of Township High School Dist.* (1968)....

This significant, albeit qualified, protection of public employees who irritate the government is understood to flow from the First Amendment, in part, because a government paycheck does nothing to eliminate the value to an individual of speaking on public matters, and there is no good reason for categorically discounting a speaker's interest in commenting on a matter of public concern just because the government employs him.... [in part on] the value to the public of receiving the opinions and information that a public employee may disclose. "Government employees are often in the best position to know what ails the agencies for which they work." *Waters v. Churchill*, (U.S. 1994).

The reason that protection of employee speech is qualified is that it can distract coworkers and supervisors from their tasks at hand and thwart the implementation of legitimate policy, the risks of which grow greater the closer the employee's speech gets to commenting on his own workplace and responsibilities. It is one thing for an office clerk to say there is waste in government and quite another to charge that his own department pays full-time salaries to part-time workers....

...[I]t stands to reason that a citizen may well place a very high value on a right to speak on the public issues he decides to make the subject of his work day after day. Would anyone doubt that a school principal evaluating the performance of teachers for promotion or pay adjustment retains a citizen's interest in addressing the quality of teaching in the schools?...Would anyone deny that a prosecutor like Richard Ceballos may claim the interest of any citizen in speaking out against a rogue law enforcement officer, simply because his job requires him to express a judgment about the officer's performance? (But the majority says the First Amendment gives Ceballos no protection, even if his judgment in this case was sound and appropriately expressed.)

Indeed, the very idea of categorically separating the citizen's interest from the employee's interest ignores the fact that the ranks of public service include those who share the poet's "object ... to unite [m]y avocation and my vocation." These citizen servants are the ones whose civic interest rises highest when they speak pursuant to their duties, and these are exactly the ones government employers most want to attract....

The interest at stake is as much the public's interest in receiving informed opinion as it is the employee's own right to disseminate it. This is...true when an employee's job duties require him to speak about such things: when, for example, a public auditor speaks on his discovery of embezzlement of public funds, when a building inspector makes an obligatory report of an attempt to bribe him, or when a law enforcement officer expressly balks at a superior's order to violate constitutional rights he is sworn to protect. (The majority, however, places all these speakers beyond the reach of First Amendment protection against retaliation.)...

Justice BREYER, Dissenting

The facts present two special circumstances that together justify First Amendment review.

First, the speech at issue is professional speech—the speech of a lawyer. Such speech is subject to independent regulation with Those canons provide an obligation to speak in certain instances....

Second, the Constitution itself here imposes speech obligations upon the government's professional employee. A prosecutor has a constitutional obligation to learn of, to preserve, and to communicate with the defense about exculpatory and impeachment evidence in the government's possession. [Exculpatory evidence is evidence that proves innocence. Ceballos believed that what he learned about the affidavit was exculpatory.]

I would apply the *Pickering* balancing test here. With respect, I dissent.

QUESTIONS

1. Dissenting Justices Souter, Stevens, and Ginsburg write: "When constitutionally significant interests clash, resist the demand for winner-take-all; try to make adjustments that serve all of the values at stake." Think about the values that underlie each portion of this opinion. Which values are most prominent for Justice Kennedy with the majority? For Justice Stevens in dissent? Which values are framed in the dissent led by Souter? What value does Breyer mention?

2. The majority adds a threshold requirement to the analysis of First Amendment claims for public employees. According to *Pickering* and its progeny (cases interpreting *Pickering*), the first determination was whether the employee spoke as a citizen on a matter of public concern. If no, then the employee would have no First Amendment protection. If yes, the balancing test would be applied to the facts. Here in *Garcetti*, the Court sets up an additional threshold barrier for plaintiffs: Where public employee speech is found to be pursuant to official duties, it lacks First Amendment protection. How does the majority argue in favor of this new requirement? What arguments do the dissenters make for alternative methods of analysis?

3. In a part of *Garcetti* not included in this text, Justice Kennedy writes that government employees can turn to "the powerful network of legislative enactments—such as whistleblower protection laws and labor codes—available to those who seek to expose wrongdoing "Dissenting Justice Souter counters that these laws are not uniform and do not exist in all states. Where they do exist, do they tend to protect employees? In Mississippi, police officers were fired for reporting that a fellow officer had beaten a "restrained prisoner." They sued under federal constitutional and state whistleblower law. The court ruled that, because they had reported through the chain of command as their job duties required, they were doing so pursuant to their official duties and their speech was not protected under *Garcetti*. And because they were reporting through the chain of command, the Mississippi state whistleblower statute too did not protect them. State law would have protected the officers had they reported the misconduct through an investigative agency such as the district attorney instead of to their commanding officers. *Williams v. Riley*, 481 F. Supp. 2d 582 (N.D. Miss. 2007).

   (a) **Research:** Find a public employee whistleblower case that made claims both under *Garcetti* and under state whistleblower law. What were the facts? Was the federal constitutional claim successful? The state law claim?

   (b) If the police officers who were fired after reporting to their supervisors that some of their co-workers were physically beating restrained prison inmates had instead gone straight to the media, their actions would not have been pursuant to their official duties. Does *Garcetti* create a perverse incentive to go public with workplace grievances and concerns?

4. Consider the following scenarios drawn from the news. If these whistleblowers sued, would they succeed in their federal constitutional free speech claims? Why or why not?

   a. The April 5, 2010 explosion at the Massey Energy's Upper Big Branch Mine in West Virginia was the worst coal mining disaster in 40 years. Fellow coal miners and family members of the 29 miners killed described the deadly conditions in the mine during the months leading up to the blast at a House of Representatives Committee on Education and Labor hearing in May 2010. Gary Quarles, a coal miner for 34 years and father of a miner killed in the blast, testified about the role of federal government inspectors at Upper Big Branch, stating that "MSHA [Mine Safety and Health Administration] inspections at Massey did little to protect miners. We absolutely looked to MSHA for leadership, particularly on safety issues, but MSHA has let us down many times." Quarles blamed MSHA for only conducting inspections during the day shift, ignoring safety during evenings, nights and weekends. A federal mine inspector complained about this to her supervisors and was fired.

   b. Gregory Williams was the football coach and athletic director at DISD's Pinkston High School. Coach Williams began asking questions about irregular budgetary procedures and confusing balance statements in his athletic budget. Unsatisfied with the answers he got from the principal and office manager, Williams sent a memo to the principal protesting the unorthodox way funds were being managed and spent at the school. Four days later, the principal removed Williams as athletic director. His contract for the next year was not renewed.

c. Adis M. Vila was the Vice President for External and Legal Affairs at Miami Dade Community College (MDCC). She told MDCC administrators (who had authority to investigate and take corrective action) about concerns regarding three potentially illegal/unethical projects at the college: (1) an advertising contract between MDCC and a vendor that was not bid competitively as required by Florida law, (2) a proposal for MDCC to purchase the Freedom Tower for $10 million, and (3) the proposed use of college funds to illustrate a poetry book for the daughter of a college trustee. Vila received notice that she would not be renewed.

d. Chief of Police proposed to change the staffing of the police department. While the supervisors were still together, Sgt. Mills voiced her objections to the plan to reduce the number of crime prevention officers under her command. Mills was on duty and in uniform at the time. She was later admonished for failure to work through the chain of command, removed from her supervisory position, and assigned to patrol duties.

e. Jennifer Green, a technician and detention officer, worked in the drug lab of a juvenile detention center. She suspected that a certain drug test was producing false positives. On her own initiative, without consulting with her superiors, she arranged a confirmation test at a nearby hospital. She also notified the Department of Human Services about her concerns. The confirmation test results showed that the test was indeed flawed, and Green then informed her supervisor. The detention center adopted a new policy requiring confirmation tests, but soon after that Green herself received a transfer and a demotion. When she failed to come to work, she was fired.

■ ■ ■

False Claims Act *Qui Tam* Whistleblowers

Physical courage is remarkably widespread in [the U.S.] population.... Moral and intellectual courage are not in nearly so flourishing a state, even though the risks they entail—financial or professional disadvantage, ridicule, ostracism—are comparatively minor.... These forms of courage suffer from the disadvantage of requiring new definitions continually, which must be generated out of individual perception and judgment. They threaten or violate loyalty, group identity.... They are, intrinsically, outside the range of consensus.

— MARILYNNE ROBINSON, Novelist and Essayist

We have seen to what extent the law might—or might not—protect whistleblowers from retaliation by their employers. But another legal approach is to give individuals an incentive to become whistleblowers in the first place, rewarding them for speaking out against wrongdoing. This is the premise of the federal False Claims Act, a more than 150-year-old response to fraud against the government. It was first enacted in 1863 during the Civil War, when profiteers were selling rancid food rations and artillery shells filled with sawdust to the Union army. Private citizens who came forward to report such abuses and successfully filed suit were eligible for fifty percent of damages.

Plaintiffs who initiate cases under the False Claims Act are called *qui tam*, an abbreviation of a Latin phrase meaning "who sues on behalf of the king as well as for himself." The law has been amended several times, including in 1986 when it was brought to light that up to ten percent of the federal budget was being drained by fraud, particularly in defense and health care contracts. Under the 1986 amendments, qui tam cases are mutually advantageous to the Justice Department, which can receive triple damages, and to whistleblowers, who can be awarded from 15 to 25 percent of the amount recovered, depending on the value of the evidence they provide.

Qui Tam and Fraud in Health Care

According to the Kaiser Family Foundation, in 2009 the U.S. spent 17.6 percent of its gross domestic product on health care, more than double the percentages spent by Spain, Italy, Australia, Britain, or Japan. American health care costs continue to skyrocket, and fraud in the health care industry contributes as much as 10 percent of these costs.

Since 1986, more than $15 billion has been recovered by the government in False Claims Act cases—nearly 75 percent of this amount from health care entities. Here are the facts of one such case: In the 1990s, protease inhibitors became available to treat HIV/AIDS and were markedly helpful in alleviating the severe wasting symptoms which beforehand had been treated with Serono Laboratories' drug Serostim. Foreseeing a drop-off in sales, the company began promoting Serostim with a medical device that produced false diagnoses of the wasting syndrome. This device, not approved by the FDA, was rigged to indicate a loss of cell mass and what the company called "hidden AIDS wasting." It came into widespread use by AIDS patients because of an aggressive marketing campaign, part of which involved all-expense-paid trips to the South of France for a "conference" for prominent physicians who agreed within six days to prescribe more than $6 million in Serostim. Serono employee Christine Driscoll filed a *qui tam* case alleging fraud, conspiracy, and false marketing. The case resulted in a $704 million settlement. Another example: In September 2009, a $2.3 billion settlement was reached with Pfizer, in a case involving illegal marketing to doctors leading to government overpayments. Former Pfizer sales representative John Kopchinski, the *qui tam* plaintiff in this case, drew attention to the way in which the company, which had already been fined for pushing off-label uses of another drug, went on to similar illegal practices with Bextra. FDA-approved for arthritis and menstrual cramps, Bextra was being promoted for treatment of acute and surgical pain at doses well above those approved, in spite of risks to the kidney, skin, and heart. "The whole culture of Pfizer is driven by sales, and if you didn't sell drugs illegally, you were not seen as a team player," said Mr. Kopchinski. His qui tam share of the Pfizer settlement will exceed $50 million.

EXPERIENCES OF *QUI TAM* WHISTLEBLOWERS AGAINST THE PHARMACEUTICAL INDUSTRY

In May 2010 three academics in public health[25] wrote an article[26] summarizing their investigation of the motivations and experiences of health care industry whistleblowers under the False Claims Act. Focusing on successful prosecutions taken up by the Department of Justice against pharmaceutical companies, they analyzed data gleaned from 40-minute interviews with 26 individuals who became *qui tam*

---

[25] Aaron Kesselheim, M.D., J.D., M.P.H., instructor at Harvard Medical School and faculty member in the Department of Medicine at Brigham and Women's Hospital, David Studdert LL.B., Sc.D., M.P.H with a joint appointment at Melbourne Law School and the Melbourne School of Population Health, and Michelle Mello, J.D., Ph.D., M.Phil Associate Director of the Program in Law and Public Health at Harvard University.

[26] "Whistleblowers' Experiences in Fraud Litigation against Pharmaceutical Companies," 362 N.E. J. Med. 19, 1832–39 (May 13, 2010).

plaintiffs between January 2001 and March 2009. Their study yields valuable insights about whistleblowers, more nuanced than the common stereotypes depicting them as either "heroes struggling against corporate greed, [enduring] hardships and retaliation," or people with questionable motives who reap excessive rewards for disloyal behavior.

Here are some of the findings: Virtually all of the "insiders"—those who worked for the company against whom they eventually became *qui tam* plaintiffs—attempted to fix the situation first from within, "talking to their superiors, filing an internal complaint, or both." These individuals were either told the behavior was legal, or had their complaints dismissed "with accompanying demands that [they] do what they were told."

As for the motivations of these whistleblowers, only six of the 26 said they had intended from the start to use the *qui tam* process; the rest were advised to do so as they considered bringing suit for other reasons—unfair employment practices, for example. None stated that financial reward was what motivated them to get involved. Instead, they reported being driven by a mix of these factors: integrity, altruism, public safety and self-preservation—with integrity the most frequently-mentioned reason. Potential risks to public health was a concern for about one third of the respondents.

The majority described the process of working with the government to gather evidence for a *qui tam* case as grueling. More than half were actively involved in these efforts, wearing wires to covertly record conversations, and secretly copying files. One respondent described spending "thousands of hours" on the case over five years; another said the first few years demanded "probably 30 hours a week."

For nearly all of the *qui tam* plaintiffs in this study, the personal toll was "substantial and long-lasting." Of those who worked for the company at the time of the investigation, 82 percent experienced retaliation with devastating effects on their careers. After settlement, only two of the 22 "inside" plaintiffs continued to work in the pharmaceutical industry. And there were harsh effects on their personal lives. Six of the respondents experienced divorce, marital stress or other family difficulties while they while going through the *qui tam* process. About half reported health disorders, including panic attacks, asthma, insomnia and generalized anxiety.

All of the respondents received a share of the damages recovered by the government. Their rewards ranged from $100,000 to $42 million; the median was $3 million. Yet for the majority, the financial payoff was not worth it "relative to the time they spent on the case and the disruption and damage to their careers."

Despite all of this, most of the respondents—22 of the 26—remained convinced that "what they did was important for ethical…psychological or spiritual reasons."

Global Norms and Internal Corporate Communication

In the next reading, Terry Morehead Dworkin, a leading authority on employment-at-will, makes intriguing connections among commercial activity, protection for whistleblowers, and world peace. Assuming the preconditions for a peaceful society are "justice, good governance, transparency, and giving individuals voice," whistleblowing protections developed by multiational corporations (MNCs) in response to legal pressures in the

United States can become valuable tools when implemented in other countries. Dworkin writes: "Whistleblowing is a procedural way to reinforce the transparency necessary to free trapped capital, encourage foreign investment, and move economies, especially transitional ones, away from reliance on personal relationships and bribes." Noting that countries rife with cronyism tend also to be plagued by violence, Dworkin argues that by protecting whistleblowing worldwide, MNCs support democratic institutions and "help deliver on the promise of peace through commerce."

WHISTLEBLOWING, MNCS, AND PEACE
Terry Morehead Dworkin[27]

Work organizations, both governmental and civil, are growing in size and complexity, and individuals are often little more than "cogs" in the organization in which they work. Individual jobs have also grown in complexity, and as a result have become more specialized and expertise-based. This, in turn, makes the detection of wrongful conduct more difficult due to both lack of knowledge and access to information. At the same time, the information and technology revolutions have increased the opportunities for significant fraud and other harmful and illegal activities. Whistleblowing is one way to obtain—or regain—societal control over the large organizations that increasingly dominate society.

The premise behind recent governmental promotion of whistleblowing is that people of conscience work within these large, complex organizations, and would normally take action against wrongdoing except for fear of losing their jobs or other forms of retaliation...

Thus, if adequately protected from retaliation, they will come forward with evidence of wrongdoing before external detection is possible. Harms from the wrongdoing could be reduced, wrongful behavior stopped, and the expense of public oversight and investigation would be reduced if such reporting occurs. Also, if whistleblowing proved a relatively common occurrence, wrongdoing would decrease because potential wrongdoers would be aware that their activities were not truly secret.

[Dworkin describes the evolution of the law related to whistleblowing in the United States, noting how catastrophes such as the 1981 Space Shuttle Challenger explosion spurred protective measures across all three branches of both state and federal government. Importantly, she points to "a shift toward encouraging internal whistleblowing and away from the almost exclusive legislative emphasis on reporting outside the organization." An organization can save litigation costs and avoid reputational damage by adopting effective internal mechanisms for reporting wrongdoing. And unlike punishment that is meted out after public exposure, internal reporting can prevent losses—of resources and even lives. Laws like the 1991 U.S. Sentencing Guidelines that allow reduced fines for wrongdoing if a company has an appropriate deterrence program in place—an ethical code supported by "a meaningful reporting system and protection of whistleblowers from reprisals"—have driven this trend to set up internal reporting systems.

The question now becomes: Is whistleblowing protection exportable?]

The Cultural Dimension

...[M]odern, non-political whistleblowing is a Western phenomenon. The countries that have adopted it have common law-based legal systems and societies that prize

[27] Terry Morehead Dworkin, "Whistleblowers, MNCs and Peace," *Vanderbilt Journal of Transnational Law* 35(2), March 2002, pp. 457–486. Reprinted by permission.

individualism. While "snitching" is not generally condoned, the idea of citizen law enforcement has long roots in the United Kingdom and the United States, and whistleblowing has been advocated as a way to control large organizations for over thirty years. In some Western countries such as France, Greece, and Luxembourg, however, whistleblowing is seen as little different from informing the government about a neighbor's dissident views. This, in turn, is frowned on at least in part because it is considered an attribute of totalitarian or Communist states....

The idea of reporting the wrongdoing of one's group is alien to many other cultures in which group membership, rather than individualism, is the norm. In Japan, for example, the traditions of consensus, company mentality, and lifetime employment make whistleblowing almost unheard of and highly risky. One employee who defied this tradition, an ex-Honda engineer who allegedly quit in a dispute over safety issues, is now a plaintiff's expert witness in the United States in suits against Honda. His testimony provides an income that he could no longer earn in Japan because of his dissent.

An explanation for these differences can be drawn from [one of] several studies that show basic differences in value systems between national cultures.[28]... [It] identifies five dimensions on which cultures vary: power distance, individualism, uncertainty avoidance, masculinity, and Confucian dynamism.... Of these five, power distance, individualism, and Confucian dynamism are most relevant to examining whistleblowing among cultures. Cultures with a high power distance are more willing to accept that power is unequally distributed among individuals and are therefore more willing to accept inequality, autocratic leadership, and centralization of authority. Cultures high in individualism have a loosely knit social framework in which people believe they are responsible for themselves and their immediate family instead of believing that they are members of an in-group which will look out for them. A society which scores high in Confucian dynamism is a dynamic, future-oriented society, while a society low in this dimension tends to be tradition bound and static.

These classifications are, of course, only tools of analysis, and countries may vary along a continuum in each dimension. Nonetheless, they may help explain why the United States, Australia, and the United Kingdom are some of the first countries with whistleblower legislation, and other countries are more reluctant to accept the idea. Japan is a low-scoring country on individualism, relatively low-scoring on dynamism, and high-scoring on power distance. People living in a low individualistic, high power distance country are less likely to challenge authority, and those in authority are less likely to tolerate challenges. Additionally, loyalty to the group will be stronger in this climate, thus making reporting on someone within the group less likely. Finally, going against societal norms to blow the whistle is less likely in a low-dynamic society.

The United States, Australia, and the United Kingdom, by contrast, are countries which score at the high end on the individualism and dynamism dimensions, and low on power distance. Thus, people in these societies are more likely to challenge authority, and doing so is more likely to be socially acceptable....

This analysis does not imply that whistleblowing procedures cannot be successfully implemented in countries like Japan. It does indicate that it will be more difficult, and MNCs will have to carefully consider and structure what they ask their employees to do if internal reporting is to be used as an ethical control mechanism. This may be easier now than it would have been even a decade ago for two reasons. First, the societies studied are dynamic. Japan, for example, is slowly moving away from lifetime employment...and independent thinking and challenges to authority are becoming more common. Second, whistleblowing is increasingly being discussed and considered on an international scale, so it is not as radical an idea as it once may have appeared....

---

[28] Gert Hofstede, *Culture's Consequences: International Differences in Work-Related Values* (abridged ed. 1984).

[Given these cultural differences, Dworkin next suggests how standards and reporting mechanisms might work.]

Reporting Procedures

A large number of studies have been conducted on whistleblowers, particularly on what distinguishes observers of wrongdoing who blow the whistle from those who do not. The most important predictor is whether there is a clear reporting procedure that is seen as effective....

In situations where great emphasis is placed on organizational conformity and loyalty to co-workers and the organization, the organization must convince employees that whistleblowing is normative and desired.... Reporting requirements, if implemented and seriously followed, will help achieve this "normative" behavior.

To have an effective compliance program, an organization should:

- Establish a written compliance program. Written compliance programs should be clearly written, easily understood, relatively brief, and lack legal verbiage. To the extent feasible, employees from all sectors of the organization should participate in the formation of the requirements....
- Train employees regarding compliance.... Policies should stress that employees can be held personally liable for failure to comply and that the organization may be legally liable for compliance failure. Corporations should stress that nonretaliation is an integral part of the policy.
- Establish a simple reporting procedure.... Establishing a special person [to receive reports] sends the message that the organization takes the issues seriously and is open to dissent. Having someone like an ombudsperson, independent of management, reinforces this message.
- Investigate and respond quickly. To the extent possible, the privacy of the parties involved should be maintained during the investigation. The response should include a report back to the whistleblower to demonstrate that the company has listened and has taken action....

Appropriate Ethical Norms and Cultural Adaptability

To foster participation, the code should concern relatively few issues that can garner wide acceptance or understanding....

The easiest norm for employees to understand is compliance with the law. Other norms on which a company could get broad agreement are fair treatment of employees, protection of the environment, and rules against bribery.

[Using the example of sexual harassment, Dworkin discusses the problem of culturally divergent attitudes. Pointing to Wharton professors Donaldson and Dunfee's notion of "hypernorms,"[29] she argues that there are ways of identifying globally shared values.]

A hypernorm is a [principle] "so fundamental to human existence that [it serves] as a guide in evaluating lower level moral norms." Because of its importance, the hypernorm is likely to be reflected in global principles that are generally recognized....

An examination of numerous global and regional declarations and other documents, such as the 1948 Universal Declaration of Human Rights, the UN Convention on the Elimination of All Forms of Discrimination Against Women, OECD Guidelines for Multinational Enterprises, the Council of Europe's 1996 Social Charter, EC Directives and Codes of Practice, as well as the laws and philosophies of particular countries, suggest there are three hypernorms relevant to harassment: personal security, respect for human dignity, and nondiscrimination. At a minimum, these hypernorms

---

[29] Thomas Donaldson and Thomas W. Dunfee, *Ties that Bind: A Social Contracts Approach to Business Ethics*, 49–81 (1999).

support global rules against...[b]eing forced to trade sexual favors for the right to employment [because this] threatens personal security, undermines human dignity, and is generally acknowledged to be discriminatory....

MNC implementation of global equal treatment standards that are reinforced by reporting procedures is not only feasible, but can help reduce conflict. Some studies indicate there is a positive correlation between gender equality and nonviolence. Creating an atmosphere where inter-group interactions are fostered under conditions of equal treatment helps reduce conflict. It can help defuse resentment and limit disruptive behavior by contributing to a feeling of psychological security and increased physical security....

[Dworkin next looks at another example, bribery.]

Despite the lack of uniformity, it is feasible for an MNC to ban bribery. Every country in the world prohibits bribery of its officials. This would be the starting point of such a code, along with compliance with local laws. However, allowance for legitimate gift-giving can be made on a [local] basis with appropriate discussion and training....

[B]ribery can cause conflict. One important reason is that it undermines free trade, and free trade helps foster peace. Corporations that adopt bribery bans and enforce them through reporting procedures potentially contribute to peace by allowing better utilization of resources. This, in turn, frees up more resources for those at the bottom of the economic rungs, and will have an increased impact in the emerging economies that are most harmed by bribery....

Contributions of Open Reporting to the Corporation and to Peace

Internal whistleblowing procedures and codes of ethics will operate more effectively when organizations operate as mediating institutions. Mediating institutions are relatively small organizations where moral identity and behavior are formed. Studies indicate that as the size of an organization increases, individual ethical decision-making behavior decreases. Thus, for large multinational corporations, the need for training in relatively small groups at the local level is heightened....

There are benefits to the organization that adopts these policies and procedures. Global strategic alliances represent a type of competitive weapon. In order to take the best advantage of the alliance, organizations must listen to multicultural perspectives. Additionally, firm-specific fairness norms promote efficiency.

Organizations that foster internal reporting and open discussion are likely to find that external reporting will be virtually nonexistent. Problems can be raised and resolved earlier if employees feel free to engage in discussion and dissent....

Conclusion

MNCs can help in the evolution of a normative global village. They can create conditions that socialize and empower individuals and give them the tools to interact more successfully in their society. To the extent that ideas such as fairness and responsibility for compliance are learned within the company and are then taken externally, organizations have the ability to have an impact far beyond their individual realm. At the same time, exporting the idea of whistleblowing helps promote transparency and good government in larger society. Organizational norms matter most when law is the weakest.

As countries shift in their commercial institutions from a "relational orientation" to a more Western "formal orientation" based on the rule of law, whistleblowing could be a helpful procedure in that transition. It is designed to allow individuals to enforce the rules despite the individual connections of those in power. In the words of Alan Watson, "In most places at most times, borrowing is the most fruitful source of legal change." Borrowing from MNCs which set the bar higher is also a fruitful source of change.

QUESTIONS

1. Dworkin builds on the notion that MNCs can best function in societies in which honest, open transactions can occur, and in which conflicts are resolved through free exchange of opinions rather than by violence. How does she link this to MNC policies and procedures on whistleblowing?

2. According to Dworkin, how might the cultural setting where an MNC operates affect its compliance policies and reporting procedures? And how might an MNC's procedures affect the society in which it operates?

3. Hold up an ethical lens to Dworkin's argument. Which ethical framework is most clearly reflected here? Begin by thinking about stakeholders. Which seem most sharply in focus?

4. Cultural imperialism, according to Wikipedia, is a pejorative phrase for "the practice of promoting, distinguishing, separating, or artificially injecting the culture or language of one nation into another. It is usually the case that the former is a large, economically or militarily powerful nation, and the latter is a smaller, less affluent one." Do Dworkin's recommendations amount to cultural imperialism? Why or why not?

5. In line with Dworkin's remarks about Japan as a "low-scoring country on individualism," is the Japanese aphorism: "The nail that sticks up gets hammered." Yet Dworkin also notes that Japan is becoming more "dynamic," and suggests change is on the way.

    Research: What can you find out about this? Has any whistleblowing legislation been passed in Japan? Any cases won? Any other signs that a cultural shift is underway around workplace norms? Look into the activities of MNCs in Japan. Is there any indication that they have been instrumental in driving change?

6. Dworkin writes: "Rules reinforced by whistleblowing can help to deliver transparency."

    Research: What is meant by "transparency" in the context of global business? Check the Web site of Transparency International. Compare corruption indices across countries. Do the countries with lower transparency rates also have weaker whistleblowing protections, reinforcing Dworkin's analysis?

Chapter Problems

1. Kenneth Abbott, a former contractor who worked for British Petroleum, claims the company violated state and federal laws and its own internal policy by failing to maintain crucial safety documents related to one of its deepwater production facilities in the Gulf of Mexico. The project, called BP Atlantis, is one of the largest and deepest underwater oil and gas platforms in the world. Abbott, who had been hired to oversee BP databases, discovered Atlantis had been operating without the majority of the engineer-certified documents required by law and by BP's own procedures, and that the platform was at risk for a catastrophic disaster even more massive than the spill that was triggered by the deadly Deepwater Horizon explosion in early 2010. Abbott reported his concerns BP management. His contract was abruptly terminated. He later made reports to a former federal judge who was serving as an ombudsman to take complaints about BP operations following a ruptured pipeline incident in Prudhoe Bay. BP has issued this statement in response to Abbott's allegations:

    As CEO Tony Hayward constantly makes clear, safe and reliable operations are his number 1 priority for BP and the company has a very strong record of safe and reliable operations in the Gulf of Mexico.... The Atlantis field has been in service since October 2007 and has safely produced many millions of barrels of oil. The platform was successfully maintained through the course of two major hurricanes in 2008. Its safety, operation, and performance record is excellent.

Assume Kenneth Abbott sues. How would he fare under the law in Maryland? New Jersey? Montana? Assume a whistleblower in the federal Minerals Management Service (MMS) reported these concerns to his supervisor. How would she fare under *Garcetti*?

2. What would you do if you were the supervisor in the following situation: Your company has a rule forbidding armored truck drivers from leaving the truck unattended. Even if pulled over by someone who appears to be a police officer, drivers are to show a card explaining that the driver will follow the police to the stationhouse. Kevin Gardner is one of your drivers. At a scheduled stop at a bank, he waited in the vehicle while his coworker was in the bank. Suddenly he spotted a woman, whom he recognized as the manager, running out of the bank screaming, "Help me!" Chasing her was a man with a knife. Seeing nobody coming to help the manager, Gardner got out of the truck, locking the door behind him. Gardner lost sight of the manager, but walked toward the suspect who had already grabbed another employee, Kathy Martin, who Gardner recognized. The suspect put the knife to Martin's throat and dragged her back into the bank. Gardner followed them into the bank where he observed his partner with his gun drawn and aimed at the suspect. While his partner distracted the suspect, Gardner and a bank customer tackled the suspect and disarmed him. The police arrived immediately thereafter and took custody of the suspect. Ms. Martin was unharmed. Find out what happened in the case on which this is based: *Gardner v. Loomis Armored Inc.*, 913 P.2d 377 (Washington 1996).

3. Jane Akre and her husband, Steve Wilson, award-winning broadcast journalists, were recruited by Fox News to do investigative reports. With a deep voice in its promotional commercial, Fox promoted the two as the Mod Squad, "The Investigators, uncovering the truth, getting results, protecting you!" Akre and Wilson were promised that Fox would support them in their work, never caving into advertisers' pressure or altering a disturbing news story. In 1997 the team began investigating the use of bovine growth hormone (BGH) in the dairy farming industry. BGH, a Monsanto product, is used to enhance production; it is controversial because it is linked to cancer. In a four-part series, Akre and Wilson uncovered information about BGH health risks and unethical marketing practices. Having learned of the series, Monsanto's legal department sent a series of threatening letters to Fox, casting aspersions of the journalists' integrity: "Consider thoroughly what is at stake and the enormous damage that can be done by the reckless presentation of unsupported speculation as fact and the equally reckless publication of unsupported accusations..." Fox had Akre re-write the BGH story 83 times over nine months, and finally fired the "Mod Squad." They sued under Florida whistleblower law, which protects employees who experience retaliation for refusing to participate in or reporting illegal activity. A jury awarded Akre and Wilson $425,000. How would they have fared under Maryland law? New Jersey? Montana? What are the ethical issues in this case? What happened on appeal? See *New World Communications of Tampa, Inc. v. Akre*, 866 So. 2d 1231 (Florida 2003).

4. Born in Mexico, Jose Castro illegally entered the United States in 1988 and got a job with Hoffman Plastic by showing false identification. In December 1988, the

United Rubber, Cork, Linoleum, and Plastic Workers of America AFL-CIO started a union-organizing campaign at his production plant, and Castro supported the effort, distributing authorization cards. In January 1989, Castro and others who had been involved in the organizing were laid off. The National Labor Relations Board (NLRB) found that Castro's layoff violated the law because Hoffman was attempting to "rid itself of known union supporters." In 2002, the Supreme Court ruled that as an undocumented "alien," Castro was not entitled to the monetary remedy (back pay) otherwise available under the National Labor Relations Act. Who are the stakeholders in this case? What impact does the ruling have on each of them? Suppose Castro had been fired after reporting health or safety violations in the workplace. Would a similar outcome—no whistleblower protection for an undocumented alien—apply?

5. What do the findings below suggest about the best way to craft a whistleblower policy for a private company?

- *A 2007 PricewaterhouseCoopers (PWC) survey of CEOs, CFOs, and executives responsible for compliance from over 5,400 firms in 40 countries found that "Fraud remains one of the most problematic issues for business worldwide," but in order to detect and combat fraud, corporations "cannot" simply "rely on" internal "controls" to "detect and deter economic crimes." The study found that "43 percent of corporate fraud was uncovered by whistleblowing related activities:" "[I]n virtually every region of the world, whistleblowing is playing a role in uncovering the activities of wrongdoers."*

- *In 2008, the Association of Certified Fraud Examiners (ACFE) released a study of nearly 1,000 cases of fraud related to American firms. The findings: "One of the primary characteristics of fraud is that it is clandestine, or hidden; almost all fraud involves the attempted concealment of the crime." Like PWC, the ACFE concluded that tipsters were more effective at uncovering fraud than internal corporate controls: "Despite increased focus on antifraud controls in the wake of Sarbanes-Oxley…our data shows that occupational frauds are much more likely to be detected by a tip then by audits, controls, or any other means."*

- *Nearly 3,000 employees from the for-profit sector participated in the Ethics Resource Center's 2009 National Business Ethics Survey. Although results indicated that most key measures had improved since 2007, retaliation against those who reported misconduct had increased. The most common form of retaliation experienced as a result of reporting misconduct was "your supervisor or management actively excluded you from decisions and work" (62 percent) and "other employees gave you the cold shoulder" (60 percent). Fifty-five percent experienced "verbal abuse by a supervisor or someone else in management" and almost half reported almost losing their jobs (48 percent). 49 percent of employees reported witnessing some type of misconduct occurring in the workplace, such as company resource abuse, abusive behavior, lying to employees, e-mail or Internet abuse, conflicts of interest, and discrimination.*

6. **Research:** Founded in 1977, the Government Accountability Project promotes "government and corporate accountability through advancing occupational free speech and ethical conduct, defending whistleblowers, and empowering citizen activists." What tips do they offer a would-be whistleblower? See *www.whistleblower.org*.

7. The Web site *www.wikileaks.org* describes itself as "a multi-jurisdictional public service designed to protect whistleblowers, journalists, and activists who have sensitive materials to communicate to the public." (a) How does WikiLeaks work? (b) Find

out what happened to Bradley Manning, an army intelligence analyst arrested in 2010 for allegedly passing classified information—including a video of a U.S. military helicopter firing on civilians in Baghdad—to WikiLeaks. (c) What are the current postings on WikiLeaks?

CHAPTER PROJECT

Stakeholder Ethics Role Play

Guidelines: Appendix D
Name the stakeholders in this business ethics dilemma. Discuss possible choices for Nash in the light of law and ethical theory.

Desperate Air[30]
Desperate Air Corporation (DAC) flies routes along the U.S. East Coast. DAC acquired a number of hotels and undeveloped properties five years ago as part of a short-lived diversification strategy. DAC has recently experienced substantial losses, has a negative cash flow. Bankruptcy looms as a possibility unless high labor costs can be reduced and consumer confidence restored.

Benton Williams has just been brought in as CEO to revitalize DAC. Williams began by cutting back on middle management and by placing a one-year moratorium on hiring MBAs. Middle managers terminated by DAC and other airlines are having a tough time finding equivalent jobs.

DAC owns a large, undeveloped oceanfront property on the east coast of Florida. Williams directs George Nash, DAC's vice president of real estate, to find a buyer for the property to generate badly needed cash. After some effort, Nash identifies Fledgling Industries, a relatively new developer of retirement villas, as a good prospect. Fledgling is interested in finding a property on which it could build a complex of high-rise retirement condos featuring elaborate walking trails and outside recreational facilities.

DAC had conducted a full environmental audit of the property six months earlier and had discovered no problems. A copy of this report was given to the Fledgling representative, who also walked over the property and discovered no problems. The representative asked, "Anything I should know about?" Nash replied, "No problems."

As the negotiations progressed with Fledgling, Nash was approached by a long-time friend at DAC, Laura Devitt, who told him that there was now some highly toxic waste on the property. She said she heard this might be true through the rumor mill at the firm and that she had been curious enough to check things out. Walking around on the property one day, she had found several partially buried metal containers marked DANGER/BIOHAZARD. RADIOACTIVE MEDICAL WASTE. The containers were rusted where they were exposed; two were cracked, and their liquid contents were seeping onto the ground. Laura told Nash she wanted him to know about this because she was worried that innocent people could be hurt if the sale went through.

---

[30] This case was written by the late and much-beloved Professor Thomas Dunfee of the Wharton School at the University of Pennsylvania and is reprinted with his permission.

Nash contacted Williams, but before he could mention the containers to him, Williams interrupted and told him it was vital that the sale closed and that it be done as soon as possible. Nash consulted with a DAC lawyer who told him that under Florida law it is not necessary to disclose the existence of hazardous waste on commercial property as long as there hasn't been a fraudulent misstatement about the condition of the property.

Nash was troubled. Should he mention the hazardous materials to the Fledgling representative before he closed the sale? He knew Fledgling had been considering some other similar properties, and Nash thought that if he mentioned the toxic spill problem Fledgling would probably not go through with the sale. At the least, disclosure could delay the sale for months while the spill was investigated and potential liability problems considered. Nash figured that he would be unlikely ever to deal with Fledgling again regarding future real estate deals because DAC did not own any other properties that fit Fledgling's business needs.

The question of whether to close the sale immediately bothered Nash enough that he talked to his wife about it, and then prayed about what to do.

CHAPTER 3

Privacy and Technology

A wonderful fact to reflect upon, that every human creature is constituted to be that profound secret and mystery to every other. A solemn consideration, when I enter a great city by night, that every one of those darkly clustered houses encloses its own secret; that every room in every one of them encloses its own secret; that in every beating heart in the hundreds of thousands of breasts there is, in some of its imaginings, a secret to the heart nearest to it!

— CHARLES DICKENS

Ladies and gentlemen, progress is like a storekeeper. You can have anything you want, but you have to pay the price. You can have the telephone, but you will lose some of your privacy, and the charm of distance. You can have the airplane, but the birds will lose their wonder and the clouds will smell of gasoline.

— CLARENCE DARROW in *INHERIT THE WIND*

You already have zero privacy—get over it.

— SCOTT MCNEALY, CEO, Sun Microsystems

Human beings must experience a degree of privacy to thrive. Yet, as they act inside organizations, they frequently need information about one another, information that may be sensitive and confidential. Employers want to find out if their workers are productive and loyal. Corporations want to know the preferences of potential customers or the strategies of their competitors. Governments want to thwart terrorists. Tension between privacy and the need to know is heightened as computer technology revolutionizes information gathering. The process has never been so fast, so efficient, or so omnipresent.

This chapter highlights the conflict between the sweeping power of technology to access and assemble information and the ongoing concerns we all share about privacy. Opening with a case involving the interception of e-mail by an employer, it broadens to look at electronic surveillance more generally, and at the legal framework that might address it. We read about the value of privacy, both for individuals and for communities. Next, we look at efforts to control employees' off-the-job behavior. Should employers be able to fire you for smoking, drinking, or other unhealthy habits? For dating someone who is married? We consider workplace testing as it intersects with privacy concerns. We look at privacy issues surrounding Facebook. We then explore, for employees in the pubic sector, the limits of privacy for text messaging. The chapter ends with a focus on the collection of sensitive health data through genetic testing and at the new Genetic Information Nondiscrimination Act, called GINA.

Surveillance at Work

E-mail Interception

In the U.S., billions of e-mails are sent every day from business settings. Because they use passcodes, employees may believe their e-mail messages are private, but the reality is that they are not. Even deleted messages are stored in archives easily accessible to employers and others.

■ ■ ■

In 1996, a district court in Philadelphia was faced with the following situation. A Pillsbury employee and his supervisor were sending e-mail messages to one another. One message, referring to sales management, mentioned plans to "kill the back-stabbing bastards." Another message described a holiday party as the "Jim Jones Kool-Aid affair." These messages fell into their boss's hands, and both men were fired for sending "inappropriate and unprofessional comments" over Pillsbury's e-mail system. One of the employees sued, claiming he was "wrongfully discharged" when he lost his well-paid position as a regional manager.

MICHAEL A. SMYTH v. THE PILLSBURY COMPANY
United States District Court, 1996 914 F. Supp. 97

WEINER, District Judge.

Defendant [Pillsbury Company] maintained an electronic mail communication system ("e-mail") in order to promote internal corporate communications between its employees. Defendant repeatedly assured its employees, including plaintiff, that all e-mail communications would remain confidential and privileged. Defendant further assured its employees, including plaintiff, that e-mail communications could not be intercepted and used by defendant against its employees as grounds for termination or reprimand.

In October 1994, plaintiff [Michael Smyth] received certain e-mail communications from his supervisor over defendant's e-mail system on his computer at home. In reliance on defendant's assurances regarding defendant's e-mail system, plaintiff responded and exchanged e-mails with his supervisor. At some later date, contrary to the assurances of confidentiality made by defendant, defendant, acting through its agents, servants, and employees, intercepted plaintiff's private e-mail messages made in October 1994. On January 17, 1995, defendant notified plaintiff that it was terminating his employment ... for transmitting what it deemed to be inappropriate and unprofessional comments over defendant's e-mail system....

[Smyth argued wrongful discharge, claiming his employer had violated public policy by committing a tort known as "invasion of privacy." One version of invasion of privacy is called "intrusion." In the first step of his analysis, the judge defines the tort of "intrusion":]

One who intentionally intrudes, physically or otherwise, upon the solitude or seclusion of another or his private affairs or concerns, is subject to liability to the other for invasion of his privacy, if the intrusion would be highly offensive to a reasonable person....

[To determine if the facts of the case fit the definition above, the judge uses a "balancing test," weighing the employee's privacy interests against the employer's need to discover information.]

[W]e do not find a reasonable expectation of privacy in e-mail communications voluntarily made by an employee to his supervisor over the company e-mail system notwithstanding any assurances that such communications would not be intercepted by management. Once plaintiff communicated the alleged unprofessional comments to a second person (his supervisor) over an e-mail system which was apparently utilized by the entire company, any reasonable expectation of privacy was lost. Significantly, the defendant did not require plaintiff, as in the case of a urinalysis or personal property search, to disclose any personal information about himself. Rather, plaintiff voluntarily communicated the alleged unprofessional comments over the company e-mail system. We find no privacy interests in such communications.

Secondly, even if we found that an employee had a reasonable expectation of privacy in the contents of his e-mail communications over the company e-mail system, we do not find that a reasonable person would consider the defendant's interception of these communications to be a substantial and highly offensive invasion of his privacy.... [T]he company's interest in preventing inappropriate and unprofessional comments or even illegal activity over its e-mail system outweighs any privacy interest the employee may have in those comments.

In sum, we find that the defendant's actions did not tortiously invade the plaintiff's privacy and, therefore, did not violate public policy.

QUESTIONS

1. How does Judge Weiner explain why Michael Smyth lost any "reasonable expectation of privacy" in his e-mail comments?

2. Is there any difference between a password-protected message sent on company e-mail and a handwritten memo sealed in an envelope marked "private" sent through company mail? Consider the judge's reasons for his ruling. Would they also apply to the memo? Suppose Pillsbury began covert audio monitoring of the area near the coffee station in order to screen employee conversations on break time. How would the judge's reasoning apply?

3. From a Kantian perspective, how ethical were the actions of Smyth? Of Pillsbury? What appears to be the ethical framework underlying the judge's ruling?

4. Corporate culture varies, and with it, corporate surveillance policies. Some companies give notice to employees that their e-mail communications are not private. Kmart's policy, for example, introduced at every employee orientation, states that "misuse of the e-mail system could result in denial of access to the Kmart computing environment or dismissal." Apple Computers, on the other hand, has an explicit policy of not monitoring employee e-mail. What might be the advantages and disadvantages of such policies from an employee's viewpoint? An employer's?

5. Suppose you were responsible for developing a surveillance policy where you worked. How would you go about setting its parameters? How would you implement it?

6. Nearly half of American workers bring work home with them regularly, according to *American Sociological Review* in December 2009. Laptop computers, cell phones, and other hand-held communication devices invite them to do more and more work outside the physical confines of the traditional office, during hours that were once considered reserved for leisure time. At the same time, people often find themselves handling personal chores during the hours they spend at the workplace. According to a study by the Center for Business Ethics at Bentley College, by 2003, virtually all

(92% of) employers allow office computers to be used—within reason—for personal purposes. As the division between work and the rest of life becomes ever more blurred, should the balancing of interests articulated in the *Pillsbury* case change?

7. Hi-tech surveillance is not solely directed by employers at workers. American businesses have always been interested in capturing confidential information and trade secrets from competitors. Today, thanks to computer technology, they are able to spy on one another with more sophisticated means than ever before. What are some of the latest developments in this area? How far can a company go in this direction without crossing the line? Visit the Web site of the Society of Competitive Intelligence Professionals at *http://www.scip.org*.

8. Should educational institutions be free to randomly monitor student and faculty e-mail? What is your school's policy on e-mail privacy? Review it and discuss it with others. Are there elements of the policy that you would change, in light of what you have read? Rewrite it.

■ ■ ■

Electronic Surveillance: The Debate

Employers have long had an interest in scrutinizing their workforces. In the 1880s, Frederick Taylor invented an approach to industrial efficiency that broke each job into many separate, measurable components. He monitored every part of the process—time per task; hand and eye movements; spacing between workers, machines, and products—and developed a system that gave managers the ability to track both the speed and the intensity of work very closely. And in the early twentieth century, Ford Motor Company hired social workers to investigate employees, to check that they had the right habits of cleanliness, thriftiness, and churchgoing to deserve what was then an impressive $5/day wage. What is different about present-day workplace oversight is the use of technology that allows workers to be observed secretly and in newly intrusive ways. Too, the rate of electronic monitoring of employees has scaled up dramatically over recent years. In 1998, the congressional Office of Technology Assessment found that only eight percent of firms were conducting monitoring. Just five years later, by 2003, nearly all (92%) of employers were using some form of electronic surveillance.[1]

SURVEY DATA SHOWS INCREASING WORKPLACE SURVEILLANCE

Since 2001 the American Management Association (AMA) has been conducting biannual studies of the employee monitoring practices of hundreds of firms. Their 2007 survey indicated that workplace surveillance—from videotaping to monitoring of blogsites to GPS tracking of vehicles—was on the rise. While AMA data from 2005 showed 25% of respondents reporting they had fired employees for misuse of email, by 2007, 28% reported having done so. In the 2005 AMA survey, 26% of respondents reported firing employees for misuse of the Internet; by 2007 that number had increased to 30%. Further 2007 findings: Nearly half of employers surveyed tracked keystrokes, content, and time spent on computers. Twelve percent monitored blogs to check for comments about the company, and 10% monitored social networking sites. In 2001, when the AMA did its first electronic monitoring survey, 33% of employers reported using video surveillance to counter theft or sabotage. By

---

[1] 2003 Center for Business Ethics at Bentley College, "Survey: You've Got Mail, and the Boss Knows."

2007 nearly half did so—48%—with 7% reporting video monitoring of job performance. According to the latest AMA survey, 12 percent of the companies that monitor do not notify their employees.

Interest in the use of software to track employee activity online is growing. Filtering software is evolving quickly and becoming increasingly sophisticated. These programs can take surreptitious "screen shots" of employee computers; track Web usage; rank individuals according to their rates of traffic to game, joke, pornography, shopping, or job-hunting sites; or examine images attached to e-mails for anything that looks like flesh. Consider for example SpectorSoft's flagship product, Spector 360, which "takes the recorded Internet and computer activities from each of your employees, feeds that information into a database, and provides you with more than 50 built-in reports and unlimited customization." About $2,000 will pay for installation on 15 computers, allowing a company to discover:

- *Which employees spend the most time surfing Web sites*
- *Which employees chat the most*
- *Who sends the most e-mails with attachments*
- *Who arrives to work late and leaves early*
- *What ... employees [are] searching for on the Internet*

This software product promises "through a first of its kind surveillance-like camera recording tool" to reveal a "level of detail so precise that you can see what an employee does each and every second."[2]

Businesses justify electronic surveillance in a number of ways. It enables supervisors to observe and improve employee performance. It both measures and encourages efficiency. It enhances the completeness and fairness of personnel evaluations. It can uncover employee disloyalty, which can take the form of stealing tangible items, such as products and supplies, or intangibles, such as trade secrets. It can flag racially or sexually harassing e-messages.

Countering all this employees claim that electronic monitoring puts them under dehumanizing pressure with computers instead of people judging their performance. Because computers measure quantity better than quality, employees who work fast might look better than those who work best. The "electronic sweatshop," they say, causes psychological stress and physical symptoms.[3] For example, a study of employees in financial institutions and government agencies found that subjecting people to monitoring negatively affected the quality of their work. And a 1993 Rutgers University study found that employees subjected to video surveillance were less able to solve complex problems.[4] Apart from the more measurable costs, employees emphasize their need to preserve at work what they expect to maintain elsewhere—a sense of dignity and self-respect.

---

[2] http://www.spectorsoft.com, last visited June 18, 2010.

[3] Peter Blackman and Barbara Franklin, "Blocking Big Brother: Proposed Law Limits Employers' Right to Snoop," *N.Y.L.J.* August 19, 1993, p. 5, citing University of Wisconsin study finding monitored telecommunications workers suffered more depression, anxiety, and fatigue than their non-monitored counterparts in the same facility.

[4] Lewis Maltby, *Can They Do That? Retaking our Fundamental Rights at the Workplace* (New York: Penguin Publishing, 2009), p. 27.

Electronic Surveillance: The Law

America lacks a comprehensive and uniform legal standard protecting privacy. No express "right to privacy" was written into the U.S. Constitution, although the Supreme Court has interpreted the First, Fourth, Fifth, and Ninth Amendments as creating certain privacy rights that cannot be violated by the government. (Later in this chapter, we explore one aspect: the right to be free of unreasonable government searches and seizures.)

In the private sector, privacy law is determined by a variety of federal and state statutes and by the common law of torts.[5] Employees may claim that electronic monitoring amounts to "intrusion," a variation on the tort of invasion of privacy. As the *Pillsbury* case indicates, intrusion involves invading another person's solitude in a manner considered highly offensive—unauthorized prying into a personal bank account or a landlord bugging the wall of his tenants' bedroom, for example. Most courts consider two main factors: (1) the obnoxiousness of the means used to intrude; that is, whether it is a deviation from the normal, accepted means of discovering the relevant information; and (2) the reasons for intruding. In one Alabama case, a man had multiple surgeries after he fell while working as a winch-truck driver. In preparation for a worker's compensation trial, and in order to collect evidence regarding the extent of his actual injuries, employer had him videotaped secretly while he was at home. The court dismissed his claim for intrusion, stating "Because the activities [the injured worker] carried on in his front yard could have been observed by any passerby," the employer's investigation was not offensive or objectionable.[6] As electronic monitoring becomes increasingly commonplace, and increasingly taken for granted, and as long as employers can point to a legitimate purpose for monitoring, it will be difficult for employees to convince courts that their privacy was invaded.

The 1968 Federal Wiretap Law, as amended by the Electronic Communications Privacy Act 1986 (ECPA), making it illegal to intercept, disclose, or access messages without authorization, would appear to protect workers from electronic eavesdropping. But there are a number of exemptions to the ECPA. For example, there is no protection for communications that are "readily accessible to the general public," such as public chat room exchanges. The law does not apply to the extent that employees give "consent" to monitoring, which would seem to eliminate ECPA coverage in the many workplaces where people are told that their communications are not private. The ECPA also allows employers to listen in on communications made in the "ordinary course of business." In other words, where business interests such as efficiency or legal liability are at stake, the surveillance would be allowed.

The Value of Privacy

Privacy is much more than just a possible social technique for assuring this or that substantive interest ... it is necessarily related to ends and relations of the most fundamental sort: respect, love, friendship, and trust. Privacy is not merely a good technique for furthering these fundamental relations, rather without privacy they are simply inconceivable. They require a context of privacy or the possibility of privacy for their existence.... To respect, love, trust, feel affection for others, and to regard ourselves as the objects of love, trust, and affection is at the heart of our notion of ourselves as persons

[5] Connecticut and Delaware have passed laws to protect employees against electronic monitoring without notice. *Conn. Gen. Stat.* Sec 31-48d, *Del. Code* tit. 19 Sec. 705.

[6] *ICU Investigations, Inc. v. Charles R. Jones*, 780 So.2d 685 (2000).

among persons, and privacy is the necessary atmosphere for those attitudes and actions, as oxygen is for combustion.

— CHARLES FRIED, "PRIVACY," 77 YALE L.J. 475 (1968)

The following excerpt describes how privacy serves a set of important human needs. The author, Columbia University Professor Emeritus Alan Westin, now a corporate consultant on privacy issues, has been in the forefront of research on the effects of technology on privacy in our society, particularly in the workplace.

THE FUNCTIONS OF PRIVACY
Alan Westin[7]

[T]he functions privacy performs for individuals in democratic societies...can [be] ... grouped conveniently under four headings—personal autonomy, emotional release, self-evaluation, and limited and protected communication....

Personal Autonomy

In democratic societies there is a fundamental belief in the uniqueness of the individual, in his basic dignity and worth as a creature of God and a human being, and in the need to maintain social processes that safeguard his sacred individuality. Psychologists and sociologists have linked the development and maintenance of this sense of individuality to the human need for autonomy—the desire to avoid being manipulated or dominated wholly by others.

[Scholars describe a] "core self,"... pictured as an inner circle surrounded by a series of larger concentric circles. The inner circle shelters the individual's "ultimate secrets"—those hopes, fears, and prayers that are beyond sharing with anyone unless the individual comes under such stress that he must pour out these ultimate secrets to secure emotional relief.... The next circle outward contains "intimate secrets," those that can be willingly shared with close relations, confessors, or strangers who pass by and cannot injure. The next circle is open to members of the individual's friendship group. The series continues until it reaches the outer circles of casual conversation and physical expression that are open to all observers.

The most serious threat to the individual's autonomy is the possibility that someone may penetrate the inner zone and learn his ultimate secrets, either by physical or psychological means. Each person is aware of the gap between what he wants to be and what he actually is, between what the world sees of him and what he knows to be his much more complex reality. In addition, there are aspects of himself that the individual does not fully understand but is slowly exploring and shaping as he develops. Every individual lives behind a mask in this manner; indeed, the first etymological meaning of the word "person" was "mask." ...

Emotional Release

Life in society generates such tensions for the individual that both physical and psychological health demand periods of privacy for various types of emotional release. At one level, such relaxation is required from the pressure of playing social roles.... On any given day a man may move through the roles of stern father, loving husband, car-pool comedian, skilled lathe operator, union steward, water-cooler flirt, and American Legion

[7] Reprinted with the permission of Simon and Schuster, Inc. from PRIVACY AND FREEDOM by Alan F. Westin. Copyright © 1967 by the Association of the Bar of the City of New York. All rights reserved.

committee chairman—all psychologically different roles.... [N]o individual can play indefinitely, without relief, the variety of roles that life demands. There have to be moments "off stage" when the individual can be "himself": tender, angry, irritable, lustful, or dream-filled. Such moments may come in solitude; in the intimacy of family, peers, or woman-to-woman and man-to-man relaxation; in the anonymity of park or street; or in a state of reserve while in a group. Privacy in this aspect gives individuals, from factory workers to presidents, a chance to lay their masks aside for rest....

Another form of emotional release is provided by the protection privacy gives to minor noncompliance with social norms.... [A]lmost everyone does break some social or institutional norms—for example, violating traffic laws, breaking sexual mores, cheating on expense accounts, overstating income tax deductions, or smoking in restrooms when this is prohibited. Although society will usually punish the most flagrant abuses, it tolerates the great bulk of the violations as "permissible" deviations.... [I]f all transgressions were known—most persons in society would be under organizational discipline or in jail, or could be manipulated by threats of such action. The firm expectation of having privacy for permissible deviations is a distinguishing characteristic of life in a free society. At a lesser but still important level, privacy also allows individuals to deviate temporarily from social etiquette when alone or among intimates, as by putting feet on desks, cursing, letting one's face go slack, or scratching wherever one itches.

Another aspect of release is the "safety valve" function afforded by privacy. Most persons need to give vent to their anger at "the system," "city hall," "the boss," and various others who exercise authority over them, and to do this in the intimacy of family or friendship circles, or in private papers, without fear of being held responsible for such comments. This is very different from freedom of speech or press, which involves publicly voiced criticism without fear of interference by government....

Still another aspect of release through privacy arises in the management of bodily and sexual functions....

Self-Evaluation

Every individual needs to integrate his experiences into a meaningful pattern and to exert his individuality on events. To carry on such self-evaluation, privacy is essential. At the intellectual level, individuals need to process the information that is constantly bombarding them, information that cannot be processed while they are still "on the go." This is particularly true of creative persons. Studies of creativity show that it is in reflective solitude and even "daydreaming" during moments of reserve that most creative "nonverbal" thought takes place. At such moments the individual runs ideas and impressions through his mind in a flow of associations; the active presence of others tends to inhibit this process....

The evaluative function of privacy also has a major moral dimension—the exercise of conscience by which the individual "repossesses himself." While people often consider the moral consequences of their acts during the course of daily affairs, it is primarily in periods of privacy that they take a moral inventory of ongoing conduct and measure current performance against personal ideals. For many persons this process is a religious exercise.... Even for an individual who is not a religious believer, privacy serves to bring the conscience into play, for, when alone, he must find a way to continue living with himself.

Limited and Protected Communication

The greatest threat to civilized social life would be a situation in which each individual was utterly candid in his communications with others, saying exactly what he knew or felt at all times. The havoc done to interpersonal relations by children, saints, mental patients, and adult "innocents" is legendary.

In real life, among mature persons all communication is partial and limited.... Limited communication is particularly vital in urban life, with its heightened stimulation, crowded environment, and continuous physical and psychological con-frontations between individuals who do not know one another in the extended, soft-ening fashion of small-town life....

Privacy for limited and protected communication has two general aspects. First, it provides the individual with the opportunities he needs for sharing confidences and intimacies with those he trusts.... "A friend," said Emerson, "is someone before ... [whom] I can think aloud." In addition, the individual often wants to secure counsel from persons with whom he does not have to live daily after disclosing his confi-dences. He seeks professionally objective advice from persons whose status in soci-ety promises that they will not later use his distress to take advantage of him. To protect freedom of limited communication, such relationships—with doctors, law-yers, ministers, psychiatrists, psychologists, and others—are given varying but impor-tant degrees of legal privilege against forced disclosure. In its second general aspect, privacy through limited communication serves to set necessary boundaries of mental distance in interpersonal situations ranging from the most intimate to the most for-mal and public. In marriage, for example, husbands and wives need to retain islands of privacy in the midst of their intimacy if they are to preserve a saving respect and mystery in the relation.... In work situations, mental distance is necessary so that the relations of superior and subordinate do not slip into an intimacy which would create a lack of respect and an impediment to directions and correction....

Psychological distance is also used in crowded settings.... [A] complex but well-understood etiquette of privacy is part of our social scenario.... We learn to ignore people and to be ignored by them as a way of achieving privacy in subways, on streets, and in the "nonpresence" of servants or children....

QUESTIONS

1. What are the functions of privacy, as described by Westin? For each, can you think of examples from your own experience?

2. Law professor and journalist Jeffrey Rosen, author of *The Unwanted Gaze: The Destruction of Privacy in America*,[8] offers this description of one of the primary values of privacy:

   Privacy protects us from being misdefined and judged out of context.... [W]hen your browsing habits or e-mail messages are exposed to strangers, you may be reduced, in their eyes, to nothing more than the most salacious book you once read or the most vulgar joke you once told. And even if your Internet browsing isn't in any way embarrassing, you run the risk of being stereotyped as the kind of person who would read a particular book or listen to a particular song. Your public identity may be distorted by fragments of information that have little to do with how you define yourself. In a world where citizens are bombarded with information, people form impressions quickly, based on sound bites, and these brief impressions tend to oversim-plify and misrepresent our complicated and often contradictory characters.

   Does Westin come close to mentioning this aspect of privacy?

3. Which functions of privacy may have been served by the e-mail messages that Michael Smyth sent while working for Pillsbury?

4. To what extent can we describe privacy as an ethical imperative? Think of the *Smyth v. Pillsbury* scenario. Who are the most affected stakeholders? Under the utilitarian approach to ethics, was intercepting the e-mail the right thing to do? Now consider the case from the deontological perspective. Again, was Pillsbury's action ethical?

---

[8] New York: Random House, 2000.

Lifestyle Control

During the early phase of the industrial revolution, it was not unusual for "company towns" to be built, communities where a single company constructed, owned and operated the entire town—not only the business enterprise itself, but also the stores, roads, parks, recreational and medical facilities, and homes for the workers. Firms would also pay for services normally provided by government, such as sewage treatment and garbage collection. In the mid-1800s, company towns were created out of self-interest, in often-remote locations where relatively dangerous operations in coal mining, timber, or construction required a stable workforce. With the many amenities came pervasive social control. Drinking, gambling, smoking, cleanliness, and morals were tightly regulated. Employees were closely watched in public and in private, and were fired for "straying from the path of virtue."[9] They could also be disciplined for minor infringements: Frank Gilchrist, the entrepreneur who built Gilchrist, Oregon, "drove around town, upbraiding those whose yards weren't clean and tidy."[10] One mill owner would walk around the workers' houses at 9:00 pm every night, knocking on doors to hurry people to turn off their lights and go to bed![11]

When he opened up his assembly line in the early 20th century, Henry Ford issued a booklet, called *Helpful Hints and Advice to Employees*, warning against drinking, gambling, borrowing money, taking in boarders, and poor hygiene (advising workers to "use plenty of soap and water in the home and upon their children, bathing frequently"). Ford deployed a vast "Sociology Department," with 150 door-to-door investigators to check the conduct of workers who were not living in houses or shopping in stores that Ford built, but whose well-being was of great interest to the entrepreneur. Once Ford instituted the famous $5 a day wage, he worried that workers would splurge their windfall; his goal was to maintain maximum productivity at the factory by keeping them healthy and stable. The company established a savings and loan to encourage thrift, and had doctors available at all times for workers and their families.[12]

Today we find such a story quaint. We might think we have reached some sort of societal consensus that what employees do on their own time, away from the workplace, should be entirely their own business. Yet we see in the 21st century a wave of corporate efforts to control employees' off-site, off-duty conduct. Rather than paternalism, this is driven by the hard facts surrounding health care in the United States. Expenses are skyrocketing, and employers carry many of them. Escalating insurance costs as well as lost productivity are affecting global competitiveness: Average health care costs to U.S. companies are 13% of total payroll, while countries like Germany, Japan or the United Kingdom spend half that proportion.

Smoking and obesity, for example, are major causes of poor health in the U.S. Recent estimates peg obese employees as costing more than $700 annually more than individuals of normal weight.[13] The Center for Disease Control found in a 2002 study that annual healthcare and productivity losses traceable to smoking were $3,391 per smoker. Consider what this means for a company like Walmart, with 2 million workers. If they smoked at the

[9] James B. Allen, *The Company Town in the American West* (Oklahoma 1966), 189.

[10] Id. at 193.

[11] Margaret Crawford, Earle S. Draper, "The Company Town in the American South," 146 in Garner, ed., *The Company Town: Architecture and Society in the Early Industrial Age* 3, 4 (Oxford 1992).

[12] Steven Watts, *The People's Tycoon: Henry Ford and the American Century* 204-05 (Knopf 2005).

[13] http://www.wbgh.org/healthtopics/bestemployerdocs/bestemployersgoldwinners617.pdf (last visited Oct 3, 2009).

average U.S. rate, each year they would cost the firm $1.4 billion in healthcare costs. Companies have tried to cut such losses with a number of strategies. Some are voluntary. IBM, for example, offers a range of rebates, and employees who agree to exercise, to eat healthy, and not to smoke are paid $150 per year—$300 if their whole family follows suit. At the other end of the spectrum is a company like Scotts Miracle-Gro, whose CEO Jim Hagedorn prefers the stick to the carrot, docking worker pay for unhealthy habits. Scotts employees take a long, extremely personal health-risk assessment, which asks, for instance, "Do you smoke? Drink? What did you parents die of? Do you feel down, sad, hopeless? Burned out? How is your relationship with your spouse? Your kids?" If they refuse to take the test, employees pay added premium costs each month.[14] Weyco, a Michigan-based, health-benefits management company, not only refuses to hire smokers, but announced a draconian no smoking policy: Effective January 1, 2005, every employee who failed the mandatory nicotine test would be terminated. Recently Weyco expanded this program to include workers' spouses; if the spouse fails the monthly nicotine test, the worker pays $80 monthly until the spouse quits. Policies like these have been aimed at a range of behaviors: Workers must keep their blood pressure and cholesterol at healthy levels, wear seat belts, and join corporate wellness programs. One Georgia developer will not employ anyone who engages in "high risk" recreational activities such as motorcycling or skydiving. The Best Lock Corporation will hire no one who admits to drinking. At the Borgata Casino in Atlantic City, New Jersey, bartenders and waitresses can be fired if they gain more than 7 percent of their body weight. Weigh-ins are mandatory, with 90-day unpaid suspensions for violators. Exceptions are made for pregnancy and other valid medical reasons. "Borgata Babes" who miss their target weight after 90 days are fired.

Whereas companies say they are cutting health care costs and lowering rates of absenteeism in these ways, organizations such as the American Civil Liberties Union (ACLU) are troubled by this drift to control off-site behavior. Former ACLU president Ira Glasser has said:

> If an employer believes your capacity to take care of yourself is in his interest, then you become like a piece of equipment. He gets to lock it up at night and control the temperature and make sure dust doesn't get into the machine, because what happens when it's not working affects how long it's going to last.

In fact, an interesting alliance between the ACLU and the tobacco industry was extremely effective in lobbying state legislatures for laws that protect employees who smoke when they are not at work.[15] Today, a majority of states have some version of off-the-job privacy protection laws. In New York, for instance, it is illegal to fire an employee for engaging in off-hours sports, games, hobbies, exercise, reading, movie- or TV-watching. This is the statute at issue in the next case.

■ ■ ■

Laurel Allen was married, but separated from her husband when she began dating Samuel Johnson, a coworker at Walmart. When the store manager found out, they were both fired. Walmart's anti-fraternization policy prohibited such relationships as inconsistent with the company's "strongly held belief in and support of the family unit." The New York attorney general entered the case on behalf of the dating couple, alleging

---

[14] The company will analyze each set of test results and will then arrange a coach and action plan for each at-risk employee.

[15] By 1996, such laws were in effect in 28 states. Virginia, a "tobacco state," was the first to pass one. It reads: "No employee or applicant … shall be required … to smoke or use tobacco products on the job, or to abstain from smoking or using tobacco products outside of the course of his employment." *VA Code Ann.* 15.1-29, 18 (1990).

that firing them violated the state law protecting the employees' right to engage in off-duty, off-premises recreational activity.

STATE OF NEW YORK v. WALMART STORES, INC.
N.Y. App. Div., 1995 621 N.Y.S.2d 158

MERCURE, Justice.

In February 1993, defendant discharged two of its employees for violating its "fraternization" policy, which is codified in defendant's 1989 Associates Handbook and prohibits a "dating relationship" between a married employee and another employee, other than his or her own spouse. In this action, plaintiff seeks reinstatement of the two employees with back pay upon the ground that their discharge violated [New York] Labor Law § 201-d(2)(c), which forbids employer discrimination against employees because of their participation in "legal recreational activities" pursued outside of work hours....

[The court must decide whether "a dating relationship" is meant to be included within the statutory definition of "recreational activities."]

[NY] Labor Law § 201-d(1)(b) defines "recreational activities" as meaning:

> ... any lawful, leisure-time activity, for which the employee receives no compensation and which is generally engaged in for recreational purposes, including but not limited to sports, games, hobbies, exercise, reading, and the viewing of television, movies, and similar material.

In our view, there is no justification for proceeding beyond the fundamental rule of construction that "[w]here words of a statute are free from ambiguity and express plainly, clearly and distinctly the legislative intent, resort may not be had to other means of interpretation," ... To us, "dating" is entirely distinct from and, in fact, bears little resemblance to "recreational activity." Whether characterized as a relationship or an activity, an indispensable element of "dating," in fact its raison d'etre, is romance, either pursued or realized. For that reason, although a dating couple may go bowling and under the circumstances call that activity a "date," when two individuals lacking amorous interest in one another go bowling or engage in any other kind of "legal recreational activity," they are not "dating."

Moreover, even if [NY] Labor Law § 201-d(1)(b) was found to contain some ambiguity, application of the rules of statutory construction does not support [the trial court's] interpretation. We agree with defendant that ... the voluminous legislative history to the enactment, including memoranda issued in connection with the veto of two earlier more expansive bills, [shows] an obvious intent to limit the statutory protection to certain clearly defined categories of leisure-time activities. Further, in view of the specific inclusion of "sports, games, hobbies, exercise, reading, and the viewing of television, movies, and similar material" within the statutory definition of "recreational activities,"... personal relationships fall outside the scope of legislative intent....

[Order in defendant's favor affirmed.]

Yesawich, Justice, dissenting.

I respectfully dissent, for I find defendant's central thesis, apparently accepted by the majority, that the employment policy at issue only prohibits romantic entanglements and not other types of social interaction, to be wholly without merit. While the majority encumbers the word "dating" with an "amorous interest" component, there is nothing in defendant's fraternization policy, its application—defendant does not allege that its two former employees manifested an intimate or amatory attitude toward each other—or even in defendant's own definition of a "date", "a social engagement between persons of opposite sex" (Webster's Ninth New Collegiate Dictionary, 325 [1988]), that leads to such a conclusion.

More importantly, I do not agree that "dating," whether or not it involves romantic attachment, falls outside the general definition of "recreational activities" found in [the law]. The statute, by its terms, appears to encompass social activities, whether or not they have a romantic element, for it includes any lawful activity pursued for recreational purposes and undertaken during leisure time. Though no explicit definition of "recreational purposes" is contained in the statute, "recreation" is, in the words of one dictionary, "a means of refreshment or diversion" (Webster's Ninth New Collegiate Dictionary, 985 [1985]); social interaction surely qualifies as a "diversion." ...

In my view, given the fact that the Legislature's primary intent in enacting Labor Law § 201-d was to curtail employers' ability to discriminate on the basis of activities that are pursued outside of work hours, and that have no bearing on one's ability to perform one's job, and concomitantly to guarantee employees a certain degree of freedom to conduct their lives as they please during nonworking hours, the narrow interpretation adopted by the majority is indefensible. Rather, the statute, and the term "recreational activities" in particular, should be construed as broadly as the definitional language allows, to effect its remedial purpose.... Here, the list, which includes vast categories such as "hobbies" and "sports," as well as very different types of activities (e.g., exercise, reading), appears to have been compiled with an eye toward extending the reach of the statute. This, coupled with the explicit directive that the definition is not to be limited to the examples given, provides further indication that the term "recreational activities" should be construed expansively.

QUESTIONS

1. The judges in this case—both majority and dissenting—are engaging in what is called **statutory construction**; they are determining the outcome of the case by trying to understand the meaning of the law passed by New York's legislature. Note the differences between them. One gives the statute a "broad" reading, the other gives it a "narrow" one. Which is which? What tools do the two judges use to interpret the law? Which interpretation do you think is most in keeping with the intent of the legislators?

2. Try to imagine yourself in Albany as this New York law was being debated. What policy issues might have been raised in favor of passing the law? Against?

3. Suppose you had the ability to rewrite the New York law, or even delete it from the statute books. How would you change it?

4. **Research:** For your state, find out if there is any legislation protecting employees' rights to engage in off-site activities. If so, are there any cases interpreting the law? Then go back to the Montana Wrongful Discharge statute in Chapter 2. What similarities can you see between it and your state's law? What differences?

■ ■ ■

Testing

Are you a homosexual? Do you know of any reason why you could be blackmailed? Do you get along with your spouse? Are you a communist? Do you have any money in the bank? Have you ever stolen anything and not been caught?

These are a few of the questions asked in a polygraph test used by the Coors Brewing Company as a preemployment screening device. The intrusive nature of that test was part of the reason for a wildcat strike at Coors in 1977. In 1986, as the U.S. Congress was considering a law that would make the use of polygraphs by employers illegal,[16] Coors replaced its polygraph with a lengthy psychological test and background check.

---

[16] *The Polygraph Act of 1988* bans such tests except for security personnel and others in extremely sensitive positions. Applicants for police force jobs, for instance, are often faced with the kinds of intrusive questions asked in the Coors polygraph test.

Today, the use of such "pen and pencil" (as opposed to electronic polygraph) honesty or integrity tests is common among employers. One major reason is that employee theft costs U.S. businesses about $10 billion annually. In addition, companies claim an interest in the ability to identify people who are not only competent and honest, but who also fit a certain psychological or moral profile.

■ ■ ■

The next case involves a challenge to the use of a psychological test known as the Minnesota Multiphasic Personality Inventory, or MMPI. The three Karraker brothers worked for a chain called Rent-A-Center and were required to pass a battery of tests before they could be considered for promotion, including the MMPI, which asked questions designed to reveal a range of mental conditions from depression to paranoia. This case is a **class action**, meaning that it was brought by the Karrakers on behalf of themselves and all the other employees at Rent-A-Centers across the country who were expected to take the MMPI test in order to get promoted. The results of a class action suit are applied across the entire similarly-affected group; if the Karrakers' claim succeeds, all Rent-A-Centers will have to alter their testing practices.

KARRAKER v. RENT-A-CENTER, INC.
U.S. Court of Appeals, Seventh Circuit, 2005
411 F.3d 831

TERENCE T. EVANS, Circuit Judge.

To prove their worth prior to the annual college draft, NFL teams test aspiring professional football players' ability to run, catch, and throw. But that's not all. In addition to the physical tests, a draft prospect also takes up to 15 personality and knowledge tests....

This case involves a battery of nonphysical tests similar to some of those given by NFL teams, though the employees here applied for less glamorous and far less well-paying positions. Steven, Michael, and Christopher Karraker are brothers who worked for Rent-A-Center (RAC), a chain of stores that offer appliances, furniture, and other household goods on a rent-to-own basis.... [T]o secure a promotion, ... an employee was required to take the APT Management Trainee-Executive Profile, which was made up of nine tests designed to measure math and language skills as well as interests and personality traits.

As part of the APT Test, the Karrakers and others were asked 502 questions from the Minnesota Multiphasic Personality Inventory (MMPI), a test RAC said it used to measure personality traits. But the MMPI does not simply measure such potentially relevant traits as whether someone works well in groups or is comfortable in a fast-paced office. Instead, the MMPI considers where an applicant falls on scales measuring traits such as depression, hypochondriasis, hysteria, paranoia, and mania. In fact, elevated scores on certain scales of the MMPI can be used in diagnoses of certain psychiatric disorders.

Applicants were asked whether the following statements were true or false: "I see things or animals or people around me that others do not see."

> "I commonly hear voices without knowing where they are coming from." "At times I have fits of laughing and crying that I cannot control."
>
> "My soul sometimes leaves my body."
>
> "At one or more times in my life I felt that someone was making me do things by hypnotizing me."
>
> "I have a habit of counting things that are not important such as bulbs on electric signs, and so forth."

All parts of the APT Test were scored together, and any applicant who had more than 12 "weighted deviations" was not considered for promotion. Thus, an applicant could be denied any chance for advancement simply because of his or her score on the MMPI. The Karrakers [claim] RAC's use of the MMPI as part of its testing program violated the Americans With Disabilities Act of 1990 (ADA). They also claimed that RAC failed to protect the confidentiality of the test results in violation of Illinois tort law....

Americans with disabilities often faced barriers to joining and succeeding in the workforce ... [including] attitudinal barriers resulting from unfounded stereotypes and prejudice. People with psychiatric disabilities have suffered as a result of such attitudinal barriers, with an employment rate dramatically lower than people without disabilities and far lower than people with other types of disabilities....

Congress enacted three provisions in Title I [of the ADA] which explicitly limit the ability of employers to use "medical examinations and inquiries"...as a condition of employment: a prohibition against using preemployment medical tests; a prohibition against the use of medical tests that lack job-relatedness and business necessity; and a prohibition against the use of tests which screen out (or tend to screen out) people with disabilities.

At its heart, the issue in this case is whether the MMPI fits the ADA's definition of a "medical examination." ...

Psychological tests that are "designed to identify a mental disorder or impairment" qualify as medical examinations, but psychological tests "that measure personality traits such as honesty, preferences, and habits" do not. Therefore, this case largely turns on whether the MMPI test is designed to reveal a mental impairment. RAC argues that, as it used the MMPI, the test only measured personality traits. For example, RAC argues in its brief that the MMPI does not test whether an applicant is clinically depressed, only "the extent to which the test subject is experiencing the kinds of feelings of 'depression' that everyone feels from time to time (e.g., when their favorite team loses the World Series)." Although that particular example seems odd to us (can an Illinois chain really fill its management positions if it won't promote disgruntled Cubs fans?), the logic behind it doesn't seem to add up, either. Repeating the claim at oral argument, RAC argued that the MMPI merely tested a "state of mood" and suggested that an applicant might, for example, score high on the depression scale because he lost his keys that morning. But why would RAC care if an applicant lost his keys the morning of the MMPI or took the test the day after another Cubs loss? Would RAC really want to exclude an employee from consideration for a promotion because he happened to feel sad on the wrong day? We see two possibilities: either the MMPI was a very poor predictor of an applicant's potential as a manager (which might be one reason it is no longer used by RAC), or it actually was designed to measure more than just an applicant's mood on a given day....

Because it is designed, at least in part, to reveal mental illness and has the effect of hurting the employment prospects of one with a mental disability, we think the MMPI is best categorized as a medical examination. And even though the MMPI was only a part (albeit a significant part) of a battery of tests administered to employees looking to advance, its use, we conclude, violated the ADA....

The Karrakers also challenge the district court's dismissal of their tort claim based on the public disclosure of private facts. To prevail, they must show that private facts were made public and that the matter made public would be highly offensive to a reasonable person.... The publicity requirement is satisfied by disclosure to a limited number of people if those people have a special relationship with the plaintiff that makes the disclosure as devastating as disclosure to the public at large.... Disclosure to persons with a "natural and proper interest" in the information is not actionable....

Much of the Karrakers' claim centered around RAC's handling of the test results, which they claim did not adequately protect their privacy. As the district court described, the test results were kept in a filing cabinet in personnel files, and anyone wishing to view the records needed permission to do so from someone in the payroll department. The filing cabinet was locked at night, and the records were eventually moved into a locked room. Although someone could have seen the test results sitting in the fax machine or in the personnel file, that possibility is not sufficient to support a claim....

[Held: Summary judgment for the plaintiffs on their claim that the MMPI is a medical examination under the ADA, and dismissing the public disclosure of private facts claim.]

QUESTIONS

1. What rights of privacy are created by the Americans With Disabilities Act? How does the ADA benefit people without disabilities?

2. According to the American Management Association, more than 40 percent of employers—including 89 of the Fortune 100—require psychological tests. The multi-million dollar psychological testing industry has been criticized for unreliability. In a case involving testing for jobs at Target Stores, for instance, expert witnesses had thrown into question both the validity and the reliability of the test used, which had a 61 percent false positive rate; in other words, more than 6 of every 10 qualified applicants failed it.[17]

   Recent studies reveal a very low correlation between good tests results and effective performance at work. Some wonder if American employers put so much stock in psychological testing out of an urge to get a quick fix on something that is impossible to quantify. As one writer put it: "We have personality in the sense that we have a consistent pattern of behavior. But that pattern is complex.... Personality is contingent: it represents an interaction between our internal disposition and tendencies and the situation that we find ourselves in."[18] Assuming psychological testing is rife with problems, what could employers do instead to screen job applicants?

3. In a 1982 Massachusetts case, salespeople for Bristol-Myers were fired for resisting an integrity test. Here the judge describes what happened:

   The questionnaire, entitled Biographical Summary, sought information which, it represented, would be held in strict confidence. The subjects covered included business experience, education, family, home ownership, physical data, activities, and aims.... Questions...concerned (a) serious illnesses, operations, accidents, or nervous disorders, (b) smoking and drinking habits, (c) off-the-job problems, and (d) principal worries, if any.... [Employee] Cort, however, gave limited answers, one of which he admitted was wrong. He was not married in 1960, 1961, and 1962. He listed his dog as a dependent. He gave no information, as the others did, about parents or siblings, if any.

   Cort answered [other] questions...largely in a flippant manner.... He wrote as to his principal strengths: "Able to leap tall bldg. at a single bound." As to his principal weaknesses: "Can't land on my feet." Activities in which he would prefer not to engage: "Filling in questions on forms of very personal nature that are no one's business but mine." He suggested "$1,000,000" as the income he would need to live the way he would like to. Answering concerning plans for the future, he wrote, "Depends on who reads this." He followed his questionnaire with a memorandum to his superiors asking the value to Bristol-Myers of answers to the following questions: "what medications I may be taking, the age and health of my mother and father, the occupations of my brothers and sisters, the value of my house and the amount of mortgage, whose support outside of my immediate family I contribute to, how much I smoke and drink each day, my wife's maiden name, and what personal problems I have outside of business."

---

[17] *Soroka v. Dayton Hudson Corporation*, 1 Cal Rptr.2d 77 (1991).

[18] Malcolm Gladwell, "Personality Plus," *The New Yorker*, September 20, 2004.

Can you see any connections between the value of privacy, as expressed in Alan Westin's essay, and Cort's answers to the test questions? His memo to his bosses?

The court decided Cort and his coworkers were at-will employees with no cause of action for privacy invasion:

> *Questions about family and home ownership were probably not of much significance to Bristol-Myers, but those questions were not improperly intrusive, sought information mostly available in public records, and...were no more intrusive than those asked on an application for life insurance or for a bank loan.*

> — *Cort v. Bristol-Myers Co.*, 431 N.E.2d 908 (1982).

Research: In your state, find a case dealing with psychological or honesty testing. What happened? What was the legal outcome? Can you identify ethical issues in the case?

4. Some tests measure abilities:

- *Can you type 200 words a minute?*
- *Can you run 1.5 miles in 12 minutes?*
- *Are you comfortable using Excel?*

Clearly, employers need the results of ability tests to make good hiring and promotion decisions. More controversial is the use of another type of test, one that asks whether you are what you say you are. These are called authenticity tests:

- *You say you don't use illegal drugs, but are you really drug-free?*
- *You say you are honest, but are you really honest?*

In his 1993 book *Testing Testing: Social Consequences of the Examined Life*, anthropologist F. Allan Hanson explores this form of testing. He begins with history from the period before the scientific method, when authenticity tests took the form of torture and witch burning. He then moves forward to modern forms of testing for truth—the polygraph, honesty test, and urinalysis drug test. Hanson is concerned with the "metamessage," an inevitable byproduct of authenticity testing. He writes:

> *[T]he metamessage of distrust conveyed by the demand that employees take authenticity tests is unmistakable, and it often erodes loyalty and morale. Essentially they are being told, regardless of your record of service, reliability, and safety, you are suspected of theft, dishonesty, or drug use, and that suspicion will be suspended only by your passing this test, and even if you pass, you will be trusted only until the next test. This engenders hostility against the company and may even spur some workers to take steps to confound or subvert the tests purely as a way to maintain a sense of autonomy and dignity in the face of a system that is aimed at systematically humiliating them.... Much more commonly, the metamessage ... destroys employee motivation to take pride in one's work and perform at a high level and engenders a passive-aggressive response marked by smoldering resentment and diminished productivity.*

Hanson goes on to mention the problem of false positives, where innocent people are wrongly judged guilty. Which ethical theory would attach significance to the points Hanson makes? Next, Hanson links his argument to a basic privacy concern:

> *To the claim that only those with something to hide need fear ... authenticity tests, the proper response is that there is a little crook in all of us.... [S]ocial interaction consists largely of a series of dramaturgical performances in which people don many masks in an effort to present themselves artfully—concealing*

certain elements of the self while highlighting and tinting others. The aim is to exercise some control over social situations by influencing others' perception of the self and thereby of the situation.... [A]uthenticity testing erodes this distinctive feature of social life. Whether test results are positive or negative is, at this level, irrelevant. The point is that testing opens the self to scrutiny and investigation in ways that the self is powerless to control. So far as the areas of knowledge covered by the tests are concerned, this transforms the person from autonomous subject to passive object.

What similarities to Alan Westin's description of the functions of privacy do you detect here? Some may claim that the fact that test results can be kept confidential changes the picture, but Hanson argues the reverse. For him, confidentiality is not a safeguard of privacy, but "yet another ingenious and highly effective technique for exercising power and discipline over the individual":

Although it is advertised as a protective measure for test takers, confidentiality completes the domination of test givers over test takers. It assures that each individual confronts the organizations that mandate testing utterly alone and therefore in the weakest possible state. Here disciplinary power has achieved the remarkable feat of perfecting the domination of people by dividing them and dealing with them singly, all the while convincing them that the arrangement is for their own good.

Do you agree with Hanson's analysis?

■ ■ ■

IMPAIRMENT TESTING VS. DRUG TESTING

Lewis Maltby, president and founder of the National Workrights Institute, has written provocatively on workplace drug testing. He tells of when he worked for Drexelbrook Engineering, which designed, manufactured, and installed control systems for companies like DuPont and Dow Chemical using the most advanced proprietary knowledge available and dealing with thousands of deadly chemicals. Obviously, there was no room for error—mistakes would have been disastrous—yet Drexelbrook did not institute a drug testing program for employees. Rather, the company created a corporate culture that—almost obsessionally—emphasized safety. As Maltby explains:

Drexelbrook had a quality control system unlike anything I've ever seen. Before an order even went to the factory, a team of engineers studied the intended applications—if they weren't certain the system would do what the customer needed, the order stopped cold and didn't go to the factory. There was no appeal. This team reported to the vice president of engineering, but even he had no authority to overrule their decision. The order went forward only once modified to the engineers' satisfaction.[19]

From there, Drexelbrook products were checked and rechecked for flaws before being sent to a Quality Assurance inspector who would not ship until satisfied that everything was exactly right. Again, the QA inspector could not be overruled—except by the CEO of the company, who never did so. This culture of quality and safety

---

[19] *Can They Do That? Retaking Our Fundamental Rights in the Workplace* (New York: Penguin Group 2009), 101.

stretched from the factory floor to the upper echelons of management at Drexelbrook. A drug testing program, Maltby says, would have drained attention and resources away from the laser-like focus the company wanted to place where it belonged—on safety.

In his recent book about the lack of civil rights for U.S. employees in the private sector, Maltby tackles the question often raised when drug testing is under debate: What about jobs where human error risks catastrophe—what about airline pilots? He suggests an alternative to drug testing, even for those who fly planes—impairment testing:

> [We should] test pilots for what really counts: their ability to fly a plane safely. The reason stoned pilots are dangerous is that their vision, reflexes, coordination and judgment are impaired. Systems are available that will test whether someone is impaired in this way in a matter of minutes. The technology for these systems was originally developed by NASA for testing astronauts. Taking the test is a lot like paying a video game. You take the test a few times to establish a baseline. Every time you take the test later, the system compares your score to the baseline. If your score is significantly lower than the baseline, the system reports that you are impaired.[20]

Maltby points out that scores indicating impairment can be caused by any number of factors beyond drug-taking—being sleep-deprived, ill, or going through a divorce, for example—but whatever the reason, the test will determine that you shouldn't fly the plane.

Although workplace drug testing occurs less frequently—the practice peaked in 1996 at 81% of firms—it is still prevalent. What do you think of Lew Maltby's suggestion? Can you imagine impairment testing for various jobs instead of drug testing?

Social Media and Privacy

The Internet is the biggest psychological and social human experience.... We make encouraging viral activity.

— CYNTHIA GORDON, Vice President of
New Media Marketing for Universal Orlando Resort

Privacy is dead, and social media hold the smoking gun.

— PETE CASHMORE, Mashable CEO

The Electronic Privacy Information Center (EPIC) advocates for consumer privacy. In 2004, it brought the privacy risks of online advertising to the attention of the Fair Trade Commission (FTC), leading to a $15 million fine against Choicepoint. Another recent EPIC complaint resulted in an FTC injunction preventing over-the-counter sales of "stalker spyware." The excerpt that follows is from a complaint filed by EPIC in 2010, challenging Facebook's privacy policies as unfair and deceptive in violation of the FTC Act.

---

[20] Id. at 105.

Complaint re. Facebook to Federal Trade Commission

This complaint concerns material changes to privacy settings made by Facebook, the largest social network service in the United States, which adversely impact users of the Facebook service. Facebook's changes to users' privacy settings disclose personal information to the public that was previously restricted…[and] also disclose personal information to third parties that was previously not available. These changes violate user expectations, diminish user privacy, and contradict Facebook's own representations….

The Importance of Privacy Protection

The right of privacy is a personal and fundamental right in the United States. The privacy of an individual is directly implicated by the collection, use, and dissemination of personal information. The opportunities to secure employment, insurance, and credit, to obtain medical services and the rights of due process may be jeopardized by the misuse of personal information.

The excessive collection of personal data in the United States coupled with inadequate legal and technological protections have led to a dramatic increase in the crime of identity theft….

Facebook's Size and Reach Is Unparalleled Among Social Networking Sites

Facebook is the largest social network service provider in the United States. According to Facebook, there are more than 350 million active users, with more than 100 million in the United States. More than 35 million users update their statuses at least once each day. More than 2.5 billion photos are uploaded to the site each month…. As of August 2009, Facebook is the fourth most-visited Web site in the world and the sixth most-visited web site in the United States.

Facebook Has Previously Changed Its Service in Ways that Harm Users' Privacy

In September 2006, Facebook disclosed users' personal information, including details relating to their marital and dating status, without their knowledge or consent through its "News Feed" program. Hundreds of thousands of users objected to Facebook's actions. In response, Facebook stated:

> We really messed this one up. When we launched News Feed and Mini-Feed we were trying to provide you with a stream of information about your social world. Instead, we did a bad job of explaining what the new features were and an even worse job of giving you control of them.[21]

[The complaint goes on to mention that in 2007, Facebook created controversy with Beacon, an advertising tool allowing its users' activities, such as retail purchases, on certain external sites to be tracked and shown as updates on Facebook. CEO Mark Zuckerberg again apologized to users and changed the site's privacy settings. In the wake of this debacle, several lawsuits were filed.]

On February 4, 2009, Facebook revised its Terms of Service, asserting broad, permanent, and retroactive rights to users' personal information—even after they

---

[21] Mark Zuckerberg, An Open Letter from Mark Zuckerberg (Sept. 8, 2006), http://blog.facebook.com/blog. php?post=2208562130.

deleted their accounts. Facebook stated that it could make public a user's "name, likeness, and image for any purpose, including commercial or advertising." Users objected to Facebook's actions, and Facebook reversed the revisions on the eve of an EPIC complaint to the Commission.

Changes in Privacy Settings: "Publicly Available Information"

Facebook updated its privacy policy and changed the privacy settings available to users on November 19, 2009 and again on December 9, 2009. Facebook now treats the following categories of personal data as "publicly available information:"

- users' names,
- profile photos,
- lists of friends,
- pages they are fans of,
- gender,
- geographic regions, and
- networks to which they belong.

By default, Facebook discloses "publicly available information" to search engines, to Internet users whether or not they use Facebook, and others. According to Facebook, such information can be accessed by "every application and Web site, including those you have not connected with...."

Prior to these changes, only the following items were mandatorily "publicly available information:"

- a user's name and
- a user's network.

Users also had the option to include additional information in their public search listing [such as profile picture, friend list, message links, and fan pages].... Facebook's original privacy policy stated that users "may not want everyone in the world to have the information you share on Facebook." ...

[The complaint goes on to state that Chris Kelly, then Chief Privacy Officer of Facebook (who ran for Governor of California in 2010) testified to Congress that Facebook users "have extensive and precise controls available to choose who sees what among their networks and friends, as well as tools that give them the *choice* to make a limited set of information available to search engines and other outside entities." As Kelly and CEO Zuckerberg were publicly touting that users were getting more control and choice with the new privacy settings, Zuckerberg himself decided to reverse these changes on his own Facebook page. Meanwhile, Facebook's Director of Corporate Communications and Public Policy, suggested that "users are free to lie about their hometown or take down their profile picture to protect their privacy." Providing false information violates Facebook's Terms of Service.]

Facebook users can indicate that they are "fans" of various organizations, individuals, and products, including controversial political causes. Under the original privacy settings, users controlled public access to the causes they supported. Under the revised settings, Facebook has made users' causes "publicly available information," disclosing this data to others and preventing users from exercising control as they had under the original privacy policy.

Based on profile data obtained from Facebook users' friends lists, MIT researchers found that "just by looking at a person's online friends, they could predict whether the person was gay." Under Facebook's original privacy policy, Facebook did not categorize users' friends lists as "publicly available information." Facebook now makes users' friends lists "publicly available information."

Dozens of American Facebook users, who posted political messages critical of Iran, have reported that Iranian authorities subsequently questioned and detained their relatives. Under the revised privacy settings, Facebook makes such users' friends lists publicly available.

According to the Wall Street Journal, one Iranian-American graduate student received a threatening email that read, "we know your home address in Los Angeles," and directed the user to "stop spreading lies about Iran on Facebook." Another U.S. Facebook user who criticized Iran on Facebook stated that security agents in Tehran located and arrested his father as a result of the postings....

Changes to Privacy Settings: Information Disclosure to Application Developers

The Facebook Platform transfers Facebook users' personal data to application developers without users' knowledge or consent.

Facebook permits third-party applications to access user information at the moment a user visits an application Web site. According to Facebook, third party applications "receive publicly available information automatically when you visit them, and additional information when you formally authorize or connect your Facebook account with them."

As Facebook itself explains in its documentation, when a user adds an application, by default that application then gains access to everything on Facebook that the user can see....

According to Facebook, [applications and Web sites have access to, among other data:]

> *your political view, your activities, your interests, your musical [television, movie and book] preferences ... your dating interests, your relationship interests, your network affiliations ... the total number of "pokes" you have sent and/or received, the total number of wall posts on your Wall, a list of user IDs mapped to your friends, your social timeline, notifications that you have received from other applications, and events associated with your profile.*

Under the revised privacy policy...Facebook allows user information that is categorized as publicly available to "everyone" to be: "accessed by everyone on the Internet (including people not logged into Facebook);" made subject to "indexing by third party search engines;" "associated with you outside of Facebook (such as when you visit other sites on the Internet);" and "imported and exported by us and others *without* privacy limitations."

Facebook states in the revised privacy policy that users can "opt-out of Facebook Platform and Facebook Connect altogether through [their] privacy settings." Facebook further states that, "you can control how you share information with those third-party applications and Web sites through your application settings."

In fact, under the original privacy settings, users had a one-click option to prevent the disclosure of personal information to third party application developers.... [This option has been replaced with two paragraphs of prose followed by fifteen boxes to check.] Under the revised settings, even when a user unchecks all boxes and indicates that none of the personal information listed above should be disclosed to third party application developers..."applications will *always* be able to access your publicly available information (Name, Profile Picture, Gender, Current City, Networks, Friends List, and Pages) and information that is visible to Everyone."

Facebook's "Everyone" setting overrides the user's choice to limit access by third-party applications and Web sites....

Users can block individual third-party applications from obtaining personal information by searching the Application Directory, visiting the application's "about" page, clicking a small link on that page, and then confirming their decision. A user would have to perform these steps for each of more than 350,000 applications in order to block all of them....

Prayer for Investigation and Relief

EPIC requests that the Commission investigate Facebook, enjoin its unfair and deceptive business practices, and require Facebook to protect the privacy of Facebook users. Specifically, EPIC requests the Commission to:

Compel Facebook to restore its previous privacy settings allowing users to choose whether to publicly disclose personal information, including name, current city, and friends;

Compel Facebook to restore its previous privacy setting allowing users to fully opt out of revealing information to third-party developers;

Compel Facebook to make its data collection practices clearer and more comprehensible and to give Facebook users meaningful control over personal information provided by Facebook to advertisers and developers; and

Provide such other relief as the Commission finds necessary and appropriate.

QUESTIONS

1. **Research:** Security experts, bloggers, consumer groups, and news organizations have opposed Facebook's privacy policy—and Facebook users have, too. Thousands have formed groups like *Facebook! Fix the Privacy Settings* and *Petition: Facebook, stop invading my privacy!* This controversy fueled a movement called Quit Facebook, and on Memorial Day 2010 thousands had agreed to do just that. What can you find out about the degree to which Facebook users care about the privacy of their personal information and about the way companies can access it to boost sales? If you use Facebook or an equivalent social networking site, how do you feel about the new privacy policy?

2. **Research:** In 2009, EPIC urged the FTC to undertake an investigation of Google and cloud computing. Read about this issue on EPIC's Web site: *http://epic.org/privacy/cloudcomputing/google/031809_ftc_ltr.pdf*

   What consumer privacy issues were raised? Find out how the FTC responded.

3. **Research:** (a) The EPIC complaint also mentions the Madrid Privacy Declaration of November 2009, which states that "corporations are acquiring vast amounts of personal data without independent oversight." What can you find out about this global effort to set universal standards for the collection and use of personal information?

   (b) In March 2010, draft legislation that would come close to the stricter privacy rules in other developed countries was introduced by Rick Boucher, Democrat of Virginia and Cliff Stearns, Republican of Florida. Find out if it has moved forward and what it requires. Would this law mandate any changes by Facebook?

4. "The fact is, the Internet is changing privacy as we know it." This was part of the address Matt Ivester, founder of the now-defunct Juicy Campus, gave in October 2008 at Georgetown University. Students there worried that his Web site, which "encourages people to post gossip anonymously...naming names and spreading detailed rumors about sex, drugs, [and] college life," could adversely affect their future careers, particularly those hoping to work for the government. Ivester responded that employers are "going to have to start developing a sense of humor." Hiring specialists are not alone in mining social networking sites to learn about applicants. According to the *Wall Street Journal*, a 2008 study of more than 500 top colleges revealed that 10% looked at students' social networking pages to help evaluate applicants. Of those, 38% said viewing applicants' pages negatively impacted their evaluation; one quarter said views produced positive impacts. What are the ethical implications of these two trends: that of college students to freely share sensitive information in social media, and that of employers and admissions officers to use what they find there to evaluate applicants?

5. **Research:** In filing this complaint, EPIC was joined by several not-for-profit organizations including: the American Library Association, the Center for Digital Democracy, the Consumer Federation of America, Privacy Activism, Patient Privacy Rights, and the U.S. Bill of Rights Foundation. Investigate each group's Web site to determine the likely reasons for their interest in the FTC taking action with regard to Facebook.

EUROPE VS. AMERICA: DIGNITY VS. LIBERTY

Yale law professor James Q. Whitman makes this broad distinction between conceptions of privacy in Europe versus America:

Continental privacy protections are, at their core, a form of protection of a right to respect and personal dignity. [They] … are rights to one's image, name, and reputation, and… to informational self-determination—the right to control the sorts of information disclosed about oneself…all rights to control your public image—to guarantee that people see you the way you want to be seen. They are, as it were, rights to be shielded against unwanted public exposure—to be spared embarrassment or humiliation.

By contrast, America, in this as in so many things, is much more oriented toward values of liberty, liberty against the state. The American right to privacy still takes much of the form that it took in the eighteenth century: It is the right to freedom from intrusions by the state, especially in one's own home. The prime danger, from the American point of view, is that the…[home] will be breached by government actors. American anxieties…tend to be about maintaining a kind of private sovereignty within our own walls.[22]

Perhaps this distinction explains the strength of the protections given to personal information by the European Privacy Directive. A "Directive" protecting the privacy of personal information as it moves across national borders was passed by the European Union on July 24, 1995. Under the Privacy Directive, each member nation must pass laws guaranteeing that personal data gathered is accurate, up-to-date, relevant, and not excessive. Information collected may be used only for the purpose for which it was collected, and can be processed only with the consent of the subject, when required by law, or to protect the "public interest" or the "legitimate interests" of a third party, unless those interests are superseded by the "fundamental rights and freedoms of the data subject." The Directive sharply limits the collection of information about "racial or ethnic origin, political opinions, religious or philosophical beliefs, trade-union membership, [or] concerning health or sex life." Data subjects must be informed that data will be taken about them, and must be notified how it will be used. Perhaps most striking of all, given the very different legal rules in the United States, the EU Directive gives Europeans the right of access to information collected about themselves, and the opportunity to correct inaccuracies. Further, each member nation must establish a data privacy "commissioner" and a national agency that monitors enforcement.

---

[22] "The Two Western Cultures of Privacy: Dignity v. Liberty," 113 *Yale L. J.* 1151 (2004).

Privacy Under the Constitution

The right of the people to be secure in their persons, houses, papers, and effects, against unreasonable searches and seizures, shall not be violated.

— FOURTH AMENDMENT, U.S. Constitution

What are the legal boundaries of an employee's privacy in this interconnected, electronic-communication age, one in which thoughts and ideas that would have been spoken personally and privately in ages past are now instantly text-messaged to friends and family via hand-held, computer-assisted electronic devices?

— DISTRICT JUDGE LARSON, *Quon v. Arch Wireless Operating Co., Inc.,* (9th Cir. 2006).

Over the years, the Supreme Court has created three strands of privacy rights through its interpretation of various Constitutional Amendments and their penumbras. One stops the government from interfering in the choices you make about your private family and sexual life—to use or not use birth control or (for adults) to engage in consensual homosexual activity, for example—without government interference. Another prevents the government from publicizing the kind of information about ourselves that we consider most intimate—our medical and sexual histories, for example. Finally, and of most importance to business, the Fourth Amendment protects the "reasonable expectations of privacy" of both individual and corporations against unwarranted and unreasonable government searches or seizures. When police frisk for drugs or test for alcohol, when a health department inspects a restaurant, or when a regulatory agency searches a business for evidence of illegal activity, there is a potential Fourth Amendment "privacy" claim.

While the Fourth Amendment does protect citizens from "unreasonable searches," it is triggered only when the government is conducting a search; there is no constitutional protection against searches or surveillance by private corporations. And while government employees might argue that electronic surveillance is a "search" in violation of the Fourth Amendment, their constitutional rights are limited by a balancing test: judges must decide which counts more weightily, an employee's privacy interest or the need of the government (as employer) to conduct a search.

In 1987, the Supreme Court decided a case involving the search of a public employee's office. Magno Ortega, a psychiatrist at a state hospital, was suspected of stealing a computer and of sexually harassing female workers. While he was on vacation, his desk and file cabinets were searched thoroughly. Investigators found, among other items, a valentine card, a book of love poetry, and a seminude photograph of a female doctor. The Court found that this search did not violate the Fourth Amendment. It explained that the employment context itself both (1) lowered the employee's legitimate privacy expectations, and (2) created a special need on the employer's part to discover work-related misconduct:

> *An office is seldom a private enclave free from entry by supervisors, other employees, and business and personal invitees. Instead in many cases offices are continually entered by fellow employees and other visitors during the workday for conferences, consultations, and other work-related visits....*
>
> *While police...conduct searches for the primary purpose of obtaining evidence for use in criminal...proceedings, employers most frequently need to enter the offices and desks of their employees for legitimate work-related reasons wholly unrelated to*

illegal conduct. Employers and supervisors are focused primarily on the need to complete the government agency's work in a prompt and efficient manner. An employer may have need for correspondence, or a file or report available only in an employee's office while the employee is away.... Or, as is alleged to have been the case here, employers may need to safeguard or identify state property or records in an office in connection with a pending investigation into suspected employee malfeasance.[23]

■ ■ ■

In June 2010, using *O'Connor v. Ortega* as precedent, the Supreme Court decided the case that follows. Jeff Quon, a member of the police special-weapons and tactics (SWAT) team in Ontario, California, had been given a text-messaging pager by his department. In an effort to determine whether it should raise its quota of free messages for employees, the department obtained a transcript of Quon's texting, and discovered that most were sexually explicit communications to his wife and mistress. Sergeant Quon challenged this search as violating his Fourth Amendment rights.

CITY OF ONTARIO, CALIFORNIA v. QUON
2010 WL 2400087 (U.S.)

Justice Kennedy delivered the opinion of the Court.

...In October 2001, the City acquired 20 alphanumeric pagers capable of sending and receiving text messages. Arch Wireless Operating Company provided wireless service for the pagers. Under the City's service contract with Arch Wireless, each pager was allotted a limited number of characters sent or received each month. Usage in excess of that amount would result in an additional fee. The City issued pagers to Quon and other SWAT Team members in order to help the SWAT Team mobilize and respond to emergency situations.

Before acquiring the pagers, the City announced a "Computer Usage, Internet, and E-Mail Policy" (Computer Policy) that applied to all employees. Among other provisions, it specified that the City "reserves the right to monitor and log all network activity, including e-mail and Internet use, with or without notice. Users should have no expectation of privacy or confidentiality when using these resources." In March 2000, Quon signed a statement acknowledging that he had read and understood the Computer Policy.

The Computer Policy did not apply, on its face, to text messaging. Text messages share similarities with e-mails, but the two differ in an important way. In this case, for instance, an e-mail sent on a City computer was transmitted through the City's own data servers, but a text message sent on one of the City's pagers was transmitted using wireless radio frequencies from an individual pager to a receiving station owned by Arch Wireless. It was routed through Arch Wireless' computer network....After delivery, Arch Wireless retained a copy on its computer servers. The message did not pass through computers owned by the City....

At an April 18, 2002, staff meeting at which Quon was present, Lieutenant Steven Duke, the OPD officer responsible for the City's contract with Arch Wireless, told officers that messages sent on the pagers "are considered e-mail messages. This means that [text] messages would fall under the City's policy as public information and [would be] eligible for auditing." Duke's comments were put in writing in a memorandum....

---

[23] *O'Connor v. Ortega*, 480 U.S. 709 (1987).

Within the first or second billing cycle after the pagers were distributed, Quon exceeded his monthly text message character allotment. Duke told Quon about the overage, and reminded him that messages sent on the pagers were "considered e-mail and could be audited." Duke said, however, that "it was not his intent to audit [an] employee's text messages to see if the overage [was] due to work related transmissions." Duke suggested that Quon could reimburse the City for the overage fee rather than have Duke audit the messages. Quon wrote a check to the City for the overage. Duke offered the same arrangement to other employees who incurred overage fees.

Over the next few months, Quon exceeded his character limit three or four times. Each time he reimbursed the City. Quon and another officer again incurred overage fees for their pager usage in August 2002. At a meeting in October, Duke told Scharf that he had become "'tired of being a bill collector.'" [Chief] Scharf decided to determine whether the existing character limit was too low—that is, whether officers such as Quon were having to pay fees for sending work-related messages—or if the overages were for personal messages. Scharf told Duke to request transcripts of text messages sent in August and September by Quon and the other employee who had exceeded the character allowance....

Duke reviewed...transcripts [provided by Arch Wireless] and discovered that many of the messages sent and received on Quon's pager were not work related, and some were sexually explicit. Duke reported his findings to Scharf, who, along with Quon's immediate supervisor, reviewed the transcripts himself. After his review, Scharf referred the matter to OPD's internal affairs division for an investigation into whether Quon was violating OPD rules by pursuing personal matters while on duty.

The officer in charge of the internal affairs review... used Quon's work schedule to redact the transcripts in order to eliminate any messages Quon sent while off duty. He then reviewed the content of the messages Quon sent during work hours. [His] report noted that Quon sent or received 456 messages during work hours in the month of August 2002, of which no more than 57 were work related; he sent as many as 80 messages during a single day at work; and on an average workday, Quon sent or received 28 messages, of which only 3 were related to police business. The report concluded that Quon had violated OPD rules. Quon was allegedly disciplined.

[Quon, his then wife, his mistress (who worked for the police department), and another member of the SWAT team brought suit against the city for violating their Fourth Amendment rights by obtaining and reading the transcript of text messages. The progress of this case through the federal courts up to the Supreme Court displays a range of interpretations of the Constitution.]

The Fourth Amendment states: "The right of the people to be secure in their persons, houses, papers, and effects, against unreasonable searches and seizures, shall not be violated." The Court discussed this principle in *O'Connor*.... All Members of the Court agreed with the general principle that "[i]ndividuals do not lose Fourth Amendment rights merely because they work for the government instead of a private employer." [Because it would be impracticable to require government employees to get a warrant to search government office, we instead established a two-step analysis.] First, because "some government offices may be so open to fellow employees or the public that no expectation of privacy is reasonable," a court must consider "[t]he operational realities of the workplace" in order to determine whether an employee's Fourth Amendment rights are implicated. On this view, "the question whether an employee has a reasonable expectation of privacy must be addressed on a case-by-case basis." Next, where an employee has a legitimate privacy expectation, an employer's intrusion on that expectation "for noninvestigatory, work-related purposes, as well as for investigations of work-related misconduct, should be judged by the standard of reasonableness under all the circumstances." ...

The Court must proceed with care when considering the whole concept of privacy expectations in communications made on electronic equipment owned by a government employer.... In [a case from 1967] the Court relied on its own knowledge and experience to conclude that there is a reasonable expectation of privacy in a telephone booth. It is not so clear that courts at present are on so sure a ground. Prudence counsels caution before the facts in the instant case are used to establish far-reaching premises that define the existence, and extent, of privacy expectations enjoyed by employees when using employer-provided communication devices....

Rapid changes in the dynamics of communication and information transmission are evident not just in the technology itself but in what society accepts as proper behavior. As one *amici* [Electronic Frontier Foundation] brief notes, many employers expect or at least tolerate personal use of such equipment by employees because it often increases worker efficiency. Another *amicus* points out that the law is beginning to respond to these developments, as some States have recently passed statutes requiring employers to notify employees when monitoring their electronic communications. At present, it is uncertain how workplace norms, and the law's treatment of them, will evolve....

[T]he Court would have difficulty predicting how employees' privacy expectations will be shaped by those changes or the degree to which society will be prepared to recognize those expectations as reasonable. Cell phone and text message communications are so pervasive that some persons may consider them to be essential means or necessary instruments for self-expression, even self-identification. That might strengthen the case for an expectation of privacy. On the other hand, the ubiquity of those devices has made them generally affordable, so one could counter that employees who need cell phones or similar devices for personal matters can purchase and pay for their own. And employer policies concerning communications will of course shape the reasonable expectations of their employees, especially to the extent that such policies are clearly communicated....

[Continuing its analysis, the Court assumes Sergeant Quon had a reasonable expectation of privacy in the text messages, and that the city's review of those messages amounted to a "search" under the Fourth Amendment. Guided by its *O'Connor* decision, the Court now must determine whether the search was yet "reasonable."]

Although as a general matter, warrantless searches "are *per se* unreasonable under the Fourth Amendment," there are "a few specifically established and well-delineated exceptions" to that general rule. The Court has held that the "'special needs'" of the workplace justify one such exception. Under the [*O'Connor*] approach, when conducted for a "noninvestigatory, work-related purpos[e]" or for the "investigatio[n] of work-related misconduct," a government employer's warrantless search is reasonable if it is "'justified at its inception'" and if "'the measures adopted are reasonably related to the objectives of the search and not excessively intrusive in light of'" the circumstances giving rise to the search.

The search was justified at its inception because there were "reasonable grounds for suspecting that the search [was] necessary for a noninvestigatory work-related purpose." As a jury found, Chief Scharf ordered the search in order to determine whether the character limit on the City's contract with Arch Wireless was sufficient to meet the City's needs.... The City and OPD had a legitimate interest in ensuring that employees were not being forced to pay out of their own pockets for work-related expenses, or on the other hand that the City was not paying for extensive personal communications.

As for the scope of the search, reviewing the transcripts was reasonable because it was an efficient and expedient way to determine whether Quon's overages were the result of work-related messaging or personal use. The review was also not "'excessively intrusive.'" Although Quon had gone over his monthly allotment a number of times, OPD requested transcripts for only the months of August and September 2002. While it may have been reasonable as well for OPD to review transcripts of all the months in which Quon exceeded his allowance, it was certainly reasonable for OPD to review messages for just two months.... And it is worth noting that during his internal affairs investigation, [the investigating officer] redacted all messages Quon sent while off duty, a measure which reduced the intrusiveness....

[A]gain on the assumption that Quon had a reasonable expectation of privacy in the contents of his messages, the extent of an expectation is relevant to assessing whether the search was too intrusive. Even if he could assume some level of privacy would inhere in his messages, it would not have been reasonable for Quon to conclude that his messages were in all circumstances immune from scrutiny. Quon was told that his messages were subject to auditing. As a law enforcement officer, he would or should have known that his actions were likely to come under legal scrutiny, and that this might entail an analysis of his on-the-job communications. Under the circumstances, a reasonable employee would be aware that sound management principles might require the audit of messages to determine whether the pager was being appropriately used. Given that the City issued the pagers to Quon and other SWAT Team members in order to help them more quickly respond to crises—and given that Quon had received no assurances of privacy—Quon could have anticipated that it might be necessary for the City to audit pager messages to assess the SWAT Team's performance in particular emergency situations.

Because the search was motivated by a legitimate work-related purpose, and because it was not excessive in scope, the search was reasonable ... [The city] did not violate respondents' Fourth Amendment rights, and the court below erred by concluding otherwise. The judgment of the Court of Appeals for the Ninth Circuit is reversed, and the case is remanded for further proceedings consistent with this opinion.

It is so ordered.

QUESTIONS

1. Trace the Fourth Amendment analysis made by Justice Kennedy. Based on that, and what you know about the law of privacy from this chapter, tell how the following would be resolved:

   (a) You work as a car salesperson. One day your boss walks over to your desk and sees that you are playing Grand Theft Auto. She says nothing about it, but later, using surveillance software, reviews your online activities over recent months and finds many more visits to video game sites. There has been no communication about whether you would be monitored. You are fired.

   (b) You work for an investment bank. You have been issued a Blackberry to do business, on- and off-site. The bank, without warning, decides to review your cell phone use and determines you have been spending too much time manipulating your own stock portfolio. You are fired.

   (c) You work for the local library. You have been told that your use of the Internet will not be monitored without notice. However, your supervisors have decided to use surveillance software anyway, without notice, and have discovered that you are having e-mail correspondence with a homeless individual who frequently sits amongst the periodicals, making strange grunting noises that sometime disturb other visitors. You are fired.

2. **Research:** As Justice Kennedy notes, "many employers expect or at least tolerate personal use of [electronic communications] equipment by employees because it often increases worker efficiency." To what extent are employees taking care of personal matters during working hours? What can you find out about the causes of this trend and the rate at which it might be increasing? Start by looking at the Web sites of some of the organizations who filed *amicus* ("friend of the court" advisory) briefs in this case: The Electronic Frontier Foundation, The Center for Democracy & Technology, The Electronic Privacy Information Center, the ACLU, etc.

3. **Research:** Delaware and Connecticut have laws requiring employers to give their workers notice before monitoring their electronic communications.[24] Check your state for a law like this. If one exists, look for cases decided under it. For one of those, what was the outcome? If there is no statute, find out if there is a common law case dealing with

---

[24] *Del.Code Ann.*, Tit. 19, § 705 (2005); *Conn. Gen.Stat. Ann.* § 31-48d (West 2003).

electronic monitoring at work. Can you forecast whether a monitoring notice law might be passed in your state?

4. In gauging the intrusiveness of the search in this case, Justice Kennedy states "[T]he audit of messages on Quon's employer-provided pager was not nearly as intrusive as a search of his personal e-mail account or pager, or a wiretap on his home phone line, would have been." Given the trend to use employer-provided communications equipment to accomplish private tasks both at work and from home, does the distinction Justice Kennedy draws make sense? What are the ethical considerations that come up when law is trying to form itself on the cusp of technological change?

■ ■ ■

Privacy in Genetic Information

Whatsoever things I see or hear concerning the life of men, in my attendance on the sick or even apart therefrom, which ought not to be noised about, I will keep silence thereon, counting such things to be as sacred secrets.

— HIPPOCRATIC OATH

One of the most disturbing flashpoints where technology has outstripped privacy protection involves the health care industry. Profoundly revealing medical information is generated by and accessible to thousands of individuals and organizations—physicians, hospitals, HMOs, insurers, pharmacies, government agencies, pension funds, and employers.

■ ■ ■

Genetic testing of tiny amounts of human tissue—strands of hair or a few drops of blood—can reveal tremendous amounts of sensitive health data. In the next case, medical privacy issues come up in the context of genetic testing. A research facility in California required all job applicants to undergo health examinations to be eligible for clerical and administrative positions. The applicants, seven African-Americans and one Latino, had completed questionnaires and given blood and urine samples, but did not realize that theirs would be among those selected to be tested for such conditions as syphilis, sickle cell trait, and pregnancy. Here, the Ninth Circuit, in a case of first impression, must decide whether citizens have a right to genetic privacy.

NORMAN-BLOODSAW v. LAWRENCE BERKELEY LABORATORY
U.S. Court of Appeals, Ninth Circuit, 1997 135 F.3d 1260

REINHARDT, Circuit Judge.

[The named plaintiffs] are current and former administrative and clerical employees of defendant Lawrence Berkeley Laboratory ("Lawrence"), a research facility operated … pursuant to a contract with the United States Department of Energy (the Department). The Department requires federal contractors such as Lawrence to establish an occupational medical program. Since 1981, it has required its contractors to perform "preplacement examinations" of employees as part of this program, and until 1995, it also required its contractors to offer their employees the option of subsequent "periodic health examinations." The mandatory preplacement examination occurs after the offer of employment but prior to the assumption of job duties. The Department actively oversees Lawrence's occupational health program, and, prior to 1992, specifically required syphilis testing as part of the preplacement examination.

[All but one of the named plaintiffs] received written offers of employment expressly conditioned upon a "medical examination."... All accepted these offers and underwent preplacement examinations.... In the course of these examinations, plaintiffs completed medical history questionnaires and provided blood and urine samples. The questionnaires asked, [among other things,] whether the patient had ever had any of sixty-one medical conditions, including "[s]ickle cell anemia,"[25] "[v]enereal disease," and, in the case of women, "[m]enstrual disorders."[26]

The blood and urine samples given by all employees during their preplacement examinations were tested for syphilis; in addition, certain samples were tested for sickle cell trait; and certain samples were tested for pregnancy. Lawrence discontinued syphilis testing in April 1993, pregnancy testing in December 1994, and sickle cell trait testing in June 1995. Defendants assert that they discontinued syphilis testing because of its limited usefulness in screening healthy populations, and that they discontinued sickle cell trait testing because, by that time, most African-American adults had already been tested at birth. Lawrence continues to perform pregnancy testing, but only on an optional basis. Defendants further contend that "for many years" signs posted in the health examination rooms and "more recently" in the reception area stated that the tests at issue would be administered.

Plaintiffs allege that the testing of their blood and urine samples for syphilis, sickle cell trait, and pregnancy occurred without their knowledge or consent, and without any subsequent notification that the tests had been conducted. They also allege that only black employees were tested for sickle cell trait and assert the obvious fact that only female employees were tested for pregnancy. Finally, they allege that Lawrence failed to provide safeguards to prevent the dissemination of the test results. They contend that they did not discover that the disputed tests had been conducted until approximately January 1995, and specifically deny that they observed any signs indicating that such tests would be performed. Plaintiffs do not allege that the defendants took any subsequent employment-related action on the basis of their test results, or that their test results have been disclosed to third parties.

On the basis of these factual allegations, plaintiffs contend...that the defendants violated the federal constitutional right to privacy by conducting the testing at issue, collecting and maintaining the results of the testing, and failing to provide adequate safeguards against disclosure of the results. They [also] contend that the testing violated their right to privacy under ... the California Constitution. Finally, plaintiffs contend that Lawrence and the Regents violated Title VII by singling out black employees for sickle cell trait testing and by performing pregnancy testing on female employees generally.

Federal Constitutional Due Process Right of Privacy

The constitutionally protected privacy interest in avoiding disclosure of personal matters clearly encompasses medical information and its confidentiality. Although cases defining the privacy interest in medical information have typically involved its disclosure to "third" parties, rather than the collection of information by illicit means, it goes without saying that the most basic violation possible involves the performance of unauthorized tests—that is, the nonconsensual retrieval of previously unrevealed medical information that may be unknown even to plaintiffs. These tests may also be viewed as searches ... that

---

[25] Sickle cell anemia is a physical affliction in which a large proportion or majority of an individual's red blood cells become sickle-shaped. Sickle cell trait is a genetic condition in which an individual carries the gene that causes sickle cell anemia. The sickle cell gene is only semi-dominant; [if paired with a non-sickle cell gene that person will not usually develop anemia.]

[26] The section of the questionnaire also asks women if they have ever had abnormal pap smears and men if they have ever had prostate gland disorders.

require Fourth Amendment scrutiny. Accordingly, we must balance the government's interest in conducting these particular tests against the plaintiffs' expectations of privacy. Furthermore, "application of the balancing test requires not only considering the degree of intrusiveness and the state's interests in requiring that intrusion, but also 'the efficacy of this [the state's] means for meeting' its needs."

One can think of few subject areas more personal and more likely to implicate privacy interests than that of one's health or genetic make-up.... Furthermore, the facts revealed by the tests are highly sensitive, even relative to other medical information. With respect to the testing of plaintiffs for syphilis and pregnancy, it is well established in this circuit "that the Constitution prohibits unregulated, unrestrained employer inquiries into personal sexual matters that have no bearing on job performance." The fact that one has syphilis is an intimate matter that pertains to one's sexual history and may invite tremendous amounts of social stigma. Pregnancy is likewise, for many, an intensely private matter, which also may pertain to one's sexual history and often carries far-reaching societal implications. Finally, the carrying of sickle cell trait can pertain to sensitive information about family history and reproductive decision-making. Thus, the conditions tested for were aspects of one's health in which one enjoys the highest expectations of privacy.

[T]here was little, if any, "overlap" between what plaintiffs consented to and the testing at issue here.... That one has consented to a general medical examination does not abolish one's privacy right not to be tested for intimate, personal matters involving one's health—nor does consenting to giving blood or urine samples,[27] or filling out a questionnaire. As we have made clear, revealing one's personal knowledge as to whether one has a particular medical condition has nothing to do with one's expectations about actually being tested for that condition. Thus, the intrusion was by no means [insignificant]....

Title VII Claims

Section 703(a) of Title VII of the Civil Rights Act of 1964 provides that it is unlawful for any employer:

> to fail or refuse to hire or to discharge any individual, or otherwise to discriminate against any individual with respect to his compensation, terms, conditions, or privileges of employment, because of such individual's race, color, religion, sex, or national origin....

The Pregnancy Discrimination Act further provides that discrimination on the basis of "sex" includes discrimination "on the basis of pregnancy, childbirth, or related medical conditions."

[P]laintiffs' Title VII claims fall neatly into a Title VII framework: Plaintiffs allege that black and female employees were singled out for additional nonconsensual testing and that defendants thus selectively invaded the privacy of certain employees on the basis of race, sex, and pregnancy.

It is well established that Title VII bars discrimination ... in the "terms" and "conditions" under which individuals may obtain employment.... [A] requirement of preemployment health examinations imposed only on female employees, or a requirement of preemployment background security checks imposed only on black employees, would surely violate Title VII.

In this case, the term or condition for black employees was undergoing a test for sickle cell trait; for women it was undergoing a test for pregnancy. It is not disputed that the preplacement exams were, literally, a condition of employment: the offers of employment stated this explicitly. Thus, the employment of women and blacks at Lawrence was

---

[27] Indeed, the Supreme Court has recognized that while the taking of a bodily fluid sample implicates one's privacy interests, "[t]he ensuing chemical analysis of the sample to obtain physiological data is a further intrusion of the tested employee's privacy interests." *Skinner v. Railway Labor Executives' Ass'n*, (1989) (allowing urine testing of railway workers for drugs).

conditioned in part on allegedly unconstitutional invasions of privacy to which white and/or male employees were not subjected. An additional "term or condition" requiring an unconstitutional invasion of privacy is, without doubt, actionable under Title VII.[28]

[Judgment of the lower court dismissing the claims is reversed.]

QUESTIONS

1. On what basis did the Ninth Circuit find that the federal Constitution had been violated by the laboratory in this case? The federal Civil Rights Act?

2. Why do you think employers are interested in the results of genetic testing of their employees? Can you think of potential problems with genetic testing, in the workplace or in any other context?

■ ■ ■

A Comprehensive Federal Statutory Response

When genetic testing revealed a young boy suffered from an inherited form of mental retardation called Fragile X Syndrome, his family's insurer claimed this was a preexisting condition and dropped his coverage. Just one week after a social worker mentioned that her mother had Huntington's disease—a fatal illness with no cure—and that she had a 50% chance of developing it, she was fired. Whether instances like these of discrimination based on genetic information have been prevalent in recent years is debatable; there have been no reported cases yet under the many state laws outlawing such discrimination. Yet the public perception is that genetic discrimination is a real threat. In 2007, a Johns Hopkins University survey indicated that 93% of respondents believed that insurers and employers should be prevented from accessing predictive genetic test results.

A variety of laws addressing genetic discrimination now exist in most states—some forbidding preemployment testing, some prohibiting discrimination only against persons with certain specific genetic traits, some regulating the use of test results—but they make up a patchwork quilt offering inconsistent protection. Until recently, federal legislation dealt only tangentially with genetic information. The 2004 *Health Information Portability and Accountability Act* (HIPAA), for example, requires consent for medical information to be accessed and shared, but does not address discrimination. The *Americans with Disabilities Act* covers those with "perceived" disability or with symptoms of inherited disability, but does not protect anyone from requests to provide genetic information to employers as part of a post-offer medical exam.

Widespread public concern gave a boost to privacy advocates, who had been working towards a comprehensive federal statute for 18 years. Their efforts finally bore fruit in the form of the *Genetic Information Nondiscrimination Act*, or GINA. This law represents a rare bipartisan effort: It passed in the House of Representatives 414 to 1; in the Senate it passed unanimously.

Before GINA, federal laws addressing discrimination were designed to end particular forms of existing harm. In the debates preceding their passage, statutes like the Civil Rights Act of 1964 looked back at lengthy histories of discrimination—300 years of legal ownership of Africans as slaves, for example. Yet when GINA passed in 2008, the technology for mining genetic data was new, and there was relatively little evidence

---

[28] An exception exists for pregnancy testing in those "instances in which … pregnancy actually interferes with the employee's ability to perform the job." No such exception is asserted here.

indicating that genetic-information discrimination posed a historical—or even a current—problem. As one commentator stated, "While GINA's opponents saw the absence of a history of discrimination as a major flaw, its advocates embraced the slim record as an exciting opportunity to preempt discrimination for the first time in American history."[29]

GENETIC INFORMATION NONDISCRIMINATION ACT OF 2008

Sec. 201. Definitions

(4) GENETIC INFORMATION.
  (A) IN GENERAL. The term "genetic information" means, with respect to any individual, information about—
    (i)   such individual's genetic tests,
    (ii) the genetic tests of family members of such individual, and
    (iii) the manifestation of a disease or disorder in family members of such individual.

  (B) INCLUSION OF GENETIC SERVICES AND PARTICIPATION IN GENETIC RESEARCH. Such term includes…any request for, or receipt of, genetic services, or participation in clinical research which includes genetic services….

(5) GENETIC MONITORING. The term "genetic monitoring" means the periodic examination of employees to evaluate acquired modifications to their genetic material, such as chromosomal damage or evidence of increased occurrence of mutations, that may have developed in the course of employment due to exposure to toxic substances in the workplace, in order to identify, evaluate, and respond to the effects of or control adverse environmental exposures in the workplace.
(6) GENETIC SERVICES. The term "genetic services" means
  (A) a genetic test,
  (B) genetic counseling (including obtaining, interpreting, or assessing genetic information),or
  (C) genetic education.

Sec. 202. Employer Practices

  (a) DISCRIMINATION BASED ON GENETIC INFORMATION. It shall be an unlawful employment practice for an employer:—
  (1) to fail or refuse to hire, or to discharge, any employee, or otherwise to discriminate against any employee with respect to the compensation, [or] … conditions of employment because of genetic information with respect to the employee; or
  (2) to limit, segregate, or classify employees…in any way that would deprive or tend to deprive any employee of employment opportunities or otherwise adversely affect the status of the employee…, because of genetic information with respect to the employee.

---

[29] Jessica L. Roberts, "Preemptive Discrimination: The Genetic Information Nondiscrimination Act," 63 *Vand L.Rev.* 440 (Spring 2010). While Roberts points out that there was slim evidence in the case law that discrimination related to genetic information existed, she states: "GINA's preemptive nature truly makes the statute unique. GINA provides a novel opportunity to stop a new form of discrimination before it takes hold. Moreover, because a socially recognized group of genetically disadvantaged people does not currently exist, GINA can preempt not only discrimination but also the formation of a new type of social stigma." *Id.* At 488.

(b) ACQUISITION OF GENETIC INFORMATION. [GINA makes it unlawful for an employer to request, require or purchase genetic information related to employees or their families. There are several exceptions to this, including:]

(2) where—

   (A) health or genetic services are offered by the employer, including such services offered as part of a wellness program;

   (B) the employee provides prior, knowing, voluntary, and written authorization;

   (C) only the employee (or family member if the family member is receiving genetic services) and the licensed health care professional or board certified genetic counselor involved in providing such services receive individually identifiable information concerning the results of such services; and

   (D) [The employer receives aggregate, not individually–identified, genetic information]....

(5) where the information involved is to be used for genetic monitoring of the biological effects of toxic substances in the workplace, but only if—

   (A) the employer provides written notice of the genetic monitoring to the employee;

   (B) (i) the employee provides prior, knowing, voluntary, and written authorization; or
       (ii) the genetic monitoring is required by Federal or State law;

   (C) the employee is informed of individual monitoring results;

Sec. 206. Confidentiality of Genetic Information

(a) TREATMENT OF INFORMATION AS PART OF CONFIDENTIAL MEDICAL RECORD. If an employer...possesses genetic information about an employee or member, such information shall be maintained on separate forms and in separate medical files and be treated as a confidential medical record of the employee....

(b) LIMITATION ON DISCLOSURE. An employer...shall not disclose genetic information concerning an employee or member except—

(1) to the employee ...(or family member if the family member is receiving the genetic services) at the written request of the employee;

(2) to an occupational or other health researcher...

(3) in response to an order of a court, except that—

   (A) the employer ... may disclose only the genetic information expressly authorized by such order; and

   (B) if the court order was secured without the knowledge of the employee..., the employer ... shall inform the employee...of the court order and any genetic information that was disclosed pursuant to such order;

[GINA similarly restricts insurers from discriminating, forbidding them from raising premiums or denying coverage on the basis of genetic information. GINA does not, however, prevent an insurance company from raising an employer's premium if an insured individual in the group actually manifests a disease or disorder.]

QUESTIONS

1. Has anyone in the following scenarios violated GINA?

   (a) Supervisor overhears Employee A say she and her sister share the same gene predictive of developing breast cancer. Supervisor gives Employee A a lower performance rating than she deserves, in preparation for letting her go with the next round of lay-offs.

   (b) A health professional working learns that Employee B has family members with breast cancer as a result of a medical interview in which Employee B participated as a requirement for joining the company's wellness program. He shares that information with Employee B's supervisor over lunch.

(c) Employer asks Employee C, who has requested Family and Medical Leave, to certify the health status of the family member she will care for, and Employee C provides evidence that her mother has breast cancer.

(d) Employee D reads the obituary of Employee C's mother, describing that she died after a long struggle with breast cancer for which she carried a predictive gene. She shares this information with Supervisor, who asks Employee C to take a genetic test.

(e) A drilling company uses vast quantities of water containing toxic chemicals in a "fracking" operation, which forces water deep underground to fracture rock and release natural gas. During routine medical check-ups given by the company that normally do not contain genetic testing, workers' blood is analyzed to find out if exposure to benzene and other toxics in this process might be causing health problems. Three employees are discovered to have a genetic tendency to develop lymphoma and are given desk jobs that pay less.

(f) Same as (e), but the tests are mandated by state law, the employees are given notice, sign consent forms, and are told the results and why they have been reassigned.

2. The 2008 GINA law protects against genetic discrimination by employers and health insurers, but there are loopholes in the legislation. Privacy advocates point out that GINA is silent on discrimination that might take place on the part of companies offering life and disability insurance. Too, it does not touch the unregulated and fast-growing market for genetic testing. At present, direct-to-consumer marketing has meant an explosive growth in this field, with millions of consumers sending in saliva samples to find out if they are at risk of developing cancer, diabetes, heart disease and other illnesses. The predictive accuracy of the reports generated by genetic testing companies are of concern, and then there is the question of where the vast amounts of genetic information being collected might be going. Testing companies can sell clients' genetic information for pure research and for commercial purposes—to pharmaceutical companies to develop drugs, for example. What ethical issues arise here?

3. In 1927, the Supreme Court legitimized state-sponsored sterilization of a young woman with alleged mental disabilities. Carrie Buck, an 18-year-old described as having the mental age of nine, was sent to the State Colony of Epileptics and the Feeble–Minded in Virginia to deliver a baby who was conceived after she had been raped by the nephew of her foster parents. At that time, Virginia allowed sterilization of people who suffered hereditary forms of insanity or imbecility, a law designed to prevent "mentally defective" people from reproducing. Against her will, Buck was ordered to be sterilized. The superintendent of the state facility petitioned the courts to enforce Virginia law, arguing that compulsory sterilization was simply analogous to compulsory vaccination.

   In an 8-1 decision, the Court agreed, stating that Carrie Buck was "feeble-minded" and "promiscuous." Justice Oliver Wendell Holmes, Jr. argued that a "pure" gene pool outweighed an individual's interest in bodily integrity:

> We have seen more than once that the public welfare may call upon the best citizens for their lives. It would be strange if it could not call upon those who already sap the strength of the State for these lesser sacrifices, often not felt to be such by those concerned, to prevent our being swamped with incompetence. It is better for all the world, if instead of waiting to execute degenerate offspring for crime, or to let them starve for their imbecility, society can prevent those who are manifestly unfit from continuing their kind. The principle that sustains compulsory vaccination is broad enough to cover cutting the Fallopian tubes.

Holmes infamously concluded that "Three generations of imbeciles are enough."[30]

In the 40 years following the Court's decision, the pseudoscience of eugenics permitted the forcible sterilization of some 60,000 Americans. What has happened to change societal attitudes (as reflected in change in the law) so significantly?

■ ■ ■

Chapter Problems

1. We have seen that, in general, workplace e-mail monitoring is legal. In the landmark *Smyth v. Pillsbury* case at the start of this chapter, employees had no recourse when they were fired for messages sent through the employer's server, even when password-protected, and even when the employer had issued assurances that they would not be read for retaliatory purposes. But what if the employer monitors messages sent on Web-hosted e-mail accounts like Yahoo? And what if the employee was already fired, and was sending those messages to his attorney, discussing strategy for the arbitration claim he was about to make regarding his termination? These are the facts alleged by Scott Sidell, who filed a suit in May 2008 against Structured Settlements in federal court in Connecticut. As his attorney put it, "It's kind of like the other side gets your playbook or they're spying on your locker room." In a case for intrusion, should these facts create a "reasonable expectation of privacy?" **Research:** Find out what happened.

2. In 1968, Thomas Watson Jr., then-chairman of IBM and son of its founder, notified his managers that off-the-job behavior should concern them only when it impaired a person's ability to perform on the job. He wrote:

   The line that separates an individual's on-the-job business life from his other life as a private citizen is at times well-defined and at other times indistinct. But the line does exist, and you and I, as managers in IBM, must be able to recognize that line.... Our primary objective as IBM managers is to further the business of this company by leading our people properly and measuring quantity and quality of work and effectiveness on the job against clearly set standards of responsibility and compensation. This is performance—and performance is, in the final analysis, the one thing that the company can insist on from everyone....

   More recently, in 2009, the company created guidelines for IBM bloggers. Consider this from the executive summary:

   Blogs, wikis, and other forms of online discourse are individual interactions, not corporate communications.... Identify yourself—name, and, where relevant, role at IBM—when you blog about IBM or IBM-related matters. Respect your audience. Don't use ethnic slurs, personal insults, obscenity, etc,. and show proper consideration for others' privacy and for topics that may be considered objectionable or inflammatory—such as politics and religion.

---

[30] *Buck v. Bell*, 274 U.S. 200, at 270 (1927). In 1979, researchers determined that Carrie Buck, her sister, who was also sterilized, and her daughter, were all of average intelligence. Virginia's sterilization procedures were not repealed until 1974.

At *http://www.ibm.com/blogs/zz/en/guidelines.html*, these Guidelines are fully listed and explained. There is a link for reporting suspected infractions and a video showing how IBM is trying to embed these values into its culture. Does this recent statement on the use of social media align with Tom Watson's memo from 1968? Do you think the 2009 Guidelines strike the right balance between privacy and corporate loyalty?

3. For years, Elizabeth Collins blogged about her personal life and about her teaching experience. Before her blogging got her fired, she was an English teacher at the Academy of Notre Dame de Namur, a private all-girls school in Villanova, Pennsylvania. Although Collins never identified the school, nor any of its employees or students by name, she did give her own name and occupation on *www.prettyfreaky.blogspot.com*. One of her posts described how she had asked her students to give a speech advocating a point of view without being hostile, and she wrote about her disappointment over the way one of her students didn't seem to understand that assignment. She then posted a sample speech defending the Obama administration. The parents of the student who had misunderstood the assignment, prominent members of the local Catholic community, were distressed by Collins' blog, which they called "an attack on a child." Their criticisms, and Collins' continued posts (she wrote about a fictional meeting with Mr. Bratwurst and Miss Petunia Fluffyglow, including thinly disguised dialogue of her actual encounters with the parents) led to her termination. What ethical issues arise in this situation? **Research:** Find out if Elizabeth Collins is still blogging. Has she gotten another teaching job? Can you find another case where an employee was fired for blogging? What were the facts? What was the outcome?

4. The National Labor Relations Act protects employees as they communicate with one another to organize and form a union, or to engage as a union in collective bargaining with their employers. Where should the line be drawn between protected "concerted activities for the purpose of collective bargaining or other mutual aid" under this law, and unprotected blogging that may disclose trade secrets, project harassment, inappropriate or disloyal attitudes about an employer? Do "concerted activities" always have to focus on working conditions? What if employees blog critically about safety or environmental issues as they also begin to organize to form a union or to negotiate a collective bargaining agreement? **Research:** First, read the following article. It will lead you to some recent cases: Katherine M. Scott, "When is Employee Blogging Protected by Section 7 of the NLRA?" 2006 *Duke L. & Tech. Rev.* 17.

5. The Supreme Court has recently grappled with the speech rights of public school students under the constitution, ruling that they can be disciplined for activities that happen outside of school if officials can prove their activities were disruptive or dangerous, and if it was foreseeable they would find their way to campus. Apply this analysis to the following:

    (a) In October 2009, two sophomore girls at Churubusco High School in Indianapolis, Illinois were banned from extracurricular activities for posting sexually suggestive photographs on MySpace during their summer vacation. The girls were also required to apologize to a team of male coaches and to undergo counseling.

    (b) High school students from western Pennsylvania ridiculed school principals on MySpace using home computers. One described his principal as a "big steroid freak" who smoked "blunts;" the other called the principal a pedophile. Neither was distributed on school property; neither disrupted school activities. They were expelled.

(c) Responding to these kinds of cases, John Palfrey, a Harvard University law professor and co-director of the Berkman Center for Internet and Society, says: "From the standpoint of young people, there's no real distinction between online life and offline life. It's just life." Do you agree? What ethical issues surface here? **Research:** Locate the actual cases and find out what happened.

6. In the summer of 1995, Gail Nelson, an employee of Salem State College in Massachusetts, suffered a severe sunburn. Several times a day when she was alone in the office, she would go to the back area, unbutton her blouse and apply sunburn medication. After discovering that she had been videotaped by a hidden camera, she sued her employer. (a) What arguments might she make? (b) How might the employer defend itself? (c) **Research:** What happened? *Nelson v. Salem State College*, 845 N.E.2d 338 (MA 2006).

7. Do Americans have a reasonable expectation of privacy that is violated when they are videotaped on public streets? In store dressing rooms? In motel rooms? In coffee bars? When cybercafés began to proliferate in Garden Grove, California, they seemed to bring with them gang activity. The police chief pushed for some control, and the city council responded by passing a law requiring cybercafés to install video surveillance systems that could be inspected by the city during business hours. When a California court denied a constitutional challenge to the video-surveillance law, one judge dissented:

> *Cybercafes allow people who cannot afford computers … the freedom of the press. They can post messages to the whole world, and, in theory (if they get enough "hits") can reach more people than read the hard copy of the New York Times every morning.… Logging on is an exercise of free speech.*
>
> *Consider that totalitarian governments have always cracked down on unrestricted access to the means of communication. When the Communists were in control of countries such as Albania and Bulgaria, each typewriter was licensed.…*
>
> *And consider that the governments of both Communist China and Vietnam have recently cracked down on cybercafes in an effort to curb the freedom of ideas that they promote—an effort that has entailed learning the identity of cybercafe owners.… Given the constitutional ramifications of the very nature of cybercafes, I will go so far as to say that there is an expectation of privacy even as to one's identity when using a cybercafé.… Vo v. City of Garden Grove, 9 Cal.Rptr.3d 257 (Court of Appeal, 2004).*

(a) Create a constitutional analysis of Garden Groves' video surveillance requirement.

(b) **Research:** The ubiquitous cameras that provide the images for Google's Street View caused a stir in Europe recently. What happened? What can you find out about the reaction in the U.S.?

8. The cost of errors in inventory management has been estimated as high as $500 billion a year in the United States. Radio Frequency Identification (RFID), the technology which enabled British flight controllers in World War II to distinguish between friendly and enemy planes and which makes the EZ Pass and similar systems through highway tollbooths possible, is the likely successor to bar code scanning. Tags can be almost as small as a grain of sand. Unlike the Universal Product Code used by bar code scanners, RFID does not require that the scanning device "see" the bars. Some RFID

sensors can operate at 100 meters. And, unlike the Universal Product Code used by bar code scanners, the Electronic Product Code (EPC) can be programmed to add specific information that may have uses in product handling prior to sale and even in research concerning customer behavior after the purchase. It is the use of RFID technology to study customer behavior that has privacy groups concerned. An RFID trial in 2003 by Procter & Gamble triggered hidden cameras, which enabled researchers in Cincinnati to watch female customers handling lipstick in a Walmart store in Oklahoma. As a California state senator said in reference to that incident, "How would you like it if … one day you realized your underwear was reporting on your whereabouts?" What are the ethical pros and cons of RFID?

9. **Research:** In June 2010, the E.U. data protection authorities released an opinion declaring that online advertisers must obtain "informed" consent before tracking consumers' Web browsing for targeted ads. Find out what the Federal Trade Commission (FTC) has to say about this practice, and then compare and contrast the American and European policies.

10. Advocating for genetic privacy in 2000, Lew Maltby warned:

> *The knowledge we gain from the genetic revolution chips away at our very sense of community. Our willingness to think of ourselves as members of a community and to act as such has two deep roots. The first is that we are inherently social animals. Nature has wired us that way. The second is people have generally been better off as members of a community.…*
>
> *Our growing ability to peer into the medical future only makes things worse. When we don't know who among us will be struck by calamity, it makes sense to stick together and take care of each other. But when we know that the curses of Job are likely to befall someone else rather than ourselves, our incentive to be a community diminishes. All of a sudden, we're not in the same boat anymore.*

How does Maltby link privacy and community? Can you draw other connections between privacy and a vibrant collective life?

CHAPTER PROJECT

Collaborative Exercise:
Writing a Model Corporate Privacy Policy

Begin with students working in teams of five. Within each group, the following roles should be represented:

- Upper management
- Mid-management
- Production/office workers
- Human resources
- Public relations

Each team should first discuss and try to reach consensus on a set of guiding values. From there, it should hammer out specific policies addressing electronic monitoring, Internet usage, mixing work and personal activities, testing policies, and so on.

Groups should write their final versions and present them to one another, arguing in support of their privacy policies to their classmates, taking questions and challenges.

A final task might be to vote on the "best" corporate privacy policy, and to compare it to the one recommended by the National Workrights Institute.

CHAPTER 4

Valuing Diversity
Stereotyping vs. Inclusion

Like and difference are quickening words, brooding and hatching. Better and worse are eggsucking words. They leave only the shell.

— URSULA LE GUIN

The case is simple. A woman with preschool children may not be employed, a man with preschool children may. The distinguishing factor seems to be motherhood versus fatherhood. The question then arises: Is this sex-related? To the simple query, the answer is just as simple: Nobody—and this includes Judges, Solomonic or life tenured—has yet seen a male mother. A mother, to oversimplify the simplest biology, must then be a woman.

— JUSTICE BROWN, Dissenting, Phillips v. Martin Marietta Corp.

The events of 9/11 made "immigrant" synonymous with "terrorist."

— RUBEN J. GARCIA, "Ghost Workers in an Interconnected World," (2003)

Despite civil rights laws and Supreme Court rulings that span half a century, the remnants of past discriminatory practices survive. They can be seen in the difficulties that continue to plague small businesses owned by minorities and women, in the wage gap between men and women, in the difference in treatment of people of color and whites, and in a national workforce in which jobs are still by and large segregated by race and gender. Stereotypes continue to create social and economic hardships for many in our society. In the early decades of the new millennium, the threat of terrorism and the globalization of business and labor have created new strains and concerns. These pressures, coupled with an economic crisis that began to unfold in 2007, has revived a national debate over immigration policies and the rights of noncitizens who live among us.

   This chapter opens with a case that is one of the most controversial in years: the ruling by the high court of Massachusetts in favor of same-sex marriage. The Equal Protection Clause of the U.S. Constitution and federal laws against discrimination based on race, religion, sex, national origin, and disability provide the legal backdrop. Readings that explore the importance of the workplace (especially to the most vulnerable) and the work/family dilemma round out the chapter.

■ ■ ■

   In 2001, gay and lesbian couples in Massachusetts—including some who had lived together for many years—applied for licenses to marry. Denied by the town clerks, they filed a lawsuit seeking a judicial declaration that the Department of Public Health's policy violated the Massachusetts Constitution. When the lower court ruled against them, the plaintiffs appealed.

GOODRIDGE v. DEPARTMENT OF PUBLIC HEALTH

Supreme Judicial Court of Massachusetts, 2003
798 N.E.2d 941

MARSHALL, C. J. (with whom IRELAND and GREANEY, J. J. Concur)

… Marriage is a vital social institution. The exclusive commitment of two individuals to each other nurtures love and mutual support; it brings stability to our society. For those who choose to marry, and for their children, marriage provides an abundance of legal, financial, and social benefits. In return it imposes weighty legal, financial, and social obligations. The question before us is whether, consistent with the Massachusetts Constitution, the Commonwealth may deny the protections, benefits, and obligations conferred by civil marriage to two individuals of the same sex who wish to marry. We conclude that it may not. The Massachusetts Constitution affirms the dignity and equality of all individuals. It forbids the creation of second-class citizens. In reaching our conclusion we have given full deference to the arguments made by the Commonwealth. But it has failed to identify any constitutionally adequate reason for denying civil marriage to same-sex couples.

We are mindful that our decision marks a change in the history of our marriage law. Many people hold deep-seated religious, moral, and ethical convictions that marriage should be limited to the union of one man and one woman, and that homosexual conduct is immoral. Many hold equally strong religious, moral, and ethical convictions that same-sex couples are entitled to be married, and that homosexual persons should be treated no differently than their heterosexual neighbors…."Our obligation is to define the liberty of all, not to mandate our own moral code." *Lawrence v. Texas (U.S. 2003)*….

The plaintiffs are fourteen individuals from five Massachusetts counties. As of April 11, 2001, … Gloria Bailey, sixty years old, and Linda Davies, fifty-five years old, had been in a committed relationship for thirty years; … Hillary Goodridge, forty-four years old, and Julie Goodridge, forty-three years old, had been in a committed relationship for thirteen years and lived with their five-year-old daughter; … Gary Chalmers, thirty-five years old, and Richard Linnell, thirty-seven years old, had been in a committed relationship for thirteen years and lived with their eight-year-old daughter and Richard's mother….

The plaintiffs include business executives, lawyers, an investment banker, educators, therapists, and a computer engineer. Many are active in church, community, and school groups…. Each plaintiff attests a desire to marry his or her partner in order to affirm publicly their commitment to each other and to secure the legal protections and benefits afforded to married couples and their children….

The benefits accessible only by way of a marriage license are enormous, touching nearly every aspect of life and death. The department states that "hundreds of statutes" are related to marriage and to marital benefits…. [S]ome of the statutory benefits conferred by the Legislature on those who enter into civil marriage include … joint Massachusetts income tax filing; tenancy by the entirety (a form of ownership that provides certain protections against creditors and allows for the automatic descent of property to the surviving spouse without probate); [inheritance rights]; … entitlement to wages owed to a deceased employee; eligibility to continue certain businesses of a deceased spouse; the right to share the medical policy of one's spouse; … access to veterans' spousal benefits …; financial protections for spouses of … fire fighters, police officers, and prosecutors … killed in the performance of duty; [property rights upon divorce or separation]; ... right to bring claims for wrongful death and loss of consortium; ... the presumptions of legitimacy and parentage of children born to a married couple; ... evidentiary rights, such as the prohibition against spouses testifying against one another about their private conversations; ... qualification for bereavement or medical leave to care for [relatives]; ... an automatic "family member" preference to make medical decisions for an incompetent or disabled spouse; ... and the right to interment in the lot or tomb owned by one's deceased spouse....

It is undoubtedly for these concrete reasons, as well as for its intimately personal significance, that civil marriage has long been termed a "civil right."

Without the right to marry—or more properly, the right to choose to marry—one is excluded from the full range of human experience and denied full protection of the laws for one's "avowed commitment to an intimate and lasting human relationship."...

For decades, indeed centuries, in much of this country (including Massachusetts) no lawful marriage was possible between white and black Americans. That long history availed not when the ... United States Supreme Court ... held that a statutory bar to interracial marriage violated the Fourteenth Amendment, *Loving v. Virginia*, (1967)....

The individual liberty and equality safeguards of the Massachusetts Constitution protect both "freedom from" unwarranted government intrusion into protected spheres of life and "freedom to" partake in benefits created by the State for the common good. Both freedoms are involved here. Whether and whom to marry, how to express sexual intimacy, and whether and how to establish a family—these are among the most basic of every individual's liberty and due process rights....

Under both the equality and liberty guarantees, regulatory authority must, at very least, serve "a legitimate purpose in a rational way." ... Any law failing to satisfy the basic standards of rationality is void....

The [lower court held] that "the state's interest in regulating marriage is based on the traditional concept that marriage's primary purpose is procreation." This is incorrect. Our laws of civil marriage do not privilege procreative heterosexual intercourse between married people above every other form of adult intimacy and every other means of creating a family.... Fertility is not a condition of marriage, nor is it grounds for divorce....

There is ... no rational relationship between the marriage statute and the Commonwealth's proffered goal of protecting the "optimal" child rearing unit.... People in same-sex couples may be "excellent" parents. These couples have children for the reasons others do—to love them, to care for them, to nurture them.... Excluding same-sex couples from civil marriage will not make children of opposite-sex marriages more secure, but it does prevent children of same-sex couples from enjoying the immeasurable advantages that flow from the assurance of "a stable family structure in which children will be reared, educated, and socialized."

The department [also argues that] broadening civil marriage to include same-sex couples will trivialize or destroy the institution of marriage as it has historically been fashioned. Certainly our decision today marks a significant change in the definition of marriage as it has been inherited from the common law, and understood by many societies for centuries. But it does not disturb the fundamental value of marriage in our society.

Here, the plaintiffs seek only to be married, not to undermine the institution of civil marriage....

The history of constitutional law "is the story of the extension of constitutional rights and protections to people once ignored or excluded." ... As a public institution and a right of fundamental importance, civil marriage is an evolving paradigm. The common law was exceptionally harsh toward women who became wives: a woman's legal identity all but evaporated into that of her husband.... Alarms about the imminent erosion of the "natural" order of marriage were sounded over ... the expansion of the rights of married women, and the introduction of "no-fault" divorce. Marriage has survived all of these transformations, and we have no doubt that marriage will continue to be a vibrant and revered institution.

The marriage ban works a deep and scarring hardship on a very real segment of the community for no rational reason. The absence of any reasonable relationship between, on the one hand, an absolute disqualification of same-sex couples who wish to enter into civil marriage and, on the other, protection of public health, safety, or general welfare, suggests that the marriage restriction is rooted in persistent prejudices against persons who are (or who are believed to be) homosexual. "The Constitution cannot control such prejudices but neither can it tolerate them...." Limiting the protections, benefits, and obligations of civil marriage to opposite-sex couples violates the basic premises of individual liberty and equality under law protected by the Massachusetts Constitution [Held: the Department of Health policy denying marriage licenses to same-sex couples violates the Massachusetts Constitution.]

SPINA, J. (dissenting, with whom Sosman and Cordy, JJ. , join).

...The power to regulate marriage lies with the Legislature, not with the judiciary.... Today, the court has transformed its role as protector of individual rights into the role of creator of rights, and I respectfully dissent....

CORDY, J. (dissenting, with whom Spina and Sosman, JJ. , join).

...Because a conceivable rational basis exists upon which the Legislature could conclude that the marriage statute furthers the legitimate State purpose of ensuring, promoting, and supporting an optimal social structure for the bearing and raising of children, it is a valid exercise of the State's police power.

The marriage statute ... does not intrude on any right that the plaintiffs have to privacy in their choices regarding procreation, an intimate partner or sexual relations. The plaintiffs' right to privacy in such matters does not require that the State officially endorse their choices in order for the right to be constitutionally vindicated...

While the institution of marriage is deeply rooted in the history and traditions of our country and our State, the right to marry someone of the same sex is not. No matter how personal or intimate a decision to marry someone of the same sex might be, the right to make it is not guaranteed by the right of personal autonomy...[nor by the] right to freedom of association....

Paramount among its many important functions, the institution of marriage has systematically provided for the regulation of heterosexual behavior, brought order to the resulting procreation, and ensured a stable family structure in which children will be reared, educated, and socialized....

The alternative, a society without the institution of marriage, in which heterosexual intercourse, procreation, and child care are largely disconnected processes, would be chaotic....

It is undeniably true that dramatic historical shifts in our cultural, political, and economic landscape have altered some of our traditional notions about marriage, including the interpersonal dynamics within it, the range of responsibilities required of it as an institution, and the legal environment in which it exists. Nevertheless, the institution of marriage remains the principal weave of our social fabric.... A family defined by heterosexual marriage continues to be the most prevalent social structure into which the vast majority of children are born, nurtured, and prepared for productive participation in civil society.

It is difficult to imagine a State purpose more important and legitimate than ensuring, promoting, and supporting an optimal social structure within which to bear and raise children. At the very least, the marriage statute continues to serve this important State purpose....

[T]he Legislature could conceivably conclude that declining to recognize same-sex marriages remains prudent until empirical questions about its impact on the upbringing of children are resolved....

As long as marriage is limited to opposite-sex couples who can at least theoretically procreate, society is able to communicate a consistent message to its citizens that marriage is a (normatively) necessary part of their procreative endeavor; that if they are to procreate, then society has endorsed the institution of marriage as the environment for it and for the subsequent rearing of their children; and that benefits are available explicitly to create a supportive and conducive atmosphere for those purposes. If society proceeds similarly to recognize marriages between same-sex couples who cannot procreate, it could be perceived as an abandonment of this claim, and might result in the mistaken view that civil marriage has little to do with procreation: just as the potential of procreation would not be necessary for a marriage to be valid, marriage would not be necessary for optimal procreation and child rearing to occur. In essence, the Legislature could conclude that the consequence of such a policy shift would be a diminution in society's ability to steer the acts of procreation and child rearing into their most optimal setting.…[I dissent.]

QUESTIONS

1. On what basis does the majority strike down the Massachusetts marriage license law? How does the dissent respond?

2. **Research**: The dissent mentions "empirical questions" about the impact of same-sex marriage on children. What can you find out about the impact—positive or negative— on those who have been raised by same-sex parents?

3. **Research**: Find *Loving v. Virginia,* the 1967 Supreme Court case that held that statutes barring marriage across racial lines were unconstitutional. Did the Court employ any of the same arguments made by the majority in *Goodridge*?

4. In your view, what is marriage really about: An intimate relationship? An economic partnership? A way to raise children? An institution that allows the state to "privatize dependency" by making spouses legally responsible for caring for each other and their children? Which judge in *Goodridge* comes closest to your own vision? To what extent does your vision affect how you feel about same sex-marriage?

5. Do you think the majority in Goodridge would have a problem with the following: (a) A statute declaring divorce illegal? (b) A law lowering the age for legitimate marriage to 11? How would the dissent react?

6. In 2002, the Netherlands became the first country in the world to open up civil marriage to same-sex couples. Since then, Belgium, Canada, Denmark, Sweden, Iceland, Finland, France, Germany, Norway, South Africa, and Spain have recognized marriage-like partnerships. What impact might wide-scale recognition of same-sex marriage have on business?

7. **Research**: By 2009, Connecticut, Iowa, Maine, New Hampshire, Rhode Island, and Vermont had joined Massachusetts in recognizing same sex marriages. A handful of other states recognize domestic partnerships but not marriage among same sex couples. Find out how your state deals with same-sex marriages or partnerships.

8. **Research**: In 1996 Congress passed the Defense of Marriage Act (DOMA)[1] defining marriage and spouse for purposes of federal law as between one man and one woman. DOMA also permits states to refuse to recognize same sex marriages performed in other states. In 2010, a federal district court judge in Massachusetts held that DOMA violates the equal protection clause, in *Gill v. Office of Personnel Management*, 699 F.Supp.2d 374 (D. Mass. 2010). Find out how the court ruled when Mary Bishop filed a similar suit in Oklahoma. Have there been any appellate rulings in either case?

■ ■ ■

---

[1] 1 U.S.C. § 7.

Equal Protection

[N]or shall any State deprive any person of life, liberty or property, without due process of law; nor deny to any person within its jurisdiction the equal protection of the law.

— FOURTEENTH AMENDMENT, United States Constitution

The Equal Protection Clause of the United States Constitution requires government to treat groups of people in the same situation similarly. As with all constitutional rights, however, the right to equal protection is not absolute. If the government can show that it has strong enough justification for treating different—but "similarly situated"—groups differently, it may do so. The justification the government must give varies depending on the type of discrimination involved.

Suppose the state of California passed a law that allowed all 16-year-olds, except those of Mexican ancestry, to apply for drivers' licenses. This law would discriminate between groups (Mexicans vs. non-Mexicans) that are similarly situated: They are all 16 years old, and they all want to get a driver's license. It distinguishes them based on a characteristic that people can do nothing to change ("immutable"), and one that has been used historically to oppress groups of people: their ethnicity. This kind of discrimination can only pass the standard of equal protection if California can show its law serves a very strong or **"compelling" state interest,** and if it is narrowly tailored to do so. In other words, if California can achieve its important goal(s) in a less discriminatory way, it must. This equal protection test is called **strict scrutiny**. It has been applied only to **suspect classifications,** such as race and ethnicity, and in cases where the classification infringes on such **fundamental freedoms** as the right of free speech or religion or the right to vote. It sets such a high barrier that few cases in our entire history have met the strict scrutiny standard. The best known case was the *Korematsu* decision, in which the Supreme Court upheld an executive order issued by President Franklin Roosevelt that sent Japanese-Americans to live in internment camps during World War II.[2]

When the government discriminates in a way that is neither based on race nor ethnicity nor involves a fundamental right, equal protection analysis is much looser and permits the **state action** so long as it has a **rational relationship** to a valid government purpose. For example, suppose Chicago passed a law specifying that restaurants of more than 1,000 square feet must be inspected by the Department of Health twice a year, while smaller restaurants need be inspected only annually. The classification—larger versus smaller eating establishments—is not suspect, and there is no fundamental right to operate an unclean restaurant. The law will probably be upheld as well tailored to promote a legitimate state goal. Most legislation can pass the rational relationship test.

Some classifications—notably gender—receive what has come to be known as **intermediate or heightened scrutiny,** a level of judicial inquiry that falls somewhere between strict scrutiny and the minimal rational relationship. When government treats males one way and females another, the courts must determine if there is a substantial government reason for the difference. If not, it will rule that the classification violates equal protection.

At times, government action that appears to be neutral, in fact may more negatively impact on one group than another. For example, a law granting veterans' preferences for government jobs would tend to favor men over women, simply because a higher percentage of men than women have served in the armed services. Under judicial interpretations

---

[2] *Korematsu v. United States,* 323 U.S. 214 (1944). In an effort to ameliorate the results of this later-regretted decision, Congress in 1988 ordered $20,000 in reparations to be paid to each living survivor of the detention camps. 50 U.S.C. App. §1989(b)(1988).

of the Equal Protection Clause, such "facially neutral" laws are acceptable unless there is proof of an intent to discriminate against the group that is harmed by them.

■ ■ ■

The city of Hazleton is nestled in the coal mining region of northeastern Pennsylvania. After the September 11, 2001 terrorist attacks, many Latino families—legal and undocumented—left New York and New Jersey, seeking a better life, employment, and affordable housing in Hazleton. The sudden influx led to a sharp rise in population from 23,000 residents in 2000 to an estimated 30,000-33,000 by 2006. Although immigrants supported the local economy as consumers, renters, and taxpayers, the City adopted a series of ordinances aimed at combating what many viewed as the problems created by the presence of "illegal aliens." The ordinances (hereinafter, IIRA) made it unlawful to employ or rent to illegal aliens.

The following lawsuit successfully challenged the IIRA on the grounds that federal immigration law "preempted" the town's right to pass its own laws. The case had been filed by multiple plaintiffs: Pedro Lozano, a lawful permanent resident of the United States, who immigrated in January 2002 after thirty-five years as an officer in Colombia's National Police; Jose Luis and Rosa Lechuga, who immigrated illegally to the United States from Mexico in 1982 to forge a better life for themselves and their children (and who became lawful permanent residents through an amnesty program in the late 1980s); and several John Does who had lived in Hazleton unlawfully for a number of years. One of them, an architect in Colombia, had moved to Hazleton with his wife of twenty-eight years. They were joined by several organizations, including the Hazleton Hispanic Business Association and others. In the following excerpt, the court addresses another argument raised by plaintiffs: that the ordinance violated the Equal Protection Clause.

LOZANO v. CITY OF HAZLETON
United States District Court, M.D. Pennsylvania, 2007
496 F.Supp.2d 477

MUNLEY, District Judge

Generally, under federal law, aliens can be present in the country as: 1) lawfully admitted non-immigrants, i.e., visitors, those in the country temporarily; and 2) lawful immigrants, lawful permanent residents, referred to sometimes as "green card holders." (Lawfully admitted for permanent residence status can be attained in various ways, including family or employment characteristics, the "green card lottery" or relief such as asylum.)

A third category of aliens present in the country are "undocumented aliens" who lack lawful immigration status. These aliens may have overstayed their time in the United States or may have entered the country illegally. The number of these individuals is approximately twelve million. Hazleton's use of the term "illegal alien" evidently is aimed at these individuals....

The equal protection "clause prohibits states from intentionally discriminating between individuals on the basis of race." "To prove intentional discrimination by a facially neutral policy, a plaintiff must show that the relevant decisionmaker (e.g., a state legislature) adopted the policy at issue 'because of,' not merely 'in spite of,' its adverse effects upon an identifiable group." ...

Plaintiffs point to the testimony of immigration expert Marc Rosenblum, Ph.D., to argue that IIRA will "exacerbate the phenomenon of 'defensive hiring,'" the practice by which employers choose not to hire individuals who "'might be illegal.'" ... Plaintiffs contend that these actions would more likely affect Latinos than members of other groups, since employers and landlords would ... operate on the assumption that illegal aliens are most likely Latinos....

No evidence indicates that Mayor Barletta approved of the ordinances because of their potential discriminatory impact.... [Therefore no] equal protection violation exists on those grounds.

As another ground for an equal protection challenge, plaintiffs have argued that IIRA improperly allows the City to consider race, ethnicity or national origin in enforcing it.... [T]he ordinances do not implicate a fundamental right or use a suspect classification ... since they declare that no complaint that uses race, ethnicity or national origin will be enforced. The plaintiffs also do not contend that they implicate a fundamental right, such as marriage. We need not examine the policy using strict scrutiny. Accordingly, our equal protection analysis must only explore whether IIRA has "a rational relationship to a legitimate state interest." We agree with the defendant that the ordinances meet this standard. As its interest in passing this legislation, the City claims that it was motivated by a desire to protect public safety by limiting the crimes committed by illegal immigrants in the city and to safeguard community resources expended on policing, education and health care. The City presented evidence that some crimes were committed by illegal aliens. Assuming that the City has the right to regulate the presence of illegal aliens in the city, the City program that provides penalties for those who employ or provide housing for undocumented persons in the City is rationally related to the aim of limiting the social and public safety problems caused by the presence of people without legal authorization in the City. We therefore find that Ordinance [IIRA] does not on its face violate the plaintiffs' right to the equal protection of the laws. [Held: the Hazleton ordinance cannot be enforced because it is preempted by federal immigration law and violates due process. Aff'd 620 F.3d 170 (3d Cir.2010)].

QUESTIONS

1. What role does stereotyping play in the challenged ordinances? Is it relevant to the court's analysis?

2. Who are the stakeholders in the Hazleton immigration debate? How does the Hazleton ordinance impact them? If you had been on Hazleton's City Council, how would you have voted? Why?

3. **Research**: The Hazleton ordinance was defended as a crime-prevention tool. Find out whether there was any statistical evidence that illegal immigrants were responsible for an increase in the crime rate. What connections can you find between crime and immigration status in your own state?

4. In 2007, when the Hazleton case was decided, 41 states adopted some kind of immigration laws. Most were aimed at discouraging undocumented immigrants—by restricting the right to obtain a driver's license or the right to medical and other state aid. But it was Arizona's tough stance, signed into law in April 2010, that revved up the national debate. Faced with an estimated 460,000 illegal immigrants, miles of desert-border with Mexico, and what it deemed inadequate federal enforcement, Arizona took matters into its own hands. The new law requires "aliens" to carry registration documents and empowers local law enforcers to question the immigration status of anyone violating a state or local law if they reasonably suspect the person is in the state illegally.

Yet some parts of the country moved in the opposite direction. A growing number of city governments—from Trenton, New Jersey to San Francisco, California—have recently adopted community identification cards. The cards are meant to make life easier for illegal immigrants by easing access to services and places that require identification: public libraries, medical centers, charitable organizations, and public recreation areas. As this book goes to press, eleven states grant in-state tuition to undocumented resident college students. In May 2010, New York's governor announced that the state would accelerate consideration of pardons to legal immigrants for old or minor criminal convictions, a move that would prevent deportation for some. What arguments can you make for and against such laws? **Research**: Find out if your state or municipality has recently adopted any immigration laws. What are they? (b) What happened in the legal challenges to Arizona's new law?

5. Illegal immigrants are not eligible for Social Security benefits or the earned income tax credit. Since 1996, however, they can get a special Individual Tax Identification Number (ITIN) that enables them to pay federal taxes without a social security number. In 2009 the IRS issued some 1.8 million ITINS, the most ever. What are the pros and cons of this approach?

6. Pew Hispanic Center reported that unauthorized immigrants account for some 4% of the nation's population and 5.4% of its workforce in 2009. While their economic status is volatile—illegals earn less than legal immigrants and have been hard hit by the recession—they nonetheless have considerable purchasing power. According to Pew Hispanic, illegal immigrant families in the United States accounted for nearly $200 billion in purchasing power in 2006. But 30 million foreign workers—legal and illegal—are said to lack bank accounts. Citigroup Inc. and Bank of America have tried to tap into that market by making credit cards available without a Social Security number. (Other safeguards are in place, such as the requirement that an applicant have a Bank of America account in good standing for at least three months.) Nonprofit worker centers in Hempstead, New York, Chicago, Los Angeles, and the New Labor Center in New Brunswick, New Jersey have begun to offer debit cards to immigrants. What problems are solved by such credit/debit cards? Created?

IS THE U.S. "POST-RACIAL"?

Post-Racial America is a theoretical environment where the United States is void of racial preference, discrimination, and prejudice. (Wikipedia, June 29, 2010)

- **Poverty rate**: The poverty rate among African Americans is no longer more than three times the rate for whites; but at no point since 1959 has the poverty rate for African Americans been less than double that of whites.
- **Income**: While the median income level of African American families has increased over the last two decades, it is still less than two-thirds that of white families. The median net worth of white households is more than ten times that of black households.
- **Home ownership**: In 2008, the gap between whites and people of color remained substantial, with ownership rates of 74.9% for whites, 59.1% for Asians, 47.5% for blacks, and 48.9% for Latinos. Even controlling for income, blacks and Latinos were twice as likely as whites to hold subprime mortgages. African Americans and Latinos have suffered the greatest declines in homeownership rates since the housing bust in 2007 and are more likely than whites to be turned down for mortgages.
- **Employment**: Although some people of color have ascended to the ranks of the professional class, African Americans and Latinos still disproportionately tend to occupy lower paying and lower status jobs while their unemployment rates exceed that of whites. The situation is most dire for African Americans, whose unemployment rate has been roughly double that of whites since the early 1970s.

Source: Mario L. Barnes, Erwin Chemerinsky, Trina Jones Essay, "A Post-Race Equal Protection?" 9 Geo. L.J. 97 (2010).

The Civil Rights Act Of 1964[3]

It shall be unlawful for an employer to fail or refuse to hire or to discharge any individual or otherwise discriminate against any individual with respect to his compensation, terms, conditions, or privileges of employment because of such individual's race, color, religion, sex or national origin.

— TITLE VII, The Civil Rights Act of 1964

Gradually, over time, the courts began to expand the meaning of equal protection—ruling in *Brown v. Board of Education* in 1954, for example, that segregated schools were unequal. But the Constitution applies only to discrimination by government. For almost a century after the Civil War, there was no federal law against discrimination by private individuals or businesses, and state laws were uneven in their scope and application.

After a decade of protest against segregation and in the wake of the assassination of President John F. Kennedy, the U.S. Congress passed comprehensive civil rights legislation that, for the first time, would address discrimination in the private sector, banning discrimination in housing, public education, public accommodations (hotels, motels, restaurants), federally assisted programs, and employment.

Title VII, the provision dealing with employment, has no mention of the hot-button issues that emerged in the decades after its passage—affirmative action, sexual harassment, and same-sex marriage. Its mandate appears to be relatively straightforward: to end discrimination. Yet Title VII has been interpreted as banning not only outright differential treatment, but also practices that appear to be neutral (height and weight standards, educational requirements, for example), but which disproportionately disadvantage members of one race, sex, or religion ("disparate impact discrimination"). It empowers courts to correct discrimination when they find it: to order companies to hire, promote, adjust raises or benefits, or otherwise compensate those who have been wronged.

Affirmative Action

Four decades ago, when the Civil Right Act was first enacted, some believed that to achieve equality within a reasonable time, the nation would have to do more than simply end past discriminatory practices. In September 1965, President Lyndon B. Johnson signed Executive Order 11246, requiring companies that contracted with the federal government to "act affirmatively" to ameliorate the effects of past race discrimination. Many employers, either because they sought federal contracts or because they wanted to avoid Title VII liability, devised plans allowing race and gender to positively affect hiring or promotion decisions.

The seminal case on affirmative action in industry reached the U.S. Supreme Court in 1979. It grew out of an affirmative action plan adopted by Kaiser Aluminum and its unions five years earlier. At the time, fewer than two percent of Kaiser's skilled craft workers were black, even though the local workforce was approximately 39 percent black, largely due to past discriminatory practices. As a remedy, Kaiser agreed to establish a program to train production workers to fill craft openings and to earmark 50 percent of the openings for blacks. During the first year, seven black and six white trainees were selected from the plant. Brian Weber, a white man, was not, despite the fact that he

---

[3] 42 U.S.C.A. § 2000(e).

had more seniority than any of the seven black trainees. He sued, arguing for a literal interpretation of the Civil Rights Act that would outlaw Kaiser's affirmative action plan because it did not treat whites the same as blacks. The Court rejected his claim in an opinion by Justice Brennan:

> The purposes of [Kaiser Aluminum's affirmative action] plan mirror those of [Title VII of the Civil Rights Act.] Both were designed to break down old patterns of racial segregation and hierarchy. Both were structured to "open employment opportunities for Negroes in occupations that have been traditionally closed to them...."
>
> At the same time, the plan does not unnecessarily trammel the interests of the white employees. The plan does not require the discharge of white workers and their replacement with new black hires.... Nor does the plan create an absolute bar to the advancement of white employees; half of those trained in the program will be white. Moreover, the plan is a temporary measure; it is not intended to maintain racial balance, but simply to eliminate a manifest racial imbalance. Steelworkers v. Weber, 443 U.S. 193 (1979).

Religion

The impetus for the passage of Title VII was clearly the movement for civil rights for African Americans, and race discrimination remains the most common claim made to the Equal Employment Opportunity Commission (E.E.O.C.), the federal agency responsible for enforcing the law. But in recent years, charges based on religion and national origin have become increasingly common.

■ ■ ■

Kimberlie Webb is a practicing Muslim, employed by the City of Philadelphia as a police officer since 1995. On February 11, 2003, Webb requested permission from her commanding officer to wear a khimar or hijaab—the traditional headcover worn by Muslim women—while in uniform and on duty. Webb's headscarf would cover neither her face nor her ears, only her head and the back of her neck. Her request was denied because Police Department Directive 78 prescribes the approved Philadelphia police uniforms and equipment, and does not authorize any religious symbols or garb as part of the uniform.

Webb filed a complaint of religious discrimination under Title VII of the 1964 Civil Rights Act. While the matter was pending, she arrived at work wearing her headscarf, refused to remove it and was sent home. After repeating this three times, she was charged with insubordination and suspended for thirteen days.

WEBB v. CITY OF PHILADELPHIA
United States Court of Appeals, Third Circuit, 2009
562 F.3d 256

SCIRICA, Chief Judge.

In this employment discrimination case, the issue on appeal is whether a police officer's request to wear religious garb with her uniform could be reasonably accommodated without imposing an undue burden upon the City of Philadelphia. On the facts presented, the District Court held it could not.... We agree....

Title VII of the 1964 Civil Rights Act prohibits employers from discharging or disciplining an employee based on his or her religion. "Religion" is defined as "all aspects of religious observance and practice, as well as belief…. To establish a prima facie case of religious discrimination, the employee must show: (1) she holds a sincere religious belief that conflicts with a job requirement; (2) she informed her employer of the conflict; and (3) she was disciplined for failing to comply with the conflicting requirement. Once all factors are established, the burden shifts to the employer to show either it made a good-faith effort to reasonably accommodate the religious belief, or such an accommodation would work an undue hardship upon the employer and its business.

Title VII religious discrimination claims often revolve around the question of whether the employer can show reasonable accommodation would work an undue hardship. An accommodation constitutes an "undue hardship" if it would impose more than a *de minimis* cost on the employer….

[Next the court refers to precedents involving challenges to dress and grooming codes. In the first, police officer Edward Johnson objected to a rule requiring male officers to wear their hair neat, clean, trimmed above their ears and without falling below the front of their headgear.]

In *Kelley v. Johnson (1976),* the Supreme Court characterized a police department's "[c]hoice of organization, dress, and equipment for law enforcement personnel…[as] a decision entitled to [a] … presumption of legislative validity."…[In another case, the Court] found "the traditional outfitting of personnel in standardized uniforms encourages the subordination of personal preferences and identities in favor of the overall group mission." [For that reason, uniform policies are allowed.]

Our most recent decision in this area is *Fraternal Order of Police Newark Lodge No. 12 v. City of Newark,* (3d Cir.1999). … The Newark police department forbade police officers from growing beards but granted medical exceptions for beards as required by the Americans with Disabilities Act…. Two Muslim police officers, whose religion required they grow beards, filed suit contending their First Amendment rights were infringed upon by the no-beards policy. We agreed, holding that the police department must create a religious exemption to its "no-beards" policy to parallel its secular [medical] one….

Webb's religious beliefs are sincere, her employer understood the conflict between her beliefs and her employment requirements, and she was disciplined for failing to comply with a conflicting official requirement. Thus, the burden shifts and the City must establish that to reasonably accommodate Webb (that is, allow her to wear a headscarf with her uniform) would constitute an undue hardship. The City offered no accommodation, contending any accommodation would impose an undue hardship.

In the City's view, at stake is the police department's impartiality, or more precisely, the perception of its impartiality by citizens of all races and religions whom the police are charged to serve and protect. If not for the strict enforcement of Directive 78, the City contends, the essential values of impartiality, religious neutrality, uniformity, and the subordination of personal preference would be severely damaged to the detriment of the proper functioning of the police department. In the words of Police Commissioner Sylvester Johnson, uniformity "encourages the subordination of personal preferences in favor of the overall policing mission" and conveys "a sense of authority and competence to other officers inside the Department, as well as to the general public."

Commissioner Johnson identified and articulated the police department's religious neutrality (or the appearance of neutrality) as vital in both dealing with the public and working together cooperatively…. Commissioner Johnson's testimony was not contradicted or challenged by Webb at any stage in the proceedings….

As a paramilitary entity, the Philadelphia Police Department requires "a disciplined rank and file for efficient conduct of its affairs." Commissioner Johnson's thorough and uncontradicted reasons for refusing accommodations are sufficient to meet the more than *de minimis* cost of an undue burden….

[The District Court's dismissal of this case is affirmed.]

QUESTIONS

1. How does Philadelphia Police Directive 78 differ from the "No beards" policy at issue in the *Fraternal Order of Police* case? Why is that difference legally significant? Does it seem ethically distinguishable to you? Why or why not?

2. How would you deal with each of the following as head of human resources: (a) L. is hired to work as a saleswoman/model, adheres to the store's "Look Policy" which directs associates to wear clothes similar to the brand sold. At the time, that consisted of very short skirts, ripped-up jeans, and slightly revealing tops—in short, sporty, laid back California beach-style clothes that were sexy, form-fitting, and designed to show off body contours. Within a relatively short time, L is promoted. However, several months later, she converts to the Apostolic religion, which has dress regulations: below-the-knee skirts, forearms covered, no revealing cleavage. She begins to come to work in long skirts and loose fitting, long-sleeved shirts. (b) Jiffy-Lube has been taken over by a new president who has decided to improve customer relations by implementing a grooming code requiring customer-contact employees to be clean-shaven and hair neatly trimmed and combed. Richard has been a practicing Rastafarian for a decade. His religion does not permit him to shave or cut his hair. He has worked as a technician at Jiffy-Lube for several years, on both the upper and lower bays. When he works on the upper bay, he also works as greeter, salesperson, and cashier. The lower bay is colder, more dangerous, and it is harder to take breaks. Richards prefers the upper bay.

3. Dress and grooming codes have also been challenged as discriminatory on the basis of sex or race. Gender-specific rules are generally acceptable if based on social norms, unless they place an unfair burden on one sex. So, for example, having a "business dress" rule that requires men to wear ties and women to wear dresses or skirts would be legal, but requiring only one sex to wear a uniform would not. What problems can you identify with any of the following? (a) A pizza company will make no exceptions to its rule that drivers must be clean shaven. Sixty percent of African-American men have a skin condition characterized by severely painful shaving bumps. The condition is cured by growing a beard. (b) Bank does not allow male employees to wear earrings. (c) Casino hires men and women as cocktail waiters. Women are required to wear three-inch high heels and make-up; men are allowed to wear any "dress shoe."

4. As we saw in the *Webb* case, Title VII requires employers to reasonably accommodate the religious practices of employees, unless doing so would cause an undue hardship to the company. How would you handle the following (a) A worker who has recently been promoted to driver for your company (United Parcel Service) has refused to make deliveries between sunset on Friday, his Sabbath, and sunset on Saturday. (b) One of your employees insists that her religion requires her to convert others; she persists in bringing religious tracts to the office, even though co-workers are annoyed when they find them in their workspace.

■ ■ ■

National Origin

During the past four decades, the United States has experienced the largest wave of immigration in its history, with at least one-third of new immigrants coming from Mexico. Census Bureau figures show that nearly 10 percent of the 304 million people living in the United States in 2008 were born somewhere else. Increasingly, the new migrants are finding homes throughout the country from the upper Midwest to the Rocky Mountain states, as well as the more traditional landing spots along the borders and coasts.

In an economy still adjusting to globalization, the information revolution, and the shift from production to services, there is widespread debate about the new influx of foreign-born workers. Here we look at one site of that contest: rules requiring English as the only language to be used at a workplace.

EEOC GUIDELINE ON ENGLISH-ONLY WORKPLACE RULES

1. an English-only rule that applies at all times is considered "a burdensome term and condition of employment," [in violation of Title VII] and
2. an English-only rule that applies only at certain times does not violate Title VII if the employer can justify the rule by showing business necessity.

Rationale for Rules

1. English-only policies may "create an atmosphere of inferiority, isolation, and intimidation" that could make a "discriminatory working environment";
2. English-only rules adversely impact employees with limited or no English skills … by denying them a privilege enjoyed by native English speakers: the opportunity to speak at work;
3. English-only rules create barriers to employment for employees with limited or no English skills;
4. English-only rules prevent bilingual employees whose first language is not English from speaking in their most effective language; and
5. the risk of discipline and termination for violating English-only rules falls disproportionately on bilingual employees as well as persons with limited English skills.

■ ■ ■

When the city of Altus, Oklahoma, adopted an English-only rule for its employees, 29 workers complained to the EEOC. All are Hispanic, the only significant national-origin minority group affected by the policy. All are bilingual, each speaking fluent English and Spanish. Unable to resolve the dispute, the EEOC granted them a right to sue. The trial court, however, threw out their case, granting summary judgment that would allow the city to enforce its new regulations. The employees appealed. Their claim: rights under Title VII of the Civil Rights Act of 1964 and the First Amendment to the U.S. Constitution were violated.

MALDONADO v. CITY OF ALTUS
U. S. Court of Appeals, Tenth Circuit, 2006
433 F.3d 1294

HARTZ, Circuit Judge.

In the spring of 2002 the City's Street Commissioner, Defendant Holmes Willis, received a complaint that because Street Department employees were speaking Spanish, other employees could not understand what was being said on the City radio. Willis informed the City's Human Resources Director, Candy Richardson, of the complaint, and she advised Willis that he could direct his employees to speak only English when using the radio for City business.

Plaintiffs claim that Willis instead told the Street Department employees that they could not speak Spanish at work at all and informed them that the City would soon implement an official English-only policy....

In July 2002 the City promulgated the following official policy:

To insure effective communications among and between employees and various departments of the City, to prevent misunderstandings and to promote and enhance safe work practices, all work related and business communications during the work day shall be conducted in the English language with the exception of those circumstances where it is necessary or prudent to communicate with a citizen, business owner, organization, or criminal suspect in his or her native language due to the person or entity's limited English language skills. The use of the English language during work hours and while engaged in City business includes face to face communication of work orders and directions as well as communications utilizing telephones, mobile telephones, cellular telephones, radios, computer or e-mail transmissions, and all written forms of communications.... This policy does not apply to strictly private communications between co-workers while they are on approved lunch hours or breaks or before or after work hours while the employees are still on City property if City property is not being used for the communication...[or to] strictly private communication between an employee and a family member.... Employees are encouraged to be sensitive to the feelings of their fellow employees, including a possible feeling of exclusion if a co-worker cannot understand what is being said in his or her presence when a language other than English is being utilized....

Plaintiffs allege that the policy created a hostile environment for Hispanic employees, causing them "fear and uncertainty in their employment," and subjecting them to racial and ethnic taunting. They contend "that the English-only rule created a hostile environment because it pervasively—every hour of every work day—burdened, threatened, and demeaned the [Plaintiffs] because of their Hispanic origin." Plaintiffs each stated in their affidavits:

The English-only policy affects my work environment every day. It reminds me every day that I am second-class and subject to rules for my employment that the Anglo employees are not subject to....

Evidence of ethnic taunting included Plaintiffs' affidavits stating that they had "personally been teased and made the subject of jokes directly because of the English-only policy...." Plaintiff Tommy Sanchez testified in his deposition that ... other employees of the City of Altus "would pull up and laugh, start saying stuff in Spanish to us and said, 'They didn't tell us we couldn't stop. They just told you.'" Sanchez also testified that an Altus police officer taunted him about not being allowed to speak Spanish by saying, "Don't let me hear you talk Spanish." As evidence that such taunting was not unexpected by management, Lloyd Lopez recounted in his deposition that Street Commissioner Willis told ... him [and an Hispanic co-worker] that he was informing them of the English-only policy in private because Willis had concerns about "the other guys making fun of [them]."

I. Discussion of Civil Rights Violations: Disparate Impact

...One might say that Plaintiffs have not been subjected to an unlawful employment practice because they are treated identically to non-Hispanics. They claim no discrimination with respect to their pay or benefits, their hours of work, or their job duties. And every employee, not just Hispanics, must abide by the English-only policy...

[But in] *Griggs v. Duke Power Co.* (1971) the Supreme Court held that Title VII "proscribes not only overt discrimination but also practices that are fair in form, but discriminatory in operation." These kinds of claims, known as disparate-impact claims, "involve employment practices that are facially neutral in their treatment of different groups but that in fact fall more harshly on one group than another and cannot be justified by business necessity."...

Plaintiffs have produced evidence that the English-only policy created a hostile atmosphere for Hispanics in their workplace....[A]ll the Plaintiffs stated that they had experienced ethnic taunting as a result of the policy and that the policy made them feel like second-class citizens....

[According to the Supreme Court in the *Griggs* case] the touchstone is business necessity. If an employment practice which operates to [discriminate against a protected minority] cannot be shown to be related to job performance, the practice is prohibited.

Defendants' evidence of business necessity in this case is scant. As observed by the district court, "[T]here was no written record of any communication problems, morale problems, or safety problems resulting from the use of languages other than English prior to implementation of the policy." And there was little undocumented evidence. Defendants cited only one example of an employee's complaining about the use of Spanish prior to implementation of the policy.... [And city officials] could give no specific examples of safety problems resulting from the use of languages other than English...." Moreover, Plaintiffs produced evidence that the policy encompassed lunch hours, breaks, and private phone conversations; and Defendants conceded that there would be no business reason for such a restriction....

In our view, the record contains sufficient evidence of intent to create a hostile environment that the summary judgment on those claims must be set aside...[and the plaintiffs may proceed to trial on their Title VII claims.]

II. First Amendment claims

... Perhaps the City's English-only rule suffers from First Amendment shortcomings. But on the evidence and contentions presented by Plaintiffs, their challenge fails.... They have not shown that their speech precluded by the English-only rule includes communications on matters of public concern. Nor have they produced evidence that the English-only rule was intended to limit communications on matters of public concern [as required by the Supreme Court precedent case, *Pickering*.]...

Here, we do not question that Plaintiffs take pride in both their Hispanic heritage and their use of the Spanish language, nor do we question the importance of that pride. What we do question, because there is no supporting evidence, is that by speaking Spanish at work they were intending to communicate that pride, much less "to inform [an] issue [so] as to be helpful ... in evaluating the conduct of government."...[Held: plaintiff's First Amendment claims are dismissed.]

SEYMOUR. J. , concurring [in Part I, Discrimination] and dissenting [in Part II, First Amendment.]

...[I] part company with the majority in determining whether Plaintiffs' speech touched on a matter of public concern.... [It is] reasonable to assume that the alleged "content" of Plaintiffs' speech, namely, their choice to converse in Spanish rather than English, is pride in their cultural and ethnic identity and heritage. Plaintiffs have thus indicated that their desire to speak Spanish is, itself, a matter of public concern.

In arguing that their choice of language is itself a statement of public concern, Plaintiffs find support in *Hernandez v. New York* (1991), [where the Supreme Court] recognized the power of language (as well as a person's decision to speak a particular language as opposed to another) to convey special meaning as well as to engender conflict and disclose bigotry.

> ...[A] person's choice of language can convey a message–and a powerful one at that.... [L]anguage choice and ethnic or cultural identity can be inextricably intertwined both in the mind of the speaker and in the minds of those who hear him....

Before litigation challenging the legality of the City's English-only policy ever commenced ... in a plea for understanding and reconciliation, Mr. Sanchez himself characterized the content of the prohibited speech as an expression of community identity and ethnic heritage, of solidarity and pride, in the face of contravening forces. In other words, an apter analogy may be wearing a tee-shirt proclaiming "proud to be a Yankees fan" to a rally for the Boston Red Sox, because that analogy describes the context as well as the content of the speech.

With respect to context, the record contains evidence of months of tension between Hispanic and non-Hispanic City employees. Prior to the adoption of the English-only policy, several Hispanic employees had filed complaints of discrimination and retaliation. The City, in response, had hired an outside human resources consultant.... Numerous individuals, both Hispanic and non-Hispanic, were involved in an ongoing and evolving discussion on race relations, and that all levels of City government were involved, including the mayor, the City administrator, the City's director of human resources, and many City department heads and supervisors.... [T]he general public was aware of and interested in the English-only policy and its effects.... In one [news] article, the mayor was quoted as referring to the Spanish language as "garbage." That he later claimed in his deposition to have been misquoted is irrelevant to the question of whether his misquote further inflamed public debate over the English-only policy and its perceived intent. Moreover, the mayor's testimony that he eventually apologized to the City council for the misquote underscores the seriousness and the pervasiveness of the whole issue, namely, the apparently degenerating relations between Hispanics and non-Hispanics in the City of Altus. At a certain point then, this dispute evolved from a situation involving City employees to a wider discussion of discrimination, race relations, and the power of expressions of ethnic identity to elicit strong emotions on either side.

In sum, this is not a case about a single employee wearing a tee-shirt proclaiming "proud to be Hispanic!" or "proud to be Irish!" or "proud to be Vietnamese!" This is a case about a large group of employees (twenty-nine Hispanic City employees) desiring to wear such tee-shirts when an even larger number of their fellow employees are wearing (or perceived to be wearing) tee-shirts proclaiming "annoyed by Hispanics!" or "sick and tired of the Irish!" or "threatened by Vietnamese!" The record suggests this was a situation in which the right to speak one's chosen language became an expression of pride and resistance and identity....

[I]t is important to remember what this case is not about. This is not a case involving the sole complaint of one employee in a City with no history of racial tensions. This not a case involving one employee's complaint against one or two of his supervisors. This is a case involving more than two dozen employees in a diverse workforce in a City with a recent history of racial and national origin discrimination complaints. This is a case in which the City, fully cognizant of that history, nonetheless adopted a broadly-sweeping policy that its director of human resources admitted in her deposition testimony could offend Hispanic employees and further inflame racial tensions. This is a case in which we have upheld, for summary judgment purposes, Plaintiffs' race and national origin discrimination claims against the City for restricting the very speech Plaintiffs want to use. In light of these facts, it seems incorrect to characterize Plaintiffs' expression of pride in their ethnic identity as reflecting merely "personal" or "internal" grievances. It is also difficult to see how that expression of pride does not add to the public debate on diversity or "sufficiently inform" the public that there are two equally vocal and passionate sides to that debate.... To the contrary, plaintiffs have expressed a desire to speak Spanish in order to sustain their community's history of linguistic and ethnic diversity and to preserve that history in the everyday details of their lives. The City's ban on Spanish from the workplace creates a public space where Spanish speakers arguably do not feel welcome. In such a context, it is not hard to imagine the power of a simple "buenos dias" to convey resistance to that effort and hope for the future....

QUESTIONS

1. Who might be hurt by English-only rules? Who tends to benefit? Can such rules create or reinforce stereotypes?

2. Articulate the kind of discrimination claim made by the plaintiffs in this case. What will they have to prove at trial? How will the city defend itself? How important is it that Plaintiffs are all bilingual?

3. Would there be a business necessity for requiring airline pilots to speak English in all air traffic communications within the United States? Having computer software salespeople speak English in all management meetings? What about an English-only rule for workers on a semiconductor assembly line or an airline baggage handling area? Is there ever a business necessity for requiring English to be spoken during non-work hours?

4. What reasons might an employer have for preferring to hire people who don't speak English? What ethical issues might arise in such circumstances?

5. Title IX of the Civil Rights Act prohibits discrimination on the basis of race, color, religion, sex, or national origin in education. Should a school be allowed to prohibit students from speaking a language other than English in school? Should it matter whether it is a public or private school? See *Rubio v. Turner Unified School District No. 202,* 453 F. Supp.2d 1295 (D. Kansas, 2006).

6. Dissenting Judge Seymour mentions the history behind the adoption of the city's English-only policy, a history fraught with conflict. Can you think of a way this litigation might have been avoided? Suppose you were the HR consultant hired to lead discussions on a possible English-only policy for the city. Who would you try to bring into the conversation? How might you enable the different stakeholders to become active, respectful participants? What information might you want to access to assist their decision-making process?

■ ■ ■

Sex Discrimination

Sexual Harassment   Sexual harassment has a familiar ring today. But the notion that any type of private discrimination based on sex could be grounds for lawsuits was new at the time the Civil Rights Act of 1964 was under consideration by Congress. Then, opponents of the law attempted to block its passage by amending it to cover "sex," a ploy they believed would expose the whole concept of the law as absurd. Their strategy backfired; the Civil Rights Act did pass, and sex discrimination became illegal almost as an ironic afterthought. Yet the law made no mention of sexual harassment and never identified it as a form of sex discrimination. By the late 1970s, successful plaintiffs had convinced the courts that what feminist lawyer Catharine MacKinnon described as the "unwanted imposition of sexual requirements in the context of a relationship of unequal power" must indeed be classified as sex discrimination—an understanding that receives widespread support today.

HIGHLIGHTS IN THE EVOLVING LAWS OF SEX DISCRIMINATION

- **Congress Sets the Stage**: In 1964, Title VII of the Civil Rights Act was passed, outlawing discrimination in hiring, firing, and terms and conditions of employment based on race, color, religion, sex, or national origin. There is no mention of sexual harassment.
- **Early Lower Court Cases**: The first reported case of sexual harassment is filed by two women who resigned because of constant sexual advances from their boss. The court denied their claim, describing the supervisor's conduct as "nothing more than a personal proclivity, peculiarity, or mannerism." *Corne v. Bausch &*

Lomb, 380 F. Supp.161 (D. Ariz., 1975). But in a breakthrough case, a woman whose job was abolished after she repulsed the sexual advances of her boss sued and won. ("But for her womanhood the woman would not have lost her job.") *Barnes v. Costle,* 561 F.2d 983 (D. C. Cir. 1977).

- **EEOC Drafts Guidelines**: By 1980, EEOC announced that two types of illegal sexual harassment existed: quid pro quo and hostile environment. Quid pro quo refers to demands for sexual favors with threats attached; either the victim gives in or loses a tangible job benefit—even the job itself. Hostile environment refers to behavior that creates an intimidating or abusive workplace atmosphere.

- **Supreme Court Speaks**: Recognizing the hostile environment form of sexual harassment, the Supreme Court allows a suit where behavior is "sufficiently severe or pervasive to alter the conditions of the victim's employment and create an abusive working environment," in *Meritor Savings Bank v. Vinson,* 106 S.Ct. 2399 (1986). In a later case, the Supreme Court explains that a victim need not prove psychological injury to win, "so long as the environment would reasonably be perceived, and is perceived, as hostile or abusive." *Harris v. Forklift Systems,* 510 U.S. 17 (1993).

- **Supreme Court and Employer Liability**: The Court clarifies that employers are liable for misuse of supervisory authority—whether or not threats are carried out. Where tangible employment retaliation—for example, termination, demotion, or undesirable reassignment—is carried out or even threatened, the employer is automatically liable. In cases where a plaintiff claims a hostile environment exists, the employer can successfully defend by proving (1) it took reasonable care to prevent and correct promptly any sexually harassing behavior, and (2) the employee "unreasonably failed to take advantage of any preventive or corrective opportunities." *Faragher v. City of Boca Raton* 118 S.Ct. 2275 (1998) and *Burlington Industries v. Ellerth,* 118 S.Ct. 2257 (1998).

- **Same-Sex Harassment**: In 1999, the Supreme Court held that Title VII protects men as well as women, and that the fact that both plaintiff and defendant are of the same sex does not necessarily prevent a claim of sex discrimination. *Oncale v. Sundowner Offshore Services, Inc.,* 118 S.Ct. 998 (1999).

- **Constructive Discharge**: When a supervisor's official act precipitates a constructive discharge—making the abusive working environment so intolerable that a reasonble person would be compelled to resign—the employer is strictly liable ("aggravated hostile environment"). *Pennsylvania State Police v. Suders,* 124 S.Ct. 2342 (2004).

- **Class Action Lawsuit**: The largest class action discrimination suit in U.S. history was filed in 2001 against Walmart, accusing the company of paying women employees less than men for the same jobs and of granting fewer promotions to women who had to wait longer for those upgrades than male counterparts. The suit, brought on behalf of more than a million female workers at some 3,400 stores across the nation, was hotly contested by Walmart. In April 2010, the Ninth Circuit Court of Appeals issued a decision that seemed to clear the way for the case to proceed to trial, although no date was scheduled as this book went to press. To win, plaintiffs will have to prove their claims that company-wide policies and practices created a culture of gender stereotyping that allowed management to discriminate. *Dukes v.Walmart Stores, Inc.,* 603 F. 3d 571 (9th Cir. 2010). (Ninth Circuit, April 21 2010).

- **Recent Developments**: Although Swiss company Novartis Pharmaceuticals was lauded by "Working Mother" magazine as one of the "100 best companies" for women for a decade, in the spring of 2010 a jury in New York awarded $3.36 million to twelve saleswomen who testified to a sexist atmosphere controlled by male district managers. One woman was wrongly fired when seven months pregnant; others were subjected to hostile remarks when pregnant and unfairly passed over for promotion. Duff Wilson, "Women Win A Bias Suit Against Novartis," THE NEW YORK TIMES May 18, 2010.

Hostile Environment: Proving a* Prima Facie *Case   What has been called "quid pro quo" harassment—sexual favors in exchange for something concrete such as a job or a raise—is generally easily identifiable as illegal sex discrimination and employers are automatically responsible for such "tangible" employment retaliation. Much harder to define and far more controversial are situations involving what has come to be known as "hostile environment" sexual harassment.

As is true in every civil lawsuit, a plaintiff's first burden is to demonstrate the possibility of winning by offering evidence to support each element of her claim. This is called a *prima facie* case. The defendant will then offer contrary evidence, witnesses who can discredit the plaintiff's allegations or support the defendant's own claims and affirmative defenses. To make out a prima facie case of hostile environment sexual harassment, a plaintiff must show that (1) she is a member of a protected group, (2) she was the subject of unwelcome sexual harassment, (3) the harassment occurred because of her sex, and, (4) the harassment was sufficiently severe or pervasive to alter the terms and conditions of her employment.

Member of a Protected Group   The first element is easy to prove in most cases. The Supreme Court has made clear that men, as well as women, are "protected" by Title VII—so long as they are targeted based on their maleness or femaleness—and that a supervisor can be responsible for sexually harassing a person of the same sex. Each of the other elements, however, have created knotty problems for the lower courts.

Unwelcomeness   Plaintiffs must prove that the behavior that creates a hostile environment is not welcome. As courts try to determine "welcomeness," they consider the entire range of circumstances. They may take into account, for example, a plaintiff's manner of speaking, behaving, or dressing. For a female plaintiff, this could mean that the tight fit of her sweaters or her taste in jokes may be viewed as "provocative," as inviting the behavior of which she complains. Even after-hours behavior can be examined: Does she go to bars alone? Have intimate relationships outside of marriage?

Some have argued that the standard used to measure hostile environment and whether a victim found it unwelcome is male-biased. While studies have repeatedly demonstrated that there is a great disparity between the way men and women view being approached sexually at work—men are typically flattered; women insulted—many in our society make the assumption that women tend to enjoy and welcome sexualized behavior. The law allows that assumption to be overcome, but the burden of proof is on the plaintiff. While in the context of a rape case the victim must prove nonconsent, in the context of a claim of sexual harassment, she must prove unwelcomeness.

Making such proof even more difficult is the tendency of females in our culture to avoid direct confrontation, to find ways to avoid conflict.

Because Of ... One's Sex   Since hostile environment suits are essentially claims of sex discrimination, a plaintiff must establish that whatever harassment took place did so "because of" her sex. This element can be proven even if the particular plaintiff is not targeted. In a recent case the court found harassment based on sex where the office atmosphere was akin to a "guys locker room," rife with sexually explicit comments not aimed directly at the plaintiff.[4]

This requirement is hardest to meet when both harasser and harassed are of the same sex. Some same-sex claims sound relatively familiar: e.g. a male supervisor makes sexual advances, motivated by sexual desire, toward a male surbordinate, or a female supervisor is professional and friendly with her male employees, but constantly treats other women in the workplace with hostility. In those cases, it is relatively easy for a judge to find that the treatment is "based on sex."

Much harder are cases involving complaints that co-workers mistreat an employee because he or she is *perceived to be gay*. Some courts consider differential treatment of an "effeminate" male to be "because of" his sex, using the logic of *Hopkins v. Price Waterhouse*[5], where the Supreme Court ruled that it was discriminatory to deny a woman a partnership because she was not sufficiently feminine and "needed to go to charm school." Other judges argue that such findings stretch Title VII beyond its intended scope by effectively outlawing discrimination based on sexual orientation.

Sufficiently Severe or Pervasive   Case law tells us that an employee does not have to put up with discriminatory intimidation, ridicule, and insult so severe or pervasive that it creates an abusive working environment. Courts are supposed to determine when this standard has been met by looking at all—the "totality" of—the circumstances including:

> [The] frequency of the discriminatory conduct; its severity; whether it is physically threatening or humiliating, or a mere offensive utterance; and whether it unreasonably interferes with an employee's work performance. [S]imple teasing, offhand comments, and isolated incidents (unless extremely serious) will not amount to discriminatory changes in the terms and conditions of employment.[6]

But which factors to consider, and how to weigh them, is a matter of dispute among the various federal courts of appeals. One federal trial judge explains:

> The question of what is "sufficiently severe" sexual harassment is complicated because: (a) courts routinely remind plaintiffs that "Title VII is not a federal civility code," (b) the modern notion of acceptable behavior—as corroded by instant-gratification driven, cultural influences (e.g., lewd music, videos, and computer games, "perversity-programming" broadcast standards, White House "internal affairs" and perjurious coverups of same, etc.) has been coarsening over time; therefore, (c) what courts implicitly ask the "Title VII victim" to tolerate as mere "boorish behavior" or "workplace vulgarity" must, once placed in the contemporary context, account for any "Slouch Toward Gomorrah" societal norms might take.

---

[4] *Gallagher v. C.H. Robinson Worldwide, Inc.* 567 F.3d 263 (6th Cir. 2009).

[5] *Hopkins v. Price-Waterhouse,* 490 U.S. 228 (1989).

[6] *Harris v. Forklift Systems, Inc.,* 510 U.S. 17 (1993).

At the same time, this entire area of law is enervated by vague, almost circular standards....[I]f behavior offends the particular judge ... then it must be "discriminatory.".....

As the case law has grown to show, determining the intensity/quantity of sexual gesturing, touching, bantering, and innuendo that it takes to render a work environment sexually hostile is now no less difficult than "trying to nail a jellyfish to the wall." ...[7]

Vicki Schultz has been a strong advocate for changes that would make the workplace more equitable and hospitable to women. In the next reading, Schultz is critical of employer attempts to wipe out sexual harassment by harshly and promptly punishing harassers—a process she dubs "sanitization," and which she believes causes problems of its own, further distancing us from real solutions to gender inequality.

THE SANITIZED WORKPLACE
Vicki Schultz[8]

...[T]he focus on sexual conduct has encouraged organizations to treat harassment as a stand-alone phenomenon—a problem of bad or boorish men who oppress or offend women—rather than as a symptom of larger patterns of sex segregation and inequality....

[T]he emphasis on eliminating sexual conduct encourages employees to articulate broader workplace harms as forms of sexual harassment, obscuring more structural problems that may be the true source of their disadvantage. Thus, women may complain about sexual jokes, when their real concern is a caste system that relegates them to low-status, low-pay positions.... Even more worrying is the prospect that some employees may make allegations of sexual harassment that disproportionately disadvantage racial and sexual minorities.... [W]hite women who enjoy sexual banter and flirtation with their white male co-workers may regard the same conduct as a form of sexual harassment when it comes from men of color. Heterosexual men who willingly engage in sexual horseplay with men whom they regard as heterosexual may be quick to label the same overtures as harassment when they come from openly gay men. [This suggests] that one-size-fits-all, acontextual prohibitions on sexual conduct may give individual employees, and management as a whole, too much power to enforce sexual conformity in the name of pursuing a project of gender equality that has been all but abandoned.

The truth is that managers cannot succeed in banishing sexuality from the workplace: They can only subject particular expressions of it to surveillance and discipline. Although some groups suffer more than others when this occurs, everyone loses.... With the decline of civil society, the workplace is one of the few arenas left in our society where people from different walks of life can come to know one another well. Because people who work together come into close contact with each other for extended periods for the purpose of achieving common goals, work fosters extraordinarily intimate relationships of both the sexually charged and the more platonic varieties.... We cannot expect diverse groups of people to form

---

[7] *Breda v. Wolf Camera, Inc.*, 148 F.Supp.2d 1371 (S.D.Ga. 2001).

[8] Vicki Schultz, "The Sanitized Workplace," 112 Yale L. J. 2061 (2003). Reprinted by permission of The Yale Law Journal Company and William S. Hein Company from The Yale Law Journal, Vol. 112, pages 2061–2193.

close bonds and alliances—whether sexual or nonsexual—if they must be concerned that reaching out to one another puts them at risk of losing their jobs or their reputations....

The larger question is whether we as a society can value the workplace as a realm alive with personal intimacy, sexual energy, and "humanness" more broadly. The same impulse that would banish sexuality from the workplace also seeks to suppress other "irrational" life experiences such as birth and death, sickness and disability, aging, and emotion of every kind. But the old Taylorist dream of the workplace as a sterile zone in which workers suspend all their human attributes while they train their energies solely on production doesn't begin to reflect the rich, multiple roles that work serves in people's lives. For most people, working isn't just a way to earn a livelihood. It's a way to contribute something to the larger society, to struggle against their limits, to make friends and form communities, to leave their imprint on the world, and to know themselves and others in a deep way.... [W]ork isn't simply a sphere of production. It is also a source of citizenship, community, and self-understanding.

Just as individual employees may express themselves or embroider intimate relations through sexual language and conduct, so too may employees as a group resort to sexual interactions to alleviate stress or boredom on the job, to create vital forms of community and solidarity with each other, or to articulate resistance to oppressive management practices. Research suggests that workplace romance may even increase productivity in some circumstances.

Contrary to prevailing orthodoxy, such uses of workplace sexuality do not always harm or disadvantage women: A lot depends on the larger structural context in which the sexuality is expressed. As a well-accepted body of systematic social science research demonstrates, women who enter jobs in which they are significantly underrepresented often confront hostility and harassment from incumbent male workers, and in some settings the men use sexual conduct as a means of marking the women as "different" and out of place. However, a new body of sociological research suggests that women who work in more integrated, egalitarian settings often willingly participate and take pleasure in sexualized interactions—probably because their numerical strength gives them the power to help shape the sexual norms and culture to their own liking. Rather than presuming that women will always find sexual conduct offensive, this research suggests that we should ensure that women are fully integrated into equal jobs and positions of authority, thus giving them the power to decide for themselves what kind of work cultures they want to have....

I would like to see organizations abandon sensitivity training in favor of incorporating their harassment policies into broader efforts to achieve integration and equality throughout the firm. Along similar lines, I urge that employers forgo measures to prohibit or discourage sexual or dating relationships among employees and refuse to intervene, just as they do with nonsexual friendships, unless there is clear evidence that a particular relationship is undermining specific organizational goals.... In my view, employees and supervisors should be free to work together to create a variety of different work cultures—including more and less sexualized ones—so long as that process occurs within a larger context of structural equality that provides all women and men the power to shape those cultures....

The contemporary drive to sanitize the workplace came about through a complex interplay of forces in which feminists, judges, HR managers, lawyers, and the news media all helped create an understanding that sexuality disadvantages women and disrupts productivity. In my view, we can only hope to halt the sanitization process by articulating a more appealing vision in which sexuality and intimacy can coexist with, and perhaps even enhance, gender equality and organizational rationality....

QUESTIONS

1. Schultz favors broad efforts to achieve integration and equality throughout the firm. What do you think she means by this? Can you give examples?

2. **Research**: Schultz mentions "the old Taylorist dream of the workplace as a sterile zone." Who was Frederick Taylor? What about his life's achievement would lead Schultz to describe his dream as "sterile"? What is Schultz's vision of work?

Sex, gender, and sexuality are terms whose meanings have been contested and re-conceptualized in the past few decades. Psychologists and feminist theorists, for example, generally use "sex" to refer to one's biological sex, labeling people "male" or "female" depending on their chromosomes, hormones, and anatomical features. Sex, they argue, is distinguishable from "gender" (whether one is masculine or feminine), because gender is the meaning that a particular society gives to one's sex. Whether one is "feminine" may depend, for example, on whether one takes care of children—even though, biologically, both males and females are capable of caring for children. This is often called the social construction of gender.

Interpreting the Civil Rights Act's ban on "discrimination on the basis of sex," courts have had to decide what Congress meant by sex. Federal courts have consistently held that "sex" refers to one's biological sex, whether discrimination occurred because one is male or female, or because of gender stereotyping. The statute has not been interpreted to protect against discrimination based on one's sexual orientation or affiliations (homosexuality, bisexuality, heterosexuality). This means that, except in those states and localities with laws banning discrimination based on sexual orientation, an employer can refuse to hire a woman because she is a lesbian, a man because he is gay.

■ ■ ■

The next case presents yet another nuance in the realm of sex discrimination. Peter Oiler alleges that he was fired from his job because he cross-dresses and impersonates a woman when he is off duty. This, he claims, illegally discriminates on the basis of sexual stereotyping.

OILER v. WINN-DIXIE LOUISIANA, INC.
U.S. District Court, Louisiana, 2002
2002 WL 31098541

AFRICK, District Judge.

In 1979, plaintiff, Peter Oiler, was hired by defendant, Winn-Dixie, as a loader. In 1981, he was promoted to yard truck driver and he later became a road truck driver. As a road truck driver, plaintiff delivered groceries from Winn-Dixie's grocery warehouse in Harahan, Louisiana, to grocery stores in southern and central Louisiana and Mississippi.

Plaintiff is a heterosexual man who has been married since 1977. The plaintiff is transgendered. He is not a transsexual and he does not intend to become a woman.... He is a male cross-dresser [or] transvestite.

When he is not at work, plaintiff appears in public approximately one to three times per month wearing female clothing and accessories. In order to resemble a woman, plaintiff wears wigs and makeup, including concealer, eye shadow, foundation, and lipstick … skirts, women's blouses, women's flat shoes, and nail polish. He shaves his face, arms, hands, and legs. He wears women's underwear and bras and he uses silicone prostheses to enlarge his breasts. When he is cross-dressed as a woman, he adopts a female persona and he uses the name "Donna."...

While cross-dressed, he attended support group meetings, dined at a variety of restaurants in Kenner and Metairie, visited night clubs, went to shopping malls, and occasionally attended church services. He was often accompanied by his wife and other friends, some of whom were also cross-dressed.

On October 29, 1999, plaintiff told Gregg Miles, a Winn-Dixie supervisor, that he was transgendered.... [W]hen plaintiff did not resign voluntarily, Winn-Dixie discharged him ... because [of concerns that] if Winn-Dixie's customers learned of plaintiff's lifestyle, i.e., that he regularly cross-dressed and impersonated a woman in public, they would shop elsewhere and Winn-Dixie would lose business. Plaintiff did not cross-dress at work and he was not terminated because he violated any Winn-Dixie on-duty dress code. He was never told ... that he was being terminated for appearing or acting effeminate at work, i.e., for having effeminate mannerisms or a high voice. Nor did any Winn-Dixie manager ever tell plaintiff that he did not fit a male stereotype or assign him work that stereotypically would be performed by a female....

In *Ulane v. Eastern Airlines, Inc.* (7th Cir. 1984) a male airline pilot was fired when, following sex reassignment surgery, she attempted to return to work as a woman.... The *Ulane* court stated that:

> *The phrase in Title VII prohibiting discrimination based on sex, in its plain meaning, implies that it is unlawful to discriminate against women because they are women and against men because they are men. The words of Title VII do not outlaw discrimination against a person who has a sexual identity disorder, i.e., a person born with a male body who believes himself to be a female, or a person born with a female body who believes herself to be male; a prohibition against discrimination based on an individual's sex is not synonymous with a prohibition based on an individual's sexual identity disorder or discontent with the sex into which they were born....*

In 1964, when Title VII was adopted, there was no debate on the meaning of the phrase "sex." In the social climate of the early sixties, sexual identity and sexual orientation related issues remained shrouded in secrecy and individuals having such issues generally remained closeted. Thirty-eight years later, however, sexual identity and sexual orientation issues are no longer buried and they are discussed in the mainstream. Many individuals having such issues have opened wide the closet doors.

Despite the fact that the number of persons publicly acknowledging sexual orientation or gender or sexual identity issues has increased exponentially since the passage of Title VII, the meaning of the word "sex" in Title VII has never been clarified legislatively. From 1981 through 2001, thirty-one proposed bills have been introduced in the United States Senate and the House of Representatives which have attempted to amend Title VII and prohibit employment discrimination on the basis of affectional or sexual orientation. None have passed....

Plaintiff argues that his termination by Winn-Dixie was not due to his cross-dressing as a result of his gender identity disorder, but because he did not conform to a gender stereotype....

After much thought and consideration of the undisputed facts of this case, the Court finds that this is not a situation where the plaintiff failed to conform to a gender stereotype. Plaintiff was not discharged because he did not act sufficiently masculine or because he exhibited traits normally valued in a female employee, but disparaged in a male employee. Rather, the plaintiff disguised himself as a person of a different sex and presented himself as a female for stress relief and to express his gender identity. The plaintiff was terminated because he is a man with a sexual or gender identity disorder who, in order to publicly disguise himself as a woman, wears women's clothing, shoes, underwear, breast prostheses, wigs, makeup, and nail polish, pretends to be a woman, and publicly identifies himself as a woman named "Donna."…

This is not just a matter of an employee of one sex exhibiting characteristics associated with the opposite sex. This is a matter of a person of one sex assuming the role of a person of the opposite sex.…

In holding that defendant's actions are not proscribed by Title VII, the Court recognizes that many would disagree with the defendant's decision and its rationale. The plaintiff was a longstanding employee of the defendant. He never cross-dressed at work and his cross-dressing was not criminal or a threat to public safety.

Defendant's rationale for plaintiff's discharge may strike many as morally wrong. However, the function of this Court is not to raise the social conscience of defendant's upper level management, but to construe the law in accordance with proper statutory construction and judicial precedent. The Court is constrained by the framework of the remedial statute enacted by Congress and it cannot, therefore, afford the luxury of making a moral judgment.…[Held: plaintiff's suit is dismissed.]

QUESTIONS

1. On what basis did Oiler lose his case?

2. Assume that this case was appealed and that the appeals court agreed with Judge Africk. Write a dissenting opinion.

3. There are a number of cases involving persons who identify themselves as transgendered or as having a "gender identity disorder" causing them to identify with a gender other than the one they were assigned at birth. How would you deal with each of these scenarios: (a) You have interviewed and decided to hire a man to work as an analyst for the Library of Congress Congressional Research Services. After you offer him the position, but before a contract as been signed, he asks to speak to you about his plans to undergo sex-transformation surgery. *Schroer v. Billington,* 577 F.Supp.2d 293 (D.D.C. 2008) (b) You are Dean at Yeshiva University, an orthodox Jewish university whose parents, alumni, and financial supporters tend to be socially conservative. One of your faculty members—a literature professor—has just been tenured after five years of teaching as a male. He writes you a letter, indicating that he will be teaching as a woman. "Jay" will be "Joy," from now on. The President of your university suggests that you place Joy on fully paid leave until she can find a position elsewhere. However, she does not want to find another job. (c) You are the human relations director at a small company in Indiana. The company has a dress code that requires male employees to maintain a "conservative, socially acceptable general appearance, with hair above the collar and without earrings or other piercings." Recently you have received customer complaints that one of your sales associates has been wearing earrings, makeup, and long hair. When you call him in to speak to you, he explains that he suffers from gender identity disorder, and has continued the transition from male to female that he began before being hired. *Creed v. Family Express Corp.* 2009 WL 35237 (N.D. Ind.)

4. In 1993 Minnesota became the first state to explicitly protect transgendered persons from discrimination. By 2007, twelve other states and many cities had passed similar laws. Find out whether or not your local or state civil rights laws protect persons who are discriminated against because of their (a) sexual orientation, (b) sexual identity (e.g. transgendered) or (c) gender performance (e.g. cross-dressing).

■ ■ ■

Work/Life Balance

There's no such thing as work-life balance.… There are work-life choices, and you make them, and they have consequences.

—JACK WELCH, Former CEO of General Electric Company

Our current system has been built upon myths of autonomy and independence and thus fails to reflect the vulnerable as well as dependent nature of the human condition.

– MARTHA ALBERTSON FINEMAN

Some economists believe that the wage gap between men and women is explained neither by discrimination nor by occupational segregation, but by the fact that many women choose to spend more time with their families than developing their careers. They point to human capital studies showing that when workers take time off (for example, to have or raise children, to care for elderly parents) they earn less money than workers who don't interrupt their careers. Not surprisingly, it is more often women who leave their jobs, work part time, and work less, and so earn lower wages.[9]

Other experts argue that the wage gap is a result of discrimination and is also affected by the degree to which women—more than men—must cope with work that takes place outside of the workplace, especially child- and elder-care. While some of this may be freely chosen, they believe, stereotyping and the lack of options factor in heavily.

Joan Williams coined the phrase "the maternal wall," a play on the "glass ceiling" as a way of describing subtle discrimination against women who become mothers. She explains that sociologists have found that our image of a "good mother" is someone who is always available to her children, while a "good father" is a man who provides for his family. As a result, a woman who works part-time to spend time with her family is often seen as only an adequate worker, but has status as a good mother; a man who does the same loses status as both worker and father. A 2009 study of Harvard College graduates seems to support that thesis, finding that women who took time off from elite careers to be fulltime caretakers suffered a salary penalty when they returned to their careers, with MBAs experiencing larger cuts (41%) than either doctors (16%) or attorneys/PHDs (29%).[10]

Legislating Family Leave

While Title VII made it illegal for employers to discriminate on the basis of gender ("sex"), the courts interpreted it as allowing employers to single out and discriminate on the basis of pregnancy. In one highly criticized case, the Supreme Court upheld an employee disability plan that provided insurance for sickness and accidents, but excluded coverage for complications arising from pregnancy. The Court explained why Title VII's ban on sex discrimination was not violated:

> [A]n exclusion of pregnancy from a disability-benefits plan providing general coverage is not a gender-based discrimination at all.…[T]he selection of risks covered by the Plan did not operate, in fact to discriminate against women.… The Plan, in effect … is nothing more than an insurance package, which covers some risks, but excludes others.…[11]

---

[9] H. Wenger, "Issue Briefing #155," April 21, 2001. Economic Policy Institute.

[10] Claudia Goldin and Lawrence F. Katz, "Transitions: Career and Family Life Cycles of the Educational Elite, " AMERICAN ECONOMIC REVIEW: PAPERS & PROCEEDINGS 2008, 98:2, 363-369; retrieved from http://www.aeaweb.org/articles.php?doi=10.1257/aer.98.2.363 pn June 10, 2010.

[11] *General Electric Co. v. Gilbert,* 429 U.S. 125 (1976).

Congress reacted to the Court's interpretation of Title VII by amending the law in 1978 to make it clear that discrimination on the basis of pregnancy was illegal. The amendments, known as the **Pregnancy Discrimination Act** of 1978, provide:

Women affected by pregnancy, childbirth, and related medical conditions shall be treated the same for all employment-related purposes, including receipt of benefits under fringe benefit programs, as other persons not so affected but similar in their ability or inability to work.

Under this law, pregnant workers are to be treated like any other workers. But an argument can be made that a law that makes it illegal to fire a woman simply because she is pregnant does not go far enough. It affords no protection, for example, to a pregnant employee who is fired for excessive absenteeism by a company that similarly dismisses ill or injured workers who miss too many days at work. Nor does it address the need for time to care for a healthy newborn or accommodate other family responsibilities.

In 1993, Congress passed, and President Clinton signed into law, the **Family and Medical Leave Act**, excerpted below. Note the format of the legislation: It begins with a section that lays out Congress' reasons for adopting it ("Findings and Purposes"), followed by the parts that create enforceable rights ("Leave Requirements.")

FAMILY AND MEDICAL LEAVE ACT
29 United States Code Annotated 2601, et seq.

Findings and Purposes

1. the number of single-parent households and two-parent households in which the single parent or both parents work is increasing significantly;
2. it is important for the development of children and the family unit that fathers and mothers be able to participate in early childrearing and the care of family members who have serious health conditions;
3. the lack of employment policies to accommodate working parents can force individuals to choose between job security and parenting;
4. there is inadequate job security for employees who have serious health conditions that prevent them from working for temporary periods;
5. due to the nature of the roles of men and women in our society, the primary responsibility for family caretaking often falls on women, and such responsibility affects the working lives of women more than it affects the working lives of men; and
6. employment standards that apply to one gender only have serious potential for encouraging employers to discriminate against employees and applicants for employment who are of that gender.

Leave Requirements

a. 1. Entitlement to leave
   [A]n eligible employee shall be entitled to a total of 12 workweeks of leave during any 12-month period for one or more of the following:

A. Because of the birth of a son or daughter of the employee and in order to care for such son or daughter.
B. Because of the placement of a son or daughter with the employee for adoption or foster care.
C. In order to care for the spouse, or a son, daughter, or parent, of the employee, if such spouse, son, daughter, or parent has a serious health condition.

D. Because of a serious health condition that makes the employee unable to perform the functions of the position of such employee.

Exceptions and Special Rules

[There are some exceptions. Those within a firm's top 10 percent of salaried employees within a 75-mile radius, for example, can be denied restoration to the job after a leave if:]

A. such denial is necessary to prevent substantial and grievous economic injury to the operations of the employer;
B. the employer notifies the employee of the intent of the employer to deny restoration on such basis at the time the employer determines that such injury would occur; and
C. in any case in which the leave has commenced, the employee elects not to return to employment after receiving such notice.

In other sections not excerpted here, the law guarantees that an employee who returns from a leave can go back to his or her position, or one with equivalent benefits, pay, and employment conditions, without losing any benefits that had accrued prior to the leave, and without gaining any seniority while they were on leave. Employees become "eligible" after they have worked a specified number of hours for twelve months.

The FMLA also provides that employees have a right to use their leave time by taking intermittent or reduced time health leaves if medically necessary. The employer, however, may temporarily transfer the employee to a different, comparably paid position. Leave for new-child care must be taken all at once, unless both employee and employer agree to some other arrangement. Employees must give whatever notice of their intention to take leave is possible and reasonable considering the circumstances (e.g., 30 days notice before birth or placement of an adopted child), and make reasonable efforts to schedule medical treatment to cause the least possible disruption to the employer. Employers are required to maintain coverage under group health plans for employees on leave.

The **Injured Servicemember Leave Act**, effective 2008, allows up to twenty-six weeks of leave in a 12-month period to care for a next-of-kin servicemember with a serious injury or illness. "Servicemember" means any current member of the armed forces including the National Guard or Reserves, or a member on temporary disability.

QUESTIONS

1. Look at the statutory provisions that explain the leave requirements. Do they seem well crafted to respond to the findings set forth by Congress in the law?

2. Does the law require employers to give paid family or medical leave? Does it permit paid leave?

3. Does Congress address any stereotypes about caregivers? How responsive is the law to changes in our ideas about family? Who benefits from the law? Is anyone harmed? Can you think of any changes that would make it more responsive to the needs of caregivers?

4. **Research**: Of 173 nations surveyed by Harvard/McGill Universities in 2007, only five did not provide some form of paid leave to all new mothers: Lesoto, Liberia, Papua New Guinea, Swaziland, and the United States. (a) Find out about an organization that advocates for or against such leave in the United States. What arguments do they give for their positions? Which is more persuasive? (b) In 2002, California became the first state to enact a comprehensive paid family leave law. The National Partnership for Women and Families has drafted a bill for a similar law. Find out the current status of similar proposals in your state.[12]

---

[12] Heymann, J., Earle, A., & Hayes, J. (2007). The Work, Family, and Equity Index: How does the United States measure up? Montreal, QC and Boston, MA: Project on Global Working Families. Retrieved June 10, 2010 from http://www.mcgill.ca/files/ihsp/WFEI2007FEB.pdf

5. **Research**: In June 2010 the Department of Labor announced that it would issue an interpretation of the FMLA that would extend it to same-sex domestic partners. Find out if the new policy has been challenged in the courts. If so, what was the result?

6. **Research**: The National Partnership for Women and Families reported that by 2010 at least 145 countries around the globe guaranteed workers paid sick days, although the United States was not among them. Nearly half of private sector employees in the United States—and nearly 80% of low-wage workers—had no paid sick leave days at a time when as many as 26 million adults might have been infected with H1N1 flu. (a) The proposed Healthy Families Act would change that. Find out whether that bill has become law. (b) Are there any laws or pending laws in your state that guarantee paid sick leave?

■ ■ ■

I know this film well. "Easter '62" was the home movie Dr. Luce talked my parents into giving him. This was the film he screened each year for his students at Cornell University Medical School. This was the thirty-five second segment that, Luce insisted, proved out his theory that gender identity is established early on in life. This was the film Dr. Luce showed to me, to tell me who I was. And who was that? Look at the screen. My mother is handing me a baby doll. I take the baby and hug it to my chest. Putting a toy bottle to the baby lips, I offer it milk.

— JEFFREY EUGENIDES, MIDDLESEX[13]

■ ■ ■

Laurie Chadwick began working for Wellpoint, an insurance company in Maine, in 1997. Two years later she was promoted to Recovery Specialist. In 2006, with the encouragement of her supervisor, Nanci Miller, Chadwick applied to be a "Team Lead," a job that would give her region-wide responsibilities. Chadwick believed she was the frontrunner—based on her experience, comments by Miller, and her most recent performance evaluation (excellent, 4.40 out of 5.0.). The other finalist, also an in-house candidate, was a woman who had been working as a Recovery Specialist for only a year and whose recent performance evaluation was not as good as Chadwick's (3.84). When Chadwick was denied the promotion she brought a claim of sex discrimination under Title VII. The district (trial court) granted summary judgment in favor of WellPoint and Chadwick appealed.

CHADWICK v. WELLPOINT, INC.
United States Court of Appeals, First Circuit, 2009.
561 F.3d 38

STAHL, Circuit Judge.

...At the time of the promotion decision, Chadwick was the mother of an eleven-year-old son and six-year-old triplets in kindergarten. There is no allegation, insinuation, or for that matter evidence that Chadwick's work performance was negatively impacted by any child-care responsibilities she may have had. Indeed, Miller, the decision maker, did not know that Chadwick was the mother of young triplets until shortly before the promotion decision was made. Apparently, Chadwick's husband, the primary caretaker for the children, stayed home with them during the day while Chadwick worked. He also worked off-hour

---
[13] (NY: Farrar, Strauss & Giroux, 2002) p. 226.

shifts, presumably nights and weekends, when Chadwick was at home with the children. During the same period, Chadwick was also taking one course a semester at the University of Southern Maine.

Chadwick alleges that WellPoint denied her the promotion based on the sex-based stereotype that mothers, particularly those with young children, neglect their work duties in favor of their presumed childcare obligations....

Title VII of the Civil Rights Act of 1964 prohibits discrimination based on sex. Notably, the Act does not prohibit discrimination based on caregiving responsibility....

The type of discrimination Chadwick alleges involves stereotyping based on sex. The Supreme Court identified sex-based stereotyping as an impermissible form of discrimination in *Price Waterhouse.* There, a woman was denied partnership at the accounting firm for which she worked and was told by the partnership that she was too aggressive and macho, should attend a charm school, and should dress and behave more femininely. *Price Waterhouse v. Hopkins,* (U.S.1989). The Supreme Court held that such remarks were evidence of sex-based stereotyping, which in turn suggested that sex discrimination was the cause of the failure to promote.... The Court pointedly said, "[W]e are beyond the day when an employer could evaluate employees by assuming or insisting that they matched the stereotype associated with their group." ...

In its 2003 decision in *Hibbs*, the Supreme Court took judicial notice of the stereotype that women, not men, are responsible for family caregiving.... It explained that Congress created the FMLA's gender-neutral twelve-week leave program in order to "attack the formerly state-sanctioned stereotype that only women are responsible for family caregiving, thereby reducing employers' incentives to engage in discrimination by basing hiring and promotion decisions on stereotypes."...

In the simplest terms, these cases stand for the proposition that unlawful sex discrimination occurs when an employer takes an adverse job action on the assumption that a woman, because she is a woman, will neglect her job responsibilities in favor of her presumed childcare responsibilities. It is undoubtedly true that if the work performance of a woman (or a man, for that matter) actually suffers due to childcare responsibilities (or due to any other personal obligation or interest), an employer is free to respond accordingly, at least without incurring liability under Title VII. However, an employer is not free to assume that a woman, because she is a woman, will necessarily be a poor worker because of family responsibilities. The essence of Title VII in this context is that women have the right to prove their mettle in the work arena without the burden of stereotypes regarding whether they can fulfill their responsibilities....

Given what we know about societal stereotypes regarding working women with children, we conclude that a jury could reasonably determine that a sex-based stereotype was behind Miller's explanation to Chadwick that, "It was nothing you did or didn't do. It was just that you're going to school, you have the kids, and you just have a lot on your plate right now." Particularly telling is Miller's comment that, "It was nothing you did or didn't do." After all, the essence of employment discrimination is penalizing a worker not for something she did but for something she simply is. A reasonable jury could infer from Miller's explanation that Chadwick wasn't denied the promotion because of her work performance or her interview performance but because Miller and others assumed that as a *woman* with four young children, Chadwick would not give her all to her job.

This inference is supported by several facts. First, the decision maker learned of Chadwick's three six-year-olds just two months before she denied Chadwick the promotion. The young age and unusually high number of children would have been more likely to draw the decision maker's attention and strengthen any sex-based concern she had that a woman with young children would be a poor worker.

Second, the decision maker's reaction upon learning of Chadwick's three small children was, "Bless you!" This statement is susceptible to various interpretations, but a jury could reasonably conclude that Miller meant that she felt badly for Chadwick because her life must have been so difficult as the mother of three young children. This conclusion could be bolstered by Miller's later explanation to Chadwick that the WellPoint interviewers, all female, would feel "overwhelmed" if they were in Chadwick's position....

Third, because a plaintiff alleging discrimination infrequently has direct evidence of bias, the discrimination can "be proven through the elimination of other plausible non-discriminatory reasons until the most plausible reason remaining is discrimination." ... In Chadwick's case, Miller explained the non-promotion in one way to Chadwick (that she had too much on her plate with her kids and school) and in a very different way in her deposition (that Chadwick had performed poorly in her interviews). A jury could reasonably question the veracity of this second explanation given that Chadwick was an in-house, long-time employee who had worked closely with her interviewers, had received stellar performance reviews, and was already performing some of the key tasks of the Team Lead position....

Given the common stereotype about the job performance of women with children and given the surrounding circumstantial evidence presented by Chadwick, we believe that a reasonable jury could find that WellPoint would not have denied a promotion to a similarly qualified man because he had "too much on his plate" and would be "overwhelmed" by the new job, given "the kids" and his school. [Held: for plaintiff.]

QUESTIONS

1. The court states that "Title VII prohibits discrimination based on sex ... not based on caregiving responsibility." How, then, does it reason that Chadwick is entitled to a trial?

2. What is a stereotype? Identify some stereotypes about men. Was Chadwick's husband challenging a stereotype about men?

3. **Research:** In 2007 the EEOC issued Guidance for Workers with Caregiving Responsibilties, supplementing it with Employer Best Practices suggestions in 2009. Find and read these. Identify which practices seem to be legally required, and which are optional.

4. Suppose a firm allows employees to schedule themselves to leave work early to engage in community service, including coaching children's league-teams. Would federal law require the company to grant similar rights to parents to spend time with their own children?

5. **Research**: Some states have mandated leave for employees to attend their children's school related activities; a dozen specifically provide leave for employees who wish to be organ, bone marrow, or blood donors. Laws have also been passed that mandate leave for victims of crime or domestic violence and for those who are volunteer emergency and/or disaster service workers. Find out what kinds of leaves are mandated by your state or municipality.

■ ■ ■

Reasonable Accommodation of Disabled Workers

Society first confined people with disabilities in almshouses, and then in institutions. Alone and ignored, people with disabling conditions experienced life in a Hobbesian state of nature: an existence, "solitary, poor, nasty, brutish, and short."...Until 1973, Chicago prohibited persons who were "deformed" and "unsightly" from exposing themselves to public view.... In 1975, when federal legislation finally required states receiving federal educational funds to serve all school-aged children with disabilities, 1.75 million children were not receiving any schooling, and an estimated 2.5 million were in programs that did not meet their needs.

— MARK C. WEBER[14]

---

[14] "Exile and the King: Integration, Harassment, and the Americans With Disabilities Act, " 63 Md.L.Rev. 162 (2004).

In 1990 Congress adopted the Americans with Disabilities Act (ADA). Hailed by some as the most important legislation since the Civil Rights Acts of 1964, the ADA is patterned on an earlier law that prohibited discrimination against persons with handicaps in government-funded programs. It is a bold stroke to eliminate barriers in employment, education, housing, transportation, and public accommodations.

The ADA also takes aim at another problem: society's accumulated myths and fears about disability and disease. The law makes it illegal for employers to discriminate against a qualified person on the basis of disability and requires firms to make "reasonable accommodation" so that the disabled are given more opportunity to enter the mainstream.

The concept of reasonable accommodation is broad and flexible—but is not intended to impose an "undue hardship" on a business. It encompasses both physical changes to buildings (e.g., broadening aisles and doorways and lowering shelves to make them accessible to those in wheelchairs) and adjustments in the ways people work (e.g., flexible work schedules or modified job descriptions). While Title VII speaks of ending discrimination, the ADA does that and more: It sometimes requires employers to alter the jobs themselves.

Wherever reasonably possible, physical obstacles—the absence of ramps to enter buildings, narrow seating in theatres, the arrangement of furniture and machinery in some workplaces—must be replaced or altered to make business and public places accessible to disabled customers, clients, and employees.

The following definitions are excerpted from the law.

EQUAL OPPORTUNITY FOR INDIVIDUALS WITH DISABILITIES (AMERICANS WITH DISABILITIES ACT)
42 United States Code Annotated Sect. 12102

The term disability means, with respect to an individual (A) a physical or mental impairment that substantially limits one or more of the major life activities of such individual; (B) a record of such an impairment; or (C) being regarded as having such an impairment.

The term **qualified individual with a disability** means an individual with a disability who, with or without reasonable accommodation, can perform the essential functions of the employment position that such individual holds or desires....[C]onsideration shall be given to the employer's judgment as to what functions of a job are essential, and if an employer has prepared a written description before advertising or interviewing applicants for the job, this description shall be considered evidence of the essential functions of the job.

The term **reasonable accommodation** may include (A) making existing facilities used by employees readily accessible to and usable by individuals with disabilities; and (B) job restructuring, parttime or modified work schedules, reassignment to a vacant position, acquisition or modification of equipment or devices, appropriate adjustment or modifications of examinations, training materials or policies, the provision of qualified readers or interpreters, and other similar accommodations....

The term **undue hardship** means an action requiring significant difficulty or expense, when considered in light of the [following]: In determining whether an accommodation would impose an undue hardship on a covered entity, factors to be considered include

(i) the nature and cost of the accommodation needed under this chapter; (ii) the overall financial resources of the facility or facilities involved in the provision of the reasonable accommodation; the number of persons employed at such facility; the effect on expenses and resources, or the impact otherwise of such accommodation upon the operation of the facility; (iii) the overall financial resources of the covered entity; the overall size of the business of a covered entity with respect to the number of its employees; the number, type, and location of its facilities; and (iv) the type of operation or operations of the covered entity, including the composition, structure, and functions of the workforce of such entity; the geographic separateness, administrative, or fiscal relationship of the facility or facilities in question to the covered entity.

In 2008, Congress amended the ADA to overturn Supreme Court decisions that had narrowed the broad scope of protection the act was supposed to offer. As amended, the law requires courts to construe the definition of "disability" in favor of broad coverage of individuals; clarifies that a person meets the definition of "disabled" if he or she has any impairment that substantially limits even one major life activity; and that persons with such impairments are covered, even if disability is episodic or in remission.

QUESTIONS

1. During the past three decades, the courts have helped define the extent to which a particular business must change to accommodate the disabled. Consider the following: The National Federation of the Blind (NFB) is a nationwide, nonprofit organization with some 50,000 members, most of whom are blind. Its mission is to aid the blind in their efforts to integrate themselves into society and to remove barriers and change social attitudes, stereotypes, and mistaken beliefs concerning the limitations created by blindness. Using JAWS screen reading software, Bruce Sexton, a legally blind man, can access the Internet to research products, compare prices, and make purchasing decisions. But when he tried to use *www.target.com*—a Web site owned by the nationwide chain store that enables customers to access information regarding Target store locations and hours, refill prescriptions, order photos, print coupons, and shop online— he could not make it work. Sexton and the NFB sued Target for violating the Americans with Disabilities Act. (a) What arguments can you make on behalf of Target? The blind plaintiffs? Find out what has happened in the actual case, *National Federation of the Blind v. Target Corporation*, 2009 WL 2390261 (N.D. Cal. 2009). (b) How important is it for the blind to be able to access ATMs independently? See *Massachusetts v. ETrade Access Inc.*, 464 F.Supp.2d 52 (2006). What were the issues and outcome in that case?

2. **Research**: In a lawsuit filed in 2006, the U.S. Treasury was accused of violating the Rehabilitation Act (the law that preceded the ADA) by failing to issue paper currency that was readily distinguishable by blind and visually impaired people. Of the 180 nations that issue paper currency, only the United States prints bills identical in size and color in all denominations. Raised symbols enable the blind to distinguish bills printed by Canada, Argentina, China, and Israel. New bills are constantly being printed— especially $1 bills—and the United States made major design changes in 1996. (a) Should the government do another redesign to address the needs the blind or visually impaired? (b) To see how the court ruled, read *American Council of the Blind v. Paulson*, 581 F.Supp.2d 1 (D.D.C. 2008).

3. **Research**: The United Nations Convention on the Rights of Persons with Disabilties, adopted in 2006, is the first human rights treaty to be adopted in the twenty-first century and the first to be signed by the United States (2009) in many years. Find it and compare its provisions to the Americans with Disabilities Act. Does the U.S. meet its treaty obligations—or is there more to be done?

■ ■ ■

The ADA has brought significant change to American society, although it has not increased the overall employment rate of Americans with disabilities. As the following reading by Michael E. Waterstone (Professor at Loyola Law School in Los Angeles) and Michael Ashley Stein (Executive Director of the Harvard Project on Disability) makes clear, this is especially true for persons with psycho-social disabilities.

DISABLING PREJUDICE[15]
Michael E. Waterstone and Michael Ashley Stein

Donald Perkl is a person with intellectual disabilities and autism spectrum disorder. After successfully working in a sheltered workshop for more than six years, he was hired as a janitor at a local Chuck E. Cheese. On Perkl's first day on the job, regional manager Donald Creasy visited the restaurant. Seeing Perkl, Creasy instructed store manager Brea Wittwer to fire Perkl on the ground that it was Chuck E. Cheese's policy not to hire "those kind of people." Creasy made a similarly dismissive statement regarding Perkl's predecessor, another individual with developmental disabilities. Wittwer attempted to resist Creasy's order by requesting additional time to sort out Perkl's position. She also faxed a plaintive note to the human resources department indicating that, although Perkl was qualified and his accommodations externally paid for, Creasy was intent on firing Perkl because of his disabilities.

Perkl continued to work at the restaurant for several more weeks, earning excellent work evaluations and the esteem and friendship of his coworkers. However, upon a later visit to Chuck E. Cheese, Creasy terminated Perkl's employment after Wittwer refused to do so. Wittwer and her entire staff resigned in protest and testified on Perkl's behalf in a subsequent lawsuit...[where] the defendant contended that Perkl's intellectual disability rendered him incapable of experiencing emotional distress from the abrupt firing.

The narrative of Donald Perkl's employment discrimination experience involves two tightly linked threads. First is the overt bigotry animating Creasy's statement that Perkl was inherently inferior and undeserving of equal treatment.... Second is the equally harmful preconception that influenced Chuck E. Cheese's contention that people with cognitive disabilities cannot feel emotional anguish, and by implication, that the legal and social standing of people with disabilities is not the same as that of other citizens....

[The authors next describe the role of unconscious or "second generation" discrimination against persons with psycho-social disabilities.]

[I]nformal norms, networking, training, mentoring systems, and evaluations all provide ample cover for decision making that is based on bias and stereotypes, [which can be understood as unintentional errors of judgment.] ...

Second generation discrimination thus quietly and invidiously prevents nonmainstream employees from equal opportunities and experiences in the workplace....

Research firmly establishes that people with mental disabilities are subjected to greater prejudice than are people with physical disabilities. For example, one study comparing attitudes regarding specific disabilities determined that people with psycho-social disabilities suffer greater stigma than people with criminal records.

Adding to this difficulty, the popular media often portray people with mental disabilities as threatening or dangerous. Moreover, pervasive cultural myths claim that psychiatric disabilities are either the fault of the impaired person (for example,

[15] Michael E. Waterstone and Michael Ashley Stein, "Disabling Prejudice," from *Northwestern University Law Review* 102(3), 2008, pp. 1351–1378. Reprinted by special permission of Northwestern University School of Law.

for not taking their medication) or that they are something other than legitimate disabilities (for example, viewing a person with severe depression as "blue" rather than as experiencing a psychiatric impairment). Positive cultural depictions are rare, with a small number of individuals with psycho-social disabilities presented as heroic exceptions for "overcoming" the mammoth impediments of mental disability.

[In the final section, the authors explain why they advocate occupational integration of people with psych-social disabilities.]

1. Social Benefits to Society. Integrating persons with mental disabilities into the workplace creates a society-wide social benefit by helping to erode existing prejudices and misconceptions regarding the group. This dynamic has long been recognized by contact theory, a key theoretical underpinning of the larger antidiscrimination project. Originally developed in the race context, contact theory posits that socially constructed stereotypes and hostility can be improved by close contact between members of different races. This notion was a key part of the assault against "separate but equal" in *Brown v. Board of Education*.

Changing attitudes are of great social benefit as part of a larger effort to make the workplace, and through it society at large, more inclusive of individuals with differences....

More trenchantly, employment is a hallmark of true citizenship because it enables individuals to participate meaningfully in society.... The workplace is the one social forum that brings diverse communities together. It is where meaningful conversations occur, where meaningful relationships form, and where loyalty to coworkers is forged. Being a part of this community is a crucial way for people with disabilities to be full members of society, and to be deemed as such. Likewise, including mentally disabled people in the workplace provides them a mechanism through which to positively affect the lives of their coworkers.

Integrating individuals with psycho-social disabilities, specifically, also counteracts a number of pervasive misconceptions.... First is the erroneous notion that mentally disabled people are a distinct and separate group, apart from the social norm. In fact, "[a]bout half of all the people in the United States will develop one or more mental disorders in their lifetimes" and in the course of "any year, one of every four people in this country fits the definition of 'mentally ill.'" A second myth ascribes permanence to mental disability....

Perhaps the most significant cultural myth is the most obvious one: the notion that group members are unable to be effective employees....

Susan Stefan argues that people with psychiatric disabilities do not just work in fast food, yard work, or as janitors. Rather, as she details, they are senators, television journalists, print journalists, clinical psychologists, and astronauts. One might also note Ludwig van Beethoven, Winston Churchill, Charles Dickens, Albert Einstein, Abraham Lincoln, or Isaac Newton. In many ways, the workplace success of individuals with mental disabilities demonstrates how real-life events are outpacing legal reform and academic discussion: large numbers of people with mental disabilities already exist in the workplace, albeit perhaps under fear of discovery....

2. Economic Benefits to Society.... Simply put, social dependency, the option when people with mental disabilities are not working, is expensive. General disability-related public assistance obligations exceed $120 billion annually; and specifically, social insurance programs are used disproportionately by persons with mental disabilities....

[E]liminating workplace discrimination against individuals with mental disabilities encourages people within that group to more fully invest in their own human capital to develop their potential, and thereby add to the talent pool of people in the workforce....

3. Benefits to Workplaces. Making employment opportunities inclusive to people with mental disabilities has several benefits that accrue to employers, nondisabled employees, and the workplace environment....

People with mental disabilities may bring abilities to a position due to the effect of their disability, for instance, an unusual degree of creativity, high level of accuracy, or attention to detail. Also accruing to the employer's benefit is the fact that many workers with disabilities have higher job retention and equal or higher performance ratings on the job than do people without disabilities....

Potential workplace modifications...[can] lead to more productive, satisfied, and safer workplaces for all workers and can increase overall economic productivity and development. In the larger disability context, employers that have made accommodations report that doing so has benefited their respective companies, including their workers without disabilities....

In addition to more readily calculable benefits, Peter Blanck also describes "ripple effects" emanating from the provision of accommodations...[including] purported higher productivity, greater dedication, and better identification of qualified candidates for promotion ... fewer insurance claims, reduced post-injury rehabilitation costs, an improved corporate culture, and more widespread use by workers without disabilities of efficiency-enhancing technologies previously utilized exclusively by their peers with disabilities.

QUESTIONS

1. The authors cite the fact that people with mental disabilities can "positively affect the lives of their co-workers." What indication do you notice that Perkl did so? Do you have any experience of this—of being positively affected by such an individual? What benefits to society and to the workplace do the authors mention?

2. What differences and what similarities can you identify between people with mental disabilities and those who suffer discrimination due to their race or gender?

3. Research: Find out what psychiatric disabilities afflicted Beethoven, Churchill, Dickens, Einstein, Lincoln, Sylvia Plath, and Virginia Woolf.

Chapter Problems

1. In a recent article discussing the call for medical research to take race into account, former law school dean Alex M. Johnson, Jr. advocates re-characterizing African-Americans as an ethnic, rather than a racial group:

    [Doing so] moves the focus from skin color, DNA, and other genetic and inheritable attributes to the social and environmental context within which this ethnicity is formed....

    Treating individuals from Atlanta, Nairobi, Kingston, London, and Rio de Janeiro similarly because they have the same skin color is as quixotic as treating individuals based on their date of birth or their height. However, treating individuals similarly who grew up in Watts or South Central Los Angeles, Harlem

Source: Alex M. Johnson, Jr. "The Re-emergence of Race as a Biological Category: The Societal Implications—Reaffirmation of Race," 94 IOWA L. REV. 1547 (2009).

in New York City, or any other inner-city ghetto—given their similar experiential histories based on their socio-economic status, their lack of access to adequate health care, poor diet, and poor educational opportunities, among other variables—makes sense as a starting point for diagnosis and treatment. Most importantly to my thesis, the focus on these other variables that produce the differential outcomes, if properly publicized and communicated, will shift the focus away from skin color and the traditional notion of "race" and racial categories and instead shift the focus toward those environmental factors that correlate to the variables that cause the differential outcomes among members of different ethnic groups.

Would such a re-characterization help to break down stereotypes? What other benefits can you imagine? Any harmful outcomes?

2. **Research**: Under the **Equal Pay Act** as interpreted by the courts, employers may not pay men and women different wages for doing the same job except to the extent that wage differentials are based on seniority, merit, or factors "other than sex." Title VII of the Civil Rights Act of 1964 prohibits discrimination in pay and other compensation based on race, sex, color, religion, or national origin. Yet there are still wage gaps. The National Committee for Pay Equity reported these statistics on its Web site in spring 2010:

   The median earnings for women working fulltime, year round was $35,745 or 77% of what men working fulltime, year round earn. The gap is even greater (67%) for African American women (67%), and for Latinas (58%).

   a. Check out the Web site of the National Committee for Pay Equity, and use its interactive map to learn if there are race and gender wage gaps in your state. (b) The proposed Fair Pay Act seeks to end wage discrimination against those who work in female-dominated or minority-dominated jobs by establishing equal pay for equivalent work. Another proposed law, the Paycheck Fairness Act, calls for voluntary guidelines to show employers how to evaluate jobs with the goal of eliminating unfair disparities. Find out the current status of these bills.

3. Let Justice Roll, a coalition of religious, labor, and anti-poverty groups, has been waging a campaign for "living-wage bills." Most require those businesses that receive government contracts to pay wages higher than the legal minimum wage. Who are the stakeholders in living wage acts? Who will benefit most from such laws? Who might be harmed by them? What ethical arguments can you make for and against living wage laws? Find out if a living wage bill has been introduced or passed in your locality.

4. A major study of low wage workers in Chicago, Los Angeles, and New York City, conducted in 2008 and published a year later, found that 26% had been victims of minimum wage, overtime, and other workplace violations. Not surprisingly, women were more vulnerable than men, Latinos more vulnerable that Whites, and African-Americans three times as likely to be victims as Whites. Violations involving foreign-born workers were double those against native-born employees. What are the implications of these findings? *Broken Laws, Unprotected Workers,* available online at *nelp.3cdn.net/1797b93ddlccdf9e7d_sdm6bc50n.pdf.*

5. **Research**: Is there still a glass ceiling in the United States? According to USA TODAY women occupied only 15% of board seats on Fortune 500 companies and were 3% of CEOS in 2010.[16] The National Venture Capitalist Association claims that only 14% of venture capitalists are women. In 2009, women received only 18% of the college degrees in computing, down from 37% in 1985. Find groups that are trying to address this issue. What do they identify as the problems? What strategies for change do these groups propose?

6. Federal fair housing laws prohibit discrimination in the rental or sale of property on the basis of race, religion, sex, color or national origin. Some state civil rights laws go further, banning discrimination on the basis of family status and sexual orientation (e.g. California, New Jersey). The Web site *www.roommates.com*, a website run out of California, helps match tenants who want to share rental housing. Users are required to provide their sex, sexual orientation, parental status, and willingness to live with children. Does this mean Roommates.com violates state housing discrimination laws? Is it fair to hold the Web service responsible for discrimination by its users? **Research**: To find out how a court ruled, find and read *Fair Housing Council of San Fernando Valley v. Roommates.com,* 521 F.3d 1157 (9th Cir. 2008).

7. **Research**: Find a company that has tried to create a corporate culture that supports men or women in caretaking responsibilities. [*Hint*: *Working Mother* magazine yearly identifies the top family-friendly companies. Warning: companies apply for this honor.] What are the characteristics of its program? Compare its work/family benefits to those of other companies in the same business sector. Now check the company's financials. Is the "progressive" firm you've located also a successful one? Is it one you would want to work for?

8. Under the ADA, special rules apply to alcoholics and drug addicts. Alcoholism is considered an "impairment," although the law explicitly allows a company to hold an alcoholic to the same standards of behavior as other employees, even if the inability to perform is related to the alcoholism. Drug addicts cannot be penalized because of their status—or history—as addicts, but employers can refuse to hire or fire those who are "current users of illegal drugs." Like alcoholics, addicts can be held to the same standards and rules as other employees. Consider the case of Jose Hernandez. After testing positive for cocaine (a violation of workplace rules), he resigned from his job at Raytheon. Two years later, he re-applied for work at Raytheon and was turned down. Assuming his work record was otherwise good, was Raytheon justified—legally and/or ethically—in refusing to hire him? What argument can you make that it was illegal and/or unethical to refuse to rehire him? See *Raytheon v. Hernandez,* 540 U.S. 44, 124 S. Ct. 513 (2003).

9. Feminist theorist Martha Abelson Fineman has written: "[S]ystems of power and privilege ... interact to produce webs of advantages and disadvantages." Can you identify systems of power and privilege that might explain your own assets and limitations? Does focusing on these structures of power—rather than on individuals—help to explain women CEOs who reject the idea that accommodations should be made for caretakers of small children or aging parents; wealthy and successful African Americans who launch campaigns against affirmative action in college admissions; Latinos who are adamant that we should deport undocumented workers?

---

[16] http://www.usatoday.com/news/opinion/forum/2010-04-15-column15_ST1_N.htm.

CHAPTER PROJECT

Alternative Dispute Resolution: Cyberbullying

Guidelines: Appendix E

Witness statement: Jonathan Scarlatti

I was thrilled when I was accepted with a full scholarship to Ratgut University last year. It was my first choice, mostly because of its music school. I've been playing oboe since I was seven. I love it. All through high school I had been performing in the band. We won two regional competitions. I had been thinking about a career as a classical musician, but I was also getting interested in jazz. My scholarship was from Ratgut's music school, one of the top five in the country. So I was happy about the financial package, and glad that Ratgut is only a half hour from home. My high school boyfriend Will and I are still close. I didn't want to break up with him just because I was going to college. I'm gay. I came out to my parents in my junior year of high school. I've been out on Facebook, and I blog about my life on a couple of LGBT sites.

I first heard about my Ratgut University roommate the summer before classes started. He sounded nice—outgoing, decent. He listed skateboarding as a hobby, and break-dancing. From the time I met Hunter Pratt he was always with a couple of other students, and about to go out somewhere, usually a party. I never saw him study. But then I never really saw him much at all. He would come in late after I was asleep. He'd be sleeping when I was awake. In the beginning of the semester, even though our room was cramped, we were managing to give each other enough space, and I felt pretty comfortable. A couple of nights, when I knew Hunter was going to be out, I had Will stay with me.

But then I found out what was really going on. My roommate is a homophobe, and cruel. He was twittering about how I was gay and I was hooking up with another "gay dude" in the dorm. And he was spying on me! He set up a webcam in our room, and while he and another student watched from their room, he was streaming video of me and Will together for the world to see.

This happened a few days ago. I've been really depressed. I feel like the whole university—the whole universe—is laughing at me. I haven't been able to study or practice. I don't want to go out of the room, but the room feels creepy too—*there's no place I want to be*. Sometimes I think of revenge—like I think of pouring pink paint all over Hunter's stuff, but that wouldn't change anything. I know this isn't over, either. He's just waiting for his next chance to humiliate me.

Witness Statement: Hunter Pratt

I'm a finance major at Ratgut University. Last year a bunch of seniors from my high school were accepted too, and we've been hanging together since we got to campus.

I'm a good student, but I'm also the kind of person who likes to be with people. I'm a great break-dancer and I'm good at most sports. In a crowd, I'm usually the one who's making people laugh. I have more friends than I can handle really, but that's a good thing. I'm a tech geek and I'm all over the net—twitter, Facebook, all that stuff.

I just pulled off my best prank ever. Before I even got to college I was checking out my roommate, Jonathan Scarlatti. He's a classical music freak, and I found out he's a fag. I have nothing against gays, it's their business. But living with one was weird! He was always either studying or playing his oboe. At first I didn't think he had any life at all, and then it turns out he's got this boyfriend, and this boyfriend is coming to Ratgut for a weekend.

So here's what I did: I tweeted the news: "Roommate asked for the room until midnight. Keep posted if you want to see him making out with a dude!" Then I set up my webcam in the room so it was aimed at Jonathan's bed but hidden. I left, I went to the game, I ate dinner, and later my friend Meghan and I watched the webcam from her dorm room. We were laughing ourselves sick. I streamed the action out to a few of our friends. People were sending each other their favorite parts. We stayed up the whole night. It was great!

Assume that Jonathan Scarlatti has complained to the Resident Assistant of his dormitory, who has in turn reported this incident to Ratgut University's Disciplinary Board.

This scenario is based on the events surrounding the suicide of Tyler Clementi, a freshman student at Rutgers University who jumped off the George Washington Bridge on September 22, 2010 after his roommate uploaded videos of him having sexual relations with a man.

CHAPTER 5

Workers' Rights as Human Rights
Health and Safety in the Workplace

There was another interesting set of statistics that a person might have gathered in Packingtown—those of the various afflictions of the workers.... [E]ach one of these lesser industries was a separate little inferno, in its way as horrible as the killing-beds, the source and fountain of them all. The workers in each of them had their own peculiar diseases. And the wandering visitor might be skeptical about all the swindles, but he could not be skeptical about these, for the worker bore the evidence of them about on his own person— generally he had only to hold out his hand.

— UPTON SINCLAIR, THE JUNGLE (1906)

Labour is not a Commodity.

— PHILADELPHIA DECLARATION OF THE INTERNATIONAL LABOUR ORGANIZATION (1994)

At the beginnings of the second decade of the twenty-first century, Americans were made painfully aware of the hazardous nature of the work that provides the energy to run our economy. In February 2010, six workers were killed in an explosion at the Kleen Energy Plant in Middletown Connecticut. A month later, an explosion at the Tesoro Refinery in Washington state killed six workers. On April 5, 2010, 29 coal miners were killed in an explosion at the Massey Energy Upper Big Branch mine in West Virginia, the nation's worst mining disaster in 40 years. Then what would become America's worst environmental disaster began with an oil-rig explosion in the Gulf of Mexico that left six BP workers dead. In this chapter we look at these tragedies through the lens of workers' rights.

From the time of the industrial revolution through today's increasingly global economy, there has been little consensus in the United States regarding the appropriate balance between risk and security in the workplace. Just how healthy and safe must a workplace be? Whose responsibility is it to set the standards to minimize harm to life, limb, and pocketbook caused by industrial accidents, occupational disease, and toxic exposure? Free-market economists believe regulation tends to stifle competition and detract from efficiency, while reformers look to the state to rein in the harshest effects of unrestrained capitalism. Some are wary of both big business and big government, arguing for maximal freedom for individuals. Similar debates arise on a transnational scale: some would allow national standards to prevail while others favor universal norms and guidance from international organizations.

This chapter begins with perspectives on work-related risks—both the avoidable and the unavoidable. The legal backdrop includes the watershed Occupational Health and Safety Act of 1970, embodying a national policy to reduce or prevent occupational harms, and laws designed to compensate those who suffer them. In the final section we explore the twenty-first-century global dimensions of workplace health and safety. Throughout, we pay particular attention those who are most vulnerable.

■ ■ ■

Confronting Risk in the Work Environment: The WTC Cleanup

In November 2004, an Army National Guard medic filed a class action against the Environmental Protection Agency (EPA), the White House Council on Environmental Quality, and the Occupational Safety and Health Administration (OSHA) on behalf of all those who worked in the immediate vicinity of the World Trade Center from September 11, 2001 to October 31, 2001. The plaintiffs claimed that statements in EPA (headed by Christine Whitman at the time) press releases issued in the wake of the disaster were made (1) to speed work at the site, (2) with the knowledge they were false or misleading, and (3) with deliberate indifference to the health risks of the workers. The court must decide if those allegations are enough to allow plaintiffs to move to the next step—a trial.

LOMBARDI v. WHITMAN
United States Court of Appeal, Second Circuit, 2007
485 F.3d 73

JACOBS, Chief Judge.
The collapse of the World Trade Center towers on [September 11, 2001] generated a cloud of debris that coated the surrounding buildings and streets of Lower Manhattan with concrete dust, asbestos, lead, and other building materials. Fires within the wreckage burned for months, emitting various metals and particulate matter in addition to such potentially harmful substances as dioxin, polychlorinated biphenyls (PCBs), volatile organic compounds, and polycyclic aromatic hydrocarbons.

The plaintiffs arrived at the site on September 11 or in the days soon after: John Lombardi is a ... medic; Roberto Ramos, Jr. is an Emergency Services Officer in the New York City Corrections Department; Hasan A. Muhammad is an Emergency Services Captain...; Rafael A. Garcia is a Deputy U.S. Marshal; and Thomas E. Carlstrom is a paramedic.... They participated in search, rescue, and clean–up work at the site, with little or no equipment to protect their lungs. They were not told by their employers or any government official about the health risks posed by the dangerous contaminants in the air, and they thought they could work at the site with little or no respiratory protection based on the information available to them, including statements of government officials indicating that Lower Manhattan's air quality presented no significant health risks to the public....

A September 13, 2001, EPA press release [i] indicated that initial environmental tests done at the site after the terrorist attacks were "very reassuring about potential exposure of rescue crews and the public to environmental contaminants"; [ii] concluded that the results of "[a]dditional sampling of both ambient air quality and dust particles ... in lower Manhattan ... were uniformly acceptable"; and [iii] expressed the EPA's intent to work with other agencies and rescue workers to provide respiratory equipment and to make sure they observed appropriate safety precautions—assistance that the plaintiffs allege (to their knowledge) never materialized....

A September 16 EPA press release reported additional good news:

"[N]ew samples confirm previous reports that ambient air quality meets OSHA standards and consequently is not a cause for public concern.... EPA has found variable asbestos levels in bulk debris and dust on the ground, but EPA continues to believe that there is no significant health risk to the general public in the coming days." ...

[A] September 18 press release [by the EPA] reported ... that the "vast majority" of air samples taken near the site measured harmful substances at below maximum acceptable levels.... [T]he highest asbestos levels were close to the site itself, where rescue and cleanup workers were supposedly being supplied with adequate equipment....

In fact, according to the EPA Inspector General, 25 percent of the bulk dust samples taken up to that point recorded asbestos at levels representing a significant health risk....

[A] September 12 internal EPA e-mail directed that all statements to the media were to be cleared by the National Security Council [through the CEQ] before release ... and in response to the CEQ's suggestions ... the EPA [i] removed a reference to recent test samples that recorded higher asbestos levels than those in previous samples and [ii] added a quote* from John L. Henshaw of OSHA assuring that it was safe to go to work in Lower Manhattan.... [*"Our tests show that it is safe for New Yorkers to go back to work in New York's financial district.... Keeping the streets clean and being careful not to track dust into buildings will help protect workers from remaining debris."]...

Under the Due Process Clause of the Fifth Amendment of the Constitution, "[n]o person shall ... be deprived of life, liberty, or property, without due process of law." This clause has been interpreted as a "protection of the individual against arbitrary action of government...." [But] government action resulting in bodily harm is not a substantive due process violation unless "the government action was 'so egregious, so outrageous, that it may fairly be said to shock the contemporary conscience.'"

Only an affirmative act can amount to a violation of substantive due process, because the Due Process Clause "is phrased as a limitation on the State's power to act, not as a guarantee of certain minimal levels of safety and security." ...It is not enough to allege that a government actor failed to protect an individual from a known danger of bodily harm or failed to warn the individual of that danger. So, to the extent the plaintiffs here allege that the defendants had an affirmative duty to prevent them from suffering exposure to environmental contaminants, their claims must fail. They cannot rely on the EPA's failure to instruct workers to wear particular equipment, its failure to explain the exact limitations of its knowledge of the health effects of the airborne substances that were present, or its failure to explain the limitations of its testing technologies.

But the complaint goes further; it alleges that defendants' affirmative assurances that the air in Lower Manhattan was safe to breathe created a false sense of security that induced site workers to forgo protective measures, thereby creating a danger where otherwise one would not have existed. "[I]n exceptional circumstances a governmental entity may have a constitutional obligation to provide ... protection, either because of a special relationship with an individual, or because the governmental entity itself has created or increased the danger to the individual." The plaintiffs allege no "special relationship" between them and federal officials.... They plead that their reliance on the government's misrepresentations induced them to forgo available safeguards, and thus characterize the harm as a state created danger....

[Plaintiffs' allegations allow the court to assume that defendants' optimistic statement caused them to experience a false sense of security that led to the harmful exposures.] But, [i]n order to shock the conscience and trigger a violation of substantive due process, official conduct must be outrageous and egregious under the circumstances; it must be truly "brutal and offensive to human dignity." ...

[D]eliberate indifference that shocks in one environment may not be so patently egregious in another....

The complaint ... recognizes what everyone knows: that one essential government function in the wake of disaster is to put the affected community on a normal footing, i.e., to avoid panic, keep order, restore services, repair infrastructure, and preserve the economy.

If anything, the importance of the EPA's mission counsels against broad constitutional liability in this situation: the risk of such liability will tend to inhibit EPA officials in making difficult decisions about how to disseminate information to the public in an environmental emergency ... [and] officials might default to silence in the face of the public's urgent need for information....

Can the goals of a government policy possibly outweigh a known risk of loss of life or bodily harm? The EPA and other federal agencies often must decide whether to regulate particular conduct by taking into account whether the risk to the potentially affected population will be acceptable. Such decisions require an exercise of the conscience, but such decisions cannot be deemed egregious, conscience-shocking, and "arbitrary in the constitutional sense," merely because they contemplate some likelihood of bodily harm....

When great harm is likely to befall someone no matter what a government official does, the allocation of risk may be a burden on the conscience of the one who must make such decisions, but does not shock the contemporary conscience.

These principles apply notwithstanding the great service rendered by those who repaired New York, the heroism of those who entered the site when it was unstable and on fire, and the serious health consequences that are plausibly alleged in the complaint.

[HELD:] Because the conduct at issue here does not shock the conscience, there was no constitutional violation. [The lower court's dismissal of the case is affirmed.]

Result

QUESTIONS

1. Plaintiffs did not allege that the defendants acted with evil intent to harm them. On what basis, then, did they claim that defendants were responsible for the harm they suffered? Why does the court dismiss that claim?

2. Do you agree with Judge Jacobs that the assurances given by the EPA were not shocking to the contemporary conscience?

3. In a sense, the judge's ruling here is in sync with the "no duty to rescue" rule discussed in Chapter 1. Which exception to the rule did the plaintiffs hope to use?

4. Identify the ethical issues that arise in this case for (a) rescue workers, (b) EPA officials, and (c) Judge Jacobs. What would have been the ethical thing for each of them to do?

5. **Research**: In the immediate aftermath of the collapse of the Twin Towers, it was fair to assume that there were safety risks at the site. Within days of the attack, Congress established a September 11 Victim Compensation Fund. Kenneth R. Feinberg, a lawyer, served as administrator, doling out more than $7 billion to the families of those who died in the WTC attacks and to rescue and cleanup workers who had already been diagnosed with respiratory ailments. After the fund expired, many others began to experience health problems. People who lived or worked near the WTC also suffered health impacts. Who are the stakeholders in this scenario? Should anyone be compensated for their injuries? How?

6. **Research**: In another lawsuit growing out of the WTC disaster, some 10,000 workers whose health was damaged at ground zero sued the City of New York, the Port Authority, and more than 100 private contractors working at the site, claiming that those in charge of the clean-up had emphasized speed over safety. A study released in April 2010 showed that rescue workers lost about 10 percent of their lung function in the year after the attack, with little or no recovery over the next six years. Two months later, after eight years of litigation, Judge Hellerstein gave tentative approval to a settlement that would establish a $712 million fund—to be administered by Feinberg—to compensate for illnesses. Payments would range from $3,250 to workers

who feared sickness ("enhanced risk") to $1.5 million to the families of those who died. The money will come from the WTC Captive Insurance fund. The proposed settlement was approved by 95% of the plaintiffs in November 2010. Find out what happened to those plaintiffs who opted out of the settlement.

7. During the attempted clean-up of the Gulf oil spill in Spring 2010, some workers expressed safety concerns. According to an environmental activist group, the National Resources Defense Council (NRDC), BP claimed that air concentrations of carcinogens such as benzene were below the limits set by the federal Occupational Safety and Health Administration (OSHA). In fact, its own data showed levels of benzene and the dispersant chemical above the Recommended Exposure Limits set by the government's research agency, the National Institute for Occupational Safety and Health (NIOSH). The NRDC noted that while NIOSH standards are not legally enforceable, OSHA had not updated its own, legally enforceable permissible exposure limits (PELS) in more than thirty years. Who should be responsible for monitoring the health of the clean up workers in the Gulf? For compensating those who suffer ill health as a result?[1]

■ ■ ■

HIGH RISK INDUSTRIES: MINING DISASTER TESTIMONY

On April 5, 2010, a massive explosion at the Massey Energy Upper Big Branch (UBB) mine in West Virginia—likely caused by a combination of methane gas and coal dust—claimed the lives of 29 miners. Mining has long been recognized to be one of the most dangerous industries in the world, and this was not the first indication of serious problems at the Massey mine.

According to the federal agency responsible for the industry, the Mine Safety and Health Administration (MSHA), there was a significant spike in safety violations at the UBB mine in 2009. Some 515 citations and orders were issued, along with 48 withdrawal orders for repeated significant and substantial violations of rules regarding ventilation, roof supports, and coal dust. Another 124 citations were issued in 2010, with proposed penalties totaling more than one million dollars. Massey contested most of them.

Nor was the UBB the only Massey mine with serious safety problems. Two miners were killed in a conveyor-belt fire at Massey's Aracoma Alma mine in 2006, leading to a criminal conviction and $2.5 million in fines. Their widows filed a wrongful death suit against Massey Energy and its CEO, Don Blankenship, blaming the company for putting production ahead of worker safety. Evidence included a 2005 memo by Blankenship to supervisors that stated "If any of you have been asked by your group presidents, your supervisors, engineers or anyone else to do anything other than run coal … you need to ignore them and run coal."[2]

On May 24, 2010, the House Committee on Education and Labor went to Beckley, West Virginia, to hear from those most affected by the UBB Mine tragedy. Below are excerpts from the testimony.

[1] http//switchboard.nrdc.org/blogs/gsolomon/osha_limits_don't_protect_gulf.html (visited 6-16-10)

[2] Briefing by the Department of Labor, Mine Safety and Health Administration on Disaster at Massey Energy's Upper Big Branch Mine-South, April 12, 2010. http://www.msha.gov/PerformanceCoal/DOL-MSHA_president_Report.pdf

Statement of Stanley "Goose" Stewart, **jack-setter and shear operator on the long wall at UBB Mine for 15 of his 34 coal-mining years.**

I am here to tell my story today because I worked at the Upper Big Branch mine until the day of the accident and was 300 feet underground the day the explosion occurred. … I know firsthand how bad conditions were at the mine and want everyone to know. In fact, last July, I told my wife, Mindi, "If anything happens to me, get a lawyer and sue the [blankety blank] out of them! That place is a ticking time bomb." Only I didn't say "blankety blank" to her because I was so scared—and mad! She told me to write down things that were wrong because she wouldn't know specifics or the terminology to convey what was happening. I began to write down things I knew were illegal or wrong.

On April 5th, I was sitting on a mantrip [shuttle used to transport workers in and out of mineshafts] at about 3 pm with several other miners approximately 300 feet underground. We were getting ready to head to the section when I felt a breeze coming from inside the mine. The intensity picked up quickly and I realized that something bad was happening so I left the mantrip and started making my way toward the outside. Before I could get out the air velocity increased to what I felt was "hurricane strength" and I felt my feet wanting to leave the ground. The air was full of dust debris and I couldn't see. Although I didn't have far to go I panicked, afraid that I might not make it out to safety.

Many things were wrong at the mine such as low air constantly. The area of the mine we were working was liberating a lot of methane. Mine management never fully addressed the air problem when it would be shut down by inspectors. They would fix it just good enough to get us to load coal again, but then it would be back to business as usual.… I was told prior to the April 5th explosion that they had experienced at least 2 fireballs on the drum of the shearer. This leads me to believe the methane was indeed building in that area, showing lack of air and ventilation problems. One question that I have is how could methane build up to that point where a fireball could start? How could this happen if the methane detectors had been working?

On July 26, 2009, on the second shift, our crew was told by management to make an air change from sweep air to split air in Head Gate 21. They knocked stoppings while crews were still working. Anything to do with changing ventilation, by law, the mine is to be evacuated because there won't be enough air. People working … will have their air short-circuited by the change in ventilation. However, the section crew was still working when the air change was made. I'm not sure MSHA was aware of the whole situation. But it scared me, and when I got home I wrote it down.

The morale around the mine for the most part was bad. No one felt they could go to management and express their fears or the lack of air on our sections. We knew that we'd be marked men and the management would look for ways to fire us. Maybe not that day, or that week, but somewhere down the line, we'd disappear. We'd seen it happen and I told my wife I felt like I was working for the Gestapo at times. They took vacation from the miners last year because they wanted a certain average of coal loaded a shift by vacation time. The conditions of the mine where we were working were so bad, it was nearly impossible to load that much coal safely.

I worked close to 20 years in the union and 15 years nonunion, so I've been on both sides of the fence long enough to know the difference in how miners feel in both types of working environments. In the union if you had safety concerns you had the right to refuse to work in unsafe conditions without fear of your job. You felt at ease and comforted by your rights. Working at a nonunion mine you do not feel that comfort. You know you have to operate with a lack of air or in unsafe conditions. They want you to load coal at all costs and I feel that mentality is handed down from top management. I used to tell the guys during an organizing drive that no amount of money is worth your rights. But Massey and Mr. Blankenship in particular ran a hands-on, anti-union campaign and threatened to shut the mine down if the union was voted in. He preached he wanted "flexibility". It didn't take me long to know what his flexibility was: do it his way or else "Massey don't need you. Get your bucket and get off the property." …

Statement of Gary Quarles, **whose son had worked the long wall at UBB Mine for 8 years before he was killed in the blast.**

…I also am a coal miner and have worked in the mines for 34 years. I worked in union mines for 23 years and have worked in nonunion mines the rest of the time. Other than working for 2 years in a saw mill, I have worked my entire adult life in the coal mining business. I have experience in all aspects of coal mining, including being a roof bolter, a long wall operator, and driving a shuttle car.…

Safety inspections were much different in the union mines I've worked at versus the nonunion Massey mines. When an MSHA inspector comes onto a Massey mine property, the code words go out "we've got a man on the property." Those words are radioed from the guard gates and relayed to all working operations in the mine. The mine superintendent and foreman communicate regularly by phone, and there are signals that require the foreman who is underground to answer the phone.… When the word goes out, all effort is made to correct any deficiencies or direct the inspector's attention away from any deficiencies.

When I worked at union mines, workers at the mine would accompany the MSHA inspectors during their inspections. I was on a safety committee and the members of the committee took turns going around with the MSHA inspectors and pointing out areas of concern. Moreover, as a union miner I was able to refuse to work in unsafe conditions without fear of retaliation.

When the MSHA inspector comes to a Massey mine, the only people accompanying him are Massey company people. No coal miner at the mine can point out areas of concern to the MSHA inspector. In fact, for a miner working for Massey, the feeling is, if an MSHA inspector fails to say anything about all of these safety problems, what right do I have to say anything about them, and I definitely would be terminated or retaliated against if I said anything.…

Statement of Alice Peters, **mother-in-law of 50-year-old Edward ("Dean") Jones who had worked 30 years as a miner, 13 in the UBB Mine when he was killed in the explosion.**

Dean told me many times that he had concerns about the ventilation at the Upper Big Branch mine. He often told me and his wife that he was afraid to go to work because the conditions at the mine were so bad. He also told me that, at least 7 times, he was told by Massey supervisors that, if he shut down production because of the ventilation problems (bad air), he would lose his job. They knew about his son [Kyle, who suffers from cystic fibrosis] and that Dean needed to keep his job to make sure his son could get the medical care he needed. On more than one occasion, I called the mine and told them there was an emergency regarding his son that he had to come home and handle in order to get him out of the mine, because I feared for his safety.…

My son-in-law was a very good miner and could have gotten a job anywhere—he had a college degree in mine engineering. However, because of the physical disability of his son and the absolute necessity of maintaining his health insurance benefits, Dean was unable to leave Massey's employment. He continued to work in that mine even though he knew it was unsafe because he was afraid of being fired and losing his health insurance coverage.

Questions

1. Congress generally responds to disasters, as it did in 2006, after 45 coal miners in the United States died on the job. The most widely publicized deaths came from an explosion in the Sago Mine in West Virginia, where a delayed rescue effort killed twelve men and severely injured the lone survivor. Three weeks later a conveyor belt fire in the Aracoma Alma Mine—also in West Virginia—killed two others. In the decade preceding these disasters, the national budget for MSHA had been cut by $2.8 million. The Sago Mine disaster was attributed to a combination of natural and man-made causes: a lightning strike touched off the methane blast, mine operators did not monitor methane levels inside the sealed section of the mine, and seals used to close off that inactive section were not strong enough to withstand the blast. Searchers did not reach the team trapped inside the mine for 40 hours. Investigations into the deaths at the Aracoma Alma mine showed that a previous fire had not been reported, a fire alarm did not work, a critical wall was missing, a waterline had no water in it, and an automatic fire sprinkler was missing. The deaths may have been caused, in part, by difficulty donning breathing devices. Federal investigators missed obvious problems before both accidents.

   In response, Congress enacted the Mine Improvement New Emergency Response Act (MINER Act) to strengthen the Mine Safety and Health Act. That legislation focused primarily on emergency responses—the problem at Sago—and enhanced penalties. Enforcement by the MSHA was also stepped up. Under the Obama administration, the agency began to develop new standards on silica and coal dust.

   After the UBB mine explosion in 2010, there were renewed calls for reform. **Research:** Find out how Congress and the Executive Branch responded.

Occupational Safety and Health Administration (OSHA)

For most people in our society, work is unavoidable. If individual workers find themselves facing unacceptable occupational risks they cannot simply withdraw from the market.... Adequate information is often lacking; the power to insist on less risk does not exist; and there is no possibility of mobility. These limitations on choices characterize occupational as opposed to recreational or aesthetic risks.

— MARK MCCARTHY, (1982)[3]

The guiding principle regarding OSHA penalties must be this: it should cost an employer more to break the law than to observe it.

— NANCY LESSIN, MASS. COALITION FOR OSH

The primary focus of lawsuits, such as that brought on behalf of WTC workers, and compensation schemes such as workers' compensation—described later in this chapter—is

---

[3] Mark McCarthy, "A Review of Some Normative and Conceptual Issues in Occupational Safety and Health," *9 Boston College Env'tl Affairs L. Rev.* 773, 778–80 (1980–82).

on paying those who have been injured or made ill. But this is not the only possible approach to workplace safety. From their earliest days, labor unions have sought greater protections for their members. During the 1937 National Silicosis Conference, for example, industry representatives argued that because exposure to silicon dust was being minimized and minimal exposure was not disabling, there was no longer a real crisis. Representing organized labor, John Frey of the American Federation of Labor disagreed. As historians Rosner and Markowitz explain:

> Frey argued silicosis was a problem for workers even before they became disabled ... because any silica in the lungs was pathological.... He maintained that ... emphasis on disability and impairment led management to rely on pre-employment physicals and periodic screening as a means of denying employment or firing diseased workers.... The real issue was not to eliminate diseased workers from the workplace but to "eliminate the silica from the air, and prevent additional infections."
>
> Unlike industry spokespeople, who sought to reduce the problem of silicosis to an engineering and cost-benefit issue that balanced the health of the work force against the cost to industry, Frey based his argument upon the older public health reformers' analysis, which emphasized protecting communities rather than individuals. "Silicosis is an industrial disease which can be eliminated as effectively as typhoid germs can be removed from the city's drinking water." ...The cost of protecting the work force was a public obligation.... Just as modern city administrators had decided that the very high cost of purifying the water supply was justified by the improvements in health of the population, so too the cost of purifying the work environment was justified by the need to protect all workers from risk of contracting a preventable condition.[4]

The union perspective did not prevail. It would be another 40 years before the AFL's goal of an expanded federal responsibility for workplace regulation and standard-setting would be realized.

With the adoption of the Occupational Safety and Health Act of 1970 (OSH Act),[5] the United States began to address the need to prevent, or minimize, workplace accidents and health hazards. Until then, although there were certain industry-specific protections such as the Coal Mine Health and Safety Act of 1969, there was no national guarantee that workers would be protected from workplace hazards.

The OSH Act created a general duty on the part of every covered employer to maintain a work environment free from "recognized hazards causing or likely to cause death or serious physical harm to employees." It also created a federal agency, the Occupational Safety and Health Administration (OSHA), empowered to oversee safety and health standards, by enforcing the general duty clause and by writing and enforcing detailed health and safety standards for each industry, and the National Institute of Occupational Safety and Health (NIOSH), to provide research, information, education, and training.

While OSHA has clearly contributed to the overall decline in national rates for workplace injuries and deaths since 1973, the agency has been at the center of controversy since its inception.

---

[4] David Rosner and Gerald Markowitz, *Deadly Dust: Silicosis and the Politics of Occupational Disease in Twentieth Century America* (Princeton U. Press, 1991).

[5] 29 U.S.C. Sections 651–678 (1970).

Dr. Michael Silverstein, who worked as the assistant director for industrial safety and health for the state of Washington for eight years, offers this critique:[6]

> *... The business community was angered at the way OSHA's first inspectors began issuing thousands of citations for non-serious violations and labor representatives were equally angered by OSHA's failure to identify and cite serious ones. The situation worsened when OSHA turned hundreds of old and sometimes laughably trivial or obsolete consensus standards into enforceable rules, exposing the new agency to public ridicule....*
>
> *The agency's political problems were compounded by trivially small appropriations and an operational strategy of using its tiny staff to inspect one workplace at a time and to regulate one new hazard at a time....*
>
> *Off to this bad start OSHA ... has never received the funding or achieved the impact Congress intended.*

Silverstein identifies the following kinds of risks that workers face on the job:

> ***First**, many dangers, such as falls from roofs or amputations from unguarded machinery, were widely recognized when the OSH Act was adopted in 1970 and should have been eliminated years ago. Simple means of correcting some of these hazards have actually been well understood for more than two thousand years, as Herodotus described the prevention of fatal trench collapses in his history of the Persian Wars. [cite omitted]*
>
> ***Second**, today's workers face hazards present in 1970 but not fully appreciated by those who wrote the OSH Act, like the forceful exertions, repetitive movements and awkward postures that can cause the work-related musculoskeletal disorders which account for more than 30% of all worker compensation claims and affect workers in virtually every industry and occupation. [cite omitted] Other examples include workplace violence and biohazards.*
>
> ***Third** are genuinely new hazards that have entered the workplace since 1970 such as diacetyl and other food flavorings that cause bronchiolitis obliterans ("popcorn lung") [cite omitted] or modern metalworking fluids that cause hypersensitivity pneumonitis. [cite omitted]*
>
> ***Fourth**, changes in the political, economic, and legal landscape of work since 1970 have brought new safety and health challenges. Globalized businesses, downsized manufacturing, increased outsourcing, reduced pension security, erosion of labor laws, an aging workforce, declining unionization, and growing numbers of recent immigrant workers have altered the nature and experience of work....[7]*

The tools available to OSHA to address these problems are relatively limited: rule setting and safety inspections. Testifying before the Senate in the wake of the West Virginia mining disaster in April 2010, Assistant Director of OSHA David Michaels called for Congress to update the OSH Act to allow the agency to adequately "plan, prevent, and protect."

First, Michaels argued for increasing the monetary penalties—raised only once in 40 years—and enhancing criminal sanctions. Serious violations that pose a substantial probability of death or serious physical harm to workers are subject to a maximum civil penalty of only $7,000. Even willful and repeated violations carry a maximum penalty of

---

[6] Michael Silverstein, "Getting Home Safe and Sound: Occupational Safety and Health Administration at 38," American Journal of Public Health 98(3), March 2008, pp. 416–423.

[7] Id.

only $70,000. That these penalties are nothing more than flea bites is evident in comparison to the power of other agencies: the Department of Agriculture, for example is authorized to impose a fine of up to $130,000 on milk processors for refusing to pay assessments to help advertise and research milk products; the Federal Communications Commission can fine a TV or radio station up to $325,000 for indecent content. Most Federal enforcement agencies have penalties automatically raised to adjust for inflation; OSHA is exempt from that law.

The original criminal penalty provisions of the OSH Act, still in force, are weaker than virtually every other safety, health, and environmental law. Criminal penalties are limited to those cases where a willful violation of an OSHA standard results in the death of a worker and to cases of false statements or misrepresentations. The maximum period of incarceration upon conviction for a violation that costs a worker's life is six months in jail, making these crimes a misdemeanor. In contrast, violators of the Clean Water or Clean Air Act can receive penalties of up to 15 years in prison.

Another major weakness in current law is that OSHA cannot force employers to fix an identified workplace hazard if the employer contests the violation until after the issue is decided, sometimes years after the original citation. Nor can the agency take immediate action to shut down the process or remove employees from harm, even if an inspector identifies an imminent danger, such as a worker in a too-deep trench or at high elevation without fall protection. Instead, the law requires OSHA to seek an injunction in Federal District Court if the employer refuses to voluntarily correct an imminent danger. As Michaels explains, "in contrast, the Mine Act treats imminent danger orders as essentially self-enforcing, requiring mine operators to evacuate miners in the affected area immediately, until the hazard is corrected, and then seek review in the Commission."

■ ■ ■

When three workers at a construction site in Houston, Texas were injured in a gas line explosion, both OSHA and the Texas state health department (TDH) investigated. The OSHA inspector found numerous violations. The most serious was a finding that Erik K. Ho, the owner of the building, had willfully violated his general duty to provide a safe workplace when he ordered a subcontractor to tap into an unmarked pipeline. On behalf of OSHA, Secretary of Labor Elaine Chao—with overall responsibility for OSHA—issued 39 violations against Ho. She also issued violations against Houston Fruitland and Ho Ho Ho Express, two corporations closely tied to Ho.

Asked to enforce the citations, the Occupational Health and Safety Review Commission instead vacated the most serious ones. Chao appealed. Below, the appeals court explains why it will not overturn the Commission's rulings.

CHAO v. OCCUPATIONAL SAFETY AND HEALTH REVIEW COMMISSION
United States Court of Appeals, Fifth Circuit, 2005,
401 F.3d 355

DeMOSS, Circuit Judge.

Background

...On October 27, 1997, Ho individually purchased a defunct hospital and medical office building in Houston to develop the property as residential housing. Ho knew there was asbestos onsite. He was also aware that any alteration to asbestos–containing materials was to be handled by personnel licensed and registered with the Texas Department of

Health ("TDH"). Ho instead hired Manuel Escobedo and Corston Tate, whose ' had previously used, to do the renovations. Escobedo hired 11 Mexican natio' were illegal immigrants, to assist. Renovations, including the removal of asbes' in January 1998.

At most, the workers were occasionally given dust masks not suitable for protec against asbestos. They were not issued protective clothing. Ho also did not provide a respiratory protection program, conduct medical surveillance, conduct asbestos monitoring, implement adequate ventilation or debris removal, inform the workers of the presence and hazards of asbestos, or provide any training whatsoever. There is no dispute that Ho was aware of the worksite conditions; he visited almost every day.

On February 2, 1998, a city inspector visited the worksite. After observing the conditions, he issued a stop-work order citing the possibility of exposure to asbestos, requiring that city approval be given before work could resume. Ho then began negotiating with a licensed contractor, Alamo Environmental, to remove the asbestos....

However, during this period of negotiation, Ho had resumed work at the site under the same conditions, except that he directed all work be performed at night. The workers ate, and some lived, at the site. The workers had no potable water and only one portable toilet.,... Ho continued to visit the worksite and was aware of these conditions.

Asbestos removal continued in this fashion until March 10, 1998. On March 11, 1998, as Ho had directed, daytime work resumed at the site. Ho had been informed that either the sprinkler system or fire hydrant valves had not been turned off and thus remained available for use. To wash out the building, Ho directed Tate to tap into an unmarked valve believed to be a water line. It turned out to be a gas line. An explosion later occurred when Tate started his truck; it injured Tate and two workers. On March 12, 1998, workers were summoned to Ho's office where they were given releases to sign, acknowledging receipt of $1000 as full payment for their work, and acknowledging receipt of $100 to release Ho from any claims that might arise from the explosion and fire. The releases were written in English, but an interpreter translated them for the workers.

After the explosion, TDH conducted an investigation. Samples of debris and the ambient air at the worksite showed levels of asbestos in excess of federal and state standards. The state notified Ho that the site remained unsafe and needed to be sealed by qualified personnel. Again, Ho used the same workers to install plywood over the windows and did not give them any protective equipment....

Piercing the Corporate Veil

[Secretary Chao challenged the OSH Review Commission's finding that there was no basis for citing the corporate entities, Ho Ho Ho Express and Houston Fruitland, Inc. The court begins by explaining the legal doctrine called "piercing the corporate veil."]

In the typical corporate veil piercing scenario, the corporate veil is pierced such that individual shareholders can be held liable for corporate acts. Here, the purpose of piercing the corporate veils of Ho Ho Ho Express, Inc. and Houston Fruitland, Inc. would be to hold the corporations liable for the acts of their individual shareholder, Ho. Therefore, this case presents a "reverse corporate veil piercing" situation. "This slight variation is of no consequence, however, because the end result under both views is the same—two separate entities merge into one for liability purposes." [cite omitted]. If alter ego is shown [i.e. the individual and the corporate are in effect, one entity], courts reverse pierce the corporate veil to treat the individual and the corporation as "one and the same."

[In a precedent case, this court] determined that an alter ego relationship for purposes of reverse veil piercing applies where "there is such unity between corporation and individual that the separateness of the corporation has ceased." [cite omitted]. Factors involved in this test for an alter ego relationship include:

[T]he total dealings of the corporation and the individual, including the degree to which corporate formalities have been followed and corporate and individual property have been kept separately, the amount of financial interest, ownership and

control the individual maintains over the corporation, and whether the corporation has been used for personal purposes....

[Next the appellate court considers the evidence in the record that led the Commission to rule that Houston Fruitland and Ho Ho Ho Express are not the alter egos of defendant Ho.]

The Secretary's contention that Ho Ho Ho Express and Houston Fruitland were "nothing more than incorporated pocketbooks for Ho's personal use" is unfounded. Although Ho clearly involved some of the corporate entities' finances in his hospital project, the record evidence indicates that Ho as the individual in charge of this particular renovation project remained distinct from the [corporations] as ongoing, formalized fruit sale and delivery entities.

While there is evidence that Ho played a role in the corporate Ho Respondents' day-to-day operations, and Ho's personal assistant employed by Ho Ho Ho Express ran some errands for Ho concerning the renovation project, Houston Fruitland and Ho Ho Ho Express still maintained entirely separate corporate identities, tax identities, bank accounts, and legitimate business operations.... [T]he record evidence here indicates that the [corporations] had a limited financial stake in Ho's renovation project, not that they functioned as his alter egos on the renovation project.

Although Ho borrowed from the [corporations] for financing of the hospital project, an admittedly personal pursuit, the record evidence indicates distinct debit ledger entries and some repayment to the corporations by Ho.... [T]here is no evidence that the corporate entities were ever treated or confused as one and the same with the individual Ho or his personal dealings....

We find substantial evidence in the record adequately supporting ... the Commission's findings that Ho Ho Ho Express and Houston Fruitland were not alter egos of Ho to support reverse corporate piercing.

Willful Violation of the General Duty Clause

[Secretary Chao's finding that Ho willfully violated the OSH Act's general duty clause was also overturned on appeal to the OSH Review Commission. Next the court must decide if it agrees with Chao's original finding or with the agency review panel.]

OSH Act requires employers to free their workplaces of "recognized hazards that are causing or are likely to cause death or serious physical harm to ... employees." The specific general duty citation here arose from the explosion of natural gas released by tapping an unmarked valve. A willful violation is one committed voluntarily, with either intentional disregard of, or plain-indifference to, OSH Act requirements.... In contrast, "[t]he gravamen of a 'serious' violation is the presence of a "substantial probability that a particular violation could result in death or serious physical harm." The employer's intent to violate an OSH Act standard is irrelevant to find a serious violation....

Though Ho's pattern of illegal work practices may have been conscious, and his asbestos–related OSH Act violations found to be willful this does not compel a finding of willfulness as to his specific instruction to open the unmarked valve. Therefore, because the Commission's legal determination as to Ho's lack of willfulness was neither arbitrary, capricious, nor an abuse of discretion, and accords with law, we accept its conclusion.

[HELD: Commission's decision is affirmed.]

EMILIO M. GARZA, Circuit Judge, dissenting:

...Courts need to look beyond formalities and records to determine the true economic relationship between the entities.... In *Jon-T Chemicals*, the court dismissed the formality of recording paid expenses as loans because "whenever [one company] could not pay its bills, [the other company] did so by writing a check." The companies shared an accounting department and "funds were transferred between the different [companies'] accounts in order to cover deficiencies." That is precisely what happened here. The Ho Entities shared one bookkeeper who notified Ho when one account was deficient; Ho would then transfer the funds to cover the deficiency of the other company.

The evidence shows that Ho has complete control over the Ho Entities. Ho owns two-thirds of the stock and is president of both companies. The Ho Entities advanced the vast majority of Ho's personal investment of the property. In addition, the Ho Entities provided funds for the workers' wages and for supplies and equipment. Converting a hospital into residential units has nothing to do with the Ho Entities' business purposes of transportation and fruit sales. While the frequent transfers among the Ho Entities and Ho were documented as debts, there were no loan documents, no interest due, no schedule for re-payment and no representation of debt repayment. Accordingly, I believe that substantial evidence supports a finding that the Ho Entities were Ho's alter egos....

Ho conceded that tapping into an unmarked pipe at a demolition site was a "recognized hazard." Instructing his employees to tap an unmarked pipe—"a recognized hazard"—evidences a plain indifference to the General Duty Clause. Even without the benefit of hindsight, it is self-evident that tapping an unmarked pipe is "likely to cause death or serious physical harm." Therefore, the Commission abused its discretion by finding Ho's violation of the General Duty Clause "serious" instead of "willful." Accordingly, I would vacate the Commission's order reducing the General Duty Clause violation to serious from willful.

For the above stated reasons, I respectfully dissent.

QUESTIONS

1. What is meant by "piercing the corporate veil?" On what basis did the majority decide not to pierce the corporate veil in this case? How does the dissent respond?

2. What is required for a "willful" violation of the OSH Act's general duty clause? For a "serious" violation? Why does the majority uphold the Commission's rule that the violation in this case was not willful? On what basis would the dissent have reversed the Commission's holding?

3. Congress is not alone in determining how government will regulate workplace safety and health. The executive branch—from the President to administrative agencies like OSHA and MSHA—also plays a role. During the Bush administration in the mid-2000s, OSHA withdrew dozens of proposed safety and health rules, including measures that would have regulated indoor air quality, glycol ethers, and lock-out of hazardous equipment in construction. Similarly, 17 safety and health rules were withdrawn at MSHA, including rules on mine rescue teams and self-contained self-rescuers. Only three significant new OSHA standards were adopted during that 8-year period, and two were issued only as a result of litigation. Despite pressure from labor and others, OSHA failed to adopt new rules regarding combustible dust or the chemical diacetyl, a butter flavoring agent used in microwave popcorn and other foods that has caused a rare and fatal lung disease ["popcorn lung"] in exposed workers. Under the Obama administration, resources for standard-setting have been increased and an ambitious regulatory agenda has been put forward, including final standards on cranes and derricks, a proposed rule on silica, and rules on diacetyl, infectious diseases, and combustible dust. What values underlie these differing approaches? Can you make an ethical argument of behalf of each approach?

4. When the UBB mine exploded in Spring 2010, the MSHA was authorized to withdraw miners or equipment from operations for imminently dangerous conditions, failure to abate a cited hazard within a specified time period, or an "unwarrantable" failure to comply with a safety rule. But the agency could not permanently shut down a mine. While MSHA can enhance penalties for a repeated pattern of violations, contested violations do not count as part of the pattern. Criminal violations are a misdemeanor, subject to a maximum one-year sentence. **Research**: Find out if Congress has done anything to address these loopholes in the mine safety laws. Have there been any changes in the executive branch, including MSHA since the UBB disaster?

■ ■ ■

Perspectives on Risk in the Workplace

Risks never exist in isolation. They are part of systems. For that reason, any effort to reduce a single risk will have a range of consequences, some of them likely unintended....

If the Occupational Safety and Health Administration ("OSHA") increases regulation of benzene, a carcinogenic substance, it might lead companies to use a less safe, or perhaps even an unsafe, substitute; it might also decrease the wages of affected workers, and decrease the number of jobs in the relevant industry. People who have less money, and who are unemployed, tend to live shorter lives and hence occupational regulation might, under certain circumstances, sacrifice more lives than it saves. Of course the unintended consequences of risk regulation might be desirable rather than undesirable as, for example, when regulation spurs new pollution-control technologies.

— CASS R. SUNSTEIN[8]

From sudden deadly accidents, like the explosion of the Deep Horizon in the Gulf of Mexico, to the gradual onset of carpal tunnel syndrome from repetitive motions such as data processing or butchering, workers face a wide array of risks. Many of the worst hazards are invisible, like the chemical exposures that threaten the reproductive capacities of both men and women. Those who work in dry cleaners and laundries face carbon disulfide and benzene. Health workers—in hospitals, clinics, and dentist offices—are exposed to infectious diseases and radiation from x-ray machines. Mercury, cadmium, coal tar, carbon tetrachloride, and vinyl chloride are risks for production line workers. Computer assemblers breathe toxic dust; taxi drivers breathe carbon monoxide.

■ ■ ■

In the following case, the court must weigh an individual's willingness to risk his own health against a company's efforts to ensure a safe working environment.

ECHAZABAL v. CHEVRON USA, INC.
United States Court of Appeals, Ninth Circuit, 2000
226 F.3d 1063

REINHARDT, Circuit Judge.

Mario Echazabal first began working at Chevron's oil refinery in El Segundo, California in 1972. Employed by various maintenance contractors, he worked at the refinery, primarily in the coker unit, nearly continuously until 1996, when the events that gave rise to this litigation occurred.

In 1992, Echazabal applied to work directly for Chevron at the same coker unit location.... A pre-employment physical examination conducted by Chevron's regional physician revealed that Echazabal's liver was releasing certain enzymes at a higher than normal level. Based on these results, Chevron concluded that Echazabal's liver might be damaged by exposure to the solvents and chemicals present in the coker unit. For that reason, Chevron rescinded its job offer. Nevertheless, Echazabal continued to work for Irwin, a maintenance contractor, throughout the refinery including at the coker unit. Chevron made no effort to have him removed from his assignment.

---

[8] "Cost-Benefit Default Principles," 99 *Mich. L. Rev.* 1651 (2001).

In 1995, Echazabal again applied to Chevron for a position at the coker unit. Again, the job offer was rescinded because of the risk that his liver would be damaged if he worked in the coker unit. This time, however, Chevron wrote Irwin and asked that it "immediately remove Mr. Echazabal from [the] refinery or place him in a position that eliminates his exposure to solvents/chemicals."

[Echazabal claimed that Chevron's refusal to allow him to work in the coker unit was illegal discrimination under the Americans with Disabilities Act (ADA) based on his disability—his diagnosed Hepatitis C. Chevron tried to raise the "direct threat defense," arguing that if Echazabal worked in the coker unit he would present a "direct threat" to his own health. The court first looks at the language of the statute:] The direct threat defense permits employers to impose a "requirement that an individual shall not pose a direct threat to the health or safety of other individuals in the workplace." On its face, the provision does not include direct threats to the health or safety of the disabled individual himself....

Although we need not rely on it, the legislative history of the ADA also supports the conclusion that the direct threat provision does not include threats to oneself....

Congress's decision not to include threats to one's own health or safety in the direct threat defense makes good sense in light of the principles that underlie the ADA in particular and federal employment discrimination law in general.... [T]he ADA was designed in part to prohibit discrimination against individuals with disabilities that takes the form of paternalism....

Chevron suggests that we must ignore Congress's clear intent because forcing employers to hire individuals who pose a risk to their own health or safety would expose employers to tort liability.... [G]iven that the ADA prohibits employers from refusing to hire individuals solely on the ground that their health or safety may be threatened by the job, state tort law would likely be preempted if it interfered with this requirement. Moreover, we note that Chevron's concern over an award of damages reflects a fear that hiring a disabled individual will cost more than hiring an individual without any disabilities. The extra cost of employing disabled individuals does not in itself provide an affirmative defense to a discriminatory refusal to hire those individuals....

[W]e conclude that the ADA's direct threat defense means what it says: it permits employers to impose a requirement that their employees not pose a significant risk to the health or safety of other individuals in the workplace. It does not permit employers to shut disabled individuals out of jobs on the ground that, by working in the jobs at issue, they may put their own health or safety at risk. Conscious of the history of paternalistic rules that have often excluded disabled individuals from the workplace, Congress concluded that disabled persons should be afforded the opportunity to decide for themselves what risks to undertake. [Held:] The district court's grant of summary judgment to Chevron on Echazabal's ADA claim is reversed.

TROTT, Circuit Judge, dissenting.

Mario Echazabal sues over not getting a job handling liver-toxic substances.... He was denied the job because he suffers from a chronic, uncorrectable, and life-threatening viral liver disease, Hepatitis C, that most likely will be aggravated by exposure to these hazardous materials to the extent that his life will be endangered.

[Under the ADA, employers are not required to hire disabled individuals unless they are "otherwise qualified" to handle the "essential functions" of the job.] ... Mr. Echazabal simply is not "otherwise qualified" for the work he seeks. Why? Because the job most probably will endanger his life. I do not understand how we can claim he can perform the essential functions of the position he seeks when precisely because of his disability, those functions may kill him. To ignore this reality is bizarre....

Our law books, both state and federal, overflow with statutes and rules designed by representative governments to protect workers from harm long before we rejected the idea that workers toil at their own peril in the workplace. "Paternalism" here is just an abstract out-of-place label of no analytical help. Whether paternalism or maternalism, the concept is pernicious when it is allowed to dislodge longstanding laws mandating work-place safety. That battle was fought and lost long ago in our legislatures. In many jurisdictions, it is a crime knowingly to subject workers to life-endangering conditions.... In effect, we repeal these laws with respect to [Echazabal], and to other workers in similar situations. So much for OSHA. Now, our laws give less protection to workers known to be in danger than they afford to those who are not. That seems upside down and backwards. Precisely the workers who need protection can sue because they receive what they need....

I believe it would be an undue hardship to require an employer to place an employee in a life-threatening situation. Such a rule would require employers knowingly to endanger workers. The legal peril involved is obvious, and as a simple human to human matter, such a moral burden is unconscionable. [I dissent.]

QUESTIONS

1. Look again at the facts offered by both the majority and the dissent. Why do you think Echazabal was willing to risk his health by working in the coker unit? Assuming he had a complete grasp of the risks involved, is it ethical to allow him to work there? For this, re-examine the frameworks for ethical decision making in Chapter 1.

2. Chevron gave certain reasons for refusing to allow Echazabal to work in the coker unit. Name them. Can you think of any other reasons the company may have had for that decision?

3. **Research**: On appeal, the Supreme Court reversed. Justice Souter explained why: "The EEOC was certainly acting within the reasonable zone when it saw a difference between rejecting workplace paternalism and ignoring specific and documented risks to the employee himself, even if the employee would take his chances for the sake of getting a job." *Chevron USA Inc. v. Echazabal*, 536 U.S. 73, 122 S.Ct. 2045 (2002). The "direct threat defense" is allowable, according to the Court, when it is based on a "'reasonable medical judgment that relies on the most current medical knowledge and/or the best available objective evidence,' and upon an expressly 'individualized assessment of the individual's present ability to safely perform the essential functions of the job....'" Find out how the lower courts applied the test when they revisited *Echazabal* on remand from the Supreme Court. Are you satisfied that Chevron's decisions were not based on the kind of pretextual stereotypes at which the ADA is aimed?

4. In this case, we see both the company and the employee between a rock and a hard place. Echazabal must choose to either further endanger his health or lose a coveted opportunity, while Chevron is caught between liability under the ADA and liability for unsafe work conditions. Suppose you were a top manager inside Chevron, responsible for strategic planning on workplace safety. Is there anything you and your firm could do to prevent or minimize the risk of this type of scenario from developing in the future?

5. In the 1990s Johnson Controls was similarly accused of paternalism for banning fertile women from working on a battery-making production line where exposure to lead could cause harm to future offspring. In *International Union v. Johnson Controls (1991)* the Supreme Court held that this restriction amounted to illegal sex discrimination under Title VII, writing that female workers should "not be forced to choose between having a child and having a job." The company had argued it was concerned about harm to future generations, but the Court wrote: "Decisions about the welfare of future children must be left to the parents who conceive, bear, support, and raise them rather than to the employers who hire those parents." Who are the stakeholders in this controversy? Are they the same as those in *Echazabal v. Chevron*?

■ ■ ■

THE STATE OF WORKERS' SAFETY AND HEALTH

"Death on the Job: The Toll of Neglect" 2010
AFL-CIO

- 5,214 workers lost their lives on the job in 2008 as a result of traumatic injury.
- 50,000–60,000 workers die of occupational illnesses every year.
- On average, every day 14 workers are fatally injured.
- More than 12,696 workers wre injured or made ill each day in 2008.
- More than 4.6 million workers across all industries, including state and local government, had work-related injuries and illnesses in 2008.
- Estimated costs of injuries and illnesses: $156 billion to $312 billion a year.
- In 2009, there were 2,218 federal and state OSHA inspectors responsible for enforcing the law at approximately 8 million workplaces.
- At its current staffing and inspection levels, it would take federal OSHA 137 years to inspect each workplace under its jurisdiction just once.
- The current level of federal and state OSHA inspectors provides one inspector for every 60,723 workers. This compares with a benchmark of one labor inspector for every 10,000 workers recommended by the International Labor Organization for industrialized countries.

Corporate Criminal Liability

Few employers in the United States have been held criminally responsible for even the most egregious workplace injuries and deaths.

For most of its history, OSHA rarely invoked its legal authority to bring criminal actions. Convictions were relatively few, and penalties light. Since the OSH Act was passed in 1970, there have been more than 360,000 workplace fatalities, but only 79 criminal prosecutions, resulting in defendants serving a total of 89 months in jail. In 2009, 11 were cases referred by the Department of Labor for possible criminal prosecution. The Department of Justice (DOJ) declined to prosecute two of these cases; the other nine were still under review in spring 2010. By comparison, there were more criminal enforcement cases brought by the EPA in 2009 (387), resulting in more jail time (76 years) and fines ($96 million) than during OSHA's entire forty-year history.[9]

In the face of weak criminal enforcement at the federal level, some state prosecutors sought indictments under state criminal laws to address the most horrific situations. The first state prosecution, *People v. O'Neil*[10] was brought after a worker extracting silver from used x-ray film died of cyanide poisoning. The employees of that company, most of whom were non-English-speaking illegal immigrants, were deceived about the hazards of working with cyanide. They were working in an area with inadequate ventilation and were supplied with virtually none of the safety equipment required by law. Both the company and its owners were initially found guilty of murder, but the convictions were overturned on technical grounds in 1990.

---

[9] Source: "Death on the Job: The Toll of Neglect" 2010. AFL-CIO.

[10] 550 N.E.2d 109 (Ill. App. Ct. 1990).

The *O'Neil* outcome is typical of cases prosecuted under state criminal codes. The president, plant manager, and foreman of Chicago-Magnet were charged with aggravated battery when they exposed 42 employees to poisonous and stupefying substances in the workplace. But, after the longest trial in Illinois history, they were acquitted. In another widely publicized case, *People v. Pymm Thermometer*, a jury found the owners of a Brooklyn-based silver reclamation company guilty of assault with a deadly weapon for knowingly exposing workers to mercury. Their sentence: weekend jail for 6 months and a $10,000 fine.

Compensation for Workplace Injury and Illness

Even under the best of circumstances, workplace injuries and illnesses are not going to disappear entirely. Most often in the United States, those who suffer such harms must look to statutory remedies provided by state laws.

For the most part, occupational injuries and illnesses are covered by state workers' compensation statutes. These statutory schemes were adopted in the United States during the period 1911–1925, first in the more industrialized states and gradually throughout the nation. Effective in ameliorating some of the conflict between management and employees over the social and economic costs of accidental injuries, the details varied from state to state. In general, however, they were designed to provide a limited, "no-fault" recovery.

Firms contribute to a workers' compensation fund that is used to pay benefits to employees accidentally injured in the workplace. Instead of suing, an employee's legal task is simplified. She need only file a claim indicating that she was hurt in the course of her employment; she need not prove the company was negligent, nor can the company raise any of the traditional defenses to negligence to defeat her claim.

Employers are willing to accept this approach because there is a trade-off: if workers' compensation covers an injury, the employee cannot choose to bring a negligence suit, hoping a jury will award large damages. This is the **exclusivity rule**, so-called because the employee's only—or "exclusive"—remedy lies with workers' compensation. Payments are set by a formula that generally provides less than the actual wages lost, and no provision is made for the kind of award that could reach high numbers in a tort suit—for pain and suffering, loss of consortium, or punitive damages.

Today, workers' compensation is widely criticized as anachronistic and unworkable. Besides the claim that the exclusivity rule is unfair where harm is intentional, there are other contentious issues: whether an injury occurred in the "course of employment;" whether a work-related disability is whole or partial, temporary or permanent; and whether an employer should pay for items not covered by workers' compensation statutes, such as property damage or mental anguish in the absence of physical harm. Whenever these issues arise, there is a chance that one party will insist on judicial resolution. In some states, workers' compensation cases languish in the courts for as many as 10 years. And, critics point out, most disability, health, and life insurance policies offer far more extensive coverage than the limited amounts available under worker's compensation, yet many firms are required to carry liability insurance to cover acts of negligence, forcing them to pay separate premiums for duplicative policies that may not even provide employees with the intended coverage.

■ ■ ■

In some states, injured construction workers may have an alternative to worker's compensation: an industry-specific remedy. Jose Raimundo Madeira, plaintiff in the next case, sued a construction site owner, Affordable Housing (Affordable) and the general contractor (Mountain) for violations of New York's Scaffold Law. Defendants, in turn, sued the subcontractor, C&L Construction Company ("C&L"), that had hired Madeira. In the case that follows, the court must address this issue: What happens, if the injured employee seeking benefits is an undocumented immigrant?

MADEIRA v. AFFORDABLE HOUSING FOUNDATION, INC.
United States Court of Appeals, Second Circuit, 2006
469 F.3d 219

RAGGI, Circuit Judge.

...Plaintiff Jose Raimundo Madeira is a citizen of Brazil who illegally entered the United States in 1998. In Brazil, Madeira had worked in a factory earning approximately $175 per month; he had also labored briefly on his parents' farm without formal remuneration. In the United States, Madeira fared better, working consistently as a construction laborer, largely through the efforts of his brother, Paulo Miranda. As a supervisor for C & L, Miranda had authority to hire workers to perform that party's subcontracts. In the years prior to the accident here at issue, Madeira was earning approximately $15 per hour in the United States and working as many as 50 hours per week....

Although Madeira was generally paid in cash for his work, he testified that he paid income taxes on his earnings by using a taxpayer identification number.... Madeira further stated that, sometime in 2000, he attempted to legitimize his work status by applying for a Social Security card and work permit but, at the time of trial in 2004, those applications had not yet been acted on.

On June 20, 2001, while working as a roofer for C & L, Madeira fell from the top of a building at a development site in Monroe, New York, sustaining serious injuries that required four surgeries and more than three months' hospitalization. At the time of trial, Madeira was still substantially disabled, particularly in walking. Following his accident, Madeira ... [sued] Affordable, the owner of the construction site, and Mountain, the development's general contractor, for their alleged failure to provide adequate safety equipment at the work site in violation of New York's "Scaffold Law." ...

The jury proceeded to find both Affordable and Mountain liable ... [and] awarded Madeira $638,671.63 in total compensatory damages, consisting of $92,651.63 in incurred expenses; $46,000 for past pain and suffering; $40,020 in past lost earnings; $230,000 for future pain and suffering (over the course of forty–two years); and $230,000 for future lost earnings (over the course of twenty–six years).... Only the past and future lost earnings awards are at issue on this appeal. From the fact that the future lost earnings award represents far more than Madeira would likely have earned in Brazil in the specified twenty–six years, but considerably less than he could have earned in the United States over the same time, one can reasonably infer that the jury concluded that, but for his injury, Madeira would have remained and worked in the United States, but only for a limited period....

[W]e note at the outset that no party here disputes the fact of Madeira's injury ... or Madeira's right to be compensated for incurred expenses and past and future pain and suffering....

[However, a]ppellants submit that, if an injured undocumented worker can recover any lost earnings, it is only at the rates he could have earned in his native country....

It is well established that the states enjoy "broad authority under their police powers to regulate ... employment relationship[s] to protect workers within the State." ...This includes "the power to enact 'laws affecting occupational health and safety.'" ... Pursuant to this power, New York, like many states, has enacted various laws to compensate workers who sustain workplace injuries.

Most obviously, New York's Workers' Compensation Law requires employers to "pay or provide compensation [to employees] for their disability or death from injury arising out of and in the course of the employment without regard to fault as a cause of the injury."
... This "statute was designed to provide a swift and sure source of benefits to the injured employee." ..."The price for these secure benefits is the [employee's] loss of the common–law tort action [against his employer] in which greater benefits might be obtained."

New York does not, however, rely only on workers' compensation awards to promote workplace safety and compensate injury. Mindful of the particular dangers of construction work, the state has long imposed absolute liability for personal injury on those site owners and general contractors who fail to provide adequate safety equipment to all persons working at construction sites.... This liability applies regardless of the fact that the injured worker may be in the direct employ of a party other than the defendant contractor or owner. As the New York Court of Appeals recently explained, [N.Y. Scaffold Law] seeks to place "ultimate responsibility for safety practices at building construction sites where such responsibility actually belongs, on the owner and general contractor, instead of on workers, who are scarcely in a position to protect themselves from accident." ...

New York law not only holds site owners and general contractors absolutely liable for personal injuries resulting from a violation of [its Scaffold Law]; it specifically extends the protections of that law to injured undocumented workers.

[The courts have created a legal rule known as federal preemption, based on the Supremacy Clause of the U.S. Constitution ("The Laws of the United States ... shall be the supreme Law of the Land."). Under this legal doctrine, Congress can "preempt" an area of law by specifically indicating that states may not adopt their own legislation. Where Congress has not specifically deprived the states of power to act, however, the courts must determine whether or not Congress nonetheless intended to preempt state laws. Here, defendants argue that the federal immigration law preempts New York state law allowing undocumented workers injured in construction accidents to recover compensatory damages for lost United States earnings. The court, however, disagrees.]

The federal government exercises supreme power in the field of foreign affairs, including "immigration, naturalization, and deportation." ...

[The Immigration Reform Control Act of 1986, or IRCA] makes it unlawful for employers knowingly to hire unauthorized aliens. To ensure against such hiring, IRCA mandates employer verification of the legal status of persons hired. Employers who fail to check their workers' immigration status or who fail to keep eligibility records face civil fines.

Employers who engage in a pattern or practice of knowingly employing undocumented aliens are subject to criminal penalties.

Not until IRCA was itself amended in 1990 did Congress provide for penalties and sanctions to be imposed directly on undocumented workers who sought employment in the United States.... Even then, however, Congress made IRCA's new sanctions applicable only to aliens who knowingly or recklessly used false documents to obtain employment. It did not otherwise prohibit undocumented aliens from seeking or maintaining employment.

Congress can convey its clear and manifest intent to preempt the exercise of state police power in three ways. First, Congress may explicitly state that it intends to preempt a state law.... Second, even absent any such explicit statement, Congress's preemptive intent may be implied "where the scheme of federal regulation is sufficiently comprehensive to make reasonable the inference that Congress 'left no room' for supplementary state regulation," in short, where Congress has manifested an intent for federal law to occupy the field.... Finally, Congress's preemptive intent may be implied from the fact that state law so conflicts with federal law that..."compliance with both federal and state regulations is a physical impossibility." ...

It is not physically impossible to comply with both IRCA and New York labor law, and appellants have failed convincingly to demonstrate that New York law, as applied in this case, stands as a definite and positive obstacle to the accomplishment and execution of the full purposes and objectives of Congress. Accordingly, we reject appellants' claim of conflict preemption as without merit and uphold the damages awarded at the first phase of trial.

QUESTIONS

1. Under what law did Madeira seek damages? On what basis did the company object? What reasons does the Court give for allowing the plaintiff to claim damages despite his status as an undocumented immigrant?

2. The construction industry has long had the largest number of fatal work injuries—many due to falls—of any sector of the economy. This remained true in 2008, although the number of deaths had declined. What might account for that decline in numbers?

3. Construction is a $26 billion industry in New York City, even in the midst of recession. In March 2008, seven people were killed when a 22-story tower crane crashed across two blocks of midtown Manhattan. Investigators found that the rigging company that was raising the crane had not inspected the nylon slings used to hoist the massive equipment and failed to follow the manufacturer's specifications. City officials ordered a sweep of all cranes in the city. Then in May 2008, two construction workers were killed when another crane collapsed. In March 2009, a construction worker who was not wearing a harness fell to his death from the tenth floor of a hotel. In June 2010, New York's former Chief Crane Inspector was sentenced to two-to-six years in prison for bribery, after approving cranes he had not inspected and issuing operating licenses to people who had not earned them. Are there special ethical issues that arise when construction companies give safety short shrift in dense urban areas?

4. The judge in the *Madeira* case mentions the Immigration Reform Control Act or IRCA, which the appellants' argued preempted New York's Scaffold Law. IRCA requires employers to pay fines if they fail to check on the immigration status of workers. **Research**: Can you find out if employers generally abide by this law? Any fines lately?

■ ■ ■

Safety Concerns in the Global Economy

Fundamentally, there are only two ways of coordinating the economic activity of millions. One is central direction involving the use of coercion—the technique of the army and of the modern totalitarian state. The other is voluntary cooperation of individuals—the technique of the marketplace.

— MILTON FRIEDMAN (1962)

Sweatshop exploitation is modern globalized capitalism stripped bare.

HTTP://WWW.NOSWEAT.ORG.UK (2004)

Labor, like capital, data and goods, crosses national boundaries with increasing ease. Products may be designed in one country, built in another (with components from still others), and then marketed around the world. Few would quarrel with the International Covenant on Economic, Social and Cultural Rights—that everyone has a right to safe and healthy working conditions, to form and join trade unions, to take other appropriate steps to safeguard the right to a livelihood. Yet, as the next series of readings makes clear, there is little consensus as to how to ensure those rights for what has become a global workforce.

Twenty-First Century Slavery

As the 2010 celebration of the Fourth of July approached, front-page headlines in THE PHILADELPHIA INQUIRER read: "Slave labor charged here."[11] Authorities indicted five Ukrainian brothers for luring mostly male migrants from the Ukraine with the promise of jobs, food and housing. Instead, they were kept in involuntary servitude, working 16-hour days cleaning at Target, Kmart, Walmart and Safeway stores throughout the northeast for seven years.

According to Kevin Bales, a scholar and activist trying to build a global coalition to end slavery, there were an estimated 27 million slaves in the world in 2002. Bales explains that this count does not include sweatshop workers or those who are just extremely poor, but "people who are controlled by violence, who cannot walk away." While this is a definition that would encompass slavery in the American pre-Civil War South, Bales notes the important difference between slavery then and now:

> Historically, the investment of purchasing a slave gave incentive for the master to provide a minimum standard of care, to ensure the slave would be healthy enough to work and generate profit for the long term. Today, slaves are extremely cheap and abundant, and thus disposable. Today the interest is not in "owning" slaves, only in controlling them—through violence or the threat of it. A slave is exploited for as long as he or she is profitable; then discarded.

The lack of legal ownership, Bales has written, is a benefit to slaveholders today, "because they get total control without any responsibility for what they own."

In the following interview, Kevin Bales discusses modern slavery and what can be done to end it. He begins by talking about why we are facing a situation where there are so many so-called "disposable people":

> Vulnerability is the key here. When subsistence farmers are driven out of the countryside because they've been replaced by cash crop agribusiness, and they end up in cardboard shacks in shantytowns around developing world cities … they don't have their temple or church, their extended family or the village network—all that gets lost.… [T]hey're economically vulnerable because they can't get work.… They're physically vulnerable because they can't protect themselves from people who have weapons, and they're legally vulnerable because the police won't enforce the law.…

SLAVERY: ALIVE AND THRIVING IN THE WORLD TODAY
Interview with Kevin Bales[12]

What Are the Most Typical Types of Modern Slavery?

Debt bondage is the most common kind of enslavement around the world, concentrating in South Asia, [most commonly] …"collateral" debt bondage: when you borrow money, you and all of your family … become collateral.… In India I've met families in their fourth generation of bondage—a great-grandfather borrowed

---

[11] Nathan Gorenstein, "Slave labor charged here," THE PHILADELPHIA INQUIRER, p.1, July 1, 2010.

[12] Slavery: Alive and Thriving in the World Today: Interview with Kevin Bales by Rachel Cernansky from SATYA MAGAZINE, January 2003. Used by permission.

$20 worth of rupees ... and because the family and all their work is collateral against the debt, there's no way that you can get the money to pay it back....

In the developing world, particularly in small communities that are not necessarily literate, a person's word and reputation are extremely important to them. It means that there's a culture of honesty ... and slaveholders will use that to trick people, to talk to them in a way that makes it sound like there's just a loan ... and it's all fair.... [Even though they] ... recognize the fact they're enslaved, they feel a responsibility to keep their word....

What Are Some Examples of Modern Slavery?

Thailand is an excellent example because it has gone through rapid changes and is highly integrated into the global economy. Here you have young women enslaved into brothels who clearly demonstrate the impact of the low cost of slaves. In world terms, they're pretty expensive—one of these women, 14 to 15 years old, costs $800 to $2,000. At that price, and because they are forced to have sex with ten to 15 people a day—what is really a kind of serial rape—they generate enormous profits, something like 850 percent profit a year for the people who procured them. But these girls ... only last two, three or four years. They become HIV positive or a cocktail of sexually transmitted diseases, they are brutalized, or their mental health diminishes to the point where they can't function anymore, or all of those things mixed together. So after three or four years, they are, in a sense, useless and are just thrown away....

It Seems so Far Removed, How Does Slavery Touch Our Own Lives?

...When you go to Walmart, for example, the stuff you find there is really cheap, so cheap that if you think about it, you think how on earth could this be?

In Brazil, we know that people are enslaved making charcoal used by the steel industry, which is a major export from Brazil. We know that American companies are invested in Brazilian steel and in the land where forests are destroyed to make charcoal. American companies are invested in beef and timber from Brazil; and slaves are used to log timber and to prepare the land for the cattle and care for them and so forth. There's two, three, five—who knows how many—links in that chain, and it's hard for us to actually trace them.

There's a parallel here with multinational corporations that subcontract out to factories using sweatshop labor, which distances them from exploitation and shifts the blame.

Slavery is even further down the line than the factories. It occurs in very small units; you rarely—if ever—find a factory full of slaves. The factory may be a sweatshop, but the raw materials or bits coming into a factory may have come up from slave labor.

Can You Give a More Specific Example of How Slavery is Linked to Our Daily Lives?

Cocoa's an easy one—the Ivory Coast is the world's largest exporter of cocoa, and it flows directly into the U.S.... [We've] discovered horrific enslavement of young men, mostly economic migrants from Mali, who'd come down looking for work and had been forced into slavery on farms growing cocoa....

Hasn't Legislation Related to that Been Passed by Congress?

This is extremely interesting. There was an amendment that would have required labeling of chocolate as slave-free; but it was withdrawn because it would have been impossible to determine—it's this problem again of tracing the product chains. It is currently impossible to determine precisely which cocoa is slave-free. Anybody who has that label wouldn't actually be able to prove that. It was also withdrawn because the chocolate industry agreed to work directly with human rights groups, antislavery organizations, and trade unions to eradicate the problem.... Now we finally have an industry that says, Yes, we take moral, economic, social responsibility for our product chain....

[A]nti-Globalization Activists ... Attack the Globalized Economy for Driving the Bottom Line at the Expense of Human Rights. Is Slavery the Epitome of that Type of Human Exploitation?

...Slavery is not essential to the global economy. The productive capacity of slaves, as I calculate it, is something like $13 billion a year in the global economy, which is nothing.... There's a positive side to globalization as well.... [T]he concepts of human rights are becoming globalized.... [W]hen I'm in rural India, where people are illiterate, and they blurt out in English, "Universal Declaration of Human Rights." They know what it means—they don't know precisely what those English words mean, but they think about human rights.

What Are International Bodies Doing?

There's a new UN convention on human trafficking giving every country that adopts it ... an agreed definition of what they're working on and suggests ways for it to be effective. A lot of countries are rewriting their laws so that they match each other's.

How Receptive Has the U.S. Government Been? What Kind of Success Have You Seen?

...Administrations change, but ... the people who actually manage the projects and programs, who work overseas, or work in the customs service to inspect for slave-made goods—to them it doesn't matter which political party's in power. They're trying very hard, they're doing very good things about slavery.

What Do You See as Hope for Change?

The number of slaves is very high, but the cost of actually helping people out of slavery is very low. Sending an activist around India, for example, to talk to people about alternatives to their bondage is very cheap. When the resources are there it can be done. It may sound crazy after talking about such huge numbers, but with sufficient mobilization this really could be the generation that brings slavery virtually to an end—for the first time in human history....

QUESTIONS

1. What impact might global slavery have on the health and safety conditions of ordinary workers?

2. In FY 2009, the Human Trafficking Prosecution Unit, a specialized anti-trafficking unit of the U.S. Department of Justice, charged 114 individuals with human trafficking, winning 47 convictions. What efforts are being made by international and nongovernmental groups to abolish this trade? Start by looking at the UN's "blue heart campaign" against human trafficking.

3. **Research**: Elsewhere in this interview, Bales talks about the fair trade movement as a means of altering the demand component of the global economic equation and of helping to eradicate modern slavery. What is the fair trade movement? How exactly might its activities impact slavery today?

4. In the mid-1990s villagers brought suit against the multinational energy giant, Unocal, for atrocities committed during the laying of a pipeline in Southeast Asia. There were allegations of land confiscation and forced labor, with the Myanmar military threatening to kill those who would resist. There was testimony that one

man was shot as he tried to escape the project, and in retaliation his wife and child were thrown into a fire; the baby died. Other witnesses described how villagers who would not work or who became too weak to work were summarily executed.

Plaintiffs brought suit under a federal statute, the Alien Tort Claims Act (ATCA), which allows non-citizens to sue in the U.S. courts for wrongs committed in violation of the law of nations. The defendants in ATCA cases are most often governments or officials accused of human rights abuses. Increasingly, however, suits have been brought against multinational corporations: Nigerian citizens sued Chevron in 1999 for human rights atrocities against activists protesting Chevron's safety and environmental record; in 2001, Exxon-Mobil was sued for killings and torture committed by the military security forces protecting and paid for by the company's operation in Indonesia.

Plaintiffs in the *Unocal* case sought to hold the company accountable for knowingly looking the other way as the military regime in Myanmar used rape and torture to intimidate local villagers into working on its pipeline.

While the *Unocal* case was ongoing, in 2004 the U.S. Supreme Court held that ATCA cases had to involve human rights violations that are "specific, universal and obligatory" under international law—crimes like genocide, enslavement, or torture. Not surprisingly, both sides predicted the precedent would benefit them. (a) What ethical theory might justify the use of U.S. courts to punish corporations for indirect involvement in human rights abuses? **Research**: (a) Find out what has happened in the *Unocal* case. (b) What other litigation involving multinational companies is discussed on the Business and Human Rights Resource Center's site?

5. Child and forced labor is widespread in agriculture in Central Asia according to a July 2010 report issued by Human Rights Watch. The group singled out Philip Morris, however, for buying tobacco from a farm in Kazakhstan, where conditions are particularly egregious: children as young as 10 develop rashes from harvesting tobacco; laborers without access to potable water drink from irrigation channels contaminated with pesticides; and tobacco field laborers are exposed to high levels of nicotine while doing their work. To what extent should a company be responsible for the working conditions of its suppliers? **Research**: Find out how Philip Morris responded to the report.

6. In what some have called the "feminization of migration," close to half of the world's 120 million legal and illegal migrants are believed to be women, who overwhelmingly work as maids, domestics, and nannies. Noreena Nesa describes her working conditions in the Washington, D.C. area in 2000:[13]

> *Imagine you are locked away in a strange home. You do not speak your captor's language. On the rare occasions when you are escorted off the premises, you are forbidden to speak to anyone. You are often fed the leftover food of the children you are required to watch while completing your around-the-clock household duties. You have never been paid for your labors, and the woman of the house physically abuses you.*

The extremes—slavery and human trafficking—can be prosecuted as criminal offenses. More common abuses—long hours, inadequate pay, unsafe conditions in the home itself—are difficult to police since domestic servants are not covered by most American labor laws. Should they be?

---

[13] Joy M. Zarembka, "America's Dirty Work: Migrant Maids and Modern-Day Slavery" in *Global Woman: Nannies, Maids, and Sex Workers in the New Economy*, Barbara Ehrenreich and Arlie Russell Hochschild, eds. (NY: Henry Holt, 2002).

The International Battle Against Sweatshop Labor

During the 1990s, student and labor activists fueled an international movement to end sweatshop labor. Tactics ranged from lobbying efforts and boycotts to street demonstrations during meetings of such established free trade groups as the World Trade Organization (WTO) and the International Monetary Fund (IMF). American-based mutlinationals responded to such pressure in a variety of ways.

■ ■ ■

Nike, for example, engaged in a public relations campaign to enhance its image. Some activists, however, were not convinced that genuine change was underway. Claiming that Nike's press releases and letters to newspaper editors misrepresented the actual working conditions under which its products were made, one activist sued Nike for unlawful and unfair business practices and false advertising in violation of California law. As we will discover in Chapter 7, commercial speech is protected by the Constitution. Although the government may place restrictions on it—banning false advertising, for example—there must be sufficient justification. Most importantly, the courts permit wider latitude to laws limiting commercial speech than those restricting political speech. They recognize that commercial speech is "hardier," more likely to reassert itself for economic reasons than speech in the political context. As you read the *Nike* case and the notes that follow, notice the way the courts struggle to characterize Nike's speech.

KASKY v. NIKE
Court of Appeals, California, 2000
93 Cal. Rptr. 2d 854

SWAGER, *Associate Justice.*

Nike, Inc., a marketer of athletic shoes and sports apparel, has grown into a large multinational enterprise through a marketing strategy centering on a favorable brand image, which is associated with a distinctive logo and the advertising slogan, "Just do it." To maintain this image, the company invests heavily in advertising and brand promotion, spending no less than $978,251,000 for the year ending May 31, 1997. The promotional activities include product sponsorship agreements with celebrity athletes, professional athletic teams, and numerous college athletic teams....

Like other major marketers of athletic shoes and sports apparel, Nike contracts for the manufacture of its products in countries with low labor costs. In Nike's case, the actual production facilities are owned by South Korean and Taiwanese companies that manufacture the products under contract with Nike. The bulk of Nike products are manufactured in China, Thailand, and Indonesia, though some components or products involving more complex technology are manufactured in South Korea or Taiwan. In 1995, a Korean company opened up a major new facility in Vietnam, giving that country also a significant share of Nike's production. The record indicates that between 300,000 and 500,000 workers are employed in Asian factories producing Nike products. The complaint alleges that the vast majority of these workers are women under the age of 24.

The company has sought to foster the appearance and reality of good working conditions in the Asian factories producing its products. All contractors are required to sign a Memorandum of Understanding that, in general, commits them to comply with local laws regarding minimum wage, overtime, child labor, holidays and vacations, insurance benefits, working conditions, and other similar matters and to maintain records documenting their compliance. To assure compliance, the company conducts spot audits of labor and environmental conditions by accounting firms. Early in 1997, Nike retained a consulting firm, co-chaired by Andrew Young, the former ambassador to the United Nations, to carry out an independent evaluation of the labor practices in Nike factories. After visits to 12 factories, Young issued a report that commented favorably on working conditions in the factories and found no evidence of widespread abuse or mistreatment of workers.

Nevertheless, Nike was beset in 1996 and 1997 with a series of reports on working conditions in its factories that contrasted sharply with the favorable view in the Young report. An accounting firm's spot audit of the large Vietnamese factory, which was leaked to the press by a disgruntled employee, reported widespread violations of local regulations and atmospheric pollution causing respiratory problems in 77 percent of the workers.... And the Hong Kong Christian Industrial Committee released an extensively documented study of several Chinese factories, including three used by Nike, which reported 11- to 12-hour work days, compulsory overtime, violation of minimum wage laws, exposure to dangerous levels of dust and toxic fumes, and employment of workers under the age of 16.

These reports put Nike under an unusual degree of public scrutiny as a company exemplifying a perceived social evil associated with economic globalization—the exploitation of young female workers in poor countries....

Nike countered with a public relations campaign that defended the benefits of its Asian factories to host countries and sought to portray the company as being in the vanguard of responsible corporations seeking to maintain adequate labor standards in overseas facilities....

The complaint alleges that, in the course of this public relations campaign, Nike made a series of six misrepresentations regarding its labor practices including ... that Nike products are made in accordance with applicable laws and regulations governing health and safety conditions....

[These misrepresentations, plaintiff claimed, constituted unlawful and unfair business practices and false advertising. Next, the court addresses the defense raised by Nike: that its press releases are protected by the First Amendment to the Constitution.]

Since extending First Amendment protection to commercial speech ... the United States Supreme Court has "been careful to distinguish commercial speech from speech at the First Amendment's core...." A line of decisions .... has sanctioned restraints on commercial speech that is false, deceptive or misleading....

[T]he speech at issue here was intended to promote a favorable corporate image of the company so as to induce consumers to buy its products. A Nike executive expressed this business objective in a letter to the editor [of a newspaper]: "Consumers ... want to know they support companies with good products and practices.... During the shopping season, we encourage shoppers to remember that Nike is the industry's leader in improving factory conditions."

[W]e think that a public relations campaign focusing on corporate image, such as that at issue here, calls for a different analysis than that applying to product advertisement.

[T]he case at bar lies in familiar First Amendment territory—public dialogue on a matter of public concern. Though drafted in terms of commercial speech, the complaint in fact seeks judicial intervention in a public debate.

The "heart of the First Amendment's protection" lies in "the liberty to discuss publicly and truthfully all matters of public concern...."

Nike exemplifies the perceived evils or benefits of labor practices associated with the processes of economic globalization.... Nike's strong corporate image and widespread consumer market places its labor practices in the context of a broader debate about the social implications of employing low-cost foreign labor for manufacturing functions once performed by domestic workers. We take judicial notice that this debate has given rise to urgent calls for action ranging from international labor standards to consumer boycotts. Information about the labor practices at Nike's overseas plants thus constitutes data relevant to a controversy of great public interest in our times.

Freedom of "expression on public issues" has always rested on the highest rung of the hierarchy of First Amendment values.... The constitutional safeguard..."was fashioned to assure unfettered interchange of ideas for the bringing about of political and social changes desired by the people." And, it represents a "profound national commitment to the principle that debate on public issues should be uninhibited, robust, and wide-open. ..."

It follows that "under the free speech guaranty the validity and truth of declarations in political disputes over issues of public interest must be resolved by the public and not by a judge." ...

The fact that Nike has an economic motivation in defending its corporate image from such criticism does not alter the significance of the speech to the "listeners," the consumers or other members of the public concerned with labor practices attending the process of economic globalization.

[The court affirms the decision of the trial judge to dismiss the complaint against Nike.]

QUESTIONS

1. The court refused to order Nike to cease its public relations campaign. Why?

2. The Supreme Court of California reversed this case and remanded it for trial. "Because the messages in question were directed by a commercial speaker to a commercial audience, and because they made representations of fact about the speaker's own business operations for purposes of promoting sales of its product," the majority found they were commercial speech, subject to California's ban on false advertising. Dissenters argued that the ruling would prohibit a business from speaking out on issues of public importance or from vigorously defending its own labor practices. *Kasky v. Nike, Inc.*, 119 Cal.Rptr.2d 296 (2002). What arguments can you make to defend the decision of the lower court? Of the state's Supreme Court? Frame your argument in terms of ethical theory.

3. **Research**: After granting a right to appeal, the United States Supreme Court issued a one-sentence unsigned order declaring that *certiorari* had been "improvidently granted." In other words, the matter was left to the California courts, where Nike would have to defend itself against Kasky's claim that it was guilty of false advertisement. Instead, in September 2003 the company agreed to pay $1.5 million to the Fair Labor Association to settle the case. In a joint statement, Nike and the FLA said the money would be used for worker education and to develop a global standard on corporate responsibility. Find out what progress FLA has made.

4. At the time of the settlement, Nike indicated that it would not disseminate its corporate responsibility report outside the company and would continue to limit its participation in public events and media engagements in California. Use ethical theory to defend Nike's decisions.

5. **Research**: The Workers Rights Consortium, sponsored by 185 universities, monitors factories to end sweatshop labor. When Russell Corporation, a subsidiary of Fruit of the Loom, announced it was closing a unionized factory in Honduras in 2009, the Consortium objected, accusing the company of systematic abuse of workers' rights of association. A dozen or more universities ended their licensing deals with Russell. Is your school one of them? Is your school a member of the Consortium? What else is it doing the to end sweatshop labor?

6. **Research**: In September 2005, toy and garment workers from Bangladesh, China, Indonesia, Nicaragua, and Swaziland brought a class-action suit against Walmart in California. All of Walmart's foreign suppliers had signed Walmart's Code of Conduct, and the plaintiffs claimed to be third-party beneficiaries of those contracts. The Code and basic human rights were violated, the plaintiffs argued, when they were forced to endure sweatshop conditions detrimental to their health and safety. And, since Walmart could have—but didn't—leverage its economic power to force better conditions

for them, the company should be held accountable. Unions representing Americans who worked for Walmart's competitors joined the suit, claiming they were harmed by Walmart's failure to enforce its suppliers' promise to pay minimum and prevailing wages. (a) Find out what has happened in this suit, *Doe v. Walmart Store*, 572 F.3d 677 (9th Cir. 2009). (b) The suit was filed by the International Labor Rights Fund (*http://www.ILRF.org*). Find out what else the ILRF has done.

■ ■ ■

Exporting Hazards

In the final reading in this chapter we consider the migration of technologies, rather than people, from the developed world to the developing world. In it, Henry Shue provides a framework for analyzing the ethics of exporting old, unsafe technology to developing nations.

─────■■■■■─────
EXPORTING HAZARDS
Henry Shue[14]

[A] general statement of the liberal no-harm principle is, "It is wrong to inflict avoidable harm upon other people, and it ought often to be prohibited by law." While harming oneself may sometimes be immoral, it is harming others that ought generally to be illegal....

No one may hurt or endanger others, except in cases of genuine necessity, in the course of justified warfare, in punishment for heinous crime, or in other quite special circumstances. Even the most one-sided advocates of freedom have rarely advocated the freedom to injure and endanger....

[Some ethicists argue that the general no-harm principle does not apply where the costs of exporting old, unsafe technology is overbalanced by the benefit to foreign workers. Shue disagrees. Below he explains why, distinguishing mere "costs" to be weighed against benefits from true "harms," which are never acceptable.]

Yes, it is granted, there are costs to the foreign workers in the form of new dangers to health and safety, but there are also new benefits that are, so to speak, part of the same package. And—this is the point—although the costs to the workers are undeniably real, ... the benefits are real too and they are greater than the costs.... The worker might be safer sitting at home, but he or she might also be unemployed....

[A cost, according to Shue, is a true harm when it involves all six of the following factors:]

The first factor is that the damage done is physical: it is life, limb, and vitality that are at stake, not, for example, reputation or lifestyle only, but the adequate, continued functioning of parts of one's body....

Second, the potential damage is not simply physical; it is serious, possibly fatal.... The bodily threat is to vital organs. Some of the malignancies are still untreatable and certainly fatal.

Third, besides being serious physical damage, the damage that is risked is irreversible. It does not "clear up," and damaged portions do not grow back....

[Fourth], the potential physical damage to the workers is undetectable for the victim without a level of medical care to which the workers have no access and [fifth] is unpredictable for the victim, even probabilistically, without a level of knowledge to which the workers have no access....

─────────

[14] "Exporting Hazards," by Henry Shue, is reprinted from BOUNDARIES: NATIONAL AUTONOMY & ITS LIMITS, P. Brown and H. Shue, eds., Rowan & Littlefield, 1981.

[Sixth,] the undetectability and unpredictability are avoidable at the choice of the firm's management.... This double point is simple but quite significant: people poor enough to work readily in the conditions we are considering will not have enough money—even if doctors are available, which is unlikely given the low effective demand—to afford routine medical examinations.... So "early detection by a doctor" is out of the question.... This is what I mean by saying the damage is undetectable for the victim: it is, for the person who has undergone it, discoverable only when it is so serious as to interfere with normal overall functioning, if not to threaten life. It is readily detectable by a physician with standard x-ray equipment. This is why the damage seems to be avoidably undetectable....

Even people who have never before seen or heard about mining ... do not need to be told that shafts sometimes collapse and so might this one.... But they would not—and generations of miners did not—realize that there is such a thing as "black lung" and that they might well be developing it.... This fifth factor is that potential victims do not know, and cannot figure out for themselves, how high the risk is, although their employers know the probabilities and keep them quiet. Thus, once again, we appear to have avoidable unpredictability....

[Finally, Shue addresses the argument that, even if harm is being inflicted in a manner that ought to be stopped, it cannot be the responsibility of individual firms acting alone to stop it: This would amount to a form of forced heroics or martyrdom. Again, Shue finds this position unpersuasive.]

It may also be suggested that firms are not in the business of protecting the interests of their workers, except when this is a means to their own goals... [and that] if the government of a poor country wants the citizens of the country to enjoy safer workplaces, the government ought to impose uniform standards upon all firms, instead of expecting isolated firms to raise their own costs while their competitors are allowed to undercut them by retaining the cheaper, less safe technology....

[B]ut no institution, including the corporation, has a general license to inflict harm, even if the infliction of harm holds down production costs. In order to maintain otherwise one must reject the traditional liberal no-harm principle. Protecting people against harm is another matter.... What the corporation is being asked to do is simply not to inflict harm: not to prefer to a safer process a manufacturing process that harms a higher percentage of the people subjected to it than other readily available processes do.

Second, the national governments of poor countries that try to protect their workers against such harms face precisely the same problem that the firms invoke— and the governments face it because of the reasoning that the firms use. They first complain that they cannot be expected to go it alone (by unilaterally introducing more expensive, safer processes) because this would put them at a competitive disadvantage. But governments of poor countries that compete for foreign investment face an exactly analogous choice....

[In the final section of this piece, Shue discusses the allocation of responsibility for preventing harms.]

Whom does this leave to defend the victims of the harm who at present cannot defend themselves? It leaves us, fellow American consumers. Why us, or, to be precise, why me?

To some degree the question answers itself. Why should I defend defenseless human beings? Because they are human beings and they are defenseless....

But there are additional ... reasons. The main reason why one particular Samaritan must decide whether to do "good" is no better a reason than that this Samaritan happened to come along this road at this time, when (a) the victim was already in the ditch and (b) the previous travelers had already passed by on the other side of the road. To this Samaritan's "why me?" there is no cosmic explanation, and there is no better answer than: "You are here and therefore in a position to help this victim—is there a stronger claim upon you now?"

The firm that has retained control ... of the harmful process [that] has inflicted the wound, and the victim's own government has usually passed by on the other side of the road. Whoever is next in a position to assist the victim has some obligation to do so, irrespective of whether he or she was previously involved, unless some stronger obligation overrides. A previous involvement with the case is not required. Call this responsibility through ability—ability to make a positive difference.

We have been considering a case in which products consumed by U.S. purchasers and formerly made by U.S. workers are now made by Mexican workers as the result of a U.S.-based firm's decision to continue to use a less safe process to which U.S. workers cannot legally be subjected. United States consumers are hardly Samaritans who just happen to be passing by an asbestos factory on the other side of the border. We pay lower prices, suffer less inflation, etc., because the health costs of the retention of the less safe technology are now borne by the Mexican workers and Mexican society. It is true, that most of us did not ask to have this arrangement made. But once we understand it, we are no longer unwilling (because unknowing) beneficiaries. We now must choose whether to continue to accept these benefits on these terms. In such situations, knowledge is not only power but also responsibility, because it places us in a position to act. Call this responsibility through complicity—complicity by continuing acceptance of benefits.

QUESTIONS

1. According to Shue, what are the six indicators that a "cost" is actually a "harm" where use of foreign labor is concerned? What does he mean by describing a harm as "unavoidably undetectable"?

2. Shue mentions (a) responsibility through ability and (b) responsibility through complicity. Consider the Unocal case. Did the company possess either form of responsibility in Myanmar? What could it have done that would be in line with the "no-harm principle?"

3. Who do you think bears responsibility for the maintenance of safe working conditions in American-owned firms located in foreign countries: the workers themselves? The corporate owners or managers? The foreign government? The U.S. government? An international safety and health organization? The individual U.S. consumer?

4. What do you think Shue would say about the actions of the EPA and other officials during the clean up of the WTC? The 2010 Gulf oil spill?

Chapter Problems

1. The most immediate consequence of the 2010 disaster at BP's Deepwater Horizon oil rig was the loss of human life: 15 men were killed in the explosion, fire, and sinking of the drill hole. Tragically, before the disaster, the Gulf had been littered with red flags signaling problems. Two months earlier, a whistleblower had complained that another BP refinery—the Atlantis, stationed at 7,070 feet of water south of New Orleans—was operating without the required engineering documents meant to serve as road maps for safely starting and halting production. BP had a long history of safety problems. Flammable liquids had overflowed at the company's Texas City oil refinery in 2005, creating a cloud of vapor that ignited, killing 15 workers and injuring 170, one of several fatal accidents during the last 35 years at BP drilling sites.

OSHA had made only one full safety-management inspection at the refinery, in 1998. (Nationally, OSHA had only enough resources to do nine such inspections in targeted industries between 1995–2005.) However, a U.S. Chemical Safety and Hazard Investigation Board (headed by former Secretary of State James Baker) reported in 2006 that most of the blame for the blast rested on the company. Cost cutting, weak leadership, and a "decentralized management system and entrepreneurial culture," which left safety processes to the discretion of managers, all contributed. Overworked employees did not report accidents and safety concerns for fear of repercussions. Internal audits were more focused on avoiding fines than on real changes that would improve safety.

Which of these problems can be resolved by voluntary actions on the part of the corporation? By changes in the law? By re-allocation of tax revenues? By individual action? How would a socially responsible corporation respond to this report? **Research**: How did Congress, Louisiana, and BP respond to the workplace safety issues connected to the 2010 explosion?

2. Assume that you are the manager of a restaurant that has been attacked by armed robbers on two occasions in the recent past—both during happy hour. Some of your employees want to change your "no firearms" rule; others are worried that guns so close to alcohol would put them at risk—especially since a worker in your city recently shot and killed five co-workers after his supervisor reprimanded him for using a cell phone. Nationally, homicide remains a leading cause of workplace fatalities. How would you resolve this dilemma? What legal issues should you consider? **Research**: A number of states have adopted laws that prohibit companies from banning firearms at work. Find out if your state is one of them.

3. What would be the costs/benefits of each of the following proposals? (a) Permitting workers whose employers have endangered them to sue for violating the OSH Act; (b) Creating labor/management safety and health committees to allow workers on the shop floor to participate in finding and fixing hazards, with authority to shut down dangerous operations; (c) Making business licenses contingent on some measure of safety and health performance, such as achieving a specified level or reduction in workplace injury rates.

4. In 2000, Human Rights Watch condemned the conditions under which hundreds of thousands of youths under 18 worked on farmlands in the United States. Ten years later, in 2010, HRW revisited farms in Florida, Michigan, North Carolina, and Texas and concluded that little had changed: children still worked under conditions described as exploitative and dangerous. Although NIOSH identifies agriculture as the most dangerous industry for young workers, the federal Fair Labor Standards Act provides fewer protections for children working in agriculture than in all other areas. Most work on family farms or with parental permission. Is it ethical for parents to encourage or allow such work? Should the government do anything to regulate? **Research**: What changes does Human Rights Watch recommend? How has the government responded? Read "Fields of Peril: Child Labor in U.S. Agriculture," available at *www.hrw.org*.

5. In July 2006, immigration officials from the Department of Homeland Security ran a sting operation in which they posed as OSHA officials. When construction workers showed up at a "mandatory OSHA meeting," the immigration officers arrested 48 workers and processed them for deportation. Is there anything unethical about

using safety and health programs as a ruse to deport undocumented immigrant workers? Why or why not?

6. Is collective bargaining by unions a better way to improve workplace safety and health than pervasive government regulation? Law professor Thomas Kohler thinks so. Despite the pervasiveness of anti-union attitudes and low union membership, Kohler argues we need unions in a time when wage and earnings distribution has become increasingly unequal and the middle class has shrunk. He writes:

> *Along with these developments has come a significant loosening of the employment bond. So-called contingent employment arrangements—part-time, temporary and contract arrangements are on the rise.... These "just-in-time" employees typically have at best highly restricted claims to pension, health and other benefits incident to employment....*
>
> *[He looks, as well, at developments on the international level:]*
>
> *[T]he remarkable transformation of what used to be called the Eastern bloc was spearheaded by an independent trade-union movement, which improbably survived despite the forces arrayed against it. Nor were the Poles left to go it alone. At a time when our own government took a wait-and-see attitude, the AFL-CIO and other unaffiliated American unions supported Solidarity from the first with funds, equipment and expertise. American unions also lobbied Western governments on Solidarity's behalf, and worked to keep the Polish situation before the public's eye.... There is also a pronounced tendency today to overlook, or to be absolutely unaware of, the domestic contributions made by the union movement. The support of unions, for example, was crucial to the passage of the Civil Rights Act of 1964. Unions also have been in the forefront of efforts to improve workplace safety and public health and to ensure pay equality for the sexes....*

Kohler speculates that unions might be more valued if people better understood the importance of collective bargaining. It is, he argues, a system of "private-law making." This is important because:

> *Individuals and societies alike become and remain self-governing only by repeatedly and regularly engaging in acts of self-government. It is the habit that sustains the condition.... [I]t is through their involvement in the collective bargaining process that average citizens can take part in deciding the law that most directly determines the details of their daily lives.* Thomas C. Kohler, "Civic Virtue at Work: Unions as Seedbeds of the Civic Virtues," 36 36 BOSTON COLLEGE LAW REV. 279 (1995).

Research: (a) Find the most recent annual report, "Death on the Job: The Toll of Neglect," posted each April on the AFL-CIO's Web site. What do you learn about the current status of occupational health and safety in your state? (b) Find out what other unions are doing today to support workers' rights in the United States and abroad.

7. The Federal Tort Claims Act (FTCA) authorizes suits against the United States or its agencies when a government worker, acting within the scope of his employment, wrongfully or negligently causes personal injury, death or property damage. So, for example, a drunk or reckless driver of a government vehicle can be sued. However, the FTCA preserves an ancient legal doctrine called "sovereign immunity" by

banning suits against the government when the injuries result from the exercise of what is considered a "discretionary function." OSHA, for example, could not be sued when an inspector exercised his discretion to perform a perfunctory workplace inspection of a shoe factory that did not uncover violations, even though a woman suffered horrific injuries when her hair was drawn into a vacuum created by a high-speed machine that should have been guarded or placed elsewhere. *Irving v. United States,* 146 F.3d 12 (1st Cir. 1998). Would it be a good idea to allow persons who are injured by OSHA's failure to inspect to sue OSHA? What arguments can you make for or against the idea?

8. **Research**: Ergonomic injuries are one of the most prevalent occupational hazards, with musculoskeletal disorders accounting for 29 percent of all serious workplace injuries in 2008. But efforts to pass a general ergonomics standard have been mired in politics for more than a decade. Find out if OSHA or your state has taken any action to limit ergonomic injuries. What are the arguments for and against government standards for ergonomics?

9. California has become a haven for professional sports figures. Anyone whose team played even one game in the state is eligible for worker's compensation; claims can be made even for injuries suffered many years ago. Scientists have recently shown that head injuries can lead to dementia as late as 40 years after the fact. Reportedly, the number of former pro-footballers moving to California to take advantage of its liberal workers' compensation laws was on the rise in 2010. Does it seem fair to expect workers' compensation to cover such claims? If not, who should pay for the person's health care?

CHAPTER PROJECT

Legislative Hearing: Reforming OSHA

Guidelines, Appendix "F"

Read through the Guidelines in Appendix "F" in preparation for class. We will be role-playing a congressional hearing on a bill that would amend the Occupational Safety and Health Act. The "Protecting American Workers Act" would make the following changes:

1. Expand the authority of OSHA to cover federal, state, and local government employees.
2. Ban employee practices and policies that discourage employees from reporting work-related injuries or illnesses.
3. Specify that time employees spend aiding inspections shall be deemed "hours worked" for which they must receive usual pay and benefits.
4. Require OSHA to investigate any incident in a place of employment that results in death or hospitalization of two or more employees.
5. Increase the civil and criminal penalties for certain OSHA violations, and allow criminal prosecutions (as a felony) of "willful" violations.

Some of you will role-play senators who serve on the Senate Health, Education, Labor, and Pensions Committee. Others will roleplay spokespersons for one of the following interest groups testifying before the Committee on the question of whether the proposed bill should become law:

Groups to be represented

1. Labor leader from the AFL-CIO
2. C.E.O. from the Business Roundtable
3. National Council for Occupational Safety and Health
4. National Association of Manufacturers
5. Bluegreen Alliance
6. The Cato Institute
7. United Support & Memorial for Workplace Fatalities (*www.usmwf.org*)
8. U.S. Chamber of Commerce
9. American Society of Safety Engineers
10. The National Labor Committee

CHAPTER 6

Global Climate Change
Responsibility and Survival

God, who hath given the world to men in common, hath also given them reason to make use of it to the best advantage of life, and convenience. The earth, and all that is therein, is given to men for the support and comfort of their being.

—JOHN LOCKE

[My] story is of all life ... and of us two-leggeds sharing in it with the four-leggeds and the wings of the air, and all green things; for these are children of one mother and their father is one Spirit.

—BLACK ELK

[The] risk of catastrophe, rather than the details of cost-benefit calculations, makes the most powerful case for strong climate policy. Current projections of global warming in the absence of action are just too close to the kinds of numbers associated with doomsday scenarios. It would be irresponsible—it's tempting to say criminally irresponsible—not to step back from what could all too easily turn out to be the edge of a cliff....

—PAUL KRUGMAN, ECONOMIST[1]

The 2010 Gulf Oil Spill, a stark reminder of how business decisions can impact an ecosystem, was the jumping-off point for our introduction to ethical theory in Chapter 1. In this chapter, we widen our lens to explore the legal, ethical, economic, and political landscape of global climate change. It opens with a novel federal case brought by residents of an Alaskan Eskimo village against a group of energy companies, alleging links between carbon emissions, global warming, and the melting of the ice that had once allowed the villagers to survive Arctic winters. The next readings examine industry resistance to developing a national policy response to global warming, and recent pressures and alliances that may be re-casting the political climate. After considering the potential—and limitations—of shareholder resolutions on climate change, we move on to consider philosophical perspectives on the natural world, and the question of whether environmental regulation is a "taking" of property requiring "just compensation" under the U.S. Constitution. We end by considering environmental justice.

■ ■ ■

---

[1] "Building a Green Economy," *NYTimes*, April 11, 2010.

The Village of Kivalina is about 70 miles north of the Arctic Circle, on the Northwest coast of Alaska, at the tip of an eight-mile-long barrier reef. The nearly 400 Inupiat Eskimo living in Kivalina brought suit in the following case, alleging that the greenhouse gas emissions of 24 defendant energy companies—Exxon, BP, Shell, Chevron among others—contributed heavily to global warming, causing the erosion of the sea ice which had protected their village from winter storms. Now that defendants have created a "public nuisance," as plaintiffs allege, Kivalina is becoming uninhabitable, and they are suing for their relocation costs estimated to be $95-$400 million.

NATIVE VILLAGE OF KIVALINA v. EXXONMOBIL CORPORATION, ET AL.
United States District Court, California, 2009
663 F. Supp. 2d 863

Opinion by Saundra Brown Armstrong.

....In recent years, much attention has been focused on the issue of global warming, which is not itself an event so much as it is a sequence of events. Generally speaking, global warming refers to the build-up of carbon dioxide and methane (commonly referred to as "greenhouse gases") in the atmosphere which, in turn, causes the temperature of the planet to increase. Both carbon dioxide and methane are products of human activity. Plaintiffs attribute the build-up of atmospheric carbon dioxide and methane to increases in the combustion of fossil fuels as well as fuel harvesting activities, such as coal mining and oil drilling.

According to Plaintiffs, carbon dioxide and other greenhouse gas levels have been increasing steadily since the beginning of the industrial revolution in the 18th century, with more than a one-third increase having occurred since 1980. The emitted gases "rapidly mix in the atmosphere and cause the increase in the atmospheric concentration of carbon dioxide levels and other greenhouse gases worldwide." These gases remain in the atmosphere for centuries and "thus have a lasting effect on [the] climate." The carbon dioxide traps heat emitted by the sun which, in turn, increases the climactic temperature on Earth. As the planet heats, the oceans become less efficient at removing carbon dioxide from the atmosphere. Likewise, the planet reflects less energy back into space which then causes "white, snowy, or icy areas" to darken and absorb more heat. The increase in the surface temperature causes seawater to expand and sea levels to rise. In addition, sea levels are rising due to the melting of ice caps and glaciers resulting from increased temperatures. Plaintiffs allege that these events have, in turn, led to the loss of [their ability to live in their village].

[Before the court can address the Plaintiff's claim for **common law nuisance**, it must address a preliminary matter. The defendant energy companies argue that this court does not have the authority to decide the case in the first place, since it lacks **subject matter jurisdiction**. The Constitution sets limits on the power of the federal courts, restricting them, for example, from hearing a case that will interfere with the separation of powers among the three branches of government. For example, it would be a violation of the **political question doctrine** for a federal court to take a case that involved making policy decisions that rightfully belong to the executive or to the legislative branch of government. Here, defendants argue that in order to resolve the Village of Kivalina's nuisance claim, this court will find itself "mak[ing] policy determinations relating to the use of fossil fuels and other energy sources and consider[ing] their value in relation to the environmental, economic, and social consequences," determinations that they claim, "are inherently political." As it evaluates its own authority to proceed, the court looks to *Baker v. Carr,* a 1962 Supreme Court case,[2] deriving three guiding principles: (1) Does the court's resolution involve "questions committed by the text of the Constitution to a coordinate branch of government"? (2) Does the case require the court to "move beyond areas of judicial expertise"? and (3) Would it be more prudent for the court not to intervene?]

...Defendants argue that allowing Plaintiffs to proceed with their global warming claim "would intrude upon the political branches' constitutionally committed authority over foreign policy." Defendants maintain that Congress and the President have declined to adopt emission caps absent an agreement from developing nations.[3] They further claim that the rationale for the United States' position is two-fold: (1) that a successful approach to global warming requires a "global" approach that includes cooperation from both industrialized and developing nations; and (2) this country could "find itself in an inferior bargaining position" with respect to future diplomatic attempts to address this issue.

[The court notes that although, in general, the executive branch must decide foreign policy, precedent warns against "sweeping statements that imply all questions involving foreign relations are political ones."]

...While Defendants have shown that global warming issues may implicate foreign policy and related economic issues, the fact that this case "touches foreign relations" does not [automatically] place it beyond the reach of the judiciary. Tellingly, none of the Defendants cite to any express provision of the Constitution or provision from which it can be inferred that the power to make the final determination regarding air pollution or global warming has been vested in either the executive or legislative branch of the government.... [T]he Court must presume that no such limitation exists.

[After deciding the first factor favorably to the Plaintiffs, the court moves to the second factor: whether it would have to move beyond its judicial expertise in resolving this dispute.]

[This factor is not a matter of] whether the case is unmanageable in the sense of being large, complicated, or otherwise difficult to tackle from a logistical standpoint. Rather, courts must ask whether they have the legal tools to reach a ruling that is "principled, rational, and based upon reasoned distinctions." ...

Plaintiffs contend that "[t]he ... manageable standards here are the same as they are in all nuisance cases" [:]...whether Defendants contributed to "an unreasonable interference with public rights[.] "Resolution of what is "reasonable," Plaintiffs assert, is to be determined by examining whether the conduct involves a "significant interference with the public health, the public safety, the public peace, the public comfort or the public convenience" and whether the conduct is "of a continuing nature" or has produced a "permanent or long lasting effect[.]" However, the flaw in Plaintiffs' argument is that it overlooks that the evaluation of a nuisance claim is not focused entirely on the unreasonableness of the harm. Rather, the fact-finder must also balance the utility and benefit of the alleged nuisance against the harm caused....

Applying the above-discussed principles here, the fact-finder will have to weigh, [among other things], the energy-producing alternatives that were available in the past, ... their reliability, ... safety, ... and the impact of the different alternatives on consumers and business at every level.... The fact-finder would then have to weigh the benefits derived from those choices against the risk that increasing greenhouse gases would in turn increase the risk of causing flooding along the coast of a remote Alaskan locale. Plaintiffs ignore this aspect of their claim and otherwise fail to articulate any particular judicially discoverable and manageable standards that would guide a fact-finder in rendering a decision that is principled, rational, and based upon reasoned distinctions.

---

[2] 369 U.S. 186, (1962).

[3] [A reference to President George W. Bush and the U.S. refusal to sign the Kyoto Protocol, the first international treaty addressing climate change.]

[Plaintffs argue that such standards had already been articulated in a lengthy history of prior cases involving air and water pollution, where it might not be certain which of several polluters had contaminated a particular waterway. Refusing to be guided by those cases as precedent, this judge distinguishes them.]

The common thread running through each of those cases is that they involved a discrete number of "polluters" that were identified as causing a specific injury to a specific area.... Plaintiffs' global warming claim is based on the emission of greenhouse gases from innumerable sources located throughout the world and affecting the entire planet and its atmosphere....

The sequence of events leading to the claimed injury also is distinguishable. In a water pollution case, the discharge in excess of the amount permitted is presumed harmful. In contrast, the harm from global warming involves a series of events disconnected from the discharge itself....

...Plaintiffs' global warming nuisance claim seeks to impose liability and damages on a scale unlike any prior environmental pollution case cited by Plaintiffs. Those cases do not provide guidance that would enable the Court to reach a resolution of this case in any "reasoned" manner. Consequently, the Court concludes that application of the second ... factor precludes judicial consideration of Plaintiff's federal nuisance claim.

[The court now moves to the third factor, asking whether resolving this case will involve policy determinations that should be made by a legislative body instead of a court.]

...[T]he resolution of Plaintiffs' nuisance claim requires balancing the social utility of Defendants' conduct with the harm it inflicts. That process, by definition, entails a determination of what would have been an acceptable limit on the level of greenhouse gases emitted by Defendants.

Plaintiffs also fail to confront the fact that resolution of their nuisance claim requires the judiciary to make a policy decision about who should bear the cost of global warming. Though alleging that Defendants are responsible for a "substantial portion" of greenhouse gas emissions, Plaintiffs also acknowledge that virtually everyone on Earth is responsible on some level for contributing to such emissions. Yet, by pressing this lawsuit, Plaintiffs are in effect asking this Court to make a political judgment that the two dozen Defendants named in this action should be the only ones to bear the cost of contributing to global warming. Plaintiffs respond that Defendants should be the ones held responsible for damaging Kivalina allegedly because "they are responsible for more of the problem than anyone else in the nation. ..." But even if that were true, Plaintiffs ignore that the allocation of fault—and cost—of global warming is a matter appropriately left for determination by the executive or legislative branch in the first instance. The Court thus concludes that the third ... factor also militates in favor of dismissal.

[The judge goes on to address another challenge made by the Defendants, that the plaintiffs lack **standing** to bring this case. Also derived from the Constitution, standing is a threshold requirement that a Plaintiff must, among other things, "adequately establish ... causation (i.e., a fairly traceable connection between the alleged injury in fact and the alleged conduct of the Defendant)." Again, analogizing to prior water pollution cases, Plaintiffs argue that the harm they have experienced is "fairly traceable" to the Defendants because the companies' activities "contributed" to their injuries. And again, the court refuses to use those precedent cases.]

Plaintiffs have not alleged that the "seed" of their injury can be traced to any of the Defendants. Plaintiffs allege that the genesis of the global warming phenomenon dates back centuries and is a result of the emission of greenhouse gases by a multitude of sources ... [and] that the level of atmospheric carbon dioxide, "the most significant greenhouse gas emitted by human activity," has been increasing steadily "since the dawn of the industrial revolution in the 18th century..." Significantly, the source of the greenhouse gases are undifferentiated and cannot be traced to any particular source ... given that they "rapidly mix in the atmosphere" and "inevitably merge[] with the accumulation of emissions in California and the rest of the world."

...[T]he pleadings make clear that there is no realistic possibility of tracing any particular alleged effect of global warming to any particular emissions by any specific person, entity, group at any particular point in time.... Thus, Plaintiffs have not and cannot show that Defendants' conduct is the "seed of [their] injury." To the contrary, there are, in fact, a multitude of "alternative culprit[s]" allegedly responsible for the various chain of events allegedly leading to the erosion of Kivalina....

The Court concludes that Plaintiffs' federal claim for nuisance is barred by the political question doctrine and for lack of standing under Article III. Accordingly, Defendants' motions to dismiss for lack of jurisdiction are granted.

QUESTIONS

1. Did Judge Armstrong resolve the underlying public nuisance claim brought by the village of Kivalina? Why/why not?

2. What were the three factors of analysis the judge used to decide whether the political question doctrine was implicated in this case, and how were they applied? Why did the plaintiffs lack standing in this case?

3. In deciding this case, Judge Armstrong made use of the factual difference between these two scenarios: (1) several companies contribute to the pollution of a stream; (2) several companies contribute greenhouse gases to the atmosphere. Do you agree that the distinction between them is significant? Or is this a "distinction without a difference"? In dismissing this case, the court notes the complexities of global warming—its lengthy timeline, its interacting chemical inputs, and its "multitude of alternative culprits," including millions of ordinary consumers. If the U.S. federal court system is not the best place to address this profoundly complicated phenomenon, what is? Why?

4. In *Comer v. Murphy Oil USA*, 2009 U.S. App. LEXIS 22772, Mississippi landowners sued energy and chemical companies for the loss of property they experienced when Hurricane Katrina hit. Plaintiffs allege defendants' greenhouse gas (GHG) emissions contributed to global warming, causing sea levels to rise and magnifying the ferocity of the storm. In *People of the State of Calif. v. Gen. Motors Corp.*, 2007 U.S. Dist. LEXIS 68547, the state sued the six largest American car manufacturers, alleging that their vehicles emissions, making up more than 20 percent of the U.S. total CO_2 emissions, were contributing significantly to global warming, degrading the resources, infrastructure and health of the citizens of California. In both cases, as in *Kivalina*, the plaintiffs' claims were dismissed under the political question doctrine. Litigation like this, alleging harm as a result of contributions to global warming, is becoming more common. Even assuming these cases are dismissed, what might be their broader societal effect?

■ ■ ■

Environmental Regulation and the New Environmental Challenge

There was a time when the United States was a global leader in regulating to protect the environment. The first Earth Day—April 22, 1970—was a dramatic signal of public concern, part of the political climate that would lead to the creation of a new federal agency, the Environmental Protection Agency (EPA) and the legislative framework in the United States—federal, state, and local regulations addressing pollution of the air, water, and land—which grew to be the most comprehensive in the world.

U.S. ENVIRONMENTAL PROTECTION STATUTES

- The **Clean Air Act of 1970**[4] regulates the emission of pollutants into the atmosphere. Under this law, national ambient air-quality standards (NAAQs) are set, and the release of certain major pollutants—particulates, toxins, and compounds that deplete stratospheric ozone, that contribute to acid rain, and that are dangerous to human health—are limited. The Clean Air Act is carried out and monitored by the states, which must submit "state implementation plans" (SIPS) for approval by the EPA. The 1990 amendments address "nonattainment" areas, the parts of the country that are not in compliance with the NAAQs, and set new deadlines—from 5 to 20 years for compliance on ozone, for example.
- The **Clean Water Act (CWA)**[5] sets the goal of ending the discharge of pollutants into navigable waters, and provides federal funding for sewage treatment plants nationwide. A 2006 Supreme Court decision and an executive decision by President George W. Bush removed small streams and wetlands from the protection of the law. Congress responded with the Clean Water Restoration Act, first proposed in 2007. In 2009 a Senate committee recommended that it be considered by the whole Senate. You can track this bill at *http://www.govtrack.us/congress/bill.xpd?bill=s111-787.*
- The **Resource Conservation and Recovery Act (RCRA)**[6] sets up a "cradle-to-grave" program for the control of hazardous waste, regulating labeling, containers, transport, and disposal sites.
- The **Comprehensive Environmental Response, Compensation, and Liability Act (CERCLA)**[7] is a liability scheme rather than a monitoring program. CERCLA created a $1.6 billion fund—**Superfund**—to finance the cleanup of toxic waste sites. For decades the government would collect from polluting companies to reimburse Superfund, but under the Bush administration most of the resources for cleanup will come from taxpayers. **Potentially responsible parties** include (1) owners or operators of hazardous waste sites, (2) those who owned or operated the sites when the hazardous material was deposited, (3) the "generators," or those who create the wastes, and (4) the transporters—those who carry it to the sites.

Other environmental laws deal with endangered species; pesticides; coastal management; the timber, mining, and oil industries; marine life; and so on. For many of these statutes, the federal version of each is either mirrored or implemented by legislation at state level. The EPA homepage, *http://www.epa.gov*, updates statutes and regulations.

Despite some success in its administration of thirteen extremely complicated national laws—improved air and water quality, restoration of contaminated land, rescue of previously endangered species to name a few—the EPA's comprehensive "**command and control**" approach came under attack. Critics charged it was cumbersome, costly,

---

[4] 42 U.S.C. 7401 (1998).

[5] 33 U.S.C. sec. 7413(a)(2)(Supp. V 1993).

[6] 42 U.S.C. Sec. 6901-6992k (1988 & Supp. V 1993).

[7] 42 U.S.C. Sec. 9601-9675 (1988 & Supp. V 1993). Amended in 1984 and 1986.

and that it was an impediment to American firms facing global competition. It would be more efficient, they argued, to make use of market incentives, integrating the profit motive with environmental goals.

This thinking was behind experiments with market-based approaches, like the **trade-able permit system**, also known as **cap and trade**. Such a plan was successful in controlling acid raid in the 1990s. Sulfur dioxide, a key culprit in producing acid rain, not only defaces buildings, but lowers the pH levels in lakes, making them uninhabitable for fish and plants. Authorized by the 1990 amendments to the Clean Air Act, the EPA issued to power plants a set number of permits for sulfur dioxide emissions each year. Firms that could install pollution controls had the incentive to do so and could sell their surplus permits. Firms which chose not to control emissions could use up their permits and buy more. Overall, sulfur dioxide emissions were capped by the fact that the government had determined the number of permits to distribute in the first place. The result: the acid rain problem was mitigated. Sulfur dioxide emissions were almost halved over time, and instead of rising, the cost of electricity fell. While cap and trade appears to offer a desirable way to reduce certain pollutants such as sulfur dioxide and smog, it may not be the best way to handle others. Mercury, for example, affects the nervous system and is particularly harmful to children and developing fetuses. Under a permit system, areas with a concentration of older plants which continue dirty operations by buying the right to pollute can create dangerous mercury "hot spots."

Through the 1990s and early 21st century, as U.S. regulators continued to make use of both "carrots" (market-based incentives) and "sticks" (injunctions, penalties) to bring environmental goals into focus, a striking shift was taking place as scientists struggled to understand newly disturbing environmental risks. The pollution the EPA dealt with initially—from factory smokestacks, landfills, and oil spills—could be traced to a few major industrial sources, and the degradation to the environment could be seen as a direct result of their actions. But as the world has come to realize, and as the *Kivalina* case makes clear, we now face an entirely different and much more complex challenge: what to do about androgenic (human-caused) global climate change. Greenhouse emissions—generated around the world by large corporations, small businesses, and by millions of individual consumers—are threatening forests, oceans, air quality, biodiversity, and human existence itself. Building fast, this problem is vast, diffuse, and potentially catastrophic.

In 1988, the hottest year on record to that date, the United Nations formed the Intergovernmental Panel on Climate Change (IPCC), composed of climate scientists from around the world. The IPCC has been producing reports at regular intervals since 1990, collecting and assessing data; the *Kivalina* judge cites the IPCC's 4th Report of 2007. By then, the Panel had found that 11 of the past 12 years were the hottest since 1850, and that the atmospheric level of CO_2, the most pervasive greenhouse gas, had reached 379 parts per million (ppm), the highest level in the past 650,000 years. The 4th Report predicted planet-wide temperature increases for the 21st century of between 2.4 and 6.4 degrees Celsius. The UN described this report as establishing "an overwhelming scientific consensus that climate change is both real and man-made."[8]

Ironically, while the international scientific consensus was solidifying that global warming was happening, and that it was caused by human activity, in the U.S. the political consensus—and the political will to respond to this problem—was eroding. Through

---

[8] The 2007/2008 UN Human Development Report, citing the IPCC 4th Report.

the 1990s, as nearly 200 countries reached agreement on the Kyoto Protocol, the world's first treaty to reduce greenhouse gas emissions, the U.S. declined to join in. The Kyoto framework commits signatory nations in the developed world to phased-in emissions reductions, with restrictions on developing countries to follow. The logic—and the ethics—behind this has to do with basic fairness: It was felt that the developed nations, with about 15 percent of the world's population but accounting for half of global GHG emissions, having had the chance to achieve high standards of living while freely using natural resources, should not expect those in the developing world to forgo the tools of their own advancement. As Henry Shue has put it:

> Even in an emergency one pawns the jewelry before selling the blankets.... Whatever justice may positively require, it does not permit that poor nations be told to sell their blankets [compromise their development strategies] in order that the rich nations keep their jewelry [continue their unsustainable lifestyles].

But in the U.S., many depicted the break Kyoto would give to the developing world as unfair to the industrialized nations. In refusing to sign Kyoto in 2002, George W. Bush said:

> I'll tell you one thing I'm not going to do is I'm not going to let the United States carry the burden of cleaning up the world's air, like the Kyoto Treaty would have done. China and India were exempted from that treaty. I think we need to be more even-handed.

U.S. resistance to Kyoto found its way into the *Kivalina* case, as the defendant energy companies argued that

> Congress and the President have declined to adopt emission caps absent an agreement from developing nations.... [A] successful approach to global warming requires a "global" approach that includes cooperation from both industrialized and developing nations...

As of this writing, the United States remains the only developed country that has not signed the Kyoto Protocol. Although the Supreme Court held in 2007 that the EPA could regulate CO_2, no such regulations have been issued. The emphasis throughout recent decades has been on voluntary efforts by industry to modify their GHG emissions.

Environmentalists, Scientists, Energy Interests: The Political Dance

With all of the hysteria, all of the fear, all of the phony science, could it be that man-made global warming is the greatest hoax ever perpetrated on the American people? It sure sounds like it.

—JAMES INHOFE, Republican senator of Oklahoma, speaking to defeat the
Climate Stewardship Act of 2003

As we look out, I believe that it's more likely than not that we'll live in a carbon-constrained world. We think we have a significant risk ... so we want to start hedging our bets.

—JAMES E. ROGERS, CEO and Chairman, Cinergy Corporation, endorsing
a national cap on greenhouse emissions

MIT Professor of Urban Studies and Planning Judith Layzer has researched the lobbying efforts of industry, particularly as they have been aimed at preventing the U.S. Congress from passing global warming legislation. She argues that energy-related corporations have employed a "three-pronged" strategy to (1) "discredit the science that underpins environmentalists' claims by portraying it as highly uncertain"; (2) "portray environmentalists as elite, misanthropic extremists"; and to (3) "draw attention to the economic costs of addressing the problem, particularly the impact of regulation on jobs and consumer prices." In this article she traces how this strategy has worked to keep global warming from becoming "widely salient"— in other words to keep it from being publicly understood as serious enough to warrant a legislative response. She points out that it was immediately after the first U.N. IPCC Assessment Report in 1990, which emphasized the role that oil and coal industries played in CO_2 emissions, that companies formed the Global Climate Coalition (GCC). The GCC has sponsored a lengthy media and advertising campaign designed to cast global warming science as inaccurate, and to turn public opinion against the idea of the U.S. signing the Kyoto Protocol. In the following excerpt, Layzer describes the interplay between these efforts and the strategies of the scientists and environmentalists, and how the business consensus on global warming began to break apart, making legislation more likely.

DEEP FREEZE: HOW BUSINESS HAS SHAPED THE GLOBAL WARMING DEBATE IN CONGRESS

Judith Layzer[9]

Even as conservative leaders in Congress and the White House adopted the arguments of global warming policy opponents, several aspects of the political context were changing in ways that divided the business community. First, the scientific consensus on the existence of, human contribution to, and threats posed by climate change was becoming unassailable. In January 2001, atmospheric concentrations of CO_2 reached a historic high of 370 ppm, and the IPPC released its third and most unequivocal report on the dangers of global warming. The report documented the unprecedented warming of the second half of the twentieth century and emphatically rejected the skeptics' primary argument—that solar activity, not human activities, was responsible for the earth's increasing temperatures. In addition, a growing mountain of scientific studies documented the impacts of global warming—from melting glaciers to changes in species' mating habits and migration patterns—many of which were occurring even faster than scientists had predicted.

Second, in the face of determined political resistance environmentalists had adjusted their tactics and begun lobbying business directly. Some of their efforts were confrontational: Greenpeace and the Rainforest Action Network launched consumer boycotts and campaigns to tarnish the reputation of big companies whose policies failed to reflect concern about global warming. In addition, environmentalists joined forces with religious groups and began submitting shareholder resolutions demanding that corporations reveal their global warming liability. Others adopted a collaborative approach: ... In March 2000, the World Wildlife Fund announced a partnership with six heavyweights, (such as Johnson & Johnson and IBM) in its Climate Savers Program, an audit program whose goal was to show that companies could

[9] Kraft, Michael, and Sheldon Kamieniecki, eds., *Business and Environmental Policy: Corporate Interests in the American Political System*, 1325 word excerpt from pages 108–125, © 2007 Massachusetts Institute of Technology, by permission of The MIT Press.

voluntarily achieve reductions that equaled or exceeded those called for under the Kyoto Protocol. Also in 2000, Environmental Defense began working with Pew, the Nature Conservancy, and at least 30 large companies to hammer out an international emissions trading scheme under its Partnership for Climate Action program.

Third, states were responding to the scientific consensus and environmental activism by enacting global warming policies of their own.... [For example, by] 2002, Massachusetts and New Hampshire had imposed CO_2 limits on power plants, and in 2003 they joined forces with seven other northeastern states and five eastern Canadian provinces to plan a regional cap-and-trade system. In July 2002, California passed a bill that made it the first state to limit greenhouse gas emissions by automobiles and light trucks. Also, in 2003, Maine passed the nation's first law calling for specific cuts in greenhouse gas emissions.

CEOs' Perceptions and Strategies Diverge

More certain science and new approaches to environmental activism, as well as action by the states, changed some senior mangers' perceptions of the costs and benefits of enacting a federal global warming policy. As a result, by the fall of 1998 the oil, automobile, and utility company coalitions were showing signs of strain.... [S]ome CEOs began to believe that carbon limits were inevitable and that being early movers would earn them a prominent role in designing the rules. Others [were] concerned about maintaining a green corporate image.... Some preferred uniform federal rules to the emerging hodge-podge of state-level requirements. So while most executives remained opposed to mandatory emissions limits, senior managers in a handful of prominent companies began to see advantages in changing their positions on the issue. Furthermore, although CEOs' motives varied, there was virtually unanimous support for a cap-and-trade system that would provide both regulatory certainty and flexibility. Therefore, they shifted their focus from blocking legislation to ensuring that Congress would adopt a market-based system whose rules would give them credit for both emissions (carbon source) reductions and forestland (carbon sink) acquisition.

In the oil industry, there was a dramatic split, with two of the largest firms— ExxonMobil and BP—taking opposite positions. Upon taking office in 1995 Exxon-Mobil's CEO, Lee Raymond, established himself as a vocal critic of global warming science and a staunch opponent of greenhouse gas emissions reductions, which he said would lead to widespread economic harm. In October 1997 Raymond urged developing countries to avoid environmental controls that would hinder their development and jeopardize foreign investment. He encouraged them not to curtail but increase their use of fossil fuels, pointing out that nature was to blame for most global warming and that changes in the Earth's temperature were commonplace. In 2002, at [an energy conference in Asia], Raymond told attendees that "we in Exxon-Mobil do not believe that the science required to establish this linkage between fossil fuels and warming has been demonstrated—and many scientists agree." To promote its position, between 1998 and 2004 ExxonMobil gave more than $15 million to conservative organizations working to influence public and policymakers' views about global warming. The company also spent $55 million between 1999 and 2004 on direct lobbying and worked closely with the [Bush] White House to craft its position on global warming and [against the U.S. signing] the Kyoto pact.

By contrast, BP withdrew from the GCC in 1997, because, according to CEO John Browne, "The time to consider policy dimensions of climate change is not when the link between greenhouse gases and climate change is conclusively proven, but when the possibility cannot be discounted and is taken seriously by the society of which we are a part." As former BP executive Steve Percy explains, large multinationals like BP recognize they have to comply with the Kyoto Protocol overseas; moreover, they prefer uniform federal regulations to an assortment of state laws.

Percy also emphasizes the potential for profitable innovation ... and the importance of maintaining a positive environmental image with both customers and shareholders.... [T]he company devised an internal cap-and-trade system that enabled it to reduce its emissions by 10 percent, at a savings of $650 million. To publicize its commitment BP undertook a $200 million public relations campaign and, in 2000, changed its corporate symbol from a shield to a sunburst and began promoting itself with the slogan "Beyond Petroleum." ...

The Ford Motor Company shook up the United States automobile industry with its highly publicized efforts to cultivate a green image. Led by its new chairman, William Clay Ford, Jr., a self-described environmentalist, in early December 1999 Ford withdrew from the GCC saying that it had begun to see its membership in the group as an impediment to pursuing its environmental initiatives credibly.... In spring 2001 Ford announced it had dropped its long-held skepticism about global warming and said that of all the ways the company would be judged in the coming years, "None will be greater than our response to climate change." Ford then took out full-page newspaper ads in the United States and Europe in May 2001 that said: "Global warming. There. We said it. Some find our stand on global warming rather unique. Mostly due to the fact that we actually have one."[10]

Adding to the chorus, a handful of companies in energy-dependent industries undertook an initiative aimed at demonstrating that a cap-and-trade system could work.... Leading the charge was DuPont, which had spent heavily to cut its greenhouse gas emissions by 40 percent between 1990 and 2000. Stung by its experience a decade earlier, when its resistance to the science linking chlorofluorocarbons and ozone loss had sparked bitter protests against the company, DuPont officials had decided to take a different tack when the global warming issue emerged.

Congress Takes up Climate Change

Activity on global warming in Congress reflected changes in the political context and the breakup of the industry coalition.... The 2003 Climate Stewardship Act failed, and a similar bill lost by an even larger margin in 2005, reflecting ... senators' continuing reluctance to act in the face of serious political uncertainty. Nevertheless, the momentum for mandatory emissions limits appeared to be growing. By 2005 many thought that greenhouse gas regulation was inevitable, and Senate leaders had begun to consider how to construct an approach that would pass muster with business and gain the endorsement of a congressional majority.

QUESTIONS

1. In the 1950s, as the popular press began publishing accounts of research linking cigarette smoking to lung cancer and heart disease, the five biggest tobacco companies responded with a media blitz. The essence of the message: the link between tobacco use and illness was controversial, and that the industry was funding a careful scientific investigation to get at the truth about smoking. Behind the scenes, the industry was working to discredit both the unwelcome scientific data and the reputations of the scientists who were bringing it to light. This strategy was effective, and was an important factor in delaying tobacco regulation for more than 50 years. As Judith Layzer reports, ExxonMobil adopted the same tactics in order to confuse the public about global warming. The company funneled millions between 1998 and 2005 to a network of 43 advocacy organizations, an overlapping collection of individuals serving as staff, board members, and

---

[10] In July 2000 Ford announced it would improve the average fuel economy of its SUV fleet 25 percent over five years (though it did not say how, and it infuriated environmentalists by continuing to lobby with the rest of the industry against increased CAFE standards).

scientific advisors that would publish and re-publish the works of a small group of climate change nay-sayers. The investigative journalist who prepared the report on this activity for the Union of Concerned Scientists, Seth Shulman, has said, "The paper trail shows that … ExxonMobil has built a vast echo chamber of seemingly independent groups with the express purpose of spreading disinformation about global warming." **Research**: The public relations titan Burston Marstellar advised both the tobacco companies in the mid 20th century and the oil companies in the 21st century. What can you find out about this firm? Who are their clients? What are they helping them to do to manage crises?

2. As Layzer notes, BP left the GCC in 1997, and reinvented itself as an environmentally-friendly company. But evidently the new green BP was also much more interested in making world-wide acquisitions while outsourcing key functions than it was in creating a culture of safety, as a string of documented blunders and accidents leading up to the massive Gulf Spill of 2010 reveal. What would an ethical analysis of this disconnect between BP's public relations effort and its actual practices look like? **Research**: Some say that ExxonMobil, having itself been responsible for a major Alaskan oil spill in 1989, has actually built up a well-functioning set of risk assessment and safety practices. What can you find out about these practices and about ExxonMobil's recent safety record?

3. As Layzer points out, once business leaders began to defect from their original hard-line resistance strategy and began to push for legislation, it was for "cap-and-trade," a system that would provide "both regulatory certainty and flexibility," and "would give [companies] credit for both emissions (carbon source) reductions and forestland (carbon sink) acquisition." Many environmentalists have favored a different legislative response to global warming—some form of carbon tax. **Research**: Find out more about cap-and-trade versus taxing emissions. What are the pros and cons of each regulatory mechanism?

4. In 2006, when the state's economy was growing and the unemployment rate was 5%, California unveiled an innovative statewide cap-and-trade plan, the first in the nation. Designed to take effect in 2012, the program would cap greenhouse gases (GHGs) from hundreds of power plants, refineries, cement plants and other big factories, allowing them to buy and sell emission permits among themselves to reach an overall goal of cutting emissions to 2005 levels by 2020. But by 2010, with the state government broke and the California jobless rate at 12.5%, the cap-and-trade plan had become hotly controversial, with regulators and industry estimating sharply different costs and benefits. In November 2010 a ballot initiative, launched by Texas oil firms Valero and Tesoro, decided the fate of this program. **Research**: What happened?

5. **Research**: The GCC was "deactivated" as of 2002. Many companies had decided to abandon their longstanding public stance against the idea that global warming was caused by human activity. Yet, in June 2010, the International Climate Science Coalition (ICSC) announced that it had 100 scientists endorsing the following statement:

We, the undersigned, having assessed the relevant scientific evidence, do not find convincing support for the hypothesis that human emissions of carbon dioxide are causing, or will in the foreseeable future cause, dangerous global warming.

This group describes itself as a "highly credible alternative to the UN's Intergovernmental Panel on Climate Change (IPCC)," offering "a more rational, open discussion about climate issues." Go to *www.climatescienceinternational.org*. What can you find out about the ICSC? Who funds them? Investigate the individuals who are prominent within the organizations. What is their expertise? What awards or achievements do they possess that would lend them credibility on this issue? If they have done research, how was it funded? Try *www.source-watch.org*, a project of the Center for Media and Democracy or the Integrity in Science project at *www.cspinet.org*. Ask the same questions of the Center for Media and Democracy and the Integrity in Science project.

6. **Research**: Has the IPCC 5th Assessment Report been published? If so, browse it to discover: (1) What has changed in terms of CO_2 levels since the 2007 Report? (2) Summarize the strategies the authors recommend national governments take to most effectively reduce greenhouse gases.

ASSESSING THE COSTS OF CLIMATE CHANGE

One of the most hotly contested issues involves the cost of responding to climate change. Many claim any comprehensive regulatory attempt to address this problem would be ruinous to the weak U.S. and global economy. Warning of lost jobs, higher taxes, and price hikes, they also point to the uncertainties of predicting what will occur.

And indeed, enormous uncertainties remain. Are we facing worst-case scenarios, where the Arctic icecaps melt, the great circulation currents of the oceans stop or slow, and the East Coast of North America experiences an ice age? Or are we just looking at the extinction of the polar bears? Will the whole western half of the United States become a dustbowl, or are we just going to have to deal with severe drought in a few areas? What is the timeline for any scenario? As of this writing, climate modelers themselves have become increasingly pessimistic. Many organizations in the forefront of this science have doubled their projections for the temperature rising over the 21st century. Their concern is "feedback effects"—like the fact that global warming will release the greenhouse gas, methane, from tundra and seabeds, and like the combined effects of rising sea levels and more intense storm activity.

But there are others, like Nobel-prize winning Princeton economist Paul Krugman, who argue "there is no credible research suggesting that taking strong action on climate change is beyond the economy's capacity." Since we are confronted with "the non-negligible probability of utter disaster" we must allow this to guide our policy choices; we cannot afford not to act. Krugman cites a Congressional Budget Office report, concluding that "strong climate policy would leave the American economy between 1.1 percent and 3.4 percent smaller in 2050 than it would be otherwise." As for the global economy, Krugman points out that experts have put the cost of acting now at about 1 to 3% of gross world product. (As one expert has estimated, to do nothing will cost far more: five to 20 percent of global GDP, depending on how bad things get.)[11] Krugman reminds us that the acid rain success story was less costly than predicted, and that "what the models do not and cannot take into account is creativity … the 'magic of the marketplace.'"

Krugman also tackles the thorny issue of the resistance of developing countries to emissions controls. He notes that China, which has recently overtaken the U.S. as

---

[11] Sir Nicholas Stern, *Stern Review: The Economics of Climate Change*, 2006. Report commissioned by the U.K. government.

the world's biggest GHG polluter (U.S. is still top per capita emitter), "currently uses energy fairly inefficiently ... and could thus achieve large energy savings at a modest cost." He favors an international cap and trade arrangement, with overall caps set at levels designed to ensure that China sells a substantial number of permits. He would combine this with carbon tariffs (probably issued by the U.S. and Europe) designed to give non-cooperating nations an incentive to cut emissions.[12]

Ethics & The U.S. Response to Climate Change

Most ethical systems and our intuitive ethical sensitivity are focused on one's responsibilities to people who are close by and who can be directly affected by one's actions. The technical power that humans now have to adversely affect people separated by time and space is a great new challenge to ethical reasoning. Yet because human-induced climate change will most hurt the poorest on the planet, seriously reduce the quality of life for future generations, and threaten plants and animals around the world, climate change and other emerging global environmental problems must be understood to raise very serious ethical issues.

—DONALD A. BROWN[13]

In his analysis of global warming, the author of the following article points to an alignment between what is ethical and what is in the best interests of the United States. He argues that influential religious groups can both help to make this alignment clear, and "can play a crucial role in establishing a political consensus to support the United States in taking a global leadership role on climate change."

THE U.S. AND ITS CLIMATE CHANGE POLICY:

ADVOCATING AN ALIGNMENT OF NATIONAL INTEREST AND ETHICAL OBLIGATIONS

John Holland[14]

...The U.S. is the world's most powerful country and by far its biggest per capita emitter of greenhouse gases. The United States' capacity to deal with the potential effects of global warming is also far greater than most countries' (both because the U.S. has more resources for adapting and because global warming will probably not affect the U.S. as much as most other countries). For these reasons ... the United States has an ethical obligation to take a leading role in addressing global warming.

American religious groups can play an important role in addressing these ethical obligations. First, religion is an obvious source of ethical principles.... Furthermore, nearly all religions contain an environmental ethic....

[The author focuses on two very politically influential religious groups in the U.S.: Catholics and evangelicals.]

---

[12] Paul Krugman. "Building a Green Economy," *New York Times*, April 11, 2010.

[13] *American Heat: Ethical Problems With the United States' Response to Global Warming* 4-5 (2002).

[14] John Holland, "The United States and Its Climate Change Policy: Advocating an Alignment of National Interest and Ethical Obligations," Notre Dame Journal of Law, Ethics & Public Policy 23(2), 2009, pp. 623–649. Reprinted by permission of the author.

The Catholic Perspective

...Global warming implicates many of the traditional concerns of the Catholic Church: the creation, redemption, stewardship of the earth, use of the world's resources for the universal common good, solidarity, concern for the poor and future generations, and respect for human life and dignity.

The U.S. Catholic Bishops have stated that "the environmental crisis is a moral challenge" ...[and in 2001] issued a statement asking the United States to take a prominent role in the global warming debate. The Bishops stated that the responsibility to lead "weighs more heavily upon those with the power to act because the threats are often greatest for those who lack similar power, namely, vulnerable poor populations, as well as future generations."

Most of the Church's recent teachings heavily emphasize the universal common good and the interdependence of the world in the age of globalization. In 1990, Pope John Paul II stated:

> The ecological crisis reveals the urgent moral need for a new solidarity, especially in relations between the developing nations and those that are highly industrialized. States must increasingly share responsibility, in complementary ways, for the promotion of a natural and social environment that is both peaceful and healthy....

The Evangelical Perspective

...The theological underpinnings of evangelical support for action on global warming are similar to those that motivate Catholics—the protection of God's creation, assisting people in the poorest countries, and overarching concerns about the sanctity of life. Reverend Richard Cizik, the former vice president of the [National Association of Evangelicals] NAE, recently described global warming as "an offense against God." At the core of this evangelical movement is "creation care"—the idea that people have the religious duty to protect God's creation and to act as stewards of the earth. Leith Anderson, the president of NAE, has said that "social issues ... relate to the sanctity of human life—before and after birth. So I would see issues like poverty, or the effects of climate change, as sanctity-of-life issues." Once a skeptic, Pat Robertson now supports action against global warming. In March 2008, Robertson agreed to appear in a TV ad in support of Al Gore's Alliance for Climate Protection. Robertson told his television audience that "it's just common sense that we ought to be good stewards of the environment and do everything within our power to protect this fragile planet that we all live on." Thus, there is a strong movement among evangelicals to break from the past and promote environmental policies. Indeed, in February 2008, a national meeting of the country's foremost evangelical leaders declared climate change "the civil-rights movement of the 21st century."

Political Influence of Catholics and Evangelicals in the United States

...[B]oth Catholics and evangelicals are powerful voting blocs in the United States....

The 47 million Catholic voters in the United States have been called "by far the largest and most important bloc of swing voters" in the American electorate. Catholics have voted for the winner of the popular vote in the last ten consecutive presidential elections.... As one writer said, however "goes the Catholic vote, so goes the country."[15]

Evangelicals are also important in American politics, but in a different way. While the Catholic vote is often up for grabs, ... the evangelical vote is a stable pillar of the

---

[15] See John Russonello & Kate Stewart, "Understanding Catholic Voters," *Conscience*, Autumn 2005, 23. In the 2008 presidential election, Barack Obama won 54% of the Catholic vote. Margaret Ramirez & Manya A. Brachear, "Obama Picks Up Religious Votes," *Chi. Trib.*, Nov. 6, 2008, at A19.

Republican Party. In 2004, seventy-eight percent of evangelical voters supported President Bush. Naturally, evangelicals are very influential within the Republican Party.... [A]n estimated twenty-five percent of American voters belong to a religious denomination that falls under the NAE umbrella.

The Possibility for Consensus Between Religious Groups and Environmentalists

....Global warming is increasingly proving its ability to make for strange bedfellows: Greenpeace and DuPont, conservative evangelicals and the Sierra Club.... Perhaps, then, it should not be surprising that religious and environmentalist organizations—who might disagree with each other on a wide variety of other issues—are uniting around the need to address global warming. Such coalitions are important since they may further solidify the foundation of political support for the American government to address climate change....

The Alignment of Morality and the National Interest

...Some American commentators seem to treat global warming as a zero-sum game between the United States and the rest of the world.... But by fulfilling its ethical duty to lead on global warming, the U.S. actually furthers its own national interest. This is true for a number of reasons. First, assuming a leadership role in promoting some immediate measures against global warming, even if that means making some unilateral emissions cuts, is a practical response to scientific uncertainty according to a purely economic risk management analysis. Second, the U.S. has a national security interest in addressing climate change, especially in the age of globalization where the collapse of societies on the other side of the world can affect the United States.

An Ethical (and Rational) Response to Uncertainty

The most common argument against addressing global warming is that of scientific uncertainty....

For a number of ethical and practical reasons, scientific uncertainty does not justify inaction.... [T]his ethical dilemma weighs heavy on the United States as the biggest per capita emitter and the country with the most resources to adapt to any future problems caused by global warming. If a country waits for the resolution of all scientific uncertainty, that nation is implicitly asking future generations, especially in the poorest regions of the world, to "bear the burden of risk in light of the fact that harm may be experienced before scientific uncertainties are resolved." ...The imposition of such a risk on the poor and future generations is inconsistent with the religious obligations to be stewards of the earth, to attempt to protect the lives of future generations, and to consider the needs of the world's poorest people.

Furthermore, from a purely economic perspective—that is, a perspective of balancing the cost of addressing global warming against the possible risk—it is rational to start addressing global warming in the face of uncertainty.... As *The Economist* summarized [The Stern Report's][16] conclusions:

> *Governments should act not on the basis of the likeliest outcome from climate change but on the risk of something really catastrophic (such as the melting of Greenland's ice sheet, which would raise sea levels by six to seven metres).*

---

[16] *The Stern Review Report on the Economics of Climate Change* (2006), study funded by U.K. government. Sir Nicholas Stern, former World Bank Chief Economist, dubbed climate change "the greatest and widest-ranging market failure ever seen" and outlined the financial risks and opportunities associated with confronting it. He projected that addressing global warming immediately would cost about 1% of the world's GDP annually, while doing nothing would raise costs to up to 20 percent of GDP "now and forever."

Just as people spend a small slice of their incomes on buying insurance on the off-chance that their house might burn down, and nations use a slice of tax-payers' money to pay for standing armies just in case a rival power might try to invade them, so the world should invest a small proportion of its resources in try-ing to avert the risk of boiling the planet. The costs are not huge. The dangers are.[17]

...Preventative measures can also have more direct economic benefits. For instance, the U.S. Clean Air Act of 1970 has "yielded estimated net health savings (benefits in excess of costs) of about $1 trillion per year, due to saved lives and reduced health costs." Also, the long-term direct economic impact of failing to address global warming may be far worse than any short-term negative impact that results from transitioning away from a carbon-reliant economy. Therefore, the ethical approach of taking some immediate action to address global warming, even in the face of uncertainty, is consistent with a rational economic risk management analysis.

Global Warming as a National Security Issue

...American history contains plenty of examples of when ethical obligations and national interest aligned. For instance.... in his inaugural address, President Kennedy said:

To those people in the huts and villages of half the globe struggling to break the bonds of mass misery, we pledge our best efforts to help them help themselves, for whatever period is required—not because the Communists may be doing it, not because we seek their votes, but because it is right.

However, Kennedy also knew that programs such as the Peace Corps were cru-cial to winning over developing countries whose allegiances were up for grabs during the Cold War.

Because of the growing interconnectedness of the world, global problems are increasingly becoming America's problems.... [According to] Professor Jared Dia-mond, winner of the Pulitzer Prize, ..."many people fear that ecocide has now come to overshadow nuclear war and emerging diseases as a threat to global civilization." One of Diamond's main concerns is that droughts, floods, lack of clean water, and unsustainable development destabilize the poorest countries (mainly in Africa) and undermine the capacity of resource-starved governments to control their populations and secure their borders. The collapse of governments and societies in places such as Rwanda, Somalia, and Afghanistan greatly increases the risk that destabilized countries will become havens for terrorists and international criminals.

For instance, the Horn of Africa now has only five percent of its original habitat remaining. The U.N. has expressed alarm over this fact, and some think that Al Qaeda hopes to open up "a new jihadist front" in the Horn. Africa, with its reliance on rain-fed farming and its already minimal clean water supply, is especially vulnera-ble to the effects of global warming....

It is evident that American political leaders are increasingly seeing climate change as a national security issue.

In response to [testimony that climate change was multiplying the stress in already-fragile Darfur region] Congress, by a wide margin of support, approved a pro-vision requiring the CIA and the Pentagon to conduct the first-ever national intelli-gence estimate on global warming and climate change....

---

[17] "Economics of Climate Change: Stern Warning," *Economist*, Nov. 4, 2006, p. 14.

Conclusion

...Nearly two decades ago, the U.S. Catholic Bishops asked, "How can the United States, as a nation, act responsibly about this ever more global problem?" Yet, the U.S.'s official policy on climate change has hardly changed since then. However, public opinion has, and it appears that Congress may soon push the U.S. into a global leadership position on global warming.... [S]uch leadership is both ethical and practical. By leading on global warming, the United States can realize an alignment of its national interest and the fulfillment of its ethical obligations.

QUESTIONS

1. Identify these separately: Holland's argument that addressing climate change now is:
   (a) ethical;
   (b) aligned with religious principles;
   (c) rational in a free market economy;
   (d) aligned with the U.S. national interest.

2. **Research**: Holland writes elsewhere in this article: "When eighty-six prominent evangelical leaders signed a "Call to Action" to address global warming, *National Geographic* declared it "the best news of the year [2009]." Find the Call to Action. Does it reflect the environmental ethics outlined in this article? Can you find more recent environmental activism among evangelicals?

3. **Research**: Although Holland looks at only Catholics and evangelicals in this piece, he states that "nearly all religions contain an environmental ethic." Choose a religion—Jewish, Muslim, Buddhist, Shinto, Sikh—or any other he did not examine, and see if you can find traces of such an ethic. Have any of its leaders made statements or become active on the issue of global climate change?

4. Elsewhere in this article, Holland points to a way in which the religious approach to environmental issues tends to focus on harms to humans as opposed to harms to other species. He writes: "Catholics and evangelicals (not to mention people of other religious beliefs) place a heavy emphasis on how climate change will threaten the quality of the lives of poor people in developing countries (in the short term) and of future generations (in the long term). These beliefs can help counter the often-raised myth that climate change advocates are only concerned about ice caps and polar bears." Indeed, opponents of environmentalists often paint them as favoring owls and beetles over jobs and the needs of people. What are the ethics, for environmental activists, of accepting the support and political "cover" of evangelicals, whose views on abortion or gender issues, for example, might be diametrically opposed to their own?

5. Has the U.S. passed comprehensive legislation to address global climate change? If so, were the voices of religious leaders heard in direct support?

Corporate Social Responsibility: A Market for Virtue?

In the next reading, David Vogel, Professor at the University of California, Berkeley, speaking at the Brookings Institute in late 2005, asks whether the market economy creates real incentives for companies to behave responsibly where environmental and human rights are concerned. He is ultimately interested to know: Do market pressures drive firms to effectively self-police in these areas? Can their voluntary behavior effectively substitute for government regulation? As he investigates a possible "market for virtue," Vogel looks first at whether ethical behavior correlates with success, as many who promote corporate social responsibility claim. He finds that there is no such relationship. While many firms are both profitable and touted as socially responsible (including BP at the time), Vogel notes companies with ethical policies are not necessarily successful, and points to a long list of profitable firms that have never been known for their ethics—ExxonMobil among them. He then looks at consumer markets, labor markets, and capital markets. If these three economic mechanisms rewarded virtuous corporate behavior, Vogel posits, "every firm would compete with every other firm to be responsible."

THE MARKET FOR VIRTUE
David Vogel[18]

[In t]he consumer market we can obviously … cite examples of cases in which people have … avoided a particular brand or store or company, because of some social environmental grievance … examples of cases where we have gone out of our way to purchase a product, a service … because we like some aspects of its social, environmental, or ethical performance…. There are cases of effective boycotts. There are cases of companies which have increased their market share by a reputation for corporate responsibility.

Unfortunately, when you add all those up, it's a very small portion of consumer spending. Basically, we buy products on the basis of price, quality, and convenience. [E]thical issues fall … by the wayside most of the time. When you [survey] people … in Britain and the U.S., do you actually take into account environmental, social, ethical concerns in your purchasing decisions? Have you gone out of your way to buy or not buy from a company because of these criteria? 70 to 80 percent say yes. When you look at actual consumer behavior, the number of people who have ever made a decision on this basis is closer to three percent….

[M]ore importantly, to the extent that corporate responsibility raises costs, consumers are unwilling to pay them. There is simply no evidence that any company can command a price premium—except very … expensive products—because they've made [their product] in a more socially responsible way.

[Turning to the labor markets, Vogel sees a similar syndrome. MBA students, when surveyed as they are about to graduate, claim they want to work for responsible firms, and claim to be willing to take wage cuts to work for them, yet when *Business Week* surveys MBAs asking them to list their most desirable employers: "You will not see a relationship between the firms listed and firms that have a good CSR reputation."]

Capital markets are in some ways the most interesting. The number of ethical mutual funds has grown … [to] about two percent of the U.S. mutual funds….upwards of $100 billion…. Ethical mutual funds now exist in every global capital market…. [T]here's no evidence that being listed by a prestigious … socially responsible fund or rating service has any impact on share prices, and the funds admit that themselves.

So we're left with … mainstream investors…. [I]n principle, if mainstream investors were to take social responsibility seriously and recognize it as a major business

---

[18] David Vogel, "The Market for Virtue," Brookings Institute Press Briefing, November 2, 2005. Reprinted by permission.

risk and opportunity, capital allocation would change, management incentives would change, the market for virtue would be clear.

Unfortunately, ... [if we] look at the business press ... stock reports with analysts talking about the prospects for a company ... what's striking is how rarely ... these reports ... mention anything to do with CSR, either positive or negative. It's simply irrelevant.

[While Vogel does acknowledge the growth of CSR over recent decades, and its accomplishments within the profit system ("When activists went to Mattel two Christmases ago, and said, we're going to start a campaign which says, buy Mattel, the company that makes toys for children by children, Mattel folded very, very quickly."), he ends with this provocative point:]

...Much writing on CSR [depicts it as if] private regulation ... can serve as an effective substitute for government regulation. And I think this is very ... distorting and quite irresponsible. We need to ... recognize the limits ... of what companies can do. [T]he only institution capable of forcing companies to internalize their externalities, to engage in socially important activities that are not profitable, that do not meet a market test is, of course, ... government and government regulation.

Now, clearly, particularly in developing countries, to the extent that there is no effective government regulation,... CSR is an effective solution. If you want to improve health and safety conditions in Vietnam, going through Nike is a much more effective strategy than going to the government of Vietnam.... If you want to improve forestry practices in Chile, going to Home Depot is much more effective than going to the government of Chile. So to the extent that one can use those con- sumer pressures and the reach of globalization to affect practices in developing countries, as long as those countries aren't willing [or able] to improve their own reg- ulations, CSR is ... a real improvement.

But [in] developed countries like the United States and Western Europe, there I think the shortcomings of CSR are important. Take the critical issue ... [of] global climate change. If you add up all the ... voluntary initiatives that companies have engaged in in the United States ... they're important. They're commendable.... [But t]hey're trivial in terms of actually ... reducing the rate of U.S. carbon emissions. If we're serious about doing that, ...there's no alternative to responsible public policies.

...[W]e need to redefine and expand the definition of corporate responsibility, and we need to [ask]...companies ... not only what are you doing on your own voluntarily, but are you supporting responsible public policies. So the company, for example, which makes no effort to improve its own carbon emissions, but supports effective government regulation of carbon emissions to require all firms to internalize this prob- lem is I think acting much more responsibly than a firm which makes enormous efforts to improve its own carbon emissions, but opposes effective public policy.

[T]he real new frontier of corporate responsibility is to ask companies which claim to be responsible to not only focus on their own internal policies, but to also think about ... chang[ing] the rules of the game and creat[ing] a more level playing field, [making] it possible for all firms to behave more responsibly....

QUESTIONS

1. Vogel does not dismiss corporate social responsibility as mere "window dress- ing," but he does recognize its limits. What are the accomplishments and limits of CSR in his view? How would Vogel redefine CSR? What would an ethical anal- ysis of his new CSR look like?

2. Elsewhere in his talk, Vogel mentions that when William Ford became CEO of Ford, he announced he was going to "green" the company. As Vogel notes, within two years he had to concede that he could not make this happen.

Ford's profits come from ... the SUV, which environmentalists would probably argue is the most irresponsible product in the history of civilization.... It's possible that there is some consumer in the United States who said, I really want to get an SUV, and it meets my price needs, [the] needs of my family and safety ... [B]ut, you know, when I think about ... global climate change ... I'm not going to buy it. It would be irresponsible. There may be some people in America who made such a choice, but ... certainly not [enough] to convince Henry Ford to change his policies.

Research: In the absence of federal regulations on carbon emissions, have consumer choices become more green-responsive in recent years? How are they trending? If the U.S. Congress has passed carbon regulations, has there been any effect on consumer choices?

GREEN TAXES, GREEN RULES

One approach to environmental protection involves creative use of taxes. Traditionally, we tax many of the things we value; we levy taxes on paychecks, income, property, sales, businesses. But because taxation tends to discourage productive activity, why not use the power to tax for what it is: a reverse incentive? Why not, many argue, tax that which we do *not* value, such as pollution, congestion, sprawl, and resource depletion? European governments do just that: Reducing taxes on the "goods," they instead tax the "bads," like toxic waste. This is called "tax shifting." A "green tax" is one that uses government taxing power to build sustainable economies and benefit the environment. In 2000, for example, the United Kingdom committed to lowering CO_2 emissions (below the Kyoto levels) to 20 percent below 1990 levels by 2010. To achieve this, the U.K. imposed a national tax on energy usage. Companies which adopted energy efficiency practices would receive energy tax refunds.

Another regulatory mechanism is to issue a uniform requirement that levels the playing field for all businesses and stimulates green markets. For example, the 2001 European Landfill Directive mandates treatment of waste before it reaches landfills, and stipulates that 50 percent of all waste producing methane (one of the most potent GHGs) must be diverted from landfills. This regulation has created a healthy market for waste processing facilities across Europe. An innovative spin-off has been the so-called waste-to-energy facilities, which turn garbage and other recyclable material into fuel. Today, more than 400 such plants cut carbon emissions and reduce energy costs across Europe.

Consider these governmental responses to climate change:

- Fines levied on companies that exceed set emission levels
- Taxing emissions
- Tradeable permit system for emissions
- Regulation like the EU Landfill Directive

Compare and contrast the three approaches. Which would you favor for business? Which would you want enforced in your neighborhood?

Corporate Governance: Shareholder Activism

Shareholders have the right to attempt to influence the actions of the management. They can do this by putting nonbinding proposals forward—called resolutions—to be voted upon at annual shareholder meetings. Until the 1970s, shareholder resolutions tended to focus on bottom line concerns. But in 1971, the Episcopal Church filed the first church-sponsored shareholder resolution, challenging General Motor's operations in the apartheid regime in South Africa, and sparking others to make proposals related to corporate social responsibility. Today, shareholder activism continues to grow, with proposals each year on a range of issues, from executive compensation to diversity to the environment.

The Proxy System   In advance of each annual meeting, shareholders are sent form ballots listing the items that are up for vote, including membership on the board of directors, choice of an outside auditor, and resolutions brought by the board or share-holders. Each share of stock generally counts as one vote.[19] Shareholders have the right to come to the annual meetings in person to cast their ballots, but few do. If they prefer, shareholders can vote by returning the "proxy card" that is mailed along with the notice of the meeting. The board of directors has the right to vote the shares of those who neither appear nor return a completed proxy vote. Given the large number of individuals who own stock in the typical publicly-owned corporation, few of whom have a big block of shares, this system assures corporate control of the majority of the votes.

Preliminary Management Resistance   Getting a shareholder resolution voted upon is not automatic. Management may strongly disagree with the proposal, and has the right to write a statement in opposition (with no length limit) that will appear on the ballot ("proxy statement"), effectively killing the proposal. In the face of outright opposition from management, shareholder proposals are often withdrawn before a vote.

Broad Policy Proposals Only   According to SEC rules regarding shareholder proposals, there are thirteen circumstances under which a corporation may "omit" or ignore the resolution.[20] For example, resolutions may not deal with "the conduct of the ordinary business operations" of a company. This means that shareholders may not make proposals dealing with how the firm is actually run, but may only offer suggestions regarding overall corporate policy. Shareholders may propose that the company review its human resource policies with regard to homosexuals, for example, but may not propose that human resource personnel hire a certain proportion of gay men and women; shareholders may propose that a company conduct an audit of its practices regarding recycling and renewable energy use, but they may not offer specifics outlining how it would carry out such a plan.

Mere Recommendations, but with Moral Authority   Even if a proposal makes it onto the ballot, and even if an impressive proportion of shareholders votes for it, the result is merely advisory—or "nonbinding." Management still has the right to respond to the issue in some different way, or to ignore the resolution altogether. However, most corporate boards realize the appropriateness of making some kind of compromise with popular shareholder measures, and shareholder resolutions have been an effective

---

[19] Most states permit corporations to issue several classes of stock. Traditionally, only common stock had voting rights, although that law has changed in some states.

[20] 17 *Code of Federal Regulations* (CFR) Ch. II, Sec. 240.14a-8.

means of forcing change even in the absence of majority shareholder approval. Recently, resolutions have brought on changes in corporate governance, accounting practices, and environmental policies.

Below is a sample shareholder resolution. It was put forward in 2004 by investors in American International Group, Inc. (AIG—Chubb Insurance its subsidiary), requesting that it assess the risks to its business presented by global climate change. The lead sponsors included "socially responsible" investment funds.[21] The insurance company decided to omit this resolution from its proxy statement.

Shareholder Resolution on Climate Change
Resolved:

The shareholders request that the Board of Directors prepare a report, at reasonable cost and omitting proprietary information, made available to shareholders by September 30, 2004, providing a comprehensive assessment of Chubb's strategies to address the impacts of climate change on its business.

Supporting Statements:

- *We believe the human contribution to climate change has become widely accepted among the scientific community. Legislation, regulation, litigation, and other responses to climate change seem likely.*
- *"In global warming, we are facing an enormous risk to the U.S. economy and retirement funds that Wall Street has so far chosen to ignore." (Philip Angelides, Treasurer of California)...*
- *In November 2003, as a part of the Carbon Disclosure Project, 87 institutional investors representing over $9 trillion in assets wrote to the 500 largest companies by market capitalization asking for relevant information concerning greenhouse gas emissions. According to the Project Coordinator, "There are potential business risks and opportunities related to actions stemming from climate change that have implications for the value of shareholdings in corporations worldwide."*
- *Munich Re's 2002 Annual Report states that climate-related catastrophes are the greatest cost to the industry. Of the 35 largest natural catastrophes that cost insurers over €1 billion, only two were not climate related. Climate change may lead to increased erratic and extreme weather events, resulting in serious environmental and public health impacts.*
- *Swiss Re sees inaction on climate change as a possible liability for directors and officers (D&O), and is considering potential coverage implications for insured companies that do not address climate change risks. As D&O liability insurance is a significant part of Chubb's business, we believe investors should know how the company is addressing this issue.*

We believe proactive behavior in the European Union, Japan, and elsewhere may put U.S. companies at a competitive disadvantage globally. Of 84 signatories to the United Nations Environmental Programme Financial Initiatives Insurance Industry Initiative, only three are North American companies. Chubb is not a signatory.

- *"Catastrophe insurers can't simply extrapolate past experience. If there is truly 'global warming,' for example, the odds would shift, since tiny changes in atmospheric*

---

[21] (Walden Asset Management, Calvert Asset Management Company, Progressive Investment Management), religious investors (Community Church of New York, Congregation of the Sisters of St. Joseph of Brighton), environmental groups (Conservation Land Trust, Tides Foundation) and government pension funds (State of Connecticut Treasurer's Office, State of Maine Office of the Treasurer).

conditions can produce momentous changes in weather patterns." (Warren Buffet, Chairman, Berkshire Hathaway, 1993)

- *With property and casualty customers in 29 countries, we believe Chubb is exposed to climate risks....*

Chubb's Annual Report has, since 1997, stated under the heading *Catastrophe Exposure*, "We also continue to explore and analyze credible scientific evidence, including the impact of global climate change, that may affect our potential exposure under insurance policies." Chubb has not responded to investor requests for additional information.

In 1990 the nonprofit organization Ceres was founded, envisioning "a world in which business and capital markets promote the well being of society and the protection of the Earth's biological systems and resources." In 2010, Ceres issued a fourth report reviewing the period 2004-07 for the mutual fund industry's practices on climate change shareholder resolutions. The data revealed that the previously "icy" attitude on climate resolutions was "beginning to thaw," and that "many on Wall Street [were] starting to realize the financial risks and opportunities from climate change." For example mutual fund votes against climate resolutions had dropped from almost 78 percent to just under two-thirds or 65.1 percent. The Ceres report also noted that some mutual funds appeared to be taking a "schizophrenic" stance. Morgan Stanley, for example, which announced a plan to invest $3 billion in GHG reduction over five years, did not support the more than 200 climate resolutions that faced their funds in the time period under analysis. On the other hand, the Ceres report depicts Goldman Sachs, starkly involved in the financial meltdown of 2006-07, as taking a leadership role, "matching its forward-thinking actions on climate (such as conducting climate-related research, establishing a company-wide environmental policy and investing in clean technology) with its increasing support of climate resolutions."

■ ■ ■

Law professor Thomas Joo considers who within the corporate structure is best situated to respond to climate change in the article below. He writes:

[T]he concentration of decision-making power at the top of the corporate hierarchy is a key reason why reformers cannot rely on shareholders to address global warming. Shareholders do not run the corporation; they are simply "along for the ride." But this hardly requires us to give up hope of reform. Rather, understanding and acknowledging the hierarchical nature of corporate governance can help create more realistic (if imperfect) approaches to reform.

In this excerpt, he explains his view that shareholders cannot make the kind of difference that public outrage can.

GLOBAL WARMING AND THE MANAGEMENT-CENTERED CORPORATION

Thomas Joo[22]

Shareholders are atomized and anonymous. They cannot be easily identified with the companies in which they invest. Shareholders also tend to have diversified portfolios made up of relatively small holdings in many different companies. All of this

[22] Thomas Joo, "Global Warming and the Management-Centered Corporation," *Wake Forest Law Review* 44, 2009, pp. 671–703. Reprinted by permission.

distances them from the companies they nominally "own" and insulates them from personal moral responsibility for the acts of these companies. Shareholders' inability to influence policy further insulates them from responsibility. Shareholding is conceived of primarily as a mechanism for building wealth, rather than as a position of influence that engenders a social responsibility. While there are certainly many "socially responsible" funds and shareholder proposals, these are relatively rare exceptions that prove the general rule.

The lack of personal moral accountability means that even as social norms change to condemn the conduct of corporations, such as carbon pollution, indeed even as shareholders themselves voice objections in their nonshareholding capacity, shareholders qua shareholders simply do not feel responsible for the conduct. Thus, reforming corporate governance to empower shareholders may be precisely the wrong approach to increasing corporate social responsibility. Even as society arrives at consensus on the threat of climate change, individual behavior is unlikely to change without some visible leadership. Because climate change is so heavily influenced by industrial production and the consumption of those products, corporate executives may be useful normative leaders.

[The author goes to emphasize that corporate law gives shareholders minimal control over the conduct of senior management.]

Based on an aversion to government control of business, corporate law does not review the actions of management (unless they are disloyal); thus, allowing management "to justify almost any action" is a fundamental aspect of corporate law. The question then, is not to whom management owes fiduciary duties, but how to restrain management discretion in the absence of any meaningful fiduciary duties. The pressure to enrich shareholders does not come from the law, but from the capital markets (including the market for corporate control). Moral accountability (together with regulatory prescriptions) can mitigate that pressure and push management to use its discretion in socially beneficial ways.

Public backlash may contribute to changes in corporate executives' behavior. Politicians can also lead reform in accordance with public opinion. But leadership from our elected officials is most likely if corporate America is also on board. The private financing of political campaigns leaves our political and corporate leaders deeply interdependent.

...[T]he existence of profit opportunities in low-carbon production does not give management any corporate-law duty to pursue them. Shareholder pressure for profits will of course motivate some management to pursue green innovations, but dirty technology will offer its own profit opportunities as long as the lack of regulation allows producers and consumers to externalize the environmental costs. Market forces and shareholder empowerment will therefore be woefully insufficient to make corporations reduce carbon emissions unless regulation reduces the profitability of carbon-intensive business activity through taxes, fines, and the like, and/or by reducing the relative costs of cleaner technology through tax breaks or direct subsidies.

Thus, the entire project of shareholder empowerment and social-responsibility disclosure may be misguided. Individuals who profess to be socially concerned may think differently when privately and anonymously making choices that would affect their retirement savings or their children's college funds. Fund managers for institutional investors may lack the anonymity of individual investors, but their jobs and compensation are dependent on attracting and satisfying anonymous, morally shielded investors who are mainly concerned with profits. Perhaps even more so than corporate officers, fund managers are typically evaluated by the short-term (quarterly) profits they generate.

As the public face of corporations, executives are much more likely to be charged with, and accept, moral accountability.... Placing moral obligation on CEOs is clearly on the rise in post-meltdown America. Politicians and the public have mobilized moral outrage (justified or not) against individual executives. The former CEO of General Motors, Rick Wagoner, took symbolic blame when the Obama administration forced his resignation as a condition of bailout assistance for GM in March 2009. The response to the bonuses paid to AIG executives in March 2009 was an even more powerful example of moral outrage. Note that the anger of politicians and the public was directed at CEO Edward Liddy (who had come out of retirement, at the government's request, to take over the job at a salary of $1) and the recipients of the bonuses, and not at AIG's board of directors or its ... shareholders.

Because the AIG incident involved executive compensation, the public outrage was consistent with traditional corporate-governance notions of loyalty to shareholders. After all, each American is, very nearly literally, an investor in AIG and other bailed-out institutions. The challenge is transferring that notion of moral accountability for profits to a social issue like climate change. This may not prove to be so difficult. Anger about AIG does not appear to be based only on the belief that our bailout investment has been squandered. It stems more fundamentally from the reason the government bailed out institutions in the first place: the fact that their enormous power meant their failure threatened the U.S. and global economies. U.S. society tolerated such power in private hands as long as it generated social benefit (mainly in the form of material wealth). Now, however, there is momentum toward holding corporate and financial America, and particularly its top executives, more responsible for abusing its power over the economy and society. At the same time, we are also coming to realize that industry has power over climate change, and it may be the moment to impose moral responsibility for the use of that power. After all, the stakes are far higher than any financial crisis. Admittedly, much of the moral responsibility currently being assigned to the financial and industrial leaders for the economic crisis is symbolic and may be too little, too late. Hopefully that need not also be true with respect to climate change.

My argument does not suppose that CEOs will spontaneously take moral responsibility and change corporate behavior. Rather, my argument is that their visibility makes them susceptible to pressure for change and that regulators should take this into account. The concentration of power at the top of the corporate hierarchy creates a focal point not only for moral accountability, but also for self-interest. ...[R]egulatory strategy can focus on pressuring the small group of corporate hierarchs by appealing both to their consciences and to their desire to maintain their grip on power and wealth.

QUESTIONS

1. Where in the corporate hierarchy does Joo place responsibility for addressing climate change? What are his reasons?

2. Consider Joo's arguments in light of the Ceres report on shareholder resolutions. Who is more convincing? **Research**: Find out if shareholder resolutions on the environment have increased or decreased in the last few years.

3. **Research**: In January, 2010, the Securities and Exchange Commission (SEC) voted to provide public companies with interpretive guidance on SEC disclosure requirements as they apply to business or legal developments related to climate change. Find out what advice the SEC has given. What impact would you expect this requirement to have on the various corporate players (CEOs, Boards of Trustees, etc.)?

Philosophical Perspectives

And the fear of you and the dread of you shall be upon every beast of the earth, and upon every fowl of the air, upon all that moveth upon the earth and upon all the fishes of the sea; into your hand are they delivered. Every moving thing that liveth shall be meat for you; even as the green herb have I given you all things.

—GOD TO NOAH, Genesis 9: 2-3

Every man ... has an equal right of pursuing and taking to his own use all such creatures as are [wild].

—W. BLACKSTONE, *Commentaries* 411 (1766)

The quotes above reflect the traditional Western Judeo-Christian understanding of the virtually unqualified right of men to control, to own, to "take" whatever can be taken from the natural world. In the late seventeenth century, political theorist John Locke wrote a justification of the natural right of each person, by dint of the labor he invested in it, to unlimited private property. Locke's thinking would greatly influence those who conceptualized and brought into existence the modern liberal democratic state, particularly those who established the American Republic.

SECOND TREATISE OF GOVERNMENT
John Locke

Of Property

§ 27. Though the earth, and all inferior creatures, be common to all men, yet every man has a property in his own person: this no body has any right to but himself. The labour of his body, and the work of his hands, we may say, are properly his. Whatsoever then he removes out of the state that nature hath provided, and left it in, he hath mixed his labour with, and joined to it something that is his own, and thereby makes it his property....

§ 28. He that is nourished by the acorns he picked up under an oak, or the apples he gathered from the trees in the wood, has certainly appropriated them to himself.... That labour ... added something to them more than nature, the common mother of all, had done; and so they became his private right....

§ 30. [W]hat fish any one catches in the ocean, that great and still remaining common of mankind ... is by the labour that removes it out of that common state nature left it in, made his property.... And ... the hare that any one is hunting, is thought his who pursues her during the chase ... whoever has employed so much labour ... as to find and pursue her, has thereby removed her from the state of nature, wherein she was common, and hath begun a property....

§ 32. As much land as a man tills, plants, improves, cultivates, and can use the product of so much is his property. He by his labour does, as it were, inclose it from the common.... God and his reason commanded him to subdue the earth, i.e. to improve it for the benefit of life....

§ 33. Nor was the appropriation of any parcel of land, by improving it, any prejudice to any other man, since there was still enough, and as good left.... So that, in effect, there was never the less left for others because of his inclosure for himself: for he that leaves as much as another can make use of, does as good as take nothing at all. No body could think himself injured by the drinking of another man, though he took a good draught, who had a whole river of the same water left him to quench his thirst....

§ 46. Now of those good things which nature hath provided in common, every one had a right ... to as much as he could use, and property in all that he could effect with his labour.... He that gathered a hundred bushels of acorns or apples, had thereby a property in them, they were his goods as soon as gathered. He was only to look, that he used them before they spoiled, else he took more than his share, and robbed others. And indeed it was a foolish thing, as well as dishonest, to hoard up more than he could make use of. If he gave away a part to any body else, so that it perished not uselessly in his possession, these he also made use of. And if he also bartered away plums that would have rotted in a week, for nuts that would last good for his eating a whole year, he did no injury; he wasted not the common stock ... so long as nothing perished uselessly in his hands. Again, if he would give his nuts for a piece of metal, pleased with its colour; or exchange his sheep for shells, or wool for a sparkling pebble or a diamond, and keep those by him all his life, he invaded not the right of others, he might heap up as much of these durable things as he pleased; the exceeding of the bounds of his just property not lying in the largeness of his possession, but the perishing of any thing uselessly in it.

§ 47. And thus came in the use of money....

Of Paternal Power

§ 57.... [The purpose] of law is not to abolish or restrain, but to preserve and enlarge freedom.... [W]here there is no law, there is no freedom: for liberty is to be free from restraint and violence from others.... [F]reedom is not ... a liberty for every man to do what he wishes: (for who could be free, when every other man's humour might domineer over him?) but a liberty to dispose, and order as he wishes, his person, actions, possessions, and his whole property, within the allowance of those laws under which he is, and therein not to be subject to the arbitrary will of another, but freely follow his own....

Of the Ends of Political Society and Government

§ 124. The great and chief [purpose] therefore, of men's uniting into commonwealths, and putting themselves under government, is the preservation of their property....

QUESTIONS

1. According to Locke, what gives a person the right to own property? Is there any limitation on that right? Why does Locke believe people form government?

2. Suppose I sell some of my wool to you in exchange for some of your sparkling pebbles. The deal, if freely agreed upon, satisfies us both. Ideally, this is how the free market works. A *laissez-faire* economic system assumes that the interplay of self-interested individuals and entities in the marketplace will result in maximal gains for both producers and consumers, and that this interplay should be, for the most part, free of government intervention. But what if a freely negotiated deal ends up causing harm to people who were not part of the deal? Suppose my wool-production pollutes the stream that runs down into my neighbor's property? Suppose your pebble-sparkler gives off toxic emissions that cause nearby children to develop asthma? These are examples of "negative externalities," costs that free markets sometimes impose on people who have not consented to them, and who are not compensated for them. Locke, writing before the Industrial Revolution, does not address them. Are there other ways in which Locke's philosophy does not appear to fit the 21st century context?

> ### INSTRUMENTALISM VS. DEEP ECOLOGY
>
> One way to understand the value of the natural world is to focus upon its usefulness to the human species. This "instrumentalist" view places worth on environmental resources to the extent that they can benefit us—materially, and also psychologically and spiritually.
>
> Some would place environmentalism on a rights-based foundation. Although the U.S. Constitution does not include the right to a livable environment, arguably we each have such a right.[23]
>
> Whether viewed as a means to human ends or as a right we each possess, we tend to conceptualize the importance of preservation of our natural world in terms of what it means to human beings. This is an **androcentric** perspective, experiencing, explaining, and reasoning always from the human vantage point.
>
> Some criticize this human-centeredness, and urge that we become **biocentric** in our approach to the environment. For them, the most profound philosophical stance is one that values the continued existence of the entire natural world *for its own sake*, not because of anything it can do for us. Supporters of what is sometimes called **deep ecology** insist that the rich diversity of life has intrinsic value, and that human beings have no right to threaten or reduce it, but rather have the obligation to change policies and behaviors that do so.

Biodiversity and Habitat Preservation

Extinction is irreversible, we lose diversity, beauty, a genetic resource, a natural wonder, a souvenir of the past. But more underlies these, really a religious reason. Life is a sacred thing, and we ought not to be careless about it. This applies not only to experienced life, but to preservation of the lesser zoological and botanical species. Species enter and exit the natural theater, but only over geologic time and selected to fit evolving habitats. Individuals have their intrinsic worth, but particular individuals come and go, while that wave of life in which they participate overleaps the single lifespan millions of times.[24]

—ROLSTON HOLMES III

Private Property, Regulation, and the Constitution

The **Fifth Amendment** to the U.S. Constitution states that "private property [may not] be taken for public use, without **just compensation**." The power to take private property for public use is called **eminent domain**. It may be exercised by local as well as federal

---

[23] Some states have amended their constitutions to mention such rights. The Constitution of Pennsylvania, for instance, now reads:

The people have a right to clean air, pure water, and to the preservation of the natural, scenic, historic and aesthetic values of the environment. Pennsylvania's natural resources ... are the common property of all the people, including generations yet to come. As trustee of these resources, the Commonwealth shall preserve and maintain them for the benefit of all the people.

[24] *Environmental Ethics: Duties to and Values in the Natural World* (Philadelphia Temple University Press, 1988).

and state government. Historically it has enabled public projects—such as the construction of highways, utility lines, parks, and rapid transit systems—to move forward in spite of private property interests that might otherwise have blocked them. Suppose your state government determines that the most appropriate route for a new expressway is right through your living room. Your family may not refuse to cooperate with the state, but the state must pay your family for this "taking" of your property; government should not be able to force a small number of citizens to bear the brunt of activities that benefit the public generally.

The Fifth Amendment is the only part of the Constitution that explicitly protects private property, owners' economic interests, and it has been an important battleground over the years as courts have had to define "public use," "just compensation," and especially in recent environmental cases, the concept of a "**taking**."

Early cases typically dealt with the confiscation of private land—as in the highway example above. By the early twentieth century, though, many of the conflicts involved local zoning laws that prevented owners from enjoying economically optimal use of their property. In a 1926 case,[25] for instance, land that had been zoned for industrial development was restricted by a new zoning ordinance to residential use, reducing its value to the owner by 75 percent. Yet the Supreme Court found that this did not amount to a taking, and the city did not have to compensate the owner for it. The Court viewed the rezoning as an exercise of the **police power**, the power of state and local governments to make laws for public health, safety, and welfare. Pointing out that commercial use of land might, in shifting circumstances under that police power, wear out its welcome and become a **nuisance**, the Court wrote:

> A nuisance may be merely a right thing in the wrong place—like a pig in the parlor instead of in the barnyard.[26]

The result in *Euclid* was reached by balancing public benefits against private loss brought on by the regulation. In a more recent test of the police power to zone, the Supreme Court held that the benefit to the public derived from preserving the beauty and historic value of a train station in New York City outweighed the cost imposed on the private owner who had planned the construction of a 53-story building on top of it.[27] Again, there was no "taking," and no need to compensate the owner.

Since the passage of the National Environmental Protection Act in 1970, **regulatory takings** challenges have been brought by private property owners who believe that environmental regulations unfairly burden them as individuals with the costs of protecting our natural resources. Here is how these cases have arisen: a government regulation designed to protect the environment impinges on an owner's freedom to use that property in some way. For instance, farmers are directed not to use certain pesticides harmful to groundwater; ranchers are told they must put their cattle at risk to protect grizzly bears; the owners of "wetlands," the marshes that harbor delicate ecosystems crucial to the natural cleansing cycle, are directed not to drain or build on their land. In each situation, the owner alleges that the environmental regulation is the equivalent of a "taking," and demands compensation. Environmentalists view these claims with alarm, because, if

---

[25] *Village of Euclid v. Ambler Realty Co.*, 272 U.S. 365 (1926).

[26] In the *Euclid* case, the pig did not wander into the parlor. By varying the zoning, the town was moving its "parlor" to surround the "pig." Even so, the Supreme Court held that a common law "nuisance" existed.

[27] *Penn Central Transportation Co. v. New York City*, 98 S.Ct. 2646 (1978).

they succeed, they have the potential of undercutting the entire regulatory network; government will not be able to afford to regulate.

■ ■ ■

In the next case, the Supreme Court deals with one of these challenges, and in the process recasts its mechanism for defining a taking under the Fifth Amendment.

LUCAS v. SOUTH CAROLINA COASTAL COUNCIL
Supreme Court of the United States, 1992
112 S.Ct. 2886

Justice SCALIA delivered the opinion of the Court.

In 1986, David H. Lucas paid $975,000 for two residential lots on the Isle of Palms ... South Carolina, on which he intended to build single-family homes. In 1988, however, the South Carolina Legislature enacted the Beachfront Management Act, which had the direct effect of barring [him] from erecting any permanent habitable structures on his two parcels.... This case requires us to decide whether the Act's dramatic effect on the economic value of Lucas's lots accomplished a taking of private property under the Fifth and Fourteenth Amendments requiring the payment of "just compensation."

South Carolina's expressed interest in intensively managing development activities in the so-called "coastal zone" dates from 1977 when, in the aftermath of Congress's passage of the federal Coastal Zone Management Act of 1972, the legislature enacted a Coastal Zone Management Act of its own. [This law] required owners of coastal zone land that qualified as a "critical area" (defined in the legislation to include beaches and immediately adjacent sand dunes), to obtain a permit from the newly created South Carolina Coastal Council prior to committing the land to a [new use].

In the late 1970s, Lucas and others began extensive residential development of the Isle of Palms, a barrier island situated eastward of the City of Charleston.... Lucas in 1986 purchased the two lots at issue in this litigation.... No portion of the lots, which were located approximately 300 feet from the beach, qualified as a "critical area" under the 1977 Act; accordingly, at the time Lucas acquired these parcels, he was not legally obliged to obtain a permit from the Council in advance of any development activity. His intention with respect to the lots was to do what the owners of the immediately adjacent parcels had already done: erect single-family residences. He commissioned architectural drawings for this purpose.

[But in 1988 new legislation directed the Council to create a line beyond which no "occupiable improvements" could be built. When this "baseline" was drawn, Lucas found he was prohibited from building on his land.]

[In *Pennsylvania Coal Co. v. Mahon* (1922), Justice Holmes recognized] that ...if ... the uses of private property were subject to unbridled, uncompensated qualification under the police power, "the natural tendency of human nature [would be] to extend the qualification more and more until at last private property disappear[ed]." These considerations gave birth in that case to the oft-cited maxim that, "while property may be regulated to a certain extent, if regulation goes too far it will be recognized as a taking."

[The Court explains that in the 70 years since the *Mahon* case, it has avoided the use of any "set formula" for determining "how far is too far," instead examining the specific facts of each case.]

We have, however, described at least two discrete categories of regulatory action as compensable without case-specific inquiry into the public interest advanced in support of the restraint. The first encompasses regulations that compel the property owner to suffer a physical "invasion" of his property. In general (at least with regard to permanent invasions), no matter how minute the intrusion, and no matter how weighty the public purpose behind it, we have required compensation. For example, in *Loretto v. Teleprompter Manhattan CATV Corp.* (1982), we determined that New York's law requiring landlords to allow television cable companies to emplace cable facilities in their apartment buildings constituted a taking, even though the facilities occupied at most only 1 1/2 cubic feet of the landlords' property.

The second situation ... is where regulation denies all economically beneficial or productive use of land....

[R]egulations that leave the owner of land without economically beneficial or productive options for its use—typically, as here, by requiring land to be left substantially in its natural state—carry with them a heightened risk that private property is being pressed into some form of public service under the guise of mitigating serious public harm....

We think, in short, that there are good reasons for our frequently expressed belief that when the owner of real property has been called upon to sacrifice *all* economically beneficial uses in the name of the common good, that is, to leave his property economically idle, he has suffered a taking....

[There are many precedent cases establishing that government may halt a use of property that is harmful to the public without paying compensation to the owner. However, Scalia argues, since none of those precedents involved regulations that completely removed all economic value from the land, that principle does not apply to the case before him. In *Lucas*-like situations, he reasons, the regulation must count as a taking—unless it simply forbids a use already forbidden under the common law.]

On this analysis, the owner of a lake bed, for example, would not be entitled to compensation when he is denied the requisite permit to engage in a landfilling operation that would have the effect of flooding others' land. Nor the corporate owner of a nuclear generating plant, when it is directed to remove all improvements from its land upon discovery that the plant sits astride an earthquake fault. Such regulatory action may well have the effect of eliminating the land's only economically productive use, but it does not proscribe a productive use that was previously permissible under relevant property and nuisance principles. The use of these properties for what are now expressly prohibited purposes was always unlawful, and ... it was open to the State at any point to make the implication of those background principles of nuisance and property law explicit.... When, however, a regulation that declares "off-limits" all economically productive or beneficial uses of land goes beyond what the relevant background principles would dictate, compensation must be paid to sustain it.

The "total taking" inquiry we require today will ordinarily entail (as the application of state nuisance law ordinarily entails) analysis of, among other things, the degree of harm to public lands and resources, or adjacent private property, posed by the claimant's proposed activities, the social value of the claimant's activities and their suitability to the locality in question, and the relative ease with which the alleged harm can be avoided through measures taken by the claimant and the government (or adjacent private landowners) alike. The fact that a particular use has long been engaged in by similarly situated owners ordinarily imports a lack of any common-law prohibition (though changed circumstances or new knowledge may make what was previously permissible no longer so). So also does the fact that other landowners, similarly situated, are permitted to continue the use denied to the claimant.

[Judgment against Lucas is reversed. The case goes back to the state courts to determine if common law principles would prevent him from building on his property. If not, he must be compensated for the environmental restriction.]

Justice KENNEDY, concurring in the judgment.

The rights conferred by the Takings Clause and the police power of the State may coexist without conflict. Property is bought and sold, investments are made, subject to the State's power to regulate. Where a taking is alleged from regulations which deprive the property of all value, the test must be whether the deprivation is contrary to reasonable, investment-backed expectations....

In my view, reasonable expectations must be understood in light of the whole of our legal tradition. The common law of nuisance is too narrow a confine for the exercise of regulatory power in a complex and interdependent society.

Justice BLACKMUN, dissenting.

Today the Court launches a missile to kill a mouse.

The State of South Carolina prohibited Lucas from building a permanent structure on his property from 1988 to 1990. Relying on an unreviewed (and implausible) state trial court finding that this restriction left Lucas' property valueless, this Court granted review to determine whether compensation must be paid in cases where the State prohibits all economic use of real estate....

I, like the Court, will give far greater attention to this case than its narrow scope suggests—not because I can intercept the Court's missile, or save the targeted mouse, but because I hope perhaps to limit the collateral damage.

In 1972 Congress passed the Coastal Zone Management Act. The Act was designed to provide States with money and incentives to carry out Congress' goal of protecting the public from shoreline erosion and coastal hazards. In the 1980 Amendments to the Act, Congress directed States to enhance their coastal programs by "[p]reventing or significantly reducing threats to life and the destruction of property by eliminating development and redevelopment in high-hazard areas."

South Carolina began implementing the congressional directive by enacting the South Carolina Coastal Zone Management Act of 1977. Under the 1977 Act, any construction activity in what was designated the "critical area" required a permit from the Council, and the construction of any habitable structure was prohibited. The 1977 critical area was relatively narrow.

This effort did not stop the loss of shoreline. In October 1986, the Council appointed a "Blue Ribbon Committee on Beachfront Management" to investigate beach erosion and propose possible solutions. In March 1987, the Committee found that South Carolina's beaches were "critically eroding," and proposed land-use restrictions. In response, South Carolina enacted the Beachfront Management Act on July 1, 1988. The 1988 Act did not change the uses permitted within the designated critical areas. Rather, it enlarged those areas to encompass the distance from the mean high watermark to a setback line established on the basis of "the best scientific and historical data" available.

Petitioner Lucas is a contractor, manager, and part owner of the Wild Dune development on the Isle of Palms. He has lived there since 1978. In December 1986, he purchased two of the last four pieces of vacant property in the development. The area is notoriously unstable. In roughly half of the last 40 years, all or part of petitioner's property was part of the beach or flooded twice daily by the ebb and flow of the tide. Between 1957 and 1963, petitioner's property was under water.... Between 1981 and 1983, the Isle of Palms issued 12 emergency orders for sandbagging to protect property in the Wild Dune development. Determining that local habitable structures were in imminent danger of collapse, the Council issued permits for two rock revetments to protect condominium developments near petitioner's property from erosion; one of the revetments extends more than halfway onto one of his lots....

The Court creates new Takings jurisprudence based on the trial court's finding that the property had lost all economic value. This finding is almost certainly erroneous. [Lucas] can still enjoy other attributes of ownership, such as the right to exclude others, "one of the most essential sticks in the bundle of rights that are commonly characterized as property." [Lucas] can picnic, swim, camp in a tent or live on the property in a moveable trailer.... Petitioner also retains the right to [sell] the land, which would have value for neighbors and for those prepared to enjoy proximity to the ocean without a house....

The Court ... takes the opportunity to create a new scheme for regulations that eliminate all economic value. From now on, there is a categorical rule finding these regulations to be a taking unless the use they prohibit is a background common-law nuisance....

I first question the Court's rationale in creating a category that obviates a "case-specific inquiry into the public interest advanced," if all economic value has been lost. If one fact about the Court's taking jurisprudence can be stated without contradiction, it is that "the particular circumstances of each case" determine whether a specific restriction will be rendered invalid by the government's failure to pay compensation. This is so because ... the ultimate conclusion "necessarily requires a weighing of private and public interests." When the government regulation prevents the owner from any economically valuable use of his property, the private interest is unquestionably substantial, but we have never before held that no public interest can outweigh it....

This Court repeatedly has recognized the ability of government, in certain circumstances, to regulate property without compensation no matter how adverse the financial effect on the owner may be. More than a century ago, the Court explicitly upheld the right of States to prohibit uses of property injurious to public health, safety, or welfare without paying compensation...... (*Mugler v. Kansas* (1887). On this basis, the Court upheld an ordinance effectively prohibiting operation of a previously lawful brewery, although the "establishments will become of no value as property." *Mugler* was only the beginning in a long line of cases.... In *Miller v. Schoene* (1928), the Court held that the Fifth Amendment did not require Virginia to pay compensation to the owner of cedar trees ordered destroyed to prevent a disease from spreading to nearby apple orchards....

In none of the cases did the Court suggest that the right of a State to prohibit certain activities without paying compensation turned on the availability of some residual valuable use. Instead, the cases depended on whether the government interest was sufficient to prohibit the activity, given the significant private cost....

[T]he Court seems to treat history as a grab-bag of principles, to be adopted where they support the Court's theory, and ignored where they do not.

QUESTIONS

1. The image of David Lucas that emerges from majority Justice Scalia's description is strikingly different from the one that Justice Blackmun creates in his dissent. What are the two contrasting stories in this case? Do you think that when Lucas bought the land at issue here, in 1986, he had reason to know that by building on it he would soon be the owner of a "pig in a parlor"?

2. According to the majority, what two types of regulatory action automatically trigger compensation as takings, without a court needing to examine the circumstances in a case-specific way? Why does the dissent object to this approach?

3. Included in the bundle of rights that go with land ownership are those of occupation, use and sale. When something is done to affect those rights—making them less valuable to the owner—the common law allows a suit for **nuisance**. A nuisance is an activity or condition that creates an unreasonable interference with a person's use and enjoyment of property. So, for example, a nuisance is created when a service station allows gasoline to leak from its holding tanks onto adjourning residential property[28] or when a farmer's seasonal irrigation system spews waste water onto his neighbors' farmlands.[29] What role does nuisance play in the majority opinion in this case? In the other *Lucas* opinions?

---

[28] *Golovach v. Bellmont*, 4 A.D.3d 730 (App.Div, N.Y. 2004); *Felton Oil Company v. Gee*, 2004 WL 119486 (Ark. 2004).

[29] *King v. Van Setten*, 2004 WL 1447736 (Mont. 2004).

4. Consider each of the following laws as potential regulatory takings:

   (a) A new Texas Open Beach Act permits public easements—a right of passage—over dry sand beaches that are privately owned. Beach erosion or sea level rises can cause those easements to move further and further inland, often closer to beach homes. *Severance v. Patternson*, 566 F.3d 490 (5th Cir. 2009).

   (b) Erosion threatens about 60% of Florida's beaches, and under a 1961 law, the state dredged sand from one area and moved it to a threatened area, extending the width of an eroding beach 80-100 feet. This new stretch of beach would then be publicly accessible. Six property owners, calling themselves Stop the Beach Renourishment Inc., claimed their deeds entitled them to the waterfront, and that members of the public should not be permitted to use the additional space. *Stop the Beach Renourishment Inc. v. Florida Dept. of the Environment*, 998 So.2d 1102 (Fl. 2008).

5. A ballot initiative passed by Oregon voters in the November 2004 election reversed a trend in that state, which had some of the most restrictive land-use rules in the country. The new measure allows owners to prove that zoning or environmental regulations will reduce the investment value of their property, forcing the government to either compensate them for those losses or exempt them from the rules. Similar ballot initiatives were put forward in California, Washington, Idaho, Nevada, and Arizona. **Research**: Were they also passed?

■ ■ ■

ENVIRONMENTAL JUSTICE

Environmental Justice refers to the ethical issues at the intersection of race/class discrimination and environmental harm or reform, as people who have suffered from discrimination or poverty are affected differently than the rest of the population, arguing that they are unfairly exposed to more environmental harms, and/or less able to gain access to important information. In general, they claim they are unfairly prevented from participating in decisions that deeply affect their health and safety in environmentally-related matters.

The movement gained momentum in the 1980s, soon after a controversy that developed in North Carolina, when a largely African American neighborhood was used as a dumping site for thousands of tons of toxic soil. The incident began in 1978 when a contractor decided to spray gallons of PCB-contaminated oil along rural highways at night instead of taking it to a recycling facility. (The contractor would spend a short time in prison.) Faced with an environmental nightmare, in 1982 the governor directed that the soil at the roadsides be moved to a rural landfill about 60 miles from Raleigh, pending clean-up when technology became available. The people living where this landfill was being created believed their county had been selected because it was mostly African American and poor. Protests began, with some people lying in the road to prevent trucks from dumping. Eventually, environmental officials admitted that the site was not ideal for hydrological reasons, and the controversy heightened, with charges of "environmental racism" made. The site was not decontaminated until 2004.

■ ■ ■

In 2001, the state environmental agency issued permits to a cement processing facility in Camden, New Jersey. About half of the people living in this mostly African American area were children, and more than half were living at or below the poverty line. Some health data for the community:

- The age-adjusted rate of death of black females in Camden County from asthma was over three times the rate of death for white females from asthma in Camden County;
- The age-adjusted rate of death of black males in Camden County from asthma was over six times the rate of death for white males from asthma in Camden County.
- The self-reported asthma rate for Waterfront South residents was 33%, more than twice the self-reported rate of asthma in other parts of the City of Camden.

The people in South Camden called for an injunction to rescind the permits and halt the cement factory project, concerned that it would add to the air pollution from which they already disproportionately suffered. *South Camden Citizens v. New Jersey Department of Environmental Protection* was a groundbreaking case, representing the first time civil rights law was applied in the context of environmental justice. It was the first time a federal judge ruled that a state agency, as a recipient of federal funds, had an obligation to investigate the ways a private project might have unfair and discriminatory effects on a subset of the community. When this case was appealed to the Third Circuit, a record number of **amicus** ("friend of the court") briefs were filed on behalf of all litigants. Both business and civil rights groups had a high stake in the outcome. **Research**: Find and read an amicus brief for each side of this dispute. What policy arguments were put forward by each interest group as it attempted to influence the Court of Appeals?

The community won the first round of the case in federal district court in 2001. On appeal, the Third Circuit found that the plaintiffs had no right to enforce Title VI's unless they could prove *intentional* discrimination.

■ ■ ■

Camden is not the only relatively powerless minority community with a concentration of heavily polluting industrial sites. In recent years, toxic waste operators have considered Indian reservations and developing countries as potential disposal sites. Sometimes environmental justice advocates are able to pressure their way towards a more equitable outcome. Living through decades of industrial explosions and toxic leaks from the Royal Dutch/Shell-affiliated plants near her neighborhood in Norco, Louisiana—and watching cancer rates there rise sharply—brought Margie Eugene-Richard to the point of activism. She spearheaded negotiations that, by 2002, resulted in Shell buying the homes of the mostly low-income African-Americans in her community, enabling them to move away. Shell also agreed to upgrade its Norco facilities. **Research**: Find out about an ongoing environmental justice project as near as possible to where you live. Which strategy is being employed—litigation, negotiation, or both?

Chapter Problems

1. Some describe polar bears, whales, white tigers, and other magnificent and endangered mammal species as "charismatic megafauna." **Research**: Find out what that means. Then find out what happened when environmental activists and a tribal government challenged an order of the Department of the Interior to approve offshore oil and gas development in an area like Kivalina which was home to endangered whales and polar bears. *Center for Biological Diversity v. U.S. Dept of Interior*, 563 F.3d 466 (D.C.Cir. 2009).

2. Cities contain 50% of the world's population, consume 75% of its energy, and are responsible for 80% of its greenhouse gas emissions. Founded in London in 2005, the Large Cities Climate Leadership Group, also known as the C40 Cities, is working to control climate change and promote sustainable development in urban centers around the world. Its third summit was in May 2009 in Seoul; its fourth will be held in 2011 in São Paulo. **Research**: What are some of this group's best practices? Is your city—or a city near you—part of this group?

3. Tom DeChristopher, an economics major at the University of Utah, committed an act of civil disobedience by deliberately disrupting an auction of federal energy leases. He bid and won $1.7 million in oil and gas lease parcels—covering about 22,000 acres— without intending to pay for them. He was prosecuted for a felony that could lead him to prison for years. A committed environmentalist, DeChristopher was particularly concerned because of the proximity of the leaseholds to national parkland. They were up for sale at the end of the Bush administration. As of this writing, the Obama administration has withdrawn these leases, and they are no longer available for sale. What are the ethics of civil disobedience related to climate change? See: *http://www. pbs.org/wnet/religionandethics/episodes/march-20-2009/civil-disobedience/2473/*.

4. In 2007, 20,000 bicycles were placed at 1,000 stations throughout Paris, in an experiment called Velib that aims to change the transportation landscape of that city. Users can pick up and use bikes, dropping them off at any one of the conveniently located stations. An advertising firm is financing the project in exchange for exclusive rights to use some 1,600 urban billboards. The city will actually make money on the deal—about $46 million over 10 years—while users pay an annual fee of about $50. The first half hour of any trip is free; additional half hours costs about $2 each. In Lyon, where a similar bicycle program has been a great success, there are now 50,000 subscribers and 4,000 bikes. Bicycle use has increased 30 percent and car use is down four percent, reversing the previous trend where automobile use was on a steady rise. Lyon calculates its program has prevented 3,000 tons of carbon monoxide from being emitted. Citywide bicycle programs are increasingly popular in Europe. **Research**: Find out if any cities in the U.S. have adopted this approach. Find the Congress for the New Urbanism and PlaNYC. What reduction in greenhouse gas emissions takes place when people choose an urban, as opposed to an exurban, lifestyle?

5. Within two weeks of the capping of the 2010 oil spill in the Gulf of Mexico, a group of government and independent scientists released a report estimating that about three-quarters of the oil had been captured directly from the wellhead, skimmed away, burned off, dispersed by chemicals or natural processes, evaporated or dissolved. The rest, about 26 percent, had been washed ashore or was still lingering in some form in the water. This report, although warning of potential long-term impact, gave the impression that the effects of the spill would be less severe than had been feared. Soon after it was made public, the government's assessment was challenged by other research scientists. Samantha Joye of the University of Georgia, who was among those who had first discovered the undersea oil-laced plumes, claimed "the idea that 75 percent of the oil is gone and is of no further concern to the environment is just incorrect." And in prepared testimony to Congress, Ian MacDonald, an oceanographer at Florida State University, said "I expect the hydrocarbon imprint of the BP discharge will be detectable in marine life for the rest of

my life." **Research:** What can you find out about the environmental after-effects of the BP Oil Spill of 2010? Does controversy over assessing it remain?

6. The United Nations declared 2010 the International Year of Biodiversity. In that year, the third Global Biodiversity Outlook (GBO-3) was published, a landmark study warning that ecosystems like rainforests, freshwater lakes, and rivers and coral reefs are approaching a "tipping point," and unless "swift, radical and creative action" is taken "massive further [species] loss is increasingly likely." According to the report, the world lost nearly one third of all vertebrate species from 1070 to 2006, for example. Nick Nuttall, a U.N. Environmental Program spokesman, put this degradation of ecosystems in economic context, stating, "In terms of land-use change, it's thought that the annual financial loss of services ecosystems provide—water, storing carbon, and soil stabilization—is about …$64 billion a year. If this continues we may well see by 2050 a cumulative loss of what you might call land-based natural capital of around $121 trillion." **Research:** What can you find out about the negotiations at the U.N. Biodiversity Summit in Nagoya, Japan in October 2010?

7. **Research:** What can you find out about the progress countries have made under the Kyoto treaty? What is a "clean development mechanism" (CDM) under Kyoto? Why has the Kyoto Protocol been criticized by environmentalists?

8. At this point in history, the destruction of habitat is the primary cause of species loss, not the actual hunting and killing of individual creatures. Although poachers still hunt the rare black rhino, for instance, much more damage to animals, birds, fish, and plants occurs indirectly, as the rapidly expanding human population of the globe makes way for itself and its drive for a high-consumption existence. This is why habitat preservation is so important—the maintenance of wetlands, forests, prairies, oceans, and rivers that naturally cleanse the water, air, and soil.

Species have been disappearing into extinction since they first existed on this planet, but the last 100 years has seen the rate of extinction leap alarmingly. Extinction should worry us for both practical and philosophical reasons. More than 50 percent of our pharmaceuticals come from various species. Until the bark of Pacific yew was discovered to contain a cure for ovarian cancer, it was considered a worthless scrub tree and was almost wiped out. We do not know what other precious essences are yet to be discovered in the multitude of species now existing, but scientists are sure that by ruining their habitats, we are cheating ourselves and our descendants of their benefits. In fact, it seems likely that the more exotically diverse habitats, such as those in the rain forests, are likely to yield, if gradually, substances of highest priority for human well being.

Research: The federal **Endangered Species Act** (ESA) went into effect in 1997. Find out how many species have been recovered since then. What is the current status of efforts to repeal the ESA?

9. As of 2010, in a world ranking of nations by environmental performance compiled biannually by researchers at Columbia and Yale, the U.S. had dropped from 39th to 61st while China had fallen from 105th to 121st. The best performance was from Iceland, which uses hydro- and geothermal energy for virtually all of its power. Other European nations were clustered at the top—Switzerland, Sweden, and Norway for instance. Developing countries also made high rankings—Costa Rica and Colombia, for example, with rainforest conservation efforts and a shift to mass-transit, respectively. **Research:** Find out where the U.S. stands now at *www.epi.yale.edu.*

10. What environmental justice issues have arisen outside the developed world? **Research**: Find out what you can about indigenous environmental activists in other countries. What has been going on, for example, with the Mapuche Indians' fight for control of the forests on their ancestral lands in Chile? What has been going on in China, where a noted Tibetan environmental activist was given a 15-year prison term? What was the result of the "water wars" in the Cochabamba region of Bolivia?

CHAPTER PROJECT

Business Ethics Fairy Tales

For the purposes of this exercise, a fairy tale is a story about how a single company was able to accomplish something "socially responsible" in the context of environmental sustainability. You will need to find an example of a company that has done what Milton Friedman would rail against—an activity that is not designed solely to increase stockholder return on investment, but is instead designed to benefit stakeholders who are not stockholders. The example you choose may in fact enhance the company's image and/or its bottom line, but the point of the exercise is to tell the story of a business which focused on environmentally responsible goals, and achieved them.

The class will be divided into teams. Each team will research and then tell a business ethics "fairy tale."

The Contest

First your team should identify a company whose tale you want to tell. Communicate your choice to your instructor as soon as you have made your selection, to avoid duplication. (Nonprofits don't count, for purposes of this project.) Your team will be presenting the company's "fairy tale" achievements by making an in-class report, distributing a written report, and perhaps by constructing a Web site.

Choose your fairy tale carefully—don't rush it. You may want to do some "dirt-digging" on a company before your team selects it. A company's own public relations description of its achievements may look wonderful, but often a little research reveals another reality. (A Web site with a perspective not susceptible to greenwashing is *www.corpwatch.org*.)

You need to check on the sincerity of your company before you select it because this competition will involve teams trying to expose flaws in one another's fairy tales. During the oral presentations, there will be an opportunity to ask questions. Your team will have to defend your company against possible accusations that it has been two-faced—promoting itself with a green image but funding fake grass-roots organizations that debunk good climate science, or fighting responsible regulation on the environment, for example. (See David Vogel on the *Market for Virtue* in this chapter.) Just as your classmates will be able to challenge the sincerity of the green achievements of your company, based on their own research, you will be able to do the same to them when it is their turn to present.

The Tasks

1. Choosing a fairy tale to tell, and letting your instructor know your choice;
2. Preparing the presentation and written report for your team's fairy tale company;
3. Researching other teams' choices in order to challenge their presentations;

4. Presenting and defending your team's fairy tale company;

5. Challenging other teams during their presentations.

6. Ultimately, the class will vote for the best fairy tale.

Evaluative Criteria

1. Effectiveness: The company's program appears to be well designed to address the goal it is trying to meet, and is succeeding in meeting its goal. (Evidence would help.)

2. Ethical consistency: The company's behavior in other areas does not appear to undercut its fairy tale goal, considering all valid criticism.

3. Originality: The company's efforts are unusual or fresh in some way.

4. Presentation: The fairy tale is told clearly and colorfully.

CHAPTER 7

Marketing and Technology
Choice and Manipulation

The drive for material goods … may be less admirable than a different … set of goals. The fact is that the system works, and that it does both motivate and reward people. If it appears to critics that the motivations are inferior, and rewards are vulgar, it must be remembered that at least the people have their own choice of what these rewards will be…. It is essentially a democratic system, and the freedom of individual choice makes it valuable to the people who do the choosing.

— JOHN CRICHTON, Morals and Ethics in Advertising[1]

It was like, "iCanBuy.com, your parents can give you an allowance and you can just go and buy whatever you want." And I said, "Ooh, that sounds cool!"

— TORI CLIFFORD, 12 years old

Good advertising does not just circulate information. It penetrates the public mind with desires and belief.

— LEO BURNETT

In the 1970s in the United States, the average city-dweller was exposed to 500 to 2,000 advertising messages a day. Today, estimates range from 3,000 to 5,000, as a constant barrage of stimuli encourage us to be consumers—from packaging, billboards, and product placements, to radio, television, and the digital media. Spending for online ads eclipsed print ads for the first time in 2010, having grown 10 percent the previous year even in the recession. By then, advertising expenditures nationally were estimated to be $368 billion, and ad spending was forecast to reach nearly $451 billion globally.

This chapter begins with the U.S. constitutional protection available to advertisers—their right to free "commercial speech." In the first case, this right was the basis of a challenge to a law banning the sale to pharmaceutical firms of data on doctors' prescribing practices—one example of the many ways in which technology has altered the landscape of marketing.

We move on to consider consumer demand: Is it created and sustained by the advertising industry, or is it already present, just waiting to be educated and informed by advertising?

---

[1] In *Ethics, Morality and the Media: Reflections on American Culture*, Lee Thayer, Ed. (New York: Hastings House, 1980), p. 113.

The chapter continues by introducing legislation responsive to deception in advertising, the Federal Trade Commission and Lanham Acts. The advertising business regulates itself, and we look at some of its own regulatory guidelines.

In classical microeconomic terms, wages and prices fluctuate in response to millions of preferences expressed by consumers as they make their purchasing choices. But do some marketing strategies warp optimal marketplace functions by manipulating consumer perceptions? We read about the marketing of junk food to children in light of rising obesity rates and about the tobacco industry, where advertising and public relations techniques have successfully reconfigured consumer perception of risk. In the same vein, a case dealing with direct-to-consumer advertising of birth control sustains the health-related theme of this chapter.

We are witnessing a sea change in marketing, where what matters is not so much the relative qualities of a product or service, but rather the mystique of its brand. In the last reading, we consider the impact branding may be having on our entire society, as the line blurs between "corporate sponsors and sponsored culture."

Free Speech and Commercial Speech

Freedom of speech is guaranteed by the First Amendment to the U.S. Constitution, but for much of our history, from the persecution of abolitionists in the nineteenth century to the jailing of socialists in the early twentieth century, the public expression of offensive or unpopular opinion could be lawfully silenced. Not until the 1920s did legal doctrines protecting speech, particularly when offensive or unpopular, begin to gel in the courts. Today, unless it is deemed defamatory, obscene, or likely to incite violence, expression—including artistic and symbolic expression—is protected in what has been dubbed "the marketplace of ideas."

Initially the Supreme Court refused to apply expanded First Amendment protection to advertising, or "commercial speech," distinguishing between the marketplace of ideas and the marketplace of goods and services. Then, in 1976, a group of discount pharmacies in Virginia claimed that a state law that prevented them from advertising cut-rate drug prices violated their First Amendment rights. The Supreme Court agreed. Apart from the advertisers' economic interest, the Court recognized the consumers' interest in hearing what the advertisers had to say. "[T]hose whom the suppression of prescription drug price information hits the hardest are the poor, the sick, and particularly the aged," it wrote. So, in *Virginia Board*,[2] the Court appeared to link the "right to receive information and ideas" with the traditional values that underlie free speech, as if well-educated consumers were the equivalent of well-educated voters. Commercial speech was protected mainly to ensure that "numerous private economic decisions" would be made on as well-informed a basis as possible. In contrast to pure political speech, though, commercial speech was considered "hardier," better able to bounce back if regulated: "Since advertising is the sine qua non of commercial profits, there is little likelihood of it being chilled."

Two years after the *Virginia Board* case, the Supreme Court again struck down a state law as a violation of the First Amendment rights of a commercial speaker. In *First National Bank v. Bellotti*,[3] a Massachusetts bank wanted to publicize its opposition to

---

[2] *Virginia State Board of Pharmacy v. Virginia Citizens Consumer Council, Inc.*, 96 S.Ct. 1817 (1976).

[3] 435 U.S. 765 (1978).

proposed legislation for a graduated income tax. State law made it a crime for a corporation to advertise to influence voters on issues that did not "materially affect" its business, adding that no law regarding taxation would "materially affect" a corporation. The Supreme Court held that this law infringed upon the bank's First Amendment rights. Drawing from its reasoning in *Virginia Board*, it found the law limited the "stock of information from which the public may draw." And, in another case upholding the right to First Amendment protection for commercial speech—this time for lawyers' advertising—the Court stated that regulation restricting the flow of information to consumers fosters the "assump[tion] that the public is not sophisticated enough to realize the limitations of advertising, and that the public is better kept in ignorance than trusted with correct but incomplete information."[4]

By 1980 the Supreme Court had developed a rule for challenges to government regulation of commercial speech. In *Central Hudson Electric Corp. v. Public Service Commission*,[5] the Court set out a four-pronged test: First, commercial speech will not be constitutionally protected if it is misleading or concerns illegal activity. Speech that qualifies as "protected commercial speech" can still be regulated, however, if three conditions are met. Then, the government must demonstrate a "substantial interest" in regulating the speech. Next, the regulation must serve its purpose and must "directly advance" whatever government interest has been asserted. Finally, the regulation must be tailored to fit its purpose and be "no more extensive than necessary."

■ ■ ■

In the following case, a federal judge must decide a commercial speech claim in the pharmaceutical marketing context. In New Hampshire, what the judge describes as "innovative legislation" has been passed to deal with the spiraling costs of health care, specifically the costs associated with brand-name drugs. That legislation is challenged here, raising "important questions that lie at the intersection of free speech and cyberspace."

IMS HEALTH INC. v. KELLY A. AYOTTE, NEW HAMPSHIRE ATTORNEY GENERAL
U.S. Court of Appeals, First Circuit, 2008
550 F.3d 42

SELYA, *Circuit Judge*.

... Pharmaceutical sales representatives, known in industry argot as "detailers," earn their livelihood by promoting prescription drugs in one-on-one interactions with physicians. A valuable tool in this endeavor, available through ... computerized technology, is knowledge of each individual physician's prescribing history. With that informational asset, detailers are able to target particular physicians and shape their sales pitches accordingly. Convinced that this detailing technique induces physicians to prescribe expensive brand-name drugs in place of equally effective but less costly generic drugs, New Hampshire enacted a law [the Prescription Information Law] that, among other things, prohibited certain transfers of physicians' prescribing histories for use in detailing. A duo of data miners promptly challenged the law as invalid on various grounds....

---

[4] *Bates v. State Bar of Arizona*, 97 S. Ct. 2691 (1977).

[5] 100 S.Ct. 2343 (1980).

Background

Modern-day detailing begins when a prescription is filled. At that moment, the pharmacy stores in its computerized database a potpourri of information about the transaction, such as the name of the patient, the identity of the prescribing physician, the drug, its dosage, and the quantity dispensed. [T]his information quickly finds its way into other databases, including those of insurance carriers and pharmacy benefit managers.

[P]laintiffs IMS Health Inc. and Verispan, LLC, are in the business of data mining.... [T]hey purchase data of the type ... described above, aggregate the entries, group them by prescriber, and cross-reference each physician's prescribing history with physician-specific information available through the American Medical Association. The final product enumerates the [physician's] identity and specialty, the drug prescribed, and kindred information. The scope of the enterprise is mind-boggling: these two plaintiffs alone record, group, and organize several billion prescriptions each year. To protect patient privacy, [the patients] names are encrypted....

These massive collections of information have great utility for ... pharmaceutical companies, whose detailers use it in marketing drugs to physicians.... Detailing involves tailored one-on-one visits by pharmaceutical sales representatives with physicians and their staffs.... [T]he detailer attempts to gain access to the physician's office, usually by presenting herself as a helpful purveyor of pharmaceutical information and research. The detailer comes to the physician's office armed with handouts and offers to educate the physician and his staff about the latest pharmacological developments....

... [D]etailers must manage their way around physicians' natural reluctance to make time for promotional presentations. To this end, detailers typically distribute an array of small gifts to physicians and their staffs ... and pass out free drug samples. From time to time, a detailer will invite a physician to attend an all-expense-paid conference or to accept a lucrative speaking engagement.

Most of these freebies cut very little ice. The free samples, however, are highly prized. Their sheer volume is astounding: in the year 2000, an estimated $1,000,000,000 in free drug samples flowed from detailers to physicians. That flood of free medications enables physicians to offer drugs free of charge to selected patients. Many physicians thus tolerate detailing visits in order to reap the harvest of samples....

Once inside a physician's office, detailers are capable of mounting an impressively sophisticated and intense marketing pitch. The detailer works to establish an ongoing relationship with the physician and, in most cases, detailers' visits become a regular occurrence. For example, the average primary care physician interacts with ... twenty-eight detailers each week and the average specialist interacts with fourteen....

[P]rescriber-identifiable information ... enables the detailer to zero in on physicians who regularly prescribe competitors' drugs, physicians who are prescribing large quantities of drugs for particular conditions, and "early adopters" (physicians with a demonstrated openness to prescribing drugs that have just come onto the market). The information also allows the detailer to tailor her promotional message....

Speech or Conduct

[The court believes that the work of the detailers is information processing, not "speech," and therefore not protected under the Constitution. Judge Selya describes it as conduct, not expression:]

[The New Hampshire] legislature sought to level the playing field not by eliminating speech but, rather, by eliminating the detailers' ability to use a particular informational asset—prescribing histories—in a particular way."

... We believe that in moving to combat the novel problems presented by detailing in the information age, New Hampshire has adopted a form of conduct-focused economic regulation that does not come within the First Amendment's scope.

[Even so, Selya proceeds to analyze the Prescription Information Law[6] under the First Amendment, demonstrating that, even if we assume that what detailers do is the equivalent of commercial speech, New Hampshire's regulation passes the *Central Hudson* test:]

First Amendment Scrutiny

... Under *Central Hudson*—so long as the speech in question concerns an otherwise lawful activity and is not misleading—statutory regulation of that speech is constitutionally permissible only if the statute is enacted in the service of a substantial governmental interest, directly advances that interest, and restricts speech no more than is necessary to further that interest....

Fiscal problems have caused entire civilizations to crumble, so cost containment is most assuredly a substantial governmental interest. As such, cost containment suffices to satisfy the first prong of the *Central Hudson* test.

The next question—whether the law directly advances that interest—is not so cut and dried. To succeed on this prong of the test, the state "must demonstrate that the harms it recites are real and that [the] restriction will in fact alleviate them to a material degree."

... [T]he state reasons that stripping detailers of the ability to use prescribers' histories as a marketing tool will decrease the quantities of (relatively expensive) brand-name drugs dispensed, increase the quantities of (relatively inexpensive) generic drugs dispensed, and thus reduce or contain overall costs....

The state's initial point is unarguable: pharmaceutical companies use detailing to promote the sale of brand-name drugs, and those drugs cost significantly more than their generic counterparts. Detailing works: that it succeeds in inducing physicians to prescribe larger quantities of brand-name drugs seems clear.... The fact that the pharmaceutical industry spends over $4,000,000,000 annually on detailing bears loud witness to its efficacy....

[T]he state ... present[ed] unrebutted testimony [at trial] to the effect that detailing tended dramatically to increase the prescription of brand-name drugs (and, thus, the cost of prescription drugs) without conferring any corresponding public health benefit.... The record also contains evidence of widespread incidents—Vioxx and calcium channel blockers are two prominent examples—that pointed in the same direction. Finally, the record contains a study that found that 11% of detailers' statements to physicians were demonstrably inaccurate....

This leaves the third *Central Hudson* question: whether the regulation is no more extensive than necessary to serve the state's interest in cost containment. The Supreme Court has [recently] explained ... "if the Government could achieve its interests in a manner that does not restrict speech, or that restricts less speech, the Government must do so."

[At this point the court looks at three alternative means by which the detailers argued the state could have achieved its goals.]

The first of the measures comprises a ban on gifts between detailers and physicians. Such a measure would target a harm that the legislature never deemed central to its aims. Some studies do indicate that detailers' gifts influence prescribing behavior, but

---

[6] The pertinent language of the statute reads: Records relative to prescription information containing patient-identifiable and prescriber-identifiable data shall not be licensed, transferred, used, or sold by any pharmacy benefits manager, insurance company, electronic transmission intermediary, retail, mail order, or Internet pharmacy or other similar entity, for any commercial purpose, except for the limited purposes of pharmacy reimbursement; formulary compliance; care management; utilization review by a health care provider, the patient's insurance provider or the agent of either; health care research; or as otherwise provided by law. Commercial purpose includes, but is not limited to, advertising, marketing, promotion, or any activity that could be used to influence sales or market share of a pharmaceutical product, influence or evaluate the prescribing behavior of an individual health care professional, or evaluate the effectiveness of a professional pharmaceutical detailing sales force.

the New Hampshire legislature only saw such gift-giving as pernicious when it occurred within the context of a high-intensity sales pitch made possible by a detailer's possession of a physician's prescribing history. Moreover, such a ban would have unintended consequences; it would necessarily cut off the flow of free samples that physicians receive from detailers and often dispense to indigent patients. New Hampshire was constitutionally entitled to attempt to regulate detailing without killing this golden goose.

The second measure comprises an envisioned campaign to educate physicians to prescribe generic drugs whenever possible. This suggested measure fails as a matter of simple economics. Pharmaceutical companies spend over $4,000,000,000 per year on detailing. Against that marketing juggernaut, the state would need to commit enormous resources to put across a contrary message. It is not a ground for striking down a commercial speech regulation that some counter-informational campaign, regardless of the cost, might restore equilibrium to the marketplace of ideas.

The third measure hinges on the thought that it would be workable for New Hampshire to retool its Medicaid program so that non-preferred drugs—such as expensive brand-name drugs for which non-bioequivalent generic substitutes exist—would only be dispensed upon a physician's consultation with a pharmacist. This suggested measure fails for impracticability, for incompleteness, and for coming too late in the prescription process. Implementing it would take extra time out of a doctor's day and, in all events, would make no inroads with respect to privately insured patients....

In sum, we find that ... the plaintiffs [have not] identified an alternative to the Prescription Information Law that promises to achieve the goals of the law without restricting speech. Consequently, we hold that the Prescription Information Law is no more restrictive than necessary to accomplish those goals.

Thus, even if one assumes that those provisions to some extent implicate commercial speech, they do not violate the First Amendment.

Conclusion

... [W]e reverse the decision of the district court and vacate the injunction against enforcement of the Prescription Information Law.

QUESTIONS

1. What is involved in "detailing" a drug? Identify the various stakeholders involved in detailing. What ethical issues are raised here?

2. How does the acquisition of prescription information facilitate the marketing of branded drugs? Why did the state of New Hampshire want to limit the practice? How did the judge apply the *Central Hudson* test?

3. A state-supported program in Pennsylvania called PACE pays a team of doctors to assess multiple scientific studies in order to give physicians objective information regarding the costs and benefits of various types of treatments. This so-called "academic detailing program" helps doctors decide which drugs are most effective and most cost-effective. Suppose the federal government supported this kind of program nationwide, and banned all pharmaceutical detailing. Would this regulation pass the *Central Hudson* test?

4. Federal law bans pharmaceutical companies from marketing drugs for uses other than those approved by the FDA. Doctors, however, may legally prescribe a drug for such "off-label" purposes. In May 2004 Pfizer paid a $430 fine and pled guilty to criminal charges over the marketing by its subsidiary Warner-Lambert of a drug called Neurontin. The marketing strategy was to pay doctors tens of thousands of dollars each if they would agree to give talks to groups of other doctors, explaining that Neurontin, which had been approved for epilepsy, could be prescribed for several other ("off-label") uses. One of these physician/lecturers was paid more than $300,000; others, including

some from prestigious medical schools, received more than $100,000 each. Neurontin became a top-selling drug, producing $2 billion in sales as doctors prescribed it for a range of maladies, including bipolar disorder and restless leg syndrome.[7] Such scandals seemed to flood the news in 2004, leading to a government crackdown on the marketing techniques of the pharmaceutical industry, with nearly every global drug company receiving subpoenas. **Research**: Has your state proposed or passed any legislation to address practices like these? Have any professional organizations like the American Medical Association (AMA) taken a stand? What evidence can you find that pharmaceutical companies have stopped giving doctors all-expense-paid conferences to exotic locales and hefty speaking fees? Have other marketing practices emerged that create ethical concerns?

■ ■ ■

NATIVE AMERICANS AND MALT LIQUOR ADVERTISING

In 1993,[8] Hornell Brewing Company decided to adopt the name Crazy Horse for one of its products, a malt liquor. This decision sparked anger among Native Americans—and their sympathizers in Washington DC. Crazy Horse was a greatly respected Oglala Sioux known for his spiritual qualities; the use of his name to sell alcohol seemed particularly outrageous in the light of a documented rate of alcoholism among Native Americans six times that of the general population. After a heated debate, Congress passed a law prohibiting the use of the name Crazy Horse on alcoholic beverages. Hornell then sued, arguing the ban violated the company's free speech rights.

Applying the *Central Hudson* test, the district judge had no difficulty finding a "substantial government interest" in protecting the health and welfare of an afflicted community, stating, "Native American infants are twenty times more likely than other United States infants of being born with fetal alcohol syndrome." Yet he was not convinced that a ban on the Crazy Horse label would "directly advance" such a worthy goal:

Indeed, the legislative record as to the offensiveness of the Crazy Horse label would seem as likely to suggest the contrary proposition, that Native Americans would be discouraged from consuming an alcoholic beverage that dishonors the name of a revered Native American leader....

The government asks the Court to make a leap of faith and logic ... by concluding that because advertising may increase consumption and a product label is a form of advertising, the mere use of the Crazy Horse label product will enhance consumption. It is true that ... a product label is a form of advertising. But that is not to say that a product label, standing alone, can have a remotely comparable effect on product consumption as would all advertising, such as print ads, billboards, and radio and television commercials.

---

[7] "I want you out there every day selling Neurontin.... Pain management, now that's money. We don't want to share these patients with everybody, we want them on Neurontin only. We want their whole drug budget—not a quarter, not half—the whole thing.... Hold their hand and whisper in their ear: 'Neurontin for pain, Neurontin for everything.' I don't want to see a single patient coming off Neurontin before they've been up to at least 4,800 milligrams a day. I don't want to hear that safety crap, either. Have you tried Neurontin? Every one of you should take one just to see there's nothing. It's a great drug!" (Transcript of a whistleblower lawsuit filed against Pfizer and Warner-Lambert in 1996 and unsealed in 2003.)

[8] *Hornell Brewing* Co., Inc. v. Brady, 819 F.Supp. 1227 (U.S. Dist. Ct. NY.) 1993.

And as for the final *Central Hudson* requirement, that a law must be tailored to fit the identified need, and be "no more extensive than necessary to further the government's interest," the judge wrote:

Finding the label ban unconstitutional as a violation of the First Amendment, the court took the trouble to explain that it did not condone or endorse Hornell's choice of Crazy Horse to name its new malt liquor:

> *The Court can well appreciate that the use of the name of a revered Native American leader, who preached sobriety and resisted exploitation under the hand of the United States government, is offensive and may be viewed as an exploitation of Native Americans throughout this country. The choice may be particularly insensitive given the ample documentation of alcohol abuse and its destructive results among Native Americans. Nevertheless, a price we pay in this country for ordered liberty is that we are often exposed to that which is offensive to some, perhaps even to many. It is from our exposure to all that is different that we best learn to address it, change it, and sometimes tolerate and appreciate it. "Freedom of speech may best serve its high purpose when it induces a condition of unrest, creates dissatisfaction with conditions as they are, or even stirs people to anger."*

The judge concluded by suggesting that those upset by the Crazy Horse label do what another judge recommended when a restaurant in Toledo, Ohio decided to call itself Sambo's:

> *If they are offended ... not only can they refuse to patronize the plaintiffs, but they, too, can erect signs, carry placards, or publish advertisements designed to persuade others to refuse to patronize the plaintiffs. That is what freedom of speech is all about.*

Advertising and Economics

Left wing economists ... hold that advertising tempts people to squander money on things they don't need. Who are these elitists to decide what you need? Do you need a dishwasher? Do you need a deodorant? Do you need a trip to Rome? I feel no qualms of conscience about persuading you to do that. [B]uying things can be one of life's more innocent pleasures, whether you need them or not. Remember your euphoria when you bought your first car?

— DAVID OGILVY, Ogilvy on Advertising

[T]he illusion arises that it is good to accumulate it without limit. By doing so, man harms both the community and himself because, concentrating on such a narrow aim, he deprives his soul and spirit of larger and more rewarding experiences.

— ARISTOTLE

Advertising ministers to the spiritual side of trade.... It is a great power ... part of the greater work of the regeneration and redemption of mankind.

— CALVIN COOLIDGE, 1926

Which came first, the advertising or the consumer craving? And what's wrong with consumer craving? Is advertising destructive of our polity? Or is it an essential driver of a healthy economy, even a form of artistic expression?

———————

THE DEPENDENCE EFFECT
John Kenneth Galbraith[9]

The theory of consumer demand, as it is now widely accepted, is based on two broad propositions, neither of them quite explicit but both extremely important for the present value system of economists. The first is that the urgency of wants does not diminish appreciably as more of them are satisfied or, to put the matter more precisely, to the extent that this happens it is not demonstrable and not a matter of any interest to economists or for economic policy. When man has satisfied his physical needs, then psychologically grounded desires take over. These can never be satisfied or, in any case, no progress can be proved. The concept of satiation has very little standing in economics. It is neither useful nor scientific to speculate on the comparative cravings of the stomach and the mind.

The second proposition is that wants originate in the personality of the consumer....

Were it so that a man on arising each morning was assailed by demons which instilled in him a passion sometimes for silk shirts, sometimes for kitchenware, sometimes for chamber pots, and sometimes for orange squash, there would be every reason to applaud the effort to find the goods, however odd, that quenched this flame. But should it be that his passion was the result of his first having cultivated the demons, and should it also be that this effort to allay it stirred the demons to ever greater and greater effort, there would be question as to how rational was his solution. Unless restrained by conventional attitudes, he might wonder if the solution lay with more goods or fewer demons.

So it is that if production creates the wants it seeks to satisfy ... then the urgency of the wants can no longer be used to defend the urgency of the production. Production only fills a void that it has itself created....

The even more direct link between production and wants is provided by the institutions of modern advertising and salesmanship. These cannot be reconciled with the notion of independently determined desires, for their central function is to create desires—to bring into being wants that previously did not exist. This is accomplished by the producer of the goods or at his behest. A broad empirical relationship exists between what is spent on production of consumers' goods and what is spent in synthesizing the desires for that production. A new consumer product must be introduced with a suitable advertising campaign to arouse an interest in it. The path for an expansion of output must be paved by a suitable expansion in the advertising budget. Outlays for the manufacturing of a product are not more important in the strategy of modern business enterprise than outlays for the manufacturing of demand for the product. None of this is novel. All would be regarded as elementary by the most retarded student in the nation's most primitive school of business administration....

But such integration means recognizing that wants are dependent on production. It accords to the producer the function both of making the goods and of making

———————

the desires for them. It recognizes that production, not only passively through emulation, but actively through advertising and related activities, creates the want it seeks to satisfy.

The businessman and the lay reader will be puzzled over the emphasis which I give to a seemingly obvious point. The point is indeed obvious. But it is one which, to a singular degree, economists have resisted. They have sensed, as the layman does not, the damage to established ideas which lurks in these relationships. As a result, incredibly, they have closed their eyes (and ears) to the most obtrusive of all economic phenomena, namely modern want creation.

This is not to say that the evidence affirming the dependence of wants on advertising has been entirely ignored. It is one reason why advertising has so long been regarded with such uneasiness by economists. Here is something which cannot be accommodated easily to existing theory. More pervious scholars have speculated on the urgency of desires which are so obviously the fruit of such expensively contrived campaigns for popular attention. Is a new breakfast cereal or detergent so much wanted if so much must be spent to compel in the consumer the sense of want? But there has been little tendency to go on to examine the implications of this for the theory of consumer demand and even less for the importance of production and productive efficiency. These have remained sacrosanct. More often the uneasiness has been manifested in a general disapproval of advertising and advertising men, leading to the occasional suggestion that they shouldn't exist. Such suggestions have usually been ill-received....

The fact that wants can be synthesized by advertising, catalyzed by salesmanship, and shaped by the discreet manipulations of the persuaders shows that they are not very urgent. A man who is hungry need never be told of his need for food. If he is inspired by his appetite, he is immune to the influence of Messrs. Batten, Barton, Durstine, and Osborn. The latter are effective only with those who are so far removed from physical want that they do not already know what they want. In this state alone men are open to persuasion....

As a society becomes increasingly affluent, wants are increasingly created by the process by which they are satisfied. This may operate passively. Increases in consumption, the counterpart of increases in production, act by suggestion or emulation to create wants. Or producers may proceed actively to create wants through advertising and salesmanship. Wants thus come to depend on output. In technical terms it can no longer be assumed that welfare is greater at an all-round higher level of production than at a lower one. It may be the same. The higher level of production has, merely, a higher level of want creation, necessitating a higher level of want satisfaction. There will be frequent occasion to refer to the way wants depend on the process by which they are satisfied. It will be convenient to call it the Dependence Effect....

The final problem of the productive society is what it produces. This manifests itself in an implacable tendency to provide an opulent supply of some things and a niggardly yield of others. This disparity carries to the point where it is a cause of social discomfort and social unhealth. The line which divides our area of wealth from our area of poverty is roughly that which divides privately produced and marketed goods and services from publicly rendered services. Our wealth in the first is not only in startling contrast with the meagerness of the latter, but our wealth in privately produced goods is, to a marked degree, the cause of crisis in the supply of public services. For we have failed to see the importance, indeed the urgent need, of maintaining a balance between the two.

This disparity between our flow of private and public goods and services is no matter of subjective judgment. On the contrary, it is the source of the most extensive comment which only stops short of the direct contrast being made here. In the years following World War II, the papers of any major city—those of New York were an excellent example—told daily of the shortages and shortcomings in the elementary municipal and metropolitan services. The schools were old and overcrowded. The police force was under strength and underpaid. The parks and playgrounds were insufficient.... Internal transportation was overcrowded, unhealthful, and dirty. So was the air....

The family which takes its mauve and cerise, air-conditioned, power-steered, and power-braked car out for a tour passes through cities that are badly paved, made hideous by litter, blighted buildings, billboards, and posts for wires that should long since have been put underground. They pass on into a countryside that has been rendered largely invisible by commercial art. (The goods which the latter advertise have an absolute priority in our value system. Such aesthetic considerations as a view of the countryside accordingly come second. On such matters we are consistent.) They picnic on exquisitely packaged food from a portable icebox by a polluted stream and go on to spend the night at a park which is a menace to public health and morals. Just before dozing off on an air-mattress, beneath a nylon tent, amid the stench of decaying refuse, they may reflect vaguely on the curious unevenness of their blessings. Is this, indeed, the American genius?...

The case for social balance has, so far, been put negatively. Failure to keep public services in minimal relation to private production and use of goods is a cause of social disorder or impairs economic performance. The matter may now be put affirmatively. By failing to exploit the opportunity to expand public production we are missing opportunities for enjoyment which otherwise we might have had. Presumably a community can be as well rewarded by buying better schools or better parks as by buying bigger cars. By concentrating on the latter rather than the former it is failing to maximize its satisfactions....

The conventional wisdom holds that the community, large or small, makes a decision as to how much it will devote to its public services. This decision is arrived at by democratic process. Subject to the imperfections and uncertainties of democracy, people decide how much of their private income and goods they will surrender in order to have public services of which they are in greater need. Thus there is a balance, however rough, in the enjoyments to be had from private goods and services and those rendered by public authority.

It will be obvious, however, that this view depends on the notion of independently determined consumer wants. In such a world one could with some reason defend the doctrine that the consumer, as a voter, makes an independent choice between public and private goods. But given the dependence effect—given that consumer wants are created by the process by which they are satisfied—the consumer makes no such choice. He is subject to the forces of advertising and emulating by which production creates its own demand. Advertising operates exclusively, and emulation mainly, on behalf of privately produced goods and services. Since management and emulative effects operate on behalf of private production, public services will have an inherent tendency to lag behind. Car demand which is expensively synthesized will inevitably have a much larger claim on income than parks or public health or even roads where no such influence operates. The engines of mass communication, in their highest state of development, assail the eyes and ears of the community on behalf of more beer but not of more schools. Even in the conventional wisdom it will scarcely be contended that this leads to an equal choice between the two.

The competition is especially unequal for new products and services. Every corner of the public psyche is canvassed by some of the nation's most talented citizens to see if the desire for some merchantable product can be cultivated. No similar process operates on behalf of the non-merchantable services of the state.... The scientist or engineer or advertising man who devotes himself to developing a new carburetor, cleanser, or depilatory for which the public recognizes no need and will feel none until an advertising campaign arouses it, is one of the valued members of our society. A politician or a public servant who dreams up a new public service is a wastrel. Few public offenses are more reprehensible.

So much for the influences which operate on the decision between public and private production. The calm decision between public and private consumption pictured by the conventional wisdom is, in fact, a remarkable example of the error which arises from viewing social behavior out of context. The inherent tendency will always be for public services to fall behind private production. We have here the first of the causes of social imbalance.

QUESTIONS

1. What are the two assumptions of consumer demand theory as Galbraith explains it? How does Galbraith undermine those assumptions?

2. According to Galbraith, the notion that production is dependent on consumer demand, which is dependent on advertising, is dangerous, because most economists would sense "the damage to established ideas, which lurks in these relationships." What does he mean by this?

3. Some would say that advertising does not create the desire to buy things, but simply taps into desires that already exist within us. According to Professor Hugh Rank, "If advertisers are often accused of peddling dreams, we must recognize first that they are our dreams: they are all genuine human desires; they are the benefits we seek." Do you agree? Why or why not?

4. Galbraith writes that we are paralyzed by a blitz "on behalf of more beer but not of more schools." Do you agree with him that advertising affects us so that we don't "want"—don't vote for—more and improved public goods and services? What would Milton Friedman and other free market economists say to this? How might a utilitarian thinker respond?

Federal versus Industry Self-Regulation

The Federal Trade Commission

The Federal Trade Commission (FTC), one of the first federal agencies, has two broad mandates: to promote competition through its enforcement of the Sherman and Clayton Antitrust Acts, and to protect consumers. The agency was established by the Federal Trade Act of 1914, which outlawed "unfair methods of competition and unfair or deceptive acts and practices," including false or misleading advertising. Since then, the FTC has issued detailed regulations that outline its interpretation of the FTC Act and later consumer-protection laws.

Deceptive advertising claims are those likely to mislead reasonable consumers, causing them to change their conduct. These can take several forms. Obvious or "express" claims must be truthful. An ad that appears to offer firsthand evidence of a product's qualities, for example, must be what it appears to be. The FTC pursued Campbell's Soup Company for having ad photos taken in which glass marbles were added to the bottom of bowls of soup, making it seem like they were brimming with vegetables.[10]

---

[10] *In re Campbell's Soup Co.*, 77 FTC 664 (1970).

Advertisers are responsible, too, for suggested, or "implied" claims—the misleading messages that consumers are led to believe. In one case, the makers of Anacin invited consumers to discover whether "medically proven" Anacin would "work better" for them. While it was true the company had proved that Anacin contained more aspirin than other nonprescription analgesics, and that Anacin was as effective as its leading competitor, the ad was deceptive because it left the reasonable consumer with the wrong impression that Anacin had been "medically proven" to work better than any other analgesic.[11]

Some ads that are literally true are deceptive because of what they don't say; they fail to disclose information a consumer would consider important. Internet service providers America Online (AOL), Prodigy, and CompuServe, for example, were all accused of deceptive advertising when their offers of "free trials" failed to mention that after the trial period, consumers would be automatically enrolled—and charged a monthly membership fee—unless they affirmatively cancelled during the free period.

Endorsements and testimonials must reflect the honest opinions or findings of the endorser. Ads that feature a named man identified as an "ordinary consumer" are deceptive unless, for example, his experience with weight loss is typical of what users of the product generally achieve. When an ad suggests that an endorser is an expert, she must have relevant expert qualifications and experience. It would be deceptive, for example, to have an "engineer" endorse a car if she were a chemical engineer and not an automotive engineer. In 2010 the FTC published guidelines for online endorsements, clarifying it had no intention of monitoring bloggers, just advertisers. In a set of FAQs, the Commission explained when online statements shade into ads: "Continuously getting free stuff from an advertiser creates an expectation of future benefits from positive reviews." Online disclosures must be sufficiently clear. "A single statement on a homepage" or a button labeled "disclosure, legal" would not be enough, but an 8 character tweet—"#paid ad--" would suffice. These FAQs lay out basic rules in simple, crisp sentences:

- *You can't talk about your experience if you haven't tried it.*
- *If you were paid to try something, and you thought it was terrible, you can't say it was great.*
- *You can't make statements about a product that would require proof you don't actually have.*

The FTC will typically investigate a complaint and attempt to settle it. One possible result is a **consent decree** that stops the ad from appearing. For example, the manufacturer of a well-known aerosol spray deodorant promoted the product as "ozone-friendly" because it did not contain or produce chlorofluorocarbons during its manufacture. What it failed to reveal was that butane, another air pollutant, was used as a substitute. The FTC barred the company from making "green" claims for products that add to air pollution. Where necessary, advertisers may be required to run new ads to correct misinformation in the original ad.

Deceptive and unfair spam practices have been an FTC target since 1987. The largest civil penalty for illegal spam resulted from a March 2006 settlement with Jumpstart Technologies. Accused of promising "free" movie tickets to consumers if they divulged the e-mail addresses of several friends and then repeatedly e-mailed those friends using the consumer's own e-mail address, Jumpstart agreed to pay a $900,000 civil penalty and promised not to engage in future e-mail campaigns with deceptive sender information or

---

[11] *American Home Products Corp. v. FTC*, 695 F.2d 681 (3d Cir. 1982).

content. *United States v. Jumpstart Techs.*, LLC, No. C-06-2079 (MHP) (N.D. Cal. filed Mar. 22, 2006). In 2009 a federal court ordered Direct Marketing Concepts to pay nearly $70 million for consumer refunds for falsely claiming its dietary supplements could treat, cure, or prevent cancer and other serious diseases.

In the wake of the financial crisis that unfolded in 2008, the FTC stepped up its law enforcement and consumer education efforts addressing mortgage foreclosure rescue scams, bogus debt relief and credit repair services, and unlawful debt collections. The agency led four federal-state enforcement sweeps to stamp out scams targeting distressed Americans, working with dozens of federal and state agencies on 387 actions. In a related action, dubbed Operation Bottom Dollar, the FTC targeted con artists who prey on the unemployed through bogus job-placement, work-at-home schemes. For example, a federal court jailed a marketer who failed to comply with a court order to stop a deceptive envelope-stuffing operation targeted at Spanish-speaking consumers throughout the United States and Puerto Rico.

Still, some critics claim the FTC's process is much too slow; its preferred method of confronting false and misleading advertising is to proceed on a case-by-case basis, and a single case may take as long as 20 years to wend its way through the system.

■ ■ ■

The following case was brought by the FTC against a company and its owner for making false and deceptive claims on Spanish-language television, as it advertised that its product would eliminate cellulite.

FTC v. SILUETA DISTRIBUTORS, INC. AND STANLEY KLAVIR
United States District Court, California, 1995
1995 WL 215313

ARMSTRONG, District Judge.

Defendants promoted the sale of a product known as Sistema Silueta through advertisement broadcasts on KDTV, Channel 14, and on other Spanish-language stations across the country. Sistema Silueta consists of a moisture lotion and diuretic tablets.... [T]he advertisement represents that Sistema Silueta will eliminate cellulite from the body and that consumer testimonials support this assertion.

The Sistema Silueta advertisement features an unidentified man sitting on the edge of a desk, positioned in front of booklined shelves. The man states: "I would like to talk to you for a few moments. Sistema Silueta is the scientific miracle of the moment." During this introduction, there is a subscript which reads: "We do not specify a determined weight loss with this product." The subscript disappears as the man continues: "Silueta is an astonishing treatment in two steps which penetrates the skin and attacks and dissolves the fat cells which are the cause of those ugly cellulite bumps, and later expels them from your body."

The commercial then switches to a swimsuit-clad woman who states: "We all know that neither diets nor strenuous exercises can get rid of cellulite, but with Sistema Silueta I did achieve it when I applied it on those areas I wanted to reduce." During the time the woman speaks, there is a subscript that reads: "To lose weight with this product, you need to eat less and follow the instructions."

The advertisement then moves into its third phase, which is comprised of illustration and narration. The illustration is of an overweight woman's body in a swimsuit. The figure rubs a cream onto corpulent and bumpy thighs. The figure then transforms and becomes thin. The next illustration apparently represents fat cells. Arrows are depicted entering into the spaces between the fat cells and the cells become smaller. Then a liquid pours over the picture, apparently washing the residue away. During this illustration phase, the narration is as follows: "Step number one—the Silueta cream penetrates underneath the surface of the skin breaking those fat and cellulite deposits and converts them into liquids that step number two takes care of by expelling them from your body."

The advertisement then returns to the unidentified man's office. He is now sitting behind the desk and the swimsuit-clad woman is perched on the edge of the desk. The woman states: "Nothing could be easier. Start today to get the figure you have always dreamed about." During this last scene, there is a subscript that reads: "Testimonials on file."

At this point, the advertisement shows an 800 number. When a consumer calls the 800 number, the consumer is told that it is possible to order the Sistema Silueta products by C.O.D. Although the advertised cost of the Sistema Silueta regimen is $34.95 plus $5.00 shipping and handling, the C.O.D. cost of the regimen is $43.95.

Liability

Section 5(a) of the FTC Act declares unlawful "unfair or deceptive acts or practices in or affecting commerce" and empowers the Federal Trade Commission (the "Commission") to prevent such acts or practices. Section 12 of the FTC Act is specifically directed to false advertising. This section prohibits the dissemination of "any false advertisement" in order to induce the purchase of "food, drugs, devices, or cosmetics...." The FTC Act defines "false advertisement" as "an advertisement, other than labelling, which is misleading in a material respect." An advertisement is misleading or deceptive if (1) there is a representation, omission, or practice that (2) is likely to mislead consumers acting reasonably under the circumstances, and (3) the representation, omission, or practice is material. Express product claims are presumed to be material. Furthermore, the use of a consumer endorsement violates Section 5 if the endorsement misrepresents that the alleged results are what consumers typically achieve.

FTC asserts that defendants' advertisement violated the FTC Act because it expressly and falsely represented that Sistema Silueta will eliminate cellulite, that Sistema Silueta has caused cellulite elimination in actual use, and that consumer testimonials support the conclusion that Sistema Silueta eliminates cellulite. Because these representations were expressly made in the advertisement, the materiality of the representations is presumed. Furthermore, because these representations relate to the very reason a consumer would purchase the product (i.e., to eliminate cellulite), these representations, if false, would clearly mislead consumers acting reasonably under the circumstances. Thus, the only issue here is whether the representations are false....

Plaintiff provides ample evidence by way of expert declaration testimony establishing that Sistema Silueta cannot eliminate cellulite. This evidence reveals that the "cream is nothing more than a moisturizer, the ingredients of which are those found in body lotions and creams generally." Furthermore, the diuretic tablets contain an herbal diuretic that cannot cause the loss of cellulite, only water loss, which will be replaced immediately upon the ingestion of water.

Because defendants have presented no evidence contradicting plaintiff's contentions regarding any of the three representations, no genuine issue of fact exists as to whether defendants' Sistema Silueta advertisement was false and violated the FTC Act. Thus, this Court grants summary judgment in favor of plaintiff on this issue.

Klavir's Liability

Klavir asserts that he is not individually liable for the violations because he did not know and should not have known of the misrepresentations. Klavir maintains that he bought Silueta from Juan Perez, who created the advertisement for Sistema Silueta.

Klavir claims that Perez stated he had verified the statements in the advertisement and Klavir had no reason to believe that Perez's verification was not accurate. Klavir claims that, except for products returned under the money-back guarantee, Klavir received no complaints about the product. Finally, he asserts that, as soon as plaintiff notified him of possible infractions of the FTC Act, defendants voluntarily stopped advertising the product. Based on these contentions, Klavir disclaims any individual liability in this case.

The policy behind the imposition of individual liability is to ensure that an individual defendant does not benefit from deceptive activity and then hide behind the corporation. Individual liability … can be predicated either on (1) having participated directly in the violative conduct, or (2) having had the authority to control the conduct. The parties do not dispute Klavir's authority to control Silueta's conduct, as he is the sole owner of Silueta. Disputed here is the issue of whether Klavir must have had knowledge of the conduct before liability attached.…

Courts requiring a showing of knowledge before imposition of individual liability apply the following standard: The Commission must show that the individual defendant possessed one of the following: (1) actual knowledge of material misrepresentations, (2) reckless indifference to the truth or falsity of such misrepresentations, or (3) an awareness of a high probability of fraud along with an intentional avoidance of truth.…

The evidence presented here reveals that 63 percent of the consumers who ordered Sistema Silueta returned the product. Such an extraordinarily high rate of return should have placed Klavir on notice that the product did not eliminate cellulite as claimed by the advertisements. This evidence causes the Court to conclude that Klavir acted with a reckless indifference to the truth or falsity of the advertisement's misrepresentations, or, at a minimum, that Klavir had an awareness of a high probability of fraud and intentionally avoided the truth. Consequently, the Court finds that imposition of individual liability on Klavir is appropriate.…

Before moving on, the Court addresses Klavir's assertions that his reasonable reliance on the alleged verification made by Perez saves him from individual liability. The Court finds Klavir's argument to be unpersuasive for several reasons.… [N]othing in the record establishes Perez as a reliable source for an endorsement of Sistema Silueta.…

[I]t was unreasonable for Klavir to rely on Perez's alleged verification, as this took place during a sales transaction between Klavir and Perez. It is unlikely that Perez would have informed Klavir, a prospective purchaser, that the advertisement was deceptive.… [T]he evidence reveals that the advertisement being challenged here was not the one created by Perez, but was one that was materially altered by Klavir. Klavir significantly edited the advertisement from a 1-minute running time to a 30-second running time. Finally, good faith reliance on another's representation is no defense to liability under the FTC Act.

[The defendant also objected to the remedy the government was seeking: not just a permanent injunction preventing Klavir from deceptively selling his product, but also "restitution and disgorgement," forcing him to give back his profits. The court ruled against Klavir on this issue also. Restitution and disgorgement are intended to prevent unjust enrichment, that is, to keep a company from benefiting from a deceptive trade practice. Klavir's firm had shipped 10,399 units of Silueta, but 6,546 were returned. Multiplying the unreturned shipments by the cost of each unit, the court required Klavir to "disgorge" $169,339.35. Then, using names and addresses provided by the defendant, the government would reimburse cheated consumers and keep in the U.S. Treasury whatever was left over.]

QUESTIONS

1. Why did Klavir claim he was not liable as an individual? How did the court respond? Note the treatment of Klavir's relationship with Perez, the creator of the ad. Why couldn't Klavir shift the responsibility for the Silueta commercial to Perez?

2. If you are led into making a contract by fraud or deception, you may sue to rescind the agreement and get your money back. Given that each of the misled customers for Silueta could have brought such a claim and won, do we need the FTC to pursue false advertisers also?

3. **Research**: Go to the FTC Web site, http://www.ftc.gov. Look for Advertising Policy Statements and Guidance. How does the agency define "deception"? "Unfairness"? What guidance is offered regarding online advertising and marketing?

■ ■ ■

Lanham Act

The Lanham Act was passed by Congress in 1946; one of a series of laws, regulating business, that were passed in reaction to the Great Depression. While the focus of the Lanham Act is trademark registration and protection, Section 43(a) gives competitors the right to sue for false or misleading advertising damaging to them. It has been interpreted to allow suits for false claims about either a company's own products or those of its rivals, and to include not only traditional advertising campaigns but infomercials, labels, and messages on telephone answering systems.

To succeed under the Lanham Act, a plaintiff must prove that the defendant made a "factual misrepresentation" about a product or service, something more than sales "puffery." (The claim that a pregnancy test kit works "in as fast as ten minutes" is asserted as a fact and must be true. The claim that a pregnancy test kit is "the most advanced equipment available" is considered mere puffery, a general statement inflating the positive quality of what is for sale.) If a company can show that its rival's ads are actually false, or likely to confuse consumers, it can win a court order stopping the ads; to win money damages it must prove that it actually lost customers because of a rival's misleading claims.[12]

■ ■ ■

GlaxoSmithKline Consumer Healthcare (GSKCH) is in the nicotine replacement therapy (NRT) market. GSKCH sells two products—Nicorette, a nicotine gum, and a skin-patch called NicoDerm CQ. In 2002, it aired two TV commercials aimed at its competitor, Pharmacia, maker of Nicotrol.

The first ad, "Revised Tough Decision," features an actor portraying a consumer deciding whether to buy Nicorette or Nicotrol. A voiceover asks: "Trying to quit smoking? According to the labels, Nicorette gum can be used whenever you need it, day or night. Nicotrol's patch can only be worn for 16 hours." Superimposed text at the bottom of the screen reads: "Use anytime. Use as directed." The announcer then states: "So much for flexibility," after which the actor chooses Nicorette. The second commercial, "Revised Smart Choice" contrasts NicoDerm and Nicotrol, based on several criteria involving consumer preferences. At the end, the announcer states "more doctors prefer the patch that gives you the choice."

Pharmacia went to court seeking to stop the ad campaign, claiming that GSKCH was violating the Lanham Act. In the case that follows, the court must decide (1) whether it is likely that GSKCH violated the law and, (2) if so, whether the court should preliminarily enjoin the ad, pending a full trial.

---

[12] Every state has its own laws banning unfair trade and consumer fraud. While federal law must be enforced by the FTC (FTC Act) or by lawsuits brought by an injured competitor (Lanham Act), some state laws, often referred to as "little FTC Acts" allow individuals harmed by false ads to sue. In addition, state tort laws offer remedies to consumers who have been harmed by the way a product has been marketed.

PHARMACIA CORPORATION v. GLAXOSMITHKLINE CONSUMER HEALTHCARE

United States District Court, D. New Jersey, 2003
292 F.Supp.2d 594

COOPER, District Judge.

… A Lanham Act false or misleading statement may be proved in one of two ways. The plaintiff must show that "the commercial message or statement is either (1) literally false or (2) literally true or ambiguous, but has the tendency to deceive consumers." … [In cases of the second kind, plaintiffs must show that a substantial portion of consumers actually understand the ad to be making the misleading claim, by producing] evidence that consumers are actually misled by the defendant's statements.…

[Discussion of Pharmacia's Likelihood of Success in Proving its Lanham Act Claims]

[The court begins by assessing Pharmacia's claims that GSKCH's ad violates the Lanham Act. The first is that the "Revised Tough Decision" ad makes an expressly false claim about Nicorette:]

While the ad tells viewers that the label states Nicorette may be used any time the consumer needs it, Pharmacia argues, the label in actuality places limitations on when Nicorette may be used. Specifically … the label instructs consumers to refrain from chewing Nicorette while eating or drinking … cautions users not to continuously chew one piece after another, and not to use more than 24 pieces per day. Pharmacia asserts that these various restrictions render "Revised Tough Decision" literally false because there are significant periods of each day during which a user may not chew Nicorette.

[The court must decide whether the claim is literally false—a "per se" violation—or merely ambiguous.]

… If the statement in question does not make an unambiguous claim, there is no Lanham Act violation absent a showing of actual consumer deception. The Court must look at the commercial as a whole when making its assessment.… ("A determination of literal falsity rests on an analysis of the message in context.")

The Court finds that GSKCH's statement makes an ambiguous claim.… "Revised Tough Decision" as a whole conveys the message that Nicorette is a more flexible aid to quitting smoking than Nicotrol. Within this context, we further find that the statement, "According to the labels, Nicorette gum can be used whenever you need it, day or night" makes an ambiguous claim. One viewer could understand the commercial to claim that Nicorette's label allows consumers to use Nicorette at times when they would be unable to use Nicotrol. Alternatively, another viewer might conclude that GSKCH is claiming that the label permits users to chew the gum whenever they feel like it, even during a meal. The statement is open to interpretation.…

[Without evidence of actual consumer confusion we] will not preliminarily enjoin GSKCH from showing "Revised Tough Decision."

Pharmacia also alleges that "Revised Smart Choice" runs afoul of the Lanham Act because it makes the expressly false claim that doctors prefer NicoDerm [because it] offers the choice of being worn for either 16 or 24 hours.…

We find … that GSKCH does not have any evidence to support its claim that doctors prefer NicoDerm over Nicotrol because it offers choice, and therefore that claim is per se false.

[Is Pharmacia Entitled to a Preliminary Injunction?]

[Having decided that Pharmacia has made a strong case that GSKCH violated the Lanham Act, the court must decide how fair it is to award a preliminary injunction.]

Harm to Pharmacia

Pharmacia can establish irreparable harm if it can "demonstrate a significant risk that [it] will experience harm that cannot adequately be compensated after the fact by monetary damages.… We find that GSKCH's own research demonstrates that a commercial nearly identical to "Revised Smart Choice" was effective at eroding Nicotrol's position in the market in 1996, and that this format was revived because GSKCH believed it would work just as well again. These findings establish a significant risk of harm to Pharmacia, because Pharmacia will likely lose market share if GSKCH is free to air "Revised Smart Choice."

Harm to GSKCH

Pharmacia must also demonstrate that the potential harm it faces without injunctive relief outweighs the harm [GSKCH] will suffer should an injunction issue.… To the extent GSKCH is injured by an injunction … that injury was caused by GSKCH's own misconduct in making a false claim. The Court therefore discounts any such harm. The likely loss of market share Pharmacia faces without injunctive relief outweighs any harm to GSKCH caused by granting preliminary relief.

Public Interest

The final factor in the preliminary injunction inquiry is whether "the public interest favors issuing the injunction." Pharmacia urges that there is a strong public policy against the dissemination of false and misleading advertising. The Court finds that the case law in the Third Circuit supports this contention, especially in the context of OTC drug advertising.…

There is a public consideration that counsels against granting an injunction, however. The public has a strong interest in free competition.… The injunctive power of the courts should not be misused by manufacturers attempting to stifle the free market that is the cornerstone of our economy. Courts should therefore be wary of producers' pleas for injunctive relief against the advertisements of their close competitors.

We nevertheless find that "[t]he public interest in truthful advertising is obviously served by a court's prohibition of advertising that is plainly false."

Equitable Considerations

… GSKCH asserts that Pharmacia has itself engaged in false advertising, and thus Pharmacia's motion should be denied under the doctrine of unclean hands.

GSKCH argues that Pharmacia comes before the Court with unclean hands because in an October 2002 press release Pharmacia stated that Nicotrol was the only 16-hour patch in the NRT market. GSKCH contends that this statement (which, the Court finds, is false because NicoDerm is also approved for 16-hour use) should preclude Pharmacia from enjoining "Revised Smart Choice."

The Court disagrees. First, GSKCH has not alleged that Pharmacia's statement caused it injury, which is a predicate to application of the unclean hands doctrine. Second … the nexus between Pharmacia's statement and GSKCH's claim in "Revised Smart Choice" is too remote. Pharmacia's claim that Nicotrol is the only 16-hour patch was made in a mere press release. The claim did not disparage NicoDerm. In contrast, [the false claim in] "Revised Smart Choice" directly attacks Nicotrol. Further, GSKCH's false statement was made in a recurring television commercial aimed at influencing millions of consumers. This is a far cry from a single press release. Pharmacia's one false statement "does not excuse current deceptive and misleading advertisements to the public." [Preliminary Injunction granted.]

QUESTIONS

1. On what basis does the court conclude that GSKCH likely violated the Lanham Act?

2. What public interests are at stake in this case?

■ ■ ■

Industry Self-Regulation and Marketing to Children

The advertising industry has established a number of mechanisms for self-regulation. For instance, all ad campaigns undergo a review process as they are conceptualized, both by the client (usually represented by a group of lawyers and other technical people) and the ad agency. Concern remains that the nature of the client/agency relationship can complicate thoughtful efforts to monitor the line between truthtelling and deception. Think, for example, of the way Perez interacted with Klavir in the *Silueta* case.

The National Advertising Division (NAD) of the Council of the Better Business Bureau is the official self-policing mechanism of the advertising industry. Set up in 1971 to preempt what might have been harsher government interference, NAD investigates about 180 disputes annually and resolves 98 percent of them. In about half the cases the challenged company is let off the hook, and the rest of the time the client company changes or agrees to stop the ad. The two percent of cases not resolved are appealed to the National Advertising Review Board (NARB), which evaluates them using standards close to those of the FTC and Lanham Acts. Although NAD and NARB have no enforcement power, they can threaten to send a case to the FTC for government investigation, and they have been successful in stemming the flow of the most openly deceptive and misleading advertising.

STANDARDS OF PRACTICE

In 1990, the American Association of Advertising Agencies adopted the following revision of its own guidelines:

We hold that the responsibility of advertising agencies is to be a constructive force in business.

We hold that, to discharge this responsibility, advertising agencies must recognize an obligation, not only to their clients, but to the public, the media they employ, and to each other. As a business, the advertising agency must operate within the framework of competition. It is recognized that keen and vigorous competition, honestly conducted, is necessary to the growth and health of American business. However, unethical competitive practices in the advertising agency business lead to financial waste, dilution of service, diversion of manpower, loss of prestige, and tend to weaken the public confidence....

To these ends the American Association of Advertising Agencies has adopted the following Creative Code....

Creative Code

We the members of the American Association of Advertising Agencies, in addition to supporting and obeying the laws of legal regulations pertaining to advertising, undertake to extend and broaden the application of high ethical standards. Specifically, we will not knowingly create advertising that contains:

a. **False or misleading statements or exaggerations, visual or verbal**
b. **Testimonials that do not reflect the real opinion of the individual(s) involved**
c. **Price claims that are misleading**
d. **Claims insufficiently supported or that distort the true meaning or practicable application of statements made by professional or scientific authority**
e. **Statements, suggestions, or pictures offensive to public decency or minority segments of the population**

We recognize that there are areas that are subject to honestly different interpretation and judgment. Nevertheless, we agree not to recommend to an advertiser, and to discourage the use of, advertising that is in poor or questionable taste or that is deliberately irritating....

Founded in 1974 to focus on responsible advertising to children, the Children's Advertising Review Unit (CARU) evaluates child-directed advertising in all media, checking for those that might be misleading or inaccurate, and seeking change where necessary by gaining the voluntary cooperation of advertising companies. CARU also created Self-Regulatory Guidelines, described as "going beyond the issues of truthfulness and accuracy to take into account the uniquely impressionable and vulnerable child audience," and claims to be scouring television, radio, print, and online media to enforce these standards.

QUESTIONS

1. **Research**: CARU boasts of a better than 95 percent compliance rate as it self-monitors advertisers. Find out what consumer advocates, like the Center for Science in the Public Interest or the Campaign for Commercial-Free Childhood, think of its work.

2. Why might children be especially vulnerable to advertising? Construct an ethical argument that advertising to children should be prohibited. Critique that argument, again using ethical tools.

Children, Obesity, and Marketing Junk Food

While there has been progress made in improving the overall health of children in the past few decades, a new and alarming menace to their well-being is emerging in the 21st century: obesity. As of this writing, it is estimated that one-third of American children and teens are overweight, and the trend has been on the rise since 1976.[13] Obesity, deeply psychologically and socially scarring in a nation that covets thin beauty, also presents a critical threat to public health, as overweight youth are at higher risk for developing hypertension, asthma, and Type-2 diabetes. The costs associated with obesity are already burdensome for the U.S. economy. According to one estimate, $117 billion annually are associated with lost productivity, health, and hospital care.[14] In another study, the care of overweight Americans accounted for more than 9 percent of all U.S. health expenditures.[15]

At the same time the so-called "obesity epidemic" has been escalating, an unprecedented burst of spending on marketing targeting children has occurred. In 1983, television was the primary venue for ads to children, and corporations spent $100 million. By

[13] Cynthia Ogden, Ph.D., and Margaret Carroll, M.S.P.H, "Prevalence of Obesity Among Children and Adolescents: United States, Trends 1963–1965 Through 2007–2008" on Centers for Disease Control Web site, http://www.cdc.gov/nchs/data/hestat/obesity_child_07_08/obesity_child_07_08.htm (last visited July 19, 2010).

[14] See Obesity Working Group, U.S. Food & Drug Admin., Calories Count 1 box 1 (2004), available at http://www.fda.gov/OHRMS/DOCKETS/ac/04/briefing/4039b1_01_calories%20count.pdf.

[15] NIH, *Economic Costs Related to Overweight and Obesity*, http://win.niddk.nih.gov/statistics/index.htm#econ (last visited March 16, 2009).

2007 money spent on marketing to kids was estimated at $17 billion,[16] and was spent in radically pervasive ways.

The following article was written by sociology professor Juliet B. Schor, author of *Born to Buy: The Commercialized Child and the New Consumer Culture*, and Margaret Ford, an honors sociology undergraduate, both from Boston College. They describe the dilemma at the intersection of these trends in vivid terms. They begin by noting how, more than ever before, children are involved "in media, celebrity, shopping, and other consumer practices."

FROM TASTES GREAT TO COOL: CHILDREN'S FOOD MARKETING AND THE RISE OF THE SYMBOLIC
Juliet B. Schor and Margaret Ford[17]

The Commercialization of Childhood

... According to the 2005 Kaiser Family Foundation study of children and media use, the average eight to eighteen year old is currently exposed to eight-and-a-half hours of media a day, almost all of which is "commercial" media. Actual media time (as opposed to media exposure, which double counts periods when more than one medium is being used simultaneously) is six hours and twenty-one minutes. Younger children, for whom the most recent data are not available, also have very high levels of media use. In a 1999 Kaiser study, children aged two to thirteen were found to watch more than two hours of television per day, and their total media time was five and a half hours per day. Although preschool children tend to have lower television viewing than school-aged children, 25% of them have televisions in their bedrooms and watch an average of two hours a day. Viewing time and exposure to junk food marketing is much higher for low-income children as well as racial and ethnic minority children, groups which also have higher rates of obesity and obesity-related illnesses. For example, in the 2005 study, black children were found to watch an average of four hours and five minutes of TV daily, compared to two hours forty-five minutes for white children....

[A] 1996 content analysis of Saturday morning cartoons[18] found that 63% of the 353 advertisements in this time slot were for food products. Among ... nearly 1,400 food ads studied between 1972 and 1996, there were no commercials advertising fruits and vegetables with the exception of a few Public Service Announcements. (The lack of fruit and vegetable advertising is due to the fact that almost none, with the prominent exception of Chiquita Bananas, are branded.)

Children are also heavily exposed to food ads during prime time viewing hours. A 1998 content analysis during the top-ranked prime-time shows for children aged two to eleven found that 23% of the commercials were for food, and 40% of those were for fast-food restaurants....[19]

[16] The amount had doubled since 1992. Christine Lagorio, "Resources: Marketing to Kids," *CBS News*, May 17, 2007. http://www.cbsnews.com/stories/2007/05/14/fyi/main2798401.shtml (last visited July 19, 2010).

[17] Juliet B. Schor and Margaret Ford, "From Tastes Great to Cool: Children's Food Marketing and the Rise of the Symbolic," *Journal of Law, Medicine, and Ethics* 35(1), Spring 2007, pp. 10–21. Reprinted by permission.

[18] M. Gamble and N. Cotuga, "A Quarter Century of TV Food Advertising Targeted at Children," *American Journal of Human Behavior* 23 (1999): 26–267, at 263.

[19] C. Byrd-Bredbenner and D. Grasso, "Prime-Time Health: An Analysis of Health Content in Television Commercials Broadcast During Programs Viewed Heavily by Children," *International Electronic Journal of Health Education* 2 (1999): 159–169.

Food marketing to children has moved beyond the television set, however. Packaging has become a form of advertisement, as companies [put] food into "cool" new containers or [add] licensed characters, games, and ads for other branded foods. Another marketing strategy is product placement, in which food companies pay producers of music videos, radio, books, comic strips, songs, plays, and movies to place the product in the setting.... Product placements ... cannot be zapped out, unlike 30-second spots.

Another common promotional technique for food is giveaways, or premiums.... McDonald's Happy Meals are arguably the most successful marketing strategy in human history and are credited with turning a visit to a fast food restaurant into a favored activity for children. The current prize for the Happy Meal is a "fun game piece" from the Disney movie Pirates of the Caribbean, which was released in the summer of 2006 to record box office revenues, and is part of a ten-year global marketing agreement Disney signed with McDonald's in 1996.

Character licensing has also become pervasive, especially for major movie releases. For example, breakfast cereal Cap'n Crunch launched a campaign with Warner Brother's 2006 Superman, creating a new cereal called "Superman Crunch" with advertisements for the movie on the box as well as in the television commercials.... Harry Potter famously "sold out," according to some, by cross-promoting with Coca-Cola.

Food corporations are also collaborating with toy companies and book publishers to launch lines of branded books and toys, especially to preschool aged children. Amazon.com sells more than 40 children's branded food counting and reading books such as: *The M&M's Brand Counting Book.... Hershey's Kisses Addition Book,* and *Reese's Math Fun: Addition 1 to 9....*

Food companies are also sponsoring events, such as music group tours, where they advertise heavily.... Food companies run promotional tours that give away free product samples on the streets of major cities with specially outfitted vehicles. Pop-Tarts sent the world's largest (branded) climbing wall touring the country for years. Motts juices sponsors concert tours by the musical group the Wiggles. Nabisco Nilla Wafers sponsored banana pudding pie eating contests at theme parks around the country.... Nestlé sponsored a "fun zone" with a number of musical groups at theme parks, air shows, fairs, camps, zoos, and sporting events, and Kellogg's has done an inline skating tour to push its Cinnamon Krunchers to tween males.

A related tactic is viral, or peer-to-peer, marketing. Children are enlisted to serve as "brand representatives" to other kids, to talk up the product, give out free samples, and help create buzz. Although originally used more for music releases, fashion, and shoes, viral marketing is now common with food products as well. Viral marketing firms enlist children to be in regular relationship with them, by constructing programs that give them titles (one firm uses the title "secret agent"), and keep in email contact. The Girls Intelligence Agency gets tween girls, beginning at about age eight, to set up slumber parties at their homes to test and give out products. Procter and Gamble's viral marketing arm, Tremor, has a reported 240,000 young people touting its products in everyday settings. Viral marketing is an increasingly popular form of marketing in the children and teen marketplace.

The Internet is another rapidly growing advertising venue.... [T]he first extensive analysis of internet food marketing [in 2005] ... reported 85% of food brands that advertise through television have branded Web sites marketing to children online. Internet advertising provides a more extensive and deeper participation by children since they are viewing the product for an unlimited and extended period of time through several different marketing vehicles. These include advergames, [on 73% of sites] which integrate the food product or characters associated with the brand, promotions or sweepstakes, clubs, email listservs, and software which allows the child to view television commercials online. [V]iral marketing ... was found on 64% of the sites.... Only about half (51%) of the Web sites had nutrition information and only 18% of the websites followed [the industry's Children's Advertising Review Unit (CARU)] specific guidelines that state that any advertising content must be clearly identified.[20]

Schools have also become a centerpiece of the marketing arsenal. In ... 2000, more than one-third of elementary schools, half of middle and junior high schools, and close to three-fourths of senior high schools had contracts giving soft drink companies the rights to sell their product at school. Fast food companies have gotten in on the action with incentive programs linked to educational activities. These include McDonald's "McSpellit Club" and Pizza Hut's "BOOK IT." By using free or discounted foods as an incentive, the companies reward children for reading or getting perfect scores on spelling tests. Another major marketing effort in schools is through Channel One, which delivers a current events program plus two minutes of pure ads to 38% of middle and high schools in the U.S. Until recently, there has been a high proportion of food ads on Channel One.... Food marketing to children has literally become a major part of public school curriculum....

Deteriorating Diets and Rising Obesity

Children's diets are now significantly deviating from the recommended diet. There has also been a dramatic rise in soft drink consumption. Between 1965 and 1996, the per capita daily soft drink consumption for boys aged eleven to eighteen rose from 179 g to 520 g, and from 148 g to 337 g for girls.... A ... study ... found a 60% increased risk of developing childhood obesity in middle-school aged children for every additional serving of soft drink consumed after controlling for potentially confounding factors.

Another important change is the growth of meals eaten outside the home, and fast food consumption in particular. In the late 1970's, children ate 17% of their meals away from home and fast food accounted for 2% of their energy intake. By the mid to late 1990s, those figures had increased to 30% and 10%.... [A]n average large-sized fast food meal contains about 2200 kcal, an amount that requires running a complete marathon to burn off.[21]

Obesity rates among children have grown rapidly.

Different Approaches to Advertising Effectiveness

... Children's marketers typically ... [seem to assume] a set of innate "needs" and attempt to create ads whose message is that the product will satisfy the need. Needs include love, mastery, power, and glamour. Food advertisers are also heavy users of reward models in which toys, prizes, or other "premia" are given in return for purchase.... It is also likely that food advertisers know much more about how to stimulate desire than they share with outsiders. Almost all of their research is proprietary and unavailable to academic researchers....

The Shift from Product Attributes to Symbolic Messages in Children's Marketing

In its early decades (1950s-1980s), children's advertising was low-budget, drew on little research or creative talent, and tended to follow well-established formulae. Children were not a lucrative market.... In general, commercials conveyed intrinsic product benefits. Toy commercials tended to show children playing with the toy, and focused on the things it could do. This strategy is part of what got many toy companies and their ad agencies into legal trouble in the 1960s and 1970s—the ads frequently portrayed toys doing things they really could not. In the case of food, the intrinsic product benefit approach meant that the ad promised the food would taste good. The implicit advertising model was thus either the economists' informational

[20] E. Moore, *It's Child's Play: Advergaming and Online Marketing of Food to Children* (Menlo Park, CA: Henry J. Kaiser Family Foundation , 2006).

[21] C. B. Ebbeling, D. B. Pawlak, and D. S. Ludwig, "Childhood Obesity: Public Health Crisis, Common Sense Cure," *Lancet* 260 (2002): 473–82.

one, or a latent stimulus/response approach in which product characteristics were assumed to trigger desire. Symbolic messaging was rare.

In contrast, adult-oriented advertising had already begun to reject the intrinsic product benefit model in the 1960s and 1970s. This was partly due to the realities of marketing commodities in a mass consumer society. If, for example, Coke and Pepsi or Nike and Reebok barely differ in terms of real product attributes, other advertising strategies are necessary to avoid damaging price cutting. In the earlier decades of the 20th century, advertisers had turned to crude appeals to status positioning and consumer insecurities (for example, consumers' fears of body odor or social isolation) to market these types of goods. But these messages became less effective as consumers' skepticism of advertising, particularly hard-sell techniques of industries such as automobiles, began to grow in the late 1950s and 1960s. Often dubbed the "creative revolution," advertisers turned instead to more symbolically and culturally driven messages, building brand value on the basis of popularly held cultural traits. They stressed brand image with campaigns designed to convince consumers that Nike equals power and athleticism or Pepsi is the brand of youth rebellion.

As Thomas Frank[22] has argued, the core of the creative revolution was an appeal to non-conformity and the counter-cultural quality of "cool." The association of a brand with "coolness" became a common strategy in adult and teen marketing....

Specific Themes in Symbolic Marketing: Junk Food as Oppositional

... [C]ool is an expansive category, which takes on a variety of specific meanings.... [P]erhaps the most important of its manifestations is the message that oppositional attitudes are cool, that junk food is oppositional, and that therefore junk food is cool. This issue has been posed most intriguingly by anthropologist Allison James, whose research was triggered by the accidental finding that the British word for children's sweets, "kets," means "rubbish" in adult dialect. "It is thus of great significance that something which is despised and regarded as diseased and inedible by the adult world should be given great prestige as a particularly desirable form of food by the child."...

Food advertisers have become sophisticated anthropologists.... Their ads build on basic social relationships and the connections of food to those relationships, and their power derives from these symbolic meanings.... [I]n our preliminary analysis of 55 commercials, 29 included both adult and child characters.

These [adult/child] ads often portray children and adults as occupying separate and frequently oppositional symbolic spaces. The strategy typically aligns the marketer (or the company) with the audience, and against adults. This "anti-adultism" is evident in commercial messages in which adults are portrayed as stupid, uncool, boring, nerdy, out of touch, controlling, or evil....

Junk Food as a "Drug"

The association of junk foods with energy, power, physiological transformation, or an altered state is another common tactic....

When one of the authors (Schor) sat in on focus groups with tweens for a sugary drink, she found that the children talked about their desire to get "hyper," or to "bounce off the walls." They ... were well versed in and took great delight in the transformative properties of sugar and caffeine. Not surprisingly, the soft drink companies have heavily promoted the concepts of high-energy and hyper. Pepsi's Mountain Dew, with its Code Red brand, is one example, with its themes of extreme sports and excess. So is the rise of "energy drinks" such as Red Bull, with their high levels of caffeine and appeals to youth.

[J]unk food is to a certain extent being positioned symbolically to children as a "drug." ... The association to drugs is partly based on the transformative

---

[22] T. Frank, *The Conquest of Cool* (Chicago: Chicago University Press, 1997).

physiological processes associated with high-sugar foods, in which they produce positive sensations (as drugs do), make the user feel differently....

Connections to Existing Research

[S]tudies look[   ] at how children respond to parental restrictions or disapproval of junk foods and discover what is colloquially known as the "forbidden fruit syndrome"—forbidden foods are more desirable. For example, [researchers] have found that maternal restrictions on high-fat, high-sugar foods lead daughters to increase their consumption of these foods when they are in environments where access is unlimited.[23] ...Another study found that preschool children are more attracted to foods that are not available to them, and that the effect was stronger with children whose mothers were more restrictive.[24] A third found that five-year-old girls are inclined to do the opposite of what they think their parents desire with respect to junk food consumption.[25]

The Debate about Food Marketing to Children

Since the publication, in late 2001, of the Surgeon General's report on the obesity epidemic, the debate about junk food marketing has heated up on a number of fronts. Medical professionals, children's advocates, and parents began to organize against in-school junk food marketing.... Soft drinks, which research had shown to have a unique impact on obesity, have been singled out for attention. School districts began to reject exclusive contracts with Coke and Pepsi.... A number of lawsuits have also been filed, claiming damages from companies such as McDonald's, for marketing harmful and addictive food to children....

[The writers describe that the industry responded initially by claiming that lack of exercise was the culprit. The Bush administration, to which industry had contributed heavily, took no steps toward regulation, and undermined a UN anti-obesity initiative. Restaurant and beverage companies funded an organization called the Center for Consumer Freedom, which mocked public health advocates as "food fascists." Schor and Ford note that these strategies mirrored those used by the tobacco industry in its early efforts to deal with the news that tobacco smoking caused lung cancer.]

More recently, some companies have realized that they cannot afford the negative reputation associated with making children fat, so they have downplayed their initial claims that food doesn't matter, and tried to position themselves as part of the solution to the obesity epidemic....

QUESTIONS

1. Describe the evolution from the "intrinsic product benefit" model for advertising and the "creative revolution." According to the authors, why did the change occur?

2. Many argue that the health dangers associated with consuming junk food are obvious and well known, and when people eat junk food they are merely exercising their freedom to choose. How would the authors respond to this claim?

---

[23] J. O. Fisher and L. L. Birch, "Mothers' Child-Feeding Practices Influence Daughters' Eating and Weight," *American Journal of Clinical Nutrition* 71 (2000): 1054–1061.

[24] J. O. Fisher and L. L. Birch, "Restricting Access to Palatable Foods Affects Children's Behavioral Response, Food Selection, and Intake," *American Journal of Clinical Nutrition* 69 (1999): 1264–1272, as cited in M. B. Schwartz and R. Puhl, "Childhood Obesity: A Societal Problem to Solve," *The International Association for the Study of Obesity: Obesity Reviews* 4 (2003): 57–71.

[25] J. L. Carper, J. O. Fisher, and L. L. Birch, "Young Girls' Emerging Dietary Restraint and Disinhibition Are Related to Parental Control in Child Feeding," *Appetite* 35 (2000): 121–129, as cited in M. B. Schwartz and R. Puhl, "Childhood Obesity: A Societal Problem to Solve," *The International Association for the Study of Obesity: Obesity Reviews* 4 (2003): 57–71.

Others stress that parents, not the government, should police their children's diets. Again, how would the authors respond?

3. In the light of what many call an obesity epidemic, in February 2010 First Lady Michelle Obama unveiled "Let's Move," an initiative with four key components: improving the information parents have about exercise and nutrition, improving the quality of food in schools, improving the access and affordability of nutritious food, and improving physical education. How effective would the authors expect this effort to be?

4. Junk food marketing proliferates in low-income communities, on billboards, store signs, targeted television, and radio. These same communities have limited access to affordable healthy food, and have—no surprise—higher obesity rates. This confluence of factors, along with recent studies showing African-American and Hispanic populations are more genetically disposed to obesity and diabetes than others, has driven grassroots strategies to raise awareness and change food choice behavior. The first step is often "food assessment," with people investigating their own neighborhoods for advertising saturation and lack of fresh food available.
Research: Find an example of a community engagement strategy designed to counter the effects of junk food marketing. Describe the plan and any results.

5. In 2003 Ashley Pelman and Jazlen Bradley, minor customers of McDonald's, claimed to have increased risk of becoming obese and developing diabetes and other medical problems as a result of the company's advertising, which gave the false impression that its food was healthy and nutritious.[26] In 2007 a doctor brought a class action against Yum Brands, parent company of KFC, alleging the chain failed to disclose the presence of trans fat and that its statement that its food could be part of a healthy lifestyle amounted to negligent misrepresentation.[27] To date, cases like these have not resulted in success for plaintiffs. Even so, might such litigation affect junk food advertisers? How?

6. The nonprofit group Children NOW has testified before the FTC in favor of a ban on interactive advertising to children. Commercial Alert has advocated a ban on all junk food sales in schools. The Center for Science in the Public Interest has petitioned the FDA to require warning labels on soft drinks.

   a. Put each of these strategies for limiting commercial speech through the *Central Hudson* test outlines in the IMS case at the beginning of this chapter. Would any of them be constitutional?
   b. Working with a partner or a small group, determine what kind of information the government would need to justify a regulation of junk food advertising under *Central Hudson*. Then try to write a law that would pass that test.

7. As the authors indicate, the public schools have been hotbeds of activism on this issue. Parents and advocacy groups have fought Channel One and banned junk food and soda. According to a 2004 U.S. Government Accountability Office report, "13 states ha[d] established laws addressing commercial activities in public schools, and at least 25 states [were] considering such legislation."

   a. Find out if your high school uses or has ever used Channel One. If it was taken out, find out how that happened.

---

[26] *Pelman v. McDonald's Corp.*, 237 F. Supp. 2d 512, 516 (S.D.N.Y. (2003).
[27] *Hoyte v. Yum Brands, Inc.*, 489 F. Supp. 2d 24, 26 (2007).

b. **Research**: Find out if your state has junk food legislation for its public schools. If not, find out if your high school has a school policy regarding food sold on premises.

c. Administrators often point to the much-needed funds and in-kind corporate resources that marketing in schools generate, while critics argue that the benefits promised are not always realized, and are not worth it, where junk food is advertised. What do you think? What ethical issues arise in this controversy?

8. In this article, the Center for Consumer Freedom is described as "a political front group." What does that mean?

a. **Research**: Locate the Center for Consumer Freedom Web site. Read some of its articles. Do they seem well-researched and reliable? Why/why not? What can you find out about how this organization is funded?

b. What ethical values underlie the CCF arguments?

9. **Research**: Regulations to fight obesity are surfacing across the nation beyond the public school context. Find out about the California Menu Education and Labeling Act (MEAL), the first such law in the U.S., which went into effect in January 2011. Have any other states or municipalities passed legislation requiring food businesses to inform the public about the caloric and nutritional qualities of their products?

10. Threatened by parents and advocacy groups with an obesity lawsuit, Kellogg announced new nutritional standards in June 2007. A single serving of any Kellogg product will contain not more than 200 calories, have no trans fats, and have limited sodium and sugar content. When the announcement was made, the company admitted that half of its products failed those standards, but Kellogg made a commitment that by 2008 all of them would meet the new guidelines. The company also promised to stop marketing to children under twelve and to stop offering branded toys.

a. What reservations might Schor and Ford have about Kellogg's announcement?

b. **Research**: Has Kellogg met its commitments?

c. **Research**: What happened in 2010 when the FTC challenged Kellogg's claims that nutrients added to Rice Krispies helped to bolster children's immune responses?

THE TOBACCO STORY

Harvard Law School professors Jon Hanson and Douglas Kysar's article, "A Case Study in Market Manipulation: The Tobacco Industry,"[28] asks whether the free market is not in fact prone to distortions caused by advertising and marketing techniques that influence how consumers perceive risk. They focus on the tobacco industry as an example of this syndrome for several reasons.

Firstly, the industry's enormous cash flow from repeat purchases of tobacco products allows the industry to spend unparalleled amounts of money on the tools of manipulation—including marketing research, promotion, public relations, and advertising. Second, the public has for some time been aware that tobacco

---

[28] Jon D. Hanson & Douglas A. Kysar, "Taking Behavioralism Seriously: Some Evidence of Market Manipulation," 112 *Harv. L. Rev.* 1420 (May 1999).

products may pose serious health risks. That awareness, coupled with the fact that cigarettes are far and away the most dangerous consumer product marketed today, means that the incentive for manufacturer manipulation of risk perceptions is perhaps nowhere more strongly felt than in the cigarette industry. Third, the concentrated nature of the industry might have a catalytic effect on the industry's ability to manipulate.

Hanson and Kysar discuss the creation of demand for cigarettes as a matter of "conveying to smokers a sense of independence, autonomy, and sexuality." Once research connecting smoking with serious health problems became public knowledge, the tobacco industry worked to discredit it, doing everything in its power to turn scientific findings into a "controversy." They also promoted filter tip and low-tar "safer" cigarettes. And in the 1970s they became particularly innovative and aggressive about recruiting new smokers—the young. As Hanson and Kysar write:

Indeed, examination of industry documents reveals a near obsession with marketing to the "pre-smoker."

The industry's chief strategy for capturing this "pre-smoker" market is pervasive, relentless advertising. Cigarettes are among the most promoted consumer products in the United States. The FTC reported to Congress that domestic cigarette advertising and promotional expenditures rose from close to $4 billion in 1990 to more than $6 billion in 1993. Tobacco imagery—product brand names, logos, and advertising messages—is ubiquitous. It can be found on or in everything from billboards to magazines, and from city buses to race cars. The effect is to convey the message "to young people that tobacco use is desirable, socially acceptable, safe, healthy, and prevalent." In fact, young people tend to buy the most heavily advertised cigarette brands, whereas many adults buy more generic or value-based cigarette brands, which have little or no image-based advertising....

In 1967 ... new advertisement campaigns [such as Philip Morris' for Virginia Slims] specifically targeting young girls coincided with a 110% jump in twelve-year-old starters....

Tobacco advertising in the United States was initially restricted as a result of a multibillion dollar settlement of a lawsuit brought by the attorneys general of most states, claiming that the industry should reimburse them for health care costs associated with caring for smokers. Then, in 2009, Congress passed the Family Smoking Prevention and Tobacco Control Act, authorizing the FDA to regulate tobacco. The law has already been challenged by the tobacco companies on First Amendment grounds. *Commonwealth Brands, Inc. v. United States*, 678 F. Supp. 2d 512 (W.D.Ky. 2010).

As Juliet Schor has pointed out, "the relationship between tobacco and junk food is not merely symbolic." She notes that Philip Morris acquired SevenUp (1978), Kraft (1988), and Nabisco (2000), as well as General Foods, Swiss confectioner Suchard, Taco Bell, and Miller Brewing Company. With the world's largest tobacco company now holding stakes in the largest junk food purveyors, it is not surprising that Schor finds "participants from the legal fights against tobacco are now active (on both sides) in struggles about junk food marketing to children."

Direct-to-Consumer Pharmaceutical Advertising

This chapter began with a case involving pharmaceutical sales techniques aimed at those who prescribe medications. This one looks at the other end of the spectrum in drug sales: marketing aimed at consumers. It was brought on behalf of women who had experienced problems with the contraceptive Norplant, an FDA-approved reversible contraceptive that can prevent pregnancy for up to five years. Wyeth Laboratories had marketed Norplant heavily to women rather than doctors, advertising on television and in women's magazines such as *Glamour*, *Mademoiselle*, and *Cosmopolitan*. The plaintiffs claim that these ads touted the convenience and simplicity of Norplant, and that none carried warnings of side effects, which, as enumerated by the majority in this appeal, included "weight gain, headaches, dizziness, nausea, diarrhea, acne, vomiting, fatigue, facial hair growth, numbness in the arms and legs, irregular menstruation, hair loss, leg cramps, anxiety and nervousness, vision problems, anemia, mood swings and depression, [and] high blood pressure." In addition, there were complications with removal of the Norplant device. Plaintiffs point to research published in medical journals. One study reported that Norplant removal was difficult for one-third of women and painful 40 percent of the time. Another found that doctors experienced difficulty in removing the implant in more than half of all instances.

SARAY PEREZ v. WYETH LABORATORIES INC.
Supreme Court of New Jersey, 1999
734 A.2d 1245

O'HERN, Judge.

Our medical-legal jurisprudence is based on images of health care that no longer exist. At an earlier time, medical advice was received in the doctor's office from a physician who most likely made house calls if needed. The patient usually paid a small sum of money to the doctor. Neighborhood pharmacists compounded prescribed medicines.... It is safe to say that the prevailing attitude of law and medicine was that the "doctor knows best."

Pharmaceutical manufacturers never advertised their products to patients, but rather directed all sales efforts at physicians....

For good or ill, that has all changed. Medical services are in large measure provided by managed care organizations. Medicines are purchased in the pharmacy department of supermarkets and often paid for by third-party providers. Drug manufacturers now directly advertise products to consumers on the radio, television, the Internet, billboards on public transportation, and in magazines.... The question in this case, broadly stated, is whether our law should follow these changes in the marketplace or reflect the images of the past.

Direct-to-Consumer Advertising

It is paradoxical that so pedestrian a concern as male-pattern baldness should have signaled the beginning of direct-to-consumer marketing of prescription drugs. Upjohn Company became the first drug manufacturer to advertise directly to consumers when it advertised for Rogaine, a hair-loss treatment. The ad targeted male consumers by posing the question, "Can an emerging bald spot ... damage your ability to get along with others, influence your chance of obtaining a job or date or even interfere with your job performance?" ...

Advertising for Rogaine was the tip of the iceberg.... [The court later mentions medicine for allergies, nail fungus, hypertension, and depression.]

Pressure on consumers is an integral part of drug manufacturers' marketing strategy. From 1995 to 1996, drug companies increased advertising directed to consumers [DTC] by ninety percent. In 1997, advertising costs of pharmaceutical products surpassed the half-billion dollar mark for the first time, "easily outpacing promotional efforts directed to physicians." ... These efforts ... [have been] extremely successful.... As of December 1998, "because of its testimonials" in print and broadcast media by renowned personalities, sales of a product that treats male impotence had increased to $788 million, with approximately 7.5 million prescriptions having been written.

[To highlight why the medical establishment has been troubled by DTC advertising, the majority next quotes from the 1999 *Harvard Law Review* article about the tobacco industry cited on p. 269]:

> The American Medical Association (AMA) has long maintained a policy in opposition to product-specific prescription ads aimed at consumers. A 1992 study by the Annals of Internal Medicine reports that a peer review of 109 prescription ads found 92 per cent of the advertisements lacking in some manner. The difficulties that accompany this [type of advertising] practice are manifest. "The marketing gimmick used by the drug manufacturer often provides the consumer with a diluted variation of the risks associated with the drug product." Even without such manipulation, "[t]elevision spots lasting 30 or 60 seconds are not conducive to 'fair balance' [in presentation of risks]." Given such constraints, pharmaceutical ads often contain warnings of a general nature. However, "[r]esearch indicates that general warnings (for example, see your doctor) in [DTC ads] do not give the consumer a sufficient understanding of the risks inherent in product use." Consumers often interpret such warnings as a "general reassurance" that their condition can be treated, rather than as a requirement that "specific vigilance" is needed to protect them from product risks[29]

[Traditionally, companies had a legal duty to warn consumers directly of dangers associated with their products. An exception developed, however, in the area of pharmaceutical drugs: Manufacturers do not have to warn consumers as long as they have warned physicians adequately. This Learned Intermediary Rule made sense in the "doctor knows best" world described at the start of this case, a setting where consumers are dependent upon their doctors for advice and information about prescription drugs.]

[T]he respected Judge John Minor Wisdom explained the rationale behind the Learned Intermediary Doctrine. His perspective reflects the then-prevalent attitude about doctor-patient relationships:

> This special standard for prescription drugs is an understandable exception to the Restatement's general rule that one who markets goods must warn foreseeable ultimate users of dangers inherent in [the] products.... Prescription drugs are likely to be complex medicines, esoteric in formula, and varied in effect. As a medical expert, the prescribing physician can take into account the propensities of the drug, as well as the susceptibilities of [the] patient. [The physician's] task [is to weigh] the benefits of any medication against its potential dangers. The choice [the physician] makes is an informed one, an individualized medical judgment bottomed on a knowledge of both patient and palliative. Pharmaceutical companies then, who must warn ultimate purchasers of dangers inherent in patent drugs sold over the counter, in selling prescription drugs are required to warn only the prescribing physician, who acts as a "learned intermediary" between

---

[29] Jon D. Hanson and Douglas A. Kysar, "Taking Behavioralism Seriously: Some Evidence of Market Manipulation," 112 *Harv. L. Rev.* 1420 (1999).

manufacturer and consumer. [Reyes v. Wyeth Labs, Inc. 498 F.2d 1264 (5th Cir. 1974)]

A more recent review summarized the theoretical bases for the doctrine as based on four considerations.

> *First, courts do not wish to intrude upon the doctor-patient relationship. From this perspective, warnings that contradict information supplied by the physician will undermine the patient's trust in the physician's judgment. Second, physicians may be in a superior position to convey meaningful information to their patients, as they must do to satisfy their duty to secure informed consent. Third, drug manufacturers lack effective means to communicate directly with patients, making it necessary to rely on physicians to convey the relevant information. Unlike [over-the-counter products], pharmacists usually dispense prescription drugs from bulk containers rather than as unit-of-use packages in which the manufacturer may have enclosed labeling. Finally, because of the complexity of risk information about prescription drugs, comprehension problems would complicate any effort by manufacturers to translate physician labeling for lay patients....*

These premises ... are all (with the possible exception of the last) absent in the direct-to-consumer advertising of prescription drugs.

First, with rare and wonderful exceptions, the "Norman Rockwell" image of the family doctor no longer exists....

Second, because managed care has reduced the time allotted per patient, physicians have considerably less time to inform patients of the risks and benefits of a drug. "In a 1997 survey of 1,000 patients, the FDA found that only one-third had received information from their doctors about the dangerous side effects of drugs they were taking."

Third, having spent $1.3 billion on advertising in 1998, drug manufacturers can hardly be said to "lack effective means to communicate directly with patients," when their advertising campaigns can pay off in close to billions....

Concerns regarding patients' communication with and access to physicians are magnified in the context of medicines and medical devices furnished to women for reproductive decisions. In *MacDonald v. Ortho Pharmaceutical Corp.*, 475 N.E.2d 65 (1985), the plaintiff's use of oral contraceptives allegedly resulted in a stroke. The Massachusetts Supreme Court explained several reasons why contraceptives differ from other prescription drugs and thus "warrant the imposition of a common law duty on the manufacturer to warn users directly of associated risks." For example, after the patient receives the prescription, she consults with the physician to receive a prescription annually, leaving her an infrequent opportunity to "explore her questions and concerns about the medication with the prescribing physician." [And] because oral contraceptives are drugs personally selected by the patient, a prescription is often not the result of a physician's skilled balancing of individual benefits and risks but originates, instead, as a product of patient choice. Thus, "the physician is relegated to a ... passive role." ...

When a patient is the target of direct marketing, one would think, at a minimum, that the law would require that the patient not be misinformed about the product. It is one thing not to inform a patient about the potential side effects of a product; it is another thing to misinform the patient by deliberately withholding potential side effects while marketing the product as an efficacious solution to a serious health problem. Further, when one considers that many of these "lifestyle" drugs or elective treatments cause significant side effects without any curative effect, increased consumer protection becomes imperative, because these drugs are, by definition, not medically necessary....

The direct marketing of drugs to consumers generates a corresponding duty requiring manufacturers to warn of defects in the product. The FDA has established a comprehensive regulatory scheme for direct-to-consumer marketing of pharmaceutical products....

[The majority holds that the plaintiffs can argue in tort that the manufacturers of Norplant misinformed them, substantially "contributing to their use of a defective pharmaceutical product...."]

POLLOCK, Judge, dissenting.

Norplant is not an over-the-counter drug; it can be obtained only with a doctor's prescription. To insert Norplant, a physician or other health care professional anesthetizes an area in a patient's upper arm, makes a one-eighth-inch incision, and implants six capsules just below the patient's skin. Similar surgery is required to remove the capsules.

The use of Norplant thus requires the significant involvement of the prescribing physician. Even Norman Rockwell would recognize the procedure as one performed in accordance with the traditional physician-patient relationship.... The invasiveness of the Norplant procedure, moreover, would give any patient pause and a physician cause to evaluate the risks....

The majority identifies four premises underlying the learned intermediary doctrine that it asserts are inapplicable when a manufacturer advertises the drug directly to consumers.... Contrary to the majority, those four considerations remain relevant to the implantation of Norplant.

First, the Norplant System must be implanted surgically. Implicit in the performance of a surgical procedure is respect for the physician-patient relationship. "[T]he physician is in the best position to take into account the propensities of the drug and the susceptibilities of the patient, and to give a highly individualized warning to the ultimate user based on the physician's specialized knowledge." Second, the physician is the only person who can communicate with the patient to obtain the patient's informed consent to the procedure. Third, a pharmaceutical company, such as Wyeth, cannot provide an adequate warning to each individual consumer about the potential side-effects and risks associated with the device. Each patient has individualized risks associated with surgical procedures. Lastly, the Norplant implant, far more than other birth control devices, is a complex contraceptive system that requires detailed instructions and warnings.

QUESTIONS

1. What is the Learned Intermediary Rule? Explain the context in which it became law.

2. On what legal grounds does the majority believe that the Learned Intermediary Rule does not apply where drugs are advertised directly to consumers? How does the dissent view this issue?

3. In the European Community, direct-to-consumer advertising of prescription drugs is prohibited. Would such a ban survive a *Central Hudson* challenge in the U.S.? **Research**: Recent proposals to regulate DTC ads have taken other forms. In July 2009 there was a proposal to rescind the tax deduction pharmaceutical companies enjoy for expenses associated with DTC ads, now estimated at $5 billion annually. It was hotly resisted by the industry. The FDA has also proposed expanded warnings of risks, to be delivered in a way that is somber, clear, and direct—the so-called "balanced manner" requirement. What happened with these attempts to regulate?

4. One theme of the *Perez* case is the degree to which consumers today are active, aware, and taking responsibility for their own health, rather than passive and in awe of medical expertise. Direct-to-consumer advertising—estimated at $5 billion as of 2010— is premised on the notion that consumers will be driven to want certain prescription drugs, and to ask for them by name when they see their doctors.

   a. From a consumer perspective, what are the pros and cons of DTC advertising?
   b. Who are the major stakeholders in the pharmaceutical direct-to-consumer scenario? Does this type of marketing create "the greatest happiness for the greatest number," in utilitarian terms? What might a deontological thinker say about DTC marketing?

■ ■ ■

The Branding of Culture

In her provocative book *No Logo*, journalist and media commentator Naomi Klein claims that a fundamental shift has occurred—from marketing as advertising of products to marketing itself as the product—to the preeminence of "the brand." She sees this shift as having profound consequences for every aspect of our culture.

NO LOGO
Naomi Klein[30]

The Beginning of the Brand

It's helpful to go back briefly and look at where the idea of branding first began. Though the words are often used interchangeably, branding and advertising are not the same process.... Think of the brand as the core meaning of the modern corporation, and of the advertisement as one vehicle used to convey that meaning to the world. The first mass-marketing campaigns, starting in the second half of the nineteenth century, had more to do with advertising than with branding as we understand it today. Faced with a range of recently invented products—the radio, phonograph, car, light bulb and so on—advertisers had more pressing tasks than creating a brand identity for any given corporation; first, they had to change the way people lived their lives. Ads had to inform consumers about the existence of some new invention; then convince them that their lives would be better if they used [it].

[Klein explains how, in the ad campaigns of the late nineteenth and early twentieth centuries, ads were more descriptive than persuasive, and rivals were not mentioned in the copy. Then things began to change.]

By the end of the 1940s, there was a burgeoning awareness that a brand wasn't just a mascot or a catchphrase or a picture printed on the label of a company's product; the company as a whole could have a brand identity....

The search for the true meaning of brands—or the "brand essence," as it is often called—gradually took the agencies away from individual products and their attributes and toward a psychological/anthropological examination of what brands means to the culture and to people's lives.

[She goes on to tell how, for companies like Nike, Apple, the Body Shop, Disney, Levi's, and Starbucks, the branding process was becoming more important than the actual products.]

They integrated the idea of branding into the very fabric of their companies. Their corporate cultures were so tight and cloistered that to outsiders they appeared to be a cross between fraternity house, religious cult, and sanitarium. Everything was an ad for the brand: bizarre lexicons for describing employees (partners, baristas, team players, crew members), company chants, superstar CEOs, fanatical attention to design consistency, a propensity for monument-building, and New Age mission statements....

[As Klein sees it, the new marketplace is marked by two important developments: "The deeply unhip big-box bargain stores that provide the essentials of life and monopolize a disproportionate share of the market (Walmart, et al.) and the extra-premium 'attitude' brands that provide the essentials of lifestyle and monopolize ever-expanding stretches of cultural space (Nike, et al.)."]

---

[30] Excerpts from *No Logo* by Naomi Klein. Copyright 1999. NY: St. Martin's Press.

Nike, for example, is leveraging the deep emotional connection that people have with sports and fitness. With Starbucks, we see how coffee has woven itself into the fabric of people's lives, and that's our opportunity for emotional leverage.... A great brand raises the bar—it adds a greater sense of purpose to the experience, whether it's the challenge to do your best in sports and fitness or the affirmation that the cup of coffee you're drinking really matters....

The Brand Expands

The effect, if not always the original intent, of advanced branding is to nudge the hosting culture into the background and make the brand the star. It is not to sponsor culture but to be the culture. And why shouldn't it be? If brands are not products but ideas, attitudes, values and experiences, why can't they be culture too? ...

The project of transforming culture into little more than a collection of brand-extensions-in-waiting would not have been possible without the deregulation and privatization policies of the past three decades.... [I]n the U.S. under Ronald Reagan and ... in many other parts of the world as well, corporate taxes were dramatically lowered, a move that eroded the tax base and gradually starved out the public sector. As government spending dwindled, schools, museums, and broadcasters were desperate to make up their budget shortfalls and thus ripe for partnerships with private corporations. It also didn't hurt that the political climate during this time ensured that there was almost no vocabulary to speak passionately about the value of a non-commercialized public sphere. This was the time of the Big Government bogeyman and deficit hysteria, when any political move that was not overtly designed to increase the freedom of corporations was vilified.... It was against this backdrop that, in rapid order, sponsorship went from being a rare occurrence (in the 1970s) to an exploding growth industry (by the mid-eighties)....

[Klein goes on to discuss the notion of "cool."]

Just as the history of cool in America is really (as many have argued) a history of African-American culture—from jazz and blues to rock and roll and rap—for many of the superbrands, cool hunting simply means black-culture hunting. Which is why the cool hunters' first stop was the basketball courts of America's poorest neighborhoods....

Tommy Hilfiger: To the Ghetto and Back Again

Tommy Hilfiger, even more than Nike or Adidas, has turned the harnessing of ghetto cool into a mass-marketing science. Hilfiger forged a formula that has since been imitated by Polo, Nautica, Munsingwear (thanks to Pu Daddy's fondness for the penguin logo), and several other clothing companies looking for a short cut to making it at the suburban mall and inner-city attitude....

Hilfiger ads are a tangle of Cape Cod multiculturalism: scrubbed black faces lounging with their windswept white brothers and sisters in that great country club in the sky, and always against the backdrop of a billowing American flag. "By respecting one another we can reach all cultures and communities," the company says. "We promote ... the concept of living the American dream." But the hard facts of Tommy's interracial financial success have less to do with finding common ground between cultures than with the power and mythology embedded in America's deep racial segregation.

Tommy Hilfiger started off squarely as white-preppy wear in the tradition of Ralph Lauren and Lacoste. But the designer soon realized that his clothes also had a peculiar cachet in the inner cities, where the hip-hop philosophy of "living large" saw poor and working-class kids acquiring status in the ghetto by adopting the gear and accoutrements of prohibitively costly leisure activities, such as skiing, golfing, even boating. Perhaps to better position his brand within this urban fantasy, Hilfiger began to associate his clothes more consciously with these sports, shooting ads at yacht clubs, beaches, and other nautical locales. At the same time, the clothes themselves were redesigned to appeal more directly to the hip-hop aesthetic. Cultural theorist Paul Smith described the shift as "bolder colors, bigger and baggier styles, more hoods and cords, and more prominence for logos and the Hilfiger name." He also plied rap artists like Snoop Dogg with free clothes and, walking the tightrope between the yacht and the ghetto, launched a line of Tommy Hilfiger beepers.

Once Tommy was firmly established as a ghetto thing, the real selling could begin—not just to the comparatively small market of poor inner-city youth but to the much larger market of middle-class white and Asian kids who mimic black style in everything from lingo to sports to music. Company sales reached $847 million in 1998—up from a paltry $53 million in 1991 when Hilfiger was still, as Smith puts it, "Young Republican clothing." Like so much of cool hunting, Hilfiger's marketing journey feeds off the alienation of the heart of America's race relations: selling white youth on their fetishization of black style, and black youth on their fetishization of white wealth.

QUESTIONS

1. How does Klein distinguish the following: marketing, advertising, branding? Which does she view as dominant today?

2. Compare Klein's article to the Galbraith reading at the beginning of this chapter. To what extent does Klein's analysis overlap or support Galbraith's? Does it contradict Galbraith in any way?

3. Klein attributes Tommy Hilfiger's financial success to the "power and mythology embedded in America's deep racial segregation." What does she mean by this? Can you argue against that view?

Chapter Problems

1. In 2010, according to the Congressional Budget Office, the pharmaceutical industry spent three times as much on detailing as it did on direct-to-consumer advertising. FDA Commissioner Margaret Hamburg, MD, in a Letter to Colleagues, asked health care providers to help in controlling misleading drug promotions by contacting the agency at BadAd@fda.gov when they notice improper sales tactics. What do you think of this program encouraging health professionals to blow the whistle on misleading pharmaceutical ads?

2. In the wake of public scrutiny and industry self-regulation of pharmaceutical detailing practices, the focus has shifted to "simple one-on-one human rapport." Former cheerleaders—female and male—are evidently joining the ranks of pharmaceutical sales reps in large numbers, and they walk into good salaries: $50,000 to $60,000 a year with bonuses, and a car. As *The New York Times* reported in 2005:

   Known for their athleticism, postage-stamp skirts and persuasive enthusiasm, cheerleaders have many qualities the drug industry looks for in its sales force. Some keep their pompoms active, like Onya, a sculptured former college cheerleader. On Sundays she works the sidelines for the Washington Redskins. But weekdays find her urging gynecologists to prescribe a treatment for vaginal yeast infection.

The article goes on to quote a cheerleading advisor at the University of Kentucky, who gets regular calls from drug company recruiters. He explains why his team is in demand:

Exaggerated motions, exaggerated smiles, exaggerated enthusiasm—they learn those things, and they can get people to do what they want.[31]

Are there ethical issues here?

3. **Research**: Over the years, the courts have dealt with First Amendment challenges to regulations aimed at the health and safety of young people. In 2002, a community college's ban on ads on its property for alcohol, tobacco, guns, and illegal drugs was found to violate the First Amendment. Find out how the *Central Hudson* test was applied in the following cases:

   a. The city of Baltimore passed an ordinance banning billboard advertising of alcoholic beverages and cigarettes near schools and playgrounds.
   b. The state of Rhode Island passed a law banning the mention of price from all advertising of alcoholic beverages.
   c. The New York State Liquor Authority banned the Bad Frog Brewery label that showed a frog with the second of its four unwebbed fingers extended in a gesture of insult.
   d. The city of Chicago banned commercial ads for "mature-content video games" from trains, buses, and related facilities.

4. What of the "aesthetic appeal" of advertising? Consider this:

During recent years, in certain circles, the surest way to silence a would-be critic of advertising has been to cite its artistic achievements. Whatever we may think of the products or the sponsors, this argument runs, we have to admit that those creative types in the agencies are ... clever, sometimes even brilliant. The only influence—far from sinister—they have exercised has been to enliven our cultural atmosphere with staccato visual and verbal rhythms of the commercial vernacular....

Since the late nineteenth century, advertising has given people who like to write, draw, or shoot film the opportunity to get paid regularly (maybe even well) for it. The industry has attracted many extraordinarily talented people. These artists and writers have served, in a sense, as emissaries between social universes, the agency-client world and the wider population; art and big business; museums and commercial culture. They have worked various boundaries, sometimes creatively reconnecting aesthetics and everyday life, more often conforming out of the necessity of agency organization. Whatever their accomplishments, they deserve more than a passing glance....[32]

And this:

Like advertising, poetry's purpose is to influence an audience; to affect its perceptions and sensibilities; perhaps even to change its mind.... [P]oetry's intent is to convince and seduce. In the service of that intent, it employs without guilt

[31] Stephanie Saul, "Cheerleaders Pep Up Drug Sales," *The New York Times*, November 28, 2005.

[32] Jackson Lears, *Fables of Abundance: A Cultural History of Advertising in America* (New York: Basic Books, 1994).

or fear of criticism all the arcane tools of distortion that the literary mind can devise. Keats does not offer a truthful engineering description of his Grecian urn. He offers, instead … a lyrical, exaggerated, distorted, and palpably false description. And he is thoroughly applauded for it, as are all other artists, in whatever medium, who do precisely the same thing successfully.

Commerce … takes essentially the same liberties with reality … as the artists, except that commerce calls its creations advertising.… As with art, the purpose is to influence the audience by creating illusions, symbols, and implications that promise more than pure functionality.…[33]

Is certain advertising art? Is all advertising art? None of it? Why or why not?

5. Nestlé ran an ad campaign aimed at parents for a drink called Boost Kid Essentials, claiming that it could prevent children from getting colds and missing school. Supposedly a substance in the straw—something similar to live yogurt culture—would have many beneficial health effects. In July 2010 the FTC found Nestlé's television, magazine, and online ads for this product deceptive, and the company agreed to "cease and desist" with Boost's boasts. Who else might sue Nestlé? On what theory? In part to counter the charge that they are implicated in rising obesity rates, food companies have been promoting "functional foods" lately, with added nutrients that they claim can produce positive health effects. Do an ethical analysis of this marketing approach. Compare and contrast it with the marketing of filter cigarettes by the tobacco companies.

6. In 1998, Coca-Cola held a contest inviting high-school students to devise promotional ideas for the company. A prize of $500 would go to the school with the best PR strategy. Greenbriar High in Evans, Georgia, was the winner. On "Coke Day," students were to attend lectures from visiting company executives, wear Coke t-shirts to school, and pose for a group photograph, spelling out the word Coke with their bodies. Senior Mike Cameron decided to play a prank. Just as the group formation photo was about to be taken, he removed his outer shirt to reveal a Pepsi t-shirt. He was suspended for being rude and disruptive. The principal explained: "We had the regional president of Coca-Cola here and people flew in from Atlanta to do us the honor of being resource speakers." Is there anything ethically troubling about this story? Is there a distinction between paid advertisements in schools and corporate sponsorship of the content of education? What would happen if Mike Cameron sued for violation of his First Amendment rights? **Research:** Find out what happened when he did.

7. By 2030 it is estimated that tobacco will be the biggest cause of death globally, killing about 10 million people annually. The fastest growing population of smokers exists in the developing world. In China, for example, there are an estimated 300 million smokers—one-third of its adult population and triple the number of 20 years ago. In the Philippines, 73 percent of adults and half the children ages 7 to 17 smoke. Africa has never been thought of as a primary growth region for smoking, but Philip Morris' profit there has been increasing at the rate of 20 percent a year. And in India, where only 12 percent of people smoke, both R. J. R. Reynolds and Philip Morris are now a presence, trying to tap the last major virgin market for tobacco consumption.

---

[33] Theodore Levitt, "The Morality (?) of Advertising," *Harv. Bus. Rev.* 48 (July–August 1970), p. 85.

a. What ethical considerations arise when tobacco companies market their products in developing countries?

b. **Research**: The first world treaty dealing with public health went into effect in February 2005. The Framework Convention on Tobacco Control bans all tobacco advertising, promotion, and sponsorship. Find out which countries ratified the treaty. Is the United States a signatory? Why or why not? What can you find out about the likely effectiveness of this global effort to reign in tobacco marketing?

8. Beginning in the 1990s, with their research pipelines drying up, the major players in the pharmaceutical industry moved to sustain profits by fighting to extend patent periods, by advertising direct-to-consumers, and by raising drug prices. The facts of a case filed recently in California reflect a blend of these strategies: As the patent for AstraZeneca's blockbuster drug for acid reflux, Prilosec, ran out, the company spent millions to persuade consumers that their new and eight-times-more-expensive product, Nexium, was more effective in treating acid reflux than Prilosec in its generic, over-the-counter form. As of late 2004, Nexium was AstraZenenca's best-selling product, ranked seventh among all prescription drug sales in the United States. With a $257 million blitz to promote Nexium, the "purple pill," in 2003, the company outspent all other pharmaceutical drug campaigns that year. AstraZeneca was sued by a coalition including senior citizens groups and the AFL-CIO. (This was the first time the union joined litigation aimed at controlling health care costs.) The plaintiffs argued that the Nexium ads were deceptive.

a. What law would be the basis for their claim? What would they have to prove to win?

b. What actions might the government have taken?

c. **Research**: Find out what happened in the actual case.

9. **Research**: Find any blog site containing advertising. What kind of buzz is the sponsor trying to generate? How would you describe the connection between the company's branding and its blogging?

10. A young, attractive couple is hanging around in Times Square. They are wearing backpacks, and they have with them a Sony-Ericsson cellular telephone with a digital camera attached. Approaching a passerby, the young man of the couple smiles and says: "Would you take a picture of me and my girlfriend?" Almost everyone is willing to, and as they do, he explains how the new gadget works. "It's easy. Look. Just push this button. This is so sweet. I just got it." …Soon the passerby is intrigued with the cell phone too. And although she'll never find out, the passerby has just had an encounter with two paid operatives in a "viral marketing" campaign, promoting a product like a virus spreads disease—silently but effectively. How would you feel if the attractive person who flirted with you at a bar asking for a light for a cigarette turned out to be hawking that cigarette? Does stealth marketing seem unethical to you? Why or why not?

11. In a meeting on commercial data privacy held in Brussels in 2010, David Bladeck, the U.S. FTC's Director for Consumer Protection, shared an anecdote. On April Fool's Day, 2010, the following optional clause was inserted in a privacy policy of a British online retailer, GameStation:

> By placing an order via this Web site … you agree to grant us a non-transferable option to claim, for now and for evermore, your immortal soul. If

you a) do not believe you have an immortal soul, b) have already given it to another party, or c) do not wish to grant us such a license, please click the link below to nullify this sub-clause and proceed with your transaction.

According to Vladeck, some 7,500 people, representing 88 percent of all shoppers that day did not click on the nullifying link. Privacy advocates have been pushing for a law that would stop Internet marketers from collecting data from users unless the user affirmatively permitted it. E-tailers claim that the data allows them to more easily send targeted online ads that are valued by consumers. **Research**: Find out the status of a proposed law that would require online advertisers to obtain "informed consent" before tracking consumers' Web browsing.

12. Scott Pasch and David Keezer ran Civic Development Group, a telemarketing project that claimed to raise money for police, fire, and veterans' charities. In 1998, the FTC charged them with misleading consumers by falsely claiming that their donations would be used to buy bulletproof vests and to provide death benefits to family survivors. A second suit, filed in 2007, claimed the defendants violated the prior FTC order when they hired telemarketers. Those callers falsely told consumers they worked directly for the charities that would receive "100 percent" of the donations. In fact, only 10 to 15 percent of the donations went to charity. **Research**: Go to the FTC's homepage to find out about other actions against telemarketers, such as the suit to stop millions of unwanted, prerecorded robocalls designed to deceive consumers into buying extended auto-warranties and worthless interest rate reduction programs.

CHAPTER PROJECT

Children's Web Site Analysis

With a partner or in a team,

a. Explore a commercial Web site directed at children, such as Webkinz, WeeWorld, Club Penguin, or YahooKids.
b. How does the site engage children?
c. How does it advertise?
d. Does it encourage consumption of junk food?
e. Locate CARU's Self-Regulatory Guidelines. Does the Web site conform to those standards?

Finally, explore Public Broadcasting's site for children at http://pbskids.org/. Compare and contrast it with the commercial site you have analyzed. How is it different?

CHAPTER 8

Allocating Risk and Responsiblities
Products Liability

... [The role tort law plays in this country] is uniquely American. A mass tort case is a passion or morality play. It speaks to the conscience of the country and asks whether we have gone badly astray. It examines values and probes motives; and when it is completed, it has a cathartic effect. When courts speak of punitive damages as reflecting a sense of outrage, they utter an important truth: when society bears witness to truly outrageous conduct it must react. Swift and certain justice is necessary not only because it will deter future wrongdoers, but also because it substantiates society's intolerance for malevolent corporate behavior that brings injury to thousands.

— AARON TWERSKI 1994[1]

Virtually every product is dangerous in some manner and to some extent, at least when put to certain uses. But most such dangers are simple facts of physics, chemistry, or biology. There is no reasonable way to avoid them. For such natural risks of life, product users, rather than product suppliers, properly bear responsibility for avoiding and insuring against any injuries that may result.

— DAVID OWEN (2004)[2]

For centuries, the phrase ***caveat emptor*** ("buyer beware") dominated the law in Britain and the United States, warning that most sellers made no enforceable promises with regard to their goods. By the middle of the twentieth century, the common law had shifted, allowing those injured by dangerous products to hold both sellers and manufacturers accountable. Today, government agencies such as the **Food and Drug Administration** (FDA), the **Consumer Product Safety Commission** (CPSC), **and the National Highway Transportation Safety Agency** (NHTSA) are charged with setting safety standards. At the same time, parties can allocate risks—with some constraints—under the **Uniform Commercial Code**. When the harm is widespread, when millions of Toyotas have sudden-acceleration problems, for example, those injured may now turn to the courts to hold manufacturers and sellers liable. In recent decades class action suits on behalf of thousands, sometimes hundreds of thousands, of injured

---

[1] Aaron Twerski, Introduction to "Symposium on Punitive Damages Awards in Products Liability Litigation: Strong Medicine or Poison Pill?" 39 *Vill. L. Rev.* 353 (1994).

[2] David G. Owen, "Proof of Product Defect," 93 *Ky. L.J.* 1 (2004–05).

plaintiffs have been brought against entire industries found to have hidden the known risks of their products: asbestos, tobacco, and lead.

The chapter opens with a recent Supreme Court case that illustrates the ongoing contest over who among the various players—federal agencies, state court juries, legislators—has responsibility to set safety standards for the products we use. We look at the regulatory agencies charged with assuring the safety of products used by Americans in an era of global free trade when a loaf of Sara Lee™ whole grain white bread contains ingredients from India, the Netherlands, China, Switzerland—along with honey from either Vietnam, Brazil, Uruguay, Canada, or Mexico and wheat gluten supplied by France, Poland, Russia, or Australia. After a consideration of tort suits—especially class actions—we turn to the warranties made under the Uniform Commercial Code. The chapter ends with a reading that offers a public-health perspective on the most deadly consumer products: tobacco, drugs, motor vehicles, food, and alcohol.

■ ■ ■

On April 7, 2000, Diana Levine—a professional musician who played bass, guitar and piano—went to her local clinic for treatment of a migraine headache. As on previous visits, she received an intramuscular injection of Demerol for her headache and Phenergan for her nausea. Still suffering, she returned later that day and a physician assistant gave her a second dose by what is called the IV-push method. Something went wrong. Phenergan entered Levine's artery, came in contact with arterial blood, and led to gangrene. Levine's doctors were forced to amputate first her right hand, and then her entire forearm. After settling claims against the health care center and clinician, Levine sued Wyeth, the company that made Phenergan. Her claims: Wyeth should have instructed clinicians to use the IV-drip method instead of the higher-risk IV-push method. Wyeth defended its Phenergan packaging labels, claiming they must be adequate because the Food and Drug Administration (FDA)—the federal agency charged with enforcing the Food, Drug and Cosmetic laws—approved them. The Vermont courts rejected that claim, letting stand a $7,400,000 jury award in Levine's favor. Wyeth appealed to the Supreme Court.

WYETH v. LEVINE
United States Supreme Court, 2009
129 S.Ct. 1187

Justice STEVENS delivered the Opinion of the Court

… Directly injecting the drug Phenergan into a patient's vein creates a significant risk of catastrophic consequences….The warnings on Phenergan's label had been deemed sufficient by the federal Food and Drug Administration (FDA) when it approved Wyeth's new drug application in 1955 and when it later approved changes in the drug's labeling. The question we must decide is whether the FDA's approvals provide Wyeth with a complete defense to Levine's tort claims. We conclude that they do not….

The evidence presented during the 5-day jury trial showed that the risk of intra-arterial injection…can be almost entirely eliminated through the use of IV-drip, rather than IV-push, administration….[Further evidence showed that in 1998, the agency instructed that Phenergan's final printed label "must be identical" to the FDA-approved package insert.]

The question presented by the petition is whether the FDA's drug labeling judgments "preempt state law product liability claims [which are] premised on the theory that different labeling judgments were necessary to make drugs reasonably safe for use."…

Our answer to that question must be guided by two cornerstones of our preemption jurisprudence. First, "the purpose of Congress is the ultimate touchstone in every pre-emption case."... Second, "[i]n all pre-emption cases, and particularly in those in which Congress has 'legislated ... in a field which the States have traditionally occupied,' ... we 'start with the assumption that the historic police powers of the States were not to be superseded by the Federal Act unless that was the clear and manifest purpose of Congress."...

In order to identify the "purpose of Congress" [in adopting the Food, Drug, and Cosmetic Act,] it is appropriate to briefly review the history of federal regulation of drugs and drug labeling. In 1906, Congress enacted its first significant public health law, the Federal Food and Drugs Act.... The Act, which prohibited the manufacture or interstate shipment of adulterated or misbranded drugs, supplemented the protection for consumers already provided by state regulation and common-law liability. In the 1930's, Congress became increasingly concerned about unsafe drugs and fraudulent marketing, and it enacted the Federal Food, Drug, and Cosmetic Act (FDCA).... The Act's most substantial innovation was its provision for premarket approval of new drugs....

As it enlarged the FDA's powers to "protect the public health" and "assure the safety, effectiveness, and reliability of drugs," Congress took care to preserve state law.

In 2007, after Levine's injury and lawsuit, Congress again amended the FDCA.... For the first time, it granted the FDA statutory authority to require a manufacturer to change its drug label based on safety information that becomes available after a drug's initial approval.... [The law also made] it clear that manufacturers remain responsible for updating their labels.

Wyeth first argues that Levine's state-law claims are pre-empted because it is impossible for it to comply with both the state-law duties underlying those claims and its federal labeling duties. The FDA's premarket approval of a new drug application includes the approval of the exact text in the proposed label.... There is, however, an FDA regulation that permits a manufacturer to make certain changes to its label before receiving the agency's approval. Among other things, this "changes being effected" (CBE) regulation provides that if a manufacturer is changing a label to "add or strengthen a contraindication, warning, precaution, or adverse reaction" or to "add or strengthen an instruction about dosage and administration that is intended to increase the safe use of the drug product," it may make the labeling change upon filing its supplemental application with the FDA; it need not wait for FDA approval....

Wyeth suggests that the FDA, rather than the manufacturer, bears primary responsibility for drug labeling. Yet through many amendments to the FDCA and to FDA regulations, it has remained a central premise of federal drug regulation that the manufacturer bears responsibility for the content of its label at all times. It is charged both with crafting an adequate label and with ensuring that its warnings remain adequate as long as the drug is on the market....

[W]hen the risk of gangrene from IV-push injection of Phenergan became apparent, Wyeth had a duty to provide a warning that adequately described that risk, and the CBE regulation permitted it to provide such a warning before receiving the FDA's approval....

[A]bsent clear evidence that the FDA would not have approved a change to Phenergan's label, we will not conclude that it was impossible for Wyeth to comply with both federal and state requirements....

Wyeth has offered no such evidence....

Congress did not provide a federal remedy for consumers harmed by unsafe or ineffective drugs in the 1938 statute or in any subsequent amendment. Evidently, it determined that widely available state rights of action provided appropriate relief for injured consumers....

If Congress thought state lawsuits posed an obstacle to its objectives, it surely would have enacted an express pre-emption provision at some point during the FDCA's 70-year history....[But it did not.]

In keeping with Congress' decision not to pre-empt common-law tort suits, it appears that the FDA traditionally regarded state law as a complementary form of drug regulation.

The FDA has limited resources to monitor the 11,000 drugs on the market, and manufacturers have superior access to information about their drugs, especially in the postmarketing phase as new risks emerge. State tort suits uncover unknown drug hazards and provide incentives for drug manufacturers to disclose safety risks promptly. They also serve a distinct compensatory function that may motivate injured persons to come forward with information. Failure-to-warn actions, in particular, lend force to the FDCA's premise that manufacturers, not the FDA, bear primary responsibility for their drug labeling at all times. Thus, the FDA long maintained that state law offers an additional, and important, layer of consumer protection that complements FDA regulation....

We conclude that it is not impossible for Wyeth to comply with its state and federal law obligations and that Levine's common-law claims do not stand as an obstacle to the accomplishment of Congress' purposes in the FDCA. Accordingly, the judgment of the Vermont Supreme Court [in favor of the plaintiff] is affirmed.

It is so ordered.

Justice ALITO, with whom THE CHIEF JUSTICE and Justice SCALIA Join, Dissenting

This case illustrates that tragic facts make bad law. The Court holds that a state tort jury, rather than the Food and Drug Administration (FDA), is ultimately responsible for regulating warning labels for prescription drugs....

[T]he real issue is whether a state tort jury can countermand the FDA's considered judgment that Phenergan's FDA-mandated warning label renders its intravenous (IV) use "safe." ... [D]uring his closing argument, [Levine's] attorney told the jury, "Thank God we don't rely on the FDA to...make the safe[ty] decision. You will make the decision.... The FDA doesn't make the decision, you do." ...

Federal law, however, *does* rely on the FDA to make safety determinations like the one it made here. The FDA has long known about the risks associated with IV-push in general and its use to administer Phenergan in particular. Whether wisely or not, the FDA has concluded—over the course of extensive, 54-year-long regulatory proceedings—that the drug is "safe" and "effective" when used in accordance with its FDA-mandated labeling. The unfortunate fact that [plaintiff's] healthcare providers ignored Phenergan's labeling may make this an ideal medical-malpractice case. But turning a common-law tort suit into a "frontal assault" on the FDA's regulatory regime for drug labeling upsets ... our conflict pre-emption jurisprudence. [The Supremacy Clause of the Constitution has been interpreted to mean that federal law will take precedence over state law, where Congress has made its intent or purpose clear.] ...

Congress made its "purpose" plain in authorizing the FDA—not state tort juries—to determine when and under what circumstances a drug is "safe."...

After the FDA approves a drug, the manufacturer remains under an obligation to investigate and report any adverse events associated with the drug, and must periodically submit any new information that may affect the FDA's previous conclusions about the safety, effectiveness, or labeling of the drug, If the FDA finds that the drug is not "safe" when used in accordance with its labeling, the agency "shall" withdraw its approval of the drug. The FDA also "shall" deem a drug "misbranded" if "it is dangerous to health when used in the dosage or manner, or with the frequency or duration prescribed, recommended, or suggested in the labeling thereof."

Thus, a drug's warning label "serves as the standard under which the FDA determines whether a product is safe and effective." Labeling is "[t]he centerpiece of risk management," as it "communicates to health care practitioners the agency's formal, authoritative conclusions regarding the conditions under which the product can be used safely and effectively." ... Neither the FDCA nor its implementing regulations suggest that juries may second-guess the FDA's labeling decisions....

By their very nature, juries are ill-equipped to perform the FDA's cost-benefit-balancing function. As we explained in *Riegel v. Medtronic, Inc.* (2008) juries tend to focus on the risk of a particular product's design or warning label that arguably contributed to a particular plaintiff's injury, not on the overall benefits of that design or label; "the patients who reaped those benefits are not represented in court."...

In contrast, the FDA ... consider[s] the interests of all potential users of a drug, including "those who would suffer without new medical [products]" if juries in all 50 States were free to contradict the FDA's expert determinations. And the FDA conveys its warnings with one voice, rather than whipsawing the medical community with 50 (or more) potentially conflicting ones....

To be sure, state tort suits can peacefully coexist with the FDA's labeling regime, and they have done so for decades. But this case is far from peaceful coexistence. The FDA told Wyeth that Phenergan's label renders its use "safe." But the State of Vermont, through its tort law, said: "Not so."

The state-law rule at issue here is squarely pre-empted. Therefore, I would reverse the judgment of the Supreme Court of Vermont.

QUESTIONS

1. Where does Justice Stevens place responsibility for assuring the safety of drugs? Why? What policy reasons does he mention to back up his analysis of the defendant's pre-emption claim? What does he mean by the "distinct compensatory function" served by state courts deciding tort claims? How does Stevens' view compare to that of dissenting Justice Alito? What policy arguments does the dissent mention? What do you think the dissent means by "tragic facts make bad law?"

2. After this case, what advice would you give to a pharmaceutical company that is deciding how to label a new drug?

3. The National Traffic and Motor Safety Vehicle Act of 1966 directs the Secretary of the Department of Transportation (DOT) to establish "minimum standard[s] for motor vehicle performance, or motor vehicle equipment performance." The DOT secretary required car manufacturers to include passive restraint system in a certain percentage of their cars built in or after 1987 but left it to carmakers to choose the type: automatic seatbelts, airbags, or any other suitable technology that they might develop.

   Alexis Geier drove her 1987 Honda Accord into a tree. Although she was wearing her seatbelt, she suffered serious injuries. She then sued Honda under state tort law, alleging that her car was negligently and defectively designed because it lacked a driver's-side airbag. The Supreme Court found Geier's state tort suit pre-empted, in part because the DOT Standard "embodies the Secretary's policy judgment that safety would best be promoted if manufacturers installed *alternative* protection systems in their fleets rather than one particular system in every car." In other words, because the federal agency had determined that a menu of alternative technologies were "safe," the pre-emption doctrine prevented a state—through law or a jury—from finding that one of those alternatives was unsafe. How might Wyeth use the *Geier* case as precedent? What argument might plaintiff Diana Levine use to distinguish the *Geier* case?

■ ■ ■

RISK MADE TRANSPARENT—OR INFORMATION OVERKILL?

In June 2010, San Francisco became the first jurisdiction in the U.S. to require retailers to display the amount of radiation emitted by their cell phones. Next to each phone, in at least 11-point type, the retailer must post the specific rate at which radio waves are absorbed (SAR) into the cell phone user's body tissue. Critics allege that there is no conclusive scientific evidence that cell phones are dangerous to human health.

The Ecology Center investigates chemicals in children's toys and cars. It maintains an online database, *www.healthystuff.org*, that reports the results of tests for lead, mercury, arsenic, or other chemicals in more than 5,000 common items. Some toxicologists believe that the mere presence of a toxic chemical in some objects may not pose a clear health danger to people or animals.

The companies that make household detergents, cleaners and furniture polish use some five billion pounds of chemicals in various secret compounds. Women's Voices for the Earth (www.womenandenvironment.org) has been pressuring companies like Procter & Gamble to voluntarily disclose all of the ingredients in their cleaning products. Some in the industry argue that the present standard—requiring companies to list on product labels only those ingredients that pose immediate risk—actually provides more useful information to consumers. Too much information, they argue, makes for cluttered labels that obscure important hazard warnings.

Government Regulation of Product Safety

Some government agencies, such as OSHA, are located within a particular executive department, like the Department of Labor, headed by persons who serve at the pleasure of the president. These are known as executive agencies. "Independent administrative agencies"—the Food and Drug Administration (FDA), the Consumer Product Safety Commission (CPSC), and the National Highway Transportation Safety Administration (NHTSA) for example—are not within any particular branch of government. They are considered independent because they are headed by a board of commissioners who are appointed for a specific term and can be removed early only for cause defined by Congress.

Regulation of product safety by the major independent agencies is spotty at best. And, not surprisingly, independent agencies are often caught in a crossfire of criticism from both consumer groups and business interests.

Food and Drug Administration (FDA)

As the Supreme Court explains in *Levine v. Wyeth,* the FDA's role has expanded since it was first created in 1906. Most of the reforms have been in response to high profile tragedies. In 1938, for example, an early "wonder drug" marketed for strep throat in children, Elixir of Sulfanilamide, was laced with a chemical used in antifreeze and killed 107 people. Public outrage led Congress to authorize the agency to require companies to prove the safety of drugs before they could be marketed and broadened its oversight to include cosmetics and therapeutic devices. Today the FDA's jurisdiction extends to additional products: dietary supplements, food additives, blood products, products that emit radiation (such as microwaves and cell phones) and—since 2009—tobacco products. At the same time, FDA's effectiveness in fulfilling its mission has been seriously questioned.

In the early 2000s, as the FDA warned against buying unregulated drugs online or from Canada, FDA-approved drugs were making headlines as unsafe. Vioxx carried cardiovascular risks, Paxil and other antidepressants increased the risk of suicide for children and teenagers, and cholesterol-lowering drugs were linked to kidney failure. Consumer advocates pointed to a striking weakness in FDA oversight of drug safety as problems surfaced in pharmaceuticals already on the market. In spite of the fact that in 2005 the FDA created a Drug Safety Oversight Board, by the time *Levine v. Wyeth* was decided, Justice Stevens would comment in a footnote:

> *In 1955, the same year that the agency approved Wyeth's Phenergan application, an FDA advisory committee issued a report finding "conclusively" that "the budget and*

staff of the Food and Drug Administration are inadequate to permit the discharge of its existing responsibilities for the protection of the American public." ... Three recent studies have reached similar conclusions. ("[T]he Agency suffers from serious scientific deficiencies ...");[3] ("... There is widespread agreement that resources for postmarketing drug safety work are especially inadequate ...");[4] ("FDA lacks a clear and effective process for making decisions about, and providing management oversight of, postmarket safety issues").[5]

The other major prong of FDA responsibility—assuring the safety of the American food supply—has become an almost impossible task. In the mid-1990s, consumer "health-consciousness" led the agency to look at the burgeoning supply of nutritional supplements—it banned Ephedra in 2004—and to exercise its new power to review the health claims of food products.

A decade later, attention had refocused on the basics: meat, fish, dairy, and produce. When 200 people became ill from E. coli—tainted spinach in 2006, the agency issued voluntary guidelines for handling produce. Critics noted that from 2001 to 2007, the only significant food safety regulations adopted by the FDA were those ordered by Congress. During that time, the corner grocery store had become a global market. With fewer than 2,000 food inspectors at ports and domestic food-production plants, the FDA could sample and inspect only a relatively small number of the roughly 9 million food shipments imported to the United States annually.

China, the world's third-largest food exporter, sends farm products worth $3 billion a year to the United States. It was the source of contaminated pet food and of toxic toothpaste discovered in spring 2007, and suffered a dairy-product crisis in 2008. Domestic producers have also been problematic. Around the same time that China was experiencing its problems, U.S. inspectors found melamine-laced ingredients for fish feed made in Toledo, Ohio, for example.

In summer 2010, the FDA recalled millions of eggs after hundreds of people contracted salmonella. Congress debated a proposed FDA Food Safety Modernization Act that would require the Secretary of Health and Human Services to establish science-based minimum standards for the safe production and harvesting of fruits and vegetables, expand the Secretary's power to inspect, and require increased inspections of information relating to food-borne contaminants.

The Consumer Product Safety Commission (CPSC)

Consumers by definition, include us all. They are the largest economic group, affecting and affected by almost every public and private economic decision. Yet they are the only important group ... whose views are often not heard.

— PRESIDENT JOHN F. KENNEDY, Declaration to U.S. Congress (1962)

The Consumer Product Safety Act of 1972 created the CPSC as an independent federal regulatory agency to protect consumers from unreasonable risk of injury, illness, or

[3] See FDA Science Board, "Report of the Subcommittee on Science and Technology: FDA Science and Mission at Risk" 2, 6 (2007), online at *http://www.fda.gov/ohrms/dockets/ac/07/briefing/2007-4329b_02_01_FDA%20Report%20on%20Science%20and%20Technology.pdf.*

[4] National Academies, Institute of Medicine, "The Future of Drug Safety: Promoting and Protecting the Health of the Public," 193–194 (2007).

[5] House Committee on Oversight and Government Reform, "Majority Staff Report, FDA Career Staff Objected to Agency Preemption Policies," 4 (2008).

death from unsafe products. Like the FDA, the agency has long been underfunded by Congress (there was only enough money for three of five potential commissioners from 1987–2007). Unsure of its mission, it was once described by consumer advocate Ralph Nader as "dormant for 15 years." For most of its existence the CPSC relied primarily on voluntary standards, ignoring its authority to adopt regulations and recall unsafe products. It was not until 2006 that the agency promulgated its first major safety standard, when it set minimum safeguards to make mattresses fire-safe.

Increasingly, the 15,000 types of consumer products over which the CPSC has jurisdiction are imported. In response to a public outcry over high-profile product recalls in 2007— especially of Chinese-made jewelry and toys painted with excess amounts of lead—Congress voted overwhelmingly for a sweeping revision of the consumer product safety laws. The Consumer Product Safety Improvement Act of 2008 (CPSIA) expands the regulatory and enforcement powers of the CPSC (e.g. greater recall authority) and imposes new obligations—including reporting requirements—on manufacturers, importers, and retailers.

Importantly, the law sets specific safety standards for children's products—lowering the permissible lead levels in painted toys and children's products, banning the use of six plasticizers, and adopting as a CPSC rule a formerly voluntary toy safety standard. It adds new requirements for children's products: testing, the use of tracking labels, and warnings in connection with advertising. Mindful of the way agencies historically avoided setting standards, Congress set some 42 deadlines for CPSC action.

Civil penalties were significantly enhanced, and appear to have real teeth. In its 2009 Annual Report, CPSC reported that it negotiated out–of–court settlements in which 38 companies voluntarily agreed to pay $9.8 million in civil penalties to the U.S. Treasury, the largest number of firms and the largest dollar amount in CPSC history. In February 2010, Schylling Associates Inc. agreed to pay a $200,000 penalty to settle CPSC claims that it violated U.S. law when it waited five years to tell the agency that it had imported Thomas and Friends, Curious George, and Winnie the Pooh toys with excessive lead levels.

By June 2010, work had begun on the development of SaferProducts.gov, a Web site that will allow consumers to report to the agency incidents of harm, search for reports on similar products, and obtain timely information on product recalls and emerging hazards.

IMPORTING LEAD-PAINTED TOYS[6]

In 2007, a U.S. toy company, RC2 Corporation, was forced to recall some 1.8 million Thomas the Tank Engine wood railway toys. The reason: the factory in China where the toys were made had used lead-based paint. In a *New York Times* article, David Leonhart wrote this backstory:

> *A typical Thomas the Tank Engine story is a little morality play about hubris. The stories take place on the fictional Island of Sodor, where train cars with faces and personalities go about their work.*
>
> *Almost inevitably, one of the trains tries to run too fast or pull too many boxcars and ends up in a big mess. By the end of the story, though, he comes to understand what he has done wrong. As the last line of "A Big Day for Thomas" puts it, "Thomas had already learned not to make the same mistake again."*

---

[6] David Leonhardt, "Economix: A Lesson That Thomas Could Teach," *The New York Times*, June 20, 2007.

> *An English clergyman named Wilbert Awdry invented the talking trains in the 1940s while trying to entertain his son Christopher, who was laid up with the measles. The first book was published in 1945, and a new one followed every year until 1972, when Mr. Awdry retired. In the 1980s, the Thomas stories became a hit television series. These days, millions of little toy Thomas trains are sold every year around the world....*

When the CPSC learned of the lead-paint problem, it advised parents to confiscate the toys. RC2 Corporation posted a notice on its website, urging customers to return the toys for lead-free replacements. Aside from this, as Leonhart pointed out, RC2 remained mum, failing to explain how the problem had happened in the first place, or what it planned to do to prevent a recurrence. Leonhart viewed the Thomas story as a failure of corporate responsibility: RC2, like other parent companies, was wrongly trying to distance itself from problems that occur during outsourcing—both the working conditions and the quality of the goods produced.

The story highlights some other concerns. When the CPSC was formed in 1974, the United States imported roughly $104 billion in goods. Three decades later, that number had increased to $2 trillion. By 2009, China had become the nation's second most important trade partner, after Canada, accounting for some 15% of total U.S. imports. Apart from the problems caused by a rising trade deficit—the U.S. imports more goods than it exports—many are alarmed at the quality of goods imported. Three quarters or more of the items recalled by the CPSC during the 21st century were made outside the United States. Some 40 million Chinese toys and other items used by children were recalled in 2007 alone—nearly one for every household with children.

The CPSC is part of the chain of government agencies responsible for the safety of imported products—a nearly impossible job given the sheer volume. There is, for example, only one CPSC employee to perform "spot checks" in the Los Angeles area ports, where some 15 million truck-sized cargo shipments enter the country each year. It should not be surprising that defective products—from dangerous toys to drywall with asbestos—make their way to American households.

National Highway Traffic Safety Administration (NHTSA)

Created in 1970 as part of the U.S. Department of Transportation, the NHTSA's mission is to reduce deaths, injuries, and economic losses resulting from motor vehicle crashes by setting and enforcing safety performance standards, investigating defects, conducting research, and educating the public. Despite this broad mandate, its specific powers are limited. The agency has no way to track safety-related problems unless it is notified by the affected industry. In the 1990s, hundreds of people were killed or injured in rollover accidents caused by tread separation on Bridgestone and Firestone tires. But the NHTSA was not notified of the tread problem by either the carmakers or the tire makers until the companies had been sued. Finally, in 2000, the NHTSA recalled 6.5 million tires.

In June 2007, on the heels of the reports of problems with toys and food imported from China, the NHTSA ordered a recall of 450,000 tires imported from China. The problem: tread separation seemingly caused two vehicle rollovers, killing two and injuring two others. Again, it was only after a lawsuit was filed that the manufacturer came forward, acknowledging that a "gum strip" was missing from the production process. Between 2007-2010, the Agency issued 524 recalls involving 23.5 million vehicles.

In 2009, the NHTSA was faced with yet another crisis: sudden acceleration of Toyotas. Federal law requires carmakers to notify the NHTSA within five days of learning about safety defects. Toyota had waited four months before it revealed what it knew about "sticky pedal" problems. In April 2010, after three recalls issued by the carmaker and a visit to Japan by the head of the NHTSA, Toyota agreed to pay $16.385 million, the largest civil penalty ever assessed against an automaker. By July 2010, the NHTSA had directed the National Academy of Science to conduct a full-scale study of unintended acceleration and electronic controls across the automotive industry, and was knee-deep in its own review of documents provided by Toyota.

■ ■ ■

But the NHTSA was not the only player to seek accountability from Toyota. The next reading is a complaint from one of the many lawsuits filed against the company.

WEIMER v. TOYOTA MOTOR NORTH AMERICA, INC.
United States District Court, E.D. Louisiana, 2010.
No. 10CV00219

1. Plaintiffs bring this class action on behalf of all persons in the United States who own Toyota vehicles of model years 2005-2010 which were subject to various recalls in January of 2010.
2. … [S]ome 5.3 million vehicles have been recalled by Toyota for defects in accelerator pedals which can unexpectedly become stuck in place and send the vehicle into a rapid, uncontrollable, and unsafe acceleration of the vehicle….
19. Toyota is the largest automobile manufacturer in the United States…. Over the last ten years, Toyota has sold over 20 million vehicles in the [U.S.]….

    [In order to move forward as a "class action," certain conditions must be met. The following section explains why the plaintiffs believe their case should be "certified" as a class action.]

Class Action Allegations

28. **NUMEROSITY**: Members of the Class are so numerous that their joinder would be impracticable. The Class includes millions of owners of Toyota vehicles. The approximate number of Class members at this time is 5.3 million. Judicial economy favors a class action mechanism instead of forcing each class member to bring a separate action individually.
29. **COMMONALITY**: Common questions of law and fact predominate over any individual questions of separate Class members. [They include the following:]
    b. Whether the defects in the vehicles recalled by Toyota render them unfit for their intended use;
    c. Whether Toyota breached their implied warranties of merchantability and fitness for a particular purpose;
    d. Whether Toyota's actions have caused damages to Plaintiffs and members of the Class…;
    g. Whether or not Toyota should be subject to punitive damages.
30. **TYPICALITY**: Plaintiffs' claims are typical of the claims of the Class Members. Plaintiffs and all Class Members have been injured by the same defective mechanism….

Source: United States District Court, E.D. Louisiana, 2010. No. 10CV00219.

Plaintiffs' claims arise from the same practices and course of conduct that gives rise to the claims of the Class Members and are based on the same legal theories.

31. **ADEQUACY**: Plaintiffs willfully and adequately assert and protect the interests of the Class. Plaintiffs have retained counsel who is experienced in class actions and complex mass tort litigation. Neither Plaintiffs nor their counsel have interests contrary to or conflicting with the interests of the Class.

32. **SUPERIORITY**: A class action is superior to all other available methods for the fair and efficient adjudication of this lawsuit because individual litigation of the claims by each of the Class members is economically unfeasible and impractical. While the aggregate amount of the damages suffered by the class is in the millions of dollars, the individual damages suffered by each of the Class members as a result of the wrongful conduct by Toyota, in many cases, are too small to warrant the expense of individual lawsuits. Even if the individual damages were sufficient to warrant individual lawsuits, the court system would be unreasonably burdened by the number of cases that would be filed....

[In the next section, plaintiffs allege several alternative causes of action on which their case rests. Those legal theories—breach of implied warranty, negligence, and strict products liability—are explained later in this chapter.]

Count I: Breach of Implied Warranty

36. At the times Toyota marketed, sold, and distributed automobiles for use by Plaintiffs and Class Members, Toyota knew of the use for which the Subject Vehicles were intended and impliedly warranted the product to be of a certain quality.

37. Toyota embarked on and carried out a common scheme of marketing and selling automobiles by falsely and deceptively representing that the vehicles were safe and without defects, specifically, that the accelerator pedal of the Subject Vehicles was fit for its intended use.

38. Said representations and warranties are false, misleading, and inaccurate in that the recalled automobiles are unsafe and unreasonably dangerous due to the defective accelerator pedals.

39. The Subject Vehicles, when sold, were defective, unmerchantable, unfit for ordinary use, and unfit for the particular use for which they were sold.

40. The Subject Vehicles contain a vice or defect which renders them either absolutely useless or renders their use inconvenient and imperfect such that Plaintiffs and Class Members would not have purchased the Subject Vehicles had they known of the vice or defect.

41. The damages in question arose from the reasonably anticipated use of the product in question.

42. Toyota breached the implied warranties of merchantability and fitness for a particular purpose when the Subject Vehicles were sold to Plaintiffs and Class Members, in that the accelerator pedals are defective and have otherwise failed to function as represented and intended.

43. As a direct and proximate cause of Toyota's breach of the implied warranties of merchantability and fitness for a particular purpose, Plaintiffs and Class Members have sustained and will continue to sustain the loss of use of their vehicles, severe emotional distress, economic losses and consequential damages, and are therefore entitled to compensatory damages and equitable and declaratory relief....

Count II: Negligence

45. Toyota had a duty to Plaintiffs and Class Members to provide a safe product in design and manufacture, to notify the NHTSA, and to warn the NHTSA of the defective nature of the accelerator pedals in the Subject Vehicles.

46. Toyota breached its duty of reasonable care to Plaintiffs and Class Members by designing the accelerator pedals of the Subject Vehicles in such a manner that

they were prone to becoming stuck in the depressed position and failing to return or returning extremely slowly to the idle position, thereby causing the vehicle to accelerate rapidly, uncontrollably, and dangerously.

47. Toyota breached its duty of reasonable care to Plaintiffs and Class Members by manufacturing and/or assembling the accelerator pedals of the Subject Vehicles in such a manner that they were prone to becoming stuck in the depressed position and failing to return or returning extremely slowly to the idle position, thereby causing the vehicle to accelerate rapidly, uncontrollably, as in para above and dangerously.

48. Toyota breached its duty of reasonable care to Plaintiffs and Class Members by failing to recall the Subject Vehicles at the earliest possible date and instead blaming the defect on a much less dangerous supposed "floor mat" defect.

49. Toyota breached its duty of reasonable care to Plaintiffs and Class Members by failing to exercise due care under the circumstances.

50. As a direct and proximate result of Toyota's negligence, ... Plaintiffs and Class Members have sustained and will continue to sustain [losses.]...

51. Toyota's egregious misconduct alleged above warrants the imposition of punitive damages against Toyota to prevent such future behavior.

Count III: Products Liability

54. Toyota knew and expected for the Subject Vehicles to eventually be sold to and operated by purchasers and /or eventual owners of the Subject Vehicles, including Plaintiffs and Class members; ...

55. The Subject Vehicles reached Plaintiffs without substantial change in their condition from time of completion of manufacture by Toyota.

56. The accelerator pedal defects in the Subject Vehicles could not have been contemplated by any reasonable person expected to operate the Subject Vehicles, and, therefore, presented an unreasonably dangerous situation ... even though ... operated by expected users in a reasonable manner.

57. Toyota should have reasonably foreseen that the dangerous conditions caused by the defective accelerator pedals in the Subject Vehicles would subject Plaintiffs and Class Members to harm resulting from the defective pedals.

59. As a direct and proximate cause of Toyota's design, manufacture, assembly, marketing, and sales of the Subject Vehicles, Plaintiffs and Class Members have sustained and will continue to sustain [losses and are] therefore entitled to compensatory relief according to proof, and entitled to a declaratory judgment that Toyota is liable to Plaintiffs and Class Members for breach of its duty to design, manufacture, assemble, market, and sell a safe product, fit for its reasonably intended use. Plaintiffs and Class Members are therefore entitled to equitable relief as described below....

Prayer for Relief

WHEREFORE, Plaintiffs, individually and on behalf of the members of the Class, demand judgment in their favor and against Toyota as follows:

a. For an Order certifying the Class pursuant to Federal Rule of Civil Procedure 23, appointing Plaintiffs as the representatives of the Class, and appointing counsel for Plaintiffs as counsel for the Class;

b. For an award of compensatory damages...;

d. For punitive or exemplary damages against Toyota, consistent with the degree of Toyota's reprehensibility and the resulting harm or potential harm to Plaintiffs and members of the Class, as well as an amount sufficient to punish Toyota and deter Toyota and others from similar wrongdoing;

e. For restitution and disgorgement of profits;

f. For an award of all costs incurred by Plaintiffs in pursuing this action;

g. For an award of reasonable attorneys' fees;

h. For an Order enjoining Toyota from implementing any fixes to the defect in the accelerator pedals of the Subject Vehicles without prior approval from NHTSA.

QUESTIONS

1. What is a class action lawsuit? Why was this suit brought as a class action? How do you think such suits might benefit the judicial system? Is anyone potentially harmed by them?

2. On what theories are the plaintiffs hoping to hold Toyota liable? What remedies do they seek?

3. In August 2010, the Associated Press reported that initial probes by the NHTSA revealed that brakes were not applied in 35 of the 58 cases studied. What impact would you expect such findings to have on the case?

4. **Research**: Find out what has happened to this case in the courts.

■ ■ ■

Elizabeth Cabraser, a partner in a major law firm, has represented plaintiffs in complex tort litigation and class actions since 1978. "The litigation system," she writes, "was conceived as a crucible of direct democracy, in which citizens would bring their disputes before a judge and a jury of their peers for adjudication in the context of community values." In the next reading, she explains why the cost of litigation must be lowered and equalized in order to restore what she calls "pragmatic due process" to the legal system. It is followed by an article written by attorneys who most often view litigation through the defendants' eyes: Victor E. Schwartz, Chairman of the Public Policy Group at Shook, Hardy & Bacon L.L.P and General Counsel of the American Tort Reform Association; Sherman Joyce, President of the American Tort Reform Association; and Cary Silverman, Of Counsel at Shook, Hardy & Bacon, L.L.P.

APPORTIONING DUE PROCESS: PRESERVING THE RIGHT TO AFFORDABLE JUSTICE

Elizabeth J. Cabraser[7]

… Sometime in the early to mid-nineteenth century, virtually unnoticed judicially, corporations happened. The modern limited liability corporation was born and somehow became a full-fledged citizen, a legal (albeit nonhuman) person with full legal rights by the courts, as a matter beyond peradventure, long before slaves were freed or women achieved constitutional recognition. The legal personhood of corporations has gone largely unquestioned for over 100 years. The limited liability corporation was an unsurpassed vehicle of capital accumulation, and the engine of our spectacular national economic growth. At the same time, however, the justice system, in according equal rights to entities which were, by definition, unequal in status (with far greater economic power and far more diffuse responsibility) than the human citizens who faced them in court, created a functional due process problem that recurs in virtually every modern civil damages case.…

It is far too late, and likely far too unwise, to disenfranchise limited liability corporations. By the same token, it is late, but not too late, to consider the economic reality of disparity of wealth, power, and influence between corporate persons and

[7] Elizabeth J. Cabraser, "Apportioning Due Process: Preserving the Right to Affordable Justice," Denver University Law Review 87(2), 2010, pp. 437–473. Reprinted by permission.

natural persons, and [to] determine whether ignoring that disparity in the civil litigation context violates due process....

There is a long-established due process solution for the smallest of claims, including those worth $20 (or less) in 2010 dollars: the class action. The class action has had a long, venerable, sometimes controversial, and recently high-profile history. It is extolled, or at least endured, when it is utilized in certain contexts, such as the enforcement of civil rights, but frequently maligned and attacked when its goal is compensatory (or to deter) and its targets are private corporations. The Class Action Fairness Act of 2005 ("CAFA"), for example, which expanded federal diversity jurisdiction to include most class actions, was promoted by business and manufacturers' groups in part to channel state court class action litigation into the federal courts where class certification standards were supposedly stricter, in order to reduce the number of class actions and to discourage their filing....

In literally "making a federal case" out of the vast majority of class actions, Congress ... complicated and marked up the price tag on the delivery of "fair and prompt recovery to class members with legitimate claims" by forcing class actions into competition for the scarce judicial resources of a well-respected, but under-populated, federal judicial community....

The reality that most plaintiffs' counsel are solo or small-firm practitioners, are thinly-capitalized, and often have no backup ... to subsidize their contingent fee work, has not prevented courts from overestimating the economic resources of plaintiffs' firms....

Attorneys billing by the hour will tend, intentionally or not, to maximize the time spent on completing assigned tasks, and to invent or elaborate tasks for which time can be billed....

The "makework" produced by time-billing attorneys generates additional work for litigation participants who do not bill by the hour: judges and plaintiffs' lawyers. Plaintiffs' lawyers typically work on contingency, which means they are not paid unless and until a monetary recovery is produced for their clients. In the meantime, they also typically advance the out-of-pocket costs of the litigation, which may also be magnified by the industry of their time-billing opposing counsel; and, in current complex civil litigation, such contingency fees are usually subject to court approval, court scrutiny, and court reduction....

[P]laintiffs' counsel can often do little or nothing to control their out-of-pocket advances ... because they are frequently responding to the fee-generating work product of the other side. Until very recently, defense counsel have had little incentive to suggest innovations, limitations, or efficiencies in discovery and other pretrial proceedings. Indeed, maximizing the cost and time consumed by such proceedings not only boosts the law firm's bottom line, but may also be a weapon intentionally selected by the corporate client in a defense strategy of litigation by attrition.

Courts, in their frustration at such tactics have often reacted, understandably but inappropriately, by reducing plaintiffs' fees. The more equitable—and effective—approach would be to also reduce or "cap" the fees to be charged, or at least the hours spent, by defendants' counsel....

Early tobacco litigation saw the perfection, if not the invention, of the strategy of litigation by attrition: the simple expedient of making litigation so expensive for the opposing side that it could not afford to win. A company, or an industry, willing and able to spend unstintingly on defense in order to avoid paying anything in compensation, can successfully deploy this strategy, unless judges [proactively manage attorney fees .... It] is expensive, exhausting, and demoralizing, but it can work....

Tobacco counsel knew how to make even nominally valuable wrongful death claims, in which a jury finding for the plaintiff might be persuaded to award $1 million or more, too expensive to pursue. As R. J. Reynolds's counsel put it:

> [T]he aggressive posture we have taken regarding depositions and discovery in general continues to make these cases extremely burdensome and expensive for plaintiffs' lawyers, particularly sole practitioners. To paraphrase General Patton, the way we won these cases was not by spending all of [RJR]'s money, but by making that other son of a bitch spend all of his.

In the *Haines v. Liggett Group, Inc.* case in which the above boast was quoted, there were over 100 motions, four interlocutory appeals, one final appeal, and two petitions for certiorari. Defendants deposed one of plaintiffs' experts, a doctor, for 22 days. The verdict for plaintiffs was $400,000. Plaintiffs expended over $500,000 in out-of-pocket costs and $2 million in lawyer and paralegal time. The defendant tobacco companies had spent an estimated $50 million in defense. Their attorneys were quoted in the press as stating, "This verdict sends a message to all plaintiff attorneys that these cases are not worth pursuing"....

Of course, the tobacco companies could have settled these individual smokers' cases for a small fraction of what they spent in each case on defense costs. The industry feared that if any cases were settled, the news of settlement would generate an endless stream of "thousands of potential claimants to whom payment—no matter how small—would be [cumulatively] prohibitive." The industry therefore demanded that its lawyers "[v]igorously defend any case; look upon each as being capable of establishing dangerous precedent and refuse to settle any case for any amount." This strategy was far from secret; its very efficacy depended on the fact that it was widely publicized [and consistently deployed]....

[T]he 1970 *Thayer* case, brought by an individual smoker, ended in a jury verdict for defendant Liggett & Myers. Afterward, the trial court—disturbed by the defendant's "overwhelming superiority in resources" and "insatiable appetite for procedural advantage"—detailed abuses that, in its view, rendered the trial a mockery. Among other things, the court noted that the defendant was evasive in discovery, "confidently risk[ed] tactics" knowing that the plaintiff "could not afford the luxury of a mistrial"....

Rather than illuminating the merits, the Federal Rules became offensive weapons in the defendant's hands—weapons that succeeded in concealing and obscuring the facts, in secreting key documents, and, in the *Thayer* court's own words, "mock[ing] the mandatory jury instruction that individuals and corporate institutions are always equal before the law"....

In early 1994, ... emboldened by the sudden exposure of tobacco industry documents revealing the industry's active role in misrepresenting and suppressing information regarding the health hazards of smoking and the addictive nature of nicotine, plaintiffs' lawyers began to file class actions. This effort included the nationwide *Castano v. American Tobacco Co.* class action, which was certified by the district court, only to be reversed by the Fifth Circuit. Efforts to certify nationwide or statewide classes for injured or addicted smokers were largely unsuccessful....

Our mass litigation system enables expert and experienced judges to employ procedures—including consolidation, bifurcation, and/or class action treatment—to fashion litigation structures that accord due process to each side, without exhausting either, and that are within the available resources of the system. The crucial question is whether our judiciary, aided by counsel of integrity, will... deploy its Constitutional powers to adopt such innovative (or under-utilized) procedures....

[P]erfect due process, from the standpoint of one side, may work as a denial of process upon the other.... Due process does not exist if it is not shared among adversaries. It must be apportioned. Each side may feel affronted, or deprived, of perfect due process if it does not receive all of the process that it wishes in a given case. But if there is a shortage of judicial resources, as indeed there is, and if the time and money of each side is finite, which it is, then due process must be allocated so that all have some, lest many have none.

WHY BUSINESSES FEAR LITIGATING IN STATE COURTS

Victor E. Schwartz, Sherman Joyce, and Cary Silverman[8]

The Judicial Hellholes report is a publication of...the educational arm of the American Tort Reform Association (ATRA). The report is an annual snapshot of where ATRA's membership, a broad-based coalition of more than three hundred businesses, corporations, municipalities, associations, and professional firms, is most concerned that the scales of justice have tipped against them. As the report states, "Judicial Hellholes are places where judges systematically apply laws and court procedures in an unfair and unbalanced manner, generally against defendants in civil lawsuits." Its focus is squarely on the judges, not juries, and its findings are limited to the civil, not criminal, justice system....

Ultimately, the purpose of the Judicial Hellholes report is to encourage courts in highlighted jurisdictions, such as West Virginia, to restore balance in their civil justice systems. Where necessary, state legislatures can also intervene to help fulfill that goal. It is important to note that although ATRA members are often defendants, the goal of the Judicial Hellholes report is for courts to be neither pro-plaintiff nor pro-defendant; what is sought is balanced decision making....

The right to appeal an adverse verdict is among the most basic safeguards that citizens expect in the civil justice system. In forty-eight states, the District of Columbia, and the federal court system, civil defendants have at least one appeal as of right.... In West Virginia, however, there is no such right, and the losing party must file a petition for appeal with the state's sole appellate court ... [which has] complete discretion as to whether to grant or deny a petition for appeal ....

The lack of appellate review is particularly concerning to out-of-state businesses that are hauled into West Virginia courts because they are placed at a distinct disadvantage against a hometown plaintiff and his or her local attorney.... This type of systemic bias against out-of-state corporate defendants and in favor of wealth redistribution, a "structural problem" stemming from the elected judiciary, led [West Virginia Supreme Court] Justice Neely to recognize a "liability crisis" and advocate... an increasing role for federal courts....

West Virginia courts have placed burdens on defendants that make it difficult, if not impossible, to fairly try cases. These practices include lumping together thousands of individual cases with diverse facts in mass consolidations, allowing cases to proceed against out-of-state defendants that have little or nothing to do with West Virginia, and permitting unorthodox trial plans that have a fact-finder consider whether

---

[8] Victor E. Schwartz, Sherman Joyce, and Cary Silverman, "Why Businesses Fear Litigating in State Courts." From Victor E. Schwartz, Sherman Joyce, and Cary Silverman, "West Virginia as Hellhole: Why Businesses Fear Litigating in State Courts," West Virginia Law Review 111(3), Spring 2009. Reprinted by permission.

the defendant's conduct warrants punitive damages even before certifying a class or determining compensatory damages. Each of these practices has a common effect: to force a defendant to settle and settle early without regard to the merits of the case....

[I]n an infamous case in 2002, the West Virginia Supreme Court of Appeals allowed a Kanawha County court to consolidate the claims of more than 8,000 asbestos plaintiffs into one legal action against more than 250 defendants. Justice Elliott Maynard explained:

> [T]his litigation involves thousands of plaintiffs; twenty or more defendants; hundreds of different work sites located in a number of different states; dozens of different occupations and circumstances of exposure; dozens of different products with different formulations, applications, and warnings; several different diseases; numerous different claims at different stages of development; and at least nine different law firms, with differing interests, representing the various plaintiffs. Additionally, the challenged conduct spans the better part of six decades.

Justice Maynard noted that these claims "migrated [to West Virginia] because of the asserted pro-plaintiff bias with which [the defendant claimed] this State handles asbestos litigation."....

[Next, the authors decry "non-traditional judicial management techniques" adopted by West Virginia courts in the 1990s when faced with an onslaught of asbestos litigation.] Instead of relieving burdened court dockets ... expedited procedures and judicial shortcuts encouraged claims. As one West Virginia trial judge handling asbestos claims observed, "We thought [a mass trial] was probably going to put an end to asbestos, or at least knock a big hole in it. What I didn't consider was that it was a form of advertising. [I]t drew more cases."....

A final example of West Virginia's procedural unfairness is the judiciary's use of a highly controversial and potentially unconstitutional procedure that permits trial courts to put the question of punitive damages before a jury prior to any determination of liability. In this practice, known as reverse bifurcation, a trial is divided into two or more phases with damages determined in the first phase followed by a determination of liability in the second phase. While such an "extraordinary" procedure is not unprecedented, and in fact is "well-recognized" in some jurisdictions as a means of encouraging settlement in complex asbestos litigation, West Virginia appears to be one of a handful of states that has permitted its use when punitive damages are at issue. The effect of reverse bifurcation is that the jury will hear the most damning evidence at the initial phase of the trial, painting the defendants as "bad actors" before the jury even considers whether (and to what extent) defendants are legally responsible for damages; for example, did the defendant's alleged wrongful conduct cause the harm? In doing so, the procedure makes it very difficult, if not impossible, for defendants to receive a fair trial, and likely violates U.S. Supreme Court due process jurisprudence that requires adequate procedural safeguards against arbitrary punitive damage awards....

[R]everse bifurcation "pose[s] an acute danger of arbitrary deprivation of property" and comes with "the potential that juries will use their verdicts to express biases against big businesses, particularly those without strong local presences."....

In addition to imposing procedural disadvantages on defendants, the West Virginia Supreme Court of Appeals, year after year, has consistently abandoned fundamental tenants of tort law. Like Hubble's Law, the liability universe in West Virginia is constantly expanding....

In 1999, the West Virginia Supreme Court of Appeals issued a landmark opinion establishing an independent cause of action for recovery of future medical monitoring costs in the absence of physical injury....

[In *Bower v. Westinghouse*], the plaintiffs, who had no present symptoms of any disease, alleged that they were exposed to thirty toxic substances as a result of defendants maintaining a pile of debris from the manufacture of light bulbs. The court, permitting recovery, "reject[ed] the contention that a claim for future medical expenses must rest upon the existence of present physical harm." This holding overruled two centuries of tort law that required physical injury to maintain a cause of action....

West Virginia stands alone in completely rejecting the learned intermediary doctrine. The closest comparison is New Jersey, which has formally adopted the learned intermediary rule, but applies a unique exception when the medication at issue was advertised directly to consumers....

[Next, the authors turn to the state's legal environment out of the courtroom.]

One of most controversial public figures in West Virginia its Attorney General Darrell McGraw, who routinely deputizes private lawyers on a contingency fee basis to pursue litigation on behalf of the state. This practice raises serious ethical and constitutional concerns because the primary incentive of the contingency fee attorney is to maximize the dollar amount of any recovery, a profit-seeking motive that is not always in step with the public's interest in assuring justice. In addition, the state may lack sufficient control over the litigation and in the accountability of the outsourced attorneys, leading to outcomes that are not in the state's best interests....

QUESTIONS

1. What is wrong with the civil litigation system according to Cabraser? How would she reform it?

2. What do Schwartz, Joyce, and Silverman mean by a "judicial hellhole"? Why did West Virginia earn that label? What aspects of the civil litigation system do they believe need to be fixed?

3. What do you think Cabraser would say about the *Toyota* class action suit? How might Schwartz, Joyce, and Silverman respond?

4. Think back to *Citizens United*, the case in Chapter 1 which held that, like people, corporations have civil rights, including the right to free speech. In this debate, the right at stake is due process, involving access to fair procedures for dispute resolution. Given the financial and power differential between a single Toyota owner and Toyota as a corporation, will affording equal due process rights put the disputants on a level playing field? If not, can you imagine a dispute resolution mechanism—other than litigation—that would provide one?

Evolution of Products Liability Law

Today, the "product liability" theory on which the Toyota plaintiffs rest their case is a common basis for lawsuits when unsafe and dangerously defective cars, toys, drugs, and other products cause injury. But that was not always so.

The early common law had allowed few exceptions to the general rule of *caveat emptor* (buyer beware), most notably for food products. In Britain, an Act of Parliament in 1266 made it a crime to sell "corrupt wine and victuals," and American law required those who sold food intended for immediate consumption to ensure its safety or pay damages to anyone injured by it. But, prior to the twentieth century, most people injured by defective goods had little legal recourse.

The most important remedy was a suit for breach of warranty against those who sold unfit goods, a legal theory described as a "freak hybrid, 'born of the illicit intercourse of tort and contract,' and partaking the characteristics of both."[9] For centuries, however, those claims were limited by a legal doctrine called "privity of contract," a rule that a buyer could sue only the entity from whom the item was purchased, not anyone further up the chain of commerce, such as a wholesale distributor or the actual manufacturer. Negligence (tort) claims against companies who breached their legal duty to be reasonably careful in the design, manufacture, and packaging of goods were hard to prove and easy for companies to defend against.

The Tort of Strict Product Liability

New York Court of Appeals Justice Benjamin Cardozo is widely considered the first to recognize that a person injured by an unsafe product has a right to bring a lawsuit based on negligence. In the early twentieth century he wrote an important decision, *MacPherson v. Buick Motor Co.,* allowing an injured person to sue the manufacturer of a car for a defect in its wheel. The wheel was wooden; when its spokes crumbled, the car collapsed and the plaintiff was thrown out and injured. Instead of suing the seller from whom he bought the car for breach of contract, the plaintiff sued the manufacturer for negligence. The jury ruled in his favor. On appeal, the court agreed that Buick was negligent because the car's "defects could have been discovered by a reasonable inspection, and that inspection was omitted."[10]

To win a suit for negligence, a plaintiff must establish that the defendant breached its duty of care, creating an unreasonable risk of harm, and that such careless behavior was the proximate cause of the plaintiff's injury. This is often difficult. Generally, a company will not be found negligent if it adhered to industry standards or the "state of the art" with regard to the engineering, selection of materials, production processes, assembly, and marketing of its product. Proof of reasonable quality control procedures is usually sufficient to negate a charge of negligence. A firm can also defend itself or limit the amount of damages it must pay by showing that its negligence was not the only cause of the injury—a car accident caused in part by faulty brakes and in part by drunk driving, for example—or that the plaintiff contributed to her own harm, either by assuming a known risk or acting carelessly.

Modern products liability law, the basis for Weiner's claim against Toyota, was born in mid-twentieth century. In 1944, a waitress injured when a bottle of Coca-Cola exploded in her face sued the local bottling company and won. This time, the jury was convinced of the company's negligence, and the California Supreme Court upheld its verdict. The most important part of the case, however, was the language of concurring Justice Traynor, which foreshadowed the development of the law of products liability:

> [I]t should now be recognized that a manufacturer incurs an absolute liability when an article that he has placed on the market ... proves to have a defect that causes injury.... [P]ublic policy demands that responsibility be fixed wherever it will most effectively reduce the hazards ... in defective products. [T]he manufacturer can anticipate some hazards and guard against the recurrence of others, as the public cannot....[11]

[9] Wiliam J. Prosser, John W. Wade, and Victor E. Schwartz, *Torts: Cases and Materials, 7th ed.* (New York: Foundation Press, 1982), p. 743.

[10] *MacPherson v. Buick Motor* Co., 111 N.E. 1050 (N.Y.).

[11] *Escola v. Coca-Cola Bottling Company of Fresno*, 50 P.2d 436 (Cal. 1944).

Eventually, the full California Supreme Court came to agree with Traynor. In a 1963 case, it adopted the rule that manufacturers should be strictly liable for selling defective products.[12] This new legal theory, referred to as the doctrine of strict liability, made it easier for injured persons to sue and harder for manufacturers to defend themselves. Described in Section 402A of the Restatement of Torts (Second),[13] strict liability recognizes that there are times when losses must be allocated between two "innocent" parties: the consumer who was hurt while using a product properly and the company that was not negligent (careless) in creating it. It places the responsibility on the company for reasons articulated here by a noted legal scholar, Prosser in "The Fall of the Citadel":

The public interest in human safety requires the maximum possible protection for the user of the product, and those best able to afford it are the suppliers...By placing their goods upon the market, the suppliers represent to the public that they are suitable and safe for use; and by packaging, advertising and otherwise, they do everything they can to induce that belief.[14]

RESTATEMENT OF TORTS (SECOND) SECTION 402A

1. One who sells any product in a defective condition unreasonably dangerous to the user or consumer or to his property is subject to liability for physical harm thereby caused to the ultimate user or consumer or to his property, if
   a. the seller is engaged in the business of selling such a product, and
   b. it is expected to and does reach the user or consumer without substantial change in the condition in which it is sold.
2. The rule stated in Subsection (1) applies although
   a. the seller has exercised all possible care in the preparation and sale of the product, and
   b. the user or consumer has not bought the product from or entered into any contractual relation with the seller.

Most states have adopted Section 402A of the Restatement, finding sellers liable for defective product designs, manufacturing ("production") defects, and failure to warn. In each case, the focus is not on the company's behavior (as it is in negligence law), but on whether the product itself is defective and unreasonably unsafe.

For example, suppose a company hires qualified engineers who design a new car using standard techniques. No one is negligent, yet the company produces a model that causes injury. Under the Restatement (Second) of Torts, a jury might conclude that there was a design defect because the harmful nature of the product outweighed its usefulness.

Or the design of a car may be perfectly safe, but something in the way a particular car is assembled causes injury—an undetected weakness in a sheet of aluminum or a glitch leading to an improperly assembled component, for example. While we expect companies to implement good quality control systems, we know that some production

---

[12] *Greenman v. Yuba Power Products, Inc.*, 377 P.2d 897 (Cal. 1963).

[13] THE RESTATEMENT OF LAW is an attempt by legal scholars to summarize and "restate" the common law based on judicial precedents from around the country. Today, there is a Third Restatement of Torts. However, most states continue to follow the Second Restatement of Torts.

[14] William Prosser, "The Fall of the Citadel' 50 MINN.L.REV 791, 799 (1966).

defects will occasionally slip through the cracks of a manufacturing process. Once again, strict liability burdens the company, not the consumer, with the loss, even when the company was not negligent.

A third kind of defect involves products that cannot be made completely safe but can be made safer by appropriately warning the consumer. The inadequate information about possible side effects of a drug or of the absence of other potential dangers posed by a product may result in a manufacturer's strict liability for failure to warn. This was the main defect in *Levine v Wyeth* and in the Norplant case discussed in Chapter 7.

In different jurisdictions, interpretations of the Restatements of Torts may vary. In every state, a person who claims injury from a defective product must prove that the product was the proximate (or legal) cause of his harm. If the injury results from some alteration in the product (e.g., by the consumer or by someone who serviced it), the seller is not held responsible. Most states allow companies to defend themselves by proving that the plaintiff misused or abused the product in a way that the manufacturer could not have foreseen.

The Restatement (Second) did not define "defective and unreasonably dangerous product," so state courts had to create their own definitions. Under what is called the "consumer expectation" test, a product is defectively dangerous if it is dangerous to an extent beyond that which would be contemplated by the ordinary consumer who purchased it with the ordinary knowledge common to the community as to the product's characteristics. Alternatively, under the danger-utility approach adopted in some states, a product is defective if, but only if, the magnitude of the danger outweighs the utility of the product. The theory underlying this approach is that virtually all products have both risks and benefits and that there is no way to go about evaluating hazards intelligently without weighing risk against utility.

Punitive Damages

Under the common law of torts, juries are free to award an injured plaintiff all sorts of damages, not only to compensate for damaged property or out-of-pocket medical expenses, but for pain and suffering, and significantly, punitive damages designed to punish companies who disregard safety, to create incentives to make safer products and deter similar wrongdoing in the future. While some state laws limit the amount of punitive damages a jury can award, others leave the jury free to award hundreds of thousands—even millions—of dollars to punish serious wrongdoing. Not surprisingly, industry lobbyists and their attorneys have targeted punitive damage awards as a goal of "tort reform."

THE FORD PINTO CASE

In 1972 a Ford Pinto hatchback unexpectedly stalled on a freeway, erupting into flames when it was rear-ended by the car behind it. The driver, Mrs. Lilly Gray, was fatally burned, and a passenger, 13-year-old Richard Grimshaw, suffered severe and permanently disfiguring burns on his face and entire body.

Harley Copp, a former Ford engineer and executive in charge of the crash testing program who had been forced into early retirement for speaking out about safety, testified against Ford. In a trial that lasted six months, plaintiffs established the Pinto was the brainchild of Lee Iaccoca, then Vice-President of Ford, who hoped to build a car at or below 2,000 pounds to sell for no more than $2,000. This was a rush job, designed to compete with European and Japanese models. Varying from the usual procedure, the Ford leadership team allowed styling to precede engineering and to dictate the design of the car.

> *"Among the engineering decisions dictated by styling was the placement of the fuel tank. It was then the preferred practice in Europe and Japan to locate the gas tank over the rear axle in subcompacts because a small vehicle has less "crush space" between the rear axle and the bumper than larger cars. The Pinto's styling, however, required the tank to be placed behind the rear axle leaving only 9 or 10 inches of "crush space," far less than in any other American automobile or Ford overseas subcompact. In addition, the Pinto was designed so that its bumper was little more than a chrome strip, less substantial than the bumper of any other American car produced then or later. The Pinto's rear structure also lacked reinforcing members known as "hat sections" (2 longitudinal side members) and horizontal cross-members running between them such as were found in cars of larger unitized construction and in all automobiles produced by Ford's overseas operations. The absence of the reinforcing members rendered the Pinto less crush resistant than other vehicles. Finally, the differential housing selected for the Pinto had an exposed flange and a line of exposed bolt heads. These protrusions were sufficient to puncture a gas tank driven forward against the differential upon rear impact.*
>
> *During the development of the Pinto, prototypes were built and tested.... The crash tests revealed that the Pinto's fuel system as designed could not meet the 20-mile-per-hour proposed [federal] standard....*
>
> *When a prototype failed the fuel system integrity test, the standard of care for engineers in the industry was to redesign and retest it. The vulnerability of the production Pinto's fuel tank at speeds of 20 and 30-miles-per-hour fixed barrier tests could have been remedied by inexpensive "fixes," but Ford produced and sold the Pinto to the public without doing anything to remedy the defects. Design changes that would have enhanced the integrity of the fuel tank system at relatively little cost per car included the following: a single shock absorbent "flak suit" to protect the tank at $4; a tank within a tank and placement of the tank over the axle at $5.08 to $5.79; a nylon bladder within the tank at $5.25 to $8; placement of the tank over the axle surrounded with a protective barrier at a cost of $9.95 per car; ... Equipping the car with a reinforced rear structure, smooth axle, improved bumper, and additional crush space at a total cost of $15.30 would have made the fuel tank safe in a 34- to 38-mile-per-hour rear end collision by a vehicle the size of the Ford Galaxie.... If the tank had been located over the rear axle, it would have been safe in a rear impact at 50 miles per hour or more.[15]*

Project engineers signed off on the design to their immediate supervisors and sent it up the chain of command, along with the crash test results. Everyone up to Mr. Iacocca approved the project, knowing the gas tank was vulnerable to puncture and that fixes were feasible at nominal cost. After a trial that lasted six months the jury awarded the plaintiffs $3.5 million in punitive damages.

---

[15] *Grimshaw v. Ford Motor Company*, 174 Cal. Rptr. 348 (Cal. Ct. App. 1981).

Contract Law

Breach of Warranty and the Uniform Commercial Code

Much of the modern American law of contracts is found in the Uniform Commercial Code (UCC), first written in 1952 and later adopted by every state in the United States as the basic law governing the sale of goods. Under the UCC, every merchant who sells a product automatically promises that it is fit for its ordinary purpose.[16] Food should not be contaminated, hair dye should not cause one's hair to fall out, rungs of ladders should not splinter, televisions should not explode. A merchant[17] who does not intend to make such a promise must adhere to specific rules in order to disclaim that implied warranty of merchantability.[18] A seller's promise that goods are fit for their ordinary purpose can be enforced not only by the purchaser, but by members of her household as well. In some states, the warranty extends even further, protecting not only the purchaser, family, and household, but "any person who may reasonably be expected to use, consume, or be affected by the goods and who is injured" as a result of the breach.[19] Historically, the "privity of contract" rule meant that an injured party could only sue his immediate seller for breach of contract or warranty, but that requirement is no longer a bar. Today, a buyer can sue retailers, wholesalers, and manufacturers when goods are not as promised.

Contract law is primarily designed to encourage commerce by assuring those who freely enter into agreements that the law will protect their expectations. If one side reneges on its bargain, the other can go to court to seek a remedy that would give the plaintiff the benefit of the bargain struck.

Since the UCC rests on a fundamental belief in the freedom to contract, the law encourages commercial parties to decide when they enter into an agreement what remedy will be available if either side breaches. If they don't make such provisions, courts deal with any breach of contract "dispassionately," giving the injured party the financial benefit it expected under the agreement—a combination of what are known as general and incidental damages. At times, the plaintiff may also win what are called "special" or consequential damages, covering the economic costs that are a "consequence" of the breach, such as lost profits while a business is shut down because a seller failed to deliver a needed machine. But juries are not free to compensate the winner for pain and suffering or to award punitive damages or attorneys' fees.

■ ■ ■

Transport Corporation of America, Inc. (TCA) operates a national trucking business out of Minnesota. In 1989, TCA decided to update the computer system it used to process incoming orders, issue dispatching assignments, and store all distribution records. TCA purchased an IBM computer system for $541,313.38 from Innovative Computing Corporation (ICC), a company that produces software and re-sells IBM computers. A year after the system was installed, it failed. Although it was ultimately repaired, TCA was without it for almost 34 hours and sued both the manufacturer (IBM) and the seller (ICC) on various tort and contract theories.

---

[16] UCC 2-314.

[17] Under UCC 2-104 a merchant includes (a) a person who deals in goods of the kind involved in the sale, for example, a car maker or car dealer when he sells cars; or (b)a person whose occupation indicates that she has special knowledge or skill regarding the good involves, e.g. an optometrist selling glasses; or (c) someone who hires a merchant (e.g. an agent) to act on his behalf.

[18] UCC 2-316 and Magnuson-Moss Warranty Act, 15 U.S.C.sections 2301, et seq.

[19] UCC 2-318.

The lower court dismissed the suit before trial, finding that the **economic loss doctrine** barred the tort claims, and that the plaintiff was not entitled to any damages for breach of contract because the computer had been repaired. The appellate court agreed, explaining why in the following excerpt.

TRANSPORT CORPORATION OF AMERICA v. IBM
United States Court of Appeals, Eighth Circuit, 1994
30 F.3d 953

McMILLAN, Circuit Judge

On December 19, 1990 ... the computer system went down and one of the disk drives revealed an error code. TCA properly contacted IBM, and IBM dispatched a service person. Although TCA requested a replacement disk drive, the error code indicated that the service procedure was not to replace any components but to analyze the disk drive. TCA had restarted the computer system and did not want to shut it down for the IBM service procedure. IBM informed TCA that replacement was not necessary under the limited warranty of repair or replace, and agreed to return on December 22, 1990, to analyze the disk drive. On December 21, 1990, the same disk drive completely failed, resulting in the computer system being inoperable until December 22, 1990.

TCA alleges that the cumulative downtime for the computer system as a result of the disk drive failure was 33.91 hours. This includes the time to replace the disk drive, reload the electronic backup data, and manually re-enter data which had been entered between 2:00 a.m. and the time the system failed. TCA alleges that it incurred a business interruption loss in the amount of $473,079.46 ($468,514.46 for loss of income; $4,565.00 for loss of data and replacement media).

Economic Loss Doctrine

Minnesota courts have consistently held that the UCC should apply to commercial transactions where the product merely failed to live up to expectations and the damage did not result from a hazardous condition....Because failure of the disk drive was contemplated by the parties and the damage was limited in scope to the computer system (into which the disk drive and its data were integrated), TCA must look exclusively to the UCC for its remedy.

IBM's Disclaimer of Implied Warranties

TCA next argues that because it was not a party to the negotiations between ICC and IBM, it is not bound by the terms of the remarketer agreement, including IBM's disclaimer of implied warranties....

The UCC as adopted in Minnesota has a privity provision that operates to extend all warranties, express or implied, to third parties who may reasonably be expected to use the warranted goods....The seller can disclaim implied warranties...[and these disclaimers] are extended to third party purchasers [like the plaintiff]....

The remarketer agreement between IBM and ICC included a disclaimer of "ALL OTHER WARRANTIES, EXPRESS OR IMPLIED, INCLUDING, BUT NOT LIMITED TO, THE IMPLIED WARRANTIES OF MERCHANTABILITY AND FITNESS FOR A PARTICULAR PURPOSE." As the district court correctly noted, this language complies with the requirements of [the UCC] (that is, it was in writing, conspicuous and mentioned merchantability) and thus effectively disclaimed all implied warranties.

IBM's Limited Remedy of Repair or Replace

[Next, the court must decide whether or not to enforce the "exclusive remedy" created by the parties to deal with a possible breach of contract. The UCC provides that the remedy should be enforced unless it "fails of its essential purpose."] Under Minnesota law, "[a]n exclusive remedy fails of its essential purpose if circumstances arise to deprive the limiting clause of its meaning or one party of the substantial value of its bargain." ... A repair or replace clause does not fail of its essential purpose so long as repairs are made each time a defect arises....

ICC's Disclaimer of Consequential Damages Liability

[Under the UCC, a] seller may limit or exclude consequential damages unless the limitation is unconscionable.... The UCC encourages negotiated agreements in commercial transactions, including warranties and limitations.... An exclusion of consequential damages set forth in advance in a commercial agreement between experienced business parties represents a bargained-for allocation of risk that is conscionable as a matter of law....

In the agreement between ICC and TCA, TCA expressly agreed to an ICC disclaimer that stated in part "IN NO EVENT SHALL ICC BE LIABLE FOR ANY INDIRECT, SPECIAL OR CONSEQUENTIAL DAMAGES SUCH AS LOSSES OF ANTICIPATED PROFIT OR OTHER ECONOMIC LOSS IN CONNECTION WITH ... THIS AGREEMENT."

[T]he disclaimer of consequential damages was not unconscionable and ... the damages claimed by TCA, for business interruption losses and replacement media, were consequential damages. Furthermore, TCA and ICC were sophisticated business entities of relatively equal bargaining power. ICC's disclaimer was not unconscionable and TCA is therefore precluded from recovering consequential damages....

[Summary Judgment for IBM and ICC is affirmed.].

QUESTIONS

1. On what grounds did the court determine that Transport Corporation was not entitled to money damages? What should the plaintiff have done to better protect itself?

2. While it is common for businesses to limit damages, as IBM did in this case, the UCC makes it unconscionable (shocking to the conscience) to limit damages for personal injury in the sale of products to consumers. So, for example, Ford could not give a warranty that limited its responsibility for injuries caused by a defect in one of its vehicles. Does it seem fair to distinguish consumer from commercial transactions in this way? To allow courts to "rewrite" a deal that two parties freely entered?

■ ■ ■

Contract Law and Tort Law

It is not uncommon for lawyers to file suit against all potential defendants (e.g., immediate seller, shipper, manufacturer, component parts maker) on several potential theories (breach of contract, negligence, and strict liability.) You can see this kind of "alternative pleading" in Weimer's complaint against Toyota. During the pre-trial discovery phase of litigation, plaintiffs can gather information about the production process, injury records, and documents indicating who knew what and when—all of which help sort out which party or parties are most likely responsible. The rules of litigation make one or another cause of action more advantageous in particular situations. In most states, for example, the time for bringing a suit ("statute of limitations") differs for tort and contract cases. And, in all states, the general rules regarding remedies are fundamentally different for contract cases, where successful plaintiffs are generally limited to damages that would give them the economic "benefit of their bargain," and tort cases, where damages are more open-ended.

■ ■ ■

In June 9, 1986, Nancy Denny slammed on the brakes of her Ford Bronco II in an effort to avoid a deer that had walked directly into the path of her vehicle. The Bronco rolled over, and Denny was severely injured. She sued Ford, asserting negligence, strict product liability, and breach of implied warranty under the Uniform Commercial Code. The jury came back with a mixed verdict; the Bronco was not unreasonably dangerous and defective, so there was no tort liability. But, they found, Ford had violated the implied warranty of merchantability—and therefore breached its contract—by selling Denny a vehicle that was not fit for its ordinary purpose. In the excerpts below, the highest court in New York has to decide whether the two legal theories—a tort action for strict product liability and a contract action for implied warranty—are really one and the same.

DENNY v. FORD MOTOR COMPANY
Court of Appeals of New York, 1995
639 N.Y.S.2d 250

TITONE, Judge

The trial evidence centered on the particular characteristics of utility vehicles, which are generally made for off-road use on unpaved and often rugged terrain. Such use sometimes necessitates climbing over obstacles such as fallen logs and rocks....

Plaintiffs introduced evidence at trial to show that small utility vehicles in general, and the Bronco II in particular, present a significantly higher risk of rollover accidents than do ordinary passenger automobiles ... [and] that the Bronco II had a low stability index attributable to its high center of gravity and relatively narrow track width. The vehicle's shorter wheel base and suspension system were additional factors contributing to its instability. Ford had made minor design changes in an effort to achieve a higher stability index, but, according to plaintiffs' proof, none of the changes produced a significant improvement in the vehicle's stability.

Ford argued at trial that the design features of which plaintiffs complained were necessary to the vehicle's off-road capabilities. According to Ford, the vehicle had been intended to be used as an off-road vehicle and had not been designed to be sold as a conventional passenger automobile. Ford's own engineer stated that he would not recommend the Bronco II to someone whose primary interest was to use it as a passenger car, since the features of a four-wheel-drive utility vehicle were not helpful for that purpose and the vehicle's design made it inherently less stable.

Despite the engineer's testimony, plaintiffs introduced a Ford marketing manual which predicted that many buyers would be attracted to the Bronco II because utility vehicles were "suitable to contemporary life styles" and were "considered fashionable" in some suburban areas. According to this manual, the sales presentation of the Bronco II should take into account the vehicle's "suitab[ility] for commuting and for suburban and city driving." Additionally, the vehicle's ability to switch between two-wheel and four-wheel drive would "be particularly appealing to women who may be concerned about driving in snow and ice with their children." Plaintiffs both testified that the perceived safety benefits of its four-wheel-drive capacity were what attracted them to the Bronco II. They were not at all interested in its off-road use.

Although the products liability theory sounding in tort and the breach of implied warranty theory authorized by the UCC coexist and are often invoked in tandem, the core element of "defect" is subtly different in the two causes of action....[T]he New York standard for determining the existence of a design defect [in strict liability cases] has required an assessment of whether "if the design defect were known at the time of manufacture, a reasonable person would conclude that the utility of the product did not outweigh the risk inherent in marketing a product designed in that manner." This standard demands an inquiry into such factors as (1) the product's utility to the public as a whole, (2) its utility to the individual user, (3) the likelihood that the product will cause injury, (4) the availability of a safer design, (5) the possibility of designing and manufacturing the product so that it is safer but remains functional and reasonably priced, (6) the degree of awareness of the product's potential danger that can reasonably be attributed to the injured user, and (7) the manufacturer's ability to spread the cost of any safety-related design changes....The above-described analysis is rooted in a recognition that there are both risks and benefits associated with many products and that there are instances in which a product's inherent dangers cannot be eliminated without simultaneously compromising or completely nullifying its benefits.... In such circumstances, a weighing of the product's benefits against its risks is an appropriate and necessary component of the liability assessment under the policy-based principles associated with tort law.

[T]he risk/utility balancing test is a "negligence-inspired" approach, since it invites the parties to adduce proof about the manufacturer's choices and ultimately requires the fact finder to make "a judgment about [the manufacturer's] judgment." ...

It is this negligence-like risk/benefit component of the defect element that differentiates strict products liability claims from UCC-based breach of implied warranty claims....

While the strict products concept of a product that is "not reasonably safe" requires a weighing of the product's dangers against its overall advantages, the UCC's concept of a "defective" product requires an inquiry only into whether the product in question was "fit for the ordinary purposes for which such goods are used." ... The latter inquiry focuses on the expectations for the performance of the product when used in the customary, usual, and reasonably foreseeable manners. The cause of action is one involving true "strict" liability, since recovery may be had upon a showing that the product was not minimally safe for its expected purpose without regard to the feasibility of alternative designs or the manufacturer's "reasonableness" in marketing it in that unsafe condition.

[Next, the court explains the distinction in terms of the history of the two doctrines: Implied warranty originated in contract law, "which directs its attention to the purchaser's disappointed expectations," while strict product liability is a tort, and tort actions have traditionally been concerned with "social policy and risk allocation by means other than those dictated by the marketplace."]

As a practical matter, the distinction between the defect concepts in tort law and in implied warranty theory may have little or no effect in most cases. In this case, however, the nature of the proof and the way in which the fact issues were litigated demonstrates how the two causes of action can diverge. In the trial court, Ford took the position that the design features of which plaintiffs complain, i.e., the Bronco II's high center of gravity, narrow track width, short wheel base, and specially tailored suspension system, were important to preserving the vehicle's ability to drive over the highly irregular terrain that typifies off-road travel. Ford's proof in this regard was relevant to the strict products liability risk/utility equation, which required the fact finder to determine whether the Bronco II's value as an off-road vehicle outweighed the risk of the rollover accidents that could occur when the vehicle was used for other driving tasks.

On the other hand, plaintiffs' proof focused, in part, on the sale of the Bronco II for suburban driving and everyday road travel. Plaintiffs also adduced proof that the Bronco II's design characteristics made it unusually susceptible to rollover accidents when used on paved roads. All of this evidence was useful in showing that routine highway and street driving was the "ordinary purpose" for which the Bronco II was sold and that it was not "fit" or safe for that purpose.

Thus, under the evidence in this case, a rational fact finder could have simultaneously concluded that the Bronco II's utility as an off-road vehicle outweighed the risk of injury resulting from rollover accidents and that the vehicle was not safe for the "ordinary purpose" of daily driving for which it was marketed and sold.... Importantly, what makes this case distinctive is that the "ordinary purpose" for which the product was marketed and sold to the plaintiff was not the same as the utility against which the risk was to be weighed. It is these unusual circumstances that give practical significance to the ordinarily theoretical difference between the defect concepts in tort and statutory breach of implied warranty causes of action.... [Held: Judgement for the plaintiff affirmed. There was no error in instructing the jury to separately consider Ford's tort liability for sale of an unreasonably dangerous product and contract liability for breach of the implied warranty of merchantability.]

SIMONS, Judge, Dissenting

In my judgment, the consumer expectation standard, appropriate to commercial sales transactions, has no place in personal injury litigation alleging a design defect and may result in imposing absolute liability on marketers of consumers' products. Whether a product has been defectively designed should be determined in a personal injury action by a risk/utility analysis....

[T]he word "defect" has no clear legal meaning....

The jury having concluded that the Bronco II was not defective for strict products liability purposes, could not logically conclude that it was defective for warranty purposes.... The warranty claim in this case was for tortious personal injury and rests on the underlying "social concern [for] the protection of human life and property, not regularity in commercial exchange." ... As such, it should be governed by tort rules, not contract rules....

Accordingly, I dissent.

QUESTIONS

1. What did Nancy Denny think she was buying? What did she buy? On what legal theories did she sue? On what basis did she win?

2. Elsewhere in the decision, dissenting Judge Simons argues that the majority imposes a kind of absolute liability on a manufacturer. Is he right? What might Ford have done differently?

3. Compare this case to the Norplant case in Chapter 7. What similarities/differences do you see in the marketing campaigns? In the lawsuits?

■ ■ ■

An Alternative Approach

The author of the reading that closes this chapter proposes an alternative way to confront the staggering degree of damage—death,[20] injury, and disease—caused by five consumer products: alcohol, tobacco, guns, motor vehicles, and junk food. "Performance-based regulation" would place responsibility on industry, but permit the sellers to figure out how to best decrease the negative public health consequences of their products.

---

[20] Sugarman estimates yearly deaths from these products at 690,000.

PERFORMANCE-BASED REGULATION: ENTERPRISE RESPONSIBILITY FOR REDUCING DEATH, INJURY, AND DISEASE CAUSED BY CONSUMER PRODUCTS

Stephen D. Sugarman[21]

In general, public health policy makers search for policy interventions on a group or population basis.... Providing communities with clean drinking water is a classic example of a population-wide measure. Mass immunization through vaccinations is another....

The typical public health perspective on problems is to promote a variety of broad policy changes designed to reduce the socially undesirable consequences. Policy changes such as banning indoor smoking, lowering speed limits, levying alcohol taxes, and restricting the number of fast food outlets in a single neighborhood are all hallmarks of conventional public health tactics aimed at these products....

Sometimes, public health leaders seek only voluntary changes by target industries. For example, a foundation connected to former president Bill Clinton recently came to an "agreement" with Pepsi, Coca-Cola, and Cadbury-Schweppes in which the three major soda companies announced that they would no longer sell certain sweetened beverages in certain schools.... Other times, rather than calling on private actors to change their behavior, public health advocates focus on the provision of new services by public agencies (like smoking cessation clinics at public hospitals, nutrition education at public schools, and safer public highways). Neither of these approaches, however, imposes legal requirements on private enterprises....

Performance-Based Regulation

In general, performance-based regulation works like this: A firm's performance target is set, either by legislation or by an administering agency running the scheme. A system of regular measurement is implemented to determine whether the firm is meeting its goal. And a penalty structure is put in place that would impose consequences if a firm fails to meet its goal....

The goal in setting the penalty levels is to induce socially efficient prevention [insofar as meeting the target may cost less for the firm than paying a fine].

In the years since the surgeon general issued his famous 1964 report on the lethal consequences of cigarettes, adult smoking prevalence rates in the United States have dropped from more than 40 percent to about 20 percent.... Earlier informational efforts have been supplemented by higher tobacco taxes, laws restricting where people can smoke, counteradvertising exposing the misconduct of tobacco companies to the public, tougher enforcement of laws barring sale to minors, restrictions on cigarette marketing campaigns, and cheaper access to more effective cessation products and programs. These policy initiatives have made a difference in curbing smoking rates.

Yet cigarettes remain widely promoted and available, and we are nowhere near the long-standing public health goal of reducing the nationwide smoking prevalence rate to below 12 percent....

Performance-based regulation attacks the issue in an altogether different way. It rests on the simple proposition that the tobacco companies themselves should be required to achieve sharply improved public health outcomes.

Imagine, then, that over, say, seven years, tobacco companies were required to cut in half the number of people who smoke their products. Reducing the smoking rate to less than 10 percent would have enormously positive public health

---

[21] Stephen D. Sugarman, "Performance-Based Regulation: Enterprise Responsibility for Reducing Death, Injury, and Disease Caused by Consumer Products," in Journal of Health Politics, Policy and Law, Volume 34, no. 6, pp. 1035–1077. Copyright, 2009, Duke University Press. All rights reserved. Reprinted by permission of the publisher.

consequences. To provide firms with the right sort of incentive, those that fail to achieve their goals would be subject to serious financial penalties.

The moral argument for this proposal is that cigarette makers—whose products kill when used as directed—should be held accountable for the death toll. The practical argument is that since tobacco companies have been so effective in enticing teens and adults to consume their products, they are also probably best positioned to figure out how to reduce the number of smokers. To be sure, cigarette makers would not be happy about having to halve the size of their businesses. But this is an industry that has been found liable for "racketeering." Besides, even if tobacco companies had only half the number of customers they now have, they could still turn a handsome profit, especially if they retained as customers their heaviest smokers....

Under my proposal, it would not matter whether a firm achieved a uniform reduction in sales from each of its brands, because the performance goal would be enterprisewide. Moreover, at least at the outset, the regulation would be indifferent as to which demographic group experienced decreased smoking rates. For example, the low-hanging fruit might consist of preventing youths from starting, keeping former smokers from restarting, and getting social smokers to quit rather than escalate to daily smoking. Notice that if firms achieved reductions in these segments of the population, they could still retain their best (i.e., heaviest-smoking) clients. Even so, the long-run public health benefits would be great.

Firms would be free to achieve their regulatory target in many different ways. One approach might be to provide smokers with subsidized access to cessation aids and programs. Alternatively, tobacco companies might increase product prices, try to convince cigarette smokers to switch to a far less dangerous alternative nicotine delivery device, or engage in advertising genuinely aimed at discouraging smoking initiation by teens. Of course, these and other tactics might be used in some combination. Given the discretion to develop their own methods, tobacco companies would likely employ some strategies that are unimaginable now. Perhaps the leading tobacco firms would cooperate in seeking to reduce smoking prevalence....

It would be possible to include a "tradable permit" feature in such a performance-based regulatory scheme.... [I]f the target reduction were 50 percent and, for example, R. J. Reynolds reduced its consumer base by more than half, it could sell that excess accomplishment to, say, Philip Morris, which could then exceed its target by the allocation it bought. Overall, the industry would have reached the public health target, and arguably in the most efficient manner....

Regulatory Alternatives

Command-and-control schemes rest on the belief that the regulator knows the best way (or at least a good way) to attack the public health problem....

[T]he major problem with this approach is that the regulator may not order the right changes, even after a number of tries, or that it will take too long to get it right. This could be because the self-interest of the regulators does not match that of the public; they may be corrupt, subject to undue influence by those being regulated, inept, or simply eager to maximize the size and budget of the agency. Even assuming the best of intentions, regulators simply may not possess or be able to acquire the information to determine the most efficient and effective changes to require. Worse yet, they may lock enterprises into outmoded and unduly costly technologies....

[Another approach is for the regulator to] try to influence the level of production or consumption of the product by imposing an excise tax or granting a subsidy.... Also in this vein, the regulator might impose a substantial license fee for a gun permit or allow consumers to claim a tax credit for purchasing a car with antilock brakes. So, too, in order to address obesity, the government might decrease subsidies for high fructose corn syrup while creating subsidies for fresh fruits and vegetables....

The success of tax and subsidy strategies in lowering the level of a dangerous activity is likely to depend [in part]...on "elasticity of demand"—how sensitive consumers are to price, which depends in part on the price and suitability of substitute products....

[Another problem is that] taxes designed to promote public health tend to have an overbreadth problem. For example, all drinkers will have to pay more for alcohol when it costs more because of tax increases, but most of those who consume less as a result are not alcoholics or irresponsible users. Thus, public-health-based taxes will frequently suffer from "target inefficiency." Even cigarette taxes—which are great to the extent they cause people to quit, not to relapse and start smoking again, and not to start in the first place—do nothing to improve public health to the extent heavy smokers respond to the higher cost by switching from premium to lower cost brands....

[Litigation] is yet another regulatory strategy that can be employed in furtherance of public health goals....

Even though a common-law tort plaintiff normally seeks money damages only after suffering harm, the regulatory theory underlying tort litigation is that firms will take health and safety precautions in advance in hopes of avoiding lawsuits (and will even more seriously address the consequences of their products after a litigant successfully sues them or their direct competitors). Indeed, sometimes the private litigants' preferred legal remedy is an injunction to prevent ongoing or future harm....

Yet litigation has its own drawbacks. For one thing, it can be quite expensive, especially the cost of the lawyers. Second, most tort litigation is not policy oriented. It is not about identifying and blocking new dangers, such as cars that are not "crashworthy" or guns that are irresponsibly marketed. Rather, most torts cases involve routine claims such as for compensation of victims of inattentive drivers or careless property owners; or they are the hundreds or thousands (or more) follow-on claims against, say, a pharmaceutical company whose drug has already been clearly shown to have been inadequately tested)....

[P]erformance-based regulation is designed to unleash private innovation and competition. The same features that we value in the production of goods in a capitalist system can now be specifically turned toward promoting safety and health....

QUESTION

1. What does Sugarman mean by "performance-based regulation?" To what alternatives does he point? What advantages do you see to each?

Chapter Problems

1. In 1999, SmithKline Beecham introduced a new FDA-approved diabetes drug, Avandia. Almost immediately, the company began a secret study, hoping to show that Avandia was safer for the heart than a competing pill, Actos. A year later, the results were clear: not only was Avandia no better than Actos, but there were signs that it was riskier to the heart. In an e-mail sent in 2001, SmithKline executive Dr. Martin I. Freed wrote: "Per Sr. Mgmt request, these data should not see the light of day to anyone outside of GSK [SmithKline's corporate successor.]"

In 2007 a cardiologist at a Cleveland Clinic, analyzing data about Avandia that GSK was forced to post on its Web site, publicly revealed the risks to the heart associated with Avandia for the first time.

Does the risk of state court litigation create an incentive for companies to fully report new safety data to the government? Would protecting whistleblowers be another way to create such an incentive? **Research**: Find out what action the FDA has taken regarding Avandia. Have any lawsuits been filed against its manufacturer?

2. In April 2010, after 6 heart patients died due to faulty defibrillators, the U.S. government charged Guidant Corporation with failing to alert doctors and patients that some of its heart defibrillators had a defect that might cause them to fail. The company was willing to plead guilty to two misdemeanors and pay a $296 million fine. A federal judge refused to accept the plea bargain. (a)What potential civil suits might arise from this scenario? (b) **Research**: Find out how the criminal case against Guidant finally ended.

3. In some states, legal options may be limited by what is known as the "**economic loss**" **doctrine**. This rule, barring a party from bringing a tort suit if the only loss suffered is economic, was applied in the *TCA v. IBM* case in this chapter. (a) Apply the economic loss rule to the following scenario: AOL released a software package, AOL 5.0, in October 1999, marketing it as "risk free," "easy to use," and providing "superior benefits." But, according to thousands of subscribers, AOL 5.0 interfered with their system's communications settings so that they could no longer connect to other ISPs, run non-AOL e-mail programs, or connect to local networks. By adding or altering hundreds of files on a user's system, AOL 5.0 was said to cause instability. Subscribers could not remove the software without doing further harm to their computers. AOL has called upon its insurance company to defend it in multiple class action suits. Its insurance contract, however, requires coverage only for bodily injury or "physical damage to the tangible property of others," such as AOL users. (b) Is there anything AOL could have done to better protect itself in the process of making an insurance deal? (c) What could it have done in the process of making/selling its software? (d) **Research**: Find out what happened in *American OnLine, Inc. v. St. Paul Mercury Insurance Co.*, 207 F. Supp.2d 459 (E.D.Va. 2002).

4. Vioxx, a nonsteroidal anti–inflammatory drug ("NSAID") was introduced to the market in 1999, approved for relief from menstrual cramps and pain caused by osteoarthritis. Its maker, Merck, promoted Vioxx as a painkiller with a safety profile superior to other NSAIDs, such as aspirin, ibuprofen, and naproxen, because it was easier on the stomach and intestines. At its peak, Vioxx was a $2.5 billion-a-year blockbuster for Merck. When its own studies revealed potential problems with Vioxx, however, Merck continued to tout the drug's "excellent safety profile" in numerous press releases and public statements. The drug was pulled from the market in 2004 because it doubled the risk of heart attacks and strokes. By then, thousands of lawsuits had been filed by injured Vioxx users. Later, shareholders also sued Merck. **Research**: Find out how the Merck product safety lawsuits have been resolved. What happened in the suit brought by investors claiming the company's failure to disclose material information about the cardiovascular risks of Vioxx led to financial loss when the truth was revealed and the stock price fell?

5. An internal Ford memo entitled "Fatalities Associated With Crash Induced Fuel Leakage and Fires" estimated the "benefits" and "costs" of design changes to its early Pinto as follows:

Benefits: Savings—180 burn deaths, 180 serious burn injuries, and 2,100 burned vehicles Unit cost—$200,000 per death, $67,000 per injury, $700 per vehicle

Total benefits: 180 × ($200,000) plus

180 × ($67,000) plus

2,100 × ($700) = $49.53 million

Costs: Sales—11 million cars, 1.5 million light trucks

Unit cost—$11 per car, $11 per truck

Total costs: 11,000,000 × ($11) plus

1,500,000 × ($11) = $137.5 million

Assume you are a safety engineer at Ford, consulted as to the wisdom of adding $11 to the cost of manufacturing the Pinto. What recommendation would you make? Can you make use of ethical theory to argue in defense of it? Against it?

6. Nokia Inc. is the world's largest manufacturer of wireless telephone headsets. Recent studies indicate that exposure to RFR from cell phones is linked to adverse health consequences, including changes in the brain, headaches, heating behind the ear, and sleep problems. What actions might be taken to hold Nokia responsible? *Zurich American Insurance Company v. Nokia, Inc.,* 268 S.W.3d 487 (Tx. 2008).

7. In July 2007, Zheng Xiaoyu, one of the most powerful regulators in China, was executed after confessing to accepting gifts and bribes from drug companies over the eight years he headed China's equivalent of the FDA. During Zheng's tenure, his agency approved over 150,000 applications for new drugs, at least six of which were fake, under a system he created. In 2002, the Chinese began to investigate charges of corruption among various drug officials. In addition to bribery, Zheng was found guilty of failing to police the drug industry and his subordinates and of creating regulatory schemes that allowed dangerous drugs to come to market. On execution day, the government announced that it was dismantling the drug approval system Zheng had created. **Research**: Find out what changes have taken place in China since 2007 to ensure greater safety of both food and drugs. What changes have taken place in the United States to ensure that imports, from China and elsewhere, are safer?

8. DDT is a cheap way to eliminate insects that threaten crops and people—including mosquitoes that spread malaria. Because it accumulates in the food chain and causes harm to humans and animals, its use has been banned in the United States since 1972. However, 23 nations continue to use it for malaria control, although most no longer use DDT for agricultural purposes. Alternative pesticides—such as pyrethroids—are two to three times more costly. By 1999, only three nations—China, Mexico, and India—still produced and exported DDT. However, when the United Nations considered a worldwide ban on DDT as part of a plan to minimize the use of 12 toxic chemicals ("persistent organic pollutants"), some members of the public health community were alarmed. There has been a resurgence of mosquito-borne malaria, with some 300 to 500 million new cases a year. Drugs to treat malaria are expensive and increasingly ineffective against the disease. Use ethical theory to articulate a response to this dilemma.

9. To fight malaria, health agencies are looking to artemisinin, a new drug derived from sweet wormwood isolated by Chinese scientists. Used in combination with other drugs, it can be a powerful treatment. But 18 companies from around the world make artemisinin in a one-drug form that can be sold cheaply in the developing world where people with fevers often take drugs without knowing for sure they

have malaria. Fearing misuse would create an incurable strain of the disease, the World Health Organization demanded that companies stop selling the drug in its monotherapy form. What ethical issues arise here?

10. In January 2010, McNeil Consumer Heath Care, a unit of Johnson & Johnson (J&J), recalled lots of Tylenol, Motrin, Benadryl, Rolaids, and aspirin in response to consumer complaints about moldy smells emanating from certain products. J&J claimed the odor was a byproduct of a chemical that leaked into the products at a company plant in Puerto Rico. FDA officials met with managers to express serious concerns about their manufacturing operations and then conducted a routine inspection of the firm's Pennsylvania plant. In May, after the FDA accused the company of using raw materials with known bacterial contamination to make certain lots of liquid Tylenol and Motrin for children in Pennsylvania, J&J issued a voluntary recall of those lots. (a) Do an ethical analysis of this scenario. (b) Can you articulate a legal claim against J&J?

11. Biotech medicines—proteins made by modifying the DNA of bacteria, yeast, or mammal cells and infused into sick patients—are the fastest growing category of health spending. Sales reached $120 billion in 2009, with hundreds of biotech products being synthesized to treat cancer, AIDS, diabetes, Alzheimer's, and a hundred other diseases. The manufacture of biotechs is more complex and costly than conventional medicine, and the cost to patients can run as high as $25,000–50,000 a year. Some members of Congress have introduced legislation that would give consumers access to lower-cost copies; one would authorize the FDA to approve safe, lower-cost versions of biotechnology drugs without the full range of tests normally required for new products. Who are the stakeholders who will be affected by such legislation? What arguments can you make for or against it?

CHAPTER PROJECT

Legislative Activism

1. For this project, you are asked to identify a proposed regulation related to product safety and to submit a written comment for or against the proposed rule.

- Begin by going to the Web site of any of the major government regulatory agencies with responsibility for product safety (the National Highway Transportation Safety Administration at *http://www.nhtsa.gov*, the Environmental Protection Agency at *http://www.epa.gov*, the Consumer Product Safety Commission at *http://www.cpsc.gov*, the Food and Drug Administration at *http://www.fda.gov*, or the Federal Trade Commission at *http://www.ftc.gov*).

- Once you have selected a government agency, locate its docket of proposed regulations. Choose one on a topic that interests you, and read through the proposal.

- Learn as much as you can about the debate for and against the proposed regulation. Check out such consumer advocacy groups such as *http://www.citizen.org*, *http://www.consumersunion.org*, or Friends of the Earth at *http://www.foe.org*. Find the business perspectives through popular business publications, by using a database such as Abinform, or through a trade association such as http://www.Phrma.org (pharmaceutical industry) or the Business Roundtable.

- Take a position for or against the new regulation, and submit a written comment to the regulatory agency that has proposed it. E-mail a copy of your comment to your professor.

CHAPTER 9

Ownership, Creativity, and Innovation
Intellectual Property

As for piracy, I love to be pirated. It is the greatest compliment an author can have. The wholesale piracy of Democracy was the single real triumph of my life. Anyone may steal what he likes from me.

—HENRY BROOKS ADAMS, 1905[1]

At its best, the Knowledge Society involves all members of a community in knowledge creation and utilization. [It] is not only about technological innovations, but also about human beings, their personal growth, and their individual creativity, experience and participation.

—THE UNITED NATIONS, "UNDERSTANDING KNOWLEDGE SOCIETIES" (2003)

Intellectual property (IP) is the work product of the human mind. Novels, paintings, computer programs, songs, and inventions are all examples. IP differs from other kinds of property (land, buildings, stocks, consumer goods) in several key ways. While often expensive and time consuming to generate, intellectual property can be quickly and easily copied. Unlike tangible items whose use has physical limitations—only one person can drive a car at a time, and a pie can be divided into only so many slices—the number of persons who can use any one item of intellectual property is boundless. A painting hung in a museum or reproduced in art books or on the Internet can be viewed by many; a poem or song can be endlessly repeated and enjoyed; the same software program can run on computers throughout the world.

The legal framework that protects intellectual property has evolved over the years, as lawmakers have sought to promote commercial progress and enrich culture by rewarding inventors and creative people for their efforts.

Today, IP law is the focus of controversy, not only in the business and legal communities, but among the general public. As intellectual property has become key to hegemony in the world economy, legal protections for those owning patents and copyright have been greatly expanded—often in conflict with the norms of cyberspace, whose founders freely shared and borrowed creative works, claiming "information wants to be free." Business interests warn that sharing has economic costs: the Business Software Alliance (BSA) estimated global losses from software piracy at $51 billion annually in 2009. For every $100

---

[1] Letter, July 11, 1905, to Brooks Adams. *Letters*, Vol. 2, Worthington Chauncy Ford, Ed. (Houghton Mifflin, 1938).

worth of legitimate software sold, an additional $75 worth of unlicensed software made its way into the market.[2] The Coalition Against Counterfeiting and Piracy is urging stronger U.S. government action to stop trafficking in counterfeit goods, pointing to the loss of hundreds of thousands of jobs and the needless exposure of consumers to dangerous and defective products (such as counterfeit pharmaceuticals and auto parts).[3] Patent law—once too technical and obscure for most of the public to notice—now commands headlines, with nearly 483,000 inventors filing patent applications in the United States in 2009 and more than 20 percent of human genes already patented. Activists caution that the "rights" created by intellectual property laws grant monopolies that can stifle not only creativity, but also the competition on which our free market economy is based.

In this chapter, we explore some critical IP issues, beginning with one of the stickiest problems: downloading music from the Internet. Traditional copyright law and relatively recent changes under the Digital Millennium Copyright Act provide the legal background. Then we turn to other kinds of IP: misappropriation, trademark, patents, and trade secrets. The ethical focus of the chapter centers on finding the delicate balance in a competitive economy between protecting individual inventiveness and stimulating a vibrant shared culture. We end with a look at the globalization of IP rights and a challenge to ensure that IP law enhances human rights.

Copyright

Article 1, Section 8 of the U.S. Constitution empowers Congress to pass legislation *"to promote the progress of science and (the) useful arts by securing for limited Times to authors and inventors the exclusive right to their respective Writings and Discoveries."*

The congressional report on the Copyright Act of 1909 articulates the tension underlying intellectual property protection in our legal system:

> *In enacting copyright law Congress must consider … two questions: First, how much will the legislation stimulate the producer and so benefit the public, and second, how much will the monopoly granted be detrimental to the public? The granting of such exclusive rights, under the proper terms and conditions, confers a benefit upon the public that outweighs the evils of the temporary monopoly.*

Tension between private and public interests, between encouraging and rewarding individual creators—authors, composers, software engineers—and improving upon, borrowing, or critiquing their works has remained a constant in an otherwise evolving legal landscape.

■ ■ ■

Bridgeport Music Inc. holds the copyright on 6,000 songs, including the works of George Clinton, leader of Parliament-Funkadelic, a key band in the 1960s and '70s funk music scene. The following case involves the rights to Clinton's 1982 single and best-known work, "Atomic Dog." It is one of hundreds of lawsuits filed by Bridgeport Music against those associated with the rap and hip-hop music industry. In 1998, Public Announcement released the song "D.O.G. in Me" on its album *All Work, No Play*. Bridgeport Music heard the song, notified the producer (UMG Recordings) that it

---

[2] *http://portal.bsa.org/globalpiracy2009/*

[3] *www.theglobalipcenter.com/pages/coalition-against-counterfeiting-and-piracy*

violated Bridgeport's copyright in "Atomic Dog," and asked UMG to either enter a licensing agreement or cease distribution of the song. UMG ignored the request, and Bridgeport Music sued. Its claim: the phrase "Bow wow wow, yippie yo, yippie yea" (the "Bow Wow refrain"), the repetition of the word "dog" in a low tone of voice at regular intervals, and the use of the sound of rhythmic panting in "D.O.G. in Me" infringed on "Atomic Dog." After a five-day trial, the jury agreed. It awarded Bridgeport Music $22,245 in actual damages and an additional $88,980 in statutory damages for willful copyright infringement. This appeal followed.

BRIDGEPORT MUSIC, INC. v. UMG RECORDINGS, INC.
United States Court of Appeals, Sixth Circuit, 2009.
585 F.3d 267

MARTHA CRAIG DAUGHTREY, Circuit Judge

Songwriters David Spradley, Garry Shider, and George Clinton created "Atomic Dog" in a recording studio in January 1982, working without a written score. As a result, the composition of "Atomic Dog" is embedded in the sound recording. Testimony at trial indicated that the song was composed spontaneously [on the set]....

According to expert testimony at trial, "Atomic Dog" "is an anthem of the funk era ... one of the most famous songs of the whole repertoire of funk and R & B." In addition to the song's continuing popularity on its own, "Atomic Dog" and other works by Clinton and Parliament-Funkadelic are said to have influenced many contemporary rap and hip-hop artists, with the most notable being the style of rap popularized by West Coast rappers such as Dr. Dre, Ice Cube, Snoop Dogg, and Coolio.... According to an expert musicologist, the Bow Wow refrain "is one of the most memorable parts of the song" and is often licensed by itself....

A. Copyright Infringement

There are two essential questions at the heart of any copyright infringement action: whether the plaintiff owned the copyrighted work and whether the defendant copied it. The federal constitution requires, moreover, that to be actionable the copying must be of elements of the copyrighted work that are "original." *See Feist Publ'ns, Inc. v. Rural Tel. Serv. Co.,* (U.S. 1991). To be original, an element must both be an independent creation of its author and involve at least minimal creativity.... To establish that it has been copied, a plaintiff must either introduce direct evidence of the defendant's copying or prove it indirectly by showing that the defendant had access to the plaintiff's work and that there is a substantial similarity between it and the defendant's work, thus giving rise to an inference of copying. Even if access cannot be proven, a plaintiff may prevail by showing a high degree of similarity between the two works....

[In most cases, the court first "filters out" elements that were not original—unprotectable ideas, standard plots, *scènes à faire*, or "stock" themes, for example—and then directs the jury to decide whether the rest of the works as a whole are substantially similar to one another.

In some cases, however, the "copying of a relatively small but qualitatively important or crucial element can be an appropriate basis upon which to find substantial similarity." Where a small fragment of a work is literally copied, but the overall theme or concept is not, the courts use what is called the "fragmented literal similarity" test to determine whether or not copyright was violated. In such situations, even a small degree of copying may support a finding of substantial similarity, depending on the context. Even a single line from a protected work might be an infringement if it is an integral part of the work and readily recognizable, such as the line "E.T., phone home" is to the film.

Here, UMG appeals the use of this fragmented literal similarity test in the court's instructions to the jury.]

[UMG] contends that the jury should not have been able to consider either the word "dog" used as musical punctuation or the rhythmic panting in "D.O.G. in Me" as infringement because those elements are not original and, thus, should have been filtered out. UMG also argues that the jury should have been instructed to consider the two songs as a whole when determining substantial similarity and, so instructed, would not have found substantial similarity due to the different mood and theme of the two songs and the limited usage of elements from "Atomic Dog" in "D.O.G. in Me." We disagree....

... [T]he standard for originality is a low one, and the "vast majority of works make the grade quite easily."... In this case, expert testimony presented at trial was sufficient to permit the jury to conclude that Clinton's use of the three disputed elements in "Atomic Dog" met this minimal standard. Additionally, there was expert testimony that these elements were not just the "mere abstract idea" of a dog or of the activity of panting because, in Clinton's composition, the word "dog" constituted a "stand-alone melody of one word" used as musical punctuation at intervals on the tonic note of the song and because the sound of panting followed the rhythm of the song. Testimony by David Spradley, a co-creator of "Atomic Dog," also demonstrated that Clinton exercised some degree of creative control over the panting by instructing the performers to create a certain rhythm....

Here, Bridgeport alleged in its complaint that UMG had copied specific elements of "Atomic Dog" and that these elements were copied literally. Thus, the overall concept or tone of the work was not relevant to the jury's task. Instead, the jury heard testimony that described the copied elements of "Atomic Dog" as unique to the song and the Bow Wow refrain, in particular, as the most well-known aspect of the song in terms of iconology, perhaps the functional equivalent of "E.T., phone home." Thus, the jury did not act unreasonably in concluding that there was substantial similarity, given evidence that the copied elements had such great qualitative importance to the song.... [Held: Judgment for plaintiff affirmed.]

QUESTIONS

1. What must a copyright holder prove to show that its rights have been violated? How did the plaintiff here meet that standard?

2. Not everything can be copyrighted, as the judge in this case indicates. Ideas, standard plot lines, and *scènes à faire* are available to all. In a footnote, Judge Daughtrey writes:

   An example of *scènes à faire*, or "stock" themes, in music is found in *Black v. Gosdin*, 740 F.Supp. 1288, 1292 (M.D.Tenn.1990), involving a dispute over a country music song about a jilted lover set in a bar with a jukebox... [In that case] these elements in the song flow directly. The court explained that these elements in the song flow directly from a common theme in country music: "Having chosen the familiar theme of a broken-hearted lover seeking solace in country music, the choice of a barroom with a jukebox as the setting in which to unfold this idea simply cannot be attributed to any unique creativity on the part of the songwriter."

   Were any parts of "Atomic Dog" copyrightable? Which ones?

3. Do either of the following practices raise legal or ethical concerns: (a) Quoting from various writers, and attributing the quotes to the authors, as part of a term paper? (b) Same as before, but without attribution?

4. Is there anything unethical about "sampling" from earlier musical compositions without naming the composer?

5. Shakespeare took whole passages from the ancient Roman writer Plutarch and used them in *Antony and Cleopatra*; the story of *Romeo and Juliet* is the basis for the Broadway

musical *West Side Story.* Is there an ethical difference between Shakespeare's actions and those of Arthur Laurents, who wrote the book for *West Side Story?* Isn't the creative process inherently derivative and/or driven by preexisting cultural creations?

■ ■ ■

Online Piracy or Culture Jamming?

If a song means a lot to you, imagine what it means to us.

—ARTISTS AGAINST PIRACY

Good artists copy, great artists steal. Steal from everyone except yourself.

—PABLO PICASSO

The enigma is this: If our property can be infinitely reproduced and instantaneously distributed all over the planet without cost, without our knowledge, without its even leaving our possession, how can we protect it? How are we going to get paid for the work we do with our minds? And, if we can't get paid, what will assure the continued creation and distribution of such work?

—JOHN PERRY BARLOW[4]

Online music sharing is now almost ubiquitous. In 1999 a 19-year-old college dropout, Shawn Fanning, released computer code that allowed his friends to share their collections of digitalized music (MP3 files) and created the Napster music sharing site. By July 2000, some five million users had visited the Napster site, and the Recording Industry Association of America (RIAA) began its campaign to stop illegal downloading. One tool in its arsenal was copyright law. As federal trial court Judge Patel saw it, the RIAA suit to shut down Napster was really about "the boundary between sharing and theft, personal use and the unauthorized worldwide distribution of copyrighted music and sound recordings." While Patel and the federal appellate court in California agreed with the recording industry that Napster illegally contributed to copyright infringement, further appeals and technical difficulties delayed the dismantling of its services.

In the meantime, music swapping had planted itself firmly in the culture. Napster-like Web sites became popular. Now joined by the movie industry, RIAA stood its ground. In a closely watched case, the Supreme Court ruled that peer-to-peer networks like Grokster and Kazaa violated copyright laws when they knowingly and intentionally distributed software that enabled users to freely download copyrighted music. Based on evidence that over 100 million copies of the software had been downloaded and billions of files shared each month, the court found that the "probable scope of copyright infringement is staggering."[5] Advertising, internal documents, and promotional materials all indicated that the P2P defendants aimed to attract Napster-users once Napster was declared illegal. That, coupled with a business model predicated on providing free software to download music financed by the sale of advertising space (the more users, the greater the revenues) and the failure to make any effort to filter or otherwise impede the sharing of copyrighted files, convinced the Court that the P2P defendants intended their product to be used to infringe on copyrights.

---

[4] John Perry Barlow, "The Economy of Ideas: A Framework for Patents and Copyrights in the Digital Age," *http://www. wired.com:/wired/archive/2.03/economy.ideas.html.*

[5] *Metro-Goldwin-Mayer Studios, Inc. v. Grokster, Ltd.,* 125 S.Ct. 2764 (2005).

Writing for the Court, Justice Souter adopted "the inducement rule" for copyright, holding that "one who distributes a device with the object of promoting its use to infringe copyright, as shown by clear expression or other affirmative steps taken to foster infringement, is liable for the resulting acts of infringement by third parties."

As the practice of music file sharing evolved, so too did efforts to stop it—using technology, the market, and law. The major industry players joined together in various ways to improve what is known as "digital rights management," systems for building copy protection into CDs and DVDs and for providing secure and compensated methods for lawful digital sharing. Sony, Apple, and RealNetworks sought a market-based solution, creating Apple iTunes, responding to music fans who claimed they wanted only selected songs, not necessarily an entire CD. Rock artist Peter Gabriel backed a British music download service, We7.com, which relied on new "Media Graft" technology and Internet marketing techniques to offer ad-sponsored music free to users.

In a wave of lawsuits, RIAA—the music industry's trade group—went after individual users. Unable to identify them initially, they sent "John Doe" subpoenas to the major Internet service providers—AOL, Verizon, universities, and so on—to learn the names of those who were downloading music. Privacy advocates and cybertarians were alarmed, but the suits had an impact: They alerted parents and school administrators to the practice and within six months, reportedly, the number of people swapping files online dropped by half.

Some critics, like the experimental music and art collective known as Negativland, argued that the problem is not infringement on rights, but rather the current structure of a music industry controlled by a handful of transnational corporations and the increasingly rigid legal regime of copyright.[6]

Yet, we might ask, should we be rethinking the norms and values that underlie our definition of intellectual property? Perhaps Negativland's view of the world as "a freely usable public domain" is more consistent with the way culture is created.

FEMINIST INTERPRETATIONS OF INTELLECTUAL PROPERTY

Debora Halbert[7]

...Two examples help highlight the values associated with women's creative work and can lead to an alternative view of the way intellectual property may look from a gendered perspective. The first example highlights the difference between craft and industrialized knowledge and illustrates the differences in knowledge construction. Knitting has long been considered a craft enterprise associated with women's work. Virtually all knitters are women. There is a long history of sharing patterns among knitters, knitting is often communicated from parent or grandparent to child, and knitting circles were a popular method of doing productive labor while enjoying the company of other women. Within the past few years, knitters have noticed changes in the world of knitting. Where once patterns were published in easy-to-share formats with little concern for copyright, today's knitting patterns come with strict prohibitions regarding sharing, copying, and producing knitted material for commercial purposes.

[6] Negativland, "Two Relationships to a Cultural Public Domain," 66 LAW & CONTEMP. PROBS. 239 (2003). This article is also available at *http://law.duke.edu/journals/66LCPNegativland.*

[7] Deborah Halbert, "Feminist Interpretations of Intellectual Property," *Journal of Gender, Social Policy, and the Law* 14(3), 2006, pp. 431–460.

In other words, copyright has entered the world of knitting patterns, a world assumed by many involved as a communal source of knowledge to share. Patterns have been appropriated into the larger industrialized process of publishing for profit....

While the knitting circles and community remain primarily female (public and shared), the ownership of knowledge about patterns has been appropriated into the dominant mode of production—it has been privatized. Patterns are sold, not to further the culture of knitting, but to maximize profit....

It is important to note that women (who need not be feminists) may operate in either paradigm and that many of those constructing these copyrighted patterns are women. Feminists, however, would argue that the women's way of knowing, illustrated by the tradition of knitting, should be used as the source for articulating and understanding a different method of constructing knowledge—one not contingent upon the abstract individual and original author, but one centered in relationships of care. After all, the pattern is only part of the creative process. The individual who does the knitting makes changes to the design, picks the colors of the yarn, and invests her unique motivation into the knitting process. The creative act of knitting transcends the pattern; yet, as copyright invades and colonizes this space, its users attempt to appropriate for themselves the claim to original creativity and seek to control the activity well beyond the construction of a pattern....

Both quilting and knitting, primarily women's ways of creating, have existed outside copyright law and developed as collective enterprises....

Once one stops privileging the abstract and rational and seeks out the relational in cultural creation and innovation, it is clear that a paradigm of intellectual property that creates rigid boundaries to sharing stands in the way of a relational approach to knowledge creation, one in which care and the work of the heart can play a role. A feminist critique from this perspective is a quite radical critique of the boundaries established by intellectual property law, which typically are boundaries that seek only to divide and control instead of facilitate exchange....

Traditional Copyright Law

In vain we call old notions fudge,
And bend our conscience to our dealing;
The Ten Commandments will not budge,
And stealing will continue stealing.

—MOTTO OF THE AMERICAN COPYRIGHT LEAGUE, 1885

Our first federal copyright law gave exclusive rights to the authors of maps, charts, and books for 14 years. During the term of copyright the copyright holder controls the right to reproduce and distribute her work. Under today's law, ideas that are "fixed in a tangible medium of expression"—such as photographs, paintings, music, movies, and computer programs—can be copyrighted, and their authors generally gain rights lasting 70 years beyond the author's life. The right attaches when the author first makes her work public: signing, dating, and using the © symbol to claim ownership. Registration with the Federal Copyright Office, necessary to sue to enforce copyright, is relatively easy; all that is required is a registration form, a fee, and a copy (or copies) of the material. By statute, the copyright holder acquires the exclusive rights to make and distribute copies, to prepare derivative works, to perform literary, dramatic, or musical works and to publicly display literary, pictorial, or sculptural work.

U.S. COPYRIGHT LAW HIGHLIGHTS

1790: First U.S. copyright law; protection available only for "maps, charts, and books,"—not music—for a 14-year term.

1831: Copyright Act amended to expand protection to musical compositions.

1909: Compulsory licensing scheme and a royalty rate created for "phonorecords."

1912: Copyright Act amended to expand protection to motion pictures.

1914: American Society for Composers and Publishers (ASCAP) formed.

1971: Copyright Act amended to extend limited protection to recordings.

1976: Major revision to U.S. copyright law; protection extended to all creations "fixed in tangible medium of expression"—including radio and television.

1984: *Sony v. Betamax* decision by the Supreme Court finds the use of VCRs by home viewers to "time-shift" television shows is a "fair use" that does not violate copyright law; Court rules that devices capable of substantial non-infringing uses are not illegal.

1994: United States signs international treaty, Trade-Related Aspects of Intellectual Property (TRIPS); Congress creates penalties for bootlegging audio recordings of live performances and music videos.

1995: Digital Rights in Sound Recordings Act gives exclusive rights to holders of sound recordings to public play of digital versions.

1997: No Electronic Theft (NET) Act expands criminal sanctions for © violations.

1998: Digital Millennium Copyright Act (DMCA) bans technologies that circumvent antipiracy measures or otherwise facilitate infringement.

1998: Sonny Bono Copyright Term Extension Act (CTEA) extends the period protecting all copyrights to author's life plus 70 years and to 95 years from creation for "works for hire" where copyright is held by a corporation.

Fair Use

In truth, in literature, in science, and in art, there are, and can be, few, if any, things, which, in an abstract sense, are strictly new and original throughout. Every book in literature, science, and art, borrows, and must necessarily borrow, and use much which was well known and used before. No man creates a new language for himself, at least if he be a wise man, in writing a book. He contents himself with the use of language already known and used and understood by others. No man writes exclusively from his own thoughts, unaided and uninstructed by the thoughts of others. The thoughts of every man are, more or less, a combination of what other men have thought and expressed, although they may be modified, exalted, or improved by his own genius or reflection.... Virgil borrowed much from Homer; Bacon drew from earlier as well as contemporary minds; Coke exhausted all the known learning of his profession; and even Shakespeare and Milton, so justly and proudly our boast as the brightest originals, would be found to have gathered much from the abundant stores of current knowledge and classical studies in their days.

—JUSTICE STORY, EMERSON V. DAVIES (1845)

In a lawsuit for copyright infringement, a defendant can avoid liability by successfully arguing **fair use**. This defense to copyright claims is based on the notion that the free flow of ideas at times requires quoting or otherwise borrowing from a copyrighted work. This can happen, for example, when critics review books, when news reporters use video clips, or when teachers make copies of articles for classroom use.[8]

■ ■ ■

Joel Tenenbaum ("Tenenbaum"), the defendant in this copyright infringement action, was accused of using Kazaa file sharing software as a college sophomore to download and distribute 30 copyrighted songs belonging to the plaintiffs. Over a period of years—before and after his activity was detected in August 2004—Tenenbaum's file sharing software made more than 800 songs available to other Kazaa users to download. When the record companies sued him, Tenenbaum did not contest these facts; he argued, instead, that they just did not matter. His copying, he argued, was a "fair use" under the Copyright Act. The plaintiffs disagreed and asked the court to rule against the fair use defense. Below, the court explains why it agreed with the music companies.

SONY BMG MUSIC ENTERTAINMENT v. TENENBAUM
United States District Court, D. Mass., 2009.
672 F. Supp. 2d 217

Gertner, District Judge

… [T]he Court was prepared to consider a more expansive fair use argument than other courts have credited—perhaps one supported by facts specific to this individual and this unique period of rapid technological change. For example, file sharing for the purposes of sampling music prior to purchase or space-shifting to store purchased music more efficiently might offer a compelling case for fair use. Likewise, a defendant who used the new file-sharing networks in the technological interregnum before digital media could be purchased legally, but who later shifted to paid outlets, might also be able to rely on the defense.

But the defendant would have none of it. Rather than tailoring his fair use defense to suggest a modest exception to copyright protections, Tenenbaum mounted a broadside attack that would excuse all file sharing for private enjoyment. It is a version of fair use so broad that it would swallow the copyright protections that Congress created, defying both statute and precedent…. In his view, a defendant just needs to show that he did not make money from the files he downloaded or distributed—i.e., that his use was "non-commercial"—in order to put his fair use defense before a jury. And every non-commercial use, to him, is presumptively fair…. Defendant's version of fair use is, all in all, completely elastic, utterly standardless, and wholly without support….

The Court is supposed to be a gatekeeper. If the defendant does not offer facts that present even a colorable legal defense of fair use, the Court is obliged to say so….

Tenenbaum did not meet this burden; in truth, he did not come close. He offered few disputed facts and little, if any, legal authority for his position. His opposition briefs were not accompanied by any affidavits, expert reports, deposition testimony, or other evidence….

---

[8] The fair use of a copyrighted work…for purposes such as criticism, comment, newsreporting, teaching (including multiple copies for classroom use), scholarship or research, is not an infringement of copyright." 17 U.S.C. § 107.

Fair Use Standard

Fair use was originally a common law doctrine developed by judges who recognized that the monopoly rights protected by copyright were not absolute. These rights were limited by their public purpose, which set out to promote the arts by offering private incentives to authors and artists. Where a use did not injure the market for the original work, and itself advanced a public purpose—like education, commentary, scholarship, or further artistic innovation—it could be considered "fair," and not infringing....

[Fair use] is the flip side of the copyright coin, embracing at its core those uses that advance public purposes without unduly diminishing the market for the original work.... At the same time, fair use may shield those types of uses that are truly *de minimis*, having little or no impact on the market for or value of the original work....

Although Section 107 [of the Copyright Act of 1974] sets out four factors that a court "shall" consider, this list was not intended to be exhaustive....

The four factors identified in the statute are: (1) the purpose and character of the use, including whether such use is of a commercial nature or is for nonprofit educational purposes; (2) the nature of the copyrighted work; (3) the amount and substantiality of the portion used in relation to the copyrighted work as a whole; and (4) the effect of the use upon the potential market for or value of the copyrighted work. Notably, the provision's introduction identifies some of those non-commercial purposes targeted by the fair use doctrine: "[P]urposes such as criticism, comment, news reporting, teaching ..., scholarship, or research." ...

The defendant has offered the Court no legal authority that file sharing of the kind he engaged in constitutes fair use. In fact, a number of courts, including the Supreme Court, have found exactly the opposite. *See Metro-Goldwyn-Mayer Studios Inc. v. Grokster, Ltd.,* (U.S.2005); *A & M Records, Inc. v. Napster, Inc.,* (9th Cir.2001); *BMG Music v. Gonzalez,* (7th Cir.2005)....

1. Fair Use: Statutory Factors
a. Purpose and Character

The parties do not dispute that the ultimate purpose of Tenenbaum's use was his own private enjoyment and that of the friends with whom he discussed and explored new music. They argue over the label that should be applied to his file-sharing activity—whether it is to be classified as "commercial" or "non-commercial." It is clear that Tenenbaum did not seek to profit from his use of file-sharing networks. He did not sell these songs, nor did he demand anything directly in exchange from those who might have downloaded them from him.... On the other hand, the plaintiffs correctly point out that the Copyright Act broadly defines "financial gain" as the "receipt, or expectation of receipt, of anything of value, including the receipt of other copyrighted works." ...

As this case reveals, the commercial/non-commercial binary is a misleading one. The purpose and character of a use must be classified along a spectrum that ranges, in reality, from pure, large-scale profit-seeking to uses that advance important public goals, like those recognized in the statute [which locates criticism, comment, news reporting, teaching, scholarship, and research at the core of fair use]. Tenenbaum's file sharing may well fall somewhere in the middle. He is not the prototypical commercial infringer, yet his use was hardly "educational." Downloading new music may have been eye-opening for him personally, but it surely did not carry any public benefit of the kind contemplated by Section 107....

Since fair use operates as an exception to the exclusive rights of the copyright holder, which broadly serve to promote artistic creation, it is critical that a proposed fair use carry its own public benefits. "The use must be productive and must employ the [copied] matter in a different manner or for a different purpose from the original." Nothing about Tenenbaum's use of these sound recordings was remotely transformative, or served other public ends.

b. Nature of the Copyrighted Work

The species of copyrighted work at issue in this case is music, which commands robust copyright protections.... Although hardly dispositive, as *Campbell* itself showed, this factor weighs against fair use.

c. Portion of the Work Used

The third statutory fair use factor requires the Court to consider the "amount and substantiality of the portion used in relation to the copyrighted work as a whole." ... Tenenbaum is alleged to have downloaded individual songs in their entirety, but not full albums. He claims that it is the albums in which the plaintiffs registered their copyrights, while the individual songs are "works made for hire." ... As a result, the defendant suggests that his use was only partial, supporting fair use.

This is the proverbial distinction without a difference. Individual songs are regularly treated as the relevant unit for evaluating the infringement or fair use of musical works....

In this context, Tenenbaum has not claimed that he just sampled individual songs as a prelude to purchasing the full albums on which those songs appeared. That could well present a compelling argument for fair use. Rather, his purpose was the enjoyment of the songs themselves, for free, which he accomplished by downloading each in its entirety. Without doubt, the reproductions that he obtained were full market substitutes for the works in question by August 2004, after the works were available on the internet for a fee. *Sony v. Betamax* (U.S.1984) acknowledged that the reproduction of an entire work has the "ordinary effect of militating against a finding of fair use." The Betamax recordings in that case proved an exception just because they allowed viewers to watch broadcast programming, already available to them for free, at a later, more convenient, time. Most users, the Court concluded, would only watch the program once, as they were otherwise entitled to do, so the reproduction amounted to mere time-shifting. As such, the copies increased access and convenience without diminishing the market for the protected product.

Not so here. First, the plaintiffs did not authorize even one free broadcast or distribution. Nor does Tenenbaum claim that he only listened to each song once. Instead, the principal advantage of Tenenbaum's downloads was the fact that they could be obtained without paying for authorized copies, and then enjoyed as much as he liked. Nothing about Tenenbaum's downloading of these songs for his private enjoyment takes this case outside the ordinary rule that use of an entire work counsels against fair use.

d. Effect on the Potential Market for the Work

... [The fourth factor focuses on the] impact on the "potential market for or value of the copyrighted work." Here, the Court considers not only Tenenbaum's conduct taken by itself, but "'whether unrestricted and widespread conduct of the sort engaged in by the defendant...would result in a substantially adverse impact on the potential market' for the original." *Campbell*. Tenenbaum argues that his file sharing made little economic difference to the plaintiffs because the songs at issue were immensely popular, and therefore widely available on Kazaa. But that is not the framework for this analysis. If thousands of others were engaged in the same activity, as he seems to acknowledge, it is the sum of that conduct that matters here.

Although the purpose of Tenenbaum's file sharing may not have been "commercial" in any classic sense, as noted above, from a consequential perspective the difference becomes harder to make out. The Court sees little difference between selling these works in the public marketplace and making them available for free to the universe of peer-to-peer users. If anything, the latter activity is likely to distribute even more copies—and therefore result in a bigger market impact—because there is no cost barrier at all. It is difficult to compete with a product offered for free. The plaintiffs provide evidence that the widespread availability of free copies of copyrighted works on the internet has decreased their sales revenue, a market reality that other courts have credited.... [T]he defendant, for his part, offered no affidavits or expert report on summary judgment to disprove or dispute this assertion....

Even if every download does not represent a lost sale, as the Court recognizes, it is plain that consumers who regularly pay for music would shift to free downloads if given the chance. Indeed, that is the very premise of Tenenbaum's sweeping argument—that this music should be free to individuals simply because it has "gone digital." He all but concedes the lost sales that would result from his version of fair use. He claims that copyright law does not protect what he labels "an outdated business model" and that the plaintiffs have other means of profiting from these works. What he seems to be arguing is that, even in the era of file sharing, the plaintiffs still make enough money from their copyrights. But the sufficiency of the plaintiffs' profits is not the measure of fair use, nor is Tenenbaum's view of what amount of profits are "enough." Congress has not capped the revenue that a copyright holder may derive from its monopoly....

To be sure, some authorities suggest that the "network effects" of making these works available for free may in fact enhance their overall value, especially for lesser-known artists, by increasing buzz and publicity.... That may be so in certain mixed systems, where some free distribution feeds demand for legitimate online sales. But Tenenbaum's version of fair use would destroy even that equilibrium. It would simply eliminate the market for digital downloads among individual consumers by transforming all file sharing for private enjoyment into fair use. Who would continue to use the iTunes Store or its equivalents, under the circumstances?...

2. Fair Use: Non-statutory Factors

a. Assumption of Risk

The defendant suggests that the plaintiffs' release of these works—in an environment where file sharing was rampant—amounts to a waiver of their copyrights and opens the door to fair use. Plaintiffs knew that these sound recordings would be shared, yet chose to produce and release them anyway.... As a result, the plaintiffs allegedly assumed the risk that their hugely popular music would be dispersed over peer-to-peer networks like Kazaa....

Nothing in the record remotely suggests that the plaintiffs foreswore any effort to enforce their copyrights or otherwise intended to surrender the rights to these sound recordings. In fact, the plaintiffs' distribution of these works with copyright notices affixed, and the aggressive litigation campaign they have pursued, suggests the opposite....

The mere act of producing and releasing artistic works where there is a known risk of piracy cannot amount to a deliberate waiver of copyright. Such a rule would hand control over copyright to counterfeiters and pirates; copyright protections would be weakest, practically and legally, precisely where piracy efforts were most concerted or successful....

b. Marketing Activities and Failure to Protect

Closely related to defendant's waiver argument is his view that the plaintiffs aggressively marketed these works, contributing to their popularity, while failing to protect them from online infringement in any meaningful way ... [because] the compact discs that these songs appeared on were not encrypted, allowing them to be easily transferred to a computer hard-drive and then over the internet....

In effect, the defendant suggests that plaintiffs all but created an "attractive nuisance" by virtue of their marketing activities and their failure to encrypt these works....

Unfortunately, this principle has no foothold in copyright law. Indeed, the idea that a copyright holder could lose the rights to his work precisely because of its popularity runs counter to the purposes of copyright. It would punish those authors and artists whose works are most attractive and pleasing to the public.

c. Availability of Paid Alternatives

Defendant also offers the difficulty of obtaining authorized digital alternatives in support of his fair-use argument. As a legal matter, he is on firmer ground here, yet again his position is defeated by the facts of this case....

Here, the defendant points out that the emergence of easy-to-use, paid outlets for digital music … lagged well behind the advent of file sharing. Before that time, it was hard to obtain individual songs in digital format; most copyrighted music was instead offered on compact disc and sold only as multi-track albums. In order to get one song, a consumer had to pay for ten to twenty separate tracks, many of which she might not want…. File-sharing software, by contrast to CDs, made individual songs directly available as digital mp3 files….

[But] by August 2004—when Tenenbaum's file sharing was detected—a commercial market for digital music had fully materialized. The iTunes Music Store debuted in April 2003, selling millions of individual digital tracks over its first months and offering a catalog of hundreds of thousands of songs. A different defendant, who was accused of file sharing prior to the iTunes Music Store's market-changing debut, might have a different case. In light of the chronology here, the unavailability of paid digital music is simply not relevant.

d. Policing Costs

Tenenbaum argues that the costs borne by parents and universities, who have to police the online activities of children and students, weigh in favor of fair use….

While the Court is very sympathetic to the parenting challenges posed by computers and the internet, the defendant has offered no proof that this task is onerous or impossible. It is often up to parents, and colleges *in loco parentis,* to teach and enforce the bounds of the law. Although the social costs of policing infringement might factor into fair use—because they diminish the overall benefits of copyright protection—these particular concerns are more appropriately part of an appeal to Congress to amend the statute….

e. The Injustice of this Action

Finally, Tenenbaum urges the Court to consider the injustice of this action in its fair use calculus—an appeal that illustrates his view of what fair use really is at its core. To him, fair use is not a legal doctrine tethered to the particular purposes of copyright, but a sweeping referendum on "fairness." It encompasses every possible inequity that might be found in the facts of this case, and owes little to precedent except—according to the defendant—its infinite elasticity.

As this Court has previously noted, it is very, very concerned that there is a deep potential for injustice in the Copyright Act as it is currently written. It urges—no implores—Congress to amend the statute to reflect the realities of file sharing. There is something wrong with a law that routinely threatens teenagers and students with astronomical penalties for an activity whose implications they may not have fully understood. The injury to the copyright holder may be real, and even substantial, but, under the statute, the record companies do not even have to prove actual damage. "Repeatedly, as new developments have occurred in this country, it has been Congress that has fashioned the new rules that new technology made necessary." It is a responsibility that Congress should not take lightly in the face of this litigation and the thousands of suits like it.

[Nonetheless, on the facts of this case, this Court grants summary judgment in plaintiff's favor on defendant's affirmative defense of fair use.]

QUESTIONS

1. Why does Tenenbaum lose this case? Does the outcome seem fair to you?

2. Shortly after the jury ruled against Tenenbaum, the "$675,000 playlist" of the songs he was guilty of downloading appeared on the notorious Swedish Web site, The Pirate Bay. Plaintiffs asked Judge Gertner to stop Tenebaum from promoting illegal file sharing, but the judge refused. How would you articulate an ethical analysis of Tenenbaum's actions? Of the music industry's attempt to silence him?

3. Using the fair use analysis from the *Tenenbaum* case, determine which of the following would be a fair use of copyrighted material:
   a. A seventh-grade teacher clips an article from the morning newspaper and makes copies for her class to discuss.
   b. A college professor collects chapters from various books and brings them to the local copy center to have them made into a "Class Anthology." She reuses the same anthology for three years.
   c. Same as above, but instead of going to the local copy center, the professor scans the articles and posts them on the course Web site.
   d. A literary critic quotes from six short stories in a scathing review of a popular author's newest collection.
   e. A painter, inspired by the poetry of a Pulitzer-prize winning poet, shows his work in a gallery installation in which he posts a different poem next to each of his two dozen paintings; the gallery publishes a guide to the show that includes the text of the poems and photos of the paintings. Neither had permission of the poet. Instead of the gallery, suppose it was a student who published an online guide to the show?

4. **Research**: Judge Gertner names a "fifth factor" not mentioned in the copyright statute, but frequently cited by courts to find a fair use: whether and to what extent the new work is "transformative," an alteration of the original work in a way that adds to its literary or artistic value. Find a case involving a "transformative use" that is deemed fair.

5. A parody—a literary or artistic work that imitates the characteristic style of an author or a work for comic effort or ridicule—is a classic example of a fair use. Parodies are considered "transformative" because they provide social benefit, shedding light on an earlier work while creating a new one. By definition, there must be some connection between the original work and the parody that borrows from it:

   [T]he heart of any parodist's claim to quote from existing material is the use of some elements of a prior author's composition to create a new one that, at least in part, comments on that author's works. Campbell v. Acu-Rose Music, Inc. *510 U.S. 569 (1994)*

   Which of the following should qualify as fair use parodies?
   a. From his fake news desk on Comedy Central's The Daily Show, Jon Stewart used a six-second excerpt from Sandra Kane's public access TV show to mock public access television, and commented on videotaped clips from network news reports.
   b. Alice Randall wrote a novel, *The Wind Done Gone*, telling the story of *Gone with the Wind* from the perspective of Cynera, a slave held by the original book's heroine, Scarlett O'Hara.

6. Consider the case involving "Atomic Dog" and "D.O.G. in Me." Can you articulate a fair use argument on behalf of Public Authority? How might the copyright holder respond?

7. J.D. Salinger is best known as the author of *Catcher in The Rye*, a critically acclaimed novel about Holden Caulfield, an adolescent coming of age. After publication of the book in 1951, Salinger did what his character did: he isolated himself. In 2010, Salinger came out of hiding to sue a Swedish writer, Fredrik Colting, who published "Sixty Years Later: Coming Through the Rye," using the name J.D. California, featuring a seventy-year old Holden Caulfield. What arguments can you make on behalf of Salinger? Colting? **Research:** What happened in the actual case? *Salinger v. Colting*, 607 F.3d 68 (2d Cir. 2010).

Joint Copyrights and Collective Rights

American copyright law creates a bundle of rights for the owner, including the right to reproduce, distribute, perform, display, or adapt the work. As with other property, the owner can sell or license some or all of her rights. Unknown authors of new books, for example, may contract to sell their copyright in exchange for royalties paid by a company that publishes the book. Others may agree to give up some, but not all, of their rights.

The copyright statute attempts to divide rights between an individual creator and the publisher of what is called a "collective work." Newspapers, magazines, and this textbook are examples. The authors of the readings in this book retain their copyright interests in the articles, although Cengage Learning holds the copyright in the overall work, *Law and Ethics in the Business Environment*. Movies, too, are collective works to which musicians, screenwriters, cinematographers, and producers all make varied contributions—with the producer holding the collective copyright, and the composer, for example, retaining her copyright to the background music.

Public Domain

The holes matter as much as the cheese.

—JAMES BOYLE, THE PUBLIC DOMAIN

Intellectual property scholar James Boyle and the author of the next reading, Lawrence Lessig, are among those who believe we should be reducing private control of culture and preserving more for our common, public use. Material that is always freely usable by anyone, without permission, is said to be **"in the public domain**." Free-floating "ideas"—as opposed to expressions that have been "fixed"—and government writings, such as judicial opinions, are available to anyone. And when copyrights expire, protected works are said to return to the public domain.

In the reading that follows, Lessig elaborates on his concerns that, left unchallenged, modern technology and changes in intellectual property law will diminish what should be a vibrant cultural commons.

THE CREATIVE COMMONS
Lawrence Lessig[9]

Everyone has heard of the Brothers Grimm. They wrote fairy tales. If you are like I was, you probably think that they wrote wonderful and happy fairy tales—the sort of stories children ought to be raised on. That's a mistake. The Grimm fairy tales are, as the name suggests, quite grim: awful, bloody, moralistic stories that should be kept far from any healthy childhood. Yet you are likely to believe that these stories are wonderful and happy, because they have been retold to us by an amazing creator called Disney.

Walt Disney took these stories and retold them in just the way our founders imagined that our culture would grow. He took the stories, and retold them in a way that would speak to his time. And most important for my purposes here, he could

---

[9] "The Creative Commons" by Lawrence Lessig from *Florida Law Review*, Vol. 55, 2003, p. 763. Reprinted by permission of Florida Law Review.

retell them because these stories lived in the public domain. Their copyright protections had lapsed. And they had lapsed because copyrights, in America at least, are for a "limited time" only. That limitation in turn builds a kind of creative commons: a resource from which anyone can draw and add and build upon because the Constitution guarantees the law's protection will end.

We can think of this "creative commons," this public domain from which others may draw, as a lawyer-free zone. No one can control what you do with material there, meaning you need never speak to a lawyer to draw material from there. The public domain is thus a resource that requires the permission of no one. And it is a resource that creators throughout history have drawn upon freely.

[But under today's law, with copyright extending 70 years beyond the life of an author, or 120 years if owned by a company as a "work for hire"] ... no one can do to the Disney Corporation what Disney did to the Brothers Grimm....

[Lessig tells another story, this one about AIBO, a robot dog created by Sony that sells for roughly $1,300.]

...As with any dog, ownership gives you the right to take the dog home and teach it how to behave—at least within limits.

One fan of the AIBO dog learned something about these limits. He took his Sony AIBO dog apart to understand how it worked. He tinkered with the dog. And after tinkering with the dog, he figured out how the code instructed the dog to operate, and he wanted his dog to operate in a somewhat different way. He wanted to teach his dog to dance jazz. On his Web site, aibopet.com, this fan of the AIBO taught others how to tinker with their pet. And one particular bit of tinkering would enable the AIBO dog to dance jazz....

[W]hen the owner of aibopet.com posted this little hack on his Web site, he got a letter from the Sony Corporation: "Your site contains information providing the means to circumvent AIBO ware's copy protection protocol constituting a violation of the anti-circumvention provisions of a law called the Digital Millennium Copyright Act."...

[To understand these stories, Lessig writes, we need to look at the technological inversion that has occurred in the United States:] ... [The original values of our copyright law] protected the public domain. They enabled a vibrant cultural commons. Yet changing technology and changing law is increasingly enclosing that commons. Tools built into the architecture of cyberspace are defeating a tradition of balanced freedom that defined our past. Yet the law has not yet recognized this inversion....

The Framers granted authors a very limited set of rights.... Our outrage at China notwithstanding, we should not forget that until 1891, American copyright law did not protect foreign copyrights. We were born a pirate nation.

In the first ten years of this copyright regime, there were some 13,000 titles that were published. Yet there were less than 1,000 copyright registrations. The aim of the original copyright regulation was to control publishers. In 1790, there were 127 publishers. This law was a tiny regulation of a tiny part of early American culture.

Most culture thus remained free of any copyright regulation. You could take a book and write an abridgement ... translate the book ... turn it into a play ... physically write out every word in that book and give it to your friends without any regulation of copyright law. The culture was free in a sense that is increasingly being demanded in debates about culture today: there was a freedom to Disnify culture, as Disney did to the Brothers Grimm ... and a freedom to tinker with the content that one finds without fear of committing a federal crime, as the fans of the AIBO wanted.

We could say, following a recent Apple ad campaign, that in our past, there was a freedom to "Rip, Mix, and Burn" culture. Regulation protected against unfair competition, but that regulation left people to develop their culture as they wished.

That past has now changed. It first changed because the law has changed. [Today, the law protects] essentially any creative work reduced to a tangible form ... [and does so] automatically.

More important than these changes in law are the changes effected by technology. Think about the life of a book.... The publisher can't control what I do with a printed book because there is no way to control pages separated from the publisher. And not only can they not control what I do physically with the book, the law, copyright law, affirmatively limits the ability of the publisher to do anything to the book, once the book is sold.

But compare then a book in cyberspace. I have ... in my Adobe eBook Reader ... *Middlemarch*—a work that is in the public domain. Even though this uncopyrighted book is in some senses free, it's not free in the Adobe eBook Reader.... [Limited permission is granted to me] to read this book aloud.... I may copy ten text sections into the computer's clipboard memory every ten days ... [and] print ten pages everyday using my computer. And here is the most embarrassing example: my most recent book, *The Future of Ideas*. My publisher released it stating I'm not allowed to copy any text sections into the memory, I'm not allowed to print any pages, and don't try to use your computer to read my book aloud, it's an offense of copyright law. Freedoms I would have with a real book get erased when this book is made virtual.

Now what makes these protections possible? In part what makes it possible is just the code built into the Adobe eBook Reader. The technology gives the publisher a control over an eBook that no publisher could ever have had over a regular book. And because of this control, the use of an eBook is regulated ... [instead of] the publishing of copyrighted material....

These controls increasingly mean that the ability to take what defines our culture and include it in an expression about our culture is permitted only with a license from the content owner. Free culture is thus transformed into licensed culture. The freedom to remake and retell our culture thus increasingly depends upon the permission of someone else. The freedom to Disnify is undermined. The freedom to counter-tell stories is weakened. The freedom to tinker, especially for the technologist to tinker, is threatened.

QUESTIONS

1. What does Lessig mean by the "freedom to Disnify"?

2. If you had the power to rewrite the law of copyright, would you want to? If so, give it a try. It may be more productive to work with a classmate or two. If not, write a critique of the revisions proposed by one or more of your classmates.

3. **Research:** Find out what you can about Lessig. What background does he bring to the debate about expanding or limiting IP rights? Who are his supporters? Detractors? What has he written or spoken about since 2003 (when this article was published)?

4. Is a Creative Commons license really "the middle ground" sought by all sides? Wikipedia, Google, MIT Open Courseware, Flickr, and the Public Library of Science all make use of creative commons licenses. What are the benefits/risks of a notice that reads "some rights reserved"?

    Research: Find out what the recording industry and RIAA attorney Hilary Rosen think of the creative commons license.

5. Apple and Microsoft have copyrighted their operating systems. This means, for example, that a software engineer who wants to write a program to run on Windows must pay Microsoft for a license to use its Windows code. Another operating system, Linux, is not copyrighted and can be freely copied. Since the 1980s, self-styled hacker Richard Stallman has promoted a "copyleft" license through his foundation, GNU. Known as a General Public License (GPL), it allows anyone

to see, modify, or redistribute the underlying computer source code as long as they publish their changes when they redistribute the software. In June 2007, Stallman's Free Software Foundation released a new version, GPL3. Anyone who contributes to GPL3-licensed software automatically licenses others to use any underlying patents. Those who buy a device that uses GPL software, like TiVo, should be free to change the software.

As the Free Software Web site explains:

Some devices are designed to deny users access to install or run modified versions of the software inside them, although the manufacturer can do so. This is fundamentally incompatible with the aim of protecting users' freedom to change the software.... Therefore, we have designed this version of the GPL to prohibit the practice for those [products made for individual use.] ...

More than 30,000 projects relied on GPL1 and GPL2, including some run by IBM and Novell. **Research**: Find out how this newest version of free software has been received. Who has been critical of it, and why?

—■———

Digital Millennium Copyright Act

"[F]or all I know, the monks had a fit when Gutenberg made his press."
—JUSTICE STEPHEN BREYER, *Oral Argument in Metro-Goldwyn-Mayer Studios, Inc. v. Grokster, Ltd.* (2005).

Once experts figured out how to digitalize movies, filmmakers found themselves in a quandary. The quality of DVDs is superior to that of videotapes, opening the door to a potentially lucrative market of home viewers. But, just as VCRs make it easy to tape a movie shown on TV, computers make it easy to copy a DVD. As the next case explains, the film industry tried to build digital walls, such as encryption codes and password protections, to prevent piracy. At the same time, they lobbied Congress for laws to make it easier to police the unlawful distribution of DVDs by combating piracy in its earlier stages, before the work was even copied. The Digital Millennium Copyright Act (DMCA) did just what the industry had hoped for: It targeted both pirates who would circumvent digital walls and anyone who would traffic in a technology primarily designed to circumvent a digital wall.

■ ■ ■

In the next case, eight motion picture studios invoke their rights under the anti-trafficking provisions of the DMCA to stop Internet Web site owners from posting computer software to decrypt DVD movies or from linking to other Web sites that made decryption software available. The defendant, publisher of a hacker magazine and its affiliated Web site,[10] argues that the DMCA violates the First Amendment.

---

[10] The court describes the hacker community as one that "includes serious computer-science scholars conducting research on protection techniques, computer buffs intrigued by the challenge of trying to circumvent access-limiting devices or perhaps hoping to promote security by exposing flaws in protection techniques, mischief-makers interested in disrupting computer operations, and thieves, including copyright infringers who want to acquire copyrighted material (for personal use or resale) without paying for it."

UNIVERSAL CITY STUDIOS, INC.
v. ERIC CORLEY

United States Court of Appeals, Second Circuit, 2001
273 F.3d 429

Newman, Circuit Judge

The improved quality of a movie in a digital format brings with it the risk that a virtually perfect copy ... can be readily made at the click of a computer control and instantly distributed to countless recipients throughout the world over the Internet....

[To minimize the piracy threat, the entertainment industry] enlisted the help of members of the consumer electronics and computer industries who in mid-1996 developed the Content Scramble System ("CSS"),... an encryption scheme that employs an algorithm configured by a set of "keys" to encrypt a DVD's contents.... [For a fee, the studios licensed these player keys to DVD-makers, who were obliged to keep them confidential and prevent any transmission from a DVD drive to any "internal recording device" such as a computer hard drive.]

With encryption technology and licensing agreements in hand, the studios began releasing movies on DVDs in 1997, and DVDs quickly gained in popularity, becoming a significant source of studio revenue....

In September 1999, Jon Johansen, a Norwegian teenager, collaborating with two unidentified individuals he met on the Internet, reverse-engineered a licensed DVD player ... and culled from it the player keys and other information necessary to decrypt CSS.... Johansen wrote a decryption program executable on Microsoft's operating system. That program was called, appropriately enough, "DeCSS."

If a user runs the DeCSS program ... with a DVD in the computer's disk drive, DeCSS will decrypt the DVD's CSS protection, allowing the user to copy the DVD's files and place the copy on the user's hard drive. The result is a very large computer file that can be played ... and copied, manipulated, and transferred just like any other computer file....

Johansen posted the executable object code, but not the source code, for DeCSS on his web site. Within months, ... DeCSS was widely available on the Internet, in both object code and various forms of source code.

In November 1999, [Defendant] Corley wrote and placed on his web site, 2600.com, an article about the DeCSS phenomenon. His web site is an auxiliary to the print magazine, *2600: The Hacker Quarterly*, which Corley has been publishing since 1984.... [T]he focus of the publications is on the vulnerability of computer security systems, and more specifically, how to exploit that vulnerability in order to circumvent the security systems. Representative articles explain how to steal an Internet domain name and how to break into the computer systems at Federal Express....

Corley's article about DeCSS detailed how CSS was cracked, and described the movie industry's efforts to shut down web sites posting DeCSS. It also explained that DeCSS could be used to copy DVDs. At the end of the article, [he] posted copies of the [computer] object and source code of DeCSS ... [because] "in a journalistic world you have to show your evidence"... [and] links ... to other web sites where DeCSS could be found....

[In the next section, the court addresses Corley's defense: that the DMCA violates the First Amendment. First, the court must decide whether DeCSS code is "protected speech":]

Communication does not lose constitutional protection as "speech" simply because it is expressed in the language of computer code. Mathematical formulae and musical scores are written in "code," i.e., symbolic notations not comprehensible to the uninitiated, and yet both are covered by the First Amendment. If someone chose to write a novel entirely in computer object code by using strings of 1's and 0's for each letter of each word, the resulting work would be no different for constitutional purposes than if it had been written in English....

Computer programs are not exempted from the category of First Amendment speech simply because their instructions require use of a computer. A recipe is no less "speech" because it calls for the use of an oven, and a musical score is no less "speech" because it specifies performance on an electric guitar....

Having concluded that computer code conveying information is "speech" within the meaning of the First Amendment, we next consider, to a limited extent, the scope of the protection that code enjoys....

[The court then quotes approvingly from the trial judge's opinion that:]

Society increasingly depends upon technological means of controlling access to digital files and systems, whether they are military computers, bank records, academic records, copyrighted works, or something else entirely. There are far too many who, given any opportunity, will bypass security measures, some for the sheer joy of doing it, some for innocuous reasons, and others for more malevolent purposes. Given the virtually instantaneous and worldwide dissemination widely available via the Internet, the only rational assumption is that once a computer program capable of bypassing such an access control system is disseminated, it will be used....

There was a time when copyright infringement could be dealt with quite adequately by focusing on the infringing act. If someone wished to make and sell high quality but unauthorized copies of a copyrighted book, for example, the infringer needed a printing press. The copyright holder, once aware of the appearance of infringing copies, usually was able to trace the copies up the chain of distribution, find and prosecute the infringer, and shut off the infringement at the source.

In principle, the digital world is very different. Once a decryption program like DeCSS is written, it quickly can be sent all over the world. Every recipient is capable not only of decrypting and perfectly copying plaintiffs' copyrighted DVDs, but also of re-transmitting perfect copies of DeCSS and thus enabling every recipient to do the same. They likewise are capable of transmitting perfect copies of the decrypted DVD. The process potentially is exponential rather than linear....

In considering the scope of First Amendment protection for a decryption program like DeCSS, we must recognize that the essential purpose of encryption code is to prevent unauthorized access. Owners of all property rights are entitled to prohibit access to their property by unauthorized persons. Homeowners can install locks on the doors of their houses. Custodians of valuables can place them in safes.... These and similar security devices can be circumvented. Burglars can use skeleton keys to open door locks. Thieves can obtain the combinations to safes....

Our case concerns a security device, CSS computer code, that prevents access by unauthorized persons to DVD movies.... CSS is like a lock on a homeowner's door, a combination of a safe, or a security device attached to a store's products.

DeCSS is computer code that can decrypt CSS. In its basic function, it is like a skeleton key that can open a locked door [or] a combination that can open a safe....

[R]egulation of decryption code like DeCSS is challenged in this case because DeCSS differs from a skeleton key in one important respect: it not only is capable of performing the function of unlocking the encrypted DVD movie, it also is a form of communication.... As a communication, the DeCSS code has a claim to being "speech," and as "speech," it has a claim to being protected by the First Amendment.... [But] the capacity of a decryption program like DeCSS to accomplish unauthorized indeed, unlawful access to [copyrighted] materials ... must inform and limit the scope of its First Amendment protection....

[Held: An injunction against posting DeCSS on the Web or linking to other Web sites that contain DeCSS is warranted. The posting restriction is justified because the government has a substantial interest in preventing unauthorized access to encrypted copyright material, and there is no less restrictive way of preventing instantaneous worldwide distribution of the decryption code. The ban on posting links is needed to regulate the "opportunity instantly to enable anyone anywhere to gain unauthorized access to copyrighted movies on DVDs."]

QUESTIONS

1. What is DeCSS? What was the defendant's legal claim, and why did he lose this case?

2. Identify the various stakeholders in the online music-swapping controversy created by Napster and its progeny. How ethical are these services from a free market perspective? A utilitarian or deontological one? What would a feminist interpretation such as Debora Halbert's bring to the table?

3. Is there a difference, ethically, between the copyright infringing activity of a music file sharing service and those who use it? Between a hacker like Johansen who created DeCSS, Corley who disseminated it, and someone who accesses and uses it to watch a movie? Is it fair that copyright law, for the most part, is enforced against the Groksters and Corleys of the digital world? Why or why not?

4. Under the DMCA, nonprofit educational service providers (e.g., state colleges) are protected when a faculty member or graduate student infringes copyright while teaching or researching if three conditions are met: (i) the activities do not involve providing recommended or instructional materials for a course taught at the institution within the preceding 3-year period; (ii) within that same time, the university received no more than two notifications of claimed infringement by the same person; and (iii) the institution provides all users with information regarding compliance with copyright law. The individual faculty member or graduate student, however, can be found liable.
   a. Why do you think the law does not apply to undergraduate infringement? Should it?
   b. Find out whether, and how, your school informs Internet users of their obligations to comply with copyright law, and evaluate the effectiveness of this policy.

5. Are any of the following in violation of the DMCA? (a) 24-year-old Jorge Romero allegedly uploaded the first four episodes of the TV show *24* to the Internet and posted links to the pirated content on other Web sites to make it easier for viewers to find them. (b) Some cites provide users with menus of links to video clips that are stored on other Web sites' computer servers. Many of those video clips are protected by copyright.

6. Viacom made news headlines when it sued YouTube and its owner, Google, for more than $1 billion, claiming YouTube had not done enough to prevent its users from posting thousands of copyrighted video clips to its site. **Research**: Find out what has happened with this lawsuit.

7. When a hacker unearthed the string of 32 digits and letters that comprise a new antipiracy code, AACS, from his movie-playing software in February 2007, he posted it on a Web bulletin board. The code spread among tech-savvy users via blogs and technology Web sites. When the code's owner (the Advanced Access Content System Licensing Administrator), sent notices to "cease and desist" posting the code in violation of the DMCA, the hacker community resisted. One 24-year-old musician improvised a melody to accompany his singing of the code and posted his song to YouTube. A Washington engineer created a Web page featuring the code, "obscured in an encrypted format that only insiders could appreciate." Is this, in the words of one news reporter, "a lesson in mob power on the Internet and the futility of censorship in the digital world"?[11]

---

[11] Brad Stone, "Antipiracy Code, Once a Secret, Spreads on Web," *The New York Times*, p.A-1, May 3, 2007.

8. According to the Business Software Alliance (BSA), globally, 41 percent of the software loaded on personal computers in 2009 was unlicensed, costing the software industry losses close to $53 billion.[12] Is there an ethical distinction between illegally downloaded music and unlicensed software? Why or why not?

■ ■ ■

A DIGITAL LIBRARY FOR THE WORLD?

Since the 1970s, Project Gutenberg (PG) has been creating a full-text, online archive of public domain documents—the first was the United States Declaration of Independence—and books. This nonprofit is run by volunteers who scan and then proofread mostly English library texts and maintain the Project's online catalog. The primary criterion is that the texts are in the public domain (i.e. copyright-free under U.S. copyright law) so that anyone can download them legally, for free. As of June 2010, PG claimed 32,000 texts in its digital library.

PG is affiliated with The Internet Archive (IA), an activist organization founded in 1996. IA's mission is to provide permanent access to the cultural artifacts of the digital age to researchers, historians, scholars, people with disabilities, and the general public. Today, working in collaboration with the Library of Congress, the Smithsonian, Project Gutenberg, and libraries around the world, IA offers free public access to its collection of public domain books (1,600,000 by Spring 2010), music, moving images (film, TV), software, and Web site images (the "wayback machine"). Unlike Project Gutenberg, the Archive pays its staff, with funding from donations, foundations, partnerships, and its Web-crawling services.

Project Gutenbeg and the IA are not the only players. Google began scanning out-of-print books in 2002 to create a kind of universal card catalogue. Many were "orphan works"—technically still under copyright, but difficult to impossible to locate the holder for permission to digitize.

In 2005, the Authors Guild and the Association of American Publishers filed class action lawsuits, claiming that Google infringed on copyright when it digitalized books without permission. Claiming fair use, Google argued that it provided only snippets—not the full text—of copyrighted material. Still, Google put its project on hold. The parties reached a complex settlement in 2008 under which Google would pay out $125 million: $45 million to rightsholders whose copyrights had been infringed and $34.5 million to create a Book Rights Registry, under which Google would collect and dispense royalties. The proposed settlement fell apart over objections from European publishers and authors, the U.S. Justice Department and others, including those with connections to the IA.

In 2009, the federal trial court in New York gave preliminary approval to a modified—but still long and complex—settlement proposal that would address some of the concerns raised and allow Google to proceed with the project. Final approval was pending as this book goes to press.

In April 2010, photographers and artists brought a new suit, claiming Google had copied, stored, and electronically displayed their work—photos, illustrations, and graphic works—without permission.

---

[12] http://global.bsa.org/internetreport2009/

Beyond Copyright: Misappropriation, Trademark, Patents, and Trade Secrets

Not every product of the human mind is—or can become—fixed in the kinds of "tangible expression" that can be copyrighted. Nor is federal copyright law the only source of protection for intellectual property. The following case involves a claim of misappropriation under California's state law.

WHITE v. SAMSUNG AND DEUTSCH ASSOCIATES
United States Court of Appeals, Ninth Circuit, 1992
971 F.2d 1395

GOODWIN, Senior Circuit Judge

Plaintiff Vanna White is the hostess of "Wheel of Fortune," one of the most popular game shows in television history. An estimated forty million people watch the program daily. Capitalizing on the fame which her participation in the show has bestowed on her, White markets her identity to various advertisers.

The dispute in this case arose out of a series of advertisements prepared for Samsung by Deutsch. The series ran in at least half a dozen publications with widespread, and in some cases national, circulation.

… Each [ad] depicted a current item from popular culture and a Samsung Electronics product. Each was set in the twenty-first century and conveyed the message that the Samsung product would still be in use by that time. By hypothesizing outrageous future outcomes for the cultural items, the ads created humorous effects. For example, one lampooned current popular notions of an unhealthy diet by depicting a raw steak with the caption: "Revealed to be health food. 2010 A.D...."

The advertisement which prompted the current dispute was for Samsung videocassette recorders (VCRs). The ad depicted a robot, dressed in a wig, gown, and jewelry which Deutsch consciously selected to resemble White's hair and dress. The robot was posed next to a game board which is instantly recognizable as the Wheel of Fortune game show set, in a stance for which White is famous. The caption of the ad read: "Longest-running game show. 2012 A.D...."

[The court must determine whether the defendants have violated Ms. White's common law right of publicity, by "appropriat[ing her] name or likeness to [their] advantage, commercially or otherwise" without her consent. Since they had not actually used Vanna White's name or her real likeness in the ad, defendants argued they did not "appropriate" her. But the Court decided not to limit the manner of appropriation in this way.]

[T]he most popular celebrities are not only the most attractive to advertisers, but also the easiest to evoke without resorting to obvious means such as name, likeness, or voice.

Consider a hypothetical advertisement which depicts a mechanical robot with male features, an African-American complexion, and a bald head. The robot is wearing black high top Air Jordan basketball sneakers, and a red basketball uniform with black trim, baggy shorts, and the number 23 (though not revealing "Bulls" or "Jordan" lettering). The ad depicts the robot dunking a basketball one-handed, stiff-armed, legs extended like open scissors, and tongue hanging out. Now envision that this ad is run on television during professional basketball games. Considered individually, the robot's physical attributes, its dress, and its stance tell us little. Taken together, they lead to the only conclusion that any sports viewer who has registered a discernible pulse in the past five years would reach: the ad is about Michael Jordan.

Viewed separately, the individual aspects of the advertisement in the present case say little. Viewed together, they leave little doubt about the celebrity the ad is meant to depict....

Television and other media create marketable celebrity identity value. Considerable energy and ingenuity are expended by those who have achieved celebrity value to exploit it for profit. The law protects the celebrity's sole right to exploit this value whether the celebrity has achieved her fame out of rare ability, dumb luck, or a combination thereof.... Because White has alleged facts showing that Samsung and Deutsch had appropriated her identity, [she is entitled to a trial on her common law right of publicity claim.]

[In the next section, the court dismisses the defendant's claim that their parody is protected under the First Amendment:]

In defense, defendants cite a number of cases for the proposition that their robot ad constituted protected speech. The only cases they cite which are even remotely relevant to this case are *Hustler Magazine v. Falwell* and *L.L. Bean, Inc. v. Drake Publishers*.... Those cases involved parodies of advertisements run for the purpose of poking fun at Jerry Falwell and L.L. Bean, respectively. This case involves a true advertisement run for the purpose of selling Samsung VCRs. The ad's spoof of Vanna White and Wheel of Fortune is subservient and only tangentially related to the ad's primary message: "buy Samsung VCRs." Defendants' parody arguments are better addressed to non-commercial parodies. The difference between a "parody" and a "knock-off" is the difference between fun and profit.... [After the appellate decision, and before the trial, the defendants sought a rehearing. They lost, but two justices agreed with them, expressing their views in this dissenting opinion:]

KOZINSKI, Circuit Judge, with Whom Circuit Judges O'SCANNLAIN and KLEINFELD Join, Dissenting

Saddam Hussein wants to keep advertisers from using his picture in unflattering contexts.... Clint Eastwood doesn't want tabloids to write about him.... The Girl Scouts don't want their image soiled by association with certain activities.... George Lucas wants to keep Strategic Defense Initiative fans from calling it "Star Wars."... And scads of copyright holders see purple when their creations are made fun of....

Something very dangerous is going on here. Private property, including intellectual property, is essential to our way of life. It provides an incentive for investment and innovation; it stimulates the flourishing of our culture; it protects the moral entitlements of people to the fruits of their labors. But reducing too much to private property can be bad medicine. Private land, for instance, is far more useful if separated from other private land by public streets, roads and highways. Public parks, utility rights-of-way and sewers reduce the amount of land in private hands, but vastly enhance the value of the property that remains.

So too it is with intellectual property. Overprotecting intellectual property is as harmful as underprotecting it. Creativity is impossible without a rich public domain. Nothing today, likely nothing since we tamed fire, is genuinely new: Culture, like science and technology, grows by accretion, each new creator building on the works of those who came before. Overprotection stifles the very creative forces it's supposed to nurture.

The Panel's opinion is a classic case of overprotection....

The ad that spawned this litigation starred a robot dressed in a wig, gown, and jewelry reminiscent of Vanna White's hair and dress ... posed next to a Wheel-of-Fortune-like game board.... The gag here, I take it, was that Samsung would still be around when White had been replaced by a robot.

Perhaps failing to see the humor, White sued, alleging Samsung infringed her right of publicity by "appropriating" her "identity." Under California law, White has the exclusive right to use her name, likeness, signature, and voice for commercial purposes. But Samsung didn't use her name, voice, or signature, and it certainly didn't use her likeness. The ad just wouldn't have been funny had it depicted White or someone who resembled her—the whole joke was that the game show host(ess) was a robot, not a real person. No one seeing the ad could have thought this was supposed to be White in 2012. The district judge quite reasonably held that, because Samsung didn't use White's name, likeness, voice, or signature, it didn't violate her right of publicity.... Not so, says the panel majority: The California right of publicity can't possibly be limited to name and likeness. If it were, the majority reasons, a "clever advertising strategist" could avoid using White's name or likeness but nevertheless remind people of her with impunity.... To prevent this,... the panel majority holds that the right of publicity must extend beyond name and likeness, to ... anything that "evoke[s]" her personality....

Intellectual property rights aren't like some constitutional rights, absolute guarantees protected against all kinds of interference, subtle as well as blatant. They cast no penumbras, emit no emanations: The very point of intellectual property laws is that they protect only against certain specific kinds of appropriation. I can't publish unauthorized copies of, say, *Presumed Innocent*; I can't make a movie out of it. But I'm perfectly free to write a book about an idealistic young prosecutor on trial for a crime he didn't commit.

So what if I got the idea from *Presumed Innocent*? So what if it reminds readers of the original?... All creators draw in part on the work of those who came before, referring to it, building on it, poking fun at it; we call this creativity, not piracy.

The majority ... [is] creating a new ... right.... It's replacing the existing balance between the interests of the celebrity and those of the public by a different balance, one substantially more favorable to the celebrity. Instead of having an exclusive right in her name, likeness, signature or voice, every famous person now has an exclusive right to anything that reminds the viewer of her....

Consider how sweeping this new right is. What is it about the ad that makes people think of White? It's not the robot's wig, clothes, or jewelry; there must be ten million blond women (many of them quasi-famous) who wear dresses and jewelry like White's. It's that the robot is posed near the "Wheel of Fortune" game board. Remove the game board from the ad, and no one would think of Vanna White.... But once you include the game board, anybody standing beside it—a brunette woman, a man wearing women's clothes, a monkey in a wig and gown—would evoke White's image, precisely the way the robot did.... The panel is giving White an exclusive right not in what she looks like or who she is, but in what she does for a living.

This is entirely the wrong place to strike the balance. Intellectual property rights aren't free: They're imposed at the expense of future creators and of the public at large. Where would we be if Charles Lindbergh had an exclusive right in the concept of a heroic solo aviator? If Arthur Conan Doyle had gotten a copyright in the idea of the detective story, or Albert Einstein had patented the theory of relativity?... Intellectual property law is full of careful balances between what's set aside for the owner and what's left in the public domain for the rest of us: The relatively short life of patents; the longer, but finite, life of copyrights; copyright's idea-expression dichotomy; the fair use doctrine; the prohibition on copyrighting facts; the compulsory license of television broadcasts and musical compositions.... All of these diminish an intellectual property owner's rights. All let the public use something created by someone else. But all are necessary to maintain a free environment in which creative genius can flourish.

The intellectual property right created by the panel here has none of these essential limitations.... Future Vanna Whites might not get the chance to create their personae, because their employers may fear some celebrity will claim the persona is too similar to her own. The public will be robbed of parodies of celebrities, and our culture will be deprived of the valuable safety valve that parody and mockery create. Moreover, consider the moral dimension, about which the panel majority seems to have gotten so exercised. Saying Samsung "appropriated" something of White's begs the question: Should White have the exclusive right to something as broad and amorphous as her "identity"? Samsung's ad didn't simply copy White's shtick—like all parody, it created something new. True, Samsung did it to make money, but White does whatever she does to make money, too; the majority talks of "the difference between fun and profit," but in the entertainment industry fun *is* profit. Why is Vanna White's right to exclusive for-profit use of her person—a persona that might not even be her own creation, but that of a writer, director, or producer—superior to Samsung's right to profit by creating its own inventions?...

The panel, however, does more than misinterpret California law: By refusing to recognize a parody exception to the right of publicity, the panel directly contradicts the federal Copyright Act. Samsung didn't merely parody Vanna White. It parodied Vanna White appearing in "Wheel of Fortune," a copyrighted television show, and parodies of copyrighted works are governed by federal copyright law....

Finally, I can't see how giving White the power to keep others from evoking her image in the public's mind can be squared with the First Amendment.... The First Amendment isn't just about religion or politics—it's also about protecting the free development of our national culture. Parody, humor, [and] irreverence are all vital components of the marketplace of ideas. The last thing we need, the last thing the First Amendment will tolerate, is a law that lets public figures keep people from mocking them, or from "evok[ing]" their images in the mind of the public....

In our pop culture, where salesmanship must be entertaining and entertainment must sell, the line between the commercial and non-commercial has not merely blurred; it has disappeared. Is the Samsung parody any different from a parody on Saturday Night Live or in *Spy Magazine?* Both are equally profit-motivated. Both use a celebrity's identity to sell things—one to sell VCRs, the other to sell advertising. Both mock their subjects. Both try to make people laugh. Both add something, perhaps something worthwhile and memorable, perhaps not, to our culture.

Commercial speech is a significant, valuable part of our national discourse....

For better or worse, we are the Court of Appeals for the Hollywood Circuit. Millions of people toil in the shadow of the law we make, and much of their livelihood is made possible by the existence of intellectual property rights. But much of their livelihood and much of the vibrancy of our culture also depends on the existence of other intangible rights: The right to draw ideas from a rich and varied public domain, and the right to mock, for profit as well as fun, the cultural icons of our time. [I dissent.]

QUESTIONS

1. Is there intellectual property at stake in this case? Explain. How might copyright law apply to the case?

2. Try to articulate the moral judgments each side uses to bolster its legal arguments. Which do you find more persuasive? Why?

■   ■   ■

Trademarks

Federal trademark law—the Lanham Trademark Act (1946) and the Federal Trademark Dilution Act of 1995—protects a company's ownership rights to the name, logo, or symbol that identifies its products. Nike's swoosh, McDonald's arches, and the Xerox name are all identifiable trademarks. The company has an economic interest in the mark it has created, and a right to prevent competitors from using it for their own benefit or in ways that would harm its rightful owner. Cases involving infringement require a showing that the use of a competitor's mark is substantially likely to confuse consumers about the source of a product, or suggest that the trademark's owner made an endorsement it didn't make. Anyone—even a noncompetitor—can be guilty of dilution if they do something to blur or tarnish a trademark, whittling away its selling power through unauthorized use on dissimilar, usually shoddy, products. But not every use is an infringement or dilution of another's trademark. For example, independent candidate for President Ralph Nader borrowed from the long-running marketing campaign known as the "Priceless Ads." Nader's ads began with a series of items showing the price of each ("grilled tenderloin for fundraiser: $1,000 a plate; "campaign ads filled with half-truths: $10 million;" "promises to special interest groups: over $100 billion"). It ends with a phrase identifying a priceless intangible that cannot be purchased ("Find out the truth: priceless. There are some things that money can't buy."). The ad was shown on television for a two-week period and appeared on Nader's Web site. When MasterCard sued the campaign for infringing and diluting its trademark, it lost. The court found that there was no infringement because viewers would not be confused into thinking MasterCard endorsed the Nader campaign, and no dilution because it was a non-commercial use that could not harm MasterCard.[13]

Patents

United States patent law protects the rights of those who discover tools, machines, processes, and other "novel, useful and non-obvious" inventions. The range of patentable ideas is enormous—from the chemical method for making pearl ash that won the first U.S. patent, to such recent inventions as Amazon.com's one-click Internet checkout ("business method"), a new variety of hybrid corn, and receptor genes on the human genome sequence.

In the United States, most patent applications—with all of the information about how to make and use the invention—are now published 18 months after the application is filed.

The patent, once acquired, gives the inventor a complete monopoly for a limited time (20 years), during which no one else may use or profit from the invention without permission. However, competitors can challenge the validity of a patent in the courts where a final determination is made as to whether a patent should have been granted.

Assume that a pharmaceutical company develops and patents a new medicine that is approved by the FDA. If the U.S. Office of Patents and Trademarks (PTO) grants a patent, the company ("inventor") will have complete control over distribution of the drug, deciding whether and how to license it to other manufacturers. Once the patent has expired, however, generic versions, based on publicly available information about its chemical makeup, can legally be sold by competitors.

In addition to utility patents, the American Inventors Protection Act allows an inventor to apply for a "design patent." These are primarily granted for ornamental designs on useful objects, and have a shorter term than utility patents (14 years.)

■ ■ ■

In 1997 Bernard L. Bilski and Rand A. Warsaw filed an application claiming a patent in a method for hedging risk in the field of commodities trading. Their claimed "business method" envisions an intermediary, the "commodity provider," that would, for example, buy coal from mining companies at a fixed price and resell coal to power plants at a different fixed price. Power plants would be protected against a huge spike in the price of coal, the coal miners against an unexpected drop in price, and the commodity provider would make a profit. According to the patent claim, the same method could be used for both commodities and options, i.e., rights to purchase or sell the commodity at a particular price within a particular timeframe. When the Patent and Trademark Office denied the patent, Bilski and Warsaw appealed to the courts.

---

[13] *MasterCard International Inc. v. Nader 2000 Primary Committee, Inc.*, 2004 WL 434404 (D. Ct. 2004).

IN RE BILSKI
United States Court of Appeals, Federal Circuit, (2008)
545 F.3d 943

MICHEL, Chief Judge

... As this appeal turns on whether Applicants' invention as claimed meets the requirements set forth in § 101 [of the Patent law] we begin with the words of the statute:

Whoever invents or discovers any new and useful process, machine, manufacture, or composition of matter, or any new and useful improvement thereof, may obtain a patent therefor, subject to the conditions and requirements of this title....

[The Supreme] Court has held that a claim is not a patent-eligible "process" if it claims "laws of nature, natural phenomena, [or] abstract ideas." ... Such fundamental principles are "part of the storehouse of knowledge of all men...free to all men and reserved exclusively to none." *Funk Bros. Seed Co. v. Kalo Inoculant Co.*, (U.S. 1948)... "Phenomena of nature, though just discovered, mental processes, and abstract intellectual concepts are not patentable, as they are the basic tools of scientific and technological work."...

The Supreme Court last addressed this issue in 1981 in *Diehr*, which concerned a patent application seeking to claim a process for producing cured synthetic rubber products. The claimed process took temperature readings during cure and used a mathematical algorithm, the Arrhenius equation, to calculate the time when curing would be complete. Noting that a mathematical algorithm alone is unpatentable because mathematical relationships are akin to a law of nature, the Court nevertheless held that the claimed process was patent-eligible subject matter....

The Court in *Diehr* ... drew a distinction between those claims that "seek to preempt the use of" a fundamental principle, on the one hand, and claims that seek only to foreclose others from using a particular "application " of that fundamental principle, on the other....

In *Diehr*, the Court held that the claims at issue did not pre-empt all uses of the Arrhenius equation but rather claimed only "a process for curing rubber...which incorporates in it a more efficient solution of the equation." The process as claimed included several specific steps to control the curing of rubber more precisely: "These include installing rubber in a press, closing the mold,... [etc.]." Thus, one would still be able to use the Arrhenius equation in any process not involving curing rubber, and more importantly, even in any process to cure rubber that did not include performing "all of the other steps in their claimed process."...

The question before us then is whether Applicants' claim recites a fundamental principle and, if so, whether it would pre-empt substantially all uses of that fundamental principle if allowed....

The Supreme Court ... has enunciated a definitive test to determine whether a process claim is tailored narrowly enough to encompass only a particular application of a fundamental principle rather than to pre-empt the principle itself. A claimed process is surely patent-eligible ... if: (1) it is tied to a particular machine or apparatus, or (2) it transforms a particular article into a different state or thing.... A claimed process involving a fundamental principle that uses a particular machine or apparatus would not pre-empt uses of the principle that do not also use the specified machine or apparatus in the manner claimed. And a claimed process that transforms a particular article to a specified different state or thing by applying a fundamental principle would not pre-empt the use of the principle to transform any other article, to transform the same article but in a manner not covered by the claim, or to do anything other than transform the specified article....

We hold that the Applicants' process as claimed does not transform any article to a different state or thing.... Given its admitted failure to meet the machine implementation part of the test as well, the claim entirely fails the machine-or-transformation test and is not drawn to patent-eligible subject matter....

Because the applicable test to determine whether a claim is drawn to a patent-eligible process under § 101 is the machine-or-transformation test set forth by the Supreme Court and clarified herein, and Applicants' claim here plainly fails that test, the decision of the Board [of Patents and Trademarks to reject the patent application] is AFFIRMED.

NEWMAN, *Circuit Judge, Dissenting*

The court today acts en banc to impose a new and far-reaching restriction on the kinds of inventions that are eligible to participate in the patent system. The court achieves this result by redefining the word "process" in the patent statute, to exclude all processes that do not transform physical matter or that are not performed by machines. The court thus excludes many of the kinds of inventions that apply today's electronic and photonic technologies, as well as other processes that handle data and information in novel ways. Such processes have long been patent eligible, and contribute to the vigor and variety of today's Information Age. This exclusion of process inventions is contrary to statute, contrary to precedent, and a negation of the constitutional mandate....

The innovations of the "knowledge economy"—of "digital prosperity"—have been dominant contributors to today's economic growth and societal change. Revision of the commercial structure affecting major aspects of today's industry should be approached with care, for there has been significant reliance on the law as it has existed, as many *amici curiae* pointed out. Indeed, the full reach of today's change of law is not clear, and the majority opinion states that many existing situations may require reassessment under the new criteria.

Uncertainty is the enemy of innovation. These new uncertainties not only diminish the incentives available to new enterprise, but disrupt the settled expectations of those who relied on the law as it existed. I respectfully dissent....

The public and the economy have experienced extraordinary advances in information-based and computer-managed processes, supported by an enlarging patent base. The PTO reports that ... there were almost 10,000 patent applications [that may not involve machine-or-transformation] filed in FY 2006 alone, and over 40,000 applications filed since FY 98 when *State Street Bank* was decided.... The industries identified with information-based and data-handling processes ... include fields as diverse as banking and finance, insurance, data processing, industrial engineering, and medicine.

Inventiveness in the computer and information services fields has placed the United States in a position of technological and commercial preeminence. The information technology industry is reported to be "the key factor responsible for reversing the 20-year productivity slow-down from the mid-1970s to the mid-1990s and in driving today's robust productivity growth."...

Bilski's patent application describes his process of analyzing the effects of supply and demand on commodity prices and the use of a coupled transaction strategy to hedge against these risks; this is not a fundamental principle or an abstract idea; it is not a mental process or a law of nature. It is a "process," set out in successive steps, for obtaining and analyzing information and carrying out a series of commercial transactions for the purpose of "managing the consumption risk costs of a commodity sold by a commodity provider at a fixed price."...

MAYER, *Circuit Judge, Dissenting*

[Mayer dissents because he believes the court should have reconsidered and overruled precedent cases. He goes on to explain his views on business method patents.]

... Business method patents do not promote the "useful arts" because they are not directed to any technological or scientific innovation. Although business method applications may use technology—such as computers—to accomplish desired results, the innovative aspect of the claimed method is an entrepreneurial rather than a technological one. Thus, although Bilski's claimed hedging method could theoretically be implemented on a computer, that alone does not render it patentable....

Methods of doing business do not apply "the law of nature to a new and useful end." Because the innovative aspect of such methods is an entrepreneurial rather than a technological one, they should be deemed ineligible for patent protection.... Although business method patents may do much to enrich their owners, they do little to promote scientific research and technological innovation....

Patents granted in the wake of *State Street* have ranged from the somewhat ridiculous to the truly absurd. See, e.g., (method of training janitors to dust and vacuum using video displays); (method for selling expert advice); (method of enticing customers to order additional food at a fast food restaurant); (system for toilet reservations).... There has even been a patent issued on a method for obtaining a patent.

There are a host of difficulties associated with allowing patents to issue on methods of conducting business. Not only do such patents tend to impede rather than promote innovation, they are frequently of poor quality. Most fundamentally, they raise significant First Amendment concerns by imposing broad restrictions on speech and the free flow of ideas.

"[T]he underlying policy of the patent system [is] that 'the things which are worth to the public the embarrassment of an exclusive patent,' ...must outweigh the restrictive effect of the limited patent monopoly."... Thus, Congress may not expand the scope of "the patent monopoly without regard to the ... advancement or social benefit gained thereby."

Patents should be granted to those inventions "which would not be disclosed or devised but for the inducement of a patent." ... Methods of doing business have existed since the earliest days of the Patent Act and have flourished even in the absence of patent protection.... Commentators have argued that "the broad grant of patent protection for methods of doing business is something of a square peg in a sinkhole of uncertain dimensions" since "[n]owhere in the substantial literature on innovation is there a statement that the United States economy suffers from a lack of innovation in methods of doing business." Instead, "the long history of U.S. business is one of innovation, emulation, and innovation again. It also is a history of remarkable creativity and success, all without business method patents until the past few years." ...

Business innovations, by their very nature, provide a competitive advantage and thus generate their own incentives. ("A business entity improves the way it does business in order to be more effective and efficient, to stay ahead of [the] competition, and to make more profit."). The rapid "growth of fast food restaurants, self-service gasoline stations, quick oil change facilities...automatic teller devices...and alternatives for long-distance telephone services" casts real doubt about the need for the additional incentive of patent protection in the commercial realm.

Business method patents, unlike those granted for pharmaceuticals and other products, offer rewards that are grossly disproportionate to the costs of innovation. In contrast to technological endeavors, business innovations frequently involve little or no investment in research and development. Bilski, for example, likely spent only nominal sums to develop his hedging method. The reward he could reap if his application were allowed—exclusive rights over methods of managing risks in a wide array of commodity transactions—vastly exceeds any costs he might have incurred in devising his "invention."....

Instead of providing incentives to competitors to develop improved business techniques, business method patents remove building blocks of commercial innovation from the public domain. Because they restrict competitors from using and improving upon patented business methods, such patents stifle innovation.... "Retarding competition retards further development." "Think how the airline industry might now be structured if the first company to offer frequent flyer miles had enjoyed the sole right to award them or how differently mergers and acquisitions would be financed...if the use of junk bonds had been protected by a patent." By affording patent protection to business practices, "the government distorts the operation of the free market system and reduces the gains from the operation of the market."

It is often consumers who suffer when business methods are patented.... Patented products are more expensive because licensing fees are often passed on to consumers.... Further, as a general matter, "quantity and quality [of patented products] are less than they would be in a competitive market."

Patents on business methods makes American companies less competitive in the global marketplace. American companies can now obtain exclusionary rights on methods of conducting business, but their counterparts in Europe and Japan generally cannot.... Producing products in the United States becomes more expensive because American companies, unlike their overseas counterparts, must incur licensing fees in order to use patented business methods...

Allowing patents to issue on business methods shifts critical resources away from promoting and protecting truly useful technological advances.... When already overburdened examiners are forced to devote significant time to reviewing large numbers of business method applications, the public's access to new and beneficial technologies is unjustifiably delayed....

The time is ripe to repudiate *State Street* and to recalibrate the standards for patent eligibility, thereby ensuring that the patent system can fulfill its constitutional mandate to protect and promote truly useful innovations in science and technology. I dissent from the majority's failure to do so.

RADER, Circuit Judge, Dissenting

... [Because the court] links patent eligibility to the age of iron and steel at a time of subatomic particles and terabytes, I must respectfully dissent....

In simple terms, the statute does not mention "transformations" or any of the other Industrial Age descriptions of subject matter categories that this court endows with inordinate importance today. The Act has not empowered the courts to impose limitations on patent eligible subject matter beyond the broad and ordinary meaning of the terms process, machine, manufacture, and composition of matter. It has instead preserved the promise of patent protection for still unknown fields of invention.

Innovation has moved beyond the brick and mortar world.... Today's software transforms our lives without physical anchors. This court's test not only risks hobbling these advances, but precluding patent protection for tomorrow's technologies. "We still do not know one thousandth of one percent of what nature has revealed to us." Attributed to Albert Einstein. If this court has its way, the Patent Act may not incentivize, but complicate, our search for the vast secrets of nature. When all else fails, consult the statute.

QUESTIONS

1. Under current U.S. patent law "Whoever invents or discovers any new and useful process, machine, manufacture, or composition of matter, or any new and useful improvement thereof, may obtain a patent therefor, subject to the conditions and requirements of this title." Under which category did Bilski and Rand apply?

2. On what basis does the majority find that the business method patent claimed by Bilski and Rand was properly denied?

3. Articulate the underlying values-conflicts between the majority and various dissenting judges. In what ways are those arguments analogous to the debates involving copyright law? How do they differ?

4. The outcome of this case was unanimously affirmed by the United States Supreme Court, 130 S.Ct. 3218 (2010) (June 28, 2010). Justice Kennedy, after suggesting that "students of patent law would be well advised to study these scholarly opinions

(referring to the case opinions you have just read) went on to reject the basic premise of Chief Judge Michel's appellate ruling. Joined by four other Justices, Kennedy stated: "This Court's precedents establish that the machine-or-transformation test is a useful and important clue, an investigative tool, for determining whether some claimed inventions are processes under … [the Patent Law. But] the machine-or-transformation test is not the sole test for deciding whether an invention is a patent-eligible "process." The case was affirmed, however, on the narrow grounds that Bilski and Warsaw claimed a patent in "unpatentable abstract ideas." Justice Stevens agreed that the patent should not have been granted. But he and three other justices argued that the Court should have gone further and ruled that a method for doing business is never patentable. **Research**: Find out how the business community reacted to this ruling by the Supreme Court.

5. Gene sequencing is used in diagnostic testing to determine whether a gene contains mutations that are associated with a particular condition. In 1991, researchers working together under the name "Myriad" sequenced newly located genes linked to an increased risk of breast and ovarian cancers (BRCA1 and 2). The isolated gene sequences were patented by Myriad, which began to offer multiple forms of BRCA 1/2 testing to the general public. At $3,000 a test, by 2008 Myriad—the sole licensor of BRCA 1/2 testing—had revenues of $222 million. In 2009, researchers at competing bio-tech research centers joined with human geneticists, oncologists, genetic counselors, breast cancer survivors, and advocates, and professional associations (the American Society for Clinical Pathology, the American College of Medical Genetics) to challenge patents given to isolated genes and gene sequence. Patients claimed their insurance would not cover the test, doctors that they could provide better—and cheaper—alternative tests, researchers that their efforts were hampered. What legal arguments for and against the patent can you articulate? What ethical issues are raised? *Association of Molecular Pathology* v. *United States Patent and Trademark Office*, 702 F. Supp. 2d 181(S.D.N.Y. 2010).

■ ■ ■

Trade Secret

One alternative to patent protection is to keep your idea to yourself, and to sue anyone who tries to use it. Under state tort laws, a lawsuit can be brought against someone who wrongfully takes ("misappropriates") or discloses a trade secret. You don't register your trade secret as you register a trademark; you don't need to go through a lengthy and costly application procedure as you do for a patent. Suppose, for example, that you create a great recipe for chocolate chip cookies. Written down, the recipe is a "fixed, tangible expression" that can be copyrighted, preventing anyone from reproducing it in other cookbooks without your permission. But the value of the recipe is in the cookies—and even if it remains unpublished, it will lose some of its allure if competitors make the same cookies. If you did not want to go through the patent process, you might still maintain a near-monopoly use of your recipe as long as (1) it has some economic value that derives from the fact that it is not generally known, and (2) you have taken reasonable steps to keep it secret. In most states, you could sue to stop anyone who wrongfully discovered your recipe from using or disclosing it. Under the Uniform Trade Secrets Act—adopted in some form by 46 states and the District of Columbia by 2010—the definition of trade secrete includes theft, bribery, misrepresentation, breach or inducement of a breach of a duty to maintain secrecy, or espionage through electronic or other means in its definition of improper means of learning a trade secret. Figuring out the recipe by taste trials ("reverse engineering"), however, would not be considered wrongful.

Inevitable Disclosure of Trade Secrets

One of the most contentious issues in current trade secret law involves former employees. What happens when a software engineer leaves one company for another—bringing with her not only her general skills and talents, but particular knowledge, including some that may be confidential, acquired over years with the first company?

■ ■ ■

William Redmond, Jr., began working for PepsiCo in 1984. In 1994, a year after he began heading the Northern California Business Unit, Redmond became the General Manager of the entire California business unit. With annual revenues of more than $500 million, the unit [PCNA] represented 20 percent of the company's U.S. profits. Earlier that year, another PepsiCo executive, Donald Uzzi, left the company to head the Gatorade division of Quaker, a PepsiCo competitor. From May until November 1994, Uzzi tried to woo Redmond away from PepsiCo. Redmond said nothing to anyone at PepsiCo until he had a firm, written offer from Quaker. When he did, PepsiCo sued to stop him from working for Quaker. The federal appeals court ruling is the most frequently cited case dealing with what is called the "inevitable disclosure rule."

PEPSICO, INC. v. REDMOND
United States Court of Appeals, Seventh Circuit, 1995
54 F.3d 1262

Flaum, Circuit Judge

The facts of this case lay against a backdrop of fierce beverage-industry competition between Quaker and PepsiCo, especially in "sports drinks" and "new age drinks." Quaker's sports drink, "Gatorade," is the dominant brand in its market niche. PepsiCo introduced its Gatorade rival, "All Sport," in March and April of 1994, but sales of All Sport lag far behind those of Gatorade. Quaker also has the lead in the new-age-drink category [with Snapple].... PepsiCo's products have about half of Snapple's market share. Both companies see 1995 as an important year for their products: PepsiCo has developed extensive plans to increase its market presence, while Quaker is trying to solidify its lead by integrating Gatorade and Snapple distribution. Meanwhile, PepsiCo and Quaker each face strong competition from Coca Cola Co., which has its own sports drink, "Power-Ade," and which introduced its own Snapple-rival, "Fruitopia," in 1994, as well as from independent beverage producers....

Redmond's relatively high-level position at PCNA gave him access to inside information and trade secrets. Redmond, like other PepsiCo management employees, had signed a confidentiality agreement with PepsiCo. That agreement stated in relevant part that he

> w[ould] not disclose at any time, to anyone other than officers or employees of [PepsiCo], or make use of, confidential information relating to the business of [PepsiCo] ... obtained while in the employ of [PepsiCo], which shall not be generally known or available to the public or recognized as standard practices.

PepsiCo filed this ... suit on November 16, 1994, seeking a temporary restraining order to enjoin Redmond from assuming his duties at Quaker and to prevent him from disclosing trade secrets or confidential information to his new employer....

The Illinois Trade Secrets Act ("ITSA"), which governs the trade secret issues in this case, provides that a court may enjoin the "actual or threatened misappropriation" of a trade secret....

The question of threatened or inevitable misappropriation in this case lies at the heart of a basic tension in trade secret law. Trade secret law serves to protect "standards of commercial morality" and "encourage invention and innovation" while maintaining "the public interest in having free and open competition in the manufacture and sale of unpatented goods." Yet that same law should not prevent workers from pursuing their livelihoods when they leave their current positions. This tension is particularly exacerbated when a plaintiff sues to prevent not the actual misappropriation of trade secrets but the mere threat that it will occur....

The ITSA [and precedent cases] lead to the same conclusion: a plaintiff may prove a claim of trade secret misappropriation by demonstrating that defendant's new employment will inevitably lead him to rely on the plaintiff's trade secrets....

PepsiCo presented substantial evidence ... that Redmond possessed extensive and intimate knowledge about PCNA's strategic goals for 1995 in sports drinks and new age drinks. The district court concluded on the basis of that presentation that unless Redmond possessed an uncanny ability to compartmentalize information, he would necessarily be making decisions about Gatorade and Snapple by relying on his knowledge of PCNA trade secrets. It is not the "general skills and knowledge acquired during his tenure with" PepsiCo that PepsiCo seeks to keep from falling into Quaker's hands, but rather "the particularized plans or processes developed by [PCNA] and disclosed to him while the employer-employee relationship existed, which are unknown to others in the industry and which give the employer an advantage over his competitors."...

Admittedly, PepsiCo has not brought a traditional trade secret case, in which a former employee has knowledge of a special manufacturing process or customer list and can give a competitor an unfair advantage by transferring the technology or customers to that competitor....PepsiCo has not contended that Quaker has stolen the All Sport formula or its list of distributors. Rather PepsiCo has asserted that Redmond cannot help but rely on PCNA trade secrets as he helps plot Gatorade and Snapple's new course, and that these secrets will enable Quaker to achieve a substantial advantage by knowing exactly how PCNA will price, distribute, and market its sports drinks and new age drinks and being able to respond strategically....

... PepsiCo finds itself in the position of a coach, one of whose players has left, playbook in hand, to join the opposing team before the big game.

For the foregoing reasons, we affirm the district court's order enjoining Redmond from assuming his responsibilities at Quaker through May 1995, and preventing him forever from disclosing PCNA trade secrets and confidential information.

QUESTIONS

1. What effect does the outcome of this case have on Redmond's ability to earn a living? Should PepsiCo have to rehire him?

2. Suppose Redmond had been terminated by PepsiCo before being hired by Quaker. Do you think this case would be decided differently? Should it be?

3. If you were offered a job by PepsiCo, what impact would cases like Redmond have on your decision?

4. Assume that you are starting a new company to produce computer software and need to hire engineers and computer analysts. What impact might decisions like this one have on your hiring process?

5. Does Redmond's willingness to sell his expertise to the highest bidder violate your sense of commercial morality? Why or why not?

■ ■ ■

Global Intellectual Property Rights (IPR)

Bioprospecting—the worldwide search for health and medicinal uses of natural substances—is a lucrative business. A 2005 report concluded that 62 percent of all cancer drugs were created from bioprospecting discoveries. The key ingredient of Taxol, owned by Bristol-Myers Squibb Company, for example, comes from the bark of the yew tree. As Gelvina Rodriguez Stevenson, author of the next reading explains, it is the traditional knowledge about the use of herbs and plants to heal, shared among native peoples, that provides a map to modern pharmaceutical companies. Stevenson explores the limitations of using patent law to protect the rights of tribal peoples to their traditional knowledge.

TRADE SECRETS: PROTECTING INDIGENOUS ETHNOBIOLOGICAL (MEDICINAL) KNOWLEDGE

Gelvina Rodriguez Stevenson[14]

Today, most major drugs are plant-derived. It is currently believed that there are approximately 35,000 plants in the developing world that have medicinal value. ... The ethnobiological knowledge of indigenous peoples can be extremely effective in focusing the search for new medicines. It is estimated that, by consulting indigenous peoples, "bio-prospectors" can increase the success ratio in trials for useful substances from one success in 10,000 samples to one success in two samples; ... [a]pproximately three quarters of the plant-derived compounds currently used as pharmaceuticals were discovered through research based on plants use by indigenous peoples. Potential cures may be lost as rain forest area diminishes. The rainforest is considered a warehouse of valuable compounds which could aid the development of useful new medicines. It is estimated that only 1,100 of the 35,000 to 40,000 plants with possible undiscovered medicinal or nutritional value for humans have been thoroughly studied by scientists.... It has been suggested that much of the orally transmitted indigenous knowledge ... will also be lost, since it is estimated that 3,000 of the world's 6,000 languages will vanish....

In 1992, the United Nations hosted a Conference on Environment and Development (UNCED) in Brazil.... [This] resulted in the United Nations Convention on Biological Diversity [CBD] which commits signatory countries to conserve biodiversity and equitably share resulting benefits. The signatories also agreed that the benefits of utilizing biodiversity, including technology, should be shared with the source country. The CBD has been ratified by 168 of the 177 countries that are parties to it ... [but has yet to be ratified by the United States.] ...

Recent advances in microelectronics and molecular biology ... enable companies to screen plants more efficiently. This has made bio-prospecting more profitable....

Recently, companies have been protecting these expanding interests by seeking patent protection for valued plant-derived drugs. This has led to an increase in biotech-related patent claims and caused a backlog at the Patent and Trademark Office.

---

[14] Gelvina Rodriguez Stevenson, "Trade Secrets: Protecting Indigenous Ethnobiological (Medicinal) Knowledge," New York University *Journal of International Law and Politics* 32(4), 2000, pp. 1122–1124, 1131–1167. Reprinted by permission.

Using U.S. Patents to Protect Indigenous Ethnobiological Knowledge

A patent is a legal certificate that gives an inventor exclusive rights to prevent others from producing, selling, using, or importing his or her invention for a limited period of time.

While patent law varies somewhat in different countries, it generally protects inventions of a particular subject matter. "Inventions" include machines and other devices, chemical compositions, manufacturing processes, and uses for such inventions that are found to be (1) new, (2) non-obvious, and (3) useful. U.S. patent law requires that an invention be new, i.e., not known or used by others in the United States or published in any country....

The non-obvious requirement establishes that ... [a claimed invention must do more than add some elements to a prior invention. New elements must not be ones that are obvious "to a person having ordinary skill in the art to which said subject matter pertains."] In other words, a patent is considered obvious if a person could have easily created the invention from what was already publicly known....

In order to satisfy the usefulness requirement, commonly known as the utility requirement, the invention must be useful to society. The patent applicant must know exactly what the invention will be useful for and must explain in the application how the invention will be useful.

A naturally occurring subject matter, often called a "product of nature," such as a plant or human cell, is not patentable. However, United States courts have held that the "discoverer" may obtain a patent on the biological matter in a purified, isolated, or altered form. The Supreme Court, in fact, has held that genetically altered living organisms are patentable as "manufactures" or "compositions of matter." Patent procurement is expensive and procedurally complex. In the United States, the only way that an inventor may obtain a patent is by filing a timely application with the Patent and Trademark Office, a federal government agency.... In general, [patents] are awarded to a natural person, but can be, and frequently are, assigned to another party or corporate entity. Patents ... may be assigned or licensed in exchange for a payment of royalties.... A patent owner may file a civil suit for infringement against anyone who, without authority, makes, uses, or sells the patented invention. The infringer need not be aware that he is infringing and is held to infringe even if he achieves the same invention independently. Under U.S. law, possible remedies include injunctions and damages, with a minimum damage award included in the statute, and attorney's fees.

It is difficult for indigenous peoples to obtain a patent on their ethnobiological knowledge for a number of reasons. All of the above-mentioned prerequisites for patentability, because they are grounded in Western notions of intellectual property, make it easier for Western pharmaceutical companies to obtain a patent on a modification of indigenous ethnobiological knowledge than for indigenous communities. Perhaps the most fundamental reason for this disparity is that patent law is based primarily on the goal of providing incentives to individuals for commercial innovation rather than the goal of protecting communal knowledge....

[The] rigid requirements that the inventor be known and be the first to invent, or the first to file in jurisdictions outside the United States, in order to receive a patent, pose an immense obstacle for indigenous communities who wish to patent their ethnobiological knowledge. Another problem with awarding a patent to a "medicine man"... or even to the indigenous community, is that the same cultural and ethnobiological knowledge is often found among several distinct indigenous societies.... It would be unfair if one community were granted a patent, because other neighboring groups which have used the same information for just as long, if not longer, would then be suddenly infringing on a patent while they continued their ancestral practices. Discovering which group was the first to discover the knowledge and first to make use of it is nearly impossible and likely to create societal disruption.

Even if [one indigenous person] were able to show that he was the inventor and were granted a patent, the individualism upon which the patent is philosophically based would still create problems for [his group.] [For example, in] 1992, a British company, The Body Shop, entered into a supply contract with Chief Paulinho Paiakan, a respected leader of the Kayapo. Chief Paiakan agreed to supply to The Body Shop 6,000 liters a year of natural oil to use in hair conditioners in exchange for a small percentage of the profits. The Body Shop gave their payment to Chief Paiakan. [According to] Stephen Corry, an indigenous rights activist and Director General of the organization Survival International... "[t]he project has caused deep divisions amongst the Kayapo exacerbated by the way Paiakan has accumulated great personal wealth and power."...

A great deal of indigenous ethnobiological knowledge has been published and documented by ethnobotanists and other scholars.... This will bar indigenous communities from satisfying the novelty requirement.

An illustration of the barrier that the utility requirement can pose is evident in the problems the National Institute of Health (NIH) has had with the patenting of genes. The NIH failed to receive a patent for gene fragments that are used as markers to aid in the mapping of genes. The Patent and Trademark Office rejected ... the NIH claim that the gene fragments satisfied the utility requirement by their use as markers in the mapping of genes.... The NIH case suggests that although much indigenous knowledge has shown its utility by the simple fact that it has led to the development of products and processes patented by pharmaceutical companies, the PTO may not consider this utility claimable under U.S. standards.

Products of nature, also known as naturally occurring subject matter, are not patentable.... [This means that] Western pharmaceutical companies that isolate an active chemical in a plant and create a genetically engineered plant or animal can receive a patent while indigenous peoples, who use the natural form of the plant, cannot....

Traditional knowledge presents unique problems in determining non-obviousness because it is difficult to determine what the prior art might have been. Presumably, the prior art would be knowledge that the indigenous people had prior to the invention. Since both prior art and claimed invention would be generations old, it would be difficult to determine at what point in time an indigenous group had acquired or developed a particular piece of knowledge, i.e., the invention....

And even if patent law was able to conceive of the entire community as the inventor, neighboring communities are likely to be aware of the plant and its use. This will automatically characterize the plant and its use as obvious. Most importantly, the mere fact that indigenous people often will have possessed the knowledge for centuries may further ensure that the knowledge is considered obvious....

Technically, patent holders have the legal right to prevent imports into the United States of products that were created using technology patented in the United States. Thus, an indigenous community in a developing country could be precluded from exporting products that were developed using existing species if that product is patented in the United States....

Finally, once an invention is patented, the characteristics of the invention are made public, enabling others to obtain the knowledge. Some of the knowledge may be sacred to indigenous communities and they may not want this knowledge shared with other cultures. A patent is effective only for [a limited time period] … and after expiration, its subject matter is freely available for use by the public.

QUESTIONS

1. What are the required elements to obtain a patent? Why is each so difficult for indigenous peoples to demonstrate? What values within indigenous cultures make it difficult or impossible for them to secure U.S. patents for their "inventions"?

2. Elsewhere in her article, Stevenson writes that "the law's preference for pure substances makes it easier for pharmaceutical companies to satisfy the non-obvious requirement and makes it difficult for indigenous communities to do so." She uses as an example: the neem plant. For centuries, farmers in India used ground neem seed as a natural pesticide. Scientists learned from the Indians how they extracted, identified, isolated, and purified the active components in the seed, and used that knowledge to synthesize the active chemical in a lab. In 1994, W.R. Grace and Agrodyne succeeded in getting a patent on the neem derivatives as an advance over the widely known prior art. Does this raise any ethical concerns?

3. Stevenson proposes that trade secret is a more advantageous route than patent law for native peoples. Articulate how trade secret law might be used to protect their rights.

4. For centuries, the Quechua Indians of the Peruvian Andes have been using the frost-resistant root of the maca plant to boost stamina and sex drive. **Research:** Find out what has happened in the lawsuit against New Jersey-based PureWorld Botanicals, granted a patent in 2001 for MacaPure, derived from the active compound in the maca plant.

5. The Ami people are the largest surviving indigenous tribe in Taiwan. Theirs is an oral culture—transmitting cultural knowledge, religion, stories, and songs for thousands of years without a written language. For much of the 20th century, an Ami tribal elder, Lifvon Guo, was a keeper of Ami traditional folksongs. In the 1990s, the Ministers of Culture of Taiwan and France invited some thirty indigenous singers, including Lifvon, to perform in Europe. Without the knowledge or consent of the Ami, the concerts were recorded. Several years later, the German rock group Enigma heard the CD, was captivated by the music, and incorporated Lifvon singing a version of the Ami's traditional *Song of Joy* into what became a worldwide hit: *Song of Innocence*. Enigma paid a nominal copyright fee to the French Ministry of Culture and sold five million copies of its song. Did Lifvon have any intellectual property interest at stake? Did the Ami people? What ethical issues arise here? Do you see any ethical problems? For the full story and a proposed change in the law, see Angela R. Riley, "Recovering Collectivity: Group Rights to Intellectual Property in Indigenous Communities," 18 *CARDOZO ARTS & ENT. L.J.* 175 (2000).

HIGHLIGHTS IN THE DEVELOPMENT OF INTERNATIONAL IPR

- **The Paris Convention (1883).** The first international agreement on IPR was founded on the principle of "national treatment." Signatories agreed to provide foreigners the same IPR protection given to their own citizens, but each nation continued to have its own rules as to what was patentable and how. The World Intellectual Property Organization (WIPO), a specialized agency of the United Nations, currently administers the terms of the Paris Convention.

- **Biodiversity Convention (1992).** An outgrowth of the global Rio Conference, the aims of this agreement are to conserve biological diversity and sustain biological resources for future generations. It recognizes states' sovereign rights over biological resources and calls for protection of the rights of communities and indigenous people to the customary use of biological resources and knowledge systems. Signatories agree to facilitate environmentally sound use of their resources by other members and to assist in the transfer of technology to developing countries so that they can capitalize on their own natural resources, even if it requires sharing innovations protected by intellectual property rights. The United States has not signed this treaty.

- **Trade-Related Aspects of IPR (TRIPS) Agreement (1994).** Strongly supported by the United States and adopted within the framework of the Uruguay Round of Multilateral Trade Negotiations that created the World Trade Organization (WTO), TRIPS incorporates IPR protection into the General Agreement on Tariffs and Trades (GATT). According to TRIPS, "the protection and enforcement of intellectual property rights should contribute to the promotion of technological innovation and to the transfer and dissemination of technology, to the mutual advantage of producers and users of technological knowledge and in a manner conducive to social and economic welfare, and to a balance of rights and obligations."

- **Doha Declaration (2001).** In recognition of the epidemics of HIV/AIDS, tuberculosis, and malaria in developing nations, WTO Ministers reaffirmed TRIPS but agreed to interpret it "in a manner supportive of WTO Members' right to protect public health, and in particular, to promote access to medicines for all." One modification of TRIPS allows countries without the capacity to produce pharmaceuticals to issue compulsory licenses to import them when urgently needed. Another extended the deadline for the least developed countries to enforce TRIPS in relation to pharmaceuticals until 2016.

Human Rights and IP

From 2003-2005, the UN convened a multistage World Summit on the Information Society. Nearly 11,000 participants from 175 countries—including 50 heads of state/governments and Vice-Presidents, 82 Ministers, and 26 Vice-Ministers, leaders of international organizations, and the private sector—held a series of meetings to agree to a set of principles to guide the development of an Information Society. The following statement grew out of one of the preliminary meetings, convened in November 2003. As you read it, see if you agree with the authors' view of the ethical use of information and communication technologies (ICTs.)

STATEMENT ON HUMAN RIGHTS, HUMAN DIGNITY
AND THE INFORMATION SOCIETY[15]

- The information and communication society benefits from new technologies, which can serve critical functions for human rights education and learning and more generally contribute to social change through the realization of human rights.
- ICTs [Information and Communication Technologies] must be put at the service of education and lifelong learning for all. In particular, as privileged instruments of human rights education and learning, they should help to enable and empower humans across the world and across generations and cultures to know, claim and own their human rights and to respect and promote those of others in a spirit of solidarity. ICTs will make a major contribution to societal development on the basis of a commonly shared culture of human rights.

Freedom of expression and information

- Full respect for freedom of expression and information by States and non-State actors is an essential precondition for the building of a free and inclusive information and communication society. ICTs must not be used to curtail this fundamental freedom. There must be no censorship and no arbitrary controls or constraints on participants in the information process, on the content of information or its transmission and dissemination.... National security legislation to combat terrorism must respect freedom of expression and information standards and be subject to judicial review, as well as international scrutiny.
- The trend to provide public access to the information produced or maintained by governments and protected under "freedom of information" legislation should be extended to all countries that do not have such legislation, ensuring that government-controlled information is timely, complete and accessible in a format and language the public can understand....

Human right to privacy

- ... The use of increasingly invasive means of surveillance and of interception of communications, of intrusive profiling and identification and of biometric identification technology, the development of communication technologies with built-in surveillance capacities, the collection and misuse of genetic data, genetic testing, the growing invasion of privacy at the workplace and the weakening of data protection regimes give rise to serious concerns from the point of view of respect for human dignity and human rights. New means must be developed to protect the human right to privacy, such as the right to know about one's personal data held by public and private institutions and to have them deleted where not strictly necessary for a legitimate purpose in a democratic society....
- It is fundamental to an understanding of the information society to recognize that information is power. Control of personal information and the deprivation of the right of privacy are ways of exercising power over individuals....

Cultural and linguistic rights and diversity

- ....ICTs can and must be used to promote diversity and respect for cultural rights and identity, including indigenous knowledge, rather than for their restriction or

---

[15] Statement on Human Rights, Human Dignity, and the Information Society: available at www.pdhre.org/wsis/statement.doc. Reprinted by permission.

suppression. This diversity is reflected positively by community radio, indigenous means of communication and local media.

- People in the information society are more than consumers; they are also providers of information and of creativity....

The public domain and intellectual property rights

- ... Everyone ... should enjoy the right, reaffirmed in article 27 of the Universal Declaration of Human Rights, freely to participate in the cultural life of the community, to enjoy the arts, and to share in scientific advancement and its benefits while at the same time having an equal right to the protection of the moral and material interests resulting from any scientific, literary or artistic production.
- Initiatives for high-quality, open-source, and public domain software and technologically neutral platforms and the development and use of open, interoperable, nondiscriminatory, and demand-driven standards that take into account needs of users, consumers, and the underprivileged should be promoted. Furthermore, a fixed percentage of spectrum, satellite, and other infrastructural bandwidth capacity should be reserved for educational, humanitarian, community and other non-commercial use.
- Concentration of ownership in the hands of a few major corporations limits the opportunities for information and communications technologies to reflect adequately the pluralism of perspectives and diversity of cultures. Legislative and other measures should avoid excessive media concentration....
- Intellectual property regimes and national and international agreements on patents, copyright and trademarks should not prevail over the right to education and knowledge. This right must indeed be exercised through the concept of fair use, that is, use for non-commercial purposes, especially education, and research. Moreover, intellectual work and ideas, including programming methods and algorithms, should not be patentable. The production and use of free and open-source software and content must thus be encouraged and covered by adequate public policy.
- Information in the public domain should be easily accessible to support the information society. Intellectual property rights should not be protected as an end in itself, but rather as a means to an end that promotes a rich public domain, shared knowledge, scientific and technical advances, cultural and linguistic diversity, and the free flow of information. Public institutions such as libraries and archives, museums, cultural collections and other community-based access points should be strengthened so as to promote the preservation of documentary records and free and equitable access to information. Scientists, universities, academic, research and other institutions have a central role in the development of the information society and the sharing of research results, scientific knowledge, and technical information.

Democratic governance

- The proper use of ICTs can strengthen democracy by improving the means and access for civil society to participate fully in public affairs. ICTs can improve access to justice and make public services more responsive, transparent and accountable. The rule of law is essential for the information society to become a space of confidence, trust, and security where human rights are fully respected.

QUESTIONS

1. **Research**: This statement was not the only one issued to influence the outcome of the World Summit on the Information Society. Find another position paper and compare the two.

2. **Research**: The World Summit on the Information Society issued its Geneva Declaration of Principles in December 2003. Find it. Do you see the influence of this manifesto on the Geneva Declaration? How do they differ?

———————

Chapter Problems

1. Avant-garde jazz flutist and composer James W. Newton wrote the song "Choir" for flute and voice, incorporating African-American gospel music, Japanese ceremonial court music, traditional African music, and classical music. In 1992, without permission from Newton, Beastie Boys sampled the opening six seconds of Newton's recording—three notes (C, D–flat, C) sung over a background C note—in their recording of "Pass the Mic." What are Newton's legal rights? What arguments can you make on behalf of Beastie Boys? Can you articulate an ethical argument on behalf of what Beastie Boys did? One that is critical of their actions? See *Newton v. Diamond* (9th Cir. 2003).

2. The Copyright Act "grants copyright owners a bundle of exclusive rights, including the rights … 'to prepare derivative works based upon the copyrighted work.' Nugroho sold over the Internet more than one hundred different works with the same title as textbooks copyrighted by Pearson Education, Inc. Each of the works was a copy of solutions manuals containing answers to problems and exercises in plaintiff's books. *Pearson Education, Inc. v. Nugroho*, 2009 WL 3429610 (S.D.N.Y. 2009). Can you articulate an ethical argument on behalf of what Nugroho did? One that is critical of their actions?

3. Shepard Fairey, an L.A. street artist, found a photo of Barack Obama using Google images. He used it to design what became an iconic image of Barack Obama looking upward, splashed in red, white, and blue, captioned with the word HOPE. Fairey released his image on his Web site and made thousands of posters. The original photo had been taken by Manny Garcia in 2006 for the Associated Press. What rights does the Associated Press have? Does Fairey have any legal rights?

4. Imagine yourself as a software developer who has written new generation peer-to-peer software. What can you do with it? What should you do with it?

5. John Facenda, a Philadelphia broadcasting legend, provided his voice to many productions of NFL Films, Inc. before his death in 1984. These well-known productions recounted tales of the National Football League with filmed highlights, background music, and Facenda's commanding narration. More than two decades after Facenda's death, NFL Films used small portions of his voice-over work in a cable-television production about the football video game "Madden NFL 06" without permission from his estate. What claims, if any, can the estate make? *Facenda v. N.F.L. Films, Inc.* 542 F.3d 1007 (10th Cir. 2008).

6. Which of the following might lead to a trademark claim? What defenses might be raised?

    (a) Artist Mark Napler created a "Barbie" Web site, using digital images and text that commented on Barbie as a cultural icon. In an interactive section, visitors could share what Barbie meant to them as they were growing up. There was also an "Alternative Barbies" section, a behind- the- scenes look at the seamy underbelly of Barbie's world, including digitally altered "Fat and Ugly Barbie" and "Mentally Challenged Barbie." Mattel, Inc. has trademarked the name Barbie.

    (b) Robert Burck is a street entertainer who performs in New York City's Times Square. The Naked Cowboy, as he's called, wears only a white cowboy hat, cowboy boots, and underpants, and carries a guitar strategically placed to give the illusion of nudity. He has registered trademarks to "The Naked Cowboy" name and likeness. The candy company, Mars, Inc. began running an animated cartoon advertisement on video billboards in Times Square, featuring a blue M&M wearing only a white cowboy hat, cowboy boots, and underpants, and carrying a guitar.

    (c) COWS, Inc. has fourteen stores that sell ice-cream, t-shirts, mugs, caps, etc., featuring caricature images of COWS with humorous word play. Shirts include ones with pictures of cows and the words "MOOVIVOR", "SPONGECOW SQUARE-MOO" and "AMOOZING RACE." Viacom owns trademarks to the TV shows and motion pictures "Sponge Bob Squarepants," "Survivor," and "The Amazing Race."

7. A family afflicted with Canavan, a rare genetic disorder, raised money, collected DNA samples, and persuaded scientists from the Miami Children's Hospital to search for the gene mutation that caused the disease. The researchers found the gene, and, without getting the consent of the parents of the children whose DNA they used, patented it for the hospital. When the hospital began to collect royalties on a genetic-screening test, patient groups were outraged. (a) Did the hospital act ethically? (b) Can you articulate any legal claims against the scientists and/or hospital? (c) **Research**: Find out what happened in the lawsuit filed against Miami Children's Hospital.

8. Misappropriation of trade secrets has been a federal crime since passage of the Economic Espionage Act (EEA) of 1996.

    Research: Find a criminal case involving wrongful taking of a trade secret in violation of this law. What kind of secret was taken? What was the outcome?

9. Barclays Capital, Merrill Lynch and Morgan Stanley provide wealth and asset management, securities trading and sales, corporate finance, and other investment services to hedge funds, private equity funds, pension funds, money managers, and wealthy individual investors for commissions. Their advice is based on hundreds of daily reports by hundreds of employees who conduct "equity research" into specific companies and entire industries. Their clients, of course, pay for these recommendations and sign agreements forbidding them to redistribute the research content.

    Since 1998, Fly has collected and published financial news, rumors, and other information flowing from Wall Street via its online subscription newsfeed. Emphasizing the timeliness of its reporting, it brags that it posts "breaking analyst comments as they are being disseminated by Wall Street trading desks," "consistently beating the news wires." Fly's Web site contains an explicit disclaimer advising users that Fly staff are not brokers, dealers, or registered investment advisors. Nevertheless, Fly's marketing materials emphasize that its service is intended to assist investors. Its online newsfeed posts Recommendations by sixty-five investment firms' research analysts, including those at Barclays, ML, and Morgan Stanley. Has Fly violated the intellectual property rights of Barclays and Morgan Stanley? Can you articulate any argument in support of Fly? *Barclays Capital Inc. V. Theflyonthe-wall.com,* 700 F.Supp.2d 310 (S.D.N.Y. 2010).

10. The HIV/AIDs pandemic continues to ravage the population of the less developed world. Nearly 80 percent of developing countries lack the capacity to produce anti-retroviral drugs and the money to pay the full costs of importing patented drugs.
    a. Is there a duty to aid the people in these nations? If so, who owes the duty and what should they do? (b) One solution would be for an industrialized country to amend its patent laws to allow the production of generics solely for export to countries in need. These cheaper drugs would not be sold in the country where they were made. Who would be the stakeholders if the United States were to consider such a change in its laws? How would each of them respond?

11. **Research**: Visit the WTO (*http://www.wto.org*) to interact with the organization on a number of topics, or to listen in on ministerial meetings through live audio stream.

CHAPTER PROJECT

Ethics Roundtable: Protecting Collective Property

Preparation
Read through the "Tivas Scenario." Students will be assigned to consider it from an "ethical perspective" or a "national perspective."

Tivas Scenario[16]
Tivas is a hypothetical indigenous community in southern Mexico that predates European contact. It is home to the Tivani people, who have had little interaction with Western industrial society. Its members maintain most of their traditional way of life. While treatments for common afflictions are generally well-known to all members of the community, the methods of preparing plants to treat serious illnesses are known solely by the community's respected "medicine man," referred to as "M" For example, many members of the community know that toenail and fingernail fungi should be treated with the green, oval shaped leaves that grow abundantly near the river. They also know that the leaves with the thickest veins and a reddish tint found primarily in the fall treat the affliction best. However, they do not know how M prepares the leaves to make the cream he applies to the nails. That secret is known only to M and other medicine men in a few neighboring indigenous communities.

The United States pharmaceutical company "BioCo," like many of its peer companies, has committed research and development money to study plants to identify

---

[16] This "Tivas Scenario" was derived from the Tivas hypothetical written by Gelvina Rodriguez Stevenson as part of "Trade Secrets: The Secret to Protecting Indigenous Ethnobiological (Medicinal) Knowledge." Reprinted with permission from 32 *N.Y.U.J. Int'l L. & Pol.* 1119, (2000), 1122–24.

useful new medicines and chemicals. It has determined that it would cut costs in half by studying the plants already used by indigenous communities to treat various afflictions. Looking specifically for medicines that treat nail fungi, and having read an article in NATURAL GEOGRAPHIC about the traditional medicinal practices of the Tivani (including their treatment of nail fungi), BioCo sends "Botanist" and "Chemist" to southern Mexico.

Botanist and Chemist move to a hotel in a small city an hour's drive from Tivas. They drive into the community and attempt to establish a relationship with M. Sensing. That M is wary of them, they explain that they are looking for a medicine that will treat people in the United States who are afflicted with nail fungi and that they understood that the Tivani had identified a plant that treats the fungi. They explain that if this plant proves useful, it will help many people. M emphasizes that the plants, and the way in which he prepares them to treat fungi, have been passed down for generations through the chain of medicine men and are extremely sacred. He does not share with them any information about the spiritual value of the plants, but does give them general information about the plant and brings the scientists directly to the antifungal plant.

The scientists stay for a couple of months, testing and collecting the antifungal and other plants. They eventually return to the United States, thanking M for his help and promising to be in touch. Upon their return, BioCo invests considerable time and resources into their efforts to isolate "frungoid," the active chemical in the newly "discovered" plant, Frundanialosis, which is actually the plant that M showed them.

After two years, BioCo isolates the active chemical, frungoid. BioCo immediately files for a patent at the United States Patent and Trademark Office (PTO). A year later they are granted a patent for frungoid and after frungoid receives FDA approval, they begin to market it. They are assured protection for their patent in all countries that are signatories to the General Agreement on Tariffs and Trade (GATT), and in Mexico and Canada under the North American Free Trade Agreement (NAFTA).

Within a year, BioCo has made $1 million in profits. BioCo sends a one-time check to M for $10,000—1 percent of the first year's profits. M has received more money than he has ever had, but this creates a number of problems.

The Ethical Roundtable
The Ethical Roundtable will take place as a fishbowl exercise. Teams of two students role-play each of the following perspectives in a discussion of the scenario:

- Global free marketers
- Utilitarians
- Deontologists
- Virtue ethicists
- Tivani people
- BioCo. shareholders
- M
- Botanist
- Chemist

Response
The rest of the class will be assigned to represent different nation-members of the World Trade Organization (WTO) as it considers policies governing intellectual property. After listening to the Ethical Roundtable, WTO members will discuss their responses from the perspectives of the nations they represent.

How to Read and Brief a Case

Common law—or case law—refers to those principles and rules of law that we can glean from studying how judges have resolved the disputes before them. The common law has been developing over centuries—since medieval times—and is still changing.

While the common law is always undergoing change, it is normally gradual, incremental change because of the important principle of **stare decisis**. Under this doctrine, judges are guided by the rules of previously decided cases, or precedent. Stare decisis gives stability to the development of the common law, as judges look to what has gone before to determine the result in the case at hand. But judges sometimes break with precedent and create a new rule of law. If not overruled on appeal, that new rule becomes part of the common law and may become the basis for even more radical changes in the law.

We learn the principles of the common law by reading "judicial opinions," the written decisions of judges. A typical appellate court decision (or case) will be signed by those justices whose views prevailed—producing what is called a "majority opinion" to affirm or reverse a trial judge's rulings. Justices who disagree with the majority sometimes feel strongly enough to write a "dissenting opinion." In this book, we have edited the cases for clarity, but where there are dissenting opinions we like to include them, to give you a richer sense of the varying perspectives within a dispute.

Cases are not the only sources of law. The elected representatives in Congress and state legislatures debate and pass laws, called statutes. These too can change over time, as legislators decide to amend them. It is up to the courts to interpret and apply statutes in disputes involving legislation.

Reading a Case

The language and logic of case law takes getting used to and requires practice and skill. Of varying lengths (from a page to more than a hundred pages) and styles (from pompous to playful), every judicial opinion includes certain basic elements:

- Facts.
  The background story: what happened in the real world to cause the parties to go to court to resolve their dispute.
- Law.
  References to relevant legal principles, precedent, statutes, or other sources of guidance for determining the outcome of the case.
- Resolution.
  Weaving together of facts and relevant law, as the judge decides the outcome of the case and explains the reasoning.

The Case Brief

To analyze a judicial opinion, lawyers write what is called a case **brief**, a summary of the important elements of a case. Following we show you how to write a brief of the first case in this book, *Yania v. Bigan*. The brief itself is in boldprint, followed by an explanation. Case brief writing is an excellent way for you to prepare for class.

Caption: *Yania* v. *Bigan*

The "caption" names the parties to the lawsuit. Usually the first name is that of the plaintiff (the party who brought the suit), and the second is the defendant (the party sued). However, in some jurisdictions, the names are reversed when a case is appealed by the defendant. Always read through the case itself to see who filed the lawsuit, as that will be the name of the "plaintiff."

Citation: Supreme Court of Pennsylvania, 1959 155 A.2d 343

The "citation" identifies the court that issued the opinion you are reading and the year the case was decided. It enables you to find the full, unedited judicial opinion. Throughout this text, you will find cases from many different courts, including state courts (like this one) and federal trial ("United States District Court") and appellate courts ("United States [Circuit] Court of Appeals" or "United States Supreme Court"). The higher the court, the more important the precedent.

Facts:

1. **Coal miner and landowner Bigan cut large trenches into his property to remove coal.**
2. **One cut contained 8–10 feet of water and a pump to remove the water, and it had side walls 16-18 feet.**
3. **Another coal miner, Yania, was on Bigan's property to discuss business. Yania was a mentally competent adult. Bigan stood near the pump and used words to "entice" Yania into jumping from the side wall of a trench.**
4. **Yania fell into the water and drowned. Bigan made no attempt to rescue him.**

Think of the "facts" of the case as everything important that happened before there was a lawsuit. Sometimes, in reality, the facts are "disputed"—that is, the parties disagree about what happened. But for purposes of a case brief, the "facts" are whatever the court determines the facts to have been. In this case, we know only what the widow claims to have happened—and the judge accepts her version as true. Your brief should also include facts gleaned from any concurring opinions (expressing agreement with the outcome but for different reasons), dissents, and those introduced by the authors of your text.

Legal History/Procedure:

1. **Yania's widow filed a suit ("complaint") against Bigan.**
2. **Bigan made a motion to dismiss.**
3. **The trial judge granted the motion to dismiss.**
4. **On appeal, the Supreme Court of Pennsylvania upheld the dismissal.**

The legal history/procedure part of a case brief begins with the lawsuit—who sued whom for what—and ends with the ruling in the case you are briefing.

Sometimes, before there is a trial, the judge will rule on what are called "pretrial motions." In *Yania* for example, the defendant made a **pretrial motion to dismiss** the complaint, and the judge granted the motion (ruling, in other words, that there should be no trial). The plaintiff appealed that decision, arguing that he should have had a trial. Here, the appellate court (the Supreme Court of Pennsylvania) disagreed, and "**affirmed**" the decision of the trial judge to dismiss the case. Had the court instead agreed with Yania's widow, the case would have been "**reversed**" and "**remanded**"—sent back to a judge for a trial.

Civil law is law that does not involve a criminal charge. In the civil context—and all of the cases in this book are civil cases—the purpose of a trial is to settle disputes. In other words, a trial is a fact-finding process, a way to determine the most credible version of "what really happened" and the fairest way to apply the law to those facts. If the facts are not contested, a judge applies the appropriate law and renders a judgment for one side or the other without a trial. This is called a **summary judgment**. In either case, the losing party has a right to appeal judicial "errors of law" (e.g., erroneous instructions to the jury or evidentiary rulings). Once the facts have been determined at a trial, however, they will not be revisited on appeal.

If there was a trial in the case you are briefing, the legal history should include the outcome of the trial (e.g., "The jury found for the plaintiff and awarded damages.") and any post-trial motions (e.g., "The trial judge overturned the jury and entered a judgment for the defendant."), as well as any rulings by the appellate courts (affirming or reversing the trial court).

Legal procedure can be quite comples, and some cases go on for years. In this text, we have tried to simplify the procedure wherever possible, so you will not always see all of the steps in the case's legal history. However, you should always be able to figure out—either from the case itself or surrounding text—who sued whom for what, and who won.

Issues (Holdings):

1. **Did Bigan "cause" Yania's death by convincing him to jump? (No) Or: Can a person legally "cause" another adult with full mental capacity to do something, by words alone? (No)**
2. **Did Bigan have a "duty to warn" Yania of the dangers of jumping into the cut that was violated by "failing to warn"? (No) or: Does a landowner have a "duty to warn" a person of a known danger on his property? (No)**
3. **Did Bigan have a "duty to rescue" Yania from drowning? (No) or: Does a landowner have a "duty to rescue" a drowning business associate on his property who voluntarily put himself in danger? (No)**

Think of the "issues" in a case as the questions of law that the judge must resolve in order to determine who should win. There are many ways to frame an issue, and you will want to practice writing both a narrow issue and a broader one. The "holding" of the case is really the answer to the question, and if you write your issues as questions that require a "yes" or "no" answer, your holdings will be easy to write. It will also make it easier for you to identify the "rule of law" that grows from the case. As you read, watch for language in the case that signals an issue ("Before us today…," "At issue…," or "The question to be determined…") or a holding ("Today we hold…" or "The court finds…").

Reasoning:

1. (Causation) Bigan did not push or touch Yania; all he did was talk. Yania was an adult, of full mental capacity, and he freely chose to jump. The court finds "no merit" in the argument that it was Bigan's fault.
2. (Duty to warn) A landowner has no duty to warn of danger that is open ("not concealed") and obvious, especially to another coal miner.
3. (Duty to rescue) There is a moral duty to rescue, but not a legal one. Bigan did nothing to cause Yania's situation—Yania brought it on himself. It would be different if Bigan had caused Yania to be at risk, but he did not.

The "reasoning" section spells out the rationale that explains the "holdings" of the court. Reasoning can be based on logic, as in the edited version of *Yania* v. *Bigan* in this text, or on:

- An interpretation of the U.S. Constitution or one of its Amendments.
- An interpretation of a statute (act) passed by Congress or a state legislature.
- The application of the precedent set by a prior, similar case (the name of the case will sometimes be omitted). When one side mentions a precedent case, the judge may choose to: (a) follow the precedent; (b) distinguish it (by deciding it is not similar enough to the case at hand) or (c) overturn it based on the unexpected consequences of the prior rulings or on changes in the business and social reality.
- Where there is no applicable statute or precedent ("**a case of first impression**") the court will need to consider political, economic, and business implications; social policy; justice; ethical or moral concerns; and basic fairness or equity.
- References to precedents from other state courts or even international law.
- Commentators (lawyers, scholars, or other authorities).
- Social science studies and literature.

Reasoning of the Dissent: (none in *Yania*)

When a case is appealed, it is always heard by a panel of appellate judges (three or more, nine on the Supreme Court) who must determine by a vote whether to affirm or reverse the lower court. When your text includes a dissent, outline the reasoning of the dissent as well.

Rule of Law:

The "rule of law" refers to the precedent set by the case. If you have carefully framed broad "issues" you can create a rule of law by turning your question into a statement.

Your Response:

For your own purposes, and to prepare for class discussion, you might want to include something that would not be included in a lawyer's case brief: your own reflections on the reasoning and the implications of the decision.

An Introduction to Legal Research

Order of Representation

I. Major Sources of U.S. Law

Under the U.S. Constitution, our government is both centralized and uniform at the national level, and decentralized and differing at the state level. As the following chart indicates, each source of law at the federal level has its counterpart at the state level.

Federal Law	State Law
Constitutional:	**Constitutional:**
U.S. Constitution	Each state has its own Constitution
Statutory:	**Statutory:**
Laws passed by the U.S. Congress	Laws passed by the state legislature

Case Law:	Case Law:
Judicial opinions of the federal District (trial) Courts, federal Circuit Courts of Appeal, and U.S. Supreme Court.	Judicial opinions from various state courts; most state judicial systems have trial, intermediate appellate, and high courts similar to federal court structure
Administrative Law:	**Administrative Law:**
Federal regulations passed by federal agencies (e.g. EPA, OSHA, FTC)	State regulations passed by each state's agencies (e.g. State Dept. of Motor Vehicles)

For a fuller introduction to the American legal system, check out the American Law Sources Online Web site at *http://www.lawsource.com/also*. This site compiles links to free legal sources online, including amicus curiae (friend of the courts) briefs, law reviews, and periodicals.

II. Citations Matter

A legal citation is an abbreviation that allows us to locate and identify legal documents—cases, laws, or articles from legal journals, for example. The same citations are used when cases appear both in print and online.

Reading the Citation to a Statute

There are three parts to a citation to a statute: an abbreviation representing the set of books (series) in which a law is published or the database in which it can be found online; a number representing the title of the law, which helps you to find the appropriate volume in the library or to identify its subject matter online; and a number that refers you to the particular section(§) of the law you are citing. Because every title contains many laws passed at different times, the section identifies a particular part of the law within that title.

Consider the citation: **42 U.S.C.A. §§2000e1–17**

Series/Database: U.S.C.A. is the abbreviation for United States Code Annotated. Most law libraries contain this set of books, which is a compilation of all of the laws passed by the U.S. Congress, arranged according to broad subjects. If you are searching online, U.S.C.A. tells you that you are looking for a federal law (i.e., one passed by the U.S. Congress). Note that each state has a set of books containing state laws. The formal citation to a state's laws requires a particular abbreviation for the series. For future reference, write the abbreviation for the series that collects your state laws. **Series:**_____

Title: The number preceding the series is called the title number. In our example, **42** is the title number for laws relating to Public Health and Safety.

Section (§): Finally, the numbers after the series (in our case, **§§2000e, et.seq.**) refer to the section(s) of the law.

In this example, **et.seq.** is used to refer to sections that begin at §2000e and continue through the end of that particular civil rights law. For online research, the easiest way to locate a specific law is to enter the database (e.g., federal statutes, or particular state statutes) and then search using the correct title and section number.

III. Locating Statutory Law

To locate the text of a statute, start by considering the information you already have.

A. Locating a Statute Using Its Legal Citation

Suppose you already have a legal citation to a particular statute. For example, assume that you know that a law prohibiting racial discrimination has the following citation: 42 U.S.C.A. §2000e-2000e-17.

On the Internet

There are a number of ways to access statutes online, and it is relatively easy if you know the citation. One of the best free online sites is the legislative service of the Library of Congress. It contains the full text and Congressional record of federal statutes, along with proposed legislation (bills) and their current status. The URL is *http://thomas.loc. gov*. Because our citation is to a federal law, this URL is a good place to start. By searching the federal laws for 42 U.S.C.A. §2000e, you should be able to find the full text of the law. Other user-friendly sites where you can find federal statutes as well as state laws include: *http://lawcrawler.findlaw.com*; *http://www.lawsource.com/also/* and *http://www. lawguru.com*. Your school library may also have Westlaw or Lexis-Nexus, two paid legal databases that are used by most attorneys.

B. Locating a Statute by Analyzing a Legal Problem

Suppose you don't have any citation or reference to a particular law. Instead, you have a problem to solve, involving discrimination in the workplace. You have heard that there are laws prohibiting such discrimination, but you have no idea where to find the text of such a law. How can you find it?

On the Internet

It can be time-consuming to try to locate a particular statute online without its citation because key words or phrases often appear in dozens, sometimes hundreds, of statutes. One of the best places to start is with a Web site that organizes American law by subject (e.g., alternative dispute, commercial law, environmental law).

C. State Statutes

The above methods work equally well for locating state statutes. Most college libraries contain the statutes for their home state and occasionally for those of neighboring states. For online searches, be sure you enter the database for the appropriate state.

IV. Locating Case Law

A. Case Reporters

The law is found not only in the text of statutes passed by Congress and state legislatures, but also in the written opinions of federal and state judges explaining their rulings in particular cases. Edited versions of such judicial opinions are found throughout this book. To find the complete case opinion and other case opinions, you need to learn something about Case Reporters—books that collect judicial opinions—and online searches for case law.

B. Locating a Case Using Its Legal Citation

Under the uniform system for referring to judicial opinions, each case is identified by the names of the parties, followed by a citation containing three parts: an abbreviation for the Reporter (or series of books in which the opinion is published) and numbers to identify the particular volume and page number where the case was published. Here, the series or Reporter corresponds to a database when searching online.

Suppose you want to read the full opinion in a case mentioned in Chapter 1, *Hurley v. Eddingfield.*

You can find it online or in the library using the names of the parties (Hurley or Eddingfield) or the citation (59 N.E. 1058). In a library, you would find the case by looking at volume 59 of a set of books called the Northeast Reporter (abbreviatied N.E.) (*Note*: Each volume of each set of reporters is numbered, beginning with 1. When the numbers get too high, the publishers begin a second series of the same Reporter, and then a third series.) You would then turn to page 1058.

Online, you can use the same case citation to locate the full text of the opinion through any of the following sites: *http://www.lawsource.com/also/* (ALSO stands for American Law Sources Online); *http://www.lawguru.com* (an Internet law library that enables you to search for cases and statutes by state); *http://lawcrawler.findlaw.com*; Westlaw; or Lexis-Nexus.

C. Common Traps to Avoid

Be sure you are using the right database—state or federal cases, trial courts (such as the federal District Courts), appellate courts (such as the federal Circuit Courts of Appeals), or the Supreme Court. (Our example is of an Indiana state court case, so you would want to be sure to use the database that includes Indiana state court cases.)

Consider how new/old your case is. Some databases require you to identify the time period (within two years? before 1945?) to be searched.

If you are searching by names of parties, be sure you are spelling the names correctly.

If you are searching by the citation, be sure you have entered each element correctly (volume number, series, page number), paying particular attention to whether the series is the first (letters only), second (letters followed by 2d) third, etc.

Some cases are only available through one or more online sources.

D. Locating a Case by Analyzing a Legal Problem

Suppose you have no particular case in mind. Instead, you know that you want to find out something about wrongful discharge of employees. You looked in your state statutes and you couldn't find any statute dealing with wrongful discharge. You know from the chapter on whistleblowing in this text that wrongful discharge is a kind of tort and that tort law is mostly judge-made law (case law). How can you find a case about wrongful discharge (or any other topic)?

Once you have located an appropriate database—federal cases if you are searching for opinions interpreting the U.S. Constitution or federal statutes and state case law in most other instances—you can search for cases by key words or phrases (such as wrongful discharge, tort, employment-at-will). As you become more experienced in reading and researching case law, you will learn to refine your search terms.

E. Locating Cases that Interpret a Particular Case

Once you identify an appropriate database (e.g. state case law), use the citation to one case as a search term to find other cases that have cited and interpreted the main case. In some databases, such as Westlaw, you will need to put quote marks around the citation to do this search. Learn the best method for whatever search tool you use most often.

V. Administrative Law

The rules and regulations promulgated by government administrative agencies are also published so that anyone can find and read them. When first adopted, federal regulations for example are published in the Federal Register. Of course, a chronological list of the latest government rules and regulations is not the easiest resource to use. Like federal statutes, federal regulations are **codified** (or arranged by subject) in the Code of Federal Regulations (CFR). This code can be searched in the same way as the United States Code or any state law code.

On the Internet (federal)

The complete Code of Federal Regulations can be accessed online through *http://www. gpoaccess.gov/cfr/index.html.*

State Administrative Law

Most states have a similar codified version of regulations adopted by state administrative agencies. Check your library to see if there is a copy of the state code of administrative rules and regulations. If there is, note here the form for citing it: _____

Check a government Web site for your state to see if the administrative code is available online.

VI. Common Abbreviations

Federal Statutory Materials

U.S.C. United States Code (the official codification of laws passed by Congress).

U.S.C.A. United States Code Annotated (U.S.C.A. contains the text of statutes, followed by notes of relevant cases and references to other materials related to the topic).

State Statutory Materials

Check to see if your library contains a copy of your state statutes. If so, locate the correct abbreviation (citation form) for the series by turning to the front of any volume to find "Cite as (abbreviation for series). (Full name of state statutes)."

Federal Case Law

1 S.Ct. 99 means: volume l, Supreme Court Reporter, page 99

U.S. Supreme Court cases can be found in each of the following:

U.S. United States Reports (official version); S.Ct. Supreme Court Reporter (Annotated case reporter) and L.Ed. United States Supreme Court, Lawyer's Edition (Annotated case reporter)

Other federal court cases can be found at:

F., Federal Reporter (oldest cases from federal Circuit Courts of Appeal); F.2d, Federal Reporter, Second Series (more recent cases); and F.3d., Federal Reporter, Third Series (most recent cases)

F. Supp., Federal Supplement (contains older decisions of federal trial courts, called District Courts); F. Supp.2d, Federal Supplement, Second Series (more recent opinions)

State Case Law

A. Atlantic Reporter, (older cases from state courts in Conn., Del., Me., Md., N.H., N.J., Pa., R.I., Vt., D.C. Munic. Ct.App.); A.2d Atlantic Reporter, Second Series (newer cases)

Cal. California Reporter

N.E., North Eastern Reporter (older cases from Ill., Ind., Mass., N.Y., Ohio); N.E.2d North Eastern Reporter, Second Series (newer cases)

N.W. North Western Reporter (older cases from Ia., Mich., Minn., Neb., N.D., S.D., Wis.); N.W.2d North Western Reporter, Second Series (newer cases)

N.Y.S. New York Supplement (older cases from N.Y. courts); N.Y.S.2d New York Supplement, Second Series

P. Pacific Reporter (Alaska, Ariz., Calif., Colo., Haw., Id., Kan., Mont., Nev., N.M., Okla., Ore., Utah, Wash., Wyo.); P.2d Pacific Reporter, Second Series

S.E. South Eastern Reporter (Ga., N.C., S.C., Va., W.Va.); S.E.2d South Eastern Reporter, Second Series

So. Southern Reporter (Ala., Fla., La., and Miss.); So. 2d Southern Reporter, Second Series

Evaluating Internet Sources

Many college and university libraries have compiled guidelines for assessing online sources. One of the best, offered by librarians Jan Alexander and Marsha Ann Tate[1], provides an extensive checklist for identifying and evaluating different kinds of Web sites:

- Advocacy (usually ending with domain .org),
- Business/marketing (.com, .net or .biz),
- Informational (.edu or .gov),
- News (usually .com) and personal.

Alexander and Tate created the following criteria:

- **Authority/Objectivity:** Look for Web sites that give the author's name, title, organizational affiliation, and contact information. This will help you identify biases, as well as expertise. Government and educational sites, along with online scholarly journals, provide such indices of authority and objectivity. Traditionally, publications that have undergone peer review or are published in scholarly journals (such as law reviews) are given greater weight than those published by the author ("vanity publications").
- **Accuracy:** Pay attention to whether information sources are cited, to how well the page has been edited for grammar/spelling, and to whether the information on a Web site can be verified by referring to other sources.
- **Currency:** Check when the Web site was last revised. Outdated links are a sign that a Web site is not current. (Laws change when amendments, new laws, or new court interpretations have occurred since a Web site was last revised.)

Another excellent place for advice about Web site evaluation is *http://www.rhetorica.net*. Some ideas from it include:

- **Beware persuasive writing:** Written advocacy for a particular view can be flawed by illogical reasoning. Learn some basics of logical analysis to monitor this. For example, check that the premises (underlying assumptions) of an argument are logical; if not, the rest should not be considered persuasive. And look for a logical connection between premises and conclusions.
- **Rev up your bias-detector:** If you identify bias, you might not necessarily dismiss a Web source as useless. But potential bias is another factor in helping you decide how to evaluate a particular Web source.

---

[1] An online version can be found at *http://www3.widener.edu/wolfgram/*.

- **Notice the "spin":** There are many subtle ways to put a spin on information. Pay special attention, for example, to the use of labels, euphemisms, and metaphors. What impression is created by the title or headline? By the writer's tone and word choice? What details are included, and do they support the overall analysis? If the text is not clear, ask yourself: Is this a deliberate attempt to confuse?
- **"Unpack" visual and audio elements:** Suppose you read a story posted on a Web "news site." Note how it is designed, its placement (front page? buried?), and the kind of material that surrounds it—textual, visual, audio, advertising. What do all of these elements—and the way they are joined—tell you about the intended audience? The point of view of the author? Consider the message being sent by such things as color choices, relative size, and the particular juxtaposition of images and text.

Web sites—or Web news sources—are posted by a person or an organization of some kind. It makes sense to find out what you can about the individual or organization in order to best evaluate what they have created online.

Art Silverblatt, Jane Ferry and Barbara Finan, in *Approaches to Media Literacy: A Handbook*, 2nd Edition (M.E. Sharpe, 2009)[2] make the following suggestions:

- **Identify ownership patterns** in the media, generally to assess how they affect media content.
- **Analyze an organization** (e.g., CNN, Fox News) to see how the ownership, resources, and internal structure (e.g., decision making) of a particular media organization influence the content of its products.
- **Uncover the "World View"** of a particular media presentation (such as a Web site) by thinking about the types of people who are depicted within it. Are characters presented in a stereotypical manner? Are they in control of their own destinies, or under the influence of others? Is there a supernatural presence in this world? Stories—and ads—reveal a world view by the way they portray what it means to be successful, how success is achieved, and what kinds of behaviors are rewarded.
- **Unpack an individual author** by finding out what you can about his or her expertise or educational background (is it relevant to the topic at hand?), employment or professional experience, and membership/leadership role in organizations or political/advocacy groups. Look for clues as to who funds/publishes his or her research. Has he or she been honored or recognized in a special way, and if so, by whom?

[2] Check out "Critical Questions for Detecting Bias," at *http://www.rhetorica.net/bias.htm*.

Stakeholder Ethics Role Play

A person faces a business ethics dilemma, with a tough decision to make. In this exercise, students play the roles of a decision maker and of several "stakeholder" advisors. After the stakeholders offer their points of view, the decision maker makes a choice and explains the reasons behind it.

The role play can be done in a "fishbowl" format, with the decision maker and the various advisors in a circle in the middle of the room and with the rest of the class arranged in a larger circle around them, observing. Or, to involve more participants, the decision maker and the different stakeholders can be represented by small groups. (Recommended size of groups is three to six students.) In another variation for larger classes, students can replicate the same exercise in separate groups, each of which has one decision maker being advised by several stakeholders.

1. First Plenary: Introduction

The decision maker defines the problem and explains the process of the role play to all.

2. Break-Out #1: Stakeholders Meet Separately

Students in each stakeholder group meet to identify their own interests and to articulate how they want to see the problem resolved (or, if they represent an ethical perspective, to articulate the direction their approach to ethics dictates and the reasons for it). Each group should appoint a "scribe" to take notes and another student to lead intra-group discussion. A "reporter" arranges the points into a cogent argument. Meanwhile, the decision maker can meet with the instructor to prepare questions for the stakeholder groups at the plenary session.

3. Plenary Session

The decision maker moderates a plenary session, asking each stakeholder representative to offer advice. As they present their interests and preferred outcomes, the decision maker asks questions to clarify or challenge a point of view. This phase of the exercise may evolve into a free-form discussion among the various stakeholders, with the decision maker acting as facilitator/referee, and with the stakeholders querying and challenging each other. The goal for the class is to achieve a refined sense of the different perspectives.

Next, the decision maker should lead a brainstorming session on options, with anyone free to suggest a means of resolving the dilemma and with no discussion of whether any one suggestion is either wise or practical. Roles are irrelevant here—the goal is to unlock creative approaches, to bring a full range of ideas to the surface. The resulting options should be listed on the board/screen before the session ends.

4. Break-Out #2: Stakeholders Regroup

While the decision maker takes time to think about what has just transpired and to weigh options, the stakeholder groups reconvene to discuss solutions and decide which to recommend, given the information they now have regarding the concerns of other stakeholders.

5. Final Plenary

The decision maker asks each group to report back its final recommendation and then explains to the class how he or she will deal with the dilemma and gives the reasons for this choice.

6. Individual Follow-Up Memo

One way to allow each student to participate more fully is to assign a brief memo, in which each person (regardless of role) recommends and justifies a solution to the dilemma.

Alternative Dispute Resolution

Since the early 1970s, the time-consuming and expensive process of litigating business disputes has been increasingly replaced by alternative forms of dispute resolution. ADR has been embraced by the Supreme Court, which has ruled that courts must refuse to hear lawsuits when a commercial contract calls for arbitration,[1] and by Congress, which has authorized federal agencies and federal courts to use informal alternatives to litigation such as mediation, conciliation, and arbitration[2]. In fact, to circumvent costly litigation, more and more companies have inserted binding arbitration clauses into employment contracts, so that disputes over pay, discrimination, misconduct, and other matters must be resolved not in court but by a panel of arbitrators.

Win-Win or Principled Negotiation

When opponents in a dispute focus only on their ultimate goals and approach one another with a "winner take all" attitude, the resulting agreement is too often one-sided and short-lived. In contrast, the concept of principled negotiation is that there is a better way, a way to reach a lasting agreement, satisfying at least some of the interests on each side. The leading resource for learning about principled negotiation is Roger Fisher & William Uri, GETTING TO YES (1991). These points summarize the process they recommend:

- Separate the people from the problem. Deal with the relationships among the parties separately from the merits of the dispute.
- Focus on interests, not positions. For example, being comfortable may be the interest at stake, not whether a window needs to be open or closed.
- Invent options for mutual gains; be creative.
- Where thorny disagreements remain, move to objective neutral criteria to ensure a fair resolution.
- Before negotiations begin, each side should develop its BATNA (best alternative to a negotiated agreement). In a legal dispute, this almost always means that if settlement fails, a party can file suit. It requires both sides to consider what they are likely to win—or lose—if the case goes to court.

---

[1] *Southland Corp.* v. *Keating*, 465 U.S. 1 (1984)

[2] Administrative Dispute Resolution Act of 1990 and Alternate Dispute Resolution Act of 1998.

Negotiation Exercise

Preparation for Assigned Disputants

Read through your assigned witness statements carefully to understand the "facts" and to get a feel for your character. Try to identify his or her real needs and interests so that you can be open to resolutions that will best satisfy those needs. Consider both long- and short-term interests, both economic and relational, business and family concerns. Rank your interests. Decide on your BATNA.

First Round

Meet with the opposition. Try to follow the rules of principled negotiation. Explain your side's interests. Listen to and question the other side carefully to develop as complete an understanding as possible of their interests.

Break-Out

Split apart. Meet with your team to develop an offer. Develop a back-up offer.

Second Round

Meet with the opposition. Exchange your offers and discuss them. If you have difficulty forming an agreement, try brainstorming alternatives.

Repeat Rounds

Continue the process of meeting with the other side and alone with your team until the negotiation is complete.

Debrief with the Whole Class

Compare the various negotiated agreements. Which one identified the largest area of mutual interest? Which one was the most balanced? Which is most likely to survive into the future? Vote for the best agreement, giving reasons for your vote.

Mediation/Arbitration Exercise

While a negotiated agreement is arrived at by opposing sides on their own, a mediator or an arbitrator is a neutral third party who is actively involved in the agreement-making process. A mediator listens carefully to both sides and then helps them discover their mutual interests, close their differences, and think of creative ways to craft an agreement. An arbitrator is more like a judge. An arbitrator listens to arguments made by each side, asks questions of each side, and then acts without further input to craft an agreement that both sides must then accept. (Before an arbitration, both sides agree that they will accept the terms of the agreement that will be decided for them.)

Preparation for Arbitrators and Mediators

In preparation for your role, learn more about alternative dispute resolution from one of the following:

- The Beginner's Guide to ADR, available through the Web site of the American Arbitration Association, *http://www.adr.org*
- National Arbitration Forum resources at *http://www.arb-forum.com*
- Arbitration: the WWW Virtual Library's section on Private Dispute Resolution, *http://www.interarb.com*

Comparative ADR Role Play

Using a single dispute, some students role play as opponents, while other students role play mediators and arbitrators. The class is evenly divided among negotiating, mediating, and arbitrating teams.

Once all the agreements have been finalized, the whole class debriefs by studying the results and discussing the comparative strengths and weaknesses of the three processes for reaching agreement.

Legislative Hearing

In this exercise some students role play legislative committee members hearing testimony on a controversial issue or bill while other students role play public witnesses offering their views on the proposed law. In larger classes, some can be assigned to role play legislative aides or news reporters.

The legislative committee sits as a panel facing the public witnesses in the middle of the room. If the class is large, the rest of the class surrounds them, to listen in, fishbowl style.

A committee chair calls each public witness, one at a time. After each speaker has finished a brief opening statement of opinion, legislators can ask a few questions of that speaker. When all of the speakers have been heard, the legislative committee members explain their positions and vote, followed by the class acting as the full legislature.

Legislators/Legislative Aides

Before the Hearing

Prepare for your role by forming your political position on the bill (for or against it), considering your own opinion and also what your "constituents" are likely to think. If you are uncertain of either, find online news coverage from your part of the state or country.

Write a list of questions to ask the various public witnesses. Try to make them provocative and interesting. Suggestions: Hypothetical questions are often very effective, setting up examples that sharpen points of disagreement. Consider asking about the long-term consequences (on business, on the nation, on particular constituents, and so on) of the proposed legislation; how new laws will impact existing state or national laws; and how proposed legislation will be implemented and enforced. Legislative Aides can assist in background research and prep for the hearing.

During the Hearing

Listen carefully to each speaker. Be prepared to vary or adapt a planned question to fit the situation at hand. Try not to give speeches during the hearing itself, as your goal is to elicit input from the public.

After the Hearing

You will have an opportunity to articulate your position for or against the proposed legislation, giving your reasons and referring to testimony that supports your position.

Public Witnesses

Remember that you are playing a role; stay in it. Avoid drifting into advocating your real-life position on the issue.

Before the Hearing

Think about the position a person in your role is likely to take on the proposed legislation, regardless of what your personal opinion may be. Find out about the group you represent, and any positions it has taken on the issue.

At the hearing, you will begin by giving a short (5 minute) statement explaining your group's view and the reasons for it. Practice a clear and crisp opening statement before class. Prepare for questions by thinking ahead about what you are likely to be asked and how you will answer.

During the Hearing

You will need to pay careful attention to other public witnesses as they may raise points you had not considered. Be prepared to address those points when it is your turn, as part of your opening statement, since you will not be able to directly question or engage with the other public witnesses. Your interaction will be limited to speaking to the legislative panel and responding to the questions they pose to you.

Writing Exercise for Reporters or Legislators

Students who do not serve as either public witnesses or legislators can be given written assignments as editorial writers covering the hearing for a newspaper or magazine or as members of the larger assembly or senate. In their editorials or absentee ballot reports, they will articulate their opinions on the proposal and their reasons for them, based on observing the legislative committee proceedings.

A

Abusive discharge   a tort, recognized in some states, committed when an employer discharges an employee in violation of a clear expression of public policy; also referred to as "wrongful discharge."

Administrative law   the rules and regulations established by government agencies, as opposed to law created by courts and legislators.

Affidavit   a written declaration or statement of facts, sworn before a person who has the authority to administer such an oath.

Affirm   the ruling by an appellate court that agrees with a lower court decision and allows the judgment to stand.

Alternative Dispute Resolution (ADR)   the resolution of disputes in ways other than through the use of the traditional judicial process; mediation and arbitration are examples of ADR.

Amicus curiae   Latin for "friend of the court;" an individual or entity that petitions the Court for permission to file a brief because of strong interest in the case.

Answer   the pleading of a defendant in which he admits or denies any or all of the facts set out in the plaintiff's complaint or declaration.

Appeal   the process by which a party to a lawsuit asks a higher court to review alleged errors made by a lower court or agency.

Appellant   the party who appeals a case to a higher court.

Appellate court   a court having jurisdiction of appeal and review.

Appellee   the party in a case against which an appeal is taken; that is, the party with an interest adverse to setting aside or reversing a judgment.

Arbitration   a process in which a dispute is submitted to a mutually acceptable person or board who will render a decision to which the parties are bound.

Arbitrator   a disinterested party who has the power to resolve a dispute and (generally) bind the parties.

Assumption of the risk   in tort law, a defense to negligence when a plaintiff has voluntarily exposed him or herself to a known risk.

B

Bill of Rights   first ten amendments to the U.S. Constitution, adopted in 1791; sets forth specific individual protections against government intrusion.

Bona fide   Latin for "in good faith;" honestly, sincerely.

Brief   in litigation, a formal legal document submitted by attorneys for each side of a dispute outlining the issues, statutes, and precedents that make up the legal arguments of each side.

Burden of proof   proof in a civil case by a fair preponderance of the evidence; proof in a criminal case beyond a reasonable doubt.

Business Judgment rule   legal doctrine that relieves directors and officers of liability for decisions that were consistent with prudent business judgment.

C

Case at bar   the particular case that is before the court.

Case of first impression   a lawsuit raising a novel question of law; without precedent in the particular jurisdiction.

Case law   the law created when an appellate court issues a written opinion in a lawsuit; sometimes referred to as common law. CONTRAST: statutory law.

Cause of action   facts which evidenced a civil wrong, thereby giving rise to a right to judicial relief.

Caveat emptor   Latin for "let the buyer beware;" the concept that the buyer bears the loss if there is any defect in the goods purchased.

Cease and desist order   an order by an agency or court directing someone to stop an unlawful practice.

Certiorari   a means of obtaining appellate review; a writ issued by an appellate court, such as the Supreme Court, to an inferior court commanding the record be certified to the appellate court for judicial review.

Chattel   personal property; tangible property that is mobile.

Claim   a cause of action.

Class action   a suit brought by or against a group with common interests in resolving particular issues of law or facts. Sometimes called a "representative action." The named plaintiff in a class action is a representative of the group.

Collective bargaining   the process whereby union representatives bargain with management on behalf of employees concerning wages, hours, and other terms and conditions of employment. The result of this process is a collective bargaining agreement.

Comity   respect or deference; the doctrine that allows an administrative agency or court to defer to the actions or decisions of another body.

Commerce clause   the clause in Article II, Section 8 of the Constitution that gives Congress power to regulate commerce among the several states.

Commercial speech   speech that proposes a commercial transaction; the Supreme Court has interpreted the First Amendment as giving more limited protection to commercial speech than to political speech.

Common law   as distinguished from law created by the enactments of legislatures, the common law is comprised of the principles and rules that derive solely from custom and from judgments and decisions of courts; also called case law or judgemade law.

Communitarianism   the belief that individual liberties depend on the bolstering of the foundations of civil society: families, schools, neighborhoods. It is through these institutions, according to communitarians, that we acquire a sense of our personal civic responsibilities, of our rights and the rights of others, and a commitment to the welfare of the whole of society.

Compensatory damages   money that compensates an injured party for the injury sustained and nothing more; such compensation as will simply make good or replace the loss caused by a wrong or injury.

Complaint   the first pleading by the plaintiff in a civil case. Its purpose is to give the defendant the information on which the plaintiff relies to support its demand. In a complaint, the plaintiff sets out a cause of action, consisting of a formal allegation or charge presented to the appropriate court.

Concurring opinion   with reference to appellate court cases, a concurring opinion is one by a judge who agrees with the majority opinion's conclusions, but for different reasons, and who therefore writes a separate opinion. CONTRAST: dissenting opinion, majority opinion.

Consent decree   a court decree entered by consent of the parties. It is not a judicial sentence but is an agreement of the parties made under the sanction of a court.

Consumer Product Safety Commission (CPSC)   an independent federal agency created in 1972 to protect the public from death or serious harm caused by dangerous products.

Contract   a legally enforceable agreement between two parties.

Copyright   protection of the original work of authors, painters, sculptors, musicians, photographers, and others who create original literary or artistic works.

Corporate Social Responsibility (CSR)   the idea that corporations have a responsibility to all major stakeholders, not only to those who own stock in the company.

Corporation   a legal entity created by statute authorizing its officers, directors, and stockholders to carry on business.

Cost-benefit analysis   a way to reach decisions in which the costs of a given action are compared with its benefits.

Counterclaim   a claim presented by a defendant that, if successful, defeats or reduces the plaintiff's recovery.

Criminal law   a set of laws, the violation of which is an offense against society. Crimes include both minor crimes (misdemeanors) and more serious felonies.

D

Damages   a monetary award granted by a court to a winning party.

Declaratory judgment   a judicial opinion that declares the rights of the parties or expresses the court's interpretation of a law without ordering anything to be done.

Deep ecology   an ethical belief system based on ecological concerns that begins with the premise that the biotic community in which we find ourselves has intrinsic value.

Defamation   the disparagement of one's reputation; a civil action (tort) involving the offense of injuring a person's character, fame, or reputation by false and malicious statements.

Default   omission to perform a legal or contractual duty; the failure of a party to appear in court or defend an action after being properly served with process.

Defendant   the party against whom an action is brought in a civil case; the accused in a criminal case.

Defense   an assertion offered by a defendant who, if successful, relieves him or her of liability, reduces the plaintiff's recovery, or defeats a criminal charge.

Deontology   the study of duty; as developed by Immanuel Kant, the notion that there are certain moral rights and duties that every human being possesses and that ethical choices derive from universal principles based on those rights and duties.

Deposition   a pretrial discovery process of testifying under oath (but not in open court) and subject to cross examination, where the testimony is recorded and intended to be used at trial.

Design defect   in product liability law, the concept that a seller should be liable for harm caused by a product that was not well designed.

Dicta/Dictum   an abbreviated form of the Latin *obiter dictum* ("a remark by the way"); an observation or remark made by a judge in pronouncing an opinion in a case, concerning some rule, principle, or application of law, or the solution of a question suggested by the court, but not necessarily involved in the case or essential to its determination.

Disclaimer of warranty   seller's claim that no promises (warranties) were made when goods were sold.

Discovery   pretrial processes that allow each side to obtain information about the case from the other side for use in preparing for trial or settlement. Discovery devices include pretrial depositions, motions to produce documents or to inspect premises, written interrogatories, and pretrial medical examinations.

Disparate impact discrimination   in an employment context, discrimination that results from certain employer practices, or procedures that, although neutral on their face, have a discriminatory effect. For example, minimum height and weight requirements for all applicants are not discriminatory on their face, but will have the effect of excluding more women than men.

Disparate treatment discrimination   in an employment context, any practice or decision that treats applicants or employees differently depending on their race, sex, religion, or national origin.

Dissenting opinion   in appellate courts, an opinion written by a judge who disagrees with the result reached by the majority, as well as its reasoning. CONTRAST: concurring opinion.

Due process   a concept embodied in the Fifth and Fourteenth Amendments to the U.S. Constitution, meaning fundamental fairness. Due process mandates that government may not take life, liberty, or property from citizens unless they are given notice and a fair opportunity to be heard.

Duty of care   in tort law, all persons have a duty to exercise reasonable care in their interactions with others.

E

Economic loss doctrine   a common law rule followed in some states that holds that a person harmed by another's breach of contract may not bring a tort action unless there was injury to a person or property other than that which was the subject of the contract.

Eminent domain   the right of the government to take privately owned land for public use, paying the owner a just compensation.

Employment-at-will doctrine   the common law rule that holds that whenever an employment relationship is of an indefinite duration, either party—the employer or the employee—may terminate the relationship at any time, for good cause or bad, in good faith or with malice.

En banc   where most appellate cases are heard by only some of the judges, a decision en banc is one heard by the full court.

Environmental Protection Agency (EPA)   the federal agency established in 1970 to oversee national environmental policy and laws.

Equal Employment Opportunity Commission (EEOC)   the five-member commission created in 1964 to administer Title VII of the Civil Rights Act by issuing interpretive guidelines, investigating, holding hearings, and keeping statistics.

Equal protection   a concept embodied in the Fifth and Fourteenth Amendments to the U.S. Constitution that government cannot treat persons in similar situations differently.

Equity   a system of justice that developed in England separate from the common-law courts. Few states in the United States still maintain separate equity courts, although most apply equity principles and procedures when equitable relief is sought. A broader meaning denotes fairness and justice.

Exclusivity rule   under workers' compensation laws, the exclusivity rule provides that workers' compensation is the only remedy available for some injuries.

Executive branch   the branch of the U.S. government that includes the president and is charged with enforcing the law; the powers of the president as established in Article II of the U.S. Constitution. Also used to refer to the governor of a state.

Expert testimony   trial testimony from an authority recognized by the court as having special knowledge.

F

Fair use   under American copyright law, the right to use limited portions of a copyrighted work, without permission, for education or criticism.

False Claims Reform Act   a federal statute that allows citizens to file a civil suit against any company known to be defrauding the government; also referred to as *qui tam*.

Federal Register   a publication providing notice of rule making by federal agencies.

Federal Trade Commission (FTC)   a bipartisan, independent administrative agency authorized by Congress to prevent unfair methods of competition and unfair or deceptive trade and advertising practices.

Federalism   the Constitutional relationship between the states and federal government whereby responsibility and autonomy is divided between them.

Feminist ethics   the notion that the right thing to do stems from a sense of responsibility for one another based on caring relationships, rather than from allegiance to abstract principles. CONTRAST: utilitarian analysis of consequences or deontological universal rights and duties approach.

Fiduciary   a person having a legal duty, created by his or her undertaking, to act primarily for another's benefit. For example, corporate officers are fiduciaries who owe fiduciary duties of loyalty and care to their shareholders; lawyers have fiduciary duties to their clients.

Fiduciary duty   the legal duty that arises whenever one person is in a special relationship of trust to another.

Food and Drug Administration (FDA)   the federal regulatory agency responsible for overseeing safety of food, drugs, and cosmetics sold in the United States.

Fundamental freedoms   those rights given special priority and protection under the U.S. Constitution, including the right to free speech, free religion, free press, the right to vote, and the freedom to travel.

G

General Agreement on Tariffs and Trade (GATT)   created in 1948 as an agreement; GATT grew to be both an agreement and an organization that negotiated international trade and tariff rules. In 1995, GATT was replaced by the World Trade Organization (WTO).

Gross negligence   a conscious or reckless act or omission that is likely to result in harm to a person or property; a higher level of culpability than simple negligence.

I

Implied warranty   a warranty or promise created by law under certain conditions. For example, when a merchant sells a good, the law implies a promise ("implied warranty of merchantability") that the good is fit for its ordinary purpose.

Indictment   a formal accusation made by a grand jury that charges a person has committed a crime.

Infringement   violating the exclusive rights of a copyright, trademark or patent holder by using the protected work or mark without permission or license.

Injunction   a court order directing someone to do or not to do something.

Instructions to the jury   directions that a trial judge gives to the jury explaining the law to be applied to the facts that the jury finds.

Intellectual property laws   copyright, patent, trademark, trade secret, and other laws that protect intangible property that is the work product of the human mind.

Intentional torts   a category of civil wrongs giving redress to the victims of willful wrongdoing. Wrongful or abusive discharge of an employee, misappropriating a trade secret, and battery are all intentional torts.

International law   law considered legally binding among otherwise sovereign, independent nations. Treaties are a form of international law.

Interrogatories   in litigation, a discovery device consisting of written questions to parties and witnesses to be answered in writing, under oath.

Intrusion   an intentional tort, committed when one party intrudes on the solitude of another in an overly offensive way. Sometimes referred to as invasion of privacy.

J

Judgment   an official ruling by a court.

Judicial branch   the branch of the U.S. government that consists of the federal courts, whose powers are set forth in Article III of the U.S. Constitution; sometimes referred to as the judiciary; Each state also has its own judiciary.

Judicial review   the process whereby a court reviews legislative action to ensure that it was Constitutional or reviews actions by a government agency to ensure that they were Constitutional, and in compliance with the agency's legal authority.

Jurisdiction   the power of the court or a judicial officer to decide a case; the geographic area of a court's authority; the power of a court over a defendant in a lawsuit.

L

Learned intermediary   a person with special training and expertise, such as a doctor, who stands between the seller of a prescription drug or other product, and the patient who uses it.

Legislation   the act of passing laws; also used as a noun to mean a statute or statutes adopted by a legislative body. CONTRAST: case law.

Legislative branch   the branch of the U.S. government that consists of Congress, whose powers are set forth in Article I of the U.S. Constitution. Each state also has its own legislature, the governmental body that enacts state laws.

Legislative history   the background and events leading up to the enactment of a statute.

Lobbyists   those who attempt to influence legislators to pass laws that favor special interests.

M

Magnuson-Moss Warranty Act   a federal statute designed to prevent deception in sales contracts by making warranties easier to understand.

Mediation   an alternative dispute resolution process in which a neutral third person helps disputing parties to adjust their positions to resolve their differences. Unlike judges or arbitrators, mediators do not impose solutions on the parties.

Misappropriation   a wrongful taking of something belonging to another, such as illegal taking of a trade secret or benefiting economically from the use of another's name or likeness, thereby misappropriating his right of publicity.

Motion a request to a judge or court for a rule or order favorable to the petitioning party, generally made within the course of an existing lawsuit.

N

National Highway Transportation Safety Administration (NHTSA) the federal agency responsible for setting standards for motor vehicle safety.

National Institute of Occupational Health and Safety (NIOSH) the government agency that conducts research into occupational health and safety

National Labor Relations Act also known as the Wagner Act; federal statute enacted in 1935 that established the rights of employees to organize unions, engage in collective bargaining and to strike.

National Labor Relations Board (NLRB) federal agency created by the Wagner Act to oversee union elections and to prevent unfair and illegal labor practices.

Negligence voluntary conduct that foreseeably exposes the interests of another to an unreasonable risk of harm; also the name of the civil (tort) action brought by a plaintiff injured by the negligence of another.

NGOs nongovernmental organizations or NGOs are voluntary and charitable not-for-profit associations, such as the Red Cross and Public Citizen.

Nominal damages minimal damages awarded for a technical injury where no actual harm was suffered.

Non-delegation doctrine interpretation of the U.S. Constitution that stops Congress from delegating too much of its power to another branch of government or to an administrative agency.

Nuisance activity that unreasonably interferes with another's use or enjoyment of his or her property.

O

Occupational Safety and Health Act of 1970 the federal statute that requires health and safety protections for employees at their places of work.

Occupational Safety and Health Administration (OSHA) the federal agency that promulgates and enforces workplace health and safety standards, conducts inspections and investigations, keeps records, and conducts research.

Order decision of an administrative law judge; final disposition of a case between the government and a private party.

P

Patent the exclusive right or privilege to make, use, or sell an invention for a limited period of time, granted by the government to the inventor.

Per curium Latin for "by the court;" used to indicate an unsigned opinion by the entire court rather than a single judge; sometimes refers to a brief statement of the court's decision unaccompanied by a written opinion.

Petitioner a party that files a petition with the court, applying in writing for a court order; a party that asks a court to hear an appeal from a judgment; a party that initiates an equity action.

Plaintiff a person or entity that brings an action or complaint against a defendant; the party who initiates a lawsuit.

Pleadings the formal allegations of the parties of their respective claims and defense, including the plaintiff's complaint, defendant's answer, and plaintiff's reply.

Police power the legal right of state government to legislate for the public health, welfare, safety, and morals.

Political Question Doctrine a rule that courts should not accept cases where the issue involves something that should be determined by one of the political (elected) branches of government.

Precedent a previously decided court case that serves to notify future litigants how subsequent similar cases will be resolved.

Preemption in federal-state relations, the concept that where there is a conflict between federal and state actions, the federal law will have priority and the state action will be void.

Prima facie Latin for "at first sight;" a fact presumed to be true unless disproved by evidence to the contrary.

Privilege in tort law, the ability to act contrary to another person's right without that person having legal redress for such actions. Privilege is usually raised as a defense.

Privity of contract   the relationship that exists between the promisor and promisee of a contract.

Probable cause   reasonable ground for supposing that an individual has committed a crime.

Procedural law   that part of the law which concerns the method or process of enforcing legal rights.

Products liability   the legal liability of manufacturers and sellers to buyers, users, and sometimes bystanders, for injuries suffered because of defects in goods sold. Liability arises when a product has a defective condition that makes it unreasonably dangerous to the user or consumer. Sometimes referred to as "strict liability."

Proximate cause   event(s) or action that, in natural and unbroken sequence, produce(s) an injury that would not have occurred absent the event(s) or action.

Public Domain   in copyright law, creative or government works that can be freely copied and used by anyone without asking permission are said to be "in the public domain."

Punitive damages   awards unrelated to the victim's injuries that are designed to punish the wrongdoer; damages awarded to a plaintiff that are greater than the amount necessary to compensate his or her loss; generally granted where the wrong involved intent, violence, fraud, malice, or other aggravated circumstances.

Q

Qualified immunity   protection from being sued that is available and is limited to certain circumstances.

Qui tam   Latin for "who as well—." A law suit brought by whistleblowers under the federal False Claims Act against those who are alleged to have defrauded the government.

Quid pro quo   Latin for "this for that;" the giving of one thing for another.

R

Regulatory takings   newly enforceable restrictions on the use of one's property, such as a newly adopted restriction on building in certain areas of wetlands.

Remand   to send back; the sending of a case back to the same lower court out of which it came for the purpose of having some action taken. For example, appellate courts often reverse a finding and remand to the trial court for a new trial.

Remedies   the aid that a court gives to a party who wins a lawsuit.

Remedies at law   court award of land, money, or items of value. CONTRAST: Remedies in equity.

Remedies in equity   relief deemed to be appropriate, based on fairness, justice, and honesty to remedy a situation, such as an injunction, restraining order, specific performance, or the like. CONTRAST: remedies at law.

Respondent   the party that contests an appeal or answers a petition.

Restatement   a book published by the American Law Institute that states its understanding of the law created by the judiciary throughout the country; each volume of the Restatement covers a different area of law, such as agency law, contracts, and torts.

Restitution   equitable remedy in which a person is restored to her original position prior to loss or injury, or is placed in the same position he or she would have been in absent a breach.

Reverse   decision of an appellate court to overthrow, vacate, set aside, void, or repeal the judgment of a lower court.

S

Shareholder   a person who owns stock in a corporation.

Shareholder derivative suit   a law suit initiated by shareholders on behalf of the corporation where the board of directors fails to do so or a demand to sue is deemed futile.

Sovereign immunity   doctrine preventing a litigant from asserting an otherwise meritorious claim against a sovereign (government).

Stakeholder   in ethical analysis, a person or group whose interests will be impacted by actions or decisions by an organization.

Standing to sue   the legal right to bring a lawsuit; in order to have standing, an individual or group must have a personal stake in the outcome of the suit.

Stare decisis Latin for "Let the decision stand." Doctrine under which courts stand by precedent and do not disturb a settled point of law. Under *stare decisis*, once a court has laid down a principle of law as applied to a certain set of facts, the court adheres to that principle and applies it to future cases in which the facts are substantially the same.

State action in Constitutional law, the term is used to designate governmental action necessary to bring a constitutional challenge to such action.

Statute an act of a legislature declaring, commanding, or prohibiting something; a particular law enacted by the legislative branch of government. Sometimes the word is used to designate codified law or legislation as opposed to case law.

Statute of limitations a law prescribing the period of time after an event within which a suit must be brought or criminal charges filed.

Stay a court order to stop, arrest, or forbear. To stay an order or decree means to hold it in abeyance or to refrain from enforcing it.

Strict liability liability without fault. A case is one in strict liability when a defendant is legally responsible without regard to his/her care or negligence, good or bad faith, knowledge or ignorance.

Strict Scrutiny in Constitutional law, government actions or laws that discriminate on the basis of race or ethnicity, or that infringe on fundamental freedoms like free speech are closely scrutinized by the courts to see if there is a compelling reason to justify the discrimination or infringement.

Subject Matter Jurisdiction the authority of a court to hear a particular kind of case; federal courts have subject matter jurisdiction over cases involving issues arising under the Constitution, treaties or federal law and lawsuits between parties of diverse citizenship (e.g. residents of different states).

Subpoena a writ ordering a person to appear and give testimony or to bring documents that are in his or her control.

Substantive law that part of the law which creates, defines, and regulates rights. CONTRAST: procedural law.

Summary judgment a pretrial decision reached by a trial court after considering the pleadings, affidavits, depositions, and other documents, on the ground that no trial is needed because no genuine issue of fact has been raised.

Supremacy clause a clause in Article VI of the U.S. Constitution which provides that all laws made by the federal government pursuant to the Constitution are the supreme laws of the land and are superior to any conflicting state law.

Supreme Court of the United States highest level of the federal judicial system, with nine justices appointed for life by the president of the United States.

Suspect classification in Constitutional law, differentiating between persons based on their race, national origin, or religion.

T

Takings term referring to government seizure, regulation, or intrusion on private property for which the owner is entitled to compensation under the Fifth Amendment to the U.S. Constitution.

Title ownership of property.

Tort French word meaning "wrong;" a civil wrong or injury, other than a breach of contract, committed against the person or property of another for which a civil court action is possible. Assault, battery, trespass, and negligence are all examples of tort actions.

Tortfeasor a person who commits a tort.

Trademark a distinctive mark, logo, or motto of stamp annexed to goods to identify their origin. Once established, a trademark gives its owner the right to its exclusive use.

Trade-Related Aspects of Intellectual Property Rights (TRIPS) Agreement a treaty adopted in 1994 that incorporates protection for intellectual property into GATT.

Trade secret something of economic value to its owner because its owner has taken reasonable steps to keep it secret (e.g. an unpatented formula or client list).

Treaty an agreement or contract between two or more nations that must be authorized (ratified) by the supreme power of each nation to become international law.

Trespass to land   entering onto or causing anything to enter onto land of another; remaining on or permitting anything or anyone to remain on land owned by another.

Trespass to personal property   sometimes called trespass to chattels; unlawful injury to (or other interference with) the personal property of another that violates the owner's right to exclusive possession and enjoyment of her property.

U

Unconscionability   against public policy; unduly harsh and one-sided; shocking to the conscience.

Uniform Commercial Code (UCC)   a comprehensive code, drafted by the National Conference on Commissioners on Uniform State Laws, which has been enacted in all the states. It includes articles governing the sale of goods, commercial paper, banking, and other commercial laws.

Utilitarianism   an approach to ethical reasoning in which ethically correct behavior is not related to any absolute ethical or moral values but to an evaluation of the consequences of a given action to those who will be affected by it. In utilitarian reasoning, a good decision is one that results in the greatest good for the greatest number of people affected by it ("stakeholders").

V

Verdict   the answer of a jury given to the court concerning the matters of fact committed to their trial and examination; it sets no precedent, and settles only the specific controversy to which it relates. It is the decision made by the jury and reported to the court, such as guilt or innocence in a criminal trial or whether the defendant is liable to the plaintiff in a civil case and the amount for which she is liable.

Virtue ethics   the ethical theory derived from Aristotle that our moral abilities (or virtues) are a matter of good habits, developed through training and repetition, within communities.

Void   null; ineffectual; having no legal force.

W

Warranty   seller's assurance to the buyers that the goods sold will meet certain standards.

Warranty of merchantability   seller's promise to the buyer that goods sold will be it for their ordinary purpose.

Whistleblowing   an employee's reporting an employer's illegal or unethical acts.

Workers' compensation   a program under which employers are required to make payments to employees who are injured during the course of their employment, regardless of negligence or fault.

World Trade Organization (WTO)   created by the Uruguay Round of GATT in 1994 to administer GATT and to resolve disputes.

Writ   a commandment of a court given for the purpose of compelling a defendant to take certain action, usually directed to a sheriff or other officer to execute it; a court order directing a person to do something.

Writ of certiorari   an order of a court to an inferior court to forward the record of a case for reexamination by the superior court. Cases are often brought to the attention of the U.S. Supreme Court when the losing party applies for a writ of certiorari. If the writ is granted, the Court agrees to allow an appeal.

Wrongful discharge   See Abusive discharge.

Z

Zoning   restrictions on land use imposed by state or local government.

Index